RUSSIAN EMPIRE

Bug

Lutsk

Vistula

San

Krakow

Przemysl • Lemberg •

• Tarnopol

G A L I C I A

Seret

Cernăuti

BUKOVINA

Miskolc •

Suceava •

Satu-Mare •

Sereth

Pruth

Dniester

E M P I R E

• Cluj

1914

Theiss

Loros

eged •

Subotica •

Maros

• Temesvár

R U M A N I A

B A N A T

Schul

Aluta

va

Danube

• Turnul-Severin

• Bucharest

Belgrade

Morava

BULGARIA

S E R B I A

NTEN-
GRO

• Scutari

• Skoplje

ALBANIA

• Bitolj

North

B. Brod •

Bosanski
Samac

DANUBE R.

SAVA R.

BELGRADE

Doboj •

Isakoviča Ada

Šabac •

Trnovo •

Priboj •

Lešnica •

Tuzla •

Loznica •

BOSNA R.

Koviljača Spa •

Zvornik •

S E R B I A

BOSNIA

Route of Princip
and Grabež

Route of Čabrinović

SARAJEVO •

Ilidže Spa •

DRINA R.

Miles

0   25   50

OTHER BOOKS BY VLADIMIR DEDIJER

THE BELOVED LAND
TITO

THE ROAD
TO
SARAJEVO

by

Vladimir Dedijer

SIMON AND SCHUSTER · NEW YORK

TO THE MEMORY OF

MARIJAN STILINOVIĆ
[1903–1959]

FRIEND AND REBEL

CONTENTS

CHAPTER I

JUNE 28, 1914

*For God's sake, let us sit upon the ground
And tell sad stories of the death of kings.*
—SHAKESPEARE, *King Richard II*

THE VISIT OF THE ARCHDUKE FRANZ FERDINAND von Österreich-Este, heir apparent to the Habsburg empire and inspector general of its armed forces, to the turbulent province of Bosnia and Hercegovina was to reach its climax on June 28, 1914.

After attending maneuvers of the 15th and 16th Army Corps in the mountains southwest of Sarajevo, the Bosnian capital, the Archduke journeyed to the nearby spa of Ilidže, where his wife was waiting for him. She had been passing the time in visiting churches, convents and orphanages and inspecting a local carpet factory. The Habsburgs' guests were staying at the Hotel Bosna, which had been reserved exclusively for the imperial party and refurnished and redecorated for the occasion.

The official program for the morning of June 28 included, first, at 9 A.M., a mass in the Hotel Bosna. At 9:25 the Archduke and his suite were to take a special train to Sarajevo. From the station they were to proceed to the nearby military barracks. Ten minutes were reserved for a short inspection of this establishment. At 10 sharp the Archduke was to drive to the *Beledija* (town hall) for a municipal welcome. From there he was to go at 10:30 to open the new premises of the State Museum—the only museum in the town, and the leading educational institution of Bosnia—in the presence of the Bosnian government. A luncheon was planned to take place in the *Konak*, the official residence of the governor of Bosnia, General Oskar Potiorek. In the afternoon, at two o'clock, the Habsburg guests were to take a sight-seeing tour, passing the Careva Džamija, the most picturesque mosque in Sarajevo, then the headquarters of the Army Inspectorate, and a carpet factory, taking the special train back to Ilidže. The rest of the afternoon, till 7 P.M., was reserved for a walk by the Archduke and his wife through the Ilidže spa. After the farewell dinner, the imperial guests were to leave Bosnia by train at nine.[1]

On the eve of the big day the Archduke was in a good mood. He had sent a telegram to his uncle, the Emperor Franz Josef, reporting on the maneuvers. In the evening there was a dinner, attended by more than forty dignitaries from Sarajevo.

The fresh mountain air had sharpened the Archduke's appetite, and he enjoyed the many elaborate dishes. There was *potage régence* (a cream soup made of rice and fish), followed by *soufflés délicieux* and *blanquettes de truites à la gelée* (trout, from the source of the river Bosna). The main course consisted of chicken, lamb and beef, with asparagus, salad and sherbet. The dinner ended with *crême aux ananas en surprise* (pineapple cream with burning brandy), cheeses, ice creams and candies.

The wine list was of an equally imposing length; it included a dry Madeira, several clarets, a Rhine wine, champagne and a Hungarian Tokay. The only representation allowed to Bosnia and Hercegovina on the bill of fare was *Žilavka*, served just before the Cognac Mestreau.[2]

When the banquet was over, the Archduke and the Duchess held court in the large foyer of the hotel.

The Duchess Sophie, a tall dark-eyed woman with an energetic chin, a little inclined to fatness in her late forties, was happily engaged in conversation. She had just received the news that her eldest child, the thirteen-year-old Maximilian, had passed his exams. She was pleased with the Ilidže spa and its natural beauties, and she was enjoying this trip with her husband. The Duchess had come to Bosnia with dark forebodings that something might happen to him. She remembered these fears when one of the leaders of the *Sabor*, the Bosnian parliament, Dr. Josip Sunarić, was presented to her. A close follower of her husband's public affairs, the Duchess knew that Dr. Sunarić had warned the Bosnian governor, General Potiorek, to cancel the Archduke's visit to Bosnia at a time when the Serbian population was in a mood of revolt.

When the politician bowed and kissed her hand she said to him: "My dear Dr. Sunarić, you are wrong, after all. Things do not always turn out the way you say they will. Wherever we have been, everyone, down to the last Serb, has greeted us with such great friendliness, politeness and true warmth, that we are very happy with our visit."

"Your Highness," answered Dr. Sunarić, "I pray to God that when I have the honor of meeting you again tomorrow night, you can repeat these words to me. A great burden will be lifted from me."[3]

When the guests had left, the Archduke, impressed by Dr. Sunarić's words, started to discuss the items on the next day's program with his entourage. Karl Freiherr von Rumerskirch, the chamberlain of the Archduke's household and senior member of his entourage on this trip, was of the opinion that the visit to Sarajevo should be canceled altogether. This would look like a rebuke to General Potiorek, the governor, and an admission of political defeat; his aide-de-camp, Lieutenant Colonel Erich von Merizzi, quickly reacted against such a suggestion.[4]

The morning of June 28, after several rainy days, was bright and sunny. After attending mass in the hotel room converted into a private chapel for their stay at a cost of 40,000 gold crowns,[5] the Archduke and his wife took a special train to Sarajevo.

Franz Ferdinand radiated serenity. He was dressed in the ceremonial uniform of an Austrian cavalry general, with a blue tunic, a high collar with three stars, and a hat adorned with pale-green feathers. He wore black trousers with red stripes down the sides and around his waist a *Bauchband*, a gold-braided ribbon with tassels. He was a stout man of fifty, with protruding, clear steel-blue eyes and an upturned hussar's mustache.

The Duchess had on a white picture hat with a veil, a white silk dress with flowers tucked into its red sash, and a fur of ermine tails over her shoulders. She carried a closed dark fan in her hand. The Archduke helped by carrying her white parasol.

They were met at the Sarajevo station by General Potiorek, a lean man in his sixties. After the guard of honor had presented arms, the party got into six waiting automobiles. The first car was reserved for the special security detectives, but an initial slip in the program occurred when only their chief officer climbed in with three local police officers, leaving behind all the others, who were in Sarajevo specifically to guard the Archduke.[6] The befezzed Lord Mayor of Sarajevo, Fehim Effendi Čurćić, got into the second car with Chief of Police Dr. Edmund Gerde.

An open sports car, a *Graef und Stift*, made by a Viennese firm, with its top folded back and with the seats covered with black leather, third in the line, was for the Archduke. The car had a very high wooden steering wheel and on the hood was flying the imperial flag—black and yellow, with a red border and the Austrian eagle in the middle. The Archduke helped the Duchess to sit down on his right, then he took his place beside her. Opposite him, on the folding seat, sat General Potiorek. Next to the driver was Lieutenant Colonal Count Franz Harrach, an officer of a transport unit. The Archduke had not brought his own automobile from Vienna and was using a military car.

The early-morning mist had cleared from the deep valley in which Sarajevo is situated. The summer sun was already strong. The inspection and briefing at the nearby military camp were soon over. Then the imperial party set out for the *beledija*, on the Appel Quay. This is a long street with houses on one side and on the other a low embankment wall along the river Miljacka, which at this time in midsummer was very shallow.

The Archduke requested that the automobiles be driven slowly, so that he could get a better look at the town. The houses were beflagged with Habsburg black-and-yellow and Bosnian red-and-yellow banners. In many windows the Archduke's portrait could be seen. A salute of twenty-four cannon salvos boomed from the fortresses on the tops of the surrounding heights, echoing among the minarets and the tall poplar trees and surging over the low tiled houses that stood on the hilly slopes around the town. As the procession moved along the Appel Quay there were a few shouts of *Živio!* (Long may he live!) from a thin crowd that stood under the shade of the houses and trees. It was very hot. The river side of the street was almost empty. In a nearby street, a huge poorly fastened black-and-yellow flag, above the ironmonger's, Racher and Babić, located opposite the Catholic cathedral, shook, wobbled and finally fell among the spectators.[7]

As the imperial car passed the central police station on the Appel Quay, General Potiorek pointed out to the Archduke the new barracks of the 15th Corps, which had taken part in the maneuvers just completed. It was 10:10 A.M. At that moment a tall young man in a long black coat and a black hat asked a policeman to tell him which car the Archduke was in;[8] seconds later he had knocked the cap of a hand grenade against a metal lamp-post by the embankment wall and hurled it at the Archduke's car. The driver, a Czech named Leopold Sojka, seeing a black object flying toward him, accelerated, and the bomb fell on the folded roof. The Archduke threw up his left arm to protect the Duchess, and the missile bounced off into the street, exploding under the left rear wheel of the next car and making a hole 11 by 12½ inches wide and 6½ inches deep.[9] The moment the bomb exploded, the Duchess jumped up in her seat. The would-be assassin in the meantime had plunged over the embankment wall into the shallow river, a drop of twenty-six feet.

The Archduke's car continued to journey toward the town hall at high speed. The Archduke ordered the chauffeur to stop, since he noticed that the other cars were not following. He asked Lieutenant Colonel Harrach to find out whether there were any dead or wounded, and the officer ran back to the scene of the explosion. The car behind had been damaged and was unable to move. Two officers, Lieutenant Colonel Erich von Merizzi (it was he who had spoken against postponement of the visit) and Lieutenant Colonel Count Alexander Boos-Waldeck, were bleeding. Merizzi had been hit by a bomb fragment on the right side of his head. A lady in waiting of the Duchess was wiping the blood from his head with her handkerchief. Policemen and detectives were running around, arresting as many onlookers as they could. People on the pavement were shouting; about twenty of them had been wounded, some of them seriously. A woman watching the parade from the balcony of her bedroom had been hit in the face, and her eardrum had been shattered by the explosion.

Lieutenant Colonel Harrach returned in a great hurry to inform the Archduke of what he had seen. The chamberlain, von Rumerskirch, came running up to order the driver to go on. The stationary car was a perfect target for a second attempt at assassination. Just then the Duchess complained that she felt a pain low down on her neck, near the shoulder blade. The Archduke examined the spot and saw that the skin had been grazed. The driver discovered that several pieces of bomb had hit his car, too—one in the upper part of the fuel tank, a second in the side of the trunk, and a third fragment in the folding roof. But the engine was not damaged.

The voice of the Archduke was heard: "The fellow must be insane. Gentlemen, let us proceed with our program."[10]

The first two cars, with the chief detective, the chief of police and the Lord Mayor, had already arrived at the town hall, an ugly building in pseudo-Moorish style on the Appel Quay. They did not know what had happened. One of them had mistaken the explosion of the bomb for a cannon salute. But the arrival of the enraged Archduke brought them face to face with reality.

The Lord Mayor was standing at the head of his councilors, who attended him in two rows—on one side, the Moslems in their conical Turkish hats, open waistcoats and baggy trousers, and on the other the Christians in tail coats, with top hats in their hands. The representative of the local Jews was also there.

Seeing the Archduke, the Lord Mayor began his speech of welcome: "Your Imperial and Royal Highness, Your Highness! Our hearts are full of happiness on the occasion of the most gracious visit with which your Highnesses have deigned to honor the capital of our land—"[11]

But the Archduke interrupted him in a harsh voice. "Herr Bürgermeister, what is the good of your speeches? I come to Sarajevo on a friendly visit and someone throws a bomb at me. This is outrageous."[12]

The Mayor was at a loss for words, but the Duchess stepped in and whispered a few words into the ear of the Archduke, who said after some hesitation: "Now, you can get on with your speech."

Somehow the bewildered Lord Mayor recovered. ". . . our deep gratitude for your Highness's graciousness and fatherly care . . . for the youngest jewel in the Holy Imperial Crown, our dear fatherland Bosnia and Hercegovina . . ."[13]

Stumbling after every sentence the Lord Mayor came to the end, and again the silence settled. It was the Archduke's turn to answer. He looked for his chamberlain, von Rumerskirch, to hand him the prepared text of the reply. He had been in the damaged car and had not yet arrived. At last he appeared, and the Archduke took the speech. He frowned for a moment; the paper was wet with the blood of the wounded officers in the chamberlain's car.

The Archduke was a man of great presence of mind and to the prepared speech he added a few words about the abortive attempt against his life:

"I received with special pleasure the assurance of your unshakable loyalty and attachment to His Royal Highness, our gracious Emperor and King, and I thank you, Herr Bürgermeister, very heartily for the enthusiastic ovations offered to me and to my wife by the population, all the more as I see in them an expression of their joy at the failure of the attempt at assassination."[14]

A crowd had assembled around the town hall to watch the ceremony. Reading quickly, the Archduke came to the end of his speech. The last few sentences were in Serbo-Croatian; he had memorized this section, and he was able to look directly at the people around him as he concluded. ". . . I ask you to give my heartiest greetings to the population of this beautiful capital city, and I assure you of my unchangeable grace and kindness."

At last the procession moved inside the town hall. The Duchess, accompanied by the Lord Mayor and by her lady in waiting, went up to the first floor to meet the Moslem ladies and their children; the Archduke waited in the vestibule with his suite and the councilors. He even joked nervously: "You mark my words! The chap will probably, in good old Austrian style, be decorated with the Order of Merit instead of being made harmless."[15] No one smiled, and he continued his monologue: "Today we shall get a few more little bullets."[16] Then he approached General Potiorek and asked him bluntly: "Do you think more attempts are going to be made against me?"[17]

There are several versions of Potiorek's answer to this question. At the inquest he said that he had replied hesitantly that he did not think so, although, despite all the necessary precautions, an attack still could take place at close range.[18] On the other hand, the Austro-Hungarian Minister of Finance Ritter Leon von Bilinski, in whose jurisdiction Bosnia was, recorded Potiorek's answer as it was transmitted by the witnesses present: ". . . Go at ease. I accept all responsibility. . . ."[19] Dr. Max Hohenberg, the Archduke's eldest son, accepted Bilinski's version, saying that Potiorek had expressed "his regrets to my parents and assured them that all danger had passed from now on."[20]

The conversation, according to Potiorek, continued with his suggestion that the plans of the imperial party should be changed. Instead of going to the museum, where the members of the government were waiting, by the narrow Franz Josef Street through the center of the city, it would be better, he thought, to proceed through the empty Appel Quay. This alteration of the Archduke's route, according to the

Governor, would also punish the population of Sarajevo by depriving them of a chance to see the Heir Apparent.[21] Some members of the entourage thought the best thing would be to change the plan altogether; some were for putting off all engagements and returning as quickly as possible to Ilidže; others asked if it would not be better to go on to the *Konak*, the Governor's official residence.

The Archduke finally came to a decision. He expressed a wish to see the wounded Lieutenant Colonel von Merizzi, who had been taken to a military hospital, and then to proceed to the museum. Before leaving the town hall, he dictated a telegram to the Emperor about the morning's unhappy incident. At that moment the Duchess returned with a bouquet of flowers, a gift from a Moslem girl. According to the official program she should not have gone to the museum to meet the government representatives, but should have driven instead to the *Konak*. In front of the whole imperial party, she said: "I will go with you to the hospital."[22]

So, at a quarter to eleven the Archduke left the town hall. He was again in the third car. Lieutenant Colonel Harrach stood on its running board, on the side of the car nearest to the river. It was from this side that the bomb had been thrown, and he wished thus to protect the Archduke should an assassination be attempted again.

The cars drove along the Appel Quay at high speed. But when the first car, with the chief detective in it, reached the corner of the Appel Quay and Franz Josef Street, it turned to the right, according to the original plan. The second car followed it with the chief of police and the Lord Mayor.

Who made this mistake, and whether it was deliberate or accidental, is one of the controversial issues of the debate on what was to happen within the next few minutes.[23]

The Czech driver of the Archduke's car was about to follow them, when the Governor shouted at him: "What is this? Stop! You are going the wrong way! We ought to go via Appel Quay."[24]

Stepping hard on the brake, the driver stopped the sports car just in front of a shop, close to the crowded pavement. At that instant a short young man with long hair and deep-set blue eyes took out a revolver. A policeman saw the danger and was on the point of grabbing his hand, when he was struck by someone standing nearby, presumably a friend of the assassin.[25] Pistol shots were heard. The killer was only a few steps from his target.

It seemed at first as though this attempt had failed, too. General Potiorek saw both the Archduke and the Duchess motionless in their places. But as the car was backing down the Appel Quay, the Duchess fell toward the Archduke and the Governor saw the blood on the Archduke's mouth. He ordered the chauffeur to drive at full speed to the *Konak*.

Count Franz Harrach, who had been standing on the opposite side, could do nothing. He recalled the scene in this way:

"As I was drawing out my handkerchief to wipe away the blood from the Archduke's lips, Her Highness cried out: 'For God's sake! What has happened to you?' Then she sank down from her seat with her face between the Archduke's knees. I had no idea that she had been hit and thought that she had fainted from shock. His Royal Highness said: 'Soferl, Soferl, don't die. Live for my children.' Thereupon I seized the Archduke by the coat collar to prevent his head from sinking forward and asked him: 'Is Your Highness in great pain?' To which he clearly answered: 'It is nothing.' His face was slightly distorted, and he repeated six or seven times, every time losing more consciousness and with a fading voice: 'It is nothing.' Then came a brief pause followed by a convulsive rattle in his throat, caused by loss of blood. This ceased on arrival at the governor's residence. The two unconscious bodies were carried into the building where their death was soon established."[26] A German Jesuit, Father Anton Puntigam, and a Franciscan father were urgently summoned.[27]

The Duchess died first. A bullet aimed at the Governor had penetrated the side of the car, her corset and her right side. The Archduke outlived her for a short time. A bullet had pierced the right side of his coat collar, severed the jugular vein and come to a stop in the spine. The fast drive from the scene of the assassination to the *Konak* must have made their condition even worse.[28]

It was 11:30 A.M., June 28, 1914. The Duchess' body was in the Governor's bedroom, where she had been brought after her death. The body of the Archduke was in an adjoining room of the secluded and walled *Konak*, a building dating from Turkish times. The Archduke's collar was open, and a gold chain from which hung seven amulets, with frames of gold and platinum, could be seen. Each of them was worn as protection against a different type of evil. His sleeves were rolled up, and on his left arm could be seen a Chinese dragon tattooed in colors. Around the neck of the Duchess was a golden chain with a scapular containing holy relics guarding her from ill health and misfortunes.[29]

The bells of all the Sarajevo churches, one after another, began to toll.

CHAPTER II

THE PERFECT
POLITICAL MURDER?

Plots, true or false, are necessary things,
To raise up commonwealths and ruin kings.
—JOHN DRYDEN, *Absalom and Achitophel*

N O OTHER POLITICAL MURDER in modern history has had such momentous consequences. The killing of the Archduke by a Bosnian student named Gavrilo Princip led to the outbreak of the First World War by a series of quick and irreversible steps—the Austrian ultimatum to Serbia on July 23, her declaration of war on July 28, Russian mobilization, Germany's declaration of war on Russia on August 1, and French and British declarations of war against Germany on August 3 and 4. This war produced the greatest carnage in world history up to that time, devastating much of Europe, and causing the death of more than ten million people. Deep social upheavals followed it. The end came to four empires and to the ancient Habsburg, Romanov, Hohenzollern and Ottoman dynasties which had ruled them for hundreds of years. This war changed the map of Europe more than any previous war in its history; from the ruins of the former empires emerged new states based on the principle of self-determination. In Russia the 1917 revolution established an entirely new order. After 1918, Europe lost its decisive power over other parts of the world which it had subjugated in earlier centuries.

The First World War moved vast armies of fighting men from all the continents to Europe. They grappled for four long years amid the birth pangs of a new epoch, whose significance few of them realized, and which even now, half a century later, is still in the process of taking shape and finding a form and style of its own.

What differentiates the Sarajevo assassination from others is, above all, the character of the international conditions under which it occurred and of the region where it took place. Gavrilo Princip fired his pistol not only at an archduke, but also at the façade of a quiet, apparently stable world. But in reality the year 1914 found Europe in a state of turmoil, rapidly approaching the end of an era. Germany, with her increasing industry and population, was challenging Britain as the leading world power. She had intensified her colonial designs and built a powerful navy. Old Franco-German and Russian-Austrian rivalries were growing. The imperalist competition was increased by the system of secret alliances. Germany, Austria and Russia practiced not only *Militarismus nach aussen* but also *Militarismus nach innen,* with military men trying to replace civilian leadership; even in Britain the Ulster generals were threatening the Crown with open rebellion.

The Balkans, a bridge between Europe, Asia and Africa, were a particularly sensitive area where the great powers clashed. The Ottoman Empire with its anachronistic feudal institutions was counting its last hours, and the great powers were quarreling over who would fill the vacuum, disregarding the right of the Balkan peoples to self-determination. The Habsburg Empire, also a product of the feudal era, wanted to establish political control over Serbia. Germany, backing the two multinational empires, Austria-Hungary and Turkey, had alienated the independent Balkan states. On the other hand, Britain, Russia and France were trying to establish a barrier to the German *Drang nach Osten* by supporting the small, economically underdeveloped Balkan states who were eager to be modernized. Leading European banking concerns were competing for the financing of armaments for the small states. The success of Serbia, Greece, Bulgaria and Montenegro in the 1912–1913 war, ending the centuries-long rule of the Ottoman Empire in Europe, had been hailed on the stock exchanges of the European capitals as a victory for Schneider-Creusot and Vickers-Armstrong over Krupp and Škoda. In the Balkans the plight of Princip's native Bosnia and Hercegovina was particularly severe; the region was living under a modern colonialism which denied both its national and its social rights.

One of the most controversial issues of contemporary history arises from the questions: What were Princip's motives and who were his instigators, if any, and his accomplices? His crime was called "the perfect political murder," in the sense that it might be impossible for the truth ever to be established. The British Foreign Secretary in 1914, Sir Edward Grey, wrote in his memoirs: "The world will presumably never be told all that was behind the murder of the Archduke Franz Ferdinand. Probably there is not, and never was, any one person who knew all there was to know."[1]

Controversy over the Sarajevo assassination has been sharpened by the long debate over responsibility for the First World War. For some, Princip's conspiracy was a cause, whether basic or immediate; for others, it was merely a pretext, the spark which detonated the mass of hatred with which the world had long been charged, and which destroyed the precarious balance of power among the empires which had dominated Europe and divided up the world.

At the very beginning of the war, the Central Powers (Germany and Austria-Hungary) claimed that its crucial cause was the Sarajevo murder. In trying to establish Serbia's role as the true instigator of the crime, they hoped to lay guilt for the war at her door and thereby implicate her allies—Russia, Britain and France.

The victorious powers, on the other hand, in Article 231 of the Peace Treaty of Versailles, and in Article 177 of the Peace Treaty of St. Germain, laid the sole responsibility on Germany and her allies. These arbitrary clauses had fateful consequences. "War guilt" became a basic issue in international relations between the two world wars, and it dominated the internal politics of Germany. Adolf Hitler's promise to free Germany from the punitive restrictions of Versailles paved his way to the Berlin Chancellery; they served him perfectly in his plans for resurrecting the driving power of German imperialism.

The historians swarmed into this controversy; by 1939 there had been some three thousand books and pamphlets published on the subject.[2] And variety was a consequence of this plenitude. Different writers have named the following countries as the hotbeds of the conspiracy which led to the assassination of the Archduke: Serbia, Russia, Hungary, Austria, Germany, France and Great Britain.

Those who accuse Serbia point out that, although Gavrilo Princip and his main accomplices were Austro-Hungarian citizens, it was in Serbia that they received their political training; that they got their weapons in Serbia, and were trained there to use them; and that in the end, it was with the help of the Serbian authorities that they traveled from Belgrade to Sarajevo to commit the assassination.

This accusation appeared for the first time in the Austro-Hungarian ultimatum to the Serbian government of July 23, 1914; it was repeated in Hitler's proclamation to the German people on April 6, 1941, when Nazi Germany and her satellites, Italy, Hungary and Bulgaria, attacked Yugoslavia.[3]

Among historians who regard Serbia as responsible for the assassination there are differing opinions as to the degree of culpability. Some have claimed that the Serbian government was actively concerned in initiating and organizing the Sarajevo conspiracy, as a direct consequence of the movement for pan-Serb expansion in the South Slav territories of the Austro-Hungarian Empire.[4]

In the United States and Great Britain there came into being a school of historians known as the "Revisionists," who expressed the opinion that the verdict of the Versailles Treaty was historically unsound and should be revised, first by historical scholars, and through them by public opinion. A leading Revisionist historian, Sidney B. Fay, has maintained that Serbia bore a heavy responsibility for the assassination of Franz Ferdinand because the Serbian government knew of the plot three weeks before it was executed, but failed to take effective steps to prevent the assassins from crossing the Serbian border, and then failed to give Austria any warning or information which might have averted the fatal crime.[5]

Among the writers who blame Serbia, opinions still differ as to who in Serbia was primarily responsible for the conspiracy. The name of the heir apparent to the throne of Serbia in 1914, Prince Alexander Karadjorjević, has been mentioned several times.[6] But most historians, whether Revisionist or anti-Revisionist, claim that the real power behind the assassins was the Serbian secret society Ujedinjenje ili Smrt ("Union or Death"), known by its enemies as the *Crna ruka* ("Black Hand"), headed by Colonel Dragutin Dimitrijević, known also by the pseudonym "Apis."[7]

Russia too has been named an instigator, because in 1914 she was Serbia's most trusted ally. Some claimed it was her policy to provoke a war to take revenge for the humiliation suffered at the hands of Austria-Hungary in 1908 and in 1913. Several writers have alleged that the Russian General Staff and the Russian secret police Okhrana were the driving forces behind Colonel Apis.[8]

A German expert on the Sarajevo assassination, Alfred von Wegerer, in 1937 suspected the Russian Bolsheviks of having been among the instigators of the deed.[9] He based his theory on the words of the Bolshevik leader Karl Radek, who, at his trial in Moscow, in January 1937, spoke of Princip as an example of a political prisoner who kept his secret until the end of his life.[10] Of the Russian Bolshevik leaders, Leon Trotsky had been in Serbia several times before 1914 and was acquainted with some members of the Bosnian secret society of which Gavrilo Princip was a member. But Trotsky was opposed in principle to the use of individual terrorism.

Others accused France and Great Britain, as allies of Russia and Serbia, of being the centers of the conspiracy. Father Anton Puntigam during the First World War alleged that the Sarajevo assassination was instigated, organized and carried out by international Freemasonry and that one of the assassins was himself a Freemason. One of the most trusted advisers of the Archduke, and in 1917 the Austro-Hungarian Minister of Foreign Affairs, Count Ottokar Czernin, claimed in his book *In the World War*, published in 1919, that the Archduke informed him "a year before the outbreak of war, that the Freemasons had resolved to kill him."[11]

Under Nazi rule this allegation was vehemently revived, and Hitler's official party newspaper, *Völkischer Beobachter*, described Gavrilo Princip as "a Jew and a Freemason."[12] In the aforementioned April 1941 proclamation, Hitler charged that behind Serbian authorities was the British Intelligence Service.[13]

Vienna, Budapest and Berlin have been accused by still others either of knowing about the preparations for the assassination of the Archduke (who was unpopular in many circles both in Vienna and in Budapest) and doing nothing to prevent it, or of actually taking part in the conspiracy through their agents in South Slav secret societies.

Wickham Steed, in an article in 1915 and in his book *Through Thirty Years*, expressed the opinion that the police authorities in Sarajevo showed a singular negligence in the organization of measures to protect the lives of the Archduke and his wife.[14] Several other writers have hinted that the Hungarian Prime Minister Count Stephen Tisza was in secret league with Colonel Apis.[15] The Archduke's eldest son, Max Hohenberg, in 1937 accused the German secret service of having been in league with the assassins in Sarajevo.[16] When Austria was occupied by the Nazis in 1938, this allegation, among other considerations, led Max Hohenberg and his younger brother to Dachau concentration camp.

So, we see that students of the First World War disagree about who was behind the assassination. They also disagree about the reasons for the murder. Political murders are committed for very complex reasons, and a study of the motives for the numerous assassinations in modern times may illuminate the complexity of the June 28, 1914, conspiracy.

The motives of most assassins between 1792 and 1914 can be grouped in the following categories:

1. *Political murders for personal reasons*. These include the killing of Spencer Perceval, Prime Minister of Great Britain, and that of James A. Garfield, President of the United States, by individuals who had personal, not political, grudges against them.

2. *Acts of individuals suffering from mental disorder* (like the assassination of the Austrian Empress Elisabeth by the Italian anarchist Luigi Luccheni). Some assassins have been legally sane but psychologically disturbed. Here it is difficult to make firm judgments; authentic documentation for each case is lacking. Criminology is a relatively new science. Assassins have often been summarily tried by judges acting in the heat of political passion. For instance, it is still a controversial issue whether or not John Wilkes Booth, who killed President Abraham Lincoln, was mentally disturbed. A similar problem exists in respect to Charles Guiteau, who assassinated President James A. Garfield, or Leon Czolgosz, the murderer of President William McKinley.[17] In England, in spite of her long juridical tradition, the issue of "responsibility of mentally abnormal political assassins" became clouded during Queen

Victoria's reign, and the treatment given them worsened after the Act of 1882. This was passed at Queen Victoria's insistence, after the seventh attempt on her life, on March 2, 1882, when Roderick MacLean fired at her with a loaded pistol at the Windsor railway station.[18]

3. *Tyrannicide.* Some assassinations are true cases of tyrannicide, an institution with deep roots in tribal society. The Old Testament mentions the cases of Ehud and Jael.[19] The European tradition of tyrannicide is based to a great extent on the classical theories of republicanism worked out in ancient Greece and Rome. The killing of a tyrant was usually praised as the noblest human deed. Aristotle, Plato, Cicero and Tacitus honored tyrannicide.[20] Its idea was connected with the whole concept of the right of resistance based on the teachings of natural law. New interpretations of tyrannicide appeared in the Christian world, when Church dignitaries came into conflict with civil power. Theologians, including John of Salisbury, Saint Thomas Aquinas, Suarez, Mariana and others, through the centuries have argued over what circumstances may justify an individual's taking the law into his own hands and killing a tyrant. The *Catholic Encyclopedia* describes tyrannicide as "the killing of a tyrant by a private person for the common good."[21] One of the basic elements in the Christian concept of tyrannicide is self-sacrifice.

There have been several cases in modern times when perpetrators of political homicide have justified their actions by the tradition of tyrannicide. On July 13, 1874, a journeyman cooper named Kullman wounded the German Chancellor, Prince von Bismarck, at Kissingen. At his trial he stated explicitly that he had tried to kill the Chancellor because of the introduction of laws against the interests of the Roman Catholic Church; "the motives were revenge and hatred in consequence of the Ecclesiastical Laws."[22] In France, as late as 1962, a heated argument was provoked over Roman Catholic dogmas on tyrannicide. A member of an O.A.S. plot against the life of the President of France, General Charles de Gaulle, declared that before the attempt he had consulted his Roman Catholic father-confessor about the permissibility of his action, and that he acted after he had received the answer "that the requisite conditions for tyrannicide were fulfilled in overabundant fashion."[23]

There is a great variety of tyrannicide theories. In countries with Germanic *Lehnrecht*, in the Middle Ages, the right of resistance (*Widerstandsrecht*), even to the point of tyrannicide, was a positive law against any king who did not keep his bonds based on the Charter of Rulership.[24]

The right of resistance, including tyrannicide, received a new interpretation during the English Revolution in the seventeenth century. In early feudal times it had been basically a defense of an established right, of divine law; with the introduction of absolute monarchy and the identification of state and religion (*cuius regio eius religio*), it often became antilegitimist. People had a right not only to remove a tyrant from power but also to alter the form of the state. A fortnight after the execution of Charles I, John Milton wrote his essay on "The Tenure of Kings and Magistrates," whose subtitle reads: "Proving that it is lawful, and hath been held so through all ages, to call to account a tyrant, or wicked king, and after due conviction, to depose, and put him to death, if the ordinary magistrates have neglected, or denied to do it. And that they who of late so much blame deposing, are the men that did it themselves."[25]

✓ John Locke, later in the same century, was the first to formulate a theory of resistance, including tyrannicide, in a precise way. His essay on civil government not only expressed the theory behind the English revolution, but also provided a pattern to be followed by many revolutions in other countries. He related his theory of resistance to the teachings of natural law and the social contract and defined it thus: "Whoever uses *force without Right* . . . puts himself into *a State of War* with those against whom he so uses it, and in that state all former ties are cancelled, all other Rights cease, and everyone has a right to defend himself and to resist *the Aggressor*."[26]

In Sweden both *Lehnrecht* and the English theory of tyrannicide were reinvoked when a Swedish nobleman and former officer, Johan Jakob Anckarström, killed King Gustavus III on March 16, 1792. He maintained that the King's murder was justified on the basis of the provisions of the Swedish constitution. Anckarström also quoted the opinions of Locke, Milton and the French Encyclopedists about the right of resistance, including assassination, against a tyrant king.

4. *Political assassinations as an expression of revolt against national or colonial oppression.* One moral aspect of classical tyrannicide—killing "for the common good"—was revived in the nineteenth century among European nations which achieved self-determination later than others (Germans, Italians, Magyars, Irishmen, East and South Slavs and others). This kind of political assassination had the purpose of drawing world public attention to the state of affairs in a nation, as in Karl Ludwig Sand's murder of August von Kotzebue in 1819, or the attempt of the Irishman O'Farrell against the Duke of Edinburgh, son of Queen Victoria, on March 12, 1868. To this category belong also political assassinations for the purpose of changing political or social systems. The conspirators against the life of Louis Philippe in 1835 believed that assassinating him would trigger an armed revolt in France. The members of Narodnaya Volya thought that the assassination of Alexander II in 1881 would provoke a revolution which would bring about the end of the absolutist Russian regime. This theory was revived at the beginning of the twentieth century by the Russian Social Revolutionaries, who relied on the heroic impulses of individuals and believed that a group of determined assassins could ignite a revolution.

Here we must distinguish between bona fide assassinations and attempted assassinations, and other violent acts organized by police agents as pretexts for the persecution of the opposition. It has been suggested that the Cato Street Conspiracy in England in 1820 was instigated by an *agent provocateur*.[27] Henri Le Caron, "Inspector General of the Irish Republican Army," was a "secret agent of the English government" and organized several terrorist acts, which ended in complete failure.[28] The Paris Prefect of Police, Louis Andrieux, in the 1890's organized acts of violence through his agents.[29] The Russian secret police Okhrana penetrated the top leadership of the Russian Social Revolutionary party in 1901 through their agent Azef, and under his directives two high Russian dignitaries were assassinated.[30] These murders were pretexts for increased terror against the revolutionaries and were used to stir up pogroms against the Jews. There is a theory that Leon Czolgosz, the murderer of President McKinley, was an *agent provocateur*.[31]

5. *Dynastic murders.* These have been organized by one dynasty to eliminate another—for example in Turkey during the nineteenth century, or in the struggle between the Karadjordjević and Obrenović dynasties in Serbia. To this category belongs assassination for so-called "reasons of state," when one political group takes power by murdering the leader of an opposing faction without any intention of introducing political or social reform. It also includes cases of classical political assassination organized by one country against a ruler or a dignitary of another country and carried out by a hired, or in some cases indoctrinated, assassin. In the eleventh and twelfth centuries a secret Mohammedan sect of the Ismailians was operating in the Middle East, committing political suicide. According to legend, its leader, Hasan ibn-al-Sabbah, gave hashish to young men in order to induce them to carry out murders he designed against public figures of that area. The Crusaders brought stories of the activities of this sect back to Europe, and the word "assassin" is derived from the Arabic *hashshashin*, a taker of the drug hashish.[32]

By 1903 there had already been many attempts at assassination which led to the accusation that they had been organized in other countries. For instance, Orsini's attempt against the life of Napoleon III in 1858 seriously strained relations between England and France and provoked rumors of impending war between the two countries. This attempt was the cause of the fall of Lord Palmerston's government in that same year. Orsini had come to Paris from England, where he had manufactured his bombs, and the French government and parliament publicly alleged "that the law of England afforded an improper degree of shelter and countenance to foreign refugees and incendiaries and that in neglecting to take means for preventing such conspiracies as that which had nearly proved fatal to the Emperor's life, England had not acted the part of a sincere and faithful ally."[33] Lord Palmerston proposed to

amend the law in relation to the crime of conspiracy to commit murder, but his bill ran into strong opposition in the House of Commons.
Roebuck warned Palmerston that "for the sake of mankind, we should
do nothing to circumscribe the liberties of England." Other M.P.'s recalled that the uncle of Napoleon III, Napoleon I, had hired Contillon
to assassinate the Duke of Wellington, and that Napoleon III had paid
Contillon's family the legacy left him by Napoleon I. In the end, Palmerston's bill was defeated by 234 votes to 215, and he resigned.[34]

In Europe two states in particular organized the assassinations of foreign dignitaries: the Venetian Republic and Spain. Philip II of Spain
(1527-1598), a member of the Habsburg dynasty, exercised what he
described as the right of tyrannicide against Protestant kings who happened also to be the sovereigns of estates in which Spain had great
interests. There is a theory that he was behind the murder of William
the Silent. Philip also sent his assassins against Queen Elizabeth I, but
she had a first-class counterespionage system and all the killers-to-be
were caught in time and executed.

It is not always simple to classify an assassination. A single homicide
may contain elements of more than one of these categories. That was,
for instance, the case in the assassination of the Serbian King Alexander
Obrenović and his wife Draga in 1903. Because of his despotic rule, he
was regarded as a tyrant by the majority of the Serbian people. But
behind some of the conspirators was the Karadjordjević dynasty, the
deadly enemy of the Obrenović family. The matter is still further complicated by the fact that both Russia and Austria-Hungary knew beforehand about the plot; some of the conspirators had their base in
Vienna and received financial and technical support from an official of
the Austro-Hungarian Ministry of Foreign Affairs, as we shall see later.

Without primary documented sources it is impossible to make any
kind of serious assessment of the motives behind a political assassination. The atmosphere surrounding the event prevents the assassins from
speaking about their deed and keeps the authorities from fully record-
ing the circumstances involved, either intentionally or out of incompe-
tence. Political expediency may lead the authorities to close the case as
soon as possible by executing the prisoner with no trial or with only a
very short and secret one. Janos Libenyi, the Magyar tailor who knifed
the Habsburg Emperor Franz Josef in the skull in 1853, was executed
so quickly that his story has never been fully revealed.

The Swedish nobleman and former officer, Johan Jakob Anckarström, who killed King Gustavus III in 1792, was described at the
time of his death as a coarse and depraved man operating from purely
personal motives. One hundred and seventy years after his execution,
Professor Stig Jägerskjöld proved that the most important parts of
Anckarström's confession had been deliberately excluded from the
published proceedings of the case. Anckarström had really acted out of

deep political conviction, believing that every Swedish subject possessed a legal right to resistance and regicide, if his sovereign violated the constitutional rights of the people.[35]

Fortunately, the assassins of Franz Ferdinand confessed their deed at once and gave long explanations of their reasons for it. Their words were recorded, both during the police investigation and at the trial. Only recently have most of these documents been made available to scholars. The various groups accused of being behind the assassins did not leave much documentation of their secret work, as is usually the case in such conspiracies. But there is now vast new source material about the governments, their public and secret agencies, and the political and secret organizations which might have had an interest in eliminating the Archduke.

Most important of all the deed itself must be seen against the background of life and conditions in Bosnia and Hercegovina for any real understanding of the character of the assassins and of the deep-rooted forces which drove them to their desperate act.

CHAPTER III

THE PRINCIPS
OF THE
GRAHOVO VALLEY

Krajina's like a blood-soaked rag;
Blood is our fare at noon, blood still at evening.
On every lip is the taste of blood,
With never a peaceful day or any rest.
—Serbian folksong

THE PRINCIPS COME of a *kmet* (serf) family which had lived for centuries in Krajina, one of the remotest parts of western Bosnia, a region where amid wooded highlands lie deep valleys—the beds of ancient glacier lakes—covered with red earth.

These valleys are the main oases of life in a thinly populated region. After long winters, lasting from October until April, when everything becomes numb and silent and when frost cracks the rocks and splits the trunks of trees, spring descends swiftly, completely inundating the valleys. When the water recedes, the rich earth is soaked so thoroughly that the grazing grounds remain dark-green throughout the hot summers.

The Princips' valley is called Grahovo Polje. It lies below the Dinara Mountain, over 6,000 feet high, which separates Bosnia from Dalmatia and the Adriatic Sea. It is situated at a height of 2,600 feet; it is only five miles long and two miles wide, and the little river Korana dawdles through it. In the northern part of Grahovo Polje is the hamlet of

Gornji Obljaj, a dozen stone houses with steep black wooden roofs, clustering together for protection. This is the home of the Princips.

The Princips were Serbs, the most numerous nationality in Bosnia and Hercegovina. Linguistically, as well as in folklore and customs, they differ little from the Croats and the Moslems, the other two groups of the country. Bosnia and Hercegovina are two of the most purely Slavonic of the South Slav provinces. Yet the Bosnians differ among themselves in religion and in specific historical development. The Serbs are Eastern Orthodox, the Croats are Roman Catholic, while a part of the Bosnian people adhere to the Moslem religion. This is due primarily to the fact that Bosnia and Hercegovina have seen many invaders, not only from the east but even more from the west and north, whose armies brought their own civilization, their own states and their own religious institutions.

Ever since the first feudal Bosnian state was formed, it suffered from the rivalry of the Roman and Byzantine churches, each of which tried to impose its own creed on the Bosnians. Their success was only partial. Eventually the majority of Bosnians rejected both churches and, under the influence of Gnostic and Neo-Manichaean teachings, which came to them from Bulgaria, established their own Bosnian Church. Although historians still argue about the character of Bosnian Bogomilism, its spread in Bosnia and Hercegovina was certainly due to sociopolitical factors. The Bosnian Church in its teachings had elements of an egalitarianism opposed to the omnipotence of the feudal state and church. It refused to own estates and declined to collect any taxes from its followers.[1] In contrast, the Roman Catholic and Eastern Orthodox churches acquired landed possessions in Bosnia and introduced the tithe, a land tax from all tenants. Both Rome and Constantinople tried to subjugate Bosnian heretics by force of arms. For more than 250 years, Hungarian kings, in the name of the Papacy, harassed Bosnia, devastating the country and imposing on the Bosnian rulers allegiance to the Roman Catholic faith. Many a Bosnian heretic was freely sold "as a slave in the Christian lands, because they were not regarded as Christian."[2] But as soon as the Hungarian armies withdrew from the Bosnian wilderness, the Bosnian Church revived, and heretics from Dalmatia and other western lands found refuge in Bosnia from persecution at home.

In 1463 the independent Bosnian state, along with the whole of the Balkan Peninsula, was conquered by the Ottoman Empire. The Bosnian Church, which had offered such resistance to the Roman Catholic and Eastern Orthodox churches, disappeared suddenly under Turkish rule. Approximately one third of Bosnia's population was either killed or enslaved. A majority of the population—aristocrats and commoners— accepted the Moslem faith.

The Turks established in Bosnia and Hercegovina a strictly centralized system of government of a military character. According to the *sheriat*, Turkish law based on the Koran and the sayings of Mohammed, all land in occupied territories belonged to God, and the Sultan exercised the right of demesne over it. He would grant rights of usage to officers who distinguished themselves in war. The converted Bosnian nobles preserved their social privileges under the new rulers. Among the Turkish grand viziers in the sixteenth century there were nine from Bosnia and Hercegovina, and Serbo-Croatian became the diplomatic language of the Ottoman court.

On the other hand, the new rulers did not interfere much in the internal life of the peasants. They demanded strict allegiance to the state, and prompt fulfillment of all obligations toward it, but the serfs were left alone to live under their own tribal forms of social organization and with their own religion. As though in a deep freeze, these ancient forms of social organization survived in Bosnia and Hercegovina for several centuries until modern times.

The *zadruga*, a familial community, was the basis of the Bosnian patriarchal society. It was both an economic and a social institution. The means of production were owned communally. Relations within each *zadruga* were regulated on the basis of old custom, which contained elements of patriarchal democracy and mutual aid. The joint family's decisions were reached through communal discussion. Complete equality prevailed among the male members. Management of the property and the division of labor and equipment were organized communally. A *staresina*, or headman, was elected. He controlled, for instance, the division of labor after it had been laid down in general terms by the members of the *zadruga*. Control of property was collective.

The Princips had lived for centuries in a *zadruga* which survived until the childhood of Gavrilo Princip. One of his biographers has recorded that his grandfather, together with his sons, their wives and their children as well as his unmarried daughters, inhabited one house.[3] The Princips' *zadruga* in Grahovo Valley lived only a few miles from Tromedja, the Junction of Three Frontiers, those of the Ottoman Empire, the Habsburg Empire and the Venetian Republic. The Princips, who were of the Jovičević clan, came to Grahovo Valley at the beginning of the eighteenth century from the rock district of Grahovo in Montenegro. They first stopped on the other side of the Dinara Mountain in Dalmatia at Polača village and from there they moved to the Grahovo Valley. They settled as the *kmets* of the feudal lords Sijerčići.

The Grahovo region was organized as a kind of military frontier, known as a *kapetanija*. The commanders were the local Bosnian feudal lords, and the soldiers were Moslems. Some Christians were also admitted to an auxiliary military service known as *matrolozi*. Members of the Princip family joined one of these frontier guard units as early as the eighteenth century.[4] From their village of Obljalj to the little town of Grahovo, a few stone houses on a hill, was a distance of only a few miles. Grahovo had a company of soldiers from the nearby *kapetanija* and was a station of caravans carrying goods on strong Bosnian mountain ponies. Besides beating off attacks from Austrian and Venetian territories, the Princips had to protect their section of the frontier against brigands and smugglers. They were familiar with the wooded country around their village. Princips knew how to pick out the most likely place through which the marauding parties from the other side of the frontier would come. They would lay in ambush and wait. For that reason the Princips' ancestors received the name of *Čeka*, meaning "lying in wait."[5] Originally this was only a nickname; later it became the family surname.

The Princips were called by the name Čeka until the beginning of the last century, when they changed it to Princip.[6] One headman of the family was called Todor; he was a big, strong, evil-tempered man, always armed. The local beys had a high esteem for his capacity as a *matroloz;* when peace reigned on the frontier he engaged a little in trade and would ride on his white horse over the border to Dalmatia and bring back red Dalmatian wine. Božidar Tomić recorded that memories about him were still alive in the Grahovo Valley:

> In the rich costume of his own region, a silver breastplate, a cap with peacocks' feathers, a short musket and a big knife in his cummerbund, he always rode a white horse. . . . When drinking he would go berserk and anyone who came into conflict with him would remember him till his dying day. The story goes that once on the festival of Saint John he was drunk and rode his white stallion through a Catholic village, piercing with his long, sharp knife the low straw-roofed huts. He snatched up the most beautiful girl from this Catholic village and kept her at his home for some time. . . . Because of his giant build, his brilliant costume, and the fear he inspired in everybody, the Moslem beys nicknamed him "Princip." All the members of his family soon changed their old name of Čeka to Princip.[7]

The word "Princip" does not exist in the Serbo-Croatian or in the Turkish language. In all probability it came from Dalmatia, on the other side of the mountain from Grahovo. There the officials spoke Italian, since Dalmatia had been under Venetian rule until the time of Napoleon. Todor's nickname seems to have come from the Italian *principe,* meaning "prince," or "chief." Italian names and titles retained their original spelling in Serbo-Croatian documents, and South Slavs, not knowing Italian, would pronounce the middle *c* as "ts" and not as "ch." Tomić writes that the wild Todor, with his fine costume, impressed the Italians so much that they called him *il principe Bosniaco.*[8] But Wladyslaw Glück mentions the possibility that the name might have come from the German word *Prinz,* which was used in the Serbo-

house he may have built, any patch of garden that his industry may have cleared among the rocks, the *Aga* seizes at his pleasure. The ordinary dues, as paid by the *kmet* to the landowner are heavy enough. He has to pay a fourth part of the produce of the ground; to present him with one animal yearly, and a certain quantity of butter and cheese; to carry for him so many loads of wood; and if the *Aga* is building a house, to carry the materials for it; to work for him gratuitously whenever he pleases, and sometimes the *Aga* requisitions one of the *kmet*'s children, who must serve him for nothing; to make a separate plantation of tobacco, cultivate it, and finally warehouse the produce in his master's store; and to plough and sow so many acres of land, the harvest of which he must also carry to his master's barn. Finally, to lodge the *Aga* in his own house when required, and to provide for his horses and dogs.[16]

But the *kmet* was also taxed by the states. The principal tax in Hercegovina paid to the central government in Istanbul consisted of an eighth of all agricultural products. Its collection was farmed out to middlemen who would appear in the villages before the harvest was gathered to fix the value of the crops at a price which was usually higher than after harvest. The *kmets* had to accept their verdict without protest, because they did not have the right to harvest before the tax was paid, and the middlemen would simply stop the harvesting, leaving the crops to rot, if they did not get as much as they demanded. The police of the Turkish authorities, called *zaptije*, would help the middlemen to collect the taxes, very often resorting to brute force. Evans recorded:

In the heat of summer men are stripped naked and tied to a tree, smeared over with honey or other sweet stuff, and left to the tender mercies of the insect world. For winter extortion it is found convenient to bind people to stakes and leave them barefoot to be frost-bitten; or at other times they are thrust into a pigsty and cold water poured on them. A favourite plan is to drive a party of serfs up a tree or into a chamber, and then smoke them with green wood. Instances are recorded of Bosnian peasants being buried up to their heads in earth, and left to repent in leisure.[17]

But besides the principal tax, there existed other central government taxes: house and land tax; cattle tax (there were three kinds of cattle tax—the *Porez*, from fifteen to twenty piastres on every head of cattle; the *Resmi Agnam*, two piastres per head of sheep and goats; and the *Donuzia*, or hog tax); and a tax paid by Christians in lieu of military service and imposed on every male member of the family between the ages of one and eighty.

To these taxes paid to the state and the landlord must be added the *corvée*, which varied in different parts of the country. The *kmets* espe-

cially objected to forced labor on the landlords' estates. In some parts of
Bosnia all the adult members of the serfs' households or *zadruga*, male
and female, had to spend three days working on the estate of the lord.
Very often there was not enough work to be done, but the lords insisted that they report "even if the serfs carried sand from one heap to
another or even if they had to spend the whole day opening and closing
the main gate of the lord's house.[18] The serfs were bitterly against this
practice, because their young wives and daughters, during these three
days on the lord's estate, were very often forced to pleasure the lord
and his aides.

Evans recorded the seven demands the *kmets* of Nevesinje laid before a commission appointed by the central Turkish authorities to investigate their grievances:

1. That Christian girls and women should no longer be molested by the
   Turks.
2. That their churches should no longer be desecrated, and that free exercise
   of their religion should be accorded them.
3. That they should have equal rights with the Turks before the law.
4. That they should be protected from the violence of the *Zaptiehs*, the local
   gendarmerie.
5. That the tithe-farmers should take no more than they were legally entitled to, and that they should take it at the proper time.
6. That every house should pay in all only one ducat a year.
7. That no forced labour, either personal or by horses, should be demanded
   by the government; but that labour, when needed, should be paid for, as
   was the case all over the world.[19]

The uprising spread to western Bosnia in August 1875, although not
with such intensity and success as in Hercegovina. The cause of rebellion in Bosnia was the tax paid to the central Ottoman government. The
middlemen were harsh in their methods of collecting this tax. The
kmets, aroused by the news of rebellion in Hercegovina, offered resistance. At the same time they revolted against their own local feudal
lords, who reacted furiously, burning down villages and killing Christians, rebels and nonrebels alike.

The Princip family, like the rest, was affected by the rebellion. Their
home town Grahovo was in the midst of the rebel territory and formed
a stronghold for the insurgents, whose main camp, Crni Potoci (The
Black Brook), was just above the Princips' home and was described by
Evans as follows:

[It is] a gap in the rocks, which forms a kind of natural gateway to the
impregnable gorge in which the low wooden sheds of the insurgents' stationary camp are built. The position is splendid and from the heights about

opened out a glorious panorama of the now snow-strewn mountains of free Bosnia. The heights are singularly bare of vegetation, like the neighbouring rock wilderness of Dalmatia and the Dinaric Alps in general; but for the purpose of defence they are admirable. Here and there the precipitous ascent to the camp and the rocky ridges around are flanked with breastworks of stone, but such artificial defences are evidently a work of supererogation.[20]

At the beginning of the revolt the Princips were in a delicate situation. The grandfather of Gavrilo Princip, old Jovo, was, in the family tradition, serving as *zaptije*, a policeman of the Turkish authorities. Whether the Princips joined the rebellion at once is not clear. One writer has recorded that the insurgents burned down the old Princip house in Obljaj.[21] He does not say clearly whether they did this to frighten the Princips into joining them or for defensive purposes against the Turkish army units stationed in nearby Grahovo.

Other sources state that the male members of the Princips joined the rebels.[22] Grandfather Jovo was in the headquarters of the insurgents at Crni Potoci along with his brother Todo, a giant of a man, of the same stamp as the famous Todor Princip. Gavrilo Princip's father Petar was also for a time among the insurgents. There is no record that he distinguished himself, but his brother Ilija took part in several battles and was awarded a medal for his bravery by Prince Petar Karadjordjević, who came to Bosnia under the war name Petar Mrkonjić and later became King Petar of Serbia.

The women and children of the Princip family crossed the border and found refuge in Austrian territory, as did the families of all the insurgents. In 1877, Arthur Evans visited the refugee camps in which they were sheltered; he was even the guest for a day of the insurgents' company in which the elder Princips were serving.

In the Austrian territory around the town of Knin there were twelve thousand refugees from the region of Grahovo Polje and its immediate environment according to an article sent to the *Manchester Guardian* by Evans on February 8, 1877. They lived under appalling conditions. Some of them were still in caves on the border of Bosnia and Dalmatia when Evans visited them.

. . . [We] found an old Bosnian, who guided us by more difficult mountain paths to a lonely glen, where a torrent divides the Austrian from the Bosnian territory, and where, on the Christian side, we descried a series of caves in the rocky mountain side, to which we now made our way. Then indeed broke upon my sight such a depth of human misery as it has fallen to the lot of few living men to witness.

We crossed a small frozen cataract, and passed the mouths of two lesser caverns, toothed with icicles three feet long and over, and then we came to the mouth of a large cave, a great black opening in the rock, from which as we climbed up to it, crawled forth a squalid and half-naked swarm of women, children and old men, with faces literally eaten away with hunger and disease. A little way off was another smaller hole outside which leant what had once been a beautiful girl, and inside, amidst filth and squalor which I cannot describe since I saw it only dimly through smoke and darkness, lay a woman dying of typhus. Others crowded out of black holes and nooks, and I found that there were about thirty in this den. In another small hole, going almost straight down into the rock, I saw a shapeless bundle of rags and part of the pale half-hidden face of another woman stricken down by the disease of hunger; another den with about a dozen, and then another more horrible than any. A black hole, sloping downwards at so steep an angle as made climbing up or down a task of some difficulty, descended thus abruptly about thirty feet, and then seemed to disappear into the bowels of the earth. The usual haggard crowd swarmed out of the dark and foetid recesses below and climbed up to seek for alms . . . Then, slowly tottering and crawling from an underground lurking place at the bottom of the pit, there stumbled into the light an old man, so lean, so wasted, with such hollow sunken eyes, that he seemed nothing but a walking skeleton; it was the realisation of some ghastly medieval picture of the resurrection of the dead . . . Not far off we passed another cave, where the bodies of some women and children had been found.[23]

Visiting several groups of refugees, Evans was surprised to find that these people still lived in a tribal, patriarchal way.

Strange as it may seem, amidst all this horror and misery, the old Slavonic *zadruga,* or family communism, has been preserved. Every cavern has its house-father and house-mother, and they have carried their little constitution underground![24]

Evans noted the rich spiritual life of the Bosnians, which was much in evidence despite the material poverty of the *zadruga:*

I was much struck at the real parliamentary capabilities of these simple armed peasants in discussing their affairs. Each speaker in turn said what he had to say in a straightforward, businesslike manner, without any oratorical vagaries, and yet with a ready flow of speech which never hesitated. I cannot believe that a party of English farm labourers could have discussed their affairs with equal readiness. These people, it is true, cannot read or write, but they have in their rude way a kind of civilisation, and even education of their own . . . The people about here are, in fact, educated in many practical ways by the hardest of all task-mistresses—necessity. Every man here is capable of building his own house, though it is true he does not aspire to a high style of architecture; and every woman can make her own clothes. At the wretched hovel of Panšavoda I was much struck with the neatness of a set of earthenware pots which the family had just been making for themselves. Nor is the more aesthetic side of education altogether wanting. The music is rude, but everybody is a musician. Literature is altogether wanting, but the poetic lore of the Bosniacs and other Southern Slavs surpasses, perhaps, in extent that of any other European people. Historians these simple Bosniacs have not, but the past lives in their heroic lays, and has not history some need to be idealized among the children and great-grandchildren of bondsmen? In much of their dress these people display great taste; and, speaking generally of South Slavonic peasants, I should say that the beauty of their costume and brilliance of its colouring are not anywhere surpassed.[25]

Traveling through the Bosnian mountains, from one company of insurgents to the other, Evans came to the Unac village, only ten miles from the Princips. He gives his description of an evening with the Bosnians:

. . . We were received, as elsewhere, with military honours by a troop of about one hundred and fifty insurgents. We were now welcomed into the hut of the local Vojvodo, Simo Kralj, and here I passed an evening which carried one back to Homeric times. The evening meal was served, as elsewhere, on a round board, on which was first set a great bowl of boiled Indian corn, from which the assembled chieftains and their guests helped themselves by means of curiously ornamented wooden spoons. This was succeeded by lumps of mutton, which we picked off the board with our fingers, one at a time, and at intervals the host handed to each in turn a silver drinking cup of curiously antique shape filled to brimming with thick Dalmatian wine. The women and children, and those of less consequence, ate afterwards, and during the meal two women held torches of resinous pinewood above our heads. Then the "ghuzla," the national lyre, was brought out, and a venerable minstrel played and sang the songs of free Bosnia, for amongst this highly poetic people the insurrection has already its unwritten epics. Then I stretched myself with the others on the hay that had been strewn, as an unusual luxury, for our common couch, with my feet towards the embers, prepared to pass from cloudland into dreamland; and last of all the chieftain, with patriarchal ceremony spread a sheepskin over me against the small hours of the night.[26]

Evans visited the company of insurgents in which were the grandfather, father and uncle of Gavrilo Princip, and he wrote in 1877 that he came to this company in "a lovely spring" and found "the whole troop assembled on a grassy lawn engaged in athletic sports." He continued:

Of course, what could an Englishman do but join them? And really but for the outlandish costume of the "muscular Christians," one might just as well have been in the vale of the White Horse. First we had "metati"—nothing else, I can ensure you, than the good old English game of "putting the stone." The insurgents showed great strength but little skill—

> Bosnian born and Bosnian bred,
> Strong i' the arm and weak i' the head—

as certain also of our own poets hath said. At any rate, though I am by no means an athlete, I found that by a little judicious knack I could throw as far as the best, and felt rather like little Jack when he did the giant! Then we had football—a primitive football, with a ball compounded of insurgent caps, and with no goal in particular—but still football. Then there was another game of "chevy," the details of which are too long to describe here; but all these sports have a real significance. I believe that there is no other people in Europe endowed so largely with the English love of field sports as these much-maligned Southern Slavs; and surely it is a most hopeful sign . . . The night I passed in this camp was miserable enough, and made one realize the hardships these poor people must undergo. The pope's shed, where I slept or tried to sleep, was a typhus hospital, without doctors. But I had finished my investigations, and was glad to be off at a very early hour next morning.[27]

Evans in this dispatch mentions explicitly the leader of the insurgents from Grahovo Polje, the priest Ilija Bilbija, who came from the Princips' village and who some twenty years later christened and chose the name for Gavrilo Princip.

The local Orthodox priests were the leaders of some of the companies of insurgents, while the bishops of the Orthodox Church in Bosnia, as Evans recorded, were on the side of the Turks.[28] These bishops were Greek—Phanariotes from Istanbul. Up to 1774 the Bosnian Orthodox Church had been under the jurisdiction of the Serbian Patriarch of Peć, but when the Turks abolished the Serbian Patriarchate, Bosnia was placed under the Greek Patriarch of Istanbul. In order to get their appointment, the bishops had to bribe the Turkish authorities, and the sees would usually go to the highest bidders in Istanbul.[29]

Evans observed also a deep conflict between the different religious groups in the country:

The intolerance of all classes of the Bosnian population is the natural off-spring of the gross ignorance in which they were steeped, and it must be confessed that the want of education is largely due to the clerical character of the schools where they exist and to the malign teachings of *odium theologicum*. "The result of the present system," says a recent observer, "is evident and is fatal. The East Orthodox children under the Iguman, the Catholics under the Franciscan priest, the Mussulmans under the *Ulema*, go to school to learn to hate each other, and in fact this is the only lesson which as men they take care to remember."[30]

Evans described a typical example of the religious intolerance and terrorism practiced by the Moslem feudal lords against the Christians in a village near the Princips' home:

Whenever Tahir beg Kulenović visited the village he rode on horseback into the church, and profaned it. After that he was in the habit of dismounting and seizing the priest's vestments, he made them into a kind of saddle, set them on the priest's back, and then mounting on it himself, made the wretched pope crawl along on all fours and serve the purpose of a beast till the poor man sank with exhaustion.[31]

Yet all the Christians were not united in the rebellion. It was an elemental uprising against the oppression of the feudal landlords. In the towns, especially in Sarajevo, there was a large number of Christian merchants and artisans, particularly Eastern Orthodox Serbs, but they did not show much enthusiasm for helping the rebellious *kmets*. Evans did not have much esteem for them:

They are, in truth, a money-grubbing, unamiable lot, interested in their own well-being. Next to the Jews, they are the richest classes in Sarajevo— richer than the Turks, for the Mahometan is incapacitated by his fatalistic want of enterprize from taking part in any but small retail trades. The Serbs, on the contrary, hold in their hands most of the external commerce of the country. But they do not make use of the wealth thus obtained either to elevate themselves or to aid their oppressed countrymen who lie outside the pale of consular protection. On the contrary, they form themselves into an exclusive caste, not only standing apart from the miserable rayah, but even pooh-poohing his cry of agony when it happens to stand a chance of being heard by Foreign Consuls or the Turkish Governor.[32]

Not having much support in the towns, the insurgent *kmets* were left to themselves. There was no coordination between the units in Hercegovina and those in Bosnia. Because of the terrain and better organization, the rebellion in Hercegovina was more successful. At the beginning, in Hercegovina the insurgents were organized along tribal-territorial lines. In each company there existed from twenty to thirty men. Later these small units were developed into a more stable military organization. The major unit became "captaincies" composed of several "hundreds," which were subdivided into "tens." There were, all together, 12,000 armed insurgents. The Ottoman government did not have many units of the regular army in Hercegovina and had to bring them from other parts of the Empire. The insurgents' commanders applied a guerrilla strategy, cutting off communications between the Turkish garrisons and even besieging some towns, as they did at Trebinje. These tactics brought good results. Of the 30,000 Turkish soldiers sent to Hercegovina in 1875, at the end of the year only one half survived. At Muratovica, after two days of fighting, on October 30 and 31, 1875, the Turks lost 1,325 soldiers, 400 horses, one gun and much ammunition.

The situation in Bosnia was different. The rebels were less organized. They formed units according to the village system, and each unit fought for itself. Often their main targets were the estates of the landlords. They also retaliated against the Moslem villages, plundering everything they could lay their hands on. A few Serb officers came to help the Bosnian rebels, but they did not have much success against the stubbornness and isolationism of the local peasant commanders.

When the winter was over, fighting continued, and the rebels both in Hercegovina and Bosnia held their own against the Ottoman troops. In the summer of 1876 the Sultan sent to Sarajevo the veil of Mohammed's shrine in Mecca with new units of the Turkish regular army. Losing hope of crushing the uprising in Hercegovina, the Turkish commander concentrated his efforts against the Bosnians, particularly against their only stronghold at Crni Potoci. The final onslaught started in the summer of 1877. The military leader of the Bosnian kmets was Colonel Mileta Despotović, a regular officer who had no esteem for guerrilla warfare. He remained at the Crni Potoci stronghold, but the Turkish units outflanked him, crossing Austrian territory, and the bastion was overrun. A hundred and fifty insurgents lost their lives, and more than 1,500 rifles were seized. In this battle, the Turkish soldiers captured Todo Princip, brother of Gavrilo Princip's grandfather Jovo. Todo was dressed in the old colorful uniform of his ancestor. He was brought in chains to Grahovo, but was not executed as were many other captured kmets. The reasons for this reprieve are not clear. According to one story, it was because the Turkish authorities were so much impressed by his strength and his personality.[33] Again, it might have been that they had in mind the former service of the Princips as frontier guards.

Gavrilo Princip's grandfather and father, Petar, fled with the other insurgents to Austrian territory, where they were disarmed. They joined their families, who had escaped earlier. The plight of the civil population was worsening rapidly. Of the more than 750,000 Christians living in Bosnia and Hercegovina, 250,000 (children, women, and aged men), it has been estimated, had to leave their homes and find refuge in Austro-Hungarian, Montenegrin and Serbian territory.[34]

The defeat at Crni Potoci did not mean the end of the rebellion in Bosnia. Other village companies were still operating around their burned-down homes. Also, many disarmed kmets on the Austrian side of the border—among them was Gavrilo Princip's grandfather—returned to Bosnia, reorganized their units and continued to harass the Moslems. Thus at the end of 1877 the situation on the military fields of Bosnia and Hercegovina was still unchanged; Istanbul was unable, despite all efforts, to cope with the guerrilla tactics of the rebels. On the other hand, the insurgents could not take the towns and achieve a complete victory. It was a stalemate, with no end in sight.

CHAPTER IV

THE CONGRESS
OF BERLIN

To me this sounds like the first cry of the cock
in the morning of a new day, full of blood,
which will bring deep mourning to humanity.
—JOSEF FREIHERR VON SCHWEGEL, diary entry.

BOSNIA AND HERCEGOVINA stepped into the limelight of international politics with the revolt of the *kmets* in 1875. For more than three hundred years the two provinces had been under Ottoman rule, playing virtually no part in European affairs. But the 1875–78 rebellion sparked off fierce controversy in the capitals of the great powers, who were keenly interested in anything affecting the gradual dissolution of the Ottoman Empire. In 1876 Montenegro and Serbia declared war on Istanbul, in support of their kinfolk, and Russia joined them six months later, her troops advancing across the Balkan Mountains to the outskirts of the Ottoman capital. Britain reacted by moving her fleet into the Straits, while Austria-Hungary mobilized, and Russia had to fall back. As a result, the Berlin Congress was convened, and the future of Bosnia and Hercegovina became one of the main bargaining points among the great powers as they argued over the division of the Ottoman possessions.

At the time of the Hercegovinian uprising, the state of affairs in most of the other parts of the Ottoman Empire did not differ much from that which existed in Bosnia and Hercegovina. The Ottoman state was identified with its feudal-military ruling caste. Unwilling and unable to reorganize itself, the Empire was in its last days. The *kmets'* rebellion increased unrest in Bulgaria and other provinces of European Turkey

where Ottoman rule was challenged by the aspirations of rising nationalities. Of 9,669,000 subjects in the European part of the Ottoman Empire, there were only about 2,000,000 Turks; in the whole Empire, of
28,500,000 inhabitants, only about 12,000,000 were Turks. The sovereignty of the Sultan stretched from Tunisia in Africa, across Libya and
Egypt, through the Arabian Peninsula, the Levant and Turkey in Asia,
and in Europe as far as the Danubian Principalities in the north and
Bosnia and Hercegovina in the west. But effective control by the Istanbul government in the days of the *kmets'* rebellion did not extend far
beyond their capital. The financial situation of the Empire was equally
bad. In 1875 the Istanbul government proclaimed partial, and in 1876
total, bankruptcy, and the payment of interest to creditors in Paris,
Vienna, London and other European financial centers was suspended.
The Ottoman state debt before 1875 was 200 million pounds, involving
an annual charge of 14 million pounds.[1] The yearly income of the Empire was 18 million pounds, of which the Sultan received 2 million
pounds for his personal expenses.

The weakening of the Ottoman Empire sharpened the hunger of the
great powers for its Balkan provinces. They formed a land bridge between Europe and Asia and their importance had increased with the
opening of the Suez Canal in 1869. Moreover, the Balkans were rich in
natural resources and provided a growing market for the goods of expanding European industries.

Among the contenders for filling the vacuum caused by the disintegration of the Ottoman Empire were not only the great powers,
Austria-Hungary, Russia, Britain and Italy, but also the small Balkan
states—Serbia and Montenegro—which had achieved a degree of autonomy before the 1875 Bosnian uprising.

Austria-Hungary had been checked in the west and in the north by
her defeats in Italy in 1859 and in Bohemia in 1866; in the 1870's,
then, she turned her attention to the south. Military circles in Vienna
urged the occupation of Bosnia and Hercegovina and other South Slav
provinces in the direction of Salonika. As early as 1856, Field Marshal
Radetzky had presented a memorandum to Emperor Franz Josef drawing his attention to the necessity of the occupation of these two South
Slav lands because they were the natural hinterland for Dalmatia,[2] a
South Slav province on the Adriatic Sea annexed by Austria after the
downfall of Napoleon. The British *Annual Register* recorded from
Vienna that Franz Josef believed it was necessary "to accede to an occupation of Bosnia and Hercegovina, or even to press further south."[3]
His conviction was attributed "first of all to his alliance with Germany,
which while it lasts makes Austria unassailable; and secondly, to his
reputation as a Habsburg who lost great provinces. He wants to die
without having injured the grand estate of the House. There can be no
objection in the West to his arrangement."[4]

The main lines of communication in the Balkans, the valleys of the

Morava and Vardar rivers, were regarded in Vienna as of vital importance. In 1870 Baron Moritz Hirsch, an enterprising financier backed by Viennese and French banks, intensified his plans for building railways through the Ottoman Empire.[5] The Orient line was partly built from Istanbul to Philippopolis; Baron Hirsch was anxious to extend it to the north via Macedonia and Serbia and link it with the Austro-Hungarian railway system. Austria-Hungary had commercial ambitions in the Balkans. Cheaper English goods had almost replaced those of the Habsburg monarchy in the markets of the Ottoman Empire. Bosnia and Hercegovina, particularly, aroused interest in industrial circles.* Bosnian gold, silver, lead and iron mines were known even in Roman times. Half of Bosnia was covered by forests of beech, oak and fir. Deposits of coal and iron ore had just been discovered. In addition to these resources, Bosnia and Hercegovina had an abundance of labor. In February 1875 the General Staff of the Austro-Hungarian Army had the whole terrain of the two provinces and even south of them as far as northern Albania thoroughly explored. At the same time, special units of the army were prepared for operations in the Balkans.

The new Austro-Hungarian foreign policy clashed with Russia's hopes of penetrating to the warmer seas through the Balkans. Just on the eve of the Hercegovinian crisis, the *Dreikaiserbündis* ("Three-Emperor Alliance") of Germany, Russia and Austria, was concluded. They agreed to discuss mutually all difficulties connected with the settlement of the Eastern question. Another important objective of this alliance was a common struggle against the revolutions, which were menacing all monarchies. Before the *Dreikaiserbündnis* was concluded, Vienna and St. Petersburg had had other agreements concerning spheres of influence in the Balkans. Emperor Joseph II had exchanged a number of letters with Empress Catherine the Great and concluded the so-called "Greek Project," on the basis of which the Balkans would be divided between Austria and Russia. The two sovereigns had met at Yalta in 1787 and discussed this grandiose plan in detail; but other European powers interested in commerce with the Levant, particularly England and the Netherlands, preferred the *status quo*, and the Ottoman Empire survived this threat.

But in the 1870's Austria and Russia were suspicious of each other. On the eve of the Hercegovinian uprising in April 1875, Emperor Franz Josef made a journey through Dalmatia, only a few miles from the borders of Bosnia and Hercegovina. Many Catholics from the two

---

* The natural wealth of Bosnia and Hercegovina did not escape the sharp eye of Sir Arthur Evans. In an article in the *Manchester Guardian*, November 25, 1878, discussing this matter with a Czech statesman in Prague, he stated: "Surely foreign capital will come to your aid in developing the marvelous resources of the country as soon as they are generally known. English capital has only been deterred hitherto from working, for instance, the rich quicksilver mines of Kresevo by Turkish maladministration."

provinces, headed by their Franciscan friars, crossed the frontier and paid homage to the Habsburg emperor. On the other hand, the Slavophile organizations in Russia increased their demand for a more active policy in the Balkans.

As at the end of the eighteenth century, England was strongly in favor of preserving the *status quo* in the Balkans. Prime Minister Disraeli brought troops from India to the Near East; he was resolved to maintain the territorial integrity of the Ottoman Empire at all costs, since it protected the British Empire's interests in the Mediterranean and safeguarded her direct access to India. In the days of the Hercegovinian uprising, Disraeli succeeded in passing through Parliament the Royal Titles bill, by which Queen Victoria was proclaimed Empress of India. At the same time, Disraeli bought from the Khedive of Egypt, who was in financial difficulties, the majority of the shares of the Suez Canal Company.

In defense of his Eastern policy, Disraeli advanced the argument of legitimism. From deep Tory convictions, he was opposed to any concessions by the Istanbul government to the insurgents in Bosnia and Hercegovina. In a personal letter to Lady Bradford, he wrote on October 1, 1875: "Fancy autonomy for Bosnia, with a mixed population: autonomy for Ireland would be less absurd, for there are more Turks in proportion to Christians in Bosnia than Ulster v. the three other provinces."[6] R. W. Seton-Watson believed "that Disraeli and Lord Derby opposed anything like full autonomy for Bosnia-Hercegovina and even the more modest reforms urged by Count Andrassy upon the Turks— and this not on the merits of the case, but simply because they saw an analogy between the details of land reform in Bosnia and the demands put forward in Ireland and were afraid to create a precedent."[7] Moreover, Disraeli was badly briefed by his ambassador in Istanbul and his consuls in Bosnia and Hercegovina on the population of the two provinces. According to the official census of 1879, the Christians numbered more than 61 per cent of the population, while the 38.7 per cent who were Moslems were almost all South Slav by race. Disraeli was also against Montenegro and Serbia increasing their territories. "As for Montenegro, it has got about that Russia is intriguing for a port under the pretence of increasing the territory of Montenegro. No such thing: we renounce the idea. Montenegro need have no port, only a little garden to grow cabbages and potatoes."[8]

Disraeli saw the agitation of secret societies as the main cause of Balkan unrest. When Serbia declared war on the Ottoman Empire in the summer of 1876, Disraeli stated in the House of Lords, "Serbia declared war upon Turkey. That is to say, the secret societies of Europe declared war upon Turkey."[9]

Like Freemasonry lodges and the Carbonari or Mazzini's Young Italy in the time of the Risorgimento, and like similar societies in Germany and Ireland during their struggles for national liberation, the secret societies in the Balkans flourished under despotism. Having no other way to express their views, the people found their outlet in secret societies. There were many different kinds of societies. Some sprang from local initiative; some were initiated from abroad, since revolutionary movements as well as the chancelleries of the great powers had their specific interests in the Balkans. For instance, in the second and third decades of the nineteenth century, *Hetaira,* a Christian secret society, had appeared in the Balkans, aiming at establishing a kind of a new Byzantine Empire there. It had support in Russia, and among its members were some of the leading figures in Rumania, Greece, Bulgaria and Serbia.

The South Slav secret societies in Bosnia and Hercegovina are of particular interest. After the Polish uprising of 1830–31, many Poles emigrated to France. Among them was Prince Adam Jerzy Czartoryski, who had been at the beginning of the nineteenth century the foreign minister of the Russian Tsar Alexander I. He was in office in 1804, during the uprising of the *kmets* in Serbia against Ottoman rule. Under the influence of an Italian Carbonaro named Scipione Piattoli, Czartoryski at that time suggested the formation of independent Slav states in the Balkans under Russian protection. Czartoryski later came into conflict with the Tsar, particularly after the Polish uprising of 1830–31. In Paris, Czartoryski opened a Diplomatic Bureau in the Hotel Lambert, with the political and financial aid of the French and English governments.[10] Oppressors of Poland were its three traditional enemies: Russia, Austria and Prussia. Neither France nor England was on friendly terms with these three powers, and Czartoryski accepted their help. He was aware that the Ottoman Empire was doomed, but his schemes were designed so that Russia and Austria should not benefit from its dissolution. He revived his idea of independent Balkan states, which would rely in their struggle for independence not on Russia or Austria but on France and England.

Czartoryski had secret agents in all the Balkan countries, and to one of them, Zwierkowski-Lenoir, he wrote that Serbia "should be the legitimate banner of all South Slavs, the center around which all others should gather." Czartoryski came into contact, through his agents, with Ilija Garašanin, a Serbian conservative statesman, whose political group was at odds with the Russian government in 1842 over internal questions of Serbian politics. The ideas of Czartoryski seemed acceptable to Garašanin. Further contacts followed and in January 1843, Czartoryski sent Garašanin his *savete,* or counsels, on how Serbia should conduct its foreign policy. He advised Garašanin that Serbia should be careful in her relations with Russia and particularly not to ask for patronage, "because the patron might become easily the master."[11] Czartoryski also warned Garašanin against any provocation against Russians—"they are our brothers by race, and one day they might become the allies of all

Slavs by rebelling against their own despotism."[12] Czartoryski was of the opinion that Belgrade should trust Austria even less, as she "wants to use the first possibility to occupy Serbia and other lands in the Balkans."[13] Czartoryski warmly urged Serbia to rely on France and England. "France has an interest in helping the Slavs in the Balkans. When the decaying Ottoman Empire comes to an end, in its place a Slav state could become the ally of France."[14] In the meantime, Serbia should adopt toward the Ottoman Empire a policy of compromise, of biding time. Czartoryski and his agents advised Garašanin to form in all the South Slav provinces a chain of secret societies, headed by *poverenici*— "men of trust"—to be ready for the final crisis of the Ottoman Empire.

Finding in Czartoryski's counsel support for his own ideas about Serbian foreign policy, Garašanin produced in 1844 a secret document called *Načertanije*, which he wrote for the Serbian prince, Alexander Karadjordjević.[15] This document became the program of Serbia's foreign policy for many generations to come. It was fully realized at the beginning of the twentieth century, when England finally changed its Disraelian course and came to the conclusion that an independent Serbia would not mean the strengthening of the Russian position in the Balkans.

Garašanin revised some of Czartoryski's original proposals. First, he was not so hostile toward Russia; he even envisaged a rapprochement with Russia against the Ottoman Empire and Austria. Secondly, instead of a Yugoslav program, the formation of a federative state of all the South Slavs, Garašanin declared himself for a pan-Serb solution, a state which would be only an enlarged Serbia, dominated by the Serbs. Thirdly, he was for revolutionary action in Turkey, but not in Austria.[16] Garašanin concentrated his efforts primarily on Bosnia and Hercegovina, which he regarded as Serb provinces, building his chain of secret societies composed of *poverenici*. They were financed from Belgrade, and their main task was gathering intelligence for the Serbian government in preparation for the day when the Serbian army would march into Bosnia. These secret societies were not of a revolutionary character. Garašanin was as conservative in his internal politics as Prince Mihailo Obrenović, who came to the Serbian throne in 1860 and increased preparations for war against the Ottoman Empire. The *poverenici* did not envisage an improvement of the social position of the *kmets*. Garašanin even tried hard to enlist the support of the Moslem feudal lords in Bosnia and Hercegovina and gave them the express guarantee that after the expulsion of the Turks and the establishment of Serbian rule, their feudal estates and their powers over the *kmets* would be safeguarded.[17]

In 1867 Garašanin resigned, and a year later Prince Mihailo Obrenović was killed in the Topčider Park near Belgrade. Although the assassination was carried out by followers of the Karadjordjević dynasty, both Turkey and Austria-Hungary were heavily involved in it. Slobodan Jovanović, historian of nineteenth-century Serbia, thinks that Turkey was directly guilty of the assassination[18] while Austria-Hungary allowed its territory to be used by the conspirators. The court in Belgrade found Alexander Karadjordjević, who lived in Budapest, guilty of the plot and sentenced him to twenty years' imprisonment. The Serbian government asked the Hungarian government to prosecute Prince Alexander. In the first instance, the Budapest court dropped the charges on the basis of "insufficient proof." However, a court of appeal then found him guilty and sentenced him to eight years in jail, on the grounds that he procured the weapons and money for the assassins. But with the deterioration of relations with Serbia, the Supreme Court of Hungary reversed this sentence and confirmed the original judgment.[19]

After Prince Mihailo's death, secret activity of the Serbian government in Bosnia and Hercegovina ceased; the initiative was left in the hands of private individuals. Yet the outbreak of rebellion in 1875 greatly stirred public opinion in Serbia, and the new ruler, Prince Milan Obrenović, was under pressure to march across the frontier into Bosnia. He was reluctant to do so at the beginning. At last, when he decided to come to the help of the rebels in Bosnia and Hercegovina, he was careful to emphasize that his action had no revolutionary character, in order to reassure conservative circles in London and other capitals.[20]

But besides the groups of *poverenici* there were other secret societies working in Bosnia and Hercegovina before the 1875 uprising. While the *poverenici* were the undercover agents of the conservative Serbian government, the other secret societies were more liberal, and some of them were revolutionary. These sprang up in the atmosphere of the Polish uprising of 1863 and the successful Italian and German struggles for unification in 1860. The first nuclei of these secret societies appeared among a few South Slav students at universities in Europe, principally in Austria. Their activities were not always clandestine; they were skilled in the use of cover organizations, like the society of Serbian students in Vienna called Zora, which performed a similar task for Princip and his secret societies in the 1900's. In 1866 Zora issued an appeal to sixteen Serbian youth societies in Austria and Hungary, as well as those in Serbia and other capitals of Europe, to attend a constitutional meeting of Ujedinjena Omladina Srpska (United Serbian Youth). The society was officially formed the same year. It resembled the German *Burschenschaft* and *Jugendbund*, the Greek *Hetaira* and Young Italy secret societies.[21] Although officially it was an educational society, it had revolutionary tasks and had its open and secret groups in all South Slav lands, including Bosnia and Hercegovina. One of its leaders, Vladimir Jovanović, had contacts with Mazzini even before the organization of Ujedinjena Omladina.[22] Both Italian and Magyar revolutionaries, in the period between 1860 and 1867, followed the events in Bosnia and Hercegovina with interest. The leader of the Hercegovinian uprising of 1861–62, Luka Vukalović, was acquainted with the revolutionary designs of the Italians and the Magyars against the Habsburgs.[23] Garibaldi was scheming to have his men in Dalmatia provoke a revolution in the Balkans. On the eve of the 1866 war against Austria, Mazzini said to Vladimir Jovanović that Italy should not rely on France in her struggle against the Habsburgs, but on the South Slavs under Vienna's rule. Revolutions were to have started simultaneously in Venice and in the Balkan provinces of Austria; the Magyar revolution which was to follow would have brought about the end of the Habsburgs. At that time even Bismarck was interested in these plans and concluded a "gentlemen's agreement with Mazzini."[24] He was preparing for his final battle against the Habsburgs and was ready to accept any allies he could find, despite his conservatism. But after his success in 1866 he quickly broke off these dangerous links. Jovanović came into contact with the Belgrade government and transmitted to them Mazzini's suggestions, but Prince Mihailo was reluctant to act, and he lost the opportunity to play a part in the 1866 events and in the defeat of the Habsburgs.[25]

Ujedinjena Omladina was not a unified organization. It was composed of many different elements, and it soon ceased to work, except for its most radical wing, headed by Svetozar Marković, a writer and socialist from Belgrade. As a student Marković went to Russia in 1866 and joined a secret society of Serbian students called Opština, which was in contact with Ujedinjena Omladina. In 1868, Marković published in a Belgrade paper an open letter addressed to Serbian youth, inviting them to be ready for the given hour, "to learn the sciences which will destroy the enemy's force, to train in weapons," and to look always to "the subjugated South Slavs."[26] From Russia Marković went to Switzerland, taking part in a congress of the League for Peace and Liberty. He met Victor Hugo, but was not much impressed by the League except in its attitude toward the Balkans—the League declared itself for the revolutionary liberation of the Balkan peoples and for the formation of a federative republic of the Slavs. Marković also made contact with Mikhail Bakunin, the Russian anarchist and one of the founders of the First International. When the Russian section of the First International was formed, Marković became its "agent-correspondent" and published several articles on Balkan affairs in the bulletin of the International.[27] Marković accused Vladimir Jovanović and other leaders of Ujedinjena Omladina of being too lenient toward the Serbian government.

Marković had accepted much of the teachings of Nikolai Chernishevsky and Pyotr Lavrov, Russian revolutionary writers of that time. Among Western European socialists he did not find much interest in the problems of the peasantry, which represented a vast majority of Serbia's population, or the problems of subjugated small nations. On the other hand, he found more understanding of these problems in Russia. Marković believed that the Russian socialism of the 1860's was far ahead of the socialism of Western Europe. He wrote:

The Russian movement is older than the European; its beginnings are to be sought in the days of Stenka Razin and Pugachev, in the peasant uprisings for land and freedom. The principles of integral Russian socialism are fuller, especially as far as family and religion are concerned, than those of the International, which are limited solely to political and economic issues. Russian revolutionary principles are more radical than those of the International. No doubt the Russians were influenced by the European doctrines and revolutionary ideas of 1789 and 1848, but they elaborated them further and brought out many new and original ideas. Today the Russian revolutionaries with their passionate hatred of the Establishment, with their radical views on marriage and God, horrify even the most radical members of the International, especially in Germany, where the sacredness of marriage and religiosity are deeply rooted among the people. There is no country in Europe with so deep a spiritual upheaval, with so much intellectual passion, as exist among the Russians. In no country is such attention devoted to the social sciences as in Russia. Today Russia has as many scientific experts in socialism as the whole of Europe taken together.[28]

At the end of this article Marković stated a practical reason why in Serbia priority had to be given to Russian socialism over European: "Serbs as Slavs have the same spiritual inclinations as Russians . . . Russian socialism is made for Russian conditions, for the Russian peasant, and owing to the fact that Serbia is in the same economic position, the only socialism which is possible and which could be realized in Serbia is Russian socialism." [29]

In his agitation Marković preached that the Serbs could not achieve their liberation from the Ottoman Empire and the Habsburgs unless they first gained their internal liberty from conservatism in Serbia. He also declared himself for the equality of all South Slav peoples and against the idea that Serbia should be a "Piedmont of the South Slavs," as the Belgrade government advocated. He stressed that there existed a marked difference between the Balkans, where there were several nationalities, religions and races, and the Apennine peninsula, where there was only one race, one religion and one nation. Therefore his aim was a republican federation of the Balkan peoples.

Marković demanded the destruction of both the Ottoman and the Habsburg empire:

We are not afraid to provoke the enmity of Austria-Hungary, because we know that she is our enemy like Turkey. We are not afraid of her, because we think that she cannot do anything against us. She will become weaker in the future as among her subjugated national groups the idea grows that an Austrian state, whether federative or nonfederative is completely unnecessary. . . . In order to solve the problem of nationalities in Austria in a real sense, we must destroy the Habsburg monarchy, which was patched up on the basis of marriages, inheritance and secret leagues, and which only survived thanks to the lies of the Jesuits and the brute force of a professional soldiery.[30]

He believed that both the Habsburg and the Ottoman Empire could be destroyed by a revolution of the South Slavs and other subjugated nationalities. When he had to leave Serbia in 1872, he went to Novi Sad, a center for the Serbs under Magyar rule. Ujedinjena Omladina in the meantime had been banned by the Budapest government, but some of its members, headed by the leader of the radical Serbs in Novi Sad, S. Miletić, founded a secret society called Družina za Ujedinjenje i Oslobodjenje Srpsko (Brotherhood for Serbian Unification and Liberation). Its task was to foment a rebellion in Hercegovina and then in Bosnia.[31] Marković came into direct contact with this secret society and helped its work. Through his brother, he even approached some of the leading statesmen in Belgrade, proposing the formation of a coalition of all Serbian progressive parties for the purpose of helping an uprising in Bosnia and Hercegovina. But the Belgrade government was afraid of such an action, particularly because of the attitude of the Russian Tsar Alexander II.[32] After that failure, Marković organized a new secret society called Centralni Revolucionarni Oslobodilački Odbor (Central Revolutionary Liberation Committee), whose sympathizers in Bosnia distinguished themselves in the 1875 uprising.[33]

Marković exchanged views with his friends among the Russian Populists about affairs in the Balkans. Althouch Marković himself died on the eve of the 1875 uprising, the Russian revolutionaries showed a marked interest in the rebellion, as had been the case in previous uprisings of South Slavs against Ottoman rule. Professor Jovan Skerlić has pointed out that Russian revolutionary circles cherished the idea of Slav solidarity a long time before it became the official line of the Slavophiles and, from time to time, of the Tsarist government. The Decembrists, in the midst of their own struggle against absolutism at home, had developed a program for the liberation of all Slavs from tyranny and for their unification through a free, federative union, based on a democratic constitution.[34] Revolutionaries from the Obshchestva Soedinjenih Slovjan (Society of United Slavs) energetically attacked the Tsarist government for neglecting the fate of the Balkan Slavs, principally the Serbs, "our faithful allies who are suffering under the yoke of Turkish brutality."[35] In 1847 the secret society Kirilo-Metodiyevsko Bratstvo (Brotherhood of Cyril and Methodius), whose members included the historian Nikolai Kostomarov and the poet Taras

Shevchenko, had asked for "the liberation of Slav peoples from foreign rule," their organization on a free federative basis, and the liquidation of "all forms of tyranny in Slav societies regardless of how cleverly disguised."[36]

Russian Populists made a distinction between the official policy of the state and the feelings of solidarity among the Russian masses for their Slav brothers in the Balkans. In the eighteenth and nineteenth centuries Imperial Russia waged nine wars under the slogan of "liberation of Slavs with the same blood and the same religion." Vasili Bogucharski has pointed out that "the Russian peasant had the same ideas about the liberation of the South Slavs as the crusaders had about the liberation of Jerusalem."[37] Bogucharski stressed the real motives of official circles in Russia on this issue. One of the Russian conservatives, Mikhail Katkov, looked at the South Slav question and a war with Turkey as a good way of combating the revolutionary movement at home. A leader of the Slavophiles, Konstantin Pobedonostsev, "the Jesuit among the Jesuits," translated William Gladstone's pamphlet on the Turkish atrocities, and General Mikhail Skobelev, the "Torquemada of modern Russia," expressed the idea that "Nihilism could be paralyzed and even uprooted by the fomenting of a war under patriotic slogans."[38]

Populists not only denounced the policies of Tsarists and the Slavophiles toward the Balkan Slavs, but at the same time gave their own support to the 1875 uprising. Skerlić recorded that the Russian Populist Michael Sazhin, who worked under the alias Armand Ross with Marković and his friends in Zurich, came to Bosnia and Hercegovina as a volunteer as soon as the uprising started.[39] Skerlić cited also the names of Sergei Kravchinsky, Dmitri Klements, editor of the clandestine paper *Zemlya i Volya*, and Eroshenko, who was killed fighting in Hercegovina. Bogucharski mentioned also the names of Ivan Debagori-Mokrayevich, Orest Gebel, Sergei Nechayev, and Pimen Enkuvatov. In 1875 a secret committee was formed in southern Russia among the Populists, which collected money and sent volunteers. One of its members was Zhelyabov, a leader of Narodnaya Volya, and one of the chief organizers of the assassination of Tsar Alexander II, on March 1, 1881.[40] Bogucharski interviewed V. F. Kostyurin, one of the members of this secret committee, who said the arrival of the first seven volunteers sent from Kiev to the Hercegovinian *kmets* was "enthusiastically greeted."[41] F. Venturi is not of that opinion, particularly as far as Ross (Sazhin) and Kravchinsky were concerned. They left Paris and came to Zagreb, where "there was a committee which provided the volunteers with arms and which helped them to cross the frontier at Dubrovnik (Ragusa) and Kotor (Cattaro). In Hercegovina they were involved in a few clashes, but their military experiences were short-lived. Like many other Russian volunteers, they were forced to admit that it was not

easy to enter a situation so new for them and adapt themselves to partisan warfare in the mountains of Dalmatia. By the time they returned
they had been completely disillusioned as to the social character of the
war. 'Religious fanaticism and love of looting'—this was what they had
seen."[42]

Svetozar Marković's followers in the Bosnian and Hercegovinian
uprisings were also aware of the difficulty of spreading their ideas
among the rebellious *kmets*. Their influence was much stronger in
northwest Bosnia than in Hercegovina, where Kravchinsky and Ross
went. Vaso Pelagić, Ugrinić and Horvaćanin, all three Socialists,
were recognized as the leaders of the uprising in northwest Bosnia.
Pelagić in his history of the 1875–78 uprising did not mention Ross
or Kravchinsky, although he spoke about the Russian volunteers. As
early as 1874 Pelagić had written a "message to the friends of the
subjugated brothers in Turkey," in which he stated that "freedom
can be achieved only by the liquidation of private property, estates,
and the entire unjust social organization of today." He called for
complete local self-government, the introduction of a jury system in
the courts, the egalitarian principle as far as salaries were concerned,
and an end to the professional army.[43]

When the uprising broke out, he prepared a document called
"Ustaško vjerovanje ili Narodno Jevandjelje" ("Insurgents' Charter
or People's Gospel"), a kind of constitution, which was to be adopted
in the event of victory. In his book on the uprising, Pelagić wrote
that this document was accepted at a meeting of several insurgent
companies (Kozaračka, Pastirevačka, Risovačka, Grmečka), "which
gave their blood oath that they would work seriously for the realization as a law of the said liberties and rights, as expressed at the meeting,
during the uprising and, after victory, in peacetime."[44]

Yet Marković's followers were not able to exercise any decisive
influence over the *kmets*, whose only goal was to rid themselves of
their feudal yoke. Vaso Pelagić also complained bitterly about the
interference of Serbian and Montenegrin dynasties in the uprising.
For Serbia's Obrenovićes as well as for Montenegro's Petrovićes the
events of 1875 were only an occasion for the advancement of the
glory of their dynasties. They had competition from the exiled
Karadjordjević dynasty as well. Prince Petar Karadjordjević was in
Bosnia with his company of *kmets*. Pelagić lamented such a state of
affairs:

This great people's uprising had just started, when different dynasties
through their lackeys tried by force, money or fair words to influence the
insurgents to proclaim this or that king as their sovereign; they were even
asked to shout the name of their candidate-king during the onslaught against
the Turks, and only if that had been done, did help come. That was the

reason why the insurgents, sons of the same people, started to quarrel among themselves, to fight and even murder one another. . . . Among the Bosnian insurgents the secret agents of seven states were intriguing, blackmailing and dividing people, four of whom were of Slav descent, and three non-Slav. With one of these Slav states the insurgents were eager to cooperate under special conditions, while they maintained contact with other states only because they were pressed to do so.[45]

Pelagić also recorded the importance of the help given by the Italian secret societies to the Hercegovinian rebels: "Among the non-Slav volunteers the greatest number were from Italy, all Garibaldi republicans and socialists. Passing through Kotor, Dubrovnik and Belgrade, they shouted in Italian 'Long live Garibaldi! Long live the Commune!' "[46] Garibaldi sent greetings to the leaders of the uprising and his special military envoy visited the battlefield in Hercegovina. He also sent a public letter to a London committee for the support of the insurgents. There were many volunteers in the uprising in Hercegovina and Bosnia; the Italians had their own brigade, composed almost entirely of Socialist Revolutionaries. One of them, Barbanti Brodano, wrote a book about his experiences.[47] Enrico Malatesta, one of the leading revolutionary figures in Italy, was among those who joined the rebels in Hercegovina. There existed other secret and public liberal societies which helped the insurgents' cause. Many committees for insurgents' relief operated in Italy, Russia, Britain, France, Austria-Hungary, Serbia, and even in northern Germany and the United States. A part of their activity was public. One of the most important relief committees operated in Dubrovnik from 1875 to 1878. It was the Comitato Secreto, headed by Pero Čingrija. Similar committees were set up in Trieste, Zadar, Vienna, Rome, Paris, London, Prague and elsewhere. The Austrian government officially announced its neutrality in the Hercegovinian uprising, but it did not hamper the work of the Comitato Secreto. The aid reached considerable proportions and took several forms: ammunition, food, clothing, money, and foreign volunteers. A Comitato Dame (Ladies' Committee) helped take care of the refugees, sick and wounded.[48]

The eastern crisis reached its climax in March 1878, when Russia, after her victory over the Turkish troops, dictated terms of the San Stefano Peace Treaty. Both Britain and Austria-Hungary regarded Russia's action as a threat to the balance of power. Bismarck was on the side of Austria-Hungary. Faced with this reaction and exhausted by a war that had cost heavily in blood and materials, Russia was obliged to give way and agree to submit the terms of the San Stefano Treaty to the consideration of a European congress. This was to convene in Berlin in June 1878.

Prior to this meeting, diplomatic negotiations proceeded with threats and counterthreats, while military preparations were not relaxed on either side. The great powers tended to negotiate with one another separately, without informing their partners in the struggle for the division of the Ottoman Empire. First an Anglo-Russian secret agreement was made, then an Anglo-Austrian one. Disraeli promised "to support any proposition with respect to Bosnia which Austria should make at the Congress,"[49] but Austria had to give assurances that she would back England against Russia, particularly in her design for the formation of a Greater Bulgaria and her claims in Asia. In addition, England undertook to influence Turkey to give up Bosnia and Hercegovina. Disraeli took advantage of the weakened position of the Ottoman Empire and in a secret convention of June 4 succeeded in obtaining Cyprus, thus greatly strengthening the strategic position of the British Empire in the Near East. The Sultan consented to assign the island to English occupation and administration. Turkey retained nominal sovereignty in Cyprus, while Britain agreed to pay a tribute of £98,000 per year for the use of the island. In return for French support over Cyprus, Disraeli agreed to countenance a French occupation of Tunisia, another province nominally under the Sultan's suzerainty. The negotiations between Russia and Austria-Hungary were more complicated; Russia gave consent to the Ottoman cession of Bosnia and Hercegovina to Austria-Hungary, but would not countenance Austrian expansion in Macedonia and Albania.

At the same time, Prince Bismarck, on the basis of the *Dreikaiserbündnis*, offered to mediate not only between the other two members of his alliance, Russia and Austria-Hungary, but between England and Russia as well. His heart was on Austria-Hungary's side. He thought that Vienna's engagement in the Balkans would be compensation for the losses she had suffered on her northern borders in 1866. Bismarck made this clear to the Habsburg heir apparent in the spring of 1878: "We should arm ourselves before the Congress in order to to be able to help you with arms in the case of any resistance by Russia. Germany will help Austria-Hungary not only morally, but also with effective forces." On May 5, 1878, he wrote to his ambassador in Vienna that he should urge Count Andrassy, the Austro-Hungarian foreign minister, to occupy Bosnia and Hercegovina immediately. On June 12 Prince Gorchakov, the Russian foreign minister, informed Andrassy that Russia would vote for the Austro-Hungarian proposal on Bosnia and Hercegovina.[50]

Thus, the fate of Bosnia and Hercegovina was settled before the Berlin Congress opened. The main bone of contention remaining was the question of Bulgaria's frontiers. Russia agreed that Bulgaria should be under Ottoman sovereignty within its natural borders, but the question of who was to hold the passes in the Balkan Mountains, the strategic key to the approaches to Istanbul, remained under dispute. The Russian-Turkish frontier in Asia was another headache for the assembled statesmen and dignitaries.

These issues took two full weeks of work at the Berlin Congress. The Russians gave way reluctantly, under the strongest pressure— amounting at one time to an ultimatum—from Disraeli.

Finally, on the afternoon of June 28, 1878, in the newly decorated rococo hall of the Radziwill Palace, the plenipotentiaries of the great European powers authorized Austria-Hungary to occupy Bosnia and Hercegovina. Disraeli has left posterity a first-class eyewitness account of what went on during these days in Berlin. Besides the official reports sent to London, he kept a special diary for Queen Victoria, which he called his "Rough Journal for One Person Only." From time to time, he would write additional letters to his sovereign or to some of his most trusted friends.

With considerable literary talent he portrayed all the leading delegates, and especially Prince Bismarck, the host and president of the Congress. When Bismarck opened the meeting, usually at 2:30 P.M., Disraeli described him as speaking in French "with a sweet and gentle voice, and with a peculiarly refined enunciation, which singularly and strangely contrasts with the awful things he says; appalling for their frankness and their audacity. He is a complete despot here, and from the highest to the lowest Prussians, and all the permanent foreign diplomats, tremble at his frown and court most sedulously his smile."[51]

Disraeli's fear of the secret societies found confirmation in events preceding the Berlin Congress. The *Annual Register* called 1878 "The Year of the Regicidal Attempts." Besides many assassination attempts against Tsar Alexander II and his statesmen in Russia and individual terrorism in Italy and Turkey, the German capital was also involved. On May 11 an attempt was made against the German Kaiser Wilhelm I in Berlin. He was not hurt, but on June 2, while he was passing through Unter den Linden, two shots were fired from a house, and the old Kaiser was seriously wounded by about thirty small splinters in his face, head, arms and back.[52] Bismarck took advantage of this attempt to introduce extraordinary measures in Prussia. "The German papers teemed with trials of persons of all classes for speaking ill of the Emperor, with a dozen daily convictions, and sentences of six months' to four years' imprisonment. Passports were re-established in Berlin, to the annoyance, as the Berlin journals truly said, only of the harmless travelers, as they alone neglect their passports. In the months of June and July 563 persons were charged with outrages upon the Emperor. Among these only 42 were acquitted; the remaining 521, of whom 31 were women, were sentenced to an aggregate imprisonment of 812 years. Not one of these trials took place by jury, but the whole of them were disposed of by magistrates appointed by the government at very small salaries," reported an English journal.[53]

These gloomy feelings were reflected at the Congress of Berlin. On its eve the Austro-Hungarian delegate Josef Freiherr von Schwegel recorded in his private diary:

Besides the announcement that the Congress should convene on June 11, the situation is completely dominated by the news of the second attempt against the life of Kaiser Wilhelm which was made yesterday in Berlin. This time the murderer has not missed his victim and it is doubtful whether the Kaiser will recover from the wounds; at the age of 81 one does not stand such a thing so easily. . . .

Yesterday's attempt may have serious consequences for Germany, if it is established that the assassin has fired his two unfortunate shots as a Social Democrat. Now there will follow a strong reaction and one must fear that this pressure will create only stronger counterpressure in response. In Germany—such lightnings prove it—the air is filled with evil elements, and social and dynastic catastrophes could not be excluded as impossibilities there. Throughout the world Communards, Internationalists, Social Democrats and Nihilists—whatever may be their name—will now have pricked up their ears at the explosion of the two shots under the trees. And perhaps the Conservatives will unite more closely because they must feel that their skin is at stake. To me this sounds like the first cry of the cock in the morning of a new day, full of blood, which will bring deep mourning to humanity. Culture and morality will vanish and leave their place to sheer force and greed. Perhaps we shall not witness it, but it will come sooner or later.[54]

This atmosphere affected Bismarck very deeply. A participant of the Congress recorded that he kept two revolvers on the writing table in his study and carried a revolver in his pocket when he walked in the garden. A few years before the Congress of Berlin, Bismarck himself had been the victim of an assassination attempt. His would-be assassin wounded him slightly in the arm.[55] But, on June 28, 1878, when the question of Bosnia and Hercegovina appeared on the agenda, he was in a better mood than before. The main problem of the Congress—the settlement of the frontiers of Bulgaria and Rumelia—was solved. As far as Bosnia and Hercegovina were concerned everything had been agreed beforehand. The texts of the speeches were ready, a sign that unanimity existed at last between the principal powers at the Congress. Germany and Britain jointly proposed that Austria-Hungary should occupy Bosnia and Hercegovina.

The first speaker was Count Andrassy. To a Russian diplomat he looked "evil and lean, with shaggy hair and hideous hands always clasped in front of him."[56] To Disraeli he was "a clean-looking knock'm-down man at a fair on Epsom Downs," although he later changed his opinion of Andrassy, reporting in a letter: "Count Andrassy is a very picturesque gentleman. I have gained him quite, and he supports me in everything . . ."[57]

Count Andrassy emphasized that it had been the events in Bosnia and Hercegovina that had led to the war in the Orient. About 250,000 people had been obliged to leave their homes.

The Imperial and Royal Government for three years was obliged to take care of them, and 10 million florins had already been used for that purpose. The population of the two provinces was composed of Moslems, Orthodox and Catholics, fanatical in the antagonism which divides them. They did not, however, live in separate localities; they mixed in the same districts, even in the same towns and villages.[58]

He further stressed that the Ottoman authorities had completely neglected the agrarian problem in Bosnia and Hercegovina:

The task of the Ottoman government should have been to unite these opposing elements with an autonomous system of government, to repatriate the refugees dispersed in Austria-Hungary and in Montenegro, to help to meet the expenses of their maintenance, and to facilitate their return to work, providing them with the necessary wheat for the sowing season and the necessary materials for the rebuilding of their houses. The task of the Ottoman government was to embark on the settlement of the agrarian question, the main cause of periodical disturbances in these countries, a problem bristling with difficulties amongst a population torn apart by religious hatred and social animosities, a problem which could be solved only by a strong and impartial power, in a country in which all the land belongs to the Moslems, while the Christians, either as laborers or as tenant farmers, represent a majority of the population.[59]

At the end of his speech, Count Andrassy said indirectly that Austria-Hungary would not tolerate the unification of the South Slavs within an independent state:

The Imperial and Royal Government had to pay close attention to the geographical situation in which Bosnia and Hercegovina would find themselves as the result of the territorial changes brought about by a new demarcation of Serbia and Montenegro. The effect of the closer proximity of the frontiers of the Principalities on the routes of communication with the Orient would be prejudicial to the commercial interests of the Monarchy.[60]

When Count Andrassy had finished reading his speech, the British Foreign Secretary, Lord Salisbury, formally proposed to the Congress that Austria-Hungary should occupy and administer Bosnia and Hercegovina. Living under the reflected glory of his Prime Minister Disraeli, whom Prince Bismarck had described as "the lion of the Congress," Lord Salisbury had not been particularly happy at Berlin. He complained in his diary: "Heat is extreme—the place detestable. At Potsdam there are mosquitoes—here there are minor powers. I don't know which is worse."[61] His task was not easy. He had to propose to the Congress that two provinces under the sovereignty of the Sultan should be occupied by a great European power. The policy of the Tories in Britain throughout the Oriental crisis had been to preserve the territorial integrity of the Ottoman Empire. Moreover, even the San Stefano Treaty had not provided for the occupation of Bosnia and Hercegovina but merely for their autonomy. Conscious of his difficult position, Lord Salisbury was forced to abandon the traditional position of Prime Minister Disraeli and to employ the arguments of his opponents in Britain, Gladstone and the Liberals. "Bosnia and Hercegovina," he said, "are the only provinces in Turkey in which the owners of the land, almost without exception, have a different religion from that of their peasants. This antagonism has provoked the rebellion which led to the war and devastated Turkey. The animosity between the classes of the population is as strong as it was three years ago."[62]

He felt more at ease arguing that the Austro-Hungarian occupation of Bosnia and Hercegovina would prevent the formation of a strong South Slav state in the Balkans:

The geographical position of the two provinces is of great political importance. If a considerable part of them were to fall into the hands of neighbouring Principalities, a chain of South Slav states would have been formed, stretching almost through the whole of the Balkans; their military force would menace the territories south of them. Such a state of affairs would without a doubt be a greater threat than anything else to the independence of Turkey. It is very probable that this danger would arise if Turkey were left to defend these two distant provinces.[63]

Unlike Disraeli, Salisbury did not enjoy a great reputation at the Congress. "The Germans did not think well of him; he made too much of details, was awkward or rude in discussion, and did not get on well with Bismarck. His frequent appeals to humanitarian feelings, when it suited the English case, rang hollow. [The Russian diplomat Alexander] Nelidov disgustedly wrote him off as a born liar and unabashed double-dealer."[64]

When Salisbury finished his speech, Prince Bismarck upheld the proposal in the name of the German Empire:

Germany, which has no direct interest in the affairs of the Orient, shares nevertheless the desire to put an end to the state of things, which, if it were prolonged, might cause new troubles among the European chancelleries. It is dangerous to have any illusions that the situation could be improved if reforms were introduced in Bosnia and Hercegovina on the basis of the institutions in existence at the present day. Only a strong power, having at its disposal sufficient forces, could re-establish order and safeguard the future of the population concerned.[65]

The position of Italy on the question of Bosnia and Hercegovina had not been clear before the Congress of Berlin; she had always kept an eye on the Balkans and did not wish to see the strengthening of Austria-Hungary in that direction. But the Italian delegate Corti was content to discuss merely procedural questions, and he made no objections to Lord Salisbury's proposal.

The atmosphere of prearranged unanimity among the delegates was marred by the opposition of the Turkish representatives. Although the Istanbul government had signed a secret convention with Britain on the eve of the Congress, accepting the occupation of Bosnia and Hercegovina, only an hour before the opening of the session of June 28 the Turkish delegates received instructions from Istanbul not to yield to the Austro-Hungarian demand. Having succeeded at Berlin in pushing back the frontiers of Bulgaria from where they had been drawn at San Stefano, the Ottoman government thought that it might also be possible to save Bosnia and Hercegovina from the Austro-Hungarian occupation, which had not even been envisaged by the San Stefano Treaty. The Turkish delegates were even advised by a special telegram, also received shortly before the beginning of the session of June 28, that they should go to Disraeli and Salisbury and ask their help in obtaining the postponement of the decision on Bosnia and Hercegovina. Disraeli told them dryly that he considered their request *"fort peu sage."*

The Turkish delegation stuck to its instructions, despite the fact that its leadership was composed of non-Turks. It was headed by Alexander Karatheodori Pasha, a Phanariote Greek scholar who had become a Turkish professional diplomat—"good-looking, full of finesse, and yet calm and plausible: a man of decided ability,"[66] as Disraeli described him to Queen Victoria. Next to Karatheodori sat a man at the sight of whom the blood always rushed to Prince Bismarck's face—he very often could not restrain himself from using the most undiplomatic language against this delegate. Although this man was in Turkish military uniform and his name was Mehemet Ali Pasha, he was a Prussian by birth. He had been a soldier in the Prussian Army who deserted and fled to Turkey, was converted to Islam, and became a well-known commander of Turkish troops. He did not live long after the Congress of Berlin; an assassin killed him in Albania about two months after the Congress ended.

The Turkish delegate particularly attacked the assertion of the other delegates that bad social conditions in Bosnia and Hercegovina had been the cause of the rebellion. He said bluntly that some great powers had deliberately provoked the uprisings.

The atmosphere of the session changed abruptly. Disraeli took the floor, although he was not on the list of speakers. He spoke in English, the only delegate to do so at the Congress. A perfectionist, he refused to speak French with a slight English accent.

First, Disraeli stressed that Turkey had never received a sufficient return for her expenditure in Bosnia and Hercegovina. He spoke at length of what he described as the dangers Turkey would have to face if Austria-Hungary did not occupy Bosnia and Hercegovina:

If the Congress leaves the two provinces in the same state of affairs in which they are at the moment, one would witness the appearance of the domination of the Slav race, a race which is little disposed to do justice to others. One should have in mind that the proposition made by Lord Salisbury had not been made for the interests of England, but only for the sake of peace of the whole of Europe.[67]

Prince Gorchakov, the chief Russian delegate, spoke from his wheel chair. He was a gentleman over eighty years old, and it seems that he did not hear the whole of Disraeli's speech. In the official minutes of the Congress, his speech was summarized as follows:

Russia is not interested in the question on the agenda, but the arguments put up by Count Andrassy, the proposals of Lord Salisbury, supported by Germany, France and Italy, and Lord Beaconsfield's explanations, *si nettes*, proved to him the expediency of the prepared resolution in view of pacific tasks the Congress intends to achieve.[68]

Count Andrassy sent a telegram the same day to Emperor Franz Josef, informing him of the course of the debate over the fate of Bosnia and Hercegovina. He stressed that Lord Beaconsfield "appealed very decidedly to the conscience of Turkey. There was no other means for the peace of Europe and the welfare of Turkey."[69] He commented as follows on Gorchakov's speech: "After the meeting Gorchakov told me that he declared himself in favor of our claim to Bosnia although his colleagues wanted to speak against it. This is what I was once told by [Russian delegate Pyotr] Shuvalov about Gorchakov."[70]

When Lord Salisbury's proposal was put to the vote, all the powers supported Austria-Hungary. The only dissent came from Turkey. Bismarck then made an onslaught on the Turkish delegates, warning them that if it had not been for the Berlin Congress they would have been faced with the full application of the San Stefano Treaty. He concluded by saying that the protocol would be left open for the Turkish delegates to join in the decision of the Congress.

Under pressure from the great powers, Turkey had to give way and accept the decision of the Berlin Congress, but only after Count Andrassy had signed a note on the eve of the last day of the Congress, July 17, 1878, to the effect that the sovereign rights of the Sultan would not suffer any diminution as a result of the Austro-Hungarian occupation of Bosnia and Hercegovina; that the occupation would be regarded as provisional; and that an agreement on the details of the occupation would be made between the two governments immediately after the closing of the Congress.[71]

In another telegram Andrassy informed Emperor Franz Josef:

The difficult and unpleasant question whether and how the territory should be included in Austria or Hungary would be for the present avoided; it would be easier to avoid undertaking responsibility for the debts of the two provinces; in view of public opinion in Turkey, it would make it easier for the Porte to accept the Austrian action without protest; Austria would attain her aims, the annexation would come about naturally in course of time, and could be proclaimed by the inhabitants.[72]

Both Count Andrassy and the prime minister of Hungary, Count Koloman Tisza, had difficulties in explaining to Magyar public opinion the decision of the Congress of Berlin on Bosnia and Hercegovina. Koloman Tisza in one speech said that "the occupation of Bosnia and Hercegovina had become necessary in order to counteract the continuous growth of pan-Slavism, by which Hungary, before all, was menaced."[73] On November 14, 1878, in the Hungarian Diet, Tisza pointed out once more that the foreign policy of Austria-Hungary was "to prevent such an adjustment of power in the East as would be contrary to the vital interests of Austria-Hungary."[74] He ended his speech with the warning to all small states in the Balkans:

If, however, any power resists the provisions and the carrying out of the Treaty of Berlin, we, who have been able to bring our interests into harmony with those of Europe, shall not stand alone in the fight which may ensue. The point to be gained by us is to instill into the minor Oriental states, and into the hearts of the races dwelling therein, the belief that, it at any time the confusion in the East cannot be controlled, the power which will have the greatest influence upon their fate will not be any other power, but Austria-Hungary alone.[75]

On April 21, 1879, after prolonged negotiations, Austria-Hungary and Turkey signed a convention which proclaimed the sovereign rights of the Sultan and gave the Austro-Hungarian government the sole right of occupation and administration of Bosnia and Hercegovina, as decided by the Congress of Berlin in its twenty-five articles.

Russia received the deliberations of the Berlin Congress with dismay. After a successful but costly war, she was forced to back down under pressure from the other great powers. As a result, the conflict between Russia and Austria-Hungary was deepened and the threat of a further outbreak of hostilities remained. Other statesmen at the Congress foresaw this possibility, particularly Disraeli. In Berlin he was fighting against more than the influence of Russia in the Balkans. With his refined political instinct, he was exploring the atmosphere of coming decades. He could not close his eyes to the fact that the unified German Empire was making a rapid industrial advance, overtaking France and swiftly approaching the level of England. German trade missions were already active in Africa, and the scramble for that vast continent was just around the corner. He realized that the continued existence of the *Dreikaiserbündnis*, an alliance of an industrially strong Germany and a vast Russia with an abundant population and rich natural resources, might definitely change the balance of power in Europe against the interest of the British Empire. He himself made this very clear in one of his letters immediately after the Congress: "Next to making a tolerable settlement for Turkey, our great object was to break up and permanently prevent the alliance of the Three Emperors, and I maintain that there never was a great diplomatic result more completely effected."[76]

After 1878 Bosnia and Hercegovina became objects of even stronger dispute among the great powers. After the 1879 alliance with Austria-Hungary, Germany identified its foreign policy with Vienna's, and Great Britain gradually realized that Germany's *Drang nach Osten* was a greater threat to her imperial interests than the advance of Russia toward the warmer seas.

At the time of the Congress of Berlin, the principles of power politics were the basis for the settlement of international relations; the open preaching of them was the practice of many a statesman of that day. International morality and the equality of large and small states were not recognized as postulates of international law. But one can find some traces of the germ of these ideas in the archives of the Congress of Berlin.

In the protocol listing petitions submitted to the Congress, there is one from the Universal Peace Union (American Branch), asking for the establishment of an international tribunal for the settlement of all international conflicts. The British and Foreign Anti-Slavery Society urged a collective declaration against slavery. Although only thirteen years had passed since the American Civil War was fought, slavery was still practiced in Brazil, Cuba, and several parts of Africa and Asia; and Spain and Portugal were involved in the flourishing slave trade in Africa.[77]

In the same protocol, under Number 12, it was recorded that "Mr.

Widowitch and several other inhabitants of Bosnia" had submitted a memorandum "asking for the reunion of Bosnia with the Principality of Serbia or the introduction of an autonomous status under the sovereignty of the Porte."[78]

Vaso Vidović was one of the leaders of the Bosnian insurgents and had had contacts with Svetozar Marković's men. Colonel Mileta Despotović, the unsuccessful defender of the *kmets* stronghold Crni Potoci, came with Vidović to Berlin. Vidović's memorandum was not read to the Congress. A historian has a few lines about him: "A Bosnian rebel leader struggled fruitlessly with his hastily acquired western costume and the refusal of any one to pay any attention to his precious memorandum on Bosnian desires."[79]

There is not much evidence of how the members of the secret revolutionary societies among the South Slavs received the decision of the Congress of Berlin. Svetozar Marković died of tuberculosis at the age of twenty-eight in a Trieste hospital before the Congress was convened. The feelings of his followers was most strikingly expressed by Jovan Jovanović-Zmaj, "a poet of action, patriotic and political, a *Programm Dichter, Freiheit Sänger*, such as are produced by the *Jung Deutschland* . . . the chief poet of the people in 1860's and 1870's, the herold of Ujedinjena Omladina Srpska."[80]

Zmaj's literary idol was Sándor Petöfi, the poet of the Magyar 1848–49 revolution.[81] Zmaj translated Petöfi, as well as Heine, Goethe, and Persian and Arabic poets. The decisions of the Congress of Berlin were a tragic blow for Zmaj. "He played in Serbian literature the same role as Victor Hugo in France; as Ernest Renan wrote: 'He was awake every hour of our century, he realized every dream of ours and gave wings to every thought.' "[82] In his paper *Ilustrovana ratna hronika*, published in Novi Sad at the time of the 1875–78 uprisings in Bosnia and Hercegovina, Zmaj printed a bitter indictment of the Berlin Congress.[83]

Austria-Hungary did not wait long for the implementation of the decisions of the Berlin Congress. On July 29, 1878, the Habsburg troops crossed the frontier at several points. The Catholics greeted them as saviors, the Serbs were hostile, and the Moslems were in state of ferment. In Sarajevo an imam, Hadži Lojo, stirred up the inhabitants by preaching that the infidel Emperor Franz Josef would destroy their mosques. He had led demonstrations against the Sultan's last vizier in Sarajevo, and issued a manifesto calling upon the Moslems to rise a hundred thousand strong to oppose the Habsburg army. "At Mostar," the capital of Hercegovina, as was recorded at the time by the *Annual Register*, "a popular rising occurred. The Kaimakam and Mufti were assassinated and an ulema appointed governor. Three Turkish battalions are said to have fraternized with the insurgents, while three others pronounced against the rising, and determined to join the Austrian troops on their arrival."[84]

Andrassy had predicted an easy occupation of Bosnia and Hercegovina "with a company of soldiers and a brass band at their head." However, the commander of the Habsburg troops, Freiherr Joseph Philippović von Philippsberg, born of a Croat family on the nearby Military Frontier, had to use more than 200,000 soldiers, who succeeded in pacifying the two provinces only after three months of fighting.

General Philippović's 13th Army Corps, whose Sixth, Seventh and Twentieth divisions advanced from the north while the Eighteenth Division marched from the west, encountered stiff resistance the moment they crossed the frontier. The regular units of the Turkish army, following orders from Istanbul, withdrew without fighting in most cases. But the Bosnian feudal lords, who had been for decades in revolt against the Ottoman government, roused the Moslem population and organized attacks on the Habsburg troops. "At Maglaj the advance was marked by serious bloodshed. Here the Kaimakam and the leading citizens expressed their unconditional submission, but the people barred the main street and opened a heavy cross fire from the houses and both banks of the river on the advancing squadron of Austrian Hussars . . . and seventy of them fell."[85] But the most serious defeat was suffered in the region of Tuzla. General Szapary, in the face of stubborn resistance and attacks from the rear, had to order a hasty retreat and wait for reinforcements.

Three more divisions were brought into Bosnia, but they were used for the march against Sarajevo, which was occupied on August 18, 1878, after hand-to-hand fighting. An official bulletin of the 13th Corps described how, after the Austro-Hungarian artillery had silenced the rebel positions, the infantry received orders to march against the town:

A ferocious and sanguinary struggle ensued; from every house, from every window, and every door, our troops were fired upon, in many instances by women. Even the sick and wounded in the military hospital took an active part in the fight, which lasted till half past one. Indescribable scenes of fanaticism are reported. Our losses are unfortunately considerable. . . . After the struggle was over and the town completely occupied, the Imperial colors were hoisted on the castle, the bands playing the National Anthem, and a salute of 101 shots was fired.[86]

The defender of the town, Hadži Lojo, had not much military experience especially against a regular army. He himself was wounded in the leg (some of his enemies said that he wounded himself) and was caught by the Austrians. He was sentenced to serve a term of five years' imprisonment in the fortress of Theresienstadt in Bohemia, which subsequently became the jail of many Bosnian rebels, including the participants in the plot against the life of the Archduke Franz Ferdinand.

Despite the capture of the rebel imam, military operations became even more intense. In northeastern Bosnia General Szapary remained in a critical position, having to bear the burden of a fortnight's incessant fighting. "In Bosnia and Hercegovina," commented the *Nineteenth Century Review,*

the resistance of the Moslems to Austrian occupation continues as obstinate and implacable as ever. All the large towns are now in the hands of General Philippović; but in the open country and in the mountains a kind of guerrilla warfare is kept up, which bodes to last fully as long as either of the Carlist wars did in the Basque provinces, the natural configuration of which is somewhat similar to that of the districts invaded by Austria. It appears that General Philippović, who is looked upon as an organ of the Jesuit camarilla of the Vienna Hofburg, treats the Roman Catholics of the provinces kindly, the Greek schismatics indifferently, and the Mahommedans very harshly. This is the safest means of keeping up a permanent war in Bosnia, which will keep the monarchy in a state of chronic bankruptcy.[87]

General Philippović had to employ four more divisions and much draconic punishment. The town of Brčko was burned down "in consequence of the treacherous conduct of the inhabitants toward the Austrian troops; and a deep and painful impression was said to have been produced throughout Serbia by the intelligence of the execution at Sarajevo, by order of General Philippović, of several Serbian merchants, on account of the assistance they rendered to the insurgents during Hadži Lojo's tenure of power," [88] the *Annual Register* of 1878 recorded.

Eventually the campaign was limited to the western parts of Bosnia. In the battle of Ključ, September 4–5, 1878, the Austro-Hungarian troops lost more than three hundred men. The regiments under the command of Major General Reinlander had orders to occupy the most remote parts of Krajina (including the Grahovo Valley in which the Princips lived). They completed the operation only on October 9, after much bloodshed and heavy losses.

In the tradition of the Habsburg army, only a few months after the end of the campaign in Bosnia and Hercegovina, the Historical Department produced a detailed history of the operations, with neat maps of each battle fought; all together 5,198 men were killed, wounded or missing, among them 178 officers.[89] The losses of the rebels were not recorded.

Thousands of Christian refugees who had found shelter from the feudal landlords' terror in Austro-Hungarian and Montenegrin territories, returned to their devastated villages. Among them was the Princip family. Gavrilo Princip's grandfather Jovo, together with his sons, gave up his arms to the new authorities and started to rebuild the old house in Gornji Obljaj, which had been burned down during the insurrection. But peace had not yet been established in Bosnia and Hercegovina. This became obvious in 1882 when a new uprising, involving both Moslems and Serbs, broke out in southern Bosnia and northern Hercegovina. One of the causes of the revolt was the order of the new authorities that the local population should furnish conscripts to the Habsburg army. Eight divisions were employed for more than six months, before the rising was put down.

The Princips remembered these hard times, too. The head of their *zadruga*, Jovo Princip, was killed one Sunday afternoon in the winter of 1881, while he was shooting wild geese and ducks in the Crni Lug marshes near his home. Božidar Tomić, one of the chroniclers of the Princip family, says "that the Princip family believed, and still believes to this day, that grandfather Jovo had been killed intentionally by the Austrian *pretstojnik*, the chief of local administration."[90] Dobrosav Jevdjević also recorded that Gavrilo Princip thought that the *pretstojnik* from Grahovo murdered his grandfather.[91] Yet at his trial, Gavrilo Princip never mentioned revenge for the assassination of his grandfather as a possible motive for his own crime.

CHAPTER V

THE HABSBURGS
AND THE
SOUTH SLAVS

*I hate this Catholic country with its hundred
races and thousand languages, governed by a
parliament which can transact no business and
sits for a week at the most, and by the most
physically corrupt royal house in Europe.*

—JAMES JOYCE

THE DECISION OF THE PLENIPOTENTIARIES of the great European
powers at the Congress of Berlin authorizing Austria-Hungary to occupy Bosnia and Hercegovina proved fatal to the multinational empire.
The inclusion of 1,200,000 South Slavs of Bosnia and Hercegovina up-
set still further an already precarious balance of nationalities within the
Austro-Hungarian Empire.

The Habsburg monarchy had entered the nineteenth century, the
era of national self-determination in Europe, as an archaic institution
with many unsolved internal problems. The first to rebel against this
state of affairs were the Magyars. The struggles of the Italians and the
Germans to achieve unification were even more threatening to the
foundations of the empire; the South Slav national liberation movement
appeared comparatively late. At the beginning of the nineteenth century the South Slavs were almost exclusively of the peasant class. They
lived under the rule of the Ottoman Empire (Bosnia and Hercegovina

and Macedonia were governed directly, while Serbia and Montenegro were vassal provinces of the Sultan), or under the rule of the Habsburgs (Slovenia, Croatia and Slavonia, Dalmatia and Vojvodina). The development of capitalism kindled their national aspirations, and eventually conflict with the two ancient dynasties was opened—conflict which was to last for more than a century.

Although differences existed in the organization and culture of the Ottoman and Habsburg empires, their institutions had certain similarities. They were both formed in the Middle Ages. The Ottoman Empire was identified with the feudal-military Ottoman caste, while the Habsburg Empire was identified with the *Erzhaus*, the "Archdynasty," as the Habsburgs called themselves; the Austro-Hungarian monarchy was essentially just one of the dynasty's possessions.

The Habsburgs had held a pre-eminent position in Europe since the time of the Renaissance. From their castle above the river Aar in Switzerland (the name Habsburg, or *Habisburg* in German, means Hawk's Castle), for more than seven hundred years this family of German aristocrats exercised their rule and acquired new territory by war, policy and dynastic marriages. Through the different branches of their family, they spread their domination from the Alps, Central Europe and the northern Balkans to the Italian peninsula (Sardinia, Naples, Sicily), to Western Europe (Alsace, the Netherlands, northern France), and to Spain and her overseas dominions on three continents.

This medieval splendor of the House of Habsburg was expressed in the imperial style and title which its reigning members held even in the twentieth century. The following titles were assembled for the Archduke Franz Ferdinand for the day when he would ascend the throne:

"Emperor of Austria, Apostolic King of Hungary, King of Bohemia, Dalmatia, Croatia, Slavonia, Galicia, Lodomeria, Rama, Bosnia and Hercegovina, Kumania; King of Illyria; King of Jerusalem, etc.; Archduke of Austria, Este, Grand Duke of Tuscany and Krakow; Duke of Lorraine, of Salzburg, Styria, Carinthia, Carniola and Bukovina; Grand Duke of Transylvania; Margrave of Moravia; Duke of Upper and Lower Silesia, of Modena, Parma, Piacenza and Quastalla, of Auschwitz, Zator, of Teschen, Friaul, Ragusa, Zara, etc.; Count of Habsburg and Tyrol, of Kyburg, Görz and Gradiška; Duke of Trient and Brixen; Margrave of Upper-and-Lower-Lausitz and of Istria; Count of Hohenembs, Feldkirch Bregenx, Samenberg, etc., Lord of Trieste, of Cattaro and above the Windische Mark; etc., etc. . . ."[1]

The constitutional and administrative relationship of these lands was very complex. The Habsburg monarchy consisted in its dying hour of two separate states: Austria and Hungary, united in a real union. Croatia-Slavonia was "an associate land" to Hungary; Austria consisted of seventeen traditional crownlands of the Holy Roman Empire. The Croats lost their national dynasty in 1102 and entered a personal union with the Magyar royal house, although Venice took possession of Dalmatia. In 1382 the Habsburgs extended their rule over the Slovenes and Trieste. By succeeding to the rule of the kingdoms of Hungary, Croatia and Bohemia in 1526 and 1527, the Habsburgs became the masters of all the Croat lands, except Dalmatia. Its possession they secured in 1797.

A special relationship between the Habsburgs and the South Slavs was introduced in the sixteenth century, when the areas immediately adjoining the Ottoman Empire were organized into a Military Frontier, in order to strengthen the defense of feudal Europe against Turkish invasions. This territory, almost half of Croatia, became a separate region under the direct jurisdiction of the Habsburg Emperor. It was mostly a depopulated area, and among the local Croats, the Habsburgs settled their Slav brothers, the Serbs who had fled from Ottoman territory. All men from sixteen to sixty were enrolled in military units. All of life was regulated on a military basis; even the time of sowing was fixed by army orders. Plowing with musket at hand, ready for use at the first sound of the bugle from the watch tower, the Slav peasants were subjected to harsh military discipline. For a serious offense the criminal law of the Cordons stipulated punishment by the severance of limbs. Yet the peasants were relieved of some feudal obligations. They possessed small farms as military fiefs and did not pay anything to their feudal lords. Sometimes when these privileges were threatened, the Frontiermen rebelled, as in 1710, 1719, 1728, 1732, 1735, 1775, and 1808.[2]

For three centuries the Military Frontier gave the Habsburg monarchy its best soldiers. Although at the beginning the officers were mostly German aristocrats, a few local men were commissioned. Among them the patrimonial rights of the Habsburgs, the *Hausmacht*, was regarded as a sacred thing; they were taught to cherish the duty of *Kaisertreue*, loyalty to the Habsburg Emperor. The Frontiermen were used not only to beat off the attacks of the Turks, but also during the Counter Reformation and the dynastic wars of Europe to quell uprisings within the monarchy. The Frontiermen were the "cossacks" of the Habsburgs, their knout against any rebel. The Serbian anthropologist and sociologist Jovan Cvijić found evidence of this role in the social psychology of the Frontier.[3] It is significant that some of the greatest military leaders in the last Habsburg era came from the regions of the Military Frontier; Feldzeugmeister Freiherr Joseph Philippović von Philippsberg, Generaloberst Freiherr Sarkotić von Lovćen, Feldmarschall Svetozar Boroević von Bojna and several others.

The Frontier was always ready to be called to the colors. When Emperor Ferdinand II wiped out the heretical Protestant faith in the Thirty Years' War, the South Slav Frontiermen were used for irregular warfare in Wallenstein's army.[4] Their cavalry would penetrate deep into enemy territory, cut off communications and plunder towns and villages. In the battle of Nördlingen, of the 40,000 Habsburg soldiers, seven regiments were from the Frontier.[5] They put into practice the command of Ferdinand II and Ferdinand III, "Better a desert than a land of heretics"—even against their Slav brothers in Bohemia and Moravia. The Reformation was once strong among the Slovenes. Primož Trubar had translated the Catechism and the New Testament into the Slovene language and had built the basis of Slovene literature and culture. Yet after the ruthlessness of the "armed commissions of religion," Protestantism was exterminated in Slovenia.

"The burden of the blood" of the Frontier was steadily increased in the dynastic wars of the Habsburgs. In the war over the Netherlands, 1672–78, four cavalry regiments went as far west as Amsterdam.[6] In the War of the Spanish Succession, 1701–14, they operated in Italy.[7] The 1733–36 war saw them again in Italy; 1740–41 in Silesia;[8] 1742–43 again in Italy;[9] 1743 in Bavaria and the Rhineland; 1746 in Provence; 1747 in the Netherlands. In the Seven Years' War (1756–63) they took part in the battle of Prague; and in October 1757, under the command of Count Hadik, they stormed into Berlin. All together, 80,000 South Slav peasants from the Frontier took part in the Seven Years' War.[10]

In the wars started by the French Revolution, the Frontiermen played an even greater role. From the battle of Valmy, in 1792, through 1801, exactly 101,692 soldiers from the Frontier were sent against France, of whom 38,583 never returned to their homes, as efficient Habsburg administration recorded.[11] When Napoleon occupied Dalmatia and Lika he too used the Frontier soldiers. Two hundred sons of officers of the Military Frontier were sent to the French military academies and learned French strategy and tactics. The First Croat Regiment was the spearhead of the Grande Armée that took Borodino on September 7, 1812.[12] In the retreat from Moscow the Third Croat Regiment under the command of General Corbineau, on November 26, secured the crossing of the river Berezina for the bulk of Napoleon's troops.[13] Their tragic fate was strikingly climaxed in the battle of Leipzig, when they fought against each other under the Habsburg and French flags. All in all, during the Napoleonic Wars, the Military Frontier lost over 100,000 men, or every ninth inhabitant.

The Habsburgs later reorganized the Frontier and used it particularly in the struggle against national movements in Italy and Hungary. The Habsburg realm was administered by a cosmopolitan aristocracy (there were many Spaniards, Italians and Frenchmen, as well as Germans), which had no sympathy for the new idea of national self-determination proclaimed by the French Revolution. They were wholeheartedly opposed to the Italian, German and Magyar national movements. Germany was divided into thirty-nine states linked by the German Confederation, which was headed by Austria. Most of Italy after 1815 had been restored to the members of the House of Habsburg. Of the ten states of Italy, the Kingdom of Lombardy and Venice was under the Habsburg Emperor, the Grand Duchy of Tuscany under the Emperor's brother, and other Habsburgs ruled the Duchy of Modena, the Duchy of Parma, and Massa and Carrara. For Prince Metternich, Italy was only a "geographical phenomenon." He proclaimed that "the Lombards must forget that they are Italians." He discarded the idea of nationality—"What is true of religious dogma is equally true of principles of government. To discuss them is often dangerous and always useless."[14]

The Inquisition helped this state of affairs. It used the confession for political purposes. "An edict of the Inquisition General Pesaro was issued in 1841 commanding all people to inform against heretics, Jews and sorcerers, those who have impeded the Holy Office or made satires against the Pope and Clergy."[15] The Habsburgs kept the Military Frontier on the alert. They unleashed the Frontiermen in 1824 when unrest took place in Italy, as well as in 1831. Frontiermen returned to their country only in 1834.[16]

When revolution broke out in Paris in the spring of 1848, it spread to Milan, Vienna, Budapest, Prague and several other cities. Metternich had to flee from Vienna concealed in a laundry cart. The Austrian Field Marshal Radetzky, after a five-day battle, from March 18 to 23, had to withdraw his forces. Among his troops were the Otočac and Ogulin battalions from the Frontier.[17] Mazzini's declaration—"Austria spells despotism in Europe. Remove Austria and it is over! 'Down with Austria!' has to be the European cry!"—was being proved.

The new Emperor Franz Josef, a boy of eighteen, at first submitted to the demands of the revolutionaries, and a new democratic constitution was promised. But once he had overcome his initial fear, the young Emperor was less compliant. He resorted to the traditional Habsburg device of playing one national group against the other.

Among the Croats, already before 1848 there had been constant opposition to the methods of Magyarization applied from Budapest (as, for instance, the attempt to introduce the Magyar language in the *Sabor*, the Croat parliament). Unfortunately, the Magyar revolutionaries, headed by Lajos Kossuth, had no understanding of the national rights of the non-Magyar people in Hungary—Rumanians, Slovaks, Croats, Serbs—but often among the popular demands in Croatia both national and social claims were made, among them a request for the abolition of serfdom in the villages. The Croat *Sabor* passed legislation to free the serfs. It also asked for the unification of all the Croat lands, the introduction of the Croat language in administration, and the opening of a university in Zagreb. Serbs from the Military Frontier also presented claims.

The Emperor Franz Josef left the impression that he would accept these demands; at the same time he asked the new Croat Ban, General

Josip Jelačić, for his help against the revolutions in Vienna and Budapest. The Frontiermen saved Vienna for the Habsburgs. A historian of the Military Frontier, Franjo Vaniček, summed up their role in this military operation: "The participation of the Frontiermen in the liberation of Vienna on October 28, 1848, was glorious; their main targets of attack were Landstrasse and Leopoldstadt."[18] Then came the turn of the Italians and the Magyars. Radetzky restored the old rule in Milan and other Italian cities. The army of the Russian Tsar Nicholas I, in the spirit of the Holy Alliance, crossed the Carpathian Mountains, and with the help of Jelačić's regiments as well as the Serb units, crushed the Magyar revolution. Kossuth and other Magyar leaders fled to Turkey. Thirteen of his generals were hanged in Arad, and 114 death sentences were carried out in other Hungarian towns.

The Croats and Serbs who helped the Habsburg dynasty against the revolution (they had 30,000 dead in 1848–49 fighting in Vienna, Hungary and Italy)[19] fared no better. The promises of greater autonomy given in 1848 were simply ignored. Karl Marx commented that they received as a reward what the Magyars received as a punishment.

The Montenegrin Prince Bishop Petar II (Petar Petrović Njegoš) described his own disappointment at the end of 1849:

The Serbs do not fight for themselves but for a foreigner. O, poor Slavs, what could Europe have done if it were not for the slaves? . . . Our tribe is owned by other people like sheer animals . . . Whoever thought that the Slavs were not born to live in servitude, let him look at their behavior today. Could there be anything more disgusting than their blindness? I have been puzzled and I am still puzzled how to some men shameless slavery can become so endearing.[20]

The Habsburgs learned no lessons from the events of 1848–49. In a circular letter in 1853, the Austrian Foreign Office gave the official view on the right of self-determination:

The claim to set up new States according to the limits of nationality is the most dangerous of all Utopian schemes. To put forward such a pretension is to break with history; and to carry it into execution in any part of Europe is to shake to its foundations the firmly organized order of States, and to threaten the Continent with subversion and chaos.[21]

Franz Josef in 1855 concluded a concordat with the Vatican which put the whole educational system, the whole matrimonial jurisdiction and the supervision of the intellectual life of the country into the hands of the Jesuit Order. Liberal opponents of the dynasty called this treaty a "printed Canossa."[22]

Field Marshal Radetzky continued his oppression in Lombardy; he was not only military chief of the Army but also head of civil affairs. He applied harsh methods against any open expression of national feelings by the Italians. In 1856 two well-known and popular actresses and singers "went to the whipping post and were subjected to a round number of strokes for having taken part in a patriotic gathering at the theater. And this instance of flogging was even carried out at the fortress in Milan, with the assistance of the authorities and in the presence of Austrian officers."[23] In 1857 Franz Josef decided to relieve Radetzky of his post, and he appointed his younger brother the Archduke Maximilian as Viceroy of Lombardy and Venice. But the situation in the two provinces did not change basically; "they remained what they had hitherto been—huge and extravagantly conducted courts."[24]

The correspondence between the Emperor Franz Josef and his brother, Archduke Maximilian, from 1857 and 1858 clearly shows that the Emperor personally controlled the Ministry of Police, which supervised the whole Empire. In 1853 he established the "Chief Office of Police," independent of the Ministry for Home Affairs and directly responsible to himself. On March 10, 1858, the Emperor wrote to his brother:

We must at the same time keep a very watchful eye upon all revolutionary mischief, so as to stifle any outbreak at its birth. This is a time of great unrest everywhere, and Italy is in a state of nervous excitement. I would therefore advise you to have recourse to severity in the event of even the smallest revolt. The Venetians are once more becoming somewhat impudent —for all that they cannot be particularly dangerous. These demonstrations in the theaters should therefore not be tolerated any longer, since they serve as preliminary practice for movements on a larger scale, and—in a city which is so greatly frequented—this sort of thing shows up their rowdiness and the all too indulgent attitude of the authorities. That demonstration of the students at Padua ought to have been prevented, for it should never be possible for some 300 students to arrange a thing of that kind without the authorities getting to know about it. Let me know the result of the inquiry, and make sure that the ringleaders do not escape their just punishment.[25]

In the same letter the Emperor gave very detailed advice as to how he should supervise the reorganization of the political police in Lombardy and Venice.[26]

But all these measures were not able to stop the unification of Italy. The Piedmontese units in cooperation with the French armies defeated the Habsburg troops in 1859, and Lombardy was liberated. After Garibaldi's march, the unification of Italy was proclaimed in 1860, and six years later the Province of Venice ceased to be a Habsburg estate.

The influence of the Habsburgs was reduced not only in the west, but also in the north. Ever since 1815 they had been engaged in a struggle with Prussia for supremacy over the German lands. In 1866 war broke out between them, and Austria was defeated. She was expelled from the German Confederation, whose leader she had been for so many decades. In 1871 Prince Bismarck proclaimed the formation of the German Empire, excluding from it the Habsburg realm.

Only when the Habsburg empire was thus threatened from without did the Emperor Franz Josef come to the conclusion that it was time to yield a little to the pressure from within, at least to the strongest nationality, the Magyars. He realized that the future of the empire would depend on strengthening his links with the higher nobility in Hungary. A compromise was arranged in 1867 with the aristocracy of Hungary; a real union was proclaimed, consisting of the sovereign states, Austria and Hungary, each with its own government and parliament, but with one Habsburg ruler (now Emperor of Austria and King of Hungary) and with a common cabinet of three members to deal with foreign affairs, finances and defense for the whole empire.

The 1867 compromise could not solve the problem of nationalities within the Habsburg empire. The two leading national groups, the Germans and the Magyars, were in the minority compared with nine other nationalities within the frontiers of the realm. According to the census of 1869, the Germans and the Magyars represented only 41.28 per cent of the total population; the rest were Czechs, Slovaks, Croats, Serbs, Slovenes, Poles, Ukrainians, Rumanians, Italians, and other smaller national groups. Eastern Slavs (Czechs, Poles, Slovaks and Ukrainians) and southern Slavs (Croats, Slovenes and Serbs) outnumbered the Germans and Magyars combined: 45.52 per cent to 41.28 per cent (German 25.27 per cent and Magyars 16.01 per cent).[27] The situation was further aggravated by the fact that these nationalities were denied the political, economic and cultural rights enjoyed by the Germans and Magyars.

The South Slavs found themselves in a particularly precarious position. Their lands were divided between Austria and Hungary. Vienna ruled over the Slovenes, dispersed in Kranjska, Štajerska Koruška, Gorica Gradiška. Dalmatia and Istria were also under Austrian jurisdiction. The Hungarian Crown was sovereign in Croatia and Slavonia, as well as in Vojvodina (Banat, Bačka and Baranja).

Although Croatia and Hungary concluded a compromise in 1868 on the basis of which a real union should have existed between them, in practice Croatia was subordinated to Hungary. It had some autonomy in internal administration, education and the administration of justice, but in fact Budapest, through the effective right to nominate the Ban, the head of the Croatian *Sabor*, dominated political and economic life in Croatia. Taxation, customs and trade, railways, post offices, recruitments for military service, commercial treaties, and maritime and commercial laws were in the hands of the Budapest authorities.

At the same time, a national awakening among the South Slavs became more evident. Despite different cultural and religious influences, there existed a feeling of unity among the South Slav peasant masses. In the sixteenth and seventeenth centuries, poets in Dalmatia and Dubrovnik were already writing in the Serbo-Croatian language as spoken by the peasantry, and they often extolled the union of all South Slavs. The appearance of capitalism caused a stratification in South Slav society; a bourgeoisie emerged from the peasant masses, and it took up the national program as the basis of its political action. Napoleon's formation in 1809 of the Kingdom of Illyria, composed of all the Slovene lands, Dalmatia and a part of the Military Frontier, contributed to the revival of plans for the unification of the South Slavs.

Among the South Slavs, as in Scandinavia, Germany, Hungary and Slovakia, Romanticism greatly influenced the struggle for national emancipation. The great literary figures of German Romanticism, like Goethe and the Grimm brothers, expressed a marked interest in South Slav folk songs and tales and encouraged the Serbian scholar Vuk Stefanović Karadžić in his pioneering work in that field.

Among the Croats in the nineteenth century a leading figure in the struggle for unification of the South Slavs was the Roman Catholic Bishop of Djakovo, Josip Juraj Strossmayer. Within the borders of his diocese were also parts of Bosnia and Serbia. Together with his friend Franjo Racki, another Roman Catholic priest, he worked on the organization of academic institutions for the study of philology, history and archaeology. The goal of these projects was to prove that the South Slavs had common ethnic and cultural roots. In 1867 he founded the Yugoslav Academy in Zagreb, and he helped with the organization of the first university among the South Slavs, also at Zagreb, in 1874. Strossmayer worked also for a broad political solution of the South Slav problem. He was a member of the Vienna Reichsrat, where he spoke out against the 1867 compromise. He was in contact with the leaders of Serbia and according to some sources he worked with Ilija Garašanin on the plans for the formation of a unified South Slav state, independent from both Austria-Hungary and Turkey.[28] At the Vatican Council of 1869–70, Strossmayer expressed his opposition to the proclamation of papal infallibility.

Under pressure from Emperor Franz Josef, Strossmayer had to leave direct political work, but he greatly influenced the development of events in all the South Slav lands. By preaching the unity of the South Slavs, he advocated at the same time closer relations among the Serbs, Croats and Slovenes.

Among the Croats, the main opposition to Strossmayer was expressed by Ante Starčević. He was also against the Act of 1868 which put Croatia into an inferior position vis-à-vis Hungary, but at the same time he was the ideologist of Croat nationalism. He did not recognize the Serbs as a national group and was against any union with them and other South Slavs. Instead, he pleaded for a unity of Croatia, Dalmatia and Bosnia and Hercegovina in a separate state under the Habsburg dynasty. Under Starčević's leadership, the Croatian Party of the Right was organized.

Both political and economic conditions in Croatia worsened after the Act of 1868. The Budapest government introduced an undemocratic franchise law. The right to vote, by open ballot to be sure, was the privilege of only 6.1 per cent of the population, that is, 27.6 per cent of all men over twenty-one years of age. The disfranchisement of nearly three-quarters of the male population was largely the result of stiff property qualifications, which were based not even on the amount of taxes paid but on the value of the property. This provision gave free rein to an arbitrary assessment of property in favor of big landed estates.[29] In Croatia the number of people who had suffrage under the Magyar rule was only 1.8 per cent of the entire population—29,045 electors out of a population of 2,200,000. In some constituencies like Karlobag the representative was elected by a ruling body of only 75 persons; at Srb by 74 and at Perušić, 61.

The distribution of seats in the Budapest parliament was even more outrageous. "The Magyars, who formed about 54 per cent of the entire population of Hungary—or, if Croatia were included, a mere 45 per cent—occupied 405 parliamentary seats. The remaining 46 per cent of the population in Hungary proper had eight seats, five allotted to the Rumanians and three to the Slovaks."[30]

In Croatia there existed a constant state of discontent against such a system of government. On October 8, 1871, a rebellion broke out in the Military Frontier, among the soldiers of the Ogulin Regiment. The leader of the revolt was Eugen Kvaternik. He proclaimed the "People's Croat Government," with the goal of complete separation of Croatia, Slavonia, Dalmatia, Slovenia and Bosnia and Hercegovina from the Habsburg monarchy and the creation of an independent Illyrian state. Kvaternik succeeded in occupying several towns, but the superior military forces of the Habsburgs crushed the revolt, and Kvaternik was killed in the fighting.

The conditions which caused the Croat discontent remained unchanged—or worsened. In 1883 the constitution was suspended and a Magyar, Count Karl Khuen-Hedervary, was appointed as the Ban of Croatia. Although economic development in Croatia was slow, the bourgeoisie coming from the Croat ranks was growing. At the same time rapid Magyarization was taking place in the Croat lands. Before the compromise of 1868 there were only 11,921 Magyars in Croatia; at the beginning of the century the number had increased to 105,948. When Franz Josef visited Zagreb in 1895, Croat students publicly burned a Magyar flag; they were protesting particularly the financial

burden imposed by Budapest. After Count Khuen-Hedervary introduced the Magyar language on the railways in Croatia in the spring of
1903, the discontent grew into an uprising, especially in the villages
near Zagreb; railway bridges were blown up and more than three thousand people were arrested.[31]

The Slovenes who dwelt in the several crownlands were both politically and economically in a position inferior to the Germans who lived
in the same crownlands. In Carinthia, although the Slovenes represented one third of the population, they had only two members in the
Reichsrat. In Kranjska the Slovenes represented 19/20 of the population, but 53 landowners of German nationality had one fourth of all
votes in the *Landtag*, the provincial diet, and blocked any pro-Slovene
measures with their veto. Although the Slovenes were in a better economic position than the Croats, they also were discriminated against in
many aspects of political, cultural and social life. For example, they
were not allowed to open a university in their own language.[32]

Bosnia and Hercegovina were governed in the first decades of the
Habsburg occupation by the military forces. Formally they were a
corpus separatum under the jurisdiction of the Joint Ministry of
Finance in Vienna, and they were treated as a colonial enterprise which
played its role in the expansion of Austro-Hungarian capital in the Balkans. With harsh measures peace and order were restored in the two
provinces and freedom of communication and commerce was established. An extensive program of modernization of the economy was
carried out.

In 1878 there were only 900 kilometers of third-rate roads. By the
end of 1914 the new authorities had built 6,960 kilometers, some of
them of good quality, although constructed by forced labor and intended predominantly for military purposes. More than 1,000 kilometers of railways were built during the same period, and new coal and
iron mines were opened, and iron and chemical industries were established. State capital was invested in these enterprises; at the same time a
state monopoly was introduced in the production of salt, tobacco, beer
and some other consumer goods. Private capital, mainly from Budapest
and Vienna, was engaged in the exploitation of the forests. More than
half the territory of the two provinces was covered with first-class forests (the Turks had not bothered to exploit these natural resources),
and of all the countries in Europe only Finland had a bigger proportion
of forest than Bosnia and Hercegovina. The firm of Steinbeis brought
Bosnian timber onto the world market, and the *Bosnische Gefahr* became a threat to many established exporters. The fact that private firms
had at their disposal a great quantity of cheap labor made possible this
competition by Bosnian timber.

All these advances in industry were counteracted by the social, cultural and national policies of the new regime. Austro-Hungarian au-

thorities preserved in Bosnia and Hercegovina the anachronistic serf-dom which had existed under the Turkish rule, and this gave rise to constant disturbances and affected all aspects of life in the two provinces.

Of the population in the villages, almost half were *kmets*, and when the Austro-Hungarian army ended Ottoman rule, the *kmets* had expected that the new Christian sovereign would eliminate the Moslem feudal agrarian relations. There was even a folk poem composed in that year announcing the end of the tribute of one third which the *kmets* had to pay to their *begs* and *agas:*

Fire the rifle from the heights,
The Turk no longer has the rights.

Although Article XXV of the Treaty of Berlin imposed no obligation on Austria-Hungary as far as the agrarian question in Bosnia and Hercegovina was concerned, Count Andrassy in his speech at the Congress of Berlin emphasized that the new authorities would solve this problem, stating that the agrarian question was the chief source of disorders in the province, that the Porte should solve it, but that it was so complicated that only a strong and impartial government could do so.[33]

In spite of this, one of the first steps of the Habsburg authorities in 1878 was to announce that the basis for agrarian relations would continue to be the Turkish Safer Decree of 1859—which the *kmets* regarded as having been imposed on them by the Bosnian feudal lords—as well as the law of February 1876 according to which *kmets* could free themselves with the consent of the feudal landlords and after paying an indemnity agreed upon with the latter.

After 1878 the *kmets* had to give one third of all their products to their feudal lords. If they did not do so in time, the efficient Austro-Hungarian authorities took measures to ensure that they complied with the law. In the Safer Decree of 1859, Point 8 gave feudal lords the right to evict a *kmet* from the land if he did not till it properly. This clause had been many times misused. In the first year of the Habsburg rule, local uprisings of the *kmets* broke out at Zvornik, Livno, Ljubuški, Bijeljina, Bileća and Stolac, as the peasants refused to pay the third.

The new authorities collected also the tribute of one tenth, which had formerly been sent to the central government in Istanbul. A commission consisting of the *desetar* ("tithe collector") appointed by the local Austro-Hungarian administration, a representative of the feudal lords, a representative of the *kmets*, as well as one local official, would evaluate the harvest and decide how much constituted one tenth. The *kmets* had to pay in money.

Such a system killed initiative among the *kmets*. During his trip through Bosnia and Hercegovina, Joseph Baernreither, a member of the

Vienna parliament, remarked: "The present *kmet* system operates against intensive cultivation of the soil. The *kmet* has, as a rule, to give the *aga* half his fodder (clover). The result is that no clover is grown, and no fodder is collected, and stable feeding is impossible. Cattle breeding suffers and cannot be improved. A system of gross deduction, of course, conduces to slackness. No one will work for somebody else's benefit. The fact that any increase in yield goes to the *aga* blocks all progress."[34]

Besides these obligations to the Austro-Hungarian state and the local feudal lords, the *kmets* had still to do *corvée*—forced labor—for the state and local authorities. All men from eighteen to sixty and all their horses and oxen had to work six days in the year on building roads. In 1893 the *corvée* was abolished, but in its place the *kmets* had to pay a new tax in money.

And this was not the end of taxation. Besides the feudal taxes, there existed other state and local taxes—on sheep, goats, pigs and houses. The *kmets* suffered greatly from the operation of the price scissors. The industrial goods which they needed in daily life were steadily growing dearer, while the prices of agricultural products were falling. That was the reason why of all the population of Bosnia and Hercegovina, the *kmets* fared worst under the Austro-Hungarian occupation. At the same time there was a population explosion among the villagers, once they were freed of the terror and the massacres of the Ottoman authorities. During the Habsburg occupation, the population of Bosnia and Hercegovina almost doubled. This further aggravated agrarian relations.

The authorities in Bosnia and Hercegovina for political reasons upheld the existing feudal order, thereby condemning the *kmets,* who represented the bulk of the agrarian population, to remain in the same economic position as before 1878. Baernreither recognized this fact in 1913: "Everywhere land development and agricultural conditions are blocked by the Turkish law of real property."[35] The spokesman of the Serbian *kmets* in the Bosnian *Sabor,* Petar Kočić, criticized the system of taxation: "Every *kmet's* income is taxed, while people in towns do not pay any taxes on the interest they get on their money in the banks nor do the feudal lords pay taxes on the one third they obtain from their *kmets.*"[36]

Agrarian strife had religious and national repercussions. The great majority of the landlords were Moslems; most of the *kmets* were Christians, chiefly Eastern Orthodox Serbs or Roman Catholic Croats.

There were several reasons why the Austro-Hungarian authorities did not reform existing feudal relations in Bosnian villages. The Habsburg empire was itself a conservative state, not inclined to introduce social changes in time. Then there was a conflict of policies between Austria and Hungary: the latter being an agrarian country had its specific interests, as we shall see later in Chapter VII. Also the conflict between the *kmets* and their Moslem landlords provided opportunities for tactical maneuvering, for playing one off against the other, especially in the period when the national awakening of the South Slavs in Bosnia and Hercegovina became a political force. The old feud between the new authorities and the Moslems, caused by the occupation in 1878, was mitigated by the very fact that the feudal order was preserved. In this way the Habsburg realm relied on Moslem feudalism and maintained the same social stratification on which the Ottoman rule had depended in the two provinces.

The mastermind behind these policies was Count Benjamin von Kallay, a Magyar aristocrat, the joint finance minister in Vienna. He ruled over Bosnia and Hercegovina for twenty-one years, from 1882 to 1903, and was called their "uncrowned king." In order to suppress the national feelings of the population, he proclaimed the notion of "Bosnian patriotism." The Serbo-Croat language was officially called *Landessprache* (language of the land), and all ties of the Serbs in Bosnia with Belgrade and of the Croats with Zagreb were discouraged. Although Kallay opened several higher educational institutions in Bosnia and Hercegovina, he neglected the villages. At the end of the Austro-Hungarian rule 88 per cent of the people over seven years of age were still illiterate.[37] Kallay's educational policy was characteristic of the attitudes of the Magyar aristocracy toward the non-Magyar peoples in Hungary, who were exposed to Magyarization and were denied any educational advantages. Kallay regarded the mass advancement of education as inimical to the interests of the ruling Budapest group.

In the spirit of *divide et impera*, by backing the existing feudal system, Kallay hoped to drive a deep wedge between the Moslems and both Serbs and Croats, and to play one against the other. Religious differences too were used by the Habsburgs for political goals. Before the occupation in 1878, the Franciscans were the only Catholic order in Bosnia and Hercegovina. They had worked for centuries under the difficult conditions of the Ottoman Empire; they were active at that time in literary activities and were the founders of Croat literature in Bosnia and Hercegovina. But when, in 1882, the Jesuit Order received permission and official backing to practice in the two provinces, its relations with the Franciscans, who were less interested in dogma, as well as with Moslems and the Eastern Orthodox, became very strained. The last two groups openly complained against proselytism of the Jesuits.[38] The Serbian Eastern Orthodox Church was denied its right, enjoyed even under the Ottoman Empire, to have its own confessional schools. The Serbian Archbishop Sava Kosanović had to leave his see in 1885, after a conflict with the Jesuits.[39] The forced conversion of a Moslem woman and her two children in 1903 caused an open conflict with the Moslems, and the *Neue Freie Presse* on March 28, 1903, denounced this Jesuit activity.

The national problem of the South Slavs was not only an internal issue of the Habsburg monarchy but an external one as well, for the frontiers of the Habsburg empire cut through the living body of the South Slavs. A great number of them lived outside the empire, either as Ottoman subjects (Macedonia, Kosovo and Metohija, Sandžak) or in Serbia and Montenegro, which had gained their independence at the Congress of Berlin.

But after 1878 most of the great powers treated Serbia as being within the Austro-Hungarian sphere of influence in the Balkans. The Russian delegation in Berlin had bluntly told the Serbian Minister of Foreign Affairs Jovan Ristić: "You not only should come to an agreement on all questions with Austria-Hungary, but should be very careful not to make at the Congress any gesture which might be against the wishes of Count Andrassy."[40]

When Ristić called on Count Andrassy, he was told that Serbia should enter into economic agreements with Austria-Hungary, especially as far as railway construction through Serbia and trade agreements were concerned. Baron Hirsch, the international financier engaged in building the railway system in the Ottoman empire, visited Ristić and told him bluntly that Serbia should construct railways through its territories, linking the Austro-Hungarian system of communications with the Ottoman one. He also suggested that he should be given the right to exploit all Serbian railways. Ristić complained that a knife was being held to the throat of Serbia. The Austrian delegate in Berlin, Josef Freiherr von Schwegel, in his diary summarized the position of Serbia as seen from the point of view of the Habsburgs: "July 12, 1878. . . . In my opinion it is crucial that the Serbian race does not achieve influence other than within our own sphere of power, and therefore it is important that we should gain a foothold in Bosnia and Hercegovina and thus establish our decisive influence in this part of the world."[41]

In the end Serbia had to yield, and an economic agreement was reached with Austria. Its main points were incorporated in the Berlin Treaty, in Article 37 (that Serbia might not raise transit customs) and in Article 38 (in return for territorial accessions Serbia was obliged to accept the responsibilities of Turkey toward Austria-Hungary and the Society for the Exploitation of the Railways in European Turkey and to build the railway line through Serbia in the course of three years).

Austro-Hungarian diplomacy also tried to bring Serbia into its political sphere of influence. It found help in that respect from the Serbian Prince Milan Obrenović. Until the Treaty of San Stefano he had been an extreme Russophile. Disillusioned by lack of support from Russia, and being a passionate man, he turned directly into the arms of Austria-Hungary. On June 16, 1881, he entered into a secret convention virtually putting the conduct of Serbia's foreign affairs into Austro-Hungarian hands. In Article IV he promised that "without a previous understanding with Austria-Hungary, Serbia will neither negotiate nor conclude any political treaty with another government, and will not admit to its territory a foreign armed force, regular or irregular, even as volunteers."[42] At the same time he renounced Serbia's rights in Bosnia and Hercegovina. Article II of the secret convention states that "Serbia will not tolerate political, religious or other intrigues which, taking its territory as a point of departure, might be directed against the Austro-Hungarian monarchy, including therein Bosnia, Hercegovina and the Sandžak of Novi Pazar."[43]

Prince Milan led the negotiations personally and informed only three members of his government about the conclusion of the secret convention. One member of the government heard about it for the first time from the Austro-Hungarian minister in Belgrade. One of the negotiators, Count Benjamin Kallay, warned his Serbian colleague that "if Austria could not bring Serbia on its side with a political convention, it would be obliged to apply protective measures, which in certain conditions might comprise also the act of occupation of Serbia."[44] On the other hand, Austria-Hungary guaranteed its support to the Obrenović dynasty and promised to back Prince Milan's efforts to proclaim himself King of Serbia.

However, the efforts of King Milan Obrenović to bring Serbia completely within the political orbit of Austria-Hungary did not succeed. By proclaiming the sovereignty of Serbia, the Congress of Berlin had made possible its independent economic and cultural life. Up to 1860 the centers of Serbian national movement were not only in Belgrade, but also in Novi Sad and to a certain extent among the Serbs in Zagreb, two towns within the Habsburg empire. After 1878 Serbia became the cradle of the Serbian national movement and also very much a kind of Piedmont for all the South Slavs.

King Milan's policy of bringing Serbia into the arms of Austro-Hungarian diplomacy hastened the downfall of his own dynasty. Within Serbia, opposition was growing against him, not only among the members of the new Radical party, representing Serbian peasants, artisans and small merchants, but also among the Eastern Orthodox clergy. The Serbian Metropolitan Mihailo was the stanchest opponent of King Milan's Austrophile policy. Besides the plain Russophiles, there were in Serbia several other pro-Russian trends. The influence of the Russian realist writers was felt among the intellectuals of that period; Populists had their followers in Serbian radical circles. Even official Russia, despite its failure to defend Serbia at the Berlin Congress, was not completely discredited. Its supporters in Belgrade repeated the words of Shuvalov, one of the Russian delegates in Berlin, when he consoled Jovan Ristić for the loss of Bosnia and Hercegovina and told him that "the occupation of Bosnia by Austria would last at the longest fifteen years and thereafter Russia would settle her accounts with Austria without fail."[45]

The Obrenović dynasty started to lose its influence in the Serbian army. A study of Serbia at the end of the nineteenth century and the beginning of the twentieth affords an illustration of the role of the army in the liberation of an economically underdeveloped country lacking any major industry and with a predominantly peasant population. Although there was a small class of merchants and prosperous artisans, society had not changed greatly since the breakup of Ottoman feudalism in the early nineteenth century, when the serfs became free farmers owning their land. Serbia was not like those countries of Western Europe where a powerful urban bourgeoisie or proletariat could take the initiative in new developments.

Until the 1890's the Serbian army was completely dominated by the monarchy and the bureaucracy, its officers recruited largely from the richest layers of society. When King Milan Obrenović abdicated in 1889, his son, Alexander, was still a minor, and a regency was established. After spending a few years in gambling and high living in Paris and Monte Carlo, Milan returned to Belgrade and took command of the regular army, with the intention of effecting a complete military reorganization.

Ex-King Milan embarked on this task with determination. He expanded the standing army, dividing the existing forces into regiments, thereby increasing the number of military units fourfold. This led to a rejuvenation of the officer cadres; young second lieutenants became commanders of companies. Meanwhile, the course of training at the military academy was cut to two years, and a profound change in the social composition of the officer cadres followed. The minister of education inadvertently hastened the process. Afraid of the so-called "intellectual proletariat," he reduced the number of high schools in Serbia. Many senior pupils, especially those of poorer parents from the villages, had no alternative but to join the military academy, thereby introducing their own ideologies into the army. Throughout Serbia at the close of the nineteenth century, the Radical party—founded by the followers of Svetozar Marković—was increasing its strength and challenging the supremacy of the bureaucracy. Through his hasty reforms of the army, King Milan unintentionally revolutionized it.

At the turn of the century both the internal and foreign affairs of Serbia were becoming increasingly difficult. The peasantry was restless, suffering from high taxation and heavy debts and resenting the arbitrary rule of the bureaucracy. Alexander carried out a successful *coup d'état* on April 1, 1893, and seized the throne before reaching his majority. He abolished the constitution and began to rule despotically. His marriage in 1900 to Draga Mašin, lady in waiting to his mother, ex-Queen Natalija, the widow of an engineer and seven years older than Alexander, provoked further trouble. He quarreled with his father, who had to leave the country and go to Vienna, where he found shelter with Emperor Franz Josef himself. Until then Serbia had been fully oriented toward Austria-Hungary, though the situation was complicated by a recent realignment of the great powers; but now, in order to gain sanction for his marriage, Alexander attempted to play off Austria-Hungary against Russia, and succeeded in alienating them both.

After the marriage Queen Draga pretended to be pregnant and the exposure of her deception was extremely damaging to the King's prestige. Dr. Snegierev, personal physician to the Russian Tsar Nicholas II, came to Belgrade and established the Queen's bad faith. Despite this, the King continued to promote a state cult of the Queen, having villages and schools and other institutions named after her. The country was in financial difficulties. In the garrisons the officers had not been paid for months, soldiers did not eat meat, and they were fed food without salt or condiments. The Queen interfered in the army, promoting the interests of her family and undermining the position of those officers who offended her. It was rumored that she intended to have her brother, Nikodije, an army officer, proclaimed as heir apparent. On April 5, 1903, demonstrations organized by students and workers took place in Belgrade against the King and his constitutional changes. The King ordered the army to intervene, but several officers fraternized with the crowd. The King then ordered the police to open fire in order to re-establish order; several youths were killed and many wounded. Among the hundred people arrested there were two officers.

Plots to depose the King had been discussed since 1901, initially among a group of young officers among whom was Dragutin Dimitrijević, a lieutenant from an artisan family, then twenty-five. He was nicknamed Apis after the Egyptian bull-god on account of his extraordinary physical strength. Apis was a man of determination and unusual charm, with a rare capacity for personal friendship. This young man soon became the *éminence grise* of the political life of Serbia.

The conspirators first thought in terms of banishment, but after the wedding of the King, they came to the conclusion that they should assassinate both of them. The violent deaths of the Italian King Umberto in 1900 and the American President McKinley in 1901 influenced their decision. The number of conspirators grew daily. Eventually 180 officers and several civilians were involved in the plot. Each one had to take an oath to the effect that they supported the deposition of the King and were prepared to kill anyone suspected of betraying the conspiracy. Various plans were considered. Poison was thought of, and even tried out, successfully, on a cat. Another idea was an attack at a ball, on the pattern of the assassination of the Swedish King Gustavus III in 1792. Finally on June 11, 1903, the officer-conspirators acted; twenty eight of them surrounded the palace with their military units, dynamited the doors and entered the royal apartments. They penetrated to the bedchamber of their victims, but the King and Queen could not be found. For almost two hours the conspirators feverishly searched the palace, fearful that the royal couple had escaped and would alert some loyal units. Apis had been wounded in the fight with the King's guard and lay, revolver in hand, ready to commit suicide if the plot failed. Alexander and Draga were eventually discovered, hiding in a concealed clothes closet. The Queen, dressed only in a petticoat, white silk stays and one yellow stocking, tried to protect the King with her body and fell under the revolver bullets of the enraged officers. The assassins emptied their pistols, then slashed their victims with their sabers and threw the bodies through the window, shouting "The tyrant is no more!"[46]

The events of 1903 in Belgrade marked the beginning of a new era in the relations between Serbia and Austria-Hungary. The predominant influence of Vienna came to an end. Serbia was strengthened economically, and her prestige among the South Slavs still under Habsburg and Ottoman rule became more marked.

In the same year an open rebellion broke out in Macedonia, strategically the most important province of the Ottoman Empire in Europe. Earlier there had been several acts of individual terrorism. Macedonian revolutionaries had plotted to assassinate Sultan Abdul-Hamid II, but were stopped by the police. Nevertheless, they made several attempts against the local Ottoman officials.[47]

Throughout their history, Macedonians had been in a more difficult situation than any other South Slav group; they had not had their own feudal state as the Serbs and the Bulgars had. Their regions were the first to fall under Ottoman rule at the end of the fourteenth century. Most of their peasants lived at the beginning of the twentieth century under a specific Ottoman feudal order called čiftlik. There were several variants of čiftlik, often administered by middlemen who imposed heavy taxation on the tenants. The serfs, čifčije, had to give up one half of their crops to the landlord and render corvée and other labor services. The uprising of August 1903 was quickly put down. In 203 skirmishes with the Turkish troops, 885 insurgents were killed, and terrorism continued unabated against the Macedonians. In the area where the outbreak occurred, 38,000 people were left homeless. More than 10,000 Macedonians fled to Bulgaria, and others found refuge in Serbia, Croatia, and as far north as Slovenia.[48] The misery of the Macedonians was increased by the fact that they had no schools in their own language, and their three neighbors, Serbia, Bulgaria and Greece, claimed that the Macedonians were not a specific national group, and each felt that Macedonia should belong to her. They organized their own guerrilla units, which operated in Macedonia, making the plight of the local population even more difficult.

Thus 1903 saw an intensification of the national struggle of the South Slavs in the Ottoman and Habsburg empires as well as in Serbia. Emperor Franz Josef reacted to the changed conditions in his own way. He dismissed Count Khuen-Hedervary as the Ban of Croatia, and Count Stefan Burian was nominated as Joint Minister of Finance and the man in charge of Bosnia and Hercegovina. But there was no basic change in policies. While Vienna made some concessions to the Poles and to a less extent to the Czechs, it remained adamant as to the position of the South Slavs. Franz Josef entered the sixth decade of his reign firmly convinced of the need to preserve the ancient institutions, as if nothing had happened within his realm.

CHAPTER VI

THE ARCHDUKE FRANZ FERDINAND AND HIS MANY ENEMIES

To do my duty in that state of life unto which
it shall please God to call me.
                    —The Book of Common Prayer

F EW PUBLIC MEN have had so many enemies, within their own countries and abroad, as the Heir Apparent to the Habsburg throne, the
Archduke Franz Ferdinand von Österreich-Este. His character and his
political ideas have been matters of great controversy among historians,
particularly after the Archduke's violent death.[1] Today, fifty years
after June 28, 1914, if one looks through his private papers, his letters
to the Emperor Franz Josef, to the German Kaiser Wilhelm II, and to
other crowned heads and dignitaries, his correspondence with his father-confessors—all these are available in the *Nachlass* of the Archduke
Franz Ferdinand[2]—and his many remarks in the margins of the reports
of his *Militärkanzlei*, one can obtain a clearer understanding of him and
his world, and why he had so many enemies.[3]

The Archduke's uncle, the Emperor Franz Josef, whose reign lasted
from 1848 until 1916, was unfortunate in his prospective successors;
four of them died before him, three by violence. Before the birth of a
direct male heir to Franz Josef, the first in line was his younger brother

Ferdinand Maximilian Josef, a restless man whose head was full of the past glory of the Habsburgs. In 1863, when a group of rich Mexican landlords of strong clerical views offered him the imperial crown of their country, he accepted it; Napoleon III was the go-between. Maximilian's Mexican adventure did not last long. Benito Juárez, the leader of the liberal opposition, organized a rebellion against the Habsburg, who was backed by French troops. The United States, just emerging from the Civil War, was determined not to allow any European power to establish itself in the American hemisphere, especially in Mexico. Washington was the more hostile because both Maximilian and Napoleon III, like most of the European courts, had counted on a victory for the South in the American Civil War. Napoleon realized the danger in time and withdrew his troops, advising Maximilian to leave Mexico before Juárez should achieve full victory. But the Habsburg refused the advice. He was captured, court-martialed and, despite protests from the Vatican, executed by a Mexcian firing squad on June 19, 1867.

Franz Josef's son Rudolf became Crown Prince on the day of his birth, in 1858, and held this title until his death on January 30, 1889, in the shooting lodge at Mayerling. His father, the Emperor, telegraphed the news of his son's death to the Pope and the crowned heads of Europe; the telegram to the Belgian king and queen read: "It is my sad task to inform you with the deepest sorrow that our Rudolf died this morning suddenly, at Mayerling, where he had gone to shoot. Probably heart failure. God strengthen us all."[4] The Empress Elisabeth showed a remarkable self-control at this time. It was she who broke the news to Franz Josef. But her health became precarious and she traveled almost without interruption, returning to Vienna very seldom. On September 10, 1898, she met her death at the hands of a lunatic, an Italian by the name of Luigi Luccheni, who was accused of being an anarchist. As she was stepping on board a steamer in Geneva, he stabbed her in the back, killing her instantly.

The third heir apparent, after Rudolf's death, was the second-youngest brother of Franz Josef, the Archduke Karl Ludwig, father of the Archduke Franz Ferdinand. He was a quiet, very pious man, "from early youth to the end of his days a docile pupil and tool of his religious teachers."[5] His father-confessors were from the Society of Jesus. In the spring of 1896 the Archduke went to Jerusalem on a pilgrimage, drank water from the river Jordan, although he had been warned not to do so, and died of typhoid on May 17.

The new heir apparent was Karl Ludwig's eldest son, Franz Ferdinand, born December 18, 1863. In him was the blood of no fewer than 112 aristocratic families, among them 71 German, 20 Polish, 8 French and 7 Italian. He was related to many European dynasties. Among his forefathers were 48 Wittelsbacher, 46 Nassauer, 29 Hohenzollern, 28 Hessen (Brabant), 27 Capetinger, 23 Welfen, 23 Habsburger, 19 Lothringer, 19 Wettiner, 19 Adenburger, 12 Askanier, and 10 Savoyard princes.[6] Franz Ferdinand inherited much of the temperament of his Bourbon ancestors on his mother's side. She was Maria Annunziata, the daughter of King Ferdinand II of the Two Sicilies, nicknamed *Re Bomba* by his own citizens for ordering the bombardment of his own towns during the rebellions of his citizens. Ferdinand was married to a Habsburg archduchess and was much influenced by her and her father-confessor, Monsignor Cocle, who pressed him to maintain his authoritarian hold over his subjects. In 1845, according to the *Annual Register*, "the soldier Agesilao Milano, from a battalion of Chasseurs, during the review at the Campo Marzo, made a thrust at him with a bayonet, which grazed the King's side and struck the holster of the saddle. Milano avowed that for six years he had cherished hatred against Ferdinand II, and that it was his intention to 'purge the earth of the monster!' "[7]

Maria Annunziata died when Franz Ferdinand was a boy of eight. His father's second wife was Maria Theresa of Braganza, daughter of King Miguel of Portugal. She treated her husband's children with care and understanding. She was one of the few persons to whom Franz Ferdinand remained attached until the end of his life.

The education of Franz Ferdinand was not envisaged as a preparation for an heir apparent. When he was born, in 1863, there was very little chance that he would become the successor of the Emperor Franz Josef. Yet his father gave him an upbringing in the strict tradition of the house of Habsburg. Among his teachers was the historian Onno Klopp, a converted Protestant, who had come to Austria after 1866 with the dethroned King George V of Hanover, who was then fleeing from the Prussians. For nine years, from February 2, 1876, to March 20, 1885,[8] Klopp taught Franz Ferdinand history and gave him general lessons in basic politics. He especially attracted the young Archduke's interest with his lecture on the methods used by Ferdinand II and Ferdinand III when they led the Counter Reformation armies in the seventeenth century.[9] Afraid that his young pupil might come into contact with some liberal thought, Klopp hesitated even to permit him to read standard historical books, because they did not do justice to the Habsburgs, and he prepared special manuscript versions himself.[10] Klopp paid great attention to describing the glory of the Habsburg dynasty. For him Bismarck and the Hohenzollern dynasty were usurpers of the rights of the Habsburgs. While teaching the Archduke Franz Ferdinand and his younger brothers Otto and Karl Friedrich, Klopp wrote essays on the military campaigns of Prince Eugen of Savoy, the Habsburg commander who pushed the Turks from Belgrade and penetrated deep into the Balkans.

Karl Ludwig paid great attention also to the religious education of his children. "Fervent Catholicism was deeply rooted in the hearts of the young princes, so that they remained until their last breath true servants of the Roman Catholic Church."[11] His biographer, Rudolf Kiszling noted that these efforts were particularly successful as far as the Archduke Franz Ferdinand was concerned.[12] Besides Onno Klopp, some of Franz Ferdinand's teachers were the suffragan Bishop Godfried Marschall, Dr. Rittner and Dr. Max Vladimir Beck,[13] a state employee who later became prime minister of Austria-Hungary. Dr. Beck started his lessons in state and constitutional law in 1882[14] and was in contact with his pupil for more than twenty-five years.

Franz Ferdinand's education was exhaustive, haphazard and superficial. He himself complained years later to his physician Victor Eisenmenger: "Everything was mixed together from morning until evening, one hour after another; we were allowed only once between two lessons to go out like good boys, holding the hand of the Chief of the Household, for a short walk. The outcome of such an education was that we were pushed to learn everything and at the end to know nothing thoroughly."[15]

According to the tradition that all the male members of the Habsburg family should start their public life in the army, Franz Ferdinand was appointed at the age of fourteen to the grade of second lieutenant of the 32nd Infantry Regiment; at eighteen he became a first lieutenant, at twenty-one a captain of cavalry, at twenty-four a major, at twenty-five lieutenant colonel, at twenty-six a colonel and at twenty-eight a major general.

The promotions were officially recorded, and a week before his first the Emperor Franz Josef in a private letter informed his young nephew that he was going to become a lieutenant. Franz Ferdinand answered, promising obedience and loyal service in the army. The copy of this letter is not in the *Nachlass* but the Emperor's acknowledgment of it, dated April 15, 1878, is extant. Franz Josef praises Franz Ferdinand's expressions of duty toward the Habsburgs and allegiance to the Emperor, "on which I will always confidently rely."[16]

Franz Ferdinand's relations with Crown Prince Rudolf were warm. Many letters were exchanged between the two cousins from October 8, 1872, when Rudolf was fourteen and Franz Ferdinand nine, until October 20, 1888, some three months before Rudolf's death. All together, there are fifty letters now in Box 5 of the *Nachlass*. Unfortunately most of them are Rudolf's; Franz Ferdinand rarely made copies of his own letters.

Franz Ferdinand's correspondence with the Archduke Albrecht, on the other hand, reveals how much the most conservative circles among the Habsburgs looked with suspicion upon these links between the two young princes and how they did everything they could to break them. Archduke Albrecht was the second cousin of Franz Josef and the oldest male member of the Habsburg house. As son of Archduke Karl Lud-

wig who defeated Napoleon at Aspern, Archduke Albrecht, under the
command of Radetzky, took part in putting down the 1848–49 revolution in Italy. He was the governor of Hungary in the years immediately after the 1849 defeat of the Magyars. During the Italian wars of
liberation, Archduke Albrecht won at Custozza one of the rare victories of the Habsburg armies. He was promoted to the rank of Field
Marshal and was appointed inspector general of the armed forces. He
was generally regarded as the leader of the military party in Austria,[17]
and he always advocated the necessity of Austria's expansion through
the Balkans. He insisted on the occupation of Bosnia and Hercegovina.

Besides these military duties, Archduke Albrecht figured as the men-
tor of the young archdukes and supervised their moral upbringing.
Like the Archduke Karl Ludwig, Franz Ferdinand's father, Archduke
Albrecht was strongly linked with the Jesuits at the Vienna court. He
was much alarmed by Rudolf's liberal behavior. In one of his letters to
Franz Ferdinand he even described the Crown Prince as an atheist.[18]
Rudolf communicated freely with Viennese liberal writers and artists
and was even suspected of associating with Freemasons, the deadly enemies of the Jesuit Order, whose activity had been banned in Austria.
Lieutenant General Count von Margutti, from 1900 to 1917 attached to
the aides-de-camp department of the imperial household, wrote in his
memoirs that the chaplain of the Royal Castle in Budapest, Abbot Kan-
ter, expressed the opinion that "Rudolf's aversion to religion was im-
puted to the influence of Freemasons."[19] This may have been another
reason why Archdukes Albrecht and Karl Ludwig tried to sever relations between Rudolf and Franz Ferdinand.

In the extant correspondence Rudolf gives the impression of being
tired of the oppressive supervision exercised by the older generation
among the archdukes. On December 18, 1883, he wrote to Franz Ferdinand:

"May today be the beginning of a life happy in every way. Enjoy
your life in full, always with moderation and intelligence. Keep your
health and do not forget that a gay youth is the only preparation for a
happy life in the future."[20]

On August 21, 1884: ". . . Look after your health and do not go
riding and hunting too early, for one has unfortunately only one body
and that body has to last a long time yet for various good and bad
purposes and pleasures. . . ."[21]

Karl Ludwig and Albrecht were determined to break off relations
between the two cousins. Rudolf's two letters of November 22 and 26,
1884, prove this clearly. In his letter of November 26, Rudolf expressed
his fear of persecution by Archduke Albrecht: ". . . I know this grand
seigneur very well and I can only hope that you do not have to endure
even half of the trouble and unpleasantness with him that I have to go
through . . ."[22]

Torn between Rudolf and the influence of the highest authorities of the Habsburg dynasty, Franz Ferdinand slowly but steadily came over to the side of the latter. Rudolf's letters became less frequent—"Can you come here today to help me to be polite—I won't be able to hold out much longer . . ." (October 4, 1885); "As you know, we have to be careful . . ." (May 3, 1886). On June 29, 1886, Rudolf was writing that Archduke Albrecht might make difficulties if Franz Ferdinand and his brother Otto were invited; and on September 27, 1888: "Just to let you know that the Emperor has ordered me to write to you to be here when the German Emperor comes; I feel very sorry for you—good stags are better than the great German Emperor . . . My only consolation is that in this boring mission you will be my companion in suffering. . . ."[23]

On the other hand, the letters of the Archduke Albrecht to Franz Ferdinand steadily increased in number. In his small handwriting on plain unheaded paper the Archduke Albrecht persevered in the task of saving Franz Ferdinand from Rudolf's influence. On February 10, 1887, for instance, Albrecht gave Franz Ferdinand a warning about his duties as an officer.[24]

Writing on August 3, 1887, Albrecht thanked Franz Ferdinand for his last letter—". . . I am very pleased with it. . . . You are on the right path . . ." Then he spoke of Rudolf, stressing the fact that Franz Ferdinand might one day be heir apparent.[25] Albrecht's advice extended to the manners of Franz Ferdinand, at that time a man of twenty-five. In a letter of April 13, 1888, he wrote to him to say that he had heard that he was not polite toward old ladies and gentlemen.[26]

Further advice followed. This time Albrecht objected to Franz Ferdinand's passion for hunting, which he shared with Rudolf and with the Emperor Franz Josef himself. There are many letters and telegrams from the Emperor describing his own hunting exploits or congratulating the Archduke on his remarkable achievements, with the greeting "*Waldmannsheil*" ("Good luck in hunting"). In this field no Habsburg for many generations could have matched Franz Ferdinand. His physician Dr. Eisenmenger made the conservative estimate that Franz Ferdinand's total kill exceeded half a million specimens. At Ringhoffer in Bohemia, during one hunt, Franz Ferdinand bagged 2,140 units of small game. In Blühnbach he shot 53 chamois in one day without hitting one single doe. Up to 1913 he had killed more than 5,000 deer.[27]

After Rudolf's death Franz Ferdinand came down definitely on the Archduke Albrecht's side as far as his general attitude on life was concerned.

Franz Ferdinand's first audience with Emperor Franz Josef after Rudolf's death was a rather cold affair. He had not yet been officially informed that he was Heir Apparent and he complained after the audience: "I shall never know officially whether I am Heir Apparent or not. It is just as if this stupidity of Mayerling were my fault. I have not been treated so coldly before. It seems that the sight of me awakens unpleasant memories."[28] The audience took place in April 1890, shortly before Franz Ferdinand went with the rank of colonel to the Hussar regiment at Ödenburg. The Emperor, knowing Franz Ferdinand's intolerance of the Magyars, "instructed him to refrain in Hungary from any public judgment on their affairs, but to study them thoroughly, as they were the most difficult in the empire. For the rest he should try to become popular in the army and to pay more attention to comradeship than in the past."[29]

Despite this warning, Franz Ferdinand could not control his bad temper, and he gave vent to his anti-Magyar feeling. "The Archduke found in this regiment much which did not conform to his wishes. Although the regiment, which was composed for the greater part of conscripts from western Hungary, the Burgenland of today, was known as the 'German one,' it was entirely Magyarized. The officers, being almost all of Hungarian nationality, conversed in their mother tongue even in the presence of the Archduke, and the Hussars, even N.C.O.'s, made all their reports in the Magyar language. The twenty-seven-year-old commander of the regiment, the Archduke, suppressed this practice energetically. The Hungarian press reacted furiously to this incident."[30] For a time it seemed that the Heir Apparent had fallen under the influence of his younger brother Otto, a handsome, arrogant and undisciplined young man, devoted to wine and women. Otto's scandalous way of life eventually became a political issue, and questions were asked in the Vienna parliament. A typical incident occurred in the Hotel Sacher, where during an orgy he took off all his clothes except for the cap on his head and walked, saber in hand, into a private room in which the British ambassador was dining decorously with his wife.[31] Otto attempted to draw Franz Ferdinand into such escapades, but the elder brother did not have much taste for them, although he raised no objections to Otto's behavior. On one occasion Otto caused a riot in the apartment of Franz Ferdinand, who at that time was with his regiment outside Vienna. The pan-Germans, who were strongly opposed to the Habsburgs, decided to make Otto's conduct an issue in the Vienna parliament. Questions about the Archduke's goings-on were asked by one of the German leaders, Engelbert Pernerstorfer. Some days later Pernerstorfer was horsewhipped in his own home by a group of Otto's friends.[32] Thereafter the private lives of both Otto and Franz Ferdinand were under constant observation on the part of the German parties as well as the Social Democrats.

One of the ways to put Franz Ferdinand on the right path was to allow him to satisfy his greatest passion next to hunting—travel. The Empress Elisabeth and the Archduke Albrecht helped him to make a journey around the world in 1892–93. Before that, at the age of twenty, he visited Italy for the first time; he had to ask special permission from the Emperor for this journey, as was the custom for all the archdukes if they wanted to travel abroad. As a boy Franz Ferdinand had inherited from the last Duke of Modena, the Habsburg Francesco V, his estates in Italy, along with the title "Österreich-Este." After this visit to Italy, Franz Ferdinand made a trip in 1885 through the Near East, visiting Egypt, Palestine, Syria and Turkey. In 1889 he was in Germany, and in 1891 in Russia.

Before starting on the journey around the world, he was advised by the Archduke Albrecht to take with him a Roman Catholic priest, because at many places on his itinerary he would not be able to find Catholic churches. A further piece of advice was to learn English, but languages were a weak point in Franz Ferdinand's education. He spoke broken French and knew a few Magyar words, and that was all. In the warship *Empress Elisabeth*, Franz Ferdinand sailed from Trieste to Suez, India, Ceylon, the East Indies, Australia and Japan, returning home by way of America on October 23, 1893, almost a year after he had sailed from Trieste. During the journey he wrote many letters to the Emperor, and in 1896 he published two volumes of his *Diaries of My Journey around the World*, each of more than five hundred pages. His onetime teacher, Dr. Max Vladimir Beck, helped him to edit the book. In the preface the Archduke described the aim of his trip; he stated that he had not made it from curiosity alone, nor simply from a love of hunting (he bagged several tigers in India), but in order to get a picture of foreign people, states, cultures and customs through personal contact. The book contains some criticism of democratic political systems, especially in America. At the same time he made a few vulgar cracks about the figures of dancing girls in New York. The introduction ends with the statement that he has seen much and that he returned home with considerable experience and with a collection of foreign objects.[33]

Franz Ferdinand presented autographed copies of his books to many a crowned head of Europe. The journey, however, had strained his health; he was prone, as were his two brothers, to tuberculosis, the disease from which their mother died. In summer 1895 he suffered from high fever, rapid loss of weight and rather extended tubercular changes at the apex of the right lung. The left lung also was under suspicion. On August 2, 1895, the Emperor Franz Josef sent him a warm letter in his own hand, urging him to take care of himself.[34] Franz Ferdinand went first to the Adriatic island of Lošinj (Lussino). Although the news of his illness had supposedly been kept secret, it spread through the Habsburg empire; he was regarded as a doomed man. Rumors went around that the Emperor was contemplating proclaiming Franz Ferdinand's brother Otto as the heir apparent.

Struggling against pulmonary tuberculosis on the lonely Adriatic island, and depressed by the bora, the cold northerly wind, and by the strict regimen imposed by his physician Dr. Eisenmenger, Franz Ferdinand reacted furiously when he heard about these rumors. Some people, Dr. Eisenmenger wrote, reported "that he had fallen into disfavor with the Emperor because of some transgression and had been sent into exile, or that it was not tuberculosis but another disease, which had made necessary long and—to add to the suspicion—finally successful cure."[35]

Worst of all, these rumors were published in the Hungarian government paper, *Magyar Hirlap*. The article began with the words "Already they are praying for him . . ." and said that the patient's family intended to make a pilgrimage to Jerusalem to restore his health. The article was full of remarks about Franz Ferdinand's dislike of the Magyars and said bluntly that in court circles in Vienna he was already regarded as a dead man. In his rage, the Archduke wrote a letter to the Emperor Franz Josef, complaining of the behavior of the Magyars. This letter, in longhand, recalls certain of Franz Ferdinand's views on key issues of the monarchy, views that he held to the end of his life.

Lussinpiccolo, October 25, 1895

Your Majesty,

I permit myself to send to Your Majesty enclosed an issue of *Magyar Hirlap* which contains a really infamous article about me, and to draw your attention to it; at the same time I appeal to you to protect me, if it is still possible, from the attacks to which I am constantly exposed in Hungary.

I was already accustomed to attacks from this quarter, because these people know very well what I think of them—these people who for the 1,000 years of their existence have constantly rebelled against the established dynasty, constantly aimed at overthrowing this dynasty and allying themselves with the enemy—these people who brought to my Emperor nothing but grievous insult, calamity and discord. One only has to call to mind the years '48, '59, '66, and finally the Compromise of '67, which shook the old, tried establishment of the monarchy to its foundations. I know that I am not popular in Hungary, and in a way I am proud of the fact, because I do not ask for the respect of such a people.

But that such a thing could be written in a country which after all still belongs to the monarchy—such an infamous outburst, where in every line unrestrained joy at my illness and probable death breaks through, this I could not have imagined before!

This hurts and enrages me all the more since this paper is in touch with the government of Your Majesty.

But one should not wonder at it, with a Freemason government which glorifies a man like Kossuth and uses him for its ends and which introduces civil marriage into a Catholic country.

To such a government a man who thinks in conservative and dynastic terms as I do is obviously an object of horror. Therefore, no confiscation, no disavowal, nothing at all resulted from the article in Hungary, and only our good *Vaterland* published a notice which I allow myself to enclose.

I remain in the hope of retaining the favor of Your Majesty; with deepest reverence,

Your Majesty's most submissive nephew
FRANZ FERDINAND[36]

There were rumors not only that the Archduke's tactless utterances showed a violent temper, but that they were caused by paralysis. This opinion was widespread in the Vienna diplomatic corps, as the French ambassador reported to Paris.[37] One of the Archduke's closest advisers, Czernin, noted "the profound lack of balance in his character, whose every feeling ran to excesses, even to mania."[38] General Conrad recorded that the Archduke told him one day bluntly: "When I am commander in chief I shall do as I wish; if anyone does anything else, I shall have them all shot."[39]

Seton-Watson, basing his opinion on Viennese sources, has recorded the suspicion that the Archduke suffered from paralysis, and that "the growth of the sinister disease was sapping his strength and found vent in occasional fits of ungovernable rage bordering for the time being upon insanity. The symptoms were most marked at shooting parties, when the Archduke fired at everything within range and was an object of general terror."[40] After the First World War several writers supported this thesis, but Karl Bardolff and the Archduke's personal physician, Dr. Eisenmenger, categorically denied rumors that the Archduke was suffering from paresis.[41] Brosch, the first head of the Archduke's *Militärkanzlei*, wrote that the Archduke acted "explosively rather than impulsively" and that he is "often sharp and strict, and also sometimes a little too fast."[42]

In front of Dr. Eisenmenger, Franz Ferdinand ridiculed the tradition that the Habsburgs should marry only in the narrow circle of the upper European aristocracy. "When somebody from our circle cares for a person, there is sure to be found some triviality in the family tree to make marriage impossible, and therefore it happens that among us a man and his wife are always twenty times related to each other. The result is that half our children are idiots or epileptics."[43] When he had built a vault for himself and his family in the Artstetten Castle he told his faithful chamberlain Janaczek, who had superintended the work: "You have managed that well. It is airy and light, as I like it. Only the entrance is not well designed. It makes too sharp a turn. Awkward bearers will knock off a corner with the coffin. Then I shall turn in my grave."[44]

Although there were signs of improvement in the Archduke's health, he was still too weak to attend the funeral of his father in Vienna at the end of May 1896. But after another year of rest in the Alps and at the seaside, the crisis was over. In the meantime, the Emperor had appointed him to the rank of *Feldmarschall-leutnant*, but the Archduke complained that he had not enough to do. In a letter dated April 7, 1897, the Emperor replied that his complaints were unjustified, since he could not fulfill his duties because of his illness.[45]

Completely out of danger by summer of 1897, the Archduke was nominated to appear officially as the successor to the throne at the sixtieth anniversary of the reign of Queen Victoria. But this trip, too, was marred by unpleasant incidents with the commander of a British ship.[46]

This was Franz Ferdinand's first visit to England; many others came afterwards, the last in 1913. His personal reports to the Emperor were full of sarcastic remarks about the other figures he met. A report from 1910, when the Archduke attended the funeral of King Edward VII, is typical:

. . . I was enraged at the behavior of the Bulgarian, who constantly tried to get me into a discussion, while at the same time he did not mention Your Majesty with a single word of gratitude, although he had just been honored with the unmerited gift of Your Majesty's picture.

Besides, I must say that this entirely unprincipled, deceitful and totally unreliable man cut a really deplorable figure in London, as he was either shunned and avoided by people or simply ridiculed. Especially on horseback he resembled a *figura porca*.

Naturally I knew almost all of the sovereigns; I allowed myself to be introduced only to the King of Portugal, while the Turkish and the Serbian Crown Prince were presented to me. The Turkish Crown Prince—it seems to me—does not yet really feel at home in his new position, for he is constantly being instructed and tutored by a very intelligent-looking colonel of the General Staff of the Turkish Army. The Serbian Crown Prince, on the other hand, looks like a bad copy of a gypsy.

The two republicans, Pichon and Rooseveldt [*sic*], who also attended the dinners on these two days, distinguished themselves by a remarkable lack of court manners, and Rooseveldt in particular was enormously witty—to put it more clearly: impertinent.

Contrary to usual English practice, the dinner was excellent, the atmosphere a very cheerful one. . . .[47]

In 1895 the Archduke thought of marrying Princess Mary, eldest daughter of the future King Edward VII. Instead, he made a marriage of love with Countess Sophie Chotek von Chotkowa und Wognin, who came from an impoverished family of the lower aristocracy, of Czech descent. She was born in Stuttgart on March 1, 1868. Her mother tongue was German, and she hardly understood Czech. He met her first in 1895 at a ball in Prague. It seems that they maintained contact throughout his illness. Dr. Eisenmenger wrote that the Archduke used to await her letters with impatience. When Franz Ferdinand recovered from tuberculosis, he saw her more often at the palace of his cousin, the Archduke Friedrich, in Bratislava, where she was employed as maid of honor to the Archduchess Isabella, Friedrich's wife. This family had several daughters, and in Vienna there were rumors that Franz Ferdinand might marry one of them.

But in 1898 the truth was discovered by accident. Franz Ferdinand had played tennis with his cousins, and, in changing his clothes, had forgotten his watch. It was brought by the servants to the Archduchess Isabella, who opened its locket, hoping to find the picture of her eldest daughter. To her surprise she saw the features of her dark-haired lady in waiting. Countess Chotek was dismissed the same evening, and the scandal exploded. A long correspondence between the Archduke Franz Ferdinand and Archduchess Isabella came suddenly to an end. It was resumed some twelve years later, but the former close relationship between the imperial cousins was never restored. In 1910, through his *Militärkanzlei*, Franz Ferdinand even ordered that the Archduke Friedrich's palace in Bratislava should be discreetly watched by the police, for fear that Magyar politicians should be paying visits to the Archduke.[48]

The Emperor Franz Josef was informed at once of the relations of his nephew and Countess Chotek. He rejected her as a possible bride for the Heir Apparent. Her family had not been recognized by the German Confederation Act of 1814 as eligible for marriage with princes of the reigning house. Court circles also inferred that she was not eligible according to the Habsburg 1839 Familien Statut, which decreed that every member of the family had to ask the permission of the head of the dynasty before entering into marriage.

In the spring of 1899, Franz Ferdinand complained to Dr. Eisenmenger about the unreasonable severity of the Habsburg family laws. According to Dr. Eisenmenger, the Archduke said: "I have at last found a woman I love and who is suited to me, and now they are making the most unheard-of difficulties, because of some trifling defect in her family tree. However, I shall overcome that."[49]

He asked his physician whether his disease might be dangerous for his wife or his future children, but Dr. Eisenmenger answered that there was no danger of infection.

The Archduke's marriage with Countess Chotek against the wish of court circles was regarded as a brave gesture by Viennese lower-middle-class society. The Archduke himself was very proud of his marriage. The French ambassador in Vienna reported to the Quai d'Orsay that the Serbian minister had had a talk with the Archduke in 1901 and had informed him that Alexander Obrenović, King of Serbia, had married Draga Mašin, a lady of nonaristocratic origin. The Archduke answered that he was delighted with the news. At the same time, the Archduke promised that he would arrange for the wife of the Serbian minister to be received by the Duchess.[50]

This did not save the Archduke from conflict with his youngest brother Karl Friedrich, when the latter married a commoner, Berta Czuber, the daughter of a university professor. "At first glance, it is surprising that the Archduke Franz Ferdinand should stand aligned with his brother's opponents in spite of all the energy with which he had justified his own misalliance. He was, after all, a convinced aristocrat, and while he was able to disregard the difference between his own rank and that of a countess of ancient lineage, the chasm between a Countess Chotek and a member of the bourgeoisie seemed to him unbridgeable. Violent scenes between the brothers ensued," wrote Dr. Eisenmenger.[51]

The brothers did not see eye to eye in many other respects. Karl Friedrich was much interested in literature and art; he was regarded as an authority on German literature. He had no esteem for his eldest brother's taste in arts, despite the fact that the Archduke was trustee of an art academy. Dr. Eisenmenger recorded a remark of Franz Ferdinand's on the unveiling of the Goethe monument in Vienna: "Goethe and Schiller get their monument, while many Austrian generals who have done more for our country are neglected."[52] Czernin expressed the following opinion about Franz Ferdinand's taste for music: "Music to him was simply a disagreeable noise, and he had an unspeakable contempt for poets. He could not hear Wagner, and Goethe left him quite cold."[53] The Archduke had his own standards in art. In the new wing of the Belvedere Palace, he kept only paintings of the post-Reformation period. He had an aversion to modern art. The Viennese Academy of Arts did not dare to elect to its membership the internationally known painter Professor Gustav Kimt and the famous Josef Hoffmann, "because the Heir Apparent was not a friend of Modern Art."[54] The brothers never met again after Karl's marriage. Karl had to renounce his title of Archduke and all other privileges of the Habsburg house. He became Ferdinand Burg and lived in Munich.[55]

In his own case the Archduke proved extremely stubborn. The Emperor tried to persuade him to give up the idea of marrying Countess Chotek; he spoke personally with him and asked several members of the imperial family to do the same. But all was in vain. Then Dr. Godfried Marschall, the Archduke's teacher of religion since he was a small boy, was asked by the Emperor to convince Franz Ferdinand that he should give up the intended marriage. Marschall also failed, and this intervention brought an end to their relationship. The Archduke said: "As long as I live, Marschall will never be anything more than a vicar of a church."[56] Marschall had been a candidate for the office of Prince Archbishop of Vienna, but his appointment never went through. In order to atone for "his sin," Marschall had to go to Jerusalem on a pilgrimage.[57]

Relations between the Emperor and his successor became strained. Franz Ferdinand informed Prime Minister Koerber that he would wait for the death of Franz Josef before he married.[58] Painful negotiations ensued. The Archduke's stepmother, the Archduchess Maria Theresa, pleaded personally with the Emperor. At last a compromise was made: the Emperor agreed to the match, but the marriage with Countess Chotek was to be morganatic. This decision was made on April 8, 1900. On June 28, Franz Ferdinand had to take an oath of renunciation in a small council room in the Hofburg Palace in the presence of the Emperor, all the archdukes, the presidents of the Austrian and Hungarian governments, and other dignitaries of the state. He had to declare his marriage with Countess Chotek a morganatic marriage; she and her descendants were dispossessed of the right to succeed to the throne, as well as of all rights, titles and privileges that belonged to eligible wives of archdukes.

Three days later, Franz Ferdinand married her. He was thirty-six and she thirty-two. No male members of the house of Habsburg, not even his brothers, attended the wedding ceremony, but his stepmother Maria Theresa was there. Franz Ferdinand was grateful to her. On July 9, he wrote her that he and his wife "owed their great happiness in the first place to her."[59] The Emperor sent a telegram with his congratulations, giving Sophie Chotek the title of Princess of Hohenberg, which seven years later was raised to Duchess of Hohenberg. The Archduke traveled under the name of Hohenberg.

The couple spent their honeymoon in the castle of Konopischt in Bohemia, but when they returned to Vienna they came up against the wall of medieval formality which had existed in Vienna since the days when the Hapsburgs were on the Spanish throne. Prince Montenuovo, the Controller of the Imperial Household, saw to it that the prescriptions of medieval Spanish etiquette were duly observed. The Princess of Hohenberg was publicly affronted many times, and refused to attend court balls. Several times her husband let his strong disapproval be publicly known. Reichspost, a Viennese newspaper very close to him, published a strongly worded article on January 17, 1911, condemning the discrimination against his wife.

Some historians have suspected that the Prince Montenuovo kept the Archduke's morganatic wife at a distance for personal reasons; but in fact he was merely carrying out the wishes of the Emperor. In 1909 she was invited, together with her husband, to attend a public ceremony in the Tirol, and the Archduke asked the Emperor's permission to accept. The answer was negative.[60]

This was confirmed again on October 1, 1909, when the Emperor informed the Archduke that his wife had been elevated to the title of "Herzogin von Hohenberg" with the predict "Highness," but the Emperor once more strictly emphasized that "at the court she has a position after the youngest archduchess."[61]

Neither the Archduke nor his wife accepted this ruling without op-position. But the vigilant Prince Montenuovo was alert all the time, as appears clearly from a letter to the Archduke informing him in very polite and evasive terms who had the right to sit in the imperial boxes in the Opera or the Burgtheater.[62] On the very eve of their death in Sara-jevo, the Archduke was obliged to cut out from his speech the words "my wife and I."[63]

On the day of his accession to the throne, the Archduke would have become not only Emperor of Austria and Apostolic King of Hungary, but head of the house of Habsburg as well. He would have had to make important decisions regarding the official position of the archdukes (there were about seventy of them) and, in particular, regarding their financial incomes. With the Renunciation Act, his wife and his children were excluded from certain material privileges of the dynasty; any ru-mors that he might repeal the act tended to strain his and his family's relations with the other members of the house of Habsburg.

Some writers, among them Count Carlo Sforza, have maintained that Sophie Chotek was a religious fanatic who believed that "Providence has given her the task of saving Franz Ferdinand's soul and the Habs-burg dynasty," that she was a tool of her Jesuit father-confessor, who implanted these ideas in her mind, and that Franz Ferdinand himself was an open-minded although religious man, and not an ultramontane clerical as he appeared to be after 1900.[64] It seems that the ultramontan-ist elements in Vienna were against Franz Ferdinand's marriage, while the Vatican circles were in favor, as Dr. Beck has recorded.[65] In the Franz Ferdinand *Nachlass*, the correspondence between Franz Ferdi-nand and Sophie Chotek is not available. Eyewitness accounts, especially those of Dr. Eisenmenger and Margutti, do not go into this question, although they confirm that Sophie Chotek was a devout and determined woman.

Dr. Eisenmenger wrote that the Duchess was far more zealous in her beliefs than the Archduke. "Even the good Prelate Lanyi, later bishop of Grosswardein, complained of the exaggerated demands which she made upon herself and those around her, especially with reference to Confession and Communion, and he was repeatedly at odds with her on that account. . . ."[66]

Margutti described the Duchess as "a woman of high intelligence, extraordinarily ambitious, resolute and yet vain, and without the slight-est intention of accommodating herself to the position of a morganatic wife kept carefully in the background. On the contrary, she strained every nerve, with a zeal which was not always coupled with the neces-sary tact—especially after she had presented her husband with a daugh-ter and two sons—to assert her full rights as the wife of the heir to the throne."[67] On the other hand, Margutti believed that the Archduke was much too honorable and too good a Catholic to break the oath of renunciation he had sworn upon the Bible. He discussed this matter once with Franz Ferdinand's former teacher, Bishop Marschall, who thought that the Duchess's influence on her husband was very strong.

The Duchess, no doubt, exercised a marked influence on the Archduke not only in matters of family life and religious beliefs, but also in his public political views. Pope Pius X once said that "the Archduke sees through the eyes of his wife."[68] Her interference in the public functions of the Archduke provoked sharp reactions in the Austrian parliament. In 1913 she accompanied her husband to the great military maneuvers in southern Bohemia. She took along her children. Sixteen German and Social Democrat legislators tabled a motion accusing the Duchess of Hohenberg of issuing orders regarding how the troops should march. It was alleged that when she decided that her children were not seeing what they should see, she asked her husband if a regiment of cavalry could make a direct charge against a gun battery in front of the imperial observation post.

The parliament also raised questions concerning the Archduke's financial affairs. In these and other matters, he was accused of using his privileges as a member of the house of Habsburg for his private benefit. Although the Archduke was one of the richest archdukes, he wished to leave his children as much as possible, particularly in view of the fact that the act of renunciation denied them any rights in the Habsburg *Familienfonds*.

The Archduke invested most of his wealth in land; he was one of the biggest landowners in Austria. In 1875 he inherited the property and the title of Herzog Francesco V of Modena in Italy. With the help of that inheritance he bought Konopischt and Chlumetz, two big estates in Bohemia. He also owned a few blocks of apartment houses in Vienna and had from the Emperor a yearly allowance of one million crowns.[69] The Archduke's wealth was estimated to be over fifty million crowns.[70] His estates in Bohemia were run on a very efficient basis. He came into conflict with the Emperor over the question of how the Habsburg family estates were conducted.[71] In a letter to the Emperor, he complained that the court treasury was ruining the estates and factories owned by the Habsburg family. He mentioned the sugar refinery in Goding, which was losing about 200,000 crowns a year because of bad management. He complained that Hapsburg lands were leased at very low prices, originally established in the 1850's. He appealed to the Emperor to change this state of affairs and introduce reforms, "because he could not look on passively as the *Familienfonds* were ruined."[72] The Emperor rejected the Archduke's complaints, saying that he could not accept any experiments "which would shake the whole system to its foundations."[73] The business transactions of the *Familienfonds* were in the hands of the Bodenkreditanstalt, behind which stood the Rothschilds, and the Archduke had plans, after his ascent to the throne, to

hand them over to the Kreditanstalt, which was the Archduke's bank.[74]
The Archduke invested a part of his wealth in the growing industries
of Austria, in the Škoda armament factory,[75] as well as in some shipping
companies.

Although the Archduke personally was a rather lonely man, spending most of his time within the circle of his family or traveling, he kept
contacts with several layers of Austrian society and had a taste for politics. The landed aristocracy of Bohemia (headed by Prince Karl
Schwarzenberg, Count Heinrich Clam-Martinic, Count Ottokar
Czernin, and Count Ernst Sliva-Taroucca) was dissatisfied with the
slow methods of the Emperor and saw in the Archduke a born leader of
extreme conservatism. Army circles also regarded the Archduke with
high hopes. At the same time, the Archduke cultivated very close relations with some organizations of the Catholic Church, and in this he
had the warm support of his wife.

The Archduke's appearance on the political scene coincided with a
revival of political influence of the Catholic Church. After the defeat
suffered as the result of the unification of Italy, the political decline of
the Vatican had been felt not only there, but in many other countries as
well, including Austria-Hungary. The 1867 Constitution gave more religious freedom in the empire, and the Jews, for instance, were granted
equal civil rights. In 1871, the Concordat of 1855, which had given
marked advantages to the Catholic Church, was abrogated.

The reappearance of the Church in political life took place under the
slogan of "defense of Christian world values." Ever since the French
Revolution, the main targets of conservative Catholicism had been liberalism and rationalism. One should not underestimate the fact that
both in Italy and Austria-Hungary the Catholic Church had great
financial interests, particularly in land. As Gaetano Salvemini has
pointed out, the Vatican suffered heavy financial losses when it tried to
convert a part of its agrarian-feudal economy into a commercial-
capitalist one, because of the keen competition of capitalists who
preached the theories of *laissez-faire* and a kind liberalism.[76] The fact
that there were some Jews among the capitalists was used by the Vatican in the 1880's as a pretext for reviving anti-Semitism. The older,
religious anti-Semitism was blended with a new economic and political
anti-Semitism. Theories were revived that the French Revolution had
been initiated by "evil" outside forces, particularly of "the Jews, Freemasons and Protestants." The idea of egalitarianism was described as a
product of Jewish tactics; they were accused of using the slogan of
equality of all men "to obtain the status of equality with other citizens
in order to rule the world." This new form of modern Catholic anti-
Semitism started to flourish under the reign of Pope Leo XIII. The
spearhead of this policy was the Jesuit Order and its paper *Civiltà Cattolica.*

Extremists among the Austrian aristocrats, in desperate conflict with the rising forces of modernization, found an alliance with the new policy of the Vatican most profitable. But if that new policy were to be successful, it had to rely on the support of at least part of the masses. To this end anti-Semitism, for a long time dormant, was revived. After Leo XIII's encyclical *Rerum novarum*, the Christian Socialist party was organized in Austria; its most dynamic leader was Dr. Karl Lueger.

One part of Austria's ruling circles looked at Dr. Lueger's activity with suspicion. They were alarmed by his efforts to bring the *petite bourgeoisie* into politics. They were not anti-Semitic; and in fact there were a few rich Jewish bankers, the *Hofjuden*, who played a vital role in the financial affairs of the palace. The Emperor was not in agreement with Dr. Lueger's violent economic and political anti-Semitism, and several times he refused to give his sanction for Dr. Lueger's election as Lord Mayor of Vienna.

On the other hand, Franz Ferdinand and the circle of fighting aristocrats around him supported Dr. Lueger. Kiszling expressed the opinion that Dr. Lueger was, in the eyes of the Archduke, the ideal political figure.[77] Franz Ferdinand had already made contacts with him in the 1890's and cherished plans of one day making him prime minister.

Dr. Lueger and Georg von Schoenerer, another Austrian politician, were among the founders of modern anti-Semitism at the end of the nineteenth century. Usually Dr. Lueger's anti-Semitism has been described as having more of a religious and economic character, while Schoenerer's anti-Semitism was racial. Yet it is difficult to draw a line between these two versions of anti-Semitism.

Dr. Lueger did not hide the fact that anti-Semitism for him was primarily a tactical move in politics. He denounced Jewish intellectuals, while at the same time, as Lord Mayor of Vienna, he cooperated with leading Viennese banks in which Jewish families like the Rothschilds were influential. Alexander Spitzmüller, head of the Kreditanstalt, asked Dr. Lueger about the logic of his anti-Semitism: "I expressed my amazement at the fact that he, despite his basic anti-Semitic attitudes, worked so well with Jews on questions of public affairs. To this the Bürgermeister replied with astonishing frankness: 'Yes, you know, anti-Semitism is a very good means of creating political agitation in order to make headway in politics; but when one is at the top, one no longer has use for it. This is a sport for the lower breeds.' " [78]

Yet in the speeches of Dr. Lueger and his followers, and in his proposals for the introduction of anti-Jewish legislation, there are not only the basic elements of religious and economic anti-Semitism, but also of racial anti-Semitism; there are even requests for the extermination of the Jews. In 1889 Dr. Lueger stated that "only fat Jews could survive the murderous competition of economic freedom. Christian folk must be protected from insatiable capitalism. . . . Anti-Semitism is not an explosion of brutality, but the cry of the oppressed Christian people for help from Church and State."[79] In a speech before the parliament in 1890 he accused the Jews of an unquenchable lust for vengeance upon anyone who questioned their activities; he likened them to wolves and lions, and denied their ability to shed their cultural heritage. Toward the end of his speech he described "with no sign of disapproval the remedy his friend Ernst Schneider had prescribed for the 'Jewish problem.' Ernst Schneider, one of the wildest of the anti-Semites, would have liked to place all Jews upon a large ship, to be sunk on the high seas with the loss of all aboard, as a great service to the world."[80]

Dr. Lueger continued his anti-Semitic propaganda even when he achieved power. It is not sheer chance that Nazi anti-Semitism of the 1930's and 1940's found not only ideological but also practical inspiration in Dr. Lueger's and Schoenerer's anti-Semitic ideas and measures. Young Hitler during his sojourn in Vienna was deeply impressed by Dr. Lueger, although he was not for the unification of Austria and Germany. In *Mein Kampf*, Hitler described Dr. Lueger as "the greatest German mayor of all times" and "if Dr. Lueger had lived in Germany, he would have ranked among the great minds of our people."[81]

As far as Franz Ferdinand's anti-Semitism is concerned, it was expressed in most of his letters dealing with political matters from the 1890's up to his death. Anti-Semitic ideas are clear in his plans for the reform of the empire as well, as we shall see in the next chapter. The second chief of the Archduke's *Militärkanzlei*, Colonel Dr. Karl Bardolff, described the Archduke's anti-Semitism in these words:

The representatives of the Jewish press never put their foot in Belvedere, because the Archduke, like myself, was no friend of the Jews. Their intrinsic being appeared to him as something entirely different and foreign. It is true that he esteemed the religious attitudes of the Orthodox Jew, but he had no liking at all for Jews who had externally adopted themselves to a foreign model. His unshakable conviction was that Freemasonry, materialism, liberalism and Marxism and everything that was connected in some way with these associations and political theories represented the danger of the time. He believed that all big capital was under the Jews.[82]

Anti-Semitism strengthened the Archduke's anti-Magyar policy, because the Jews played an influential role in the political and cultural life of Hungary. The Archduke could not forget that the Hungarian parliament passed an act in 1894 declaring civil marriage obligatory and introducing state registration, thereby making possible intermarriage of Christians and Jews. The Archduke greatly favored Dr. Lueger's hostility toward "Judaeo-Magyarism."[83] Dr. Lueger was an enemy of the 1867 Compromise, which, as he said, "made Austria a tributary of Hungary." During the 1906 crisis with the Magyars, fifteen thousand supporters of Dr. Lueger, whom the *Annual Register* described as "anti-Semites," demonstrated in Vienna. They were addressed by Dr. Lueger, "who abused 'Judaeo-Magyars' and ended by exclaiming: '*Los von Ungarn!* (Separate from Hungary!).' The mob then went into the street opposite the Hungarian Ministry, carrying a placard representing Kossuth on the gallows, smashed the windows, and threw knives into the hall where the Hungarian delegates were assembled. Apologies were afterward made by the Austrian premier and the minister of interior, but it naturally created a very bad impression in Hungary."[84]

Dr. Lueger was the stanchest supporter of the unity of the Habsburg empire under the Germans. In that respect he identified the Habsburgs in the history of the Germans with the Roman Catholic Counter Reformation. The Roman Catholic Church with its supranational and conservative ideas was the main bastion of the Habsburgs. These conceptions strongly united the Archduke Franz Ferdinand, Dr. Lueger and those organizations of the Catholic Church which inspired this whole policy.

At the same time, Dr. Lueger fought against pan-German forces, led by Georg von Schoenerer, who preached *Anschluss* between Germany and Austria. The issue had religious aspects as well. The unified German Empire of 1871 had been created by Protestant Prussia, and the Habsburgs in German history had always been identified with Roman Catholicism. In order to spur *Anschluss*, Schoenerer advocated the conversion of nine million Germans in Austria-Hungary from Catholicism to Protestantism. He organized a movement called *Los-von-Rom*, which did not have much success; by 1911 only about 75,000 Catholic Austrians had been converted to Protestantism.[85] The activities of the *Los-von-Rom* movement boomeranged by creating in Vienna a kind of Counter Reformation, led by the Jesuit Order, Dr. Lueger's party and the circles around Franz Ferdinand.

The *New York Herald*, April 18, 1901, reported, under the headline "Extraordinary Speech by Archduke Franz Ferdinand" and the subhead "He gives expression of extreme Ultramontane views and denounces Protestantism," the following:

Tonight the *Reichspost* publishes a sensational speech by the Archduke Franz Ferdinand, heir to the Austrian throne, addressed to the president and vice-president of the political body known as the Clerical Society.

The Archduke, who was elected honorary president of the body in question, gave expression to extreme, almost violent, ultramontane views. He attacked Protestants, who, he said, sought to pervert Catholics from their faith, and gave his auditors the assurance that he was on the side of the militant clericals.

This excursion of the heir to the throne into politics has caused a sensation, and an interpellation in the Reichsrat is probable.

The *St. Petersburger Zeitung,* on April 21, quoted from Franz Ferdinand's speech:

Already for a long time I have followed the activity of the Katholischer Schulverein with great satisfaction . . . I support its patriotic and religious work, especially in the time of the *Los-von-Rom* movement, which is at the same time a *Los-von-Österreich* movement and against which we have to fight. The Katholischer Schulverein may be assured not only that I am its Protector, but that I will help it with all my might as well.

The Liberal *Neue Freie Presse,* on April 18, first questioned the authenticity of the speech:

One cannot but doubt this information, as it is too obviously in contrast with everything that has up to now been the tradition of Austria and the Imperial House. Such a case could have no precedent. It has never happened that a member of the Imperial House, and especially one so close to the throne as the Archduke Franz Ferdinand, should enter into such a relation with a society directly involved in the political struggle and, as it is alleged, by recognition and approbation of its activities should make the aims of the society his own. The Katholischer Schulverein fights in the front ranks of the Church militant. Its aim is to substitute the interconfessional school which was sanctioned by the Emperor 30 years ago by the confessional school. Its activity is contrary to existing laws. The public and confessional peace suffers through this fight and, as the Imperial House has always been above parties and intrigues, it sounds incredible that a member of this house should have become its patron.

The Archduke Franz Ferdinand will one day become the Emperor. How shortsighted and dangerous would it be, if he bound himself to one extreme political tendency! In particular, what difficulties would this create in the case of Hungary! This statement of the Archduke would arouse distrust and dangers in Hungary and would constitute, as it were, an *attentat* against dynasty and monarchy.

The chief paper of the Christian Socialists, the *Reichspost,* stated on April 19, that the Archduke had a perfect right to fight against "liberals, Jews and Freemasons as anti-Austrian and anti-Catholic elements":

. . . It is now as characteristic as it is interesting that the liberal press protests against this action and its motive. If the patriotism of the Freemasons and liberals were genuine, they could not but approve the action of the Archduke; for it is a demonstration against an anti-Austrian, antidynastic movement which has only assumed the "anticlerical" garb. Instead of which the leading papers of the liberals, Jews and Freemasons find in reply only words of indignation and open threats, the threats taking the cowardly form of warning and advice.

The Socialist *Arbeiter Zeitung* on April 20, attacked the Archduke for his tendencies toward absolutism:

This is the Archduke Franz Ferdinand's first public political action. His profession of Catholicism is the first political word which has been heard from him. He has recited his political credo: he wants to leave Austria in no doubt as to his way of thinking. We should be most thankful to him. The activity of the Katholischer Schulverein is directed against all modern evolution: to bring Austria back to the position of a dominion of the Roman hierarchy. Franz Ferdinand supports a point of view which rejects the entire bourgeois development of the Austrian state. Franz Ferdinand has shown his peoples that he regards himself as a clerical, that he desires to act as a clerical, that he looks upon clericalism as the unchangeable basis of this state. But Austria is a constitutional state and Franz Ferdinand can never be an absolute ruler.

In the lower house of the Vienna parliament, the Social Democrats introduced an urgent motion demanding an amendment to the penal code, providing that criticism of members of the Imperial House should no longer be considered an offense of insult and libel. The motion was discussed on April 18 and 24. In the meantime, Dr. Lueger organized demonstrations in Vienna in support of the Archduke. He attacked what he called "the anti-Austrian elements: Socialists and pan-Germans," saying that "these despicable people constantly criticize me and the Archduke Franz Ferdinand as well. The Archduke has to endure these attacks. But the more these people attack him, the more he wins our hearts . . . I want to tell him only: 'Stay firm, Archduke Franz Ferdinand, remain firm and inflexible and protect us who are living here in Austria, so that at last the right may be granted to us to be and to remain Austrians in Austria.'"

On April 22, 1901, the Duchess of Hohenberg took part in a street demonstration in favor of her husband. The special correspondent of the *Daily Mail* reported from Vienna the next day:

The Catholic movement and the subsequent denunciations of the Archduke Franz Ferdinand are assuming threatening proportions. Last Sunday a procession of some 6,000 Catholics marched through the principal streets carrying a cross and compelling all passers-by to bow to it.

A sensation was caused yesterday by a similar procession of 200 fashionable and aristocratic ladies, led by the Duchess Hohenberg, the morganatic wife of the Archduke. They marched to several churches, and later on were addressed by the Jesuit Father Kolb in an inflammatory sermon. . . .

The debate in the parliament was one of the most bitter in years. Prime Minister Koerber simply stated "that the Government had no knowledge of the Archduke's intention to state his views in the matter, and that his speech must therefore be regarded as an expression of his personal opinion for which the Government could not be held constitutionally responsible." Dr. Pernerstorfer, who had suffered some years before at the hands of the Archduke Otto's friends, led the attack, saying that the alliance of the Archduke Franz Ferdinand and Dr. Lueger, the leader of the big clerical party, was a challenge to the country. He stressed particularly that "Jesuit Ultramontanism, which splits up nations and countries, forces democracy to take up the cudgels against clericalism, which in Austria is embodied in the person of the Archduke Franz Ferdinand." His speech was interrupted several times. Dr. Lueger was especially enraged. One of his supporters, Sten, shouted at the opposition: "Don't get excited, you Jewish bastard." The session was suspended.

A motion to amend the penal code in relation to criticism of members of the imperial family was eventually defeated, but the bitterness persisted both in Vienna and in Budapest. The *Hamburger Nachrichten* commented from Budapest that the Archduke's speech had stirred up strong emotions—"It is stressed here that in Hungary an ultramontane rule is impossible and that the Hungarian constitution is strong enough to resist ultramontane tendencies from any side. Such tendencies could quite well lead to regrettable collisions, but not to success."

Rumors began to appear in the press that the Archduke Franz Ferdinand's life was in danger and that the Vienna police were taking special security measures. In the Franz Ferdinand *Nachlass* a clipping is preserved from a Le Havre paper, *Le Courrier de la Patrie*, which reported on April 24:

The Archduke Franz Ferdinand, the Heir Apparent, did not without deliberation pronounce his words which have caused so much noise and which have aroused against him all the reptiles of the Triple Alliance. The *Vaterland*, the organ of high aristocratic society [in Vienna], stated this openly: "The Prince knew perfectly well to what dangers he was exposing himself in putting himself so resolutely at the head of the Austro-Hungarian patriots against pan-Germans of all kinds; he is a man who does not lack courage." One already hears of mortal threats addressed to him every day. He is reminded of the sad fate of the Archduke Rudolf. It should be expected, the *Vaterland* remarked, that the Archduke will find himself exposed to thousands of traps, mean machinations and even *attentats*. Extraordinary measures have been taken to protect the Prince.

The same report was published by two other provincial newspapers in France. The French Catholic press came out strongly on the side of Franz Ferdinand. On April 20, *La Libre Parole*, of Paris, commented:

For a long time, the Archduke has been treated as an object of hatred by the Prussian-Hungarian clique . . . A furious campaign is being organized against him because of his decision not to play the role of a dummy . . . The Judaeo-Prusso-Masonic clique is determined to go even further and to attack all the members of the imperial family who are suspected of possessing the will, energy and ideas suitable to their ranks and their mission . . . there is even pressure on the Emperor to disavow the Archduke.

The *Daily Express* and several papers in France, Switzerland and Belgium reported that the Emperor had rebuked the Archduke and suggested that he should withdraw his patronage of the Katholischer Schulverein. The Viennese *Neues Wiener Tageblatt* and several other papers reported that the Emperor had ordered the Archduke in the future not to give his patronage without imperial permission.

These reports were not true. The Emperor agreed with the Archduke's action and with his sentiments; he objected only to the way he pronounced them as the following letter, of April 20, shows:

DEAR FRANZ,

Thank you very much for yesterday's letter. I can only answer it briefly today and shall keep a more detailed consideration for the occasion of your next visit. I do not doubt that you had the best intentions in taking on the sponsorship of the Katholischer Schulverein and in making your statement to the newspapers, and I have always been convinced of the usefulness of this association, so that I support everything which you may have said to its members. Nevertheless, your somewhat demonstrative action was particularly apt to provoke new disturbances and excitement in the Reichsrat, after an initial improvement and partial calming down of the situation, considering your exceptionally high position, considering also your future, and considering the coming debate in parliament about the Act of Renunciation given on the eve of your marriage.

With the best regards I remain

Your faithful uncle,
FRANZ JOSEF[86]

In the meantime, on May 8, *Le Temps* in France and several other papers reported that Pope Leo XIII had sent a letter to the Archduke, thanking him "for the useful initiative he had taken for the sake of religion by proclaiming himself against the rupture with Rome and by accepting the patronage of the Katholischer Schulverein." The Rome correspondent of *Neue Freie Presse*, on May 10, reported that the Vatican issued a statement that neither the Pope, nor the State Secretary, nor any other official of the Vatican had sent a letter to the Archduke Franz Ferdinand. But the Curia was indeed very satisfied with the Archduke's action and statements. The Papal Nuncio in Vienna received instructions to express to Franz Ferdinand the thankful feelings of the Pope.

The Archduke seemed not to need any encouragement. He wrote to Dr. Max Vladimir Beck on April 20: "I stand by my opinions, and I ask you to see to it that no placatory communiqué is issued without my knowledge, which I would definitely not permit."[87]

Despite the scandal of 1901 with Katholischer Schulverein, the Archduke continued to practice intolerance toward the Protestants. General Conrad recorded: "It happened that good officers were barred from certain positions in the army because they were Protestants."[88] The Archduke "forbade his officers to marry rich Jewesses," according to Colonel Bardolff.[89]

In the *Nachlass* there is a vast collection of letters between the Archduke and his father-confessors and other members of the Catholic Church. Some of them, like the letters of Marschall, deal solely with religious and moral questions; on the other hand there are many more concerned exclusively with political matters, supporting the Archduke in his intolerance. Suffragan Bishop Dr. Lanyi, for a time his principal domestic ecclesiastic and his teacher of the Magyar language, on August 27, 1908, begged him to allow the Catholic Baron Bakoczy to remain in a particular department of the Hungarian Ministry of Culture, "because his minister Apponyi wants to transfer him . . . to another department on the request of Freemasons, Jews and Protestants. . . . In no ministry are there so many and such dangerous Freemasons and Protestants as in the Ministry of Culture; there are hardly three good Catholics there . . ."[90] Another letter contains a warning against the influence of the Freemasons at the Budapest medical faculty.

Count Augustin Galen, then a priest in the Prague Benedictine Society of St. Boniface, exercised a great influence on the Archduke. His many letters, in longhand, dealt solely with political problems. On October 15, 1907, he recommended to the Archduke Count Reinhold Boos-Waldeck and Count Beaufut as "both completely independent men who could also work against treasonable policy and other Jewish agitations."[91] Galen explained this request thus: "Would Your Imperial Majesty with your usual kindness forgive my interference in this affair, but it is due above all to my convictions that I can thereby serve Your Imperial Majesty and the Fatherland, and it is also of the greatest importance for the Church that believing men are given positions in the ministries instead of Jewish freethinkers."[92] Another letter stated briefly that Tassilo Testetich had said that "the Archduke is too weak."[93] Galen denounced certain artists for their liberalism. The Archduke was warned not to drive too fast in his car. Again comes mention of the "almighty Jews" and a report of Galen's trip to Rome, with assurances from there that all the Archduke's wishes would be fulfilled.[94] On December 8, 1909, came strong attacks on the Magyars and "their absolutist system." On January 31, 1910, came another long letter, requesting help for the Slovak clergy against the Magyars; it expressed the wish that the Archduke intervene in Rome against certain Magyar bishops and drew attention to the need for religious literature to combat the "revolutionary, atheistic spirit" in the army.[95]

The Archduke listened to what his father-confessors said and quite frequently acted on their advice. He was informed that in southern Austria the civil authorities had refused to finance the remodeling of a Roman Catholic church. The matter was even brought to the law courts. The Archduke intervened and demanded that the president of the law court rule that the state give the money. The judge refused to acquiesce to this demand. Enraged, Franz Ferdinand asked for an audience with the Emperor Franz Josef. According to Franz Ferdinand's adviser Spitzmüller, the Archduke complained to the Emperor that it was impossible in Catholic Austria that a Roman Catholic church could not be restored by public funds.[96] The Emperor answered that the judge had reacted correctly, since his legal position necessitated that he refuse any interference.

Besides letters and memorandums, some of the clerical advisers of the Archduke prepared for him elaborate theses on political issues. Father Herman Gruber, S.J., wrote a *Denkschrift* in three volumes about "the role of Freemasons in contemporary revolutionary movements since 1776," with all the necessary footnotes and references.[97] Repeating the opinion that the French Revolution had been the product of Protestants and Freemasons, Father Gruber asserted that there existed an international revolutionary secret society of Freemasonry which was fomenting revolutionary action in all parts of the world. He claimed that the revolution in Brazil in 1889, the uprisings in Cuba in 1899, the revolution of the Young Turks in 1908, and the revolution in Portugal in 1910 were all organized by Freemasonry. He put particular blame on French Freemasonry and its Grand Orient lodge, "which after 1789 was the main factor provoking revolutionary movement in the whole of the world, and its most trusted helper was Italian Freemasonry."[98]

To support his allegation, Father Gruber quoted John Strachan, whom he described as a leading English Freemason—"Indeed, Freemasonry is in such bad odor on the continent of Europe, by reason of it being exploited by socialists and anarchists, that we may have to break off relations with more of the Grand Bodies who have forsaken our landmarks."[99]

The Archduke was not just a tool of the Jesuit Order and the Vatican. Margutti emphasized that he was a strict Catholic, but that he came into conflict with the Catholic Church over policy in Hungary.[100] In the *Nachlass* there exists only one letter of Pope Pius X, that of July 30, 1906, to the Archduke, and it shows that the Archduke had some difference of opinion with the Roman Catholic hierarchy in Hungary and that he had asked for Papal intervention.[101]

The Archduke did not identify his policies completely with those of the Christian Socialist party of Dr. Lueger, although their main paper, *Reichspost*, particularly after 1905, became the mouthpiece of Belvedere. On some basic internal political issues, the Archduke's sympathies were closer to the views of the aristocracy than to those of Dr. Lueger. To Count Ottokar Czernin, his confidant and a big landowner in Bohemia, he said: "There is no getting away from the fact that the sovereign has to rely first of all on the united nobility. Even if *unfortunately* the times of feudalism and absolutism have passed, nobility with the Emperor at the top still must play the first role and must act as the determining factor in all affairs of the empire."[102]

On the question of the prerogatives of aristocracy and its financial and economic postion, the Archduke disagreed with Dr. Lueger. In the first decade of the twentieth century, when social changes were taking place in the empire as a result of industrialization, there was a readiness among leading industrialists in Austria-Hungary to accept some kind of electoral reform. The Russian Revolution of 1905 had frightened leading capitalist circles in Austria; they realized that in order to avoid a similar revolution in their own country, adequate reforms must be carried out. The Archduke's former teacher, Max Vladimir Beck, who was prime minister at that time, pushed through a general suffrage bill in Austria. Although the Germans in Austria were still greatly favored, especially in comparison with the Slavs (one parliamentary seat was granted for every 40,000 Germans, every 50,000 Slovenes, every 52,000 Poles, every 55,000 Croats, every 55,000 Czechs and every 102,000 Ukrainians),[103] the strongest opposition against the measure came from the landed aristocracy in Austria, headed by the Archduke personally, himself one of the biggest landowners in Bohemia. The Archduke's mobilization of the aristocracy could not block the introduction of general suffrage. When the new parliament was opened in Vienna in the presence of the Emperor, the Heir Apparent expressed his indignation and refused to attend it.[104]

The fury of the Archduke was turned against the Prime Minister, who carried through the electoral reform. He became his die-hard enemy. The Archduke complained about Beck—"If only the political situation were slightly better. But it looks so bleak, and the famous Beck, who relies on Social Democrats, Jews, Freemasons and Magyars, has got the cart only more deeply stuck in the mud."[105] The Archduke did his best to bring about Beck's downfall, and he finally succeeded in 1908.

Of all the Habsburg institutions, the Archduke relied primarily on the army. In that respect Franz Ferdinand was following the advice of Archduke Albrecht, who had been the leader of the military party in Austria for many decades before Franz Ferdinand gained that position. "The dynasty and the army are the only defense against separatist tendencies; otherwise the monarchy is lost."[106] Although Franz Ferdinand wanted to have a strong army for the foreign policy goals of the Habsburgs, he understood its importance in internal politics. As early as 1896 he had sent a memorandum to the then Chief of the General Staff, General Friedrich Beck-Rzikowski, about the employment of the army against the inner enemies of the dynasty. He discarded the possibility of a foreign war—"it seems to me much less likely than a revolution"—and therefore "a dependable, nationally indifferent army with an obligation solely to the Emperor" appeared to him as the "life condition of the empire, of the existence of the dynasty."[107]

The Archduke spent most of his energies on plans for the modernization of the army and the building of a powerful navy. As the Heir Apparent, he had no official function in the administration, and the only office he ever held was that of Inspector General of the Armed Forces, which he obtained only in 1913. But during the long years in which he waited to ascend the throne he acquired not so much formal, but actual, power. He achieved this gradually through the medium of his own *Militärkanzlei*, headed from 1905 by Colonel Alexander Brosch von Aarenau. Although the *Militärkanzlei* should strictly have been only an office through which the Archduke could exercise some influence on the reorganization of the army and the navy, in fact it was something more. Colonel Brosch, who appears from their correspondence as an ardent Ultramontanist, with the same intolerance against liberals, Jews, Freemasons and Social Democrats as the Archduke, had, unlike his chief, a cool mind and considerable tact.[108] The *Militärkanzlei* established contact with all the ministries in Vienna, asking them for reports on their work and the principal political issues. Before the *Militärkanzlei* was opened, the Archduke had complained "that he had to learn everything from the newspapers, that the Emperor never listened to him, and that he was told less than 'the under-footman in Schönbrunn.'"[109] Under the subtle leadership of Colonel Brosch, the *Militärkanzlei* became a first-class observation post from which to survey events in the empire.

Similar direct links were established with many politicians, who regularly sent confidential reports to Colonel Brosch. The Archduke read all the reports carefully and added his remarks on their margins. Colonel Brosch sent him daily appreciations, written in his own hand. He organized a daily digest of about thirty of the leading newspapers of the empire and other countries. Colonel Brosch knew how to place the Archduke's opinion not only in the Austrian papers, like *Reichspost* and other newspapers and reviews of similar political shade, but also in some of the foreign press, as French diplomats complained in 1914.[110] Even when he had left Belvedere in 1911, Brosch's influence did not diminish. He became commander of a regiment and when the World War broke out, Brosch fell near Rawa Ruska on September 6, 1914, four months after the death of Franz Ferdinand.

The Archduke's actual influence in the empire's politics was derived from his power over appointments to key posts. For instance, in 1906 he succeeded in effecting the nomination of his protégés to some of the most important posts in the administration. To replace the seventy-six-year-old General Beck-Rzikowski, the energetic Franz Conrad von Hötzendorf became chief of the General Staff. In place of Count Agenor von Goluchowski, the Archduke saw that the post of foreign minister went to Count Alois Lexa von Aehrenthal. Count Franz von Schönaich became minister of war, and the Archduke's teacher and friend Max Vladimir Beck was appointed prime minister.

Yet with most of them the Archduke was soon in conflict. The reason was not only the Archduke's bad temper and lack of tact; the new appointees had to follow the instructions of the Emperor Franz Josef and not those of the Archduke. Relations between the Emperor's Schönbrunn and Franz Ferdinand's Belvedere became strained, and the Habsburg empire was threatened with the existence of two central governments. The conflict was not secret and was publicly commented on. For instance, on March 16, 1910, one of the Austrian Social Democrat leaders, Dr. Karl Renner, said in parliament:

We no longer have a monarchy, a single authority; we have a dyarchy, a state of competition between Schönbrunn and Belvedere; and we know that all those who serve Schönbrunn fall immediately into the deepest disfavor with Belvedere, and that very able administrative officials who enjoy the recognition of the whole house and the recognition of history, are being persecuted from Belvedere with a petty, satanic hatred, such as is not worthy of such "high" circles, with a petty hatred which has, it could almost be said, intellectually and morally diseased features. This is particularly obvious when one sees how the pupil, hardly grown to adulthood, vents his spite particularly on his teachers—for instance, on the teacher of religion, the former provost Marschall, who has now undertaken a journey to Jerusalem, presumably in order to pray there to the Almighty to enlighten and purify his former pupil. This satanic hatred on the part of Belvedere pursues every single official who has once served the state. . . .[111]

The Archduke reacted strongly to this and similar attacks by the Social Democrats and their press. Through his *Militärkanzlei*, as his own handwriting on a document confirms, he demanded that *Arbeiterwille*, of Graz, should be confiscated because it published on January 20, 1911, a criticism of the appointment of Count Franz Thun-Hohenstein, a big landowner and a protégé of the Archduke, as governor of Bohemia:

This governorship is rising up in Prague like a threatening cloud. It is said that the archreactionary, feudal-clerical Count Thun, has been nominated against the will of the Prime Minister; he is supposed to be the nominee of the Heir to the Throne . . . A black shadow is threatening Austria . . . but the working class fears nothing, neither Bienerth nor the Austrian Duke of Alba. . . .[112]

A study of the papers of the *Nachlass* and *Militärkanzlei* creates the impression that the Archduke Franz Ferdinand was above all a true Habsburg, brought up strictly in the spirit of some of their most renowned representatives, particularly the Emperors Ferdinand II and Ferdinand III. His energies were directed primarily to restoring to the *Erzhaus* the prestige and dignity it had enjoyed over past centuries. He was a lonely man endowed with a quickness of mind above the average and an understanding of political tactics. During his long decades as heir apparent, in his struggle against the flow of history, he alienated himself from many layers of Austro-Hungarian society. He was in deep conflict not only with his uncle Emperor Franz Josef, his powerful chamberlains, with most of the archdukes and archduchesses, but also with the Magyars and the South Slav national groups in the Habsburg realm.

CHAPTER VII

REORGANIZATION OF THE EMPIRE

My people are estranged one from another and this is all for the good. They do not contract the same illness at the same time. In France when the plague comes, all of you catch it on the same day. I send the Magyars to Italy and the Italians to Hungary. Each of them watches his neighbor; they do not understand each other and they hate each other. Out of their mistrust order is born and from their mutual hatred a lasting peace arises.

—EMPEROR FRANZ *I* OF AUSTRIA (to the French ambassador at Vienna)

O F ALL THE DISPUTES AMONG HISTORIANS over the Archduke Franz Ferdinand's personality, his attitude toward the reorganization of the empire has been most passionately debated. The main difficulty in assessing the Archduke's reform plans is the fact that he was killed before he came to the throne with a real opportunity to work out a program. His basic political philosophy was well known during his lifetime; it provides no sure answer as to just what reforms he would have pressed. He possessed a talent for tactical maneuvering in politics, and he was not politically isolated. The less extreme conservatives regarded him as their leader. It is an open question whether the realities of power would have induced him to adapt his ultraconservative position to political necessities.

Being heir apparent for eighteen years, the Archduke had enough time to work on the measures he intended to apply on the day of his ascension to the Habsburg throne. His uncle, the Emperor Franz Josef, was a man of advanced age; bronchitis threatened his life several times in the last decade of his reign. In the *Nachlass*, Section I, *Persönliche Dokumente und Schriften*, there is a special collection of documents called *Programm für den Thronwechsel*, which is the most authentic historical source for assessment of the Archduke's planned reforms.[1]

The Emperor Franz Josef and his nephew Franz Ferdinand differed fundamentally in their conceptions of reform. For the Emperor, the Compromise of 1867 represented the cornerstone of the monarchy; for the Archduke, it represented a humiliation of the *Erzhaus* at the hands of the Magyar gentry.

The Emperor adhered strictly to the 1867 Compromise, rejecting pressures for its basic revision coming from the Magyar Independent groups on one side, and from the Austrian generals and aristocracy in favor of a more centralized monarchy and against dualism, on the other. Yet the main provisions of the 1867 Compromise were reopened every ten years. The basic principles of the Compromise were that the two states (Austria and Hungary) were to have a joint ruler and were obliged to help each other in national defense. The army, foreign affairs, and finances were considered common affairs, and their management was in the hands of joint ministries. A common body called Delegations determined the budget for these common affairs. Expenses were divided proportionally between Austria and Hungary by a so-called Quota Committee; Budapest's share was fixed, at the beginning, at 30 per cent. Also, all customs and commercial agreements had to be renewed every ten years on the basis of new negotiations.

During these negotiations the very basis of dualism was often threatened, particularly when the army budget was discussed. Although the army was common to both, the Emperor retained a very large measure of control over it and it continued to be the strongest instrument of the house of Habsburg. He appointed the generals and supervised the inner organization of the army, but the Delegations had their say in such matters as recruiting, the number of conscripts to be called, and supplementary manpower drafts.

In general, between 1867 and the end of the century, the revision of the economic clauses of the Compromise did not cause as much controversy as did army questions, because the Magyars wanted their own army.

The turn of the century brought an intensification of the struggle of nationalities and, therefore, a new crisis in the relations between Vienna and Budapest; the whole dualistic concept based on the 1867 Compromise was endangered. Although in 1897 revision of the Compromise gave the Magyars some concessions in the economic and financial field, no headway was made in questions concerning the central army, particularly because of Budapest's insistence on introduction of the Magyar language.

In 1902 Minister of War General Geza Fejervary de Komlos Keresztes proposed a bill augmenting the joint Austro-Hungarian forces by 22,000 each year and the *Honvédség* (Hungarian home defense army) by 18,000. The opposition in the Budapest parliament, headed by the Independent party, began filibustering. It made demands for an independent Magyar army and the introduction of the Magyar language in all regiments of the joint army stationed in Hungary, although of forty-seven regiments in Hungary only five were purely Magyar.[2] In the spring elections of 1905, the opposition in Hungary won a complete victory, but the Emperor Franz Josef appointed a caretaker government of officials headed by General Fejervary. The opposition refused to form a government if the Emperor would not give them concessions in questions of the army. The Emperor countered with a threat to introduce universal suffrage with a secret ballot. Fejervary's Minister of the Interior Kristoffy proposed a bill to increase the number and the influence of the non-Magyar political parties in the Budapest parliament. The opposition deputies organized further obstructions. The Archduke advocated strong measures.[3] The Emperor decided to show a firm hand and on February 19, 1906, General Alexander von Nejiri appeared with a battalion of the *Honvédség* in the parliament, reading out a decree of prorogation and expelling all the deputies.

The Emperor did not wish to push matters to extremes and to the disappointment of the Archduke a *modus vivendi* was reached. The opposition got no concessions as far as the army was concerned, but Kristoffy's bill was dropped, although the new government, headed by Alexander Wekerle and composed of the opposition parties, agreed in principle to prepare an electoral reform bill. After long negotiations a revision of the Compromise was achieved in 1907. The military questions remained as before, but the Magyars received some concessions in economic and financial joint affairs, some privileges in concluding commercial treaties, and approval for the organization of a separate Hungarian bank.

In this way, the Emperor succeeded in celebrating the fortieth anniversary of the 1867 Compromise in conditions of relative peace with Budapest. But he had to face a strong opposition in Austria, centered around Belvedere and composed of the hard-core generals, the ancient landed nobility, and Dr. Lueger's Christian Socialist party, which was strongly oriented against the Magyars. The extent to which relations between the Emperor and Franz Ferdinand were strained over the question of dualism is evident in their correspondence at that time. The Emperor tried to force the Archduke to accept his policy on Hungary and ordered him to go to Budapest to attend the fortieth-anniversary celebration. For the Archduke, who at that time found strong support in the army for his stand on the Magyar question, the Emperor's decision was a heavy blow, and he drafted an answer of which a copy written in the Archduke's own hand exists in the *Nachlass;* it is dated "July 1907." Among other things, he said:

> Your Majesty has commanded *me to go to Pest.* I obey the command. Please do not misunderstand me, but I must tell your Majesty the truth, because I consider it my duty to do so—this celebration is really a *confusion of concepts,* this 40 years Jubilee of the *Ausgleich* at a moment when *these people* rule, people whom I can only describe as traitors and who constantly *agitate* against *everything*, Dynasty, Empire, Army etc. etc. . . .[4]

Despite this protest, the Archduke had to go to Budapest. Yet he demonstrated his opposition to the Emperor's policy on Hungary by being absent from the last part of the celebrations.

If one looks at the personal documents of the Archduke as they exist in the *Nachlass* and at his political correspondence, one gains the impression that he was a man of above-average intelligence, with an ability to state his political views precisely and with facility. Numerous drafts of letters, penciled summaries of thoughts, written in his big, hard, military handwriting, show that he did not need ghost writers. On the other hand, unlike the Emperor, the Archduke knew how to listen to the opinions of people with whom he shared the same general political philosophy. Colonel Brosch was a mastermind in organizing the *Militärkanzlei* into a kind of instrument for following the political climate in Austria-Hungary and abroad and gathering the views of political and legal experts for the *Thronwechsel* plans.

The Archduke's political advisers came from five different categories. There were, first, those members of the government who had been appointed at the Archduke's initiative. Among them, for instance, was the Archduke's teacher in his young days, Beck, who later became prime minister.

The Archduke's relations with Foreign Minister Aehrenthal went through a similar process. He was the Archduke's appointee, and in 1907 he had already given the Archduke political and technical advice for the take-over of the throne. In a letter of October 16, 1907, Aehrenthal sent a report of Baron Schuster (one of his experts) to the Archduke. This report contained advice concerning what should happen in the first days of the *Thronwechsel.*[5] On October 22, 1907, Aehrenthal forwarded remarks concerning policy toward Hungary in the *Thronwechsel,* made by his chief of division, Wolf. He also forwarded the texts of the proclamations of the Emperor Ferdinand when he ascended the throne in 1835 and of Franz Josef in 1848. Aehrenthal added that these two documents should not be treated as though they constituted a pattern; he enclosed in addition "a few confidential reports," advising the Archduke to read them.[6]

Yet conflict broke out between the Archduke and Aehrenthal because the latter had to follow the Emperor's directives. On December 26, 1908, Aehrenthal submitted a memorandum to the Archduke, proposing the need for military concessions to the Magyars in order to strengthen the empire during the crucial international crisis caused by the annexation of Bosnia and Hercegovina.[7] In a special letter to the Emperor, on January 5, 1909, the Archduke argued against each of Aehrenthal's points.[8] In the summer of the same year, the Emperor sent Aehrenthal to the Archduke's estate, Konopischt, but the meeting produced no results. In a letter written to the Emperor, without a date (but before August 17, 1909), the Archduke again disputed Aehrenthal's position, point by point.[9]

The most trusted political advisers of the Archduke came from the ranks of the army, particularly after the 1903 crisis broke out over the request of the Magyar Independents for a less centralized joint army. The hard-core leadership of the army regarded these requests as acts of rebellion aimed against the integrity of the empire. Their idea was to introduce an even more centralized system, in view of the general rearmament of the whole of Europe at that time and the need to modernize the imperial army. But, the generals complained that every step in that direction was hampered by Budapest, which controlled the number of recruits, the army's budget, and expenditures for rearmament.

The Archduke knew the arguments of the military leadership of the army from the days when Archduke Albrecht had been the undisputed leader of the so-called Vienna military group. The crisis with the Magyars in 1903 brought him even closer to these views. Military leaders found in the Archduke an energetic representative, particularly after 1906, when the Archduke succeeded in convincing the Emperor that he ought to dismiss old General Beck-Rzikowski as Chief of the General Staff and appoint General Conrad von Hötzendorf in his place. They worked together for eight years, until the Archduke was killed. Although there were periods when they did not see eye to eye on all problems, they never made a final break, as was the case with many other protégés of the Archduke. The main reason for this was that, on the problems of army unity and reorganization, Conrad agreed with the Archduke rather than with the old Emperor.[10]

Both the Archduke and Conrad understood that the reorganization of the army could not be achieved without taking away from Budapest the right to interfere in the affairs of the joint army. Conrad defended this policy in a memorandum handed to the Emperor and the Archduke in 1907, stressing the "intolerable situation" and saying that "the army is in danger every year, because the Hungarian parliament refuses to provide them with recruits and money." At the end he suggested ways to hinder the dissolution of the monarchy and to consolidate the state.[11] At the same time, Conrad advised the Archduke how to proceed with the reorganization of the empire and how to deal with the Magyars. He strongly advised the use of military might to solve constitutional disputes.[12] Conrad also suggested to the Archduke the idea of a Great Austria federalization.[13]

Conrad came into conflict with Aehrenthal and with Minister of War Schönaich, who shared the views of the old Emperor and wished to preserve the 1867 basis of the empire. In the autumn of 1911, Conrad was obliged to resign. The character and the extent of his special relationship with the Archduke can be seen from a letter which the Archduke wrote to the Emperor before November 1911, in which he pleaded that Conrad not be dismissed. After enumerating Conrad's qualities as a military leader and a man with excellent ideas, the Archduke begged the Emperor to support Conrad in his controversies with Schönaich and Aehrenthal:

First, I would be disgraced, because the whole Army knows that Conrad was graciously nominated by Your Majesty on my proposal and at my request, against the wish of the other high military personalities, and that I am responsible for him. I should prefer to disregard this, for me unpleasant, fact if it were in the interest of the Army to do so; but it is precisely in this interest, in my opinion, not to think of replacing Conrad, since he enjoys the complete confidence of the Army, and has my full confidence, and I am for the time being destined to bear responsibility for the Army in war and, indirectly, in peace as Your Majesty's senior general.[14]

Despite this intervention Conrad was forced to resign on December 3, 1911. Foreign Minister Aehrenthal came out strongly against him, a fact which was to alienate him from the Archduke for the rest of his life. But the Archduke succeeded in bringing Conrad back to his post a year later.[15]

The Archduke found similar support for the reorganization of the empire among the German aristocracy from Bohemia. Its main spokesman in Belvedere was Count Ottokar Czernin. He was a friend of the Duchess of Hohenberg's family and a neighbor of the Archduke; his estate Winar was near Konopischt. In 1905 Czernin published a pamphlet against the franchise reform in Austria; the pamphlet strengthened his relations with the Archduke.[16]

Czernin was one of the Archduke's principal political advisers on reform of the empire. He wrote four special memorandums on the different aspects of the reforms, and he wrote many letters to the Archduke. The first memorandum dealt with some basic ideas about reform of the monarchy and was submitted as early as 1908.[17] The second, in February 1909, approached the problem of personalities in the

Archduke's take-over regime.[18] The last two memorandums, one in July 1910 and the other in January 1911, were on the Magyar question.[19] At the proposal of the Archduke, Czernin was appointed a life member of the Herrenhaus, the upper house of the Austrian parliament, in 1912. For a time, Czernin fared very well in Belvedere, and the Archduke envisaged for him the leading post during the *Thronwechsel* process. Yet Czernin had conflicts with some of the other political advisers of the Archduke, and his role in internal affairs diminished. After 1913 he concentrated mainly on foreign relations problems, particularly in relation to Rumania.

Czernin's memorandums and letters show that his political philosophy was almost identical with the Archduke's. He supported the Archduke's idea of a strong central government, which would take away from the Magyars the right to make decisions concerning joint affairs, particularly those of the army. Although on two occasions, in June 1912 and August 1913, Czernin was more flexible toward the Magyars (advising the Archduke to give Stephen Tisza an audience), he shared the view that Hungary should be reduced to the status of an Austrian province.[20] Czernin also supported the Archduke in his views about the role of aristocracy in the empire, anti-Semitism, and the need to strengthen the German element in the monarchy.[21] He especially favored the use of the army as the best instrument for the settlement of internal political controversies.

A fourth group of political advisers represented Dr. Lueger and some clerical figures around Belvedere. The fifth and last group was composed of politicians among the national minorities in Hungary. Among them were several Rumanians, headed by the members of the Budapest parliament, Alexandru Vaida-Voevod and Aurel Popovici. The latter wrote in 1906 a book, *The United States of a Great Austria,* which Conrad recommended highly to the Archduke.[22] The Slovak leader, Milan Hodža, was in constant touch with Colonel Brosch and supplied the Archduke's office not so much with memoranda as with frequent confidential political reports.[23] The leader of the German Volkspartei in Hungary, Edmund Steinacker, was also consulted.

The head of the *Militärkanzlei,* Colonel Brosch, kept contact with all these groups of political advisers and legal experts, and in 1911 the first documents of the accession program were assembled. They consisted of the internal political instructions on how the change-over should proceed, the proclamation to the people by the new sovereign, and the order of the day to the army.

One version of these three documents was published in *Neues Wiener Journal* on December 31, 1923, and January 1, 1924. Because the work on the *Thronwechsel* continued until 1914, after Brosch had left Belvedere, there is a difference between Brosch's versions of these three documents and the documents from 1914 as they exist in the

Nachlass. For instance, in the Internal Political Instructions the order of the points is not the same and there are some stylistic changes. But the main political ideas and the spirit of the document are not changed.[24]

These three documents give an insight into the reforms the Archduke intended to make in the empire after the accession to the throne, although one should also take into consideration the precise instructions for the take-over which were made after 1911 and which also exist in the *Thronwechsel* collection. These precise instructions speak primarily about the methods of implementation of the Archduke's reform plans and they complement the three above-mentioned documents.

A centralized organization of the monarchy, with a much stronger position for the Crown, was clearly envisaged. This document stated clearly that "Dr. Beck's suggestion to call the empire 'both states of the monarchy' will not be used any longer, instead the term '*Reich*' is preferred."[25] The institution of *Reichskanzler* was introduced.

The rights of Budapest in joint affairs were cut considerably in regard to passing the budget on foreign affairs, the conclusion of commercial contracts, and the affairs of the army. The principle of the empire as an economic unit was proclaimed, and this ended the specific customs advantages which Hungary had enjoyed on the basis of the 1867 Compromise. But the Hungarian quota of expenses of the joint budget was decreased.

The Archduke's ideas about a unified army under the sole command of the Emperor were proclaimed. In the order of the day to the armed forces it was said: "The glorious old army has been for centuries the first and most reliable support of the throne, in good and bad times, during war and peace; it has been the noblest guarantor of the great power of the monarchy."[26]

Any idea of concessions to the Magyars in the army was discarded. The Archduke proclaimed the principle of German as the state language for all joint institutions, including the army. Also it was explicitly stated that no Hungarian Army exists, only troops which train themselves in Hungary.[27]

All in all, the Archduke intended to reduce the status of Hungary drastically, making out of it a kind of imperial crownland. One of the means for effecting this was reliance on the non-Magyar national groups in Hungary. In his proclamation to the people the Archduke proclaimed the introduction of universal suffrage in Hungary and expressed a wish to treat all nationalities, all classes and all religious groups on an equal footing: "We want to meet all nations of the monarchy, all social layers and all religious professions that have been acknowledged by law, with the same love. Whether noble or common, whether poor or rich, all shall have equal rights before our throne." But in the internal political instructions, the Archduke expressed at several places his antidemocratic and antiliberal philosophy. Speaking for instance about the Jews in Hungary he said: "The Jew is always on the side of the strongest party, he is—if he can profit by it—even anti-Semitic and is therefore not to be feared."[28] The Archduke, under the pretense of breaking "the influence of Jewish newspapers," intended to curtail the rights of free press in the monarchy.

The Archduke also clearly stated that he wanted to use the army as an instrument for settling the controversial political issues in the monarchy. Although the internal political instructions mention "constitutional government" under the heading "J" as one of its guiding principles, the same document speaks later about octroi and *coup d'état* as possible alternative methods for pushing through the Archduke's reforms.

The Archduke's legal advisers found a legal trick which would enable the new Emperor to take the coronation oath at once and thus give him a period of six months to push through his plans. In the document "Aide Mémoire to His Imperial Highness," obviously worked out after Colonel Brosch left the *Militärkanzlei*, the legal procedure of the take-over was fixed with utmost precision.[29] The *aide-mémoire* envisaged two possibilities—first, that the Budapest government would yield and accept the Archduke's demands; and second, that it would reject them. In the latter case, the Constitution of the Empire was to be decreed through an Imperial Octroi.[30]

It seems that the Archduke expected that the Hungarian Prime Minister Count Stephen Tisza would reject his dictum; therefore, as early as 1913, he took steps for the gradual withdrawal of the Magyar military units from Hungary and for their replacement by non-Magyar units, particularly from the Tirol and Croatia.[31] At the Archduke's suggestion, General of Cavalry Karl Terstyansky von Nadas, was appointed commander of the Budapest corps.[32] Terstyansky was an energetic man, known to be loyal to the Archduke. He should have performed the same role as General Fejervary did in 1905, when he crushed the Magyar opposition by force.

In the event of a *coup d'état*, in the *Thronwechsel* there is a copy of the written order of the new Emperor to Minister of War General Alexander von Krobatin, informing him that the Prime Minister has rejected "my Proclamation and now I ask you to make immediately the necessary arrangements through the officers under your command so that the Imperial orders can be carried out through the military organs."[33] This document was typed, the year 1914 was inserted, and only the signature of the new Emperor and the exact date had to be affixed.

In addition to this order, the *Militärkanzlei* prepared the drafts of the orders which the minister of war was to send to the commanders of the army corps to use "force against anyone who does not fulfill the provisions of the Imperial Proclamation."[34]

That the Archduke Franz Ferdinand intended to use military force against the Magyars has been contested by some writers. Friedrich

Funder, former editor of the Christian Socialist paper, *Reichspost,* and one of the close political collaborators of both Dr. Lueger and Archduke Franz Ferdinand, challenged this thesis in his book *Vom Gestern ins Heute,* published after the end of the Second World War in German, and in an American edition, *From Empire to Republic,* in 1963. He rejected the idea that the Archduke would have used force against the Magyars. "Was force to be used, and bayonets drawn, to scare off the latter-day Ludwig Kossuths? He has been credited with such plans; an impetuous phrase perhaps indicated such a course, but it was certainly never considered in earnest."[35]

The documents in the *Nachlass* put this issue in a proper historical light. The Archduke himself expected that he would be obliged to use military force in Hungary. In the internal political instructions it was stated that a revolution might be expected in Hungary.[36] This confirms the validity of a conversation between the Archduke and the German Kaiser at their meeting at Konopischt in June 1914, when the Archduke spoke very bitterly not only against the Independents and other opposition parties in Hungary, but against the Hungarian Prime Minister Stephen Tisza, who was himself in conflict with the Independents. The Archduke said "that Hungary was maintained in downright medieval conditions by a tiny oligarchy, and that every Magyar was working against Austria and the monarchy as a whole."[37] The Kaiser Wilhelm was not of that opinion, and he ventured to praise Count Tisza, but the Archduke retorted that Tisza was really a dictator in Hungary and would like to be the same in Vienna, that he was working for a separate Hungarian army, and that if foreign policy went wrong a large measure of blame should be attached to Tisza for his ill-treatment of the Rumanians in Hungary.[38]

These feelings of the Archduke were publicly known. The German ambassador in Vienna, Tschirschky, informed Berlin on May 10, 1914, that the Archduke had said that "he would not let Tisza stay twenty-four hours at the head of the government, because of the risk that the latter would organize a revolution against him within forty-eight hours."[39]

Tisza knew from several sources about the Archduke's preparations for a *coup d'état* and his answer was: "If Franz Ferdinand as Emperor Franz II uses force against me, I will start a national revolution against him, and the last word will be mine."[40]

The Archduke's violent death denied Tisza the opportunity to show what he really would have done if the Archduke had carried out a *coup d'état.* Even on the eve of June 28, at his last dinner party at Ilidže, in front of all the dignitaries of Bosnia and Hercegovina, among them several Magyar civil servants, the Archduke raged against Tisza and Budapest. When the Archduke had retired, Governor Potiorek had to ask all present to forget what they had heard.[41]

Bosnia and Hercegovina were another focal point of sharp disagreement between the Archduke and Prime Minister Tisza. Nowhere else in the Habsburg empire was there such a conflict of interests between Vienna and Budapest. From the first days of the occupation of the two provinces in 1878, their rule through the Joint Ministry of Finance, was based on a tacit agreement between Austria and Hungary. The local civil service was predominantly in the hands of the Magyars, but Vienna had a slight advantage, because Bosnia and Hercegovina were primarily under military administration and the Habsburgs controlled the army.

As time went by and the industrialization of the country was accelerated, competition between Austrian and Magyar banks and commercial enterprises in the exploitation of mineral wealth and timber, in railroad building, and in other business activities increased. The 1908 annexation intensified the clash of interests. The question of the constitutional position of Bosnia and Hercegovina within the Habsburg monarchy had to be settled. The Magyar aristocracy claimed that Bosnia and Hercegovina should be possessions of the Crown of St. Stephen, because a part of the two provinces had been under the sovereignty of the Magyar kings in the Middle Ages.

The disagreement over dualism between Emperor Franz Josef and the Archduke had its repercussions in the affairs of Bosnia and Hercegovina. In August 1908 the Archduke wrote to Brosch:

If the annexation has to be realized, I give my assent under only one condition, that both provinces should join the Empire and the crownlands. If Hungary demands that these provinces belong to St. Stephen's Crown—and this will happen—we should not yield under any conditions, even if it means evading the annexation and leaving things as they are. But in this case we must put a stop to Burian's dangerous system. . . .[42]

The Archduke was particularly concerned with preventing Magyar capital from getting the upper hand in Bosnia and Hercegovina. In 1909 he issued strict instructions to his *Militärkanzlei* to block Burian's efforts to give privileges to the Pester Komercialbank and its branch in Sarajevo.[43] The Archduke was also partly responsible for the dismissal of Burian, but he did not get along with the new Joint Minister of Finance, Leon von Bilinski, a nobleman of Polish decent. In 1913 and 1914 the competition between Viennese and Budapest banks for control of the economy of Bosnia and Hercegovina became even sharper. Bosnia's mineral wealth became the object of a fierce struggle. In northern Bosnia the Ljubija mines started to produce a high quality iron ore and the Hungarian Prime Minister Lukacs tried to take this mine under Budapest control, but the Joint Minister of Finance Bilinski was against this. At last a compromise was reached on April 1, 1914,[44] but Franz Ferdinand remained dissatisfied. He was in general disagreement with

Bilinski's policy, especially with his unwillingness to support the Minister of War's requests for high military credits.[45]

Relations between the Archduke and Bilinski deteriorated even more seriously over the building of railways in Bosnia and Hercegovina. The *Militärkanzlei* sent a letter on April 1, 1913, to Bilinski saying that the Archduke would be opposed to the railways in Bosnia and Hercegovina being built under the leadership of the Bodenkreditanstalt and would prefer their construction under the domination of the Kreditanstalt.[46] Bilinski complained against such pressure and said that he was unwilling to give concession to any monopoly. This act, he said, "brought upon me the disfavor of the Archduke."[47] The building of railways through Bosnia and Hercegovina was connected with the general plans of Germany to build railways in the southeastern area of Europe and in neighboring Asian regions. Bilinski finally gave concessions to the German Dresdner Bank, and just before the outbreak of the First World War he reached an agreement for a loan of sixty million crowns.[48]

For all the above-mentioned reasons, the Archduke Franz Ferdinand paid great attention to Bosnia and Hercegovina in his *Thronwechsel* plans. In a list of the most urgent political goals of the take-over of the throne, under Part "K," the "regulation of Bosnia's place in the monarchy" was mentioned.[49] Section 8 of the *Thronwechsel* speaks about this in more detail and in the internal political instructions the Archduke defined his policy:

Hungary would never allow Bosnia and Hercegovina to be attached to Austria. This would have the consequence of strengthening the Slav majority in Austria, which would surely be of no advantage. But their attachment to Hungary would likewise not be possible, in view of the resistance which such an idea would create, not only in Austria, but also in Bosnia. Hungary cannot repair the sacrifice in money and blood which Austria has brought with the occupation and administration of these countries; on the other hand, the Bosnians will defend themselves tooth and nail against becoming Hungarian subjects and thus being as politically suppressed as the other non-Magyar nationalities enjoying the blessings of Hungarian administration. Through the attachment of the annexed lands to Hungary its economic and political influence within the monarchy would increase even more, but Austria would be cut off from the Balkans, where the monarchy sees its future. Even now Austria cannot obtain direct railway communication to Bosnia and Hercegovina; but what will it be like afterwards? Moreover, Dalmatia would lose her hinterland, which she only acquired so recently, and would finally gravitate toward Hungary, which, according to the King's title, already lays theoretical claims to this territory. Finally, Austria would even lose the Dalmatian Coast, but our future lies—at least partially—on the seas. A partition of the annexed lands between the two parts of the Empire is more likely to be discussed, but the Bosnians would protest against this, and in any case Austria would be worse off, because naturally she would get the Karst territories of Hercegovina, while Hungary would receive the fertile Posavina and Bosnia, which is rich in timber and ores. . . .[50]

As far as the status of Bosnia was concerned, the Archduke envisaged that Bosnia and Hercegovina should remain a *Reichsland*, a crownland, with the right to send its representatives to the Delegations.[51]

The instructions further mentioned the regulation of the question of the coat of arms and of the flags of Bosnia and Hercegovina.

The *Thronwechsel* documents do not go into concrete detail concerning the future of the other nationalities in the monarchy and what their political, cultural and economic status would be. The only exception was the status of the Czechs.[52] The greater part of the *Thronwechsel* deals with reforms in the relations with Hungary, and the other nationalities are mentioned primarily in connection with this problem.

In the proclamation to the people which was to have been read at the moment of his accession to the throne, the Archduke promised universal suffrage to the non-Magyar nationalities in Hungary. He expressed general ideas about the rights of nationalities in the Empire and the need for peace with foreign powers, "so that nations of the monarchy can devote themselves undisturbedly to cultural and economic tasks which we shall always foster as much as possible."[53] After this general statement he proclaimed the introduction of the general franchise in Hungary:

It is according to our principle of equality of all nations and social layers that we shall make the effort to guarantee every individual nation of the monarchy its own national development, as long as this be done within the monarchy; and we shall exert ourselves for the decree of a just election franchise for all social layers and professional classes to take part in legislative activity, as far as this has not yet been done.[54]

In his correspondence with the Emperor, the Archduke stressed the need to use non-Magyar minorities in Hungary against Budapest, as in the 1848–49 revolution. This was most emphatically stressed in a letter of November 24, 1908:

At the moment, the nationalities are only being oppressed politically; in the army they still have fully equal rights. They are therefore still loyal and dynastically minded. I doubt whether this will remain so if Andrassy's electoral reform, with plurality and public voting, is introduced. But even if the army agrees eventually to Magyarize, one can be quite sure that Germans, Rumanians, Slovaks and Serbs will in event of war show neither love for the common army nor enthusiasm for Emperor and Empire.

Up to now the Magyars—this must be stated truthfully and this is taught by world history and military history on every page—have for hundreds of years always conspired with the enemies of the house of Habsburg and of the monarchy. The recent past has proved that there has been no change in this; so one has to reckon with similar circumstances in the future. For the tendencies and final aims of Kossuthism, and therefore of the now dominant Independent party, yet even of the coalition, are antidynastic and directed against ruler and empire.

It would therefore be a mistake to hand over to the Magyars the nationalities, who have always in difficult times been a pillar of loyalty to the Emperor—may I recall the year '48?—and so drive them also into the antidynastic and Irredentist camp.[55]

Although the Archduke relied on Rumanian and Slovak minorities in his Hungarian policy, he also counted a great deal on the South Slavs, particularly the Croats. For a time he even advocated the idea of trialism, making the South Slavs a third unit in the monarchy, side by side with Austria and Hungary.

The idea of trialism existed long before the Archduke tried to use it. The Slovene scholar Kopitar had advanced a kind of cultural trialism as early as 1830, under the influence of German Romanticism.[56] As a political thesis it appeared in 1848–49 among some Croats influenced by František Palacký's ideas on the reform of the Habsburg Empire and the need for an increased role for Slavs within it.

At the turn of the twentieth century, when the Croat and Slovene bourgeoisies increased in number and economic strength, trialism took on new meaning. With the incorporation of Bosnia and Hercegovina —much less economically developed than Croatia and Slovenia—the young Croat and Slovene industrialists had a field for the expansion of business. The Croat Pure Right party accepted the idea of trialism in its 1894 program asking for the formation of a third unity within the Habsburg monarchy composed of all the Croat lands. This party came into sharp conflict with the pan-Serb movement with its center in Belgrade, which propagated the unification of all Serbs with Serbia. The Pure Right party believed that Croats should have complete predominance in the new state and regarded the Serbs in Croatia (between one fourth and one third of the population) as intruders on pure Croat territory. The Pure Right party was backed by some orders of the Roman Catholic Church and found a natural ally in Vienna in court and military circles. It was at the same time hostile toward Budapest because of its imposition of absolutism in Croatia.

The Archduke began to pay attention to trialism in 1903, when the crisis broke out over the Magyar request for reorganization of the Habsburg army. Under the influence of Dr. Lueger, the Archduke backed the idea of trialism as the best means of intimidation and pres-

sure against the Magyar nobility.[57] For a time the Archduke propagated
this idea, and in 1903 he told the Russian Tsar Nicholas II that he had
sympathy for the formation of a South Slav state unit within the Habsburg Empire.[58]

But events in Croatia and other South Slav lands soon turned the
Archduke away from the idea. The Croat struggle for independence in
1903–5 was directed not only against Budapest, but against Vienna as
well. Liberal Croat politicians from Dalmatia favored a rapprochement between the Croats and Serbs. They realized that in view of the
events in Hungary (the pro-Habsburg military government of General
Fejervary) and the increasing dependence of Vienna on Kaiser Wilhelm's Germany, the disintegration of the Habsburg empire was a
question of time and that the South Slavs should seek an alliance with
the Magyars. A meeting at Rijeka in 1905, attended by all the Croat
members of parliament except those belonging to the Pure Right party,
proposed a common front with the Serbs in Croatia. They appealed
also to the Magyar Independent party to join them in a common struggle against the Habsburgs. They passed a resolution backing up the
requests of the Magyars for independence, stressing that their demand
was just—"because every people has the right to decide freely and independently about its interests and its fate. The Croats and the Magyars
should rely on each other, and their struggle is a common one." At the
same time, the Croat legislators asked for a new election law, freedom
of the press, freedom to hold political meetings, and the unification of
Dalmatia and Croatia. The Serbian political parties accepted in Zadar
the main points of the Rijeka resolution, and soon a Croat-Serbian coalition was formed on the basis of the Rijeka and Zadar programs.

The Rijeka resolution represented a blow to the Archduke's policy.
"The Rijeka resolution bewildered the Heir Apparent very much, because up to then he had believed that all Croats were loyal to the Emperor and opposed to the Magyars. As a consequence he withdrew
from the idea of trialism, insofar as it can be said that it ever had a
definite shape," wrote Kiszling.[59]

The victory of the Croat-Serbian coalition in the elections in Croatia,
political unrest, strikes and protests in all parts of Croatia, and particularly the hostile demonstrations against the Archduke in Dalmatia and
Hercegovina during his journey through these South Slav provinces in
1906 opened his eyes as to the real feelings of the South Slavs.

Because the Emperor Franz Josef was ill, the Archduke attended the
maneuvers in September 1906, in Dalmatia and Hercegovina. His visit
was greeted by the members of the Pure Right party as a gesture which
would speed the realization of trialism and annexation of Bosnia and
Hercegovina to the monarchy. *Hrvatski Dnevnik*, of Sarajevo, on September 13 sent a telegram to the Archduke "with warm wish to unite
us, through the Kingdom of Croatia, with the Habsburg monarchy."

But both in Hercegovina and Dubrovnik (Ragusa) the Archduke was received with silence, although the authorities did their best to organize demonstrations in his honor. According to a confidential report to Vienna, the authorities in Trebinje, Hercegovina, paid thirty crowns to every citizen who agreed to cheer the Archduke.[60]

The demonstrations in Dubrovnik were even more hostile. The mayor, Peter Čingrija, refused to greet the Heir Apparent, and the chief of police had to take his place. The authorities named Fran Supilo, one of the leaders of the Croat-Serbian coalition, as the instigator of the demonstrations. Although Supilo as a fourteen-year-old boy had taken part in demonstrations against Prince Rudolf, then the heir apparent, when he visited Dubrovnik in 1886, and for that had been excluded from all high schools in the empire for one year, he denied that he was the organizer of the demonstrations against the Archduke Franz Ferdinand, insisting that the demonstrations were spontaneous.

The Archduke was hurt by the demonstrations, and his physician, Dr. Eisenmenger, who followed him on this journey, described the Archduke's feeling in this way:

The further stay at Ragusa was taken up with the official duties of the successor to the throne. Crown Prince Danilo of Montenegro came on a visit, and the Archduke drove to meet him. The streets were decorated with flags, but exclusively with flags in the national colors of Croatia. Not a single imperial black-and-yellow flag was among them, not even at the headquarters of the commanding officer of the district. On the drive, there was a cheer only now and then from the crowd which lined both sides of the street. But when the Archduke returned with Prince Danilo at his side, the progress of the carriage was accompanied by enthusiastic acclamations. The reception of the deputation which consisted entirely of handsome men of powerful stature in resplendent uniforms was rather frigid and short, and soon Crown Prince Danilo, who was also a handsome man of commanding figure, started on his return trip accompanied by the mighty cheers of the crowd. . . .[61]

The visit to Hercegovina ended in a similar way:

Count Burian, the Captain General of Bosnia and Hercegovina, arrived and Trebinje, the capital of Hercegovina, was visited. The receptions there were reeled off with indifferent haste. Only the unique costumes and the martial figures of the natives were interesting.

On the return through the terribly poor and rocky country, I became, in the saloon car, an involuntary witness of a conversation between the Archduke and a major. I did not care to listen, but the closing sentence was spoken in such a loud voice that I could not help hearing it: "You know how matters stand here, and every sensible man knows it; only the government has no idea of it . . ." The Archduke reported to the Emperor the disloyal attitude of the population, complained about the make-believe and false statements of the facts on the part of the local political authorities and demanded radical disciplinary punishment of the guilty persons.[62]

The Archduke protested to the Emperor and to the Prime Minister of Austria, complaining against the "scandalous event."[63] In a letter to Brosch he described the behavior the people of Dubrovnik and Trebinje as "infamous."[64]

One could suppose that this first direct encounter of the Archduke with the South Slav population influenced him against trialism; but, understanding political tactics, the Archduke never publicly denounced the idea. On the contrary, his political advisers, particularly those from Dr. Lueger's party, kept the legend of trialism alive, as a first-class weapon against the Magyars as well as against the Serbs. As late as 1914 there was a heated argument in different Croat, Magyar and Serb political groups about the merits of trialism; this discussion fomented friction between them.

In the *Nachlass* there are many documents which confirm this evolution of the Archduke's policy toward trialism. For instance, Brosch wrote to the Archduke, on June 17, 1910:

. . . One must not play with the slogan of trialism if it is given out from *below*, because this could have very unpleasant—at the moment hardly forseeable—consequences.

Who can guarantee, by the way, that the new state unit of Croatia, Bosnia, Dalmatia and Carinthia, which cuts Austria off from the sea, will carry out a really loyal policy which is faithful to the Emperor, and will support Austria and dynastic interests? A new Fiume Resolution could come overnight, and even now the Croats are completely in the hands of the Hungarian government. Moreover, would Bohemia watch calmly if a state unit arose in the south, while the old independent kingdom remained a province?

I must confess frankly that I consider trialism extremely dangerous, for to get taxes and recruits through three parliaments would certainly be a still more difficult job than it is now. The slogan trialism is quite useful to *frighten* the Magyars, but it should go no further than that.[65]

Similar opinions were held by other advisers to the Archduke.[66]

The Archduke accepted the advice of his experts and in the internal political instructions of the *Thronwechsel* the project of trialism was discarded, although it was agreed that the threat of trialism could be still useful in making the Magyars yield to the Archduke's plans for reform. The internal political instructions said about trialism:

Trialism is looked upon as a means of subordinating Hungary. But, in my opinion, it is simply a reasonable instrument for frightening the Magyar chauvinists, but without bringing at the same time any real advantages to the dynasty or to Austria.

First it must be stated that the South Slavs are all more or less unreliable politicians. One can observe this in Croatia and lately in Bosnia as well. And who would guarantee that this state unit within the monarchy, consisting of Croatia, Bosnia and Hercegovina, Dalmatia and the Littorals, to which also Carniola, and perhaps a piece of Styria as well, might have to be added, will always be on the side of Austria . . . It is possible that the difficulties would simply be doubled, if three ministries, three parliaments, three Delegations had to work together, and that the Slav state unit would be often on the side of Hungary, where surely the interests of the Crown were never to be sought.[67]

But Belvedere, through some of the trusted friends of the Archduke, like Prince Karl Schwarzenberg, through its newspapers, and through some of the right-wing Croat and Slovene politicians, continued to advance the idea of trialism as the pet project of the Archduke. These tactics brought certain political goals. The Magyar political parties were frightened, and the cleavage between pan-Croat and pan-Serb groups deepened. But it also brought many negative results for the Archduke. Some of his most die-hard enemies, particularly among the pan-Serbs, firmly believed in the Archduke's intention to make "Great Croatia" a third unit of the Habsburg empire, thus hampering their own dream of pan-Serb rule in this area.

The Archduke kept his real intentions regarding the treatment of the South Slavs in his reformed empire for the closed circle of his political allies and advisers. The most vital document in the *Nachlass* about the trialism controversy is a letter from the Archduke to the German Kaiser Wilhelm. In the midst of the international crisis caused by the annexation of Bosnia and Hercegovina, the Kaiser expressed his dissatisfaction with the Archduke's attitude toward the Magyars and the rumors of trialism. For Wilhelm the main danger for Germany and Austria-Hungary was the Slavs. In his answer the Archduke admitted this, but he emphasized that the chief troublemakers within the Habsburg realm were the Magyars, teachers of rebellion for all the other nationalities; once they were bridled, the Slavs would be docile. In the same correspondence, the Archduke explicitly disavowed trialism; it was being used only as a tactical move to frighten the Magyars.

The argument over this issue was opened by Kaiser Wilhelm in his letter of February 12, 1909:

The dangers for the future internal development of the Monarchy which you foresee arising from relations with Hungary have been of great interest to me. It is certain that the Magyar is not easy to manage, with his chauvinism and his vanity; and, as you explain, these qualities have been further strengthened by too much give-in, so that it is difficult to set a firm limit to concessions. It goes without saying that such concessions must not be made at the expense of the army, which by this would lose homogeneity and strength.

On the other hand, in the last month the Slav danger has surprisingly revealed itself in all its blindness and violence. According to your own description the maneuvers of Belgrade and Prague are based on a firm program, which is secured by money gifts. Behind them both stands Moscow; to what extent Cracow and Lemberg are engaged in this, I cannot judge. Now for Austria this pan-Slav danger seems to be the greater of the two, since it has leverage in your country itself, with the Czechs being against Austria and its Imperial House, and can endanger the existence of the Monarchy, because it involves the *newly incorporated Slav countries* and thereby is becoming a *second Slav great power* alongside holy Slav Russia.

It seems likely that one can expect, in the future, a much greater degree of this pan-Slav enmity, stirred up by the other great powers, and out of fear of competition and the division of total Slav power between herself and you, Russia will always regard it with suspicion.

The best support against the old Slav danger and intrigue is (a) a good firm relationship with Rumania, (b) ditto with Bulgaria, and (c) with Turkey. In addition, the hatred of the Magyars for everything which is pan-Slavistic would make them a good support in the south against all Slav velleities. For Magyar chauvinism springs from a burning patriotism, even if of a particularist coloring; and if well directed, it could be used for the general welfare of the fatherland.[68]

The Archduke answered this letter some months later, after his return from a visit to Rumania. When he was passing through the parts of Hungary inhabited by Rumanians, Rumanian politicians organized the local peasants to come to the stations past which the Archduke's train was passing and greet him and his wife. The Hungarian government ordered the gendarmerie to use their bayonets, and crowds of Rumanian peasants were dispersed in the presence of the Archduke. This infuriated him, and in his letter (undated) written after his return from Rumania he took up the Magyar question with Kaiser Wilhelm. Describing the brutality of the Hungarian gendarmerie, the Archduke said:

This yet again for the thousandth time proved what I have always said: that the so-called noble, gentlemanly Magyar is a most infamous, antidynastic, lying, unreliable fellow, and that all the difficulties which we have in the Monarchy arise exclusively from the Magyars.

You have, Your Majesty, stated in your last kind letter that you consider the Slav danger as the most serious of all for our country. I permit myself completely to be of your opinion. I also regard as highly dangerous this pressing and pushing forward of the Slavs, this violent policy of constant demands, this political blackmailing, this artificial creation of difficulties in all the operations of the state, etc., etc. But where is the root of the evil? Who served as teacher for all these elements? Who are the people who achieve everything by revolutionary pressure and blackmail? The Magyars.

Who, even a few years ago, had heard of the Young Czechs or the radical antimilitarist Czechs; who had heard of the Slovene question, of trialism, of Czech schools, of the South Slav question, of Slavization of entire communities and counties etc., etc.? Prague, for instance, was a German town; now you are half-killed if you speak a word of German, etc. The Slavs behave in this way only because they copy the disrespectful behavior of the Magyars and see how they achieve everything by their shameless methods. I am completely convinced, and could go bail for it, that the moment a stop is put to these shameless Magyar intrigues (which would be quite easy to do, since the Magyar as a true Hun and Asiatic always boasts but then gives way in the face of energetic action) the Slavs would end their violent onrush and would again submit calmly and quietly to the culturally far superior Germans.

If we want peace and quiet in the Austrian Monarchy, if we want the chance to conduct a strong foreign policy, beneficial to all nations, in association with our Allies, there is only one way and one necessity, and that is to smash the *preponderance* of the Magyars. Otherwise we shall with absolute certainty become a Slav Empire, and trialism, which would be a misfortune, will be achieved.[69]

This correspondence throws light on what the Archduke intended to do after he had settled the problem of the Magyars. It also contributes to an understanding of his conception of the rights of nationalities. He started to think about this phenomenon only under the pressure of political events, but his political philosophy, his whole feudal upbringing, did not permit him to understand the concept of the right of nationalities in any full sense. He treated these rights as an imperial gift which he could bestow, rather than as something which the people themselves possessed. Basically, he looked at the South Slavs as faithful Frontiermen, who performed their duties towards the Habsburg dynasty, since among the South Slavs nothing had changed from the beginning of the nineteenth century, when they were composed mainly of illiterate peasantry.

Brought up in the feudal tradition of the Habsburgs, he had no ear for the rights of nationalities. For the Archduke the solution of the national problem was not connected with democracy. His intention to introduce general suffrage in Hungary was just a tactical political move. In his internal political instructions he stated: "The Crown has only one instrument of power against the opposition Magyars: general suffrage."[70] The absence of any inclination toward democracy is proved by the fact that the Archduke in 1906–7 was the ardent opponent of

general suffrage in Austria, that he rallied the landed Austrian aristocracy against that change, and that the Austrian Prime Minister Beck
forfeited his confidence because he introduced general suffrage in
Austria.

In 1914 the Archduke adhered to the idea of general suffrage in Hungary only to get the non-Magyar national groups on his side. What he
intended to do after the pacification of the Magyars was revealed in his
letter to Kaiser Wilhelm. In his internal political instructions, he envisaged, as a consequence of electoral reform in Hungary, a kind of dead-
lock in the Budapest parliament, and benefits for his absolutist tendencies of government.[71]

The most effective means of curtailing the power of the Magyar aristocracy over their tenants—of whom the majority were of non-
Magyar nationality—would have been an agrarian reform. In Hungary
24,000,000 hectares of arable land was divided among approximately
2,800,000 landholders, while a mere 4,000 Magyar aristocrats owned
almost one third of it—roughly 7,500,000 hectares—another third
being shared by 2,400,000 small farmers. The 324 largest estates, averag-
ing 41,000 acres each, covered not less than 19.3 per cent of the whole
agricultural area of the country.[72] In the southern parts of historical
Hungary, where the South Slavs lived, 1,200,000 peasants owned 2,000,-
000 *jochs* of land, while 3,700 landlords had the same amount.[73] (A hec-
tare is the metric equivalent of 2½ acres. A *joch*, or yoke, is a little
bigger than an acre.)

Yet in the whole *Thronwechsel* documentation there is no mention
of agrarian reform. One of the collaborators of the Archduke among
the Rumanian minority in Hungary, Vaida-Voevod, commented about
this shortcoming of the Archduke's policy: "Anyone who brought
about agrarian reform would win the whole people of Hungary, Magyar as well as non-Magyar. And to tackle this problem the Archduke
just did not have the courage."[74]

At the same time, the *Thronwechsel's* outline of economic and financial policies for the empire, particularly the plan to form one economic
unit out of the whole empire, was not directed only against Magyar
financial circles; it would have increased the already uneven industrial
development of the monarchy in favor of Vienna. The South Slav lands
found themselves at the very bottom of the industrialization scale.

Practically all industrial and mining enterprises, and a portion of railroads
which were privately owned, in the South Slav lands within the Dual Monarchy were owned and managed by Austrians and, to a much lesser degree,
by the Magyars. The same applied to banks and insurance companies. Austrian and Hungarian investments in the South Slav areas prior to 1918 were
only partly financed by Austrian and Hungarian capital, while the other
part was financed by Western European capital loaned to Viennese and

Budapest industrial concerns and banks. Furthermore, almost the entire wholesale trade was in the hands of Viennese and Budapest firms.[75]

Per capita income in the South Slav lands was much lower than that in Austria and in Hungary proper. The disposable average per capita income in the Austrian half of the monarchy during the period 1911–13 was estimated at 531 crowns, but this income averaged as follows:[76]

Territory included in	Crowns per capita
Austria	695
Czechoslovakia	666
Poland	298
Italy	495
Rumania	343
Yugoslavia	350

In the economic policies of both Vienna and Budapest, the South Slav lands were to be kept

as sources of agricultural products and raw materials and as markets for industrial products. Among those industrial products textile and various metal products played the most important role. The South Slav lands also offered opportunities for Austrian and Hungarian investments, and for the employment of entrepreneurial talent, traders, skilled workers and bureaucrats. Thus, generally speaking, Austria and Hungary conducted toward their respective subject nations a policy of political and economic imperialism and treated them essentially as colonies, a policy which did not serve the interests of the latter nations and constituted the basic reason for the tendency of all these nations to liberate themselves from Austro-Hungarian rule.[77]

In the final version of the *Thronwechsel*, to which Dr. Alfred Eichhoff, an official of the Ministry of the Interior, together with Bardolff and Kristoffy, put the last touches, the old absolutist idea of the return of *Gesamtmonarchie*, of a unified empire, was emphasized.[78] The Archduke did not go far from his political program as he had expressed it in 1899—"I exist for the unity of Austria, and as the means of unification of her people I count on the dynasty, the Catholic religion and especially the German language as *Kulturträger* and the universal means of communication."[79] Although for a time he toyed with the idea of *Kronenföderalismus* (a federation of seventeen crownlands, the historicopolitical entities of the Habsburg realm with their feudal estates and constitutions) and for a very short period with trialism, he returned quickly and definitely to the Greater Austria scheme.

Basically, the Archduke intended to introduce a system of centralist rule by the German element in the empire. This issue has been clouded by the controversy over responsibility for the outbreak of the First World War. Sidney B. Fay, leader of the Revisionists, took such a position:

The Archduke was criticized by the Magyars and German dominant factions for wishing to favor small nationalities. It was a reproach which did honor to his wisdom and sense of justice. Here again he differed from the aged Emperor Francis Joseph as inclined to half-measures and compromise. He regarded himself as the author of the Austro-Hungarian Compromise of 1867 and had no thought of modifying it. Franz Ferdinand, however, seems to have regarded this dual organization of the Empire as an unfortunate mistake, because it gave in practice so much power into the hands of the Magyar magnates. He therefore seems to have been quite ready to see the *Dualism* of 1867 replaced by some kind of *Trialism* when he himself should come to the throne.[80]

In order to prove the Archduke's intention to federalize the monarchy, Sidney Fay has stated that the Archduke "had heard with great interest expositions of the American federal system of Professor J. W. Burgess," of Columbia University, New York, who "had been invited to return to Vienna to give further information on the subject and was on the point of again sailing for Europe to do so at the moment the Archduke was assassinated."[81]

Sidney Fay did not explain what the views of J. W. Burgess were. The writings of Burgess show clearly that he was a propagator of racialism and anti-Semitism and that he believed in the predominance of Teutonic peoples in modern society. For instance, in his main work, *Political Science and Comparative Constitutional Law*, he stated that the national state was "the creation of Teutonic political genius," which "stamps the Teutonic nations as the political nations par excellence and authorizes them in the economy of the world, to assume the leadership in the administration of states."[82] For Burgess, as for the Archduke, federalism meant the leadership of the Teutonic element:

In a state whose population is composed of a variety of nationalities, the Teutonic element, when dominant, should never surrender the balance of political power, either in general or local organization, to the other elements. Under certain circumstances, it should not even permit participation of the other elements in political power.[83]

For Burgess, as for the Archduke, the Slavs were a kind of lesser breed. The idea of equality of nation-peoples was discarded:

The Teutonic nations can never regard the exercise of political power as a right of man. The mission of the Teutonic nations must be that they are called to carry the political civilization of the modern world into those parts of the world inhabited by unpolitical and barbaric races, i.e., they must have a colonial policy. It should not be troubled in its conscience about the morality of this policy when it becomes manifestly necessary. It violates thereby no rights of these populations which are not petty and trifling in comparison with the transcendent right and duty to establish political and legal order everywhere. There is a great deal of weak sentimentality abroad in the world concerning this subject . . . History and ethnology offer us this elevated ground, and they teach us that the Teutonic nations are the political nations in the modern era; that, in the economy of history, the duty has fallen to them to organize the world politically; and that, if true to their mission, they must follow the line of this duty as one of their chief practical policies.[84]

No doubt such opinions matched the Archduke's ideas for reform of the Habsburg empire. The Archduke, as a man with a lucid mind, came to realize that unless the empire was reformed, it was doomed. Yet to achieve this reorganization the Archduke looked to the past for inspiration. His upbringing and his environment, composed of the most conservative layers of the monarchy, induced him to close his eyes to the simple fact that the survival of the multinational monarchy depended on whether its medieval institutions could be reorganized to satisfy the rising demand of its many nationalities for national self-determination. The Habsburg state institutions were, as Karl Kautsky remarked, incompatible with the modern democracy which was developing irresistibly under the influence of modern means of communication.[85]

Franz Ferdinand's failure to grasp these essential facts was to bring about his own violent death, and only a few years later, the distintegration of the Habsburg empire. The relentless drive for the self-determination of peoples, spreading across Europe, found no serious obstacles in the feudal institutions of the Habsburgs.

CHAPTER VIII

THE ARCHDUKE
FRANZ FERDINAND—
MAN OF PEACE
OR WAR

The imperial house must grow; that which the
sire
Has gloriously begun, the son must finish.
This puny people is a stumbling-stone—
This way or that, it must be thrust aside.
—Gessler, in SCHILLER's *Wilhelm Tell*

THE ARCHDUKE FRANZ FERDINAND's IDEAS about foreign policy and his practical steps in that field can be understood only in the context of his basic philosophy of life and the amount of power he actually wielded. Historians do not agree on the extent to which the Emperor Franz Josef allowed him to take part in policy decisions.[1] Yet it is logical to assume that the Archduke's influence became greater as time went by. The general goals of the Habsburg empire and the role of different internal elements within the monarchy in the last resort determined the foreign policy of the state. Its foreign relations were also profoundly shaped by the international constellation of great powers on the eve of 1914 and by the reliance of Austria-Hungary on her stronger partner Germany.

While German foreign policy goals were global in scope—rivalry with Britain for world domination, for leadership in world trade, for colonial expansion in Africa, and for naval power on the high seas— Austria-Hungary was obsessed primarily with targets on her southern borders, the Balkans and the Adriatic Sea. This area was of utmost importance for Austria-Hungary's expanding industry and commerce. Viennese and Budapest capital was invested in railroad construction as far away as Turkey. The Austrian Lloyd was one of the leading steamship companies in handling traffic from Trieste and Fiume to the Middle East, and Trieste was successfully competing with some of the greatest European ports.

Although in the first decade of the twentieth century Germany and Austria-Hungary came closer together in a common front against other rival powers, particularly France, Russia and Britain, the differences in foreign policy objectives between the two Germanic empires produced sharp differences in their respective reactions on some of the most important international issues.

In both Moroccan crises (1905 and 1911), Austria-Hungary did not back Germany strongly, because Vienna was less interested in African problems. On the other hand, in 1911 when Italy attacked the Ottoman Empire, Austria-Hungary became very hostile to Italy, while Germany sided with Rome. Germany did not always see eye to eye with Austria-Hungary on Balkan affairs. There was serious commercial and financial competition between Germany and Austria-Hungary in that area. When Austria-Hungary tried to apply economic sanctions against Serbia, in order to subjugate this South Slav kingdom which held the strategic key to the Balkans, Germany opposed this policy and helped Serbia find new markets in Germany to replace those she had lost in Austria-Hungary. Thus Germany succeeded Austria-Hungary as Serbia's biggest trading partner. Fierce competition was going on between Germany and Austria-Hungary in the Ottoman Empire, in both economic and political fields. Vienna tried in 1913–14 to obtain a sphere of influence in southern Anatolia, but the Deutsche Bank and the German General Staff prevented this. Kaiser Wilhelm had his own preferences in Balkan policies. Although he was not the sole factor in determining German foreign policy, his family relations with the Greek dynasty often ran counter to Austro-Hungarian schemes.

Yet, with time, Austria-Hungary's dependence on Germany increased. One half of Austria-Hungary's exports went to Germany. German capital, loans and credit had gained a controlling hand in Vienna. The whole imperialist expansion of Austria-Hungary required Germany's cooperation.

The conflict of interests between the two rival groups of European great powers was intensifying on the eve of 1914 and forcing Germany and Austria-Hungary toward a common policy in the Balkans. France and Germany were competing actively in this area by offering state loans and armament contracts to the Balkan states. At the same time, Russia increased her influence by advocating an alliance of Serbia, Bulgaria, Greece and Montenegro not only against the Ottoman Empire but also against Austria-Hungary. During the last half year before the outbreak of the First World War, the differences between Berlin and Vienna over Balkan affairs, particularly as far as Serbia was concerned, almost completely disappeared.

Yet this coordination of foreign policy moves by the two empires did not proceed smoothly. Within each of them there were different forces fighting for leadership in the foreign-policy field. The first real agreement took place between military circles in Berlin and Vienna, headed by the two chiefs of staff, Generals Helmuth von Moltke and Franz Conrad von Hötzendorff. Both believed that a great European conflict could not be avoided and that Germany and Austria-Hungary should not postpone the ultimate reckoning.

The Austro-Hungarian Army had a decisive influence on the foreign policy of the monarchy. This was particularly true after the defeats of 1859 and 1866, with their losses in Italy and in the north, when military circles had urged expansion southward in the Balkans. It was the military group headed by Archduke Albrecht which urged Emperor Franz Josef to occupy Bosnia and Hercegovina in 1878.

When General Conrad became chief of the General Staff in 1906, he was the strongest advocate of an expansionist policy. In December 1907 Conrad stated that the Habsburg monarchy should dominate the Adriatic, the Balkan Peninsula, the eastern shores of the Mediterranean and North Africa.[2] To this end he devoted all his energies to reorganizing and modernizing the armed forces of the empire. Conrad realized how closely internal problems of the empire were connected with its foreign policy objectives. The rising struggle of the South Slavs within the monarchy could be checked only by an attack on Serbia, which at the same time would open up the road to Salonika. In the autumn of 1906 Conrad wrote a memorandum to the Emperor in which he stated that "the future of the monarchy is to be sought in the Balkans, that moreover the occupation of Serbia and Montenegro must ensue—first of all, to ensure to the monarchy decisive influence in the Balkans; secondly, however, to prevent a sovereign Serbia from becoming a dangerous enemy and a point of attraction for the South Slav territories of the monarchy."[3]

General Conrad became the most consistent advocate in Austria-Hungary of the need for a preventive war against Serbia and a "settlement" of the South Slav question by military force. He believed that the monarchy could be saved only by such a war. As time progressed, Conrad's determination increased, particularly when Count Leopold von Berchtold became foreign minister. He saw eye to eye on this question with Conrad and the other generals who advocated a reckless foreign policy. According to Sidney Fay's calculation, "not counting the period 1906–1912, covered by the first two volumes of his memoirs, it may be noted that in the seventeen months from January 1, 1913, to June 1, 1914, the Chief of Staff, according to his own statements, urged war against Serbia no less than twenty-five times."[4]

One of Conrad's strongest supporters in this policy was the German Chief of Staff General von Moltke. Vienna did not inform Berlin about its intention to annex Bosnia and Hercegovina in October 1908, but once Wilhelm got over his initial anger at this mistrust shown by his closest ally, he fully backed Austria-Hungary through the crisis which followed. Germany went even farther than Austria-Hungary and threatened Russia with force if she did not accept the unilateral Austrian move.

The general staffs of Germany and Austria-Hungary kept very close contact throughout the crisis. Conrad and Moltke opened negotiations for the conclusion of a formal military convention. Historians have reached different verdicts on the character of their relations. Some think that this personal agreement between Conrad and Moltke, with the knowledge of Kaiser Wilhelm, changed the defensive nature of the Dual Alliance to an offensive one. The evidence for this is a passage from a letter of Moltke's on January 21, 1909, in which he said that it could be seen that the moment could come when Austria's forbearance in the face of Serbian provocation would end, in which case the monarchy would hardly have an alternative to marching into Serbia. "I believe that only this march of Austria into Serbia can precipitate an eventual active participation of Russia. This would be a *casus foederis* for Germany. . . . At the moment when Russia mobilizes, Germany will also mobilize, with its whole army."[5] Fay discounts the importance of this agreement, because of its informal, personal nature. He interprets this correspondence as a discussion of the political situation, but does not find it binding, because it was never incorporated into formal written protocols.[6]

The fact is that in 1909 Moltke could not get the full support of all determining factors of German foreign policy. Conrad found himself in a similar position. In a letter to Moltke on February 14, 1914, Conrad regretted that there had been hesitation in 1908 and 1909, and again in 1913, to take matters into their own hands in order to "break the ring that once again threatens to enclose us."[7] But he urged that now they no longer should ignore or hide the danger, but do all possible to meet it.

Can Conrad's views on foreign affairs be identified with those of the Archduke Franz Ferdinand? What was the attitude of the Archduke on the role of Austria-Hungary as a great power? Did he see the Balkans as the only field of penetration, or did he have broader views? And particularly what were the relations between the Archduke and the German Kaiser?

The Archduke and Conrad had been closely associated in the reorganization of the Austro-Hungarian armed forces, especially in building the role of the army in the internal affairs of the empire. Both fought for a unified and centralized army as the best instrument for the preservation of the *Erzhaus* and the empire against domestic and foreign enemies. Of all Franz Ferdinand's political protégés, Conrad was the only one who never definitely broke with his benefactor.

The Archduke, like Conrad, was fully aware of the necessity for the Habsburg empire to assert itself in the world as a big power, not only in Europe but on the other continents as well. On August 25, 1900, during the Boxer Rebellion in China, the Archduke complained to Beck: "It is scandalous that we did not send any troops to China, while such small, ridiculous states as Belgium and Portugal had their troops there."[8]

But the Archduke did not always share Conrad's opinions on tactics and timing. As he was in internal problems of the empire a defender of legitimism and the established order, so in international relations he cherished the idea of unity among all monarchs, a kind of revival of the Holy Alliance. But the Europe of Emperors Franz I and Alexander I differed greatly from the Europe of 1914, with its deep imperialist antagonisms. General Conrad suffered much less from a hangover of imperial legitimism; he was a reckless imperialist in the modern sense of the word. Often he differed with his benefactor over whether a preventive war against Serbia could be localized or whether it would provoke an intervention of the great powers, creating a world conflagration. The Archduke thought that "only the unanimous solidarity of the conservative powers could maintain the established monarcho-feudal order, and that a conflict between the imperial powers must inevitably lead to the overthrow of the monarchic regimes."[9]

On the eve of the First World War, which was to cost four dynasties their thrones, Franz Ferdinand extolled the principle of legitimism: "A full concord with Russia, a League of Three Emperors [*Dreikaiserbündnis*], the maintenance of peace, and the strengthening of the monarchical principle—this is my life's ideal, for which I shall ever be enthusiastic and shall work with all my strength."[10]

And once more: "I shall never lead a war against Russia. I shall make sacrifices to avoid it. A war between Austria and Russia would end either with the overthrow of the Romanovs or with the overthrow of the Habsburgs—or perhaps the overthrow of both."[11]

Franz Ferdinand's attitude toward France and Italy was also influenced primarily by his legitimist beliefs. He regarded France as the cradle of revolutionary ideas, dominated by Freemasons and antimonarchists. He observed the alliance between France and Russia with great anxiety: "The power of the Romanovs rests upon feet of clay and through his alliance with the French Freemasons Nicholas breaks his own neck."[12]

His dislike of Italy was derived from the same roots. "His Imperial Majesty," Brosch reported, "hated the Italians because they have stolen Rome."[13] The Archduke wrote to Conrad on February 26/27, 1913: "Our main enemy is Italy, against which we will have a war one day, and we have to regain Venetia and Lombardy."[14] Theodor von Sosnosky expressed the opinion that "the Archduke would have tried to reconstruct the Vatican State, in the event of a successful war."[15] The Archduke even dreamed of restoring the Bourbon Kingdom of the Two Sicilies of the King Ferdinand II (*Re Bomba*), his grandfather on his mother's side.

There was another consistent line in the Archduke's conception of foreign affairs. In view of the growing discontent within the Habsburg monarchy, he thought that he could extend its life by relying on the legitimist forces outside its frontier, as had been done in 1848–49, when the Russian Tsar Nicholas I saved the Habsburgs by quelling the Magyar Revolution.

In 1891 the Emperor had entrusted the Archduke with his first diplomatic mission, a visit to Russia. The Archduke was received with great pomp and ceremony. The Archduke later told Margutti "that the autocratic Russian system was in his eyes an admirable model."[16] The official Russian press greeted the Archduke's visit, emphasizing that Bismarck "through a series of artificial machinations had made of Austria a simple vassal of Prussia" and that "now Austria has a chance to return to its historical role."[17] Wishing the Archduke a happy return home, the paper stressed that he had established "a bond of mutual sympathies between the two countries."[18] The Archduke kept up his Russian contacts and established personal relations with the young Tsar Nicholas II. Margutti recorded that in 1895 the Archduke was full of admiration for Russia, regarding "a close association with the Tsar's empire as the way of salvation for the future development of the monarchy, and cherished the greatest hopes that through his personal efforts the young Tsar Nicholas II, who at that time had not been long on the throne and was a clean slate, so to speak, would become a real friend of Austria-Hungary."[19]

Faced with rising Magyar nationalism at the beginning of the twentieth century, the Archduke tried to find support for his policies of monarchical legitimism when he met Tsar Nicholas II at Mürzsteg in 1903. But he did not get much help. "His Imperial Highness had been astonished and even shocked by the Archduke's outspoken language about his future Hungarian subjects."[20] The Tsar was also cool to the Archduke's suggestion that trialism might lead to a kind of rapprochement with Russia and make the Habsburg empire less dependent on Ger-

many. But the Archduke did not lose hope of winning the Russian mon-
arch to his side. He continued cordial personal relations. When Grand
Duke Sergei, an uncle of the Tsar, was assassinated in Moscow in 1905,
the Archduke drafted a personal letter of condolence expressing his
"deep sorrow."[21] Even when relations with Russia deteriorated markedly, particularly after the annexation of Bosnia and Hercegovina in
1908, the Archduke still tried to find a common platform with the Russian Tsar. The French ambassador to St. Petersburg reported at the end
of 1911 that the Archduke instructed Berchtold, at that time the Habsburg ambassador in Russia, to explore the possibility of a revival of the
Dreikaiserbündnis.[22] He had this idea even in 1913, when he said to his
wife and Bardolff: "A war with Russia would be the end of us. If we do
anything against Serbia, Russia will back her and we shall have war
with Russia. Should the Emperor of Austria and the Tsar push each
other from the throne and open the road to revolution?"[23]

Even after the death of Franz Ferdinand, Kaiser Wilhelm wrote on
the margin of one of the reports: "The Archduke was Russia's best
friend. He wanted to revive the *Dreikaiserbündnis*."[24]

Under the influence of what he learned as a young boy, the Archduke despised the Hohenzollerns, regarding them as usurpers.[25] Relations between them became even more strained when the Archduke
refused to receive the officers of a German military unit which bore the
name of the Emperor Franz Josef on a courtesy visit to Vienna. In the
correspondence between the Swedish King Gustavus V and the Archduke in the *Nachlass* there is a letter, written in 1891, in which the
Swedish Crown Prince suggested that the Archduke, on his return
from his visit to Russia should stop off to see Wilhelm in Berlin, "because it is indeed so important that nothing stands between you two."[26]
The Archduke did not follow this advice.

Franz Ferdinand was influenced also by religious considerations. In
1901 the Archduke showed his feelings toward the Prussians in his reaction to the activities of the *Los-von-Rom* movement, which was obviously guided from Berlin, to convert the Austrian Catholics to Protestantism. It was significant that the Archduke accepted the patronage of
the Katholischer Schulverein and delivered his anti-Protestant speech in
1901 at the time of the German Crown Prince's visit to Vienna.

Yet under the pressure of political necessity, Franz Ferdinand slowly
changed his attitude toward the Hohenzollerns and Germany. In international relations in the first decade of the twentieth century Austria-
Hungary was becoming more and more dependent on German industry and finance capital. The formation of the alliance among Britain,
France and Russia was pushing Austria-Hungary even more firmly into
the arms of Germany.

It has been assumed that the Archduke's marriage gave Wilhelm an
opportunity to reduce the tension between them. The Kaiser, it has

been said, impressed the Archduke when he asked him in 1903, at the railway station in Vienna: "When shall I have the honor of bowing before your wife?"[27] But how difficult it was for the Kaiser to express such a wish is shown by his own comments in the margins of reports on the Archduke's marriage, which the German ambassador in Vienna, Prince Lichnowsky, sent regularly from the autumn of 1899 until the end of the affair. When Lichnowsky reported on October 2, 1899, that the Emperor Franz Josef had given his approval of a morganatic marriage and that the Archduke intended to make Countess Chotek the Habsburg empress when he ascended the throne, Kaiser Wilhelm added a sarcastic comment: "*Donnerwetter!* A Chotek the successor of Maria Theresa!"[28] In another report Lichnowsky described the feelings of the ordinary Viennese about the Archduke's marriage, citing also the jokes about the love affairs of other members of the Habsburg dynasty, about Frau Katharina Schratt, an actress from the Burgtheater, and Emperor Franz Josef, and about the many sweethearts of Franz Ferdinand's younger brother Otto. Wilhelm again commented: "*Donnerwetter!* This is almost *fin de siècle* as in 1789 in France! Poor Austria!"[29]

There were also some remarks of a political character, particularly on the reports from the German consul in Budapest on Magyar reaction to the Archduke's marriage. The consul reported on November 3, 1900, that "not without worry does one see in the activities of the Magyar chauvinists the beginning of an endless series of conflicts and difficulties which the marriage of the Archduke has provoked." And Wilhelm added his comment: "But this is in the first place his own fault."[30]

The uproar over the Archduke's support for the Katholischer Schulverein in 1901, his open statement against Protestantism, and the participation of the Duchess of Hohenberg in street demonstrations provoked anger in the German Kaiser. On February 15, 1902, Lichnowsky sent a report saying that in Budapest a Jesuit priest named Abel was active in promoting the Archduke's policies. Wilhelm made several comments. On the left side of the report, where Abel was mentioned, he added that he was influenced "naturally through the wife of the Archduke"; and on the right side he commented on the activities of the Jesuit Order—"Dirty swines have their filthy paws in everything."[31] Lichnowsky ended the report by saying that Abel's action had not achieved any results; and the Kaiser wrote his last remark: "It is good."[32]

These feelings were not easily forgotten, and it took several years for Wilhelm and Franz Ferdinand to establish a more cordial relationship. The grave crisis with the Magyars at the beginning of 1907 induced the Archduke to ask for German support. On January 18, 1907, he received the German military attaché in Vienna, Major Count Karl Kaganeck, and after discussing some military matters, the Archduke, as Kaganeck informed his superiors, expressed himself in a most aroused manner about conditions in Hungary. According to Kaganeck, the Archduke said: "The ministers are all pure criminals; Polonyi has committed all possible crimes—with the exception of suicide, which is to be regretted. One will accomplish nothing if one always yields to the Magyars, as is unfortunately the practice. The army is, as a result, the part that suffers."[33] The German ambassador in Vienna forwarded Kaganeck's report to Prince Bernhard von Bülow on January 25, 1907, adding his own comment that "he would not pay special attention to the Archduke's remarks, except that he knows that the Archduke has expressed the desire to seek the closest relations with the Kaiser and German policy."[34] After stating that the Archduke's attitude was something to rejoice over, the ambassador added that it appeared to him that a certain caution was in order: "One must keep in mind that the Archduke recently stated that 'one must conquer Hungary once more with the help of Russia.' Since Russia could not be used now for this purpose, we can assume that the Archduke by appealing to the monarchical principle would like to use German help against the revolting Magyars."[35]

The ambassador ended by proposing a rejection of the Archduke's request: "I would consider this participation on our side a great error. The Magyars even at this date have not forgotten Russian intervention, not to speak about the kind of gratitude Russia got from Austria."[36]

At a court dinner on January 27, 1907, the Archduke met the German ambassador and once more complained bitterly against the Magyars. The ambassador reported to Berlin that the Archduke "was seeking a closer dependence on Kaiser Wilhelm and Germany in order to gain support against Hungary."[37] The Archduke on this occasion stated in vulgar language that he did not agree with the attitude of the Emperor Franz Josef toward the Magyars.

Franz Ferdinand completely failed to win Wilhelm over to his side. They argued over this issue time after time. The Kaiser stood firmly behind the Hungarian prime minister, Count Stephen Tisza. At the same time he backed the Magyars against the Archduke's impending empire reforms. Wilhelm knew that the Archduke wanted to crush any Magyar opposition.[38] How Wilhelm would have reacted to such disturbances within his most important ally is a question which has given rise to much speculation. The Archduke's son, Count Max Hohenberg, has made the charge that his father was killed at the instigation of anti-Habsburg forces in Germany which wanted by all means to stop his reforms within the empire.[39]

Yet the question of the Magyars became a minor issue in the relations between Wilhelm and the Archduke. The relentless deepening of the conflict between the two blocs of great powers in Europe on the eve of 1914 brought the two closer, if involuntarily, together. The crisis of 1908-9—over Austria-Hungary's annexation of Bosnia and Hercegovina

—was proof of this. The war party in Vienna initiated this crisis by a unilateral breach of the agreement reached at the Berlin Congress of 1878. It was to prove that she was a great power that Austria-Hungary provoked this international crisis which led almost to the outbreak of a general war.

Kaiser Wilhelm was informed about the Act of Annexation only at the same time as other great powers, much to his anger. Since the Emperor Franz Josef kept the Archduke out of basic foreign policy decisions as much as he could, the Archduke himself heard about the annexation only on September 6, 1908, a month before it was carried out. At first Emperor Franz Josef was even against revealing the secret at this stage to the Archduke, because he was afraid that he would inform the Kaiser about it. But at the insistence of Aehrenthal, the Emperor changed his mind.

From a letter of the Archduke to Brosch, in October 1908, it seems the Archduke was much more concerned about the possibility that Bosnia and Hercegovina would be incorporated into Hungary than about the act itself.[40] In the *Nachlass* there is little new evidence which could throw more light on the Archduke's attitude toward the annexation question, except the two letters which the Archduke and Kaiser Wilhelm exchanged in April 1909 when the crisis was over and when both Russia and Serbia had to back down and accept the unilateral action. This correspondence supports the belief that the Archduke had not been just a passive onlooker during these crucial days. The Archduke expressed his thanks to the Kaiser for his help during the crisis:

. . . I cannot describe to you, but I believe you would be glad, if you could see yourself, what gratitude is felt for you throughout Austria and how in all circles of the population all hearts enthusiastically rejoice for you. Everywhere people speak only of you and praise the admirable manner in which you have put the Alliance into practice. It is true, we here have gone through very hot and exciting times; we were all standing ready to march to the Lower Danube. Aehrenthal has, I believe, done his job very well, and my Conrad has been a very good support to me in all our preparations for war. Your warm sympathy will surely appreciate what a consolation it was for me that after all the sad political vicissitudes which we have lately had to experience in the Monarchy, all the military measures were carried out smoothly and without a hitch, and that everywhere, in all lands and provinces, the same patriotic enthusiasm was displayed. In most army units more reservists reported than had been called up, and begged hard to be taken as well. Everything functioned without the least difficulty when suddenly, after Serbia's last impertinent note, we mobilized within a few hours 30,000 men from all provinces. . . .[41]

Kaiser Wilhelm answered on April 9, 1909, saying among other things:

Yesterday I received your kind letter and I hasten to thank you with all my heart. These past months have been extremely interesting, and their outcome must be valued very highly, even if it did not bring a solution with the bayonet. It was a real pleasure for me to be able to be a good second to you and to prove to the world, *ad oculos*, by unshakable loyalty to our alliance, that Europe *must* listen to the two Imperial Powers if they stand together. And the secret of this bloc is the granite foundation of its two allied armies. If the two best armies in the world stand side by side, determined to accept no slight and to make the interests of their countries respected, this is a fact which all other diplomats as well as states just have to accept, whether it suits them or not. As the Tappenheimer cuirassier says in *Wallensteins Lager*, "Why can we laugh about it? Because there are a lot of us." And that must always remain so! Then Europe also will keep quiet! In these weeks the value of the alliance has again been thoroughly demonstrated to the two nations, and the recognition of our attitude which all the races of your Fatherland has expressed has filled me with satisfaction even as your warm, unrestrained acknowledgment of it has deeply moved me. Of course, I can well imagine that from a purely military, technical point of view, Conrad, you and the entire army had hoped to march into battle, and that for the Lieutenant [General Conrad] the result should have been a different one. On the other hand, you have managed to have a wonderful tryout for the real thing, to ascertain whether everything will function properly. And it has worked brilliantly. Everyone—of whatever race—has hastened to the colors, and the prompt and exact functioning of the whole military mechanism is a great success for your General Staff, War Ministry and the whole army. You have shown what you are able to do as allies, and you are highly esteemed accordingly. So highly that the probable enemies renounced a countertest! Bravo! For this I express my warmest congratulations! What I once declared has been confirmed: "When the Emperor of Austria mounts his horse, all nations follow him!!!" Mr. M. P. Kramarz, who would prefer to sweep us Germans off the earth, once said: "The German-Austrian alliance is an old, worn-out piano out of which one cannot get any melodies." With permission, the gentleman is wrong. The facts proved this to have been lies; the piano is still in good order and has wonderful marching tunes in reserve, whose effect never fails, they are: The Radetzky March and Yorck's March to the Attack! . . .[42]

The events of 1908–9 in connection with the annexation crisis broke the ice in the relations between Kaiser Wilhelm and Archduke Franz Ferdinand. From that period their real correspondence started, as the *Nachlass* collection shows. They exchanged letters on serious international problems and established closer personal relations as well. The Archduke comes out in this correspondence a greater *grand seigneur* than the Kaiser, who sometimes described, in his small, almost illegible handwriting (on postcards bearing his own portrait) his feelings not only about hunting and flowers, but also about dancing and the beauty of the wives of some young Austrian diplomats.

Through the gradual development of closer political relations between 1908 and 1914, Kaiser Wilhelm and the Archduke discovered some common positions in politics, internal as well as external. The Kaiser's thoroughly militarist outlook and his contempt for civilians were hardly alien to the Archduke. Their conceptions of anti-Semitism were not far apart. The German model of a unified and centralized army was most welcome to the Archduke. He also fully shared Wilhelm's advocacy of a strong navy.

The Archduke's personal policy in the Balkans, in particular toward independent Serbia and Montenegro, is another controversial issue among historians. Did the Archduke advocate Austro-Hungarian penetration into the Balkans, and if so did he envisage achieving this by armed force, as Conrad advocated, or by peaceful infiltration? And to what extent did the Archduke coordinate his stand on this issue with the policies of Germany, especially from the end of 1913, when the danger of a European general conflict was increasing?

While military circles around the Archduke advised solely military measures in order to break South Slav resistance, Dr. Lueger, who had such an influence on the Archduke, as early as the 1890's cherished the idea of incorporating all the South Slavs of the Balkans into the Habsburg monarchy. He summed up the problem thus: "In the Balkans, Austria has to seek out and preserve extremely important interests, especially economic ones . . . In the Balkans, people outside the monarchy should be attracted to the monarchy and thus be drawn into it. Austria has to fulfill a mission."[43]

Dr. Lueger's idea that the Habsburg empire should attract the South Slavs outside its frontiers was accepted also by Franz Ferdinand, according to Margutti, who claims that the Archduke as far back as 1896 explained to him that "the Slav problem would solve itself. The Czechs would be separated from the Germans of Bohemia and enjoy autonomy. So would the Croats, the Slovenes and the Hungarian Serbs. Then all these peoples would exercise so strong an attraction—by their very mass—on the Serbs of the Kingdom [Serbia] that the latter would seek national unity within the monarchy—i.e. in a centripetal sense, and not in a centrifugal sense by the incorporation of our South Slavs with the Serbs of the Kingdom. And that even though our South Slavs are far superior to the Serbs and Montenegrins from the point of view of culture."[44]

On July 10, 1909, during his visit to the Rumanian King Carol, in talks with the Rumanian Prime Minister Ion Bratianu about Hungary and the treatment of the Rumanians there, the Archduke mentioned that in a federal Greater Austria, Rumania would have the position of Bavaria in the German Empire.[45] Five years later, in March 1914, the

Rumanian statesman Nicolai Filipescu proposed to Czernin that Transylvania should be joined to Rumania and that Rumania in turn should unite with the Austrian monarchy. Czernin welcomed the suggestion with enthusiasm and hoped for its realization on the accession of Franz Ferdinand, whose foreign minister he was to be and who approved of the project.[46]

Kristoffy, the Archduke's chief expert on the Magyar question, in 1928 published the so-called Political Testament of the Archduke Franz Ferdinand, which to some extent confirmed Margutti's thesis. Kristoffy's summary of that document reads as follows:

1) Just as he expected that in Austria general suffrage would bring about the emergence of a Great Austria characterized by the entity of the Austrian emperorship along with the hegemony of Austrian Germanism, so too he hoped that in Hungary it would both remove the issues resulting from 1848 and 1867, and would eliminate the national problem. Behind this conception was concealed the idea of a "Greater Hungary," enlarged through the reconquest of the Eastern provinces of Ludwig [Lajos] the Great and Matthias [Matthias Corvinus, or Mátyás Hollos] and in this great Hungarian Empire, he envisaged the hegemony of "democratic Hungarianism" as against the "historical" class which had constantly undermined the basis of the Monarchy with a wedge of "state rights."

2) In foreign policy he was guided by his *Drang nach Osten* tendency, with Salonika as the destination. He did not, for the time being, aim at a division of the Balkans—this is proved by the withdrawal of troops from Sandzak—but he wanted, above all, stabilized conditions in the Peninsula so that the economic policy of the Monarchy might develop freely in the Balkans. This was the opposite of Russian, English and Italian policy, which caused instability and was directed toward conquest. But his ultimate aim was the reunification of Serbia, Bosnia, Bulgaria, Rumania and Albania under the Hungarian Empire, as Joseph the Second, too, had planned. Thus did Franz Ferdinand hate Hungary.

3) With respect to the army, the model which served him for his plans of reform was, from the point of view of "Unity and organization," the German Army. The proof that he was thus going in the right direction was evinced in the German Army's unparalleled organization, with which after all (indeed) it has, so to speak, won the World War from the military point of view. He was a born army leader and soldier-emperor. In every matter of foreign policy his aim was to rely on the support, through universal suffrage, of a democratic army, because he knew that the best cannons and rifles are those that are loaded with enthusiasm and gratitude toward the dynasty." [47]

The authenticity of this summary of the Archduke's ideas has been challenged.[48] It may be that Kristoffy wrote this document himself in order to justify his own role in the Belvedere, particularly as Fejervary's minister of interior, for this position had won him much hatred from the great majority of Magyars. Yet this document does express a desire to reconcile the legitimist feelings of the Archduke with the legitimism of the Magyar aristocracy; it also expresses the possibility of providing a platform for a future common policy in Vienna and Budapest. These ideas were not entirely alien to the Archduke.

Brosch in his appraisal of the Archduke written in 1913 confirms much of Kristoffy's views about the Balkans as a sphere of penetration for Austria-Hungary. Brosch stressed that the rapid improvement of the navy was due to the Archduke's care—"I hope the Archduke will succeed in asserting himself further, because our future lies also on the seas, paticularly after the Balkan war that has been so disastrous for Austria and which has deprived us of our capability for historical developments toward Salonika."[49]

On the Archduke's decision whether Serbia should be subjugated by armed force or be incorporated within the Habsburg empire's sphere of influence by other means, the events of October 1913 had a marked impact. At that time the prestige of Serbia in the Balkans was strong; she had come successfully through two Balkan wars, and her main rival, Bulgaria, had been defeated. At the end of September a rebellion broke out among the Albanians in Kosovo and Macedonia, inflicting very heavy losses on the Serbian troops. Belgrade accused Austria-Hungary of fomenting this trouble, and after the mutiny was put down, units of the Serbian army crossed over into Albania. Austria-Hungary issued an ultimatum to Serbia on October 17, 1913, demanding that the troops be withdrawn.

This October crisis marked a basic change in the German government's attitude toward a possible conflict between Austria-Hungary and Serbia. On several occasions between 1908 and 1913 Kaiser Wilhelm had advised Vienna to restrain its pressure on Serbia, presumably out of anxiety that a local conflict might grow to involve all Europe.[50] But in the October crisis the Kaiser changed his attitude. What the reasons for this new policy were is a controversial question. Did Wilhelm come to the conclusion that he could risk a conflict with Russia and France, or did he think that Serbia would give way without resistance?

The first man to hear about the German support of Austria-Hungary's policy toward Serbia was General Conrad, when he spoke with Kaiser Wilhelm on October 18, 1913, at the centennial of the Battle of Leipzig. The Kaiser "encouraged Austria to invade Serbia, and he expressed his belief that the other powers would intervene."[51] Immediately after the Leipzig celebration Wilhelm visited Vienna, and on his way he stopped at Konopischt to be the guest of the Archduke Franz Ferdinand from October 23 to 25.

In the *Nachlass* documents about this meeting are materials which speak only about the hunting and social side of the meeting. However, in the archives of the German Ministry of Foreign Affairs there are dispatches which speak of conversations both before the meeting and at Konopischt. In a letter of September 7, the Archduke wrote to the Kaiser, extending an invitation to come to Konopischt, and stating explicitly:

Hopefully you will find a substitute for this renunciation [referring to a Corfu trip, which was given up] in the success of your policy, which I have again, as always, followed with the *greatest* admiration, and with which, if I may say in all modesty and the deepest respect, I completely identify. Allow me, Your Majesty, to say how much I long to discuss the recent political events with you, either in Leipzig, where I will have the honor to see you again, or in Konopischt. I could share with you much that is in my modest opinion very interesting.[52]

Wilhelm answered with the following telegram:

I am grateful to you with my whole heart for your friendly and lovely lines. You know how infinitely gladly I come to you and how I look forward to being with you in your beautiful home—the home created by you. Hopefully it will suit you if I meet you immediately after the birthday celebration of my wife, which appears favorable in relation to weather and climate. Perhaps Eulenburg can get in touch with Rumerskirch concerning the day and hour of my arrival.

I too seek with great interest and satisfaction the happy occasion to speak with you of so many things and am happy over the friendly agreement that you express in your dear letter.[53]

On October 1, 1913, the Kaiser sent another letter to the Archduke; he spoke first about their personal relations, and then observed that "the situation in the Balkans is confused again." He continued:

Albania driven by the Turks (Ismet Pasha and his consorts in Adrianople, Albanians) attacks Serbia to gain these cities without which it cannot exist; and to tie Serbia down for the Turks at the same time, so that the latter cannot assist Greece when the Turks together with the Bulgarian *komite* will attack Greece to take Casalla from them. Casalla shall be given to Bulgaria on behalf of Adrianople; perhaps Dedéagach taken back in exchange. Ferdinand takes advantage of the situation in a very smart way by having the Turks reconquer what he could not maintain. The Young Turks are overly confident and due to their success at Adrianople they are exorbitant in their requirements. 300,000 men are concentrated in Thrace and all kinds of reinforcements are passing by Istanbul, particularly at night. The king has therefore returned to Athens. Hopefully, Istanbul will be reasonable. But it seems that the decision remains with the army, i.e., with Ismet Pasha, of whom the grand vizier is afraid. At any rate, Ferdinand has once again schemed very nicely.

With hearty *Waldmannsheil* and a *Handküss* to your wife.

Your faithful friend and cousin,
WILHELM M.P.

Kaiser Wilhelm ended this letter with a postscript: "I am very happy that Conrad remains. I have seen him a lot during the maneuvers and have learned to appreciate him. He is a remarkable character; this is very rare nowadays."[54]

Neither in the *Nachlass* nor in the archives of the German Ministry of Foreign Affairs are there any documents which speak directly about the agenda or the substance of the talks, although there are indirect summaries. From Konopischt the Kaiser went to Vienna, where he met Emperor Franz Josef and had a long talk with Berchtold. In a dispatch from Vienna to the Foreign Office in Berlin, it was stated: "Their Majesties were completely in agreement . . . As far as I can judge, everything in Konopischt and here went well. His Majesty spoke for a long time alone with Berchtold, who appears to be very taken by our Most Gracious Lord."[55]

According to George P. Gooch, who relied for his description of these talks on Conrad's memoirs and the German and Austrian documents, Kaiser Wilhelm inquired of Berchtold what could be done to prevent future trespasses by Serbia.

Austrian policy, replied the Foreign Minister, aimed at playing off the Balkan states against one another in order that each might hold the rest in check. A Serbo-Bulgar rapprochement, which could only take place at Austria's expense, must be averted. Bulgaria was angling for an alliance, which would be acceptable if it did not affect the relations between Vienna and Bucharest. At this point the Kaiser explained his views. The power of the Slavs, and in particular of the Slav states in the Balkans, had increased in a formidable degree. War between East and West was ultimately inevitable, and in such an event a Serbian attack might be disastrous. The Slavs were born to serve, not to rule. The only possible relation to Serbia and Austria was that of the dependence of the lesser on the greater, like a planet on the sun. She should be attracted by money, military training and commercial privileges. On the other hand Serbian troops must be placed at the disposition of Austria, so that no danger to her southern frontier could occur. When Berchtold suggested that the ineradicable animosity of the Serb race was an obstacle, the Kaiser rejoined that Serbia would be ready for defense against attack. If she declined, force should be applied. "If His Majesty the Emperor Francis Joseph makes a demand, the Serbian Government must obey. If not, Belgrade must be bombarded and occupied till his will is fulfilled. And rest assured that I am behind you, and am ready to draw the sword whenever your action requires." As he uttered these swelling words, his hand moved to the hilt of his sword. Berchtold protested that the obligation to defend Serbia might drag Austria into controversies which did not affect her interest. After discussing the relations of the Central Powers to Turkey and Bulgaria, the Kaiser declared that Russia, though hostile, could not fight for six years. If war were to come, Austria could absolutely rely upon him. Whatever the Ballplatz decided was for him a command. This emphasis on the solidarity of the alliance, concluded Berchtold's report, ran like a scarlet thread through his declarations. The interviews with Conrad and the Foreign Minister in October 1913 can hardly have been without influence in the decisions of the following summer.[56]

The Kaiser and the Archduke had two more meetings before June 28, 1914. The first one took place at Miramare, near Trieste, on March 27, and the second one at Konopischt on June 12–14. In the *Nachlass* there are blank spots as far as these two meetings are concerned. Nothing is mentioned about the political character of the meetings or their agenda. There are a few postcards and telegrams of a purely personal or technical character. The last telegram sent by the Kaiser to the Archduke on June 14, 1914, at the end of the second Konopischt meeting, after thanking the Archduke for his hospitality, ends with the words: "The roses in my garden are blooming. Rhododendrons are also blooming despite three weeks of rain. *Waldmannsheil*. Many greetings to all. W."[57]

From the German and Austro-Hungarian documents it appears that at Miramare and Konopischt among the political topics discussed were the questions of the Magyars, Italy, and the Balkans, including the Serbian problem.[58] But they do not speak about the possibility of an Austro-Hungarian attack on Serbia. On the other hand, Conrad has recorded two conflicting versions of the Konopischt decision as far as Serbia was concerned.[59] Conrad had an audience with the Emperor Franz Josef on July 5, 1914:

I expressed to His Majesty my view of the inevitability of a war with Serbia . . . His Majesty looked at me questioningly and said: "Are you sure of Germany?" He had, he said, enjoined on the Heir Apparent, Archduke Francis Ferdinand, to ask at Konopischt for a statement from the German Kaiser whether we could in future count unconditionally on Germany. The German Kaiser evaded the question and did not return an answer.[60]

But on returning to his office after the audience, Conrad recorded:

I outlined the main issues to Colonel Metzger, Chief of the Operational Section. When I spoke of doubts about German cooperation in the event of a war being forced on us and mentioned His Majesty's mistrust, Metzger interposed that on the last evening at Ilidže Archduke Francis Ferdinand had assured him Kaiser Wilhelm at Konopischt had said in reference to that very case: "If we did not attack, the position would get worse."[61]

Luigi Albertini is of the opinion that the behavior of Kaiser Wilhelm in July 1914 makes it seem likely that Metzger's version is the right one.[62]

The attitude of the Archduke Franz Ferdinand on this crucial issue can be deduced from the Internal Political Instructions of the *Thronwechsel* collection, prepared in April and May 1914. They speak, first, about the annexation of Serbia as a future, faraway goal of the Archduke. In speculating about the advantages of trialism, which he rejected in favor of a Greater Austria federalism, the Archduke said: "The only advantage of trialism can be seen in relation to an attempt at a later annexation of Serbia and Montenegro to the monarchy. But it would be quite risky to jeopardize the interests of the monarchy for this distant goal."[63]

Faithful to his conceptions of legitimism and fearful of risking a big war with the great powers at a time when his own state was not yet stabilized, the Archduke outlined, in the opening sentences of the Internal Political Instructions, the foreign policy he would follow when he ascended to the throne: "Foreign countries have to be assured that a policy of peace will be preserved, with the maintenance of our trusted alliances, especially the one with Germany."[64] But he added also: "A revolution in Hungary, war with Italy, and perhaps with Serbia and Montenegro, are expected with certainty."[65]

There are some contradictions in this statement of policy. On the one hand, the Archduke spoke about "the maintenance of our trusted alliances,"[66] but on the other, he looked on war with Italy as a certainty, even though Italy was a member of the Triple Alliance with Germany and Austria-Hungary.

In the Internal Political Instructions there is another indication of the Archduke's intentions toward Serbia. In Brosch's version of 1911, when the imperial and royal titles of the Archduke Franz Ferdinand as the future Emperor Franz II were discussed it was said that "the title 'King of Serbia and Bulgaria' can be renounced, because Serbia and Bulgaria possess a sovereignty recognized in international law."[67] But in the 1914 version mention of Serbia was deleted, showing that the Archduke had changed his mind concerning the position of Serbia.

Future historical research may throw more light on this issue. But it is clear that by the decisions taken at the first Konopischt meeting in October 1913, as well as during Kaiser Wilhelm's visit to Vienna, Austria-Hungary had received from Germany carte blanche for an invasion of Serbia.

CHAPTER IX

THE REVIVAL OF TYRANNICIDE IN THE HABSBURG EMPIRE

Austria-Hungary is the best school for assassins.
—LUKA JUKIĆ *at his police inter-*
rogation after the attempt against
the Governor of Croatia on June 8,
1912.

THE ARCHDUKE FRANZ FERDINAND was the first heir apparent to the Habsburg throne to fall victim to political homicide. Violence and individual terrorism against the members of the *Erzhaus* and the dignitaries of the Habsburg state had not been common throughout their long history. But it increased suddenly when a wave of national aspirations swept over the ancient empire. Denying the right to self-determination and using force to defend its institutions, the Habsburgs were faced not only with mass revolutionary movements, as in Italy and Hungary, but also with a new version of tyrannicide.

As the first nationality to rebel against the Habsburgs in the nineteenth century, the Italians used tyrannicide. The leader of the Italian republican nationalist movement, Giuseppe Mazzini, urged his compatriots and the other subjugated nationalities within the Habsburg empire to practice political assassination against their harsh masters, as a means of opening the way to national liberation through insurrection.

Archduke Franz Ferdinand. *At left,* in his youth in hunting costume. *At bottom,* with his wife, the Duchess of Hohenberg, and their three children.

Above, the Archduke, the Duchess and General Potiorek on the morning of June 28, 1914. *At right*, a view of the Miljacka River and the Appel Quay in Sarajevo. *Below*, the royal party leaves the Town Hall just a few minutes before the assassination.

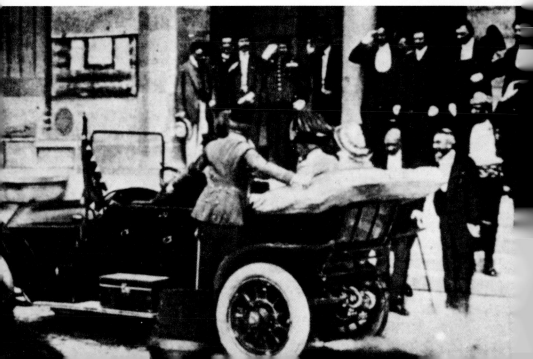

At left, Gavrilo Princip, aged 16. *Above*, his parents. *Below, left to right*, Trifko Grabež, Djuro Šarac and Gavrilo Princip in Belgrade's Kalmegdan Park in May 1914.

Above, Nedeljko Čabrinović *(left)* with his pal Tomo Vučinović. To leave his picture for posterity, Čabrinović had
this photograph taken one hour before his assassination attempt. *Below*, members of Young Bosnia in Tuzla.

Gavrilo Princip in his cell during the investigation.

Colonel Apis *(seated)* with his aides.

Above, from left to right, Grabež, Čabrinović, Ilić and Princip on their way to the courtroom. *Below,* the trial. *First row, left to right,* Grabež, Čabrinović, Princip, Ilić, Veljko Čubrilović. *Second row,* Miško Jovanović, Jakov Milović.

The gallows in Trebinje, Hercegovina, where Serbs were hanged in reprisal for the Archduke's assassination.

One should not overlook the literary contribution of the German poet Johann Christoph Friedrich von Schiller to the romantic conception of nineteenth-century tyrannicide. Schiller, unlike Mazzini, was not primarily a political leader; he was one of the leading figures of the Romantic movement in Germany. No other literary trend in modern Germany contributed so much to the national awakening of the Germans, as well as to similar movements in other parts of Europe, as German Romanticism. With an interest in humanity and aspiring idealism, looking for the natural and spontaneous in the literature of his day and the past, Schiller chose for the subject of his verse-drama *Wilhelm Tell* a revolt of Swiss peasants against the tyranny of their Habsburg governors. The struggle was uneven and lasted several decades until the Habsburgs finally had to admit the loss of their Swiss possessions. The main character of Schiller's drama, Wilhelm Tell, is a legendary figure in Swiss folklore. The story goes that his assassination of Gessler, the Habsburg bailiff (governor) of Schwyz and Uri, led to the uprising of the Swiss farmers.

Schiller finished *Wilhelm Tell* in 1804, just a year before his death. From it can be clearly seen the differences and similarities between classical and medieval conceptions of tyrannicide and the nineteenth-century version, which can be described as the romantic one. From classical republicanism Schiller inherited the idea that tyrannicide was a moral duty based on natural law. Schiller's *Wilhelm Tell* contains the same element of homicide executed for "the common good" as the ancient Greek ode to Harmodios and Aristogeiton, which reads as follows:

> *Your fame will last forever in the world,*
> *Dearest Harmodios and Aristogeiton,*
> *For you slew the tyrant*
> *And made Athens a city of equal rights.*[1]

Schiller expressed the same idea with these verses:

> *No, there's a barrier to the despot's might.*
> *When the oppressed for justice cries in vain,*
> *When tyranny can no more be borne—he lifts*
> *His heart aloft, lays hold on Heaven itself,*
> *And fetches down his everlasting rights*
> *That hang on high all indestructible,*
> *Unalienable as the fixed stars—*
> *The old primeval state comes round again,*
> *When man confronted man for nature's rights—*
> *As a last refuge, when all others fail,*
> *She puts the sword into her children's hands.*

Our dearest right we may, we must defend
Against oppression. In the van we stand,
Our homes, our wives, our children in the rear![2]

As in all classical conceptions of tyrannicide, Schiller drew a very clear line between tyrannicide and ordinary assassination. When John the Parricide tried to equate his own assassination of his uncle, the Emperor, with Tell's killing of Gessler, Tell answered angrily:

Wretched man!
Canst thou confound ambition's bloody guilt
With the just wrath a father's anguish wakes?
Hast thou been called a family to defend?
To guard thy hearth and home, and from thy kin
Ward off the last and terrible agony?
I lift to heaven hands free from stain of guilt,
To curse thee and thy deed. I have avenged
The sacred rights of nature which thy hand
Has shamelessly profaned—and nought have I
In common with thee—thou art an assassin,
I the defender of my dearest rights.[3]

As in ancient Greece Harmodios and Aristogeiton were praised, Schiller glorified the assassin's act:

Where now is Tell? Must he alone be missing,
The founder of our Freedom? He has dealt
The noblest, and has borne the heaviest blows.
Come all—come, let us to his house door throng
And bid our great Deliverer hail in loud, triumphant song.[4]

But here Schiller introduced new elements to the concept of tyrannicide. Wilhelm Tell is not the hero in the classical sense of the word. His personal fate is not the center of the drama; the real hero is the Swiss people who rebelled against the Habsburgs. When Tell ambushed Gessler on the Küssnacht road and pierced him with his arrow, it was a signal for the peasants to storm the fortress of Zwing Uri and other Habsburg strongholds in Schwyz and Unterwalden. Later the Italian Carbonari, Russian Populists, Irish Fenians and South Slavs shared this theory of tyrannicide as the main factor in initiating a rebellion. In Schiller's interpretation the tyrant is the symbol of all the injustices in a society; he sensed the interrelationship of national oppression and social reality:

Go, speed thee to Lucerne, *and* there *inquire*
How under Austria's sway the Cantons groan!

Ere long they'll come to count our flocks and herds,
To measure out our Alps by line and rule,
To banish from our forests wild and free,
Whatever skims the air or scours the plain,
To bar our bridges, bolt our doors, and pay
Out of our poverty their bills of land,
No, if our life-blood is to be the price,
In our behalf be't paid—'tis cheaper far
Freedom to buy than bondage![5]

While classical tyrannicide described action against a domestic tyrant, Schiller emphasized fighting "a foreign tyrant's rod."[6] In a way
he extended the ideal of equality between individuals into the principle
of equality between nation-states. Schiller also stressed the role of the
peasantry, whereas the medieval notion of tyrannicide had included
only the upper strata of society, on the basis of *Lehnrecht,* as executors
of tyrannicide. When the Baron of Attinghausen asked the conspirators: "The nobles—are they, too, within the league?" the Schwyz peasant Werner Stauffacher answered, "We look for their support when
need shall be; thus far, the peasantry alone is sworn."[7]

The conditions of Schiller's time, which molded his conception of
tyrannicide, were similar to the circumstances which influenced the
Germans, Italians, Magyars and other nationalities to adopt romantic
concepts of tyrannicide. The case of Schiller's compatriot, theology
student Karl Ludwig Sand, proves this to a large extent, although in
Sand's interpretation of tyrannicide, in addition to the element of romantic violence there is also something of the Judaeo-Christian teaching of martyrdom, bordering on the notion of political homicide done
as an act of utter desperation. These feelings existed among the members of the German student clubs of that time. Karl Ludwig Sand assassinated August Friedrich von Kotzebue, the German dramatic writer
and spy for Alexander I of Russia, at Jena in the summer of 1819. The
atmosphere surrounding this assassination was one of repression in
many of the small German states by the feudal kings and princes, right
after the short period of liberalism and hopes for German unification
engendered by the French Revolution. Kotzebue reported daily to
Alexander I—firm pillar of the Holy Alliance—about the work of German radicals. Sand stabbed him in the heart, and afterward, as the *Annual Register* recorded in 1819, "walked calmly into the street and,
falling on his knees with his hands raised to heaven, exclaimed: '*Vivat
Teutonia!*' and plunged a dagger into his heart."[8]

Saint Thomas Aquinas was inspired in his theories of tyrannicide by
the brutal practices of his contemporary Ezzelino da Romano, the despot of Verona and Padua. The number of tyrants increased in the days
of the Renaissance. Venice excelled in the organization of so-called
diplomatic assassinations, plotting the murder of many a foreign ruler.

Count Vittorio Alfieri, a precursor of Italian unity, gave tyrannicide a new interpretation.[9] Besides his devotion to personal liberty, Alfieri had in mind also the conditions in which Italy found herself at the end of the eighteenth century. The many Italian tyrants, among whom were several Habsburgs, who made the life of free men miserable were the chief obstacles to national unity.[10] "In Alfieri we find the development of ideas which historically prepared the way for modern Italian nationalism: hatred of tyranny, lay and religious; love of freedom, individual and national."[11] In his poem *Etruria Avenged*, Alfieri "described the killing of the Renaissance tyrant, Alessandro de' Medici, by his cousin Lorenzo. He exalted tyrannicide and defended the 'theory of the dagger' as one of the most effective means of destroying oppression.' "[12]

At the beginning of the nineteenth century the Italian secret societies of Carbonari preached Alfieri's theory of tyrannicide against both the representatives of foreign rule and the traitors among their own ranks. In 1819 Guglielmo Pepe, one of the Carbonari leaders, made an audacious plan to capture both the Habsburg Emperor Franz I and his powerful Chancellor, Prince Metternich, at Avellino in the Kingdom of Naples. The Italian Carbonari had influence in other countries living under conditions of feudal absolutism. During the trial of the participants of the December 14, 1825, revolt against the Russian Tsar Nicholas I, one of the conspirators, Krakovsky, stated that they did not exclude the possibility of using the *tsareubiistvenny kinzhal*, the "regicide dagger." The conspirators were under the direct influence of the Carbonari (the Decembrist Poggio was of Piedmontese origin), as well as being mindful of the Russian tradition of regicide—Tsar Peter III had been assassinated in 1762 and Paul I in 1801. The right of resistance was formulated in Russia as early as the end of the fifteenth century by Yosif Volotsky, the abbot of Volokolamsk Monastery, who preached that the people should resist their rulers if they violated the moral laws.[13] During the reign of Tsar Nicholas I (1825-55), the idea of regicide was alive among the Russian people, as the following folksong proves:

> *We will give the Russian people some fun,*
> *And at the stake of shame*
> *With the guts of the last priest*
> *We will strangle the last Tsar.*

In Mazzini's political theology, tyrannicide, as the first step of putschism, played an important role. Mazzini's conception of political homicide was markedly influenced by Saint Thomas Aquinas's teachings on the subject. For Mazzini, "the act of tyrannicide was not primarily a matter of political expediency, but a revindication of the moral order on which the despot had trampled. It could be justified, therefore, only if it came from an unselfish conscience."[14] In 1833 Mazzini gave his consent for Antonio Gallenga, a member of the Giovane Italia, to kill King Carlo Alberto of Sardinia, but only after he had questioned Gallenga to find out whether he had any personal grudge against the king. Being assured that Gallenga was moved only by moral reasons to eliminate a tyrant "for the common good," Mazzini gave him a dagger.[15] Although Mazzini and Felice Orsini had many disagreements, Mazzini hailed Orsini's attempt against the life of Napoleon III because "Italian patriots regarded him as the chief cause of Italian disunity."[16] Even Victor Hugo urged the assassination of Napoleon III: "You can kill that man with tranquillity."[17] Orsini was inspired by Mazzini's theories of tyrannicide. In a letter to Daniele Manin, in 1856, Mazzini gave a clear exposition of his ideas on tyrannicide:

Holy in the hand of Judith is the sword which cut the life of Holofernes; holy is the dagger which Harmodius crowned with flowers, holy is the dagger of Brutus; holy is the poniard of the Sicilian who initiated the Vespers; holy is the arrow of Tell. When justice is extinguished and the terror of a single tyrant denies and obliterates the conscience of the people and God, who wished them to be free, and when a man unblemished by hatred and base passion, solely for the Fatherland and for the external right incarnate in him rises against the tyrant, and exclaims: "You torture millions of my brothers, you withhold from them that which God has decreed theirs, you destroy their bodies and corrupt their souls; through you my country is dying a lingering death; you are the keystone of an entire edifice of slavery, dishonor, and vice; I overthrow that edifice by destroying you,"—I recognize in that manifestation of the tremendous equality between the master of millions and a single individual, the finger of God. Many feel in their hearts as I do, and I express it.[18]

Among the Magyars the tradition of tyrannicide was not so strong as among the Italians. But during the 1848 revolution in Hungary it was alive in left-wing groups of revolutionaries, "where social oppression was coupled with the absolutism of the Habsburgs."[19] The poet of the Magyar Revolution, Sándor Petőfi, expressed these feelings:

A knife in the heart of Lamberg, a rope around the neck of Latour,
And after them others may follow;
You begin to be mighty, O people!
This is all right, this is perfectly fine,
But this has achieved little.
Hang the kings.[20]

In 1853, in the atmosphere of gloom and despair engendered by the repressions following the defeat of the revolution, a Magyar tailor's apprentice, Janos Libenyi, struck the Emperor Franz Josef on the head with a knife in an attempt to assassinate him while he was walking with his aide-de-camp, Count O'Donnell, on the ramparts of Vienna. Josef Redlich described conditions at the time of the attempt as follows: "The prisons in Hungary were full of men suspected of subversive conspiracy, and Mazzini's agents had carried through a series of notably treacherous assaults on Austrian officers and soldiers in Milan."[21] The *Annual Register* contains a description of Libenyi's attack from a letter which the Emperor's great-uncle, Archduke Rainer, had sent to Archduke Albrecht, on February 18, 1853:

MY DEAR ALBRECHT,

I am writing you a few lines in a great hurry, on events here. I was sitting at my table, reading, on the 18th, about half past twelve in the day, when my chasseur rushed into the room, and exclaimed, "His Majesty is coming up stairs, bleeding; he must have had a fall." I told him to get linen and cold water, and rushed out just as his Majesty entered the ante-room. He said to me, "They have been trying their Milan tricks on me now." I was almost petrified when he showed me his handkerchief soaked with blood, which he had been holding to the back of his head. . . . We then placed his Majesty in a carriage, and drove him to the Belaria. His Majesty told me, whilst I was applying the cold water, that he had received a blow on the head like the shot of a pistol; that it made the eyes flash, and that when he looked around he saw O'Donnell struggling with a man on the ground. . . . His Majesty said to me, "O'Donnell has saved my life . . ." Everything was in commotion, everybody in despair. The lines were immediately closed, the railway stations occupied, the troops consigned to their barracks, two batteries telegraphed for. At the *Te Deum* an immense crowd gathered. Every one showed the warmest sympathy. . . . At Milan, two of Kossuth's emissaries have been arrested, each provided with 30,000 francs. They were trying to enter the town the day after the row. . . . His Majesty is getting on well; the wound is closed. To-day his headache has subsided, or is only felt when he coughs; but there are symptoms of a slight concussion of the brain. . . .[22]

The assassin Libenyi was executed, by hanging, within a few days of "his diabolic attempt," as an English newspaper recorded at the time. "He denied to the last that he had any confederates, and that this was the belief of the Austrian Government may be inferred from the fact of his speedy execution." The Russian Nicholas I, whose troops had saved the Habsburg throne in 1849 by crushing the Magyar revolt, wrote a letter to the young Emperor: "Thy life does not belong to thee but to thy country and us all. Great God, what would become of thy country if it were to lose thee, above all at such a moment?"[23] A few weeks after Libenyi's execution, the Emperor Franz Josef granted "a small pension to Libenyi's mother, left destitute by the execution of the son on whom she was dependent."[24] Ever since 1853, in the schools of the Habsburg realm the children were reminded of this attempt against the Emperor. In the boyhood of Gavrilo Princip, "in the reading books in the fourth grade in primary school there was a longish article describing 'how God saved the Emperor when a Magyar tried to kill him with his knife, in godless hatred.' "[25]

Libenyi's attempt confirms the view that political assassination may often be an act of despair by oppressed national religious or social groups. It is significant that individual terrorism receded in Hungary after 1867, when the Habsburgs had to change their policy toward the Magyars, giving them more rights through the Compromise of that year. From that time political homicide almost disappeared from Magyar political life. The only notable exceptions were attempts against the lives of the Tisza family. On November 26, 1878, a bomb exploded in front of the palace of the Prime Minister Count Koloman Tisza, where he had been giving a *soirée* to celebrate the pacification of Bosnia and Hercegovina.[26] The second outburst occurred the same day on the steps of the Liberal Club, the club of Tisza's political party, where Tisza was dining with Count Andrassy, minister of foreign affairs at that time.[27]

Count Koloman Tisza's son, Count Stephen Tisza, who also became prime minister of Hungary (1903–5 and 1913–17) was the victim of several attempts against his own life. On June 5, 1912, in the Hungarian parliament, Julius Kovacz, who disagreed with Tisza's political tactics, fired a pistol at him, but missed. When the left-wing Socialist leader, Friedrich Adler, after the defeat of the Habsburg empire in 1916, contemplated killing a leading bureaucrat of the empire, he wavered for a time between Tisza and Austrian Prime Minister Count Karl von Stürgkh. Finally he chose Stürgkh, whom he assassinated on October 21, 1916, in the Austrian parliament. At the end of 1918, Tisza was murdered by two soldiers in his own flat.

To what extent individual terrorism is caused by oppressive social and political conditions is demonstrated by the sudden upsurge of terrorism in Vienna itself in the 1880's. With rapid industrialization, the number of workers in Vienna increased, but their wages and long hours of work caused much dissatisfaction. At that time the influence of Johann Most, a bookbinder by profession and a former member of the German Reichstag, was felt in Austria. He preached the necessity of using individual terror against oppression. After his expulsion from the Reichstag for his radical views, Most emigrated to England, where he edited the German-language paper *Die Freiheit*, which was smuggled into the German-speaking parts of Europe. Under his influence several conspiratorial groups were formed in Germany. One such group, led by a printer named Reinsdorf, plotted to throw a bomb at Kaiser Wilhelm I in 1883. They were unsuccessful, but all of them were executed.[28]

When news came of the assassination of Tsar Alexander II in 1881, Most devoted to it "an editorial of gloating enthusiasm and was sent to prison for eighteen months. The comrades he left in charge of *Die Freiheit* had no desire to appear less courageous than their leader, and when the Irish rebels assassinated Lord Cavendish in Phoenix Park, they loudly proclaimed their solidarity with the killers."[29] The offices of *Die Freiheit* were raided, the paper was suppressed, and Most, after serving his sentence, left England for America.

In Vienna itself a man of similar ideas, Joseph Peuker, was publishing a paper called *Die Zukunft*. When the Vienna police started to arrest workers and suppress their meetings, there was strong resistance and several policemen were killed. The situation in Vienna was described by the *Annual Register* as follows:

An active group of terrorists operated carrying out sundry acts of violence including a plan to assassinate the Emperor Franz Joseph and to burn down Vienna. They organized clubs and made collections for various purposes connected with the organization including the purchase of arms and in March, 1883, they had three secret sittings at which it was decided to assassinate the Emperor by means of bombs during his visit to Gratz in that year. These meetings were presided over by a Michael Kappauf, who read a letter from New York, signed "Justus Schwab," announcing that the bombs were already on the way, and urged those present to draw lots in order to fix upon the persons who were to carry out the decision. The project was foiled, however, by the police, and a number of arrests were made. In July a young man was arrested on suspicion of being connected with the dynamiters, and on him were found a large dynamite bomb, two awls with their points poisoned with prussic acid, and a revolver. He was sentenced to ten years' penal servitude. These incidents, coupled with the frequent cases of incendiarism in the Austrian capital, were alleged by the Government in justification for the proposal it brought before the Reichsrat in December to renew the decrees issued in January for the suspension of trial by jury in Vienna, and to extend them to the surrounding districts.[30]

A state of siege was proclaimed in Vienna and special decrees were promulgated against social revolutionaries. One of their leaders, Hermann Stellmacher, was arrested in January and hanged on August 6, 1884.[31] One of the members of his group, a Serb by the name of Mihailo Kumić, was arrested earlier in Pforzheim, but he was banished from Austria. Other members of Stellmacher's circle were sentenced to long jail terms. But these strong measures did not subdue the Vienna workers. Terrorism continued to flare up from time to time. The *Annual Register* of 1893 was still quoting cases of assassinations and dynamite attacks. On September 23, 1893, the police arrested fourteen persons charged with participation in "an Anarchist plot." It appeared, from inquiries made by the police, "that the object of this society was to bring about a social and political revolution in Austria for the purpose of overthrowing the dynasty and making attempts on the lives of great nobles and capitalists. Among the bylaws of the society is one declaring that 'traitors to the cause shall die by the dagger.' "[32]

The flare-up of individual terrorism in Austria coincided with the "era of assassination" in many other European countries living under conditions of feudal absolutism or national and social oppression. In Russia the Tsar Alexander II was killed in 1881. In Italy between the first attempt against King Umberto in 1877 and his death at the hand of an assassin in 1900, there were repeated acts of individual terrorism. The same thing happened in Spain. In France from 1881 when a statue of Thiers, "the butcher of 35,000 Communards," was blown up, until the assassination of President Carnot in 1894, the country witnessed scores of acts of individual terrorism. In Ireland and in other countries where the Irish lived, the Fenians and other secret societies intensified their individual acts of violence against English rule.

What caused such a forceful appearance of terrorism in Europe in the nineteenth century? Jean Maitron thinks that the introduction of terrorist methods in French political life had definite social and economic causes; they represented, as he said, "a stroke of the gong, which awoke the French proleteriat from the prostration and despair caused by the massacre after the Commune of 1871."[33] Prince Kropotkin gave a similar explanation in an article which was published in *Freedom*, an anarchist paper in London, in December 1893. After rejecting the popular equation of anarchism with terrorism he emphasized the basic principles of anarchism as "a moral urge aiming at the destruction of authority in order to create a society held together by free and natural bonds of fraternity." He also wrote:

We hate murder with a hatred that may seem absurdly exaggerated to apologists for Matabele massacres, to callous acquiescers in hangings and bombardments, but we decline, in such cases of homicide or attempted cases of homicide as those of which we are treating, to be guilty of the cruel injustice of flinging the whole responsibility for the deed upon the immediate perpetrator. The guilt of the homicides lies upon every man and woman who, intentionally or by cold indifference, helps to keep up social conditions that drive human beings to despair.[34]

Events after 1893 confirmed some of the points of Kropotkin's thesis. With the lessening of poverty among the workers of France, Germany and Austria, and the appearance of their first mass political and trade-union organizations, came a decline of individual terrorism. The doctrines of socialist parties also contributed to the disappearance of the ideology and practice of individual terrorism. Individual action was re-

placed by mass action. Social change and transformation relied more on
social and economic means. The idea of tyrannicide was depersonal-
ized; its moral urge to eliminate tyranny for "the common good" remained, but it was applied against society as such. The destruction of
an individual cannot effect new trends in society. Individual acts of
terrorism under these conditions bring only damage to the mass movements. The most daring revolutionaries with their acts of political homicide alienated themselves from the revolutionary movement; they detached themselves from the main tasks of proleteriat and they distorted
the goals of the struggle, often playing into the hands of the pillars of
society.

The truth of this theory is proved by the survival of terrorism in
Italy, Russia, Spain, Ireland, and the parts of the Habsburg empire
where political and social reforms were not adequate. In Italy proper,
despite the fact that liberation and unification were achieved in the
1860's, terrorism did not disappear at once. The unsettled social conditions, especially the persistence of feudal relations in the countryside,
gave rise to individual acts of violence. It is significant that the most
vigorous apostles of terrorism came from those areas in Italy in which
poverty was endemic. In 1861, in the newly united Italy, only 418,000
of its 26,000,000 inhabitants had the right to vote—that is only 2 per
cent. Eighty-three per cent of the population was illiterate. The tradition of tyrannicide in Italy was stronger, perhaps, than among any
other people of Europe except the South Slavs. One of the apostles of
tyrannicide in Italy at the end of the nineteenth century, Andrea Costa,
defined the urge for political homicide: "Violent action was considered
a necessity to pose the problem, to show the new ideal above the old
ones."[35] The Italian terrorists at the turn of the nineteenth century became the teachers of many other nationalities in that field of activities.
The Italian emigree worker Santo Caserio killed the French President
Carnot in 1894; the Italian Michele Angiollelo went to Spain and assassinated the Spanish Prime Minister Antonio Cánovas del Castillo. The
killer of the Habsburg Empress Elisabeth, Luigi Luccheni, was also an
Italian.

The tradition of tyrannicide remained alive among Italians living
outside their motherland. The Habsburgs at one time ruled over 5,000,-
000 Italians, but after the liberation of Lombardy and Venice, only
600,000 of them remained inside the empire, living in the Tirol, Goricia
and Gradiska, Istria, Trieste and Dalmatia. Although in many ways
they were better off politically and socially than most of the nationalities in Austria-Hungary, they resorted to individual terrorism. A plot
to kill the Emperor was organized by a group of Italian Irredentists,
headed by a twenty-year-old student from Trieste named Guglielmo
Oberdank (the illegitimate son of a Slovene girl). Oberdank had
studied engineering in Vienna but in 1877 he fled from Austria-Hun-

gary to Rome to avoid being drafted into the Habsburg army, which was then about to march into Bosnia and Hercegovina. Oberdank was, by his political convictions, a sympathizer of the Republican Army. He schemed to return to his native Trieste and assassinate the Emperor Franz Josef when he came in 1882 to celebrate the five-hundredth anniversary of the annexation of that city. The Habsburgs had a well-organized espionage system, and Oberdank was arrested with the bombs before he could use them. He was sentenced to death. Leading personalities of Europe, among them Victor Hugo, pleaded with the Emperor to pardon Oberdank, but to no avail. Oberdank was hanged on December 20, 1882, in the yard of the Caserno Grande in Trieste, and according to the official report, he shouted before his execution: "Long live Italy, long live free Trieste, foreigners go home!"[36]

Oberdank was hailed as a national hero of Italy. Several towns in Italy named streets and squares after him. Venice built a monument to him. Several hymns and many poems were composed, glorifying his plot in the spirit of classical tyrannicide.

Oberdank's cult was alive long after his death. In 1913 Mario Stele published a pamphlet praising Oberdank, and the Vienna court sentenced the writer to five years' imprisonment. This provoked public demonstrations against Austria-Hungary in many Italian towns. The University of Rome had to be closed, and an Italian legislator publicly offended the Emperor Franz Josef in a speech in parliament.[37] When the Italian troops entered Trieste in 1918 a monument was erected to Oberdank.

Among the several conspiracies against the Emperor Franz Josef and other members of the house of Habsburg which the Vienna police discovered, some, it is interesting to note, originated in the United States. In addition to the Italians who emigrated to America for social reasons, there were many who had to leave their country for political reasons. This began in the nineteenth century with the exodus of several members of the Carbonari and Mazzini groups. These people brought with them their hatred for the Habsburgs and gladly joined any secret group which plotted against the rulers in their old home.

At the same time, around the turn of the century, there were several terrorists from Europe living in the United States. Among them was Johann Most, who had left England after the suppression of his radical paper, *Die Freiheit*. In America he reopened his paper in 1882 and embarked on a lecture tour through all the cities where revolutionary groups existed, advocating violence in a manner that rivaled Nechayev's.[38] He secretly found employment in an explosives factory in Jersey City, and wrote a pamphlet *Revolutionäre Kriegswissenschaft*, a manual "on the making and use of bombs, on burglary and arson for the good of a cause, and on certain aspects of toxicology already known to the Borgias."[39] Most, until his death in 1906, continued to publish his paper and was involved in many cases of violent action in America. He exercised his influence predominantly among the emigrees from the eastern parts of Europe, particularly from Austria-Hungary; he found much understanding among the Italian terrorists who fled to America at the same period.

In the archives of Vienna there exist many confidential reports from the beginning of the twentieth century about the activities of secret societies among former Habsburg subjects in the United States. The tragic death, in 1898, of the Emperor Franz Josef's wife, Empress Elisabeth, at the hands of Luigi Luccheni, intensified the countermeasures of the Habsburg police. Their intelligence service in the United States tried to infiltrate the secret societies among the emigrees. The assassination of the Italian King Umberto in 1900 showed that the plotters were energetic in their preparations. His assassin, Gaetano Bresci, had come from the United States shortly before the assassination. George Woodcock is of the opinion that he might have been a "chosen agent of an anarchist group in Paterson, New Jersey,"[40] which was linked with Most.

The Vienna police were literally flooded with reports about the new conspiracies originating among Italians, Poles, Magyars, South Slavs and other former Habsburg subjects in the United States, who had contacts with their compatriots in Europe. Here are a few of these reports:

In September 1900 information was received from the Austro-Hungarian consul in New York, Nuber, that attempts were planned "by Italian anarchists in New York" against the lives of the Russian Tsar and the Emperor Franz Josef. Nuber obtained this information from the Russian Embassy, who in turn got it from Louis Dubois, an Italian salesman in New York (his real name was Francesco Trentini). He had previously informed the Italian Prime Minister Pelloux that a plot was being prepared to kill the Italian King Umberto.[41]

The Austrian ambassador from Istanbul reported on August 27, 1900, that he had been given information by the first secretary of the Sultan "that the Turkish Embassy in Washington had found out that Italian anarchists planned the assassination of Emperor Franz Josef, the Emperor Wilhelm of Germany and the King of Greece." These anarchists were said to have had connections with Bresci, the assassin of King Umberto. The anarchists had left the United States in order to assassinate the rulers mentioned above.[42] Paul Boegner, whose real name was Louis Tournier, reported on September 19, 1900, to the Austrian Embassy in Switzerland that a certain Lodovico Ghiltoni, who had been connected with Bresci, intended to assassinate the Emperor Franz Josef. Ghiltoni was arrested in Milan and was sentenced to two days in jail and fined 25 liras; but he denied the accusations. He was released and kept under the surveillance of the police in Basel and Paris.[43]

The Austrian secret service in the United States succeeded in recruiting a man who used the name of Erasmus Dziubaniuk; he mingled among radical-minded emigrees from Austria-Hungary, and reported on March 24, 1900, the preparation of several plots against Habsburg dignitaries. Through Consul Nuber on March 24, 1900, he denounced Adalbert Lazarowicz as a member of a Polish Revolutionary Committee which planned to assassinate the Emperor Franz Josef. This committee was reported to have branches in Chicago, Buffalo, Milwaukee, Cleveland and Pittsburgh. Dziubaniuk also reported that Lazarowicz had left for Lwow with a friend by the name of Nicinsky. They both were said to be members of the student association Polskie Kolko Akademicki. "The newspaper *Die Freiheit*, the international organ of the Communist Anarchists in the German language, which was edited by Johann Most, was believed to be the center of the conspiracy."[44] Socialist workers in Lemberg (Lwow), Prague, Krakau (Krakow), Olmütz (Olomouc) and Vienna were said to have connections with this committee in America.[45]

In the reports of the Habsburg secret agents in the United States the name of Most was mentioned several times. In Chicago there was a Czech group called Novy Cult and in New York one called Svobodna Obec, both of which, according to a report to Vienna from Chicago, were connected with *Die Freiheit*, and were planning an attempt on the Emperor Franz Josef in 1901.[46] According to this information, a young female anarchist called Sophie Adelaide Schum was going to Vienna to try to kill the Emperor during an audience.[47]

Several reports from the Austro-Hungarian representatives in the United States, as well as from Trieste and Dalmatia, speak of cooperation between Italian and South Slav secret societies in planning joint actions against the leading figures of the Habsburg realm. In this respect the name of the Slovene Vidmar was mentioned several times in 1901; he supposedly should have left Chicago for Bohemia to assassinate the Emperor Franz Josef in the summer of 1901. Dziubaniuk was again the main informer. But there were reports from other sources about the whereabouts of Vidmar. He was seen in Paris, then in Prague, and a letter of his was intercepted in which he wrote to some of his friends that "it was impossible to reach him," meaning the old Emperor.[48]

From the village of Nabrežina, just east of Trieste, the Viennese police were informed on June 18, 1901, that the anarchist Vincenzo Matera was accused of taking part in a meeting of a secret society at Nabrežina at which it was decided to take action against the Emperor. Matera was arrested and questioned. He admitted that a meeting of an anarchist group had taken place, but denied that they had any plot.[49] In August 1903, P. Gasparutti, a priest of Udine, informed Vienna that eight students from Trieste, Padua and Udine were scheming to kill Emperor Franz Josef.[50] The same year another Italian priest Don Carlo Sabol sent a confidential report to the authorities that a man from

Udine by the name of Pignat together with three men from Trieste, Bambin, Marchier and a student, would try to kill the Emperor Franz Josef and the German Kaiser Wilhelm.[51]

There are in the Vienna archives many other reports about conspiracies against the members of the Habsburg house in the first decade of the twentieth century. Not all of these reports were true; some were just rumors. But, as we shall see later from the South Slav archives, the Habsburg police, despite their clever work, were ignorant of many other plots.

But the acts of individual terrorism in the Habsburg empire prove one point very clearly. Political homicide receded among the national groups which gained greater political freedom (the Italians and Magyars) and increased among the nationalities which were in the worst political, cultural and social plight—among Ukrainian and Rumanian peasantry and especially among the South Slav kmets.

In 1908 a twenty-year-old Ukrainian student, Miroslav Sičinsky, assassinated the Governor of Galicia, Count Potocki, in Lwow, shouting: "This is the punishment for our sufferings."[52] Sičinsky was sentenced to death, but the sentence was commuted to twenty years' imprisonment. In 1912 he escaped from his jail in Stanislawow with the help of the jailers. He emigrated to the United States, where he lived until the end of the Second World War and had a successful career as a businessman in New York State.

In March 1914, in the artificial Magyar Uniat bishopric at Hajdudorog in Transylvania, which had been set up by the Magyar government to Magyarize the Rumanian Uniats, the vicar general was killed by a time bomb sent through the mail by Rumanian terrorists.

An old concept of tyrannicide was being vigorously rejuvenated.

CHAPTER X

PRIMITIVE REBELS
OF BOSNIA

*My life resembles the swan's flight through the
fog toward some distant but compelling light.*
—VLADIMIR GAĆINOVIĆ

THE ASSASSINS of the Archduke Franz Ferdinand belonged to a
group of secret societies, made up mostly of students of peasant origin,
collectively called the Young Bosnians.[1] They were not a single, centralized, hierarchical organization with a written program. They were a
part of the spontaneous revolutionary movement among the South Slav
youth, existing both within Austria-Hungary—especially in Croatia,
Dalmatia and Slovenia—and in Serbia and Montenegro, and even
among the South Slav emigrants in the United States. A common goal
brought all these groups together: the revolutionary destruction of the
Habsburg empire.

Yet they were not exclusively nationalists. The hard core of the
Young Bosnians was committed not only to throwing off foreign rule
but also to overcoming the primitivism of their own society; they challenged the authority of existing institutions of state, school, church and
family, and they believed in egalitarianism and the emancipation of
women. For that reason ethics became a field of special interest for
them.

They were also engaged in other spiritual and intellectual activities.
On the eve of the First World War, they were identified among South
Slavs as the most active literary group opposing academism and advo-
cating modernism.

In 1902 there were only thirty Bosnians and Hercegovinians with a university education.[2] These came from the towns, because only rich people could afford to send their sons to Vienna and other universities of the Habsburg empire. Their political outlook was on the whole conservative; they were satisfied with minor administrative posts, and their demands did not exceed a kind of autonomy for the two provinces within the Habsburg empire.

At the turn of the century an intelligentsia of another kind appeared in Bosnia and Hercegovina, deriving entirely from the villages or from the first generation of peasants born in towns. Historical circumstances had retarded the development of Bosnian society in contrast with that of other parts of Europe. The Austro-Hungarian authorities, finding this lag, systematically sustained tribal and feudal relations in the villages and paid no attention to mass education. But among the students were a number of peasant boys. They often worked as servants in the richer homes in order to attend high school. At that time Prosvjeta, a welfare society of Serbs, was organized for the advancement of education, and started to give scholarships to poor but talented pupils. With the help of Prosvjeta many a *kmet's* son not only completed high school but attended the university in Vienna, Prague, Zagreb or Belgrade. The Serbian government also gave a number of scholarships to Bosnian and Hercegovinian students. At the universities, this new intelligentsia came into closer contact with the mainstream of European thought. Most of them, however, never cut themselves off from their villages; they returned to their homes during summer vacations or when they could not find work after graduating, and they continued to share the peasant way of life and its hardships. They brought back modern political doctrines but had difficulties applying them at home. The Habsburg authorities did not permit any kind of political liberty in Bosnia and Hercegovina. Besides, young Bosnians were faced with the parochialism of their villages. With the introduction of a money economy the peasant society underwent substantial change. Nevertheless, traditional forms of political struggle survived, such as spontaneous uprisings followed by years of complete apathy or sporadic individual agrarian terrorism. Thus the Young Bosnians were caught between two conflicting patterns of political action.

One of the intellectual cradles of the Young Bosnians was the high school in Mostar, the capital of Hercegovina. It was founded in 1893 and among its students were many peasant boys. The Habsburg authorities did not permit the organization of any student society, even an athletic one. The schoolboys were also forbidden to take part in any public society, either as members or as guests. They were not allowed to attend court proceedings. The students who violated these rules were expelled from the high school.[3] These rules were enforced throughout Bosnia and Hercegovina. The only youth society permitted by the Habsburgs was St. Mary's Congregation, headed by the Jesuit Father Anton Puntigam, a man who enjoyed the confidence of the Archduke Franz Ferdinand and the Duchess of Hohenberg.[4]

Having no chance to organize openly, the schoolboys formed secret societies, as far back as 1899.[5] These societies differed as to the subject of their work. Dimitrije Mitrinović, a gifted student, born in the village Poplat, in Hercegovina, in 1888, provided the initiative in 1904 for the organization of a secret library, where the schoolboys could read all the books they wanted. The interest in literature among Mostar youth was great; Mostar itself was one of the established centers of Serbo-Croat literature. At the turn of the century it had its literary review, *Zora* ("Dawn"); Aleksa Šantić and Jovan Dučić ranked among the leading poets among South Slavs. Out of Mitrinović's secret library a secret literary society grew up and was called Matica ("Mainstream").

At the same time, another secret society was formed, called Sloboda ("Freedom"), headed by Bogdan Žerajić, the son of a small free peasant, who had difficulties in providing for his family of nine. Other prominent members of the society were Špiro Soldo, Pero Slijepčević, Ljubo Mijatović, and Vladimir Gaćinović, all born in the nearby villages.

Sloboda was more concerned with problems of ethics and politics. The members of Matica and Sloboda knew each other and attended the meetings of both societies. There existed a marked tolerance between them. They discussed various problems of literature, ethics and politics, but held different views. Some of them, at that stage, like Vladimir Gaćinović, regarded themselves as ultra-Serbian nationalists, while Dimitrije Mitrinović described himself as a Yugoslav federalist. He thought that a common Serbo-Croat literature was the best means for the unification of Serbs and Croats.

Despite a short life and the great difficulties and strains under which he lived and worked, Gaćinović succeeded in leaving enough written material—essays and articles—to show the development of his views on nationalism, revolution and socialism.[6] Those who knew Gaćinović intimately, like the Croat poet and revolutionary Tin Ujević, described him as "an intuitive rather than a doctinaire revolutionary," whose most interesting trait was that "he carried to extremes a tendency to feel the sufferings of the society in which he lived as though they were his own."[7]

The agrarian problem obsessed Gaćinović, Žerajić and their friends in Mostar High School, although as Gaćinović himself later said: "All of us at that time did not have clear notions about that issue."[8]

The events connected with the Russian Revolution of 1905 revived the interest among the Young Bosnians in the solution of the agrarian problem in Russia, as well as in Russian literature and history in general. "Chernishevsky's *What Is to Be Done?* was passed from hand to hand. Whole pages from it were copied and learned by heart. Besides Chernishevsky, the most esteemed writers were Bakunin, Herzen, Dostoyevsky (particularly *Crime and Punishment*) and Maxim Gorky. . . ."[9]

"Special study was devoted to the Italian and German liberation movements. Mazzini was 'the real and great man.' . . ."[10] Italian revolutionary tradition from the period of *Risorgimento* was not accidental. In Hercegovina, particularly in the uprising of 1861 and 1875–78, the rebellious *kmets* maintained links with Garibaldi's supporters, and in the latter revolt many Italians actually fought alongside the rebels. Gaćinović, as a fifteen-year-old boy, called himself "a Garibaldino"[11] and read much *Risorgimento* literature. Even the title "Young Bosnia" was modeled on that of Mazzini's Giovane Italia. In *Zora*, the review published by Serbian students in Vienna, Gaćinović's friend Vasilj Popović published a history of the Italian liberation movement in several installments.[12] *Zora* also published Mazzini's revolutionary oath, "which for us was not a historical document, but a hymn of struggle," as Gaćinović later wrote in an article which he prepared at Leon Trotsky's request.[13] There is no doubt that Mazzini's idea that the youth should be the main supporters of the liberation of a country, with the mission of building men of a new type, self-denying crusaders prepared for sacrifice, contributed much in the first years of the Young Bosnians to shaping their ideas and program. During their trial in October 1914, both Gavrilo Princip and Nedeljko Čabrinović on several occasions cited Mazzini as their example for the unification of the South Slavs.[14] In the papers of two Young Bosnians, M. Stojanović and T. Ilić, arrested immediately after June 28, 1914, the following comment of Mazzini was found written after the Archduke's death: "There is no more sacred thing in the world than the duty of a conspirator, who becomes an avenger of humanity and the apostle of permanent natural laws."[15]

When the pupils of Mostar High School graduated or left it for other educational institutions, they carried their ideas and methods of work to other towns of Bosnia and Hercegovina. Dimitrije Mitrinović in 1906 helped the organization of secret societies in Sarajevo.[16] After finishing his sophomore year in high school in 1907, Vladimir Gaćinović joined the Serbian Eastern Orthodox Seminary in Reljevo, near Sarajevo. He came from a family of village priests, had a Church stipend, and should have become a priest himself. At the seminary in Reljevo, Gaćinović organized a secret revolutionary society named after the Serbian patron saint, Sava.

In the meantime, several of the Mostar High School graduates, among them Dimitrije Mitrinović, entered universities in Vienna, Prague and Zagreb. They were attracted by the philosophical and sociological teachings of Thomas Masaryk, as was the case with the academic youth from Croatia, Dalmatia, Slovenia and other South Slav lands.[17] They liked Masaryk's rationalism and denunciation of clericalism. They accepted Masaryk's idea that a man does not commit high treason if he fights for the liberation of his own people. They also followed his advice about the methods of political struggle, the so-called "realistic tactics." These consisted of a rejection of any revolutionary means and the steady cultural revival of the South Slavs through "day-to-day work" by individuals in illiteracy and temperance societies and in cultural clubs. If every intellectual would concentrate on this work, "the joint efforts, when added together, will in the end give great results." Thus, the South Slavs would achieve liberation through the cultural reawakening.

Masaryk's influence among the South Slav academic youth was for a time considerable. The review *Hrvatski Djak* ("Croat Student") became the mouthpiece for Masaryk's ideas. One of the Young Bosnians described it in this way: "We accepted his ideas in our souls and hearts, and we brought them back to our homeland in order to sow them and to reap the fruits of freedom and popular culture."[18] It was strongly influential not only in Bosnia but also in Hercegovina. Under the impact of Masaryk's teachings, the Young Bosnians changed their methods of struggle for several years. Vladimir Gaćinović and Bogdan Žerajić, as well as Dimitrije Mitrinović, advocated the methods of cultural revival of the South Slavs and the necessity of "day-to-day work."[19]

But the trend of political events in the Habsburg monarchy weakened the teachings of Masaryk's gradualism among the Young Bosnians. In October 1908 the annexation of Bosnia and Hercegovina touched off a new wave of unrest among the youngest generation of Young Bosnians. Vladimir Gaćinović and several of his other friends fled to Montenegro and then to Serbia in order to join the Serbian Army as volunteers.[20] Among the Young Bosnians at the Vienna University the opinion was expressed that Masaryk's political methods were too slow for the ensuing crisis. These students had a cultural society called Rad ("Work"), but after the news of the annexation of Bosnia and Hercegovina in October 1908, they decided to organize a secret society to wage a struggle against Austro-Hungarian authorities.[21] The students declared that they would never recognize the annexation of Bosnia and Hercegovina, that "it represents a sheer plunder, and if Austria-Hungary wants to swallow us, we shall gnaw its stomach."[22] The first members of this society were Božidar Zečević, Pero Slijepčević, Dimitrije Mitrinović, Mihajlo Blagojević, Veljko Besarović and Aco Bogdanović. Each of them headed a *kruzhok*, a secret group, composed of three members according to the practice of Russian revolutionaries. No member outside a *kruzhok* knew about the other members. The rules and goals of the secret society were not written, nor were the minutes of the meetings recorded, in order to preserve the utmost secrecy. Correspondence between different *kruzhoks* was carried on in code.[23]

One of the leaders of the new secret society, Božidar Zečević, went to Belgrade and came into contact with Major Milan Pribićević, a former Austro-Hungarian officer, who had fled to Serbia in 1906 because of his revolutionary activities, and later became the general secretary of Narodna Odbrana (National Defense).[24] Pribićević told Zečević that for the final struggle against Austria-Hungary people in Bosnia and Hercegovina should first be ideologically prepared. For that purpose the best way would be to organize secret societies and links from one village to another. In such a way the directives from above could be spread; in addition, these links would facilitate the gathering of information about the feelings of the people, as well as information on the movements of the Austro-Hungarian troops.[25] On his return to Vienna, Zečević informed his secret society, which accepted Pribićević's proposal. Pero Slijepćević had to organize the secret links in Hercegovina, Vasilj Grdjić in Sarajevo and Sarajevo district, Vojo Kećmanović and Dimitrije Zakić in Bosanska Krajina, Mihajlo Blagojević and Aco Bogdanović in northeastern Bosnia.[26] The new secret societies sprang up in Bosnia and Hercegovina by December 1908. Zečević had informed the president of Narodna Odbrana, General Boža Janković, that a number of students from Vienna were willing to come to Serbia and train themselves in guerrilla activities, but General Janković rejected this offer. Zečević succeeded in convincing another member of Narodna Odbrana, Živojin Rafajlović, of the necessity for that activity, and a number of young Bosnians and Hercegovinians from Vienna, Prague and Zagreb universities, as well as from Bosnia and Hercegovina, went to Serbia for that training.[27]

The new secret society also decided to come into contact with "all— progressive and revolutionary—elements which understand our national aspirations," particularly with "revolutionary, anarchist and nihilist organizations which exist in the world."[28] Zečević left for Russia in January 1909 in order to contact "Russian revolutionaries and learn their methods of secret work."[29] Zečević and other members from Vienna established communications with Viennese Social Democrats and their paper, *Arbeiter Zeitung,* giving them information about events in Bosnia and Hercegovina.[30]

The work of the new society was slowed down in January 1909, when one of their members was arrested in Croatia as he was trying to obtain some explosives.[31] In 1910 a greater number of students from Bosnia and Hercegovina came to study in Vienna. Among them was Vladimir Gaćinović. He had been graduated from high school in Belgrade and had entered Belgrade University, attending courses on Serbo-Croat literature given by Professor Jovan Skerlić, whose teachings influenced revolutionary youth in all the South Slav lands. After one term in Belgrade, Gaćinović, together with about thirty youths from Bosnia and Hercegovina, received a stipend from the Serbian government and entered Vienna University.[32] Here he found many of his friends from Mostar High School's secret societies. They continued their work, but in a more organized way. In 1911 Gaćinović joined the secret society of Ujedinjenje ili Smrt ("Unification or Death"), in Belgrade, as well as Narodna Odbrana.[33] During summer vacations he often visited Bosnia and Hercegovina, organizing *kruzhoks* and secret links from one village to another for the gathering of military intelligence to benefit Serbia. All together, Gaćinović had organized five *kruzhoks* in Sarajevo, two in Vienna, one in Zagreb and one in Pakrac in Croatia.[34] The review *Zora* carried detailed instructions for the work of students' secret societies in Bosnia and Hercegovina.[35]

For the first time in 1911, Vladimir Gaćinović visited Switzerland and established firm links with the Russian revolutionaries living there. Gaćinović entered Lausanne University in 1913 and made Switzerland his base of operations.[36] In Lausanne, Gaćinović met Mark Andreyevich Natanson-Bobrov, a pioneer of Russian revolutionary thought. Natanson helped Gaćinović study the history of Russian Populism. In long discussions with Natanson, new horizons were opened for young Gaćinović.

Natanson made a deep impression on Gaćinović. In a letter to his friend Mirko Damjanović, on June 2, 1911, Gaćinović wrote: "How much I have lived through these last few days! One whole faith has collapsed and withered away and in its place is growing a new ideology which is seething chaotically in my mind, an ideology vigorous and intense but still obscure and imprecise."[37]

Natanson, like Bakunin, had sympathy for the struggle of the South Slavs against the Habsburg empire. The neo-Slavism of the Social Revolutionaries, their interest in national questions, and the emphasis on the liberation of the peasantry as the main goal of their revolutionary activity were close to the heart of Gaćinović. Ujević described Gaćinović as a "left-wing Social Revolutionary, if not actually a member, since he was not a Russian, then a co-opted member. With such a position he had contact with many Russians, exchanging letters, frequenting their meetings and lectures, even contributing to the Russian Socialist press."[38] Through Natanson, Gaćinović came into contact with some of the leading Russian Social Democrats, both Mensheviks and Bolsheviks. In Natanson's Lausanne home he met Lunacharsky and Martov.[39]

From these days a new controversy arose in Gaćinović; he started to waver between the positions of the Russian Social Revolutionaries and the Social Democrats. One of the reasons for this change was the fact that his idol Natanson underwent the same evolution. In this transformation of Gaćinović's views, Trotsky played an important role. Gaćinović knew him from Serbia in 1913, and they continued their contacts in Paris in the first days of 1915. After a short period as a volunteer in the French Navy, Gaćinović returned with Ujević to Paris at the end of 1914 without any means of livelihood. He was a newsboy for a few days, selling *L'Humanité*. Ujević and he later made some money by digging trenches in the Paris suburbs and then tried to work as truck drivers. They did not have much to eat and all their free time was spent in the Bibliothèque Nationale, reading books. Gaćinović continued his connections with the Russian revolutionaries who were in Paris at the time. He met there his good friend from Switzerland Serge Kibalchich, the son of Nikolai Kibalchich, the member of the Narodnaya Volya, who was executed in 1881 for taking part in the conspiracy against Tsar Alexander II. Gaćinović was on such good terms with young Kibalchich that they were *pobratim*, an old South Slav institution of sworn brotherhood.[40]

At that time the differences between the various Russian revolutionary parties were not great, and their members used to meet together and discuss their mutual problems. Gaćinović used to visit the offices of the paper *L'Anarchie*, where Kibalchich worked. He also met Trotsky during his stay in Paris, late in the autumn of 1914. Ujević recorded that they often visited Trotsky in his hotel Odessa in the Rue d'Odessa, not far from the Montparnasse station. They attended lectures given by Trotsky and Lunacharsky in the Hall of Learned Societies and had heated discussions afterward. During one of these discussions Trotsky once said to Gaćinović that he did not regard him as a socialist. Ujević, who witnessed this discussion, said that Trotsky practiced his own party's exclusiveness, and that he relied solely on the urban proletariat in revolution, while Gaćinović as a left-wing Social Revolutionary was more ready to rely on the peasantry.

Despite these sharp words and arguments, there existed a kind of friendship between Trotsky and Gaćinović. In one of his articles Trotsky called Gaćinović "my young friend."[41] Ujević remembers that Gaćinović several times "argued vehemently with Trotsky for the victims among the anarchists arrested because of the conspiracy against the Tsar Nicholas II."[42] Trotsky also persuaded Gaćinović to write articles on the Sarajevo assassination and on his experience as a French sailor. Gaćinović wrote them and Trotsky published them later in Kiev's liberal paper, *Kievskaya Mysl* ("Kiev Thought"), whose main contributors were Mensheviks. As an introduction to the first article Trotsky wrote:

In a corner of the Café Rotonde, beside me, in the cloud of smoke which one cannot find anywhere else, is sitting a young Serb. Despite the very strange crowd, one's eyes must rest on him even against one's will. He is one of these types which are born to provoke a feeling of uneasiness among orderly people. Tall, thin, but strong, with an expression of restlessness and energy in his eyes and in the lines of his face, he watches everything and everybody with such intelligence, for greedy impressions of other people's lives, but still capable of saving himself from being drawn into them. This young man, barely out of his teens—he is hardly 23—has his goal. He is Bosnian, an intimate friend of Princip and Ilić.

Around us are the remnants of all the foreign colonies in Paris. A small, today still unknown sculptor, with a large dog, well known in the Latin Quarter; a freshly shaven Spaniard, who never takes off his mantle with its red-green lining; a stranger of unknown nationality, *habitué de la maison*, who is collecting donations for a funeral wreath for the owner of the café who died yesterday; a white-haired Italian with his wife in a velvet blouse, admired, no doubt, by all the models who frequent this café; two little Rumanians or Greeks in patent-leather shoes, with diamond rings on their fingers and with the manners of false dancing masters; the girls from the *Quartier des cigales*, who sing in low voices love songs that are not so popular these days—in this milieu my comrade is telling me about the South Slav youth, about its hopes and struggles; he gives a short character sketch of personalities, whose names we had heard from the newspapers at the end of July.

"Do you know what," I suggested to him, "do write your reminiscences. At least tell what can be publicly told now. I think that this will greatly interest the Russian reading public."

After two days my young friend brought me his manuscript. It is a reflection of the writer and his views and judgments for which I cannot take responsibility. But this is a human document, and it would not be proper to correct it or to add anything to it. I simply bring it as translated.[43]

Trotsky soon left Paris, as did Gaćinović, and they never met again. But in Switzerland, where Gaćinović settled during the war, he continued to keep contacts with Russian revolutionaries. It seems that he met Karl Radek at this time. According to a statement by his brother Vojislav, Gaćinović met Lenin in Switzerland, but this has not been confirmed by other sources.[44] After the Russian Revolution in 1917, Natanson decided to return to Russia via Germany, together with Lenin and other Russian revolutionaries. Natanson proposed that Gaćinović should go with him. Pero Slijepčević confirmed this, but said that Gaćinović rejected the offer, because "his socialism did not go so far as to accept the service of his war enemy."[45] Gaćinović's brother Vojislav gives different reasons for Gaćinović's rejection of Natanson's offer— that he was full of enthusiasm for the project, but was afraid that the Germans would arrest him because of his participation in the Sarajevo conspiracy, as well as for the fact that his name was mentioned several times at the Banja Luka trial in which more than three hundred Serbs from Bosnia were tried.[46]

When Natanson went to Russia through Germany, supposedly he

took Gaćinović's archives with him. In an undated letter to his brother, Vojislav said: "I am sure that the Old Man has already sent his news. Could you go to the house and ask whether any telegram has arrived?"[47]

Gaćinović remained in Switzerland, where he met his death in August 1917. The causes of his death are not clear. According to some versions he was poisoned by the secret agents of the Serbian and French governments or by the Austro-Hungarian secret service.[48] There exists a contrary opinion that he was a victim of Ujedinjenje ili Smrt, of which he had been a member for a time.[49]

Although Vladimir Gaćinović was one of the chief leaders of the Young Bosnians, after 1912 his influence began to fade. After the summer of that year, he could not return to his native land, because he had refused to serve in the Habsburg army. At the same time, a new revolutionary generation was springing up at home among the schoolboys. Gaćinović's influence was not nearly as overpowering as it had been with the previous generation.[50]

Nevertheless, Gaćinović kept casual contacts with Bosnia and Hercegovina through Danilo Ilić, a teacher and writer, who was a year older than Gaćinović. Danilo Ilić became a kind of bridge between different generations of Bosnian revolutionaries. He knew Gaćinović and other Bosnian students in Switzerland and in Vienna. At the same time, he was linked with many Bosnian students who had fled to Serbia, either to join the *komite*, guerrilla units, preparing for action against the Ottoman and Habsburg empires, or to study in Belgrade. Being almost constantly in Sarajevo, Ilić knew the youngest generation of Bosnian revolutionaries.

Ilić was the only son of a cobbler who died when Ilić was five years old, and his mother supported the boy by washing laundry. Being a good pupil, Ilić was sent to the Merchants School, from which he graduated in 1905. He could not find work and lived for three years as a newsboy and then as a prompter in a traveling theater, functioning at the same time as a copyist of the texts of the plays and as an usher. After he was kicked out of the theater he wandered through Bosnia on foot, working as a laborer, a porter at the railway stations, an apprentice in a quarry and then a longshoreman on the Sava.[51] Such a life was ruining his health and he returned to Sarajevo, where he received a scholarship and graduated in 1912 from the Teachers College, four years older than all the other graduates. He was a tall, quiet man, "always in a dark tie as a reminder of death." Out of nine Serb pupils in his class, six joined the *komite*.[52] In the autumn of 1912 Ilić served for a time as a teacher in Avtovac in Hercegovina and then in Foča in Bosnia. He fell ill (he was suffering from a stomach ulcer) and returned to Sarajevo, where he worked until June 1913 as a clerk in the Serbian National Bank. In June 1913, Gaćinović asked him to come to Switzerland, and he did, using the passport of a painter named Ilija Sudar,[53] a member of the Social

Democratic party, who looked much like Ilić. Having little money, Ilić traveled in Switzerland mostly on foot, visiting several of the Russian left-wing Social Revolutionaries.[54] At the news of the Second Balkan War, after his return to Sarajevo, Ilić walked to Serbia in order to join the Serbian army as a volunteer. He was accepted as a male nurse and took care of wounded soldiers stricken with cholera. At the end of the war, he returned to Sarajevo and spent a month and a half in hospital. His friends listened to his accounts of his meetings in Switzerland and Serbia "as Moslems listen to their pilgrims returned from Mecca." That was how he got the nickname Hadžija (or Hadji).[55] From the end of 1913 until June 28, 1914, Ilić was a proofreader on the local Serb paper *Srpska Riječ,* and from the middle of May 1914 the editorial writer of the paper *Zvono.* At the same time, Ilić translated extensively —Gorky's "The Burning Heart" and "Greetings to the Liberated Humanity"; Wilde's essays on art and criticism; Andreyev's *The Dark Horizon;* Bakunin's *The Paris Commune and the Idea of the State;* Petrus Ramus's *Le Mensonge du parlamentarisme;* and the work of several other writers and political philosophers.

Ilić was fond of his mother, and he lived in her small house on 3 Oprkanj Street in Sarajevo. She no longer washed laundry, but rented rooms to schoolboys. One day a peasant boy who had never before been in Sarajevo was brought to her by his older brother. She liked the thirteen-year-old boy who had been enrolled in the Merchants School, and he shared a room with her son Danilo. The name of the boy was Gavrilo Princip, and he became the best friend of Danilo, who was four years older and who in 1914 became the chief organizer of the Sarajevo assassination.

The Princip family provides an illustration of the disintegration of the *zadruga,* the joint family, under the new social and economic order. The *zadrugas* under Turkish rule had been self-sufficient, the greater part of their income coming from agricultural sources. For them, markets and the use of money were of secondary importance. They paid their tributes in kind, and produced at home everything they needed, except for a few commodities such as salt.

The Princips' *zadruga* was relatively big in Turkish times,[56] but after 1878 it dwindled quickly. After the murder of Jovo Princip in 1881, his second son Petar-Pepo, the father of Gavrilo, became its head at the age of thirty. Petar was the last head of the Princip *zadruga* before it was dissolved and the property divided among its members. Petar got about two hectares, approximately four acres of land, most of it meadow. Their harvest consisted of corn and *karišik,* a mixture of oats and barley, and it provided them with barely enough foodstuff for two months of the year. Therefore they had to find additional income by undertaking different types of work. Another reason why they needed money was that they had to pay the one-third tribute to their *beg,* Sijerčić in

eastern Bosnia, not in kind but in cash. He lived far away from Grahovo, and it was too expensive for him to send his *subaša*, assessor; so he
made a contract with the Princips that they should pay their tribute in
money.[57]

Some of the members of the family, who under the Turkish regime
had served as *matrolozi*, frontier guardsmen and, later, as *zaptije*, gendarmes, continued to serve under the Habsburgs. This fact has been
confirmed by several contemporary historians. Božidar Tomić wrote
that Todo, brother of the murdered Jovo, served after 1878 "as an Austrian *redar* [policeman] until the end of his life."[58] And Gavrilo Princip's uncle Ilija, the eldest brother of his father Petar, was for a time an
Austro-Hungarian gendarme. Vladimir Lebedev, a Russian publicist
and a member of the Kerensky government who tried his hand at a
biography of Gavrilo Princip, wrote "how Ilija together with his
friends, six gendarmes, one Christmas morning visited the family of his
brother Petar and how they sang Christmas carols together."[59] The tradition that there should be a gendarme in the Princip family lasted until
June 28, 1914. "About ten o'clock in the evening, Gavrilo Princip's parents were disturbed in their first sleep by a gendarme, a member of the
Princip family, who ordered Gavrilo's father, Petar, to report at once
to the police station in Grahovo, because it was reported that Gavre
[the nickname of Gavrilo] had murdered Verdinanda [as the Bosnian
peasants pronounced the name of Franz Ferdinand]."[60]

In jail, Gavrilo Princip wrote a few pages about his own life at the
request of Dr. Martin Pappenheim, a Viennese psychiatrist. At one
point he recorded that his father was "a peasant, but engages in business."[61] Even Princip's grandfather Jovo, after being turned down in his
application to continue to serve as a gendarme, made some money by
carrying passengers and mail on his wagon between Grahovo and
different Dalmation towns. Princip's father Petar continued to do this
work.

Petar married rather late. He had tried his luck during his father's
lifetime and had fallen in love with a Catholic girl from the Šarić family. In his father's eyes, marriage with a Catholic was impossible, and he
simply ordered his son to stop seeing this girl. Petar tried to argue, but
his father threatened to kill him.[62] That was the end of his love for the
Catholic girl.

In 1882, after his father's death, Petar at last found the girl of his
choice. Her name was Maria, or Nana, and she came from the Mićić
family of the Bilbija clan in the nearby village of Mali Obljaj. She was
fourteen years younger than her husband. She had a stepmother who
maltreated her, and marriage was a way of saving herself from an intolerable life at home. Nana was an energetic girl, with curly hair and
enough vitality for "two or three other women," as Tomić recorded.
She sang "like an angel." "Petar was quite different from his young

wife. Very short and bony, with a red weather-beaten face, in both appearance and character he counterbalanced the sharp features of his bride. Nature played with this couple in a strange way; she enriched the woman with the qualities of a man and gave to him soft, feminine features,"[63] wrote Tomić, who knew Gavrilo Princip's parents personally.

Petar and Nana had nine children, five sons and four daughters, of whom six died as babies. They lived in the old family house, made of wood, with a steep black roof, in a style described by one writer as Bosnian Gothic. The house and its interior had not changed for hundreds of years. It remained virtually unchanged until 1939, when Tomić described it:

In the old house the doors are small, and so very low that you can enter the house only by bowing your head. Inside it is dark. The house has no windows; instead of floor only beaten earth. To the left from the door is a stone bench on which a wooden barrel for water was standing; behind this, on a shelf, some cooking utensils, earthenware pots; a big round low table was hanging against the wall. On the other side of the door were three wooden chests, a box for keeping flour, a sieve and another shelf. Deep on the right side there was a low door leading to a small room in which stood a bed. On the left side of the main part of the house was an open hearth, burning day and night, surrounded by a low stone wall. Above it stood a *verige*, an iron chain hanging from the ceiling, on which were metal cauldrons hooked above the fire. Smoke went through a *badza*, a hole in the roof above the open fireplace. The only light in the house came through it.[64]

In these conditions, without doctors or midwives, newly born babies could not long survive; when Gavrilo Princip was born on July 13, 1894, his mother did not believe he would live long.[65] It was a very hot day, even at such a high altitude as Grahovo Polje. The mother had been working all day long in the meadow, gathering grass which had just been cut. She had to make big bundles of hay, each of them weighing sixty pounds. When this work was over she went back home and washed linen in the brook. After milking a cow, she felt labor pains and ran toward the house. She was not allowed to make any sign that she was going to have a baby, not to cry or shout. She had only enough strength to enter through the low door. She fell on the earth floor by the open hearth, and in a very short time the boy was born, falling on the stones formed around the fireplace.[66] Nana's mother-in-law rushed into the house, bit the cord, and washed the newly born child in a wooden bowl and wrapped him in a coarse hemp cloth. She built up the fire, brought in a bale of barley straw for the mother, and soon the house was filled with relatives, who were served with plum brandy. They toasted the newborn boy. Petar was not at home; he was again at his work. Late at night he returned, and one of his sisters came running toward him, shouting: "A scarf for me, and a boy for you."[67]

This was the second son born to Petar Princip, seven years after the first, Jovo. The new baby was rather weak, and a girl was sent to the home of the priest Ilija Bilbija, to arrange for a *znamenje*, the first part of christening. Mother Nana sent word that she wanted to give the boy the name of Spiro, her dead brother. The priest did not approve of women choosing names. He took the calendar and said: "The boy was born on the day of Saint Gabriel, and therefore he is going to be called Gavrilo."[68]

The girl ran back to the Princips' home with the priest's ruling. No one dared to contradict it, not even the energetic Nana. Ilija was not only a clergyman, he was the military leader of all the Serbs living in Grahovo Polje and had a fine record in the uprising of 1875. His exploits had been hailed by Sir Arthur Evans in his articles in the *Manchester Guardian* and in his book on the Bosnian rising. Besides, Ilija was a giant of a man weighing 275 pounds and had a voice as "strong as the trumpet of the Archangel Michael."[69] Furthermore, he was the head of the Bilbija clan, Nana's clan. Therefore, she did not wish to irritate the old priest, and she accepted his decision.

The boy was baptized a month later. Ilija was helped in his administrative duties by Miloš Bilbija, a young priest from his own clan, who was very absent-minded. He recorded in the Parish Register that Gavrilo Princip was born on July 13, 1894, and in the Civil Register, which was also kept by the parish, June 13, 1894. Twenty years later this aberration of the local priest was the cause of serious legal disputes demanding the expertise of some of the highest civil servants of the Habsburg empire to determine which of the two records was right. On their decision depended the punishment of Gavrilo Princip at his trial as an assassin; if he was under twenty on the day of his crime, he could not be sentenced to death according to Austro-Hungarian law.

The young Princips were unable to obtain a living from the land. The eldest son of the family, Jovo, as a boy of fifteen left the Grahovo Valley *"trbuhom za kruhom"*—seeking food by the urge of his stomach, as a Serb proverb says. He worked first as a scribe, then as a driver for a merchant, settling at last in the village of Hadžići near Sarajevo, where he was for a time a waiter, then an assistant to a trader whose job was to transport timber from the nearby forests. Jovo was in charge of several pairs of horses which hauled logs from the deepest parts of the forests to the railway station. With the vitality of a highlander, Jovo soon became his own boss; at the age of twenty-one he owned several pairs of horses and was thinking of starting a little sawmill of his own. Yet he did not break away completely from his family. He sent money to his father and took care of the education of his brothers, Gavrilo and

Nikola, who was two years younger. The old bonds of *zadruga* life had not disappeared completely. Gavrilo Princip himself, years later, when he was answering the questions of Dr. Pappenheim, confessed that he had been thinking a lot about his parents and all the members of the old *zadruga*. He suffered because he had no news from them; he even confessed to homesickness and tried to excuse himself for such feelings by saying "that they must exist in everybody."[70]

Although Gavrilo Princip's father was a very pious man, even by standards of the Grahovo Valley *kmets*, who kept all the prescribed fasts and never missed a mass, his wife did not share this attitude. She looked on religion as a part of traditional custom. Under her influence, Gavrilo developed the same attitude. He said to Dr. Pappenheim that "even as a child he was not particularly religious."[71]

Petar was in many ways an exceptional man in the Grahovo Valley. He never drank, never swore, and he made a hobby of planting trees around his house, in his village, and even along the road from Obljaj to Grahovo. He took his duty as a postman seriously; in the winter, when the snow was too deep for the wagon, he would carry the mail, some sixty pounds, on his back. Yet the people in the Grahovo Valley did not altogether esteem him, and some of them liked to ridicule him. Tomić wrote that "old Petar would bet that he could run in the middle of winter, dressed only in his shirt and trousers and without shoes, the distance between Grahovo and the village of Popovo Brdo and back, almost a mile distance."[72] Once on a dangerous curve on the mountain road over the Dinara Mountain his horses bolted, and Petar, trying to save the mail and the passengers, jumped out of the wagon and stopped the horses, but broke his leg.

There are few authentic facts about the childhood of Gavrilo Princip, except that he was the image of his mother, had her curly hair, her blue eyes, pointed chin and also, as a boy, a soprano voice with double ranger. Božidar Tomić, a school friend of Gavrilo's, wrote about these days:

In his early childhood Gavrilo showed exceptional signs of development. He started to walk very early, in his ninth month, and as a child was very alert and active. As a boy he did not like to play much with his mates; he preferred to tend the calves and to watch the *kmets* working in the fields. Even before he went to school, as he walked behind his calves, he liked to pretend that he was a schoolboy, carrying a bag on his back with some old books. When playing with children he was very rough, often striking boys stronger than he, especially if he felt that they were doing wrong to him or that the stronger ones were slighting him.[73]

Gavrilo Princip speaking about his childhood said to Dr. Pappenheim: "I was always a quiet, sentimental child, always earnest, with books, pictures."[74] His mother said to Gligorije Božović: "Gavrilo was a quiet boy, but every blow he received he would return twofold. He read much and kept silent most of the time."[75]

The Princips were lucky in that two miles from their village there was a primary school in Grahovo. But Gavrilo Princip nearly missed going to school. His father Petar was against it; he needed a shepherd who would guard his sheep. Only through the intervention of his mother was the boy sent to school, at the age of nine. In the first class he was not very successful, but from "the second to the fourth classes he had excellent marks and for his hard work he received from his teacher a collection of Serbian heroic folk poetry, which he read in his father's home to the assembled *kmets* at the evening parties called *selo*."[76]

Gavrilo Princip left Grahovo Valley at the age of thirteen, when he finished primary school. His brother Jovo had read in an advertisement that the Military School in Sarajevo was accepting healthy boys of fourteen as cadets. Tuition, food and uniforms were free. The cadets wore the Moslem fez, a red cylindrical cap with a black tassel. He wrote to his father that this would be a good opportunity for Gavrilo to become an officer. Old Petar, who as Gavrilo Princip wrote later to Dr. Pappenheim, "was not interested in political matters,"[77] accepted this idea at once.

From Grahovo Valley to the nearest railway station at Bugojno, where they could get a direct train to Sarajevo, Petar and little Gavrilo, with the red round cap of the Grahovo highlander on his head, had to ride on horseback for three days.

Did the Grahovo Valley and the life of its *kmets* leave any lasting impression on Gavrilo Princip? This quiet but extremely sensitive boy left several pieces of evidence on this point. To one of his intimate friends he admitted some years later that the *selo*, the evening meetings in the village, left on him the most painful memories:

The wet logs on the open fire gave the only light to the closely packed *kmets* and their wives, wrapped in thick smoke. If I tried to penetrate the curtain of smoke, the most that I could see were the eyes of the human beings, numerous, sad and glaring with some kind of fluid light coming from nowhere. Some kind of reproach, even threat, radiated from them, and many times since then they have awakened me from my dreams.[78]

When the thirteen-year-old Gavrilo came to Sarajevo, one August night of 1907, he was sleepy and frightened. "Looking for a place to spend the night, father Petar and Gavrilo came to a Moslem *han*, a kind of inn. But the boy, seeing the strange Moslem dress of the innkeeper, jumped up and fled from the *han*, shouting: 'I do not wish to sleep there. They are Turks.' His father had to find another *han*, a Christian one," Tomić has reported.[79]

The next morning, Petar and Gavrilo proceeded to Hadžići and met Petar's eldest son, Jovo. He promised his father he would take Gavrilo to the military school, and the old man returned satisfied to Grahovo Valley to drive his postman's wagon over the Dinara Mountain.

Although Jovo too was not much interested in politics, he began to wonder whether it was right to send his brother to a Habsburg military school. He came with Gavrilo to Sarajevo and on the way to the school stopped at Jovo Pešut's shop to buy the boy a pair of underpants and some shirts, the first new ones he had ever had. Jovo Pešut knew the Princip family, and he was very much against sending Gavrilo to the military school. According to Tomić, Pešut said to Jovo Princip:

Do not give the child to an institution in which he will be uprooted and become an executioner of his own people. If there is no other way, it would be better to bring him back at once to his own village, and let him live as his ancestors did. But if you want to listen to me as a friend, send him to the Merchants School. This school quicker than any other will bring him bread and profit, and what a profit![80]

Jovo was impressed by the advice of Pešut, who offered to help arrange for Gavrilo's admission to the Merchants School.

Thus the fate of Gavrilo Princip was settled on that August morning in 1907. He missed becoming a Habsburg officer simply by the accidental meeting with the merchant Pešut. Now he was destined to become a rich trader. He was duly enrolled the same day, and Jovo went around the town to find a room where his younger brother could stay. Some acquaintances told him that the old widow Stoja Ilić might be willing to accept the boy. An agreement was reached; Jovo paid a month's rent in advance and went to attend his business in Hadžići after sending a short letter to his father saying that Gavrilo had joined the Merchants School and had been settled satisfactorily in the home of the widow Stoja Ilić. Jovo did not know anything about old Stoja's son Danilo, whose collection of books made an impression on young Gavrilo.

The first three years in the Merchants School were rather uneventful for Gavrilo. He was a good pupil. The business of his brother did not always go well, and there was not enough money for Gavrilo's room. The boy returned to his brother's home and commuted from the village of Hadžići to Sarajevo. In the summer Gavrilo would go to his village, working in the field and mowing hay with other members of his family. Gavrilo was a rather reserved boy, very fond of reading. This brought him into conflict with his sister-in-law and her mother, who always grumbled that he should help his brother in counting logs or doing something else useful, instead of reading all day long. At that age Gavrilo showed some typical features of his psyche. He had a feeling of inferiority. There were several reasons for this. "He did not like it, because of his small build, when his friends called him Gavrica [little Gavrilo]; he longed to be nicknamed Gavroche, like Victor Hugo's boy hero in *Les Miserables*," his biographer and childhood friend Dragoslav Ljubibratić has reported.[81] He described Princip as a boy with a longish face, dark bushy hair, high wrinkled forehead, a very pointed chin, prominent cheekbones, and his nose a little twisted from an accident at school. "The whole appearance radiated energy and determination. Light-blue eyes softened the expression of his face . . . At first sight quiet and silent, in discussions he would sometimes become cynical and tough; stubborn but not pigheaded. I remember once when we were young schoolboys and we discussed the youth movement and youth leaders, I said about someone that he was a brave man; Princip retorted at once: 'We are all brave men, too.' He liked to make jokes and had a sense of humor. In his heart a good and devoted comrade. Very neat and paying attention to his dress."[82] In this respect he was unlike Gaćinović, who used to wrinkle his new trousers before wearing them.

Princip was also tormented by being a student at the Merchants School. Among his friends the idea of being a merchant, a money-maker, was frowned upon as the basest possible profession, particularly because of their detestation of Čaršija, the business district of Sarajevo. At the end of the third year of the Merchants School, Princip decided to transfer to the classical high school. But first he had to pass additional exams, and then, more importantly, he had to convince his brother of the necessity for transferring. At first his brother refused to discuss the matter. He was himself a small entrepreneur, and Gavrilo's wish to leave the Merchants School hurt him personally. But at last he gave in to Gavrilo's insistence. He did not understand the boy's idealism, but reckoned that Gavrilo as a lawyer or professor might fare better than as a merchant. Jovo engaged a student of medicine, Marko Maglov, to help Gavrilo prepare for the examinations in Latin and Greek in order to enter the high school. In August 1910, Gavrilo went to Tuzla, a town in northern Bosnia, and successfully passed the exams and was enrolled in the fourth grade of high school the same autumn. The first morning Gavrilo attended his new school he carried Caesar under his arm.[83]

Princip's friends from these days, Božidar Tomić, Radovan Jovanović and Vid Gaković, remembered him as a boy who preferred the company of older pupils, because he was several years older than his classmates. His main hobby was billiards. The schoolboys of the lower high school played *Russish* with five balls in the middle of the table; the older boys enjoyed the more complicated *Karambol*. Jovanović wrote that Gavrilo was very temperamental in the game—often, quarreling with his friends over "whether the stroke was clean or not, he would suddenly end the argument by hitting his opponent with the stick."[84] He would apologize quickly. He neither drank nor smoked. At that time, Gavrilo did not yet take part in political debates; he was a "passionate reader," as another school friend of his recorded. He read everything he could lay his hands on—Alexandre Dumas, Walter Scott, and also the exploits of Sherlock Holmes and Nick Carter, which were published in a series of weekly pamphlets.[85] He had considerable trouble with his professor—"I was badly treated by the professors," he complained to Dr. Pappenheim.[86] In those days pupils were not allowed to frequent the cafés or to play billiards. Gavrilo detested churchgoing. During the first year of his schooling in Sarajevo he had come into conflict for that reason with his teacher of religion.[87] The same thing happened in Tuzla High School. During an Eastern Orthodox fast, which was obligatory for all Serb boys, he demonstratively ate ćevapčići, a meat dish, on the evening before taking Holy Communion.[88] Gavrilo missed many classes, about twenty in the first two months, and in order to avoid expulsion, which was automatic after twenty-five unauthorized absences, he asked for a transfer to the high school in Sarajevo, where he moved at the end of 1910. Vaso Čubrilović, himself a student at that time in Tuzla and one of the conspirators in the Sarajevo plot, described Gavrilo as a stuha, a slightly satiric designation, signifying a restless spirit, who could never settle down, always wishing to roam around.[89]

Gavrilo graduated from the fourth grade in June 1911. He was a boy of seventeen, and his way of life changed. Literature became the world of Princip and his fellows. At his trial, a witness who knew Princip from high school testified that "Gavrilo always claimed that no one knew literature better than he and that he was the best among us in that field."[90] Princip himself in his talks with Dr. Pappenheim emphasized time after time what books meant for him from his childhood until his last days in jail, when he suffered so much through having no chance to read. Dr. Pappenheim noted:

Always earnest, with books, pictures etc. . . . Solitary, always in libraries . . . Always a reader and always alone, not often engaging in debates . . . Read much in Sarajevo . . . Had a nice library, because he always was buying books. "Books for me signify life." Therefore now it is hard without books . . . Read many anarchistic, socialistic, nationalistic pamphlets, belles lettres and everything. Bought books himself; did not speak about these things . . . It is very hard in solitary confinement, without books, with absolutely nothing to read . . . Always accustomed to read, suffering most from not having anything to read . . . If he had something to read for only 2-3 days, he could then think more clearly and express himself better. . . .[91]

To be a poet was regarded as a special mark of distinction among the Sarajevo youth. Princip did not have much talent for poetry, although he wanted very much to be a poet. Twice, as is known, he tried to show his verses to his trusted friends. The first time was to Dragutin Mras: "Trembling like a child Princip brought Mras his poems about roses which were blossoming deep at the bottom of the sea for the beloved one."[92] Mras's comment was negative. The second time Princip tried to approach Ivo Andrić, telling him that he had written a poem. Andrić told him to bring it to him, but Princip did not dare to do so. When Andrić asked him why he had not brought it, Princip answered casually that he had destroyed it.[93]

The texts of Princip's poems have not been preserved, except for a few verses. While awaiting trial, he wrote a few verses with his spoon on the back of a metal prison plate and at the very end of his life, when one arm had been amputated, he nevertheless succeeded in scribbling his last verses on the wall. Only after Princip's death was a full lyrical text of his found. He had written in 1911 in the souvenir book of the tourist hut of Bjelašnica Mountain, near the village of Hadžići. He had visited the hut with a group of school friends in 1911, when he was in the fifth grade of Sarajevo High School. It reads as follows:

Gone are the days of annoyance and boredom behind the dirty scribbled desks—holidays are here. After three days of celebration at home, we decided to enliven these hot and boring days—and travel somewhere—let us go to the Bjelašnica Mountain and beyond; no sooner said than done. We left Hadžići at sunset when the western sun was blazing in purple splendor, when the numberless rays of the blood-red sun filled the whole sky and when the whole of nature was preparing to sleep through the beautiful, dreamy summer evening in the magic peace—that beloved, ideal night of the poet. Walking briskly, we reached the foot of the Bjelašnica Mountain, boasting of our speed and wiping large beads of sweat from our brows. After a short rest and a bite at the edge of the forest, we started to climb . . .

Without a word we progressed hesitantly through the forest, entranced by the magic, deep silence, listening to the whisperings of the sweet-smelling flowers and motionless trees. Following our noses, we struggled upward through the thick forest; we looked at each other despairingly when we were surrounded by hellish darkness, which seemed like the laughter of ugly monsters. A light, faint shudder went through our rather weary limbs, and we continued to march upward in silence, lumbering over fallen trunks and scattered branches. Heavens, how many times the thought went through my mind that I would be hurled into some bottomless precipice.

We could go no further. We ate our frugal supper. We built a fire—the best sight I ever saw. No poet has ever described it well enough. Oh, if you could have seen what beautiful and ever-changing scenes were made by the lively red fire and black . . . hellish darkness, the whispering of the tall, black fir trees, and this hideous Night, the protector of hell and its sons; it seemed to me like the whisperings of bedeviled giants and nymphs, as if we were hearing the song of the four sirens and the sad aeolian harp or divine Orpheus.

My companions fell asleep around the fire. I could not. I was sleepy, I dozed, but how could one sleep in this empire of brooding illusions. A little storm—the wild winds howled sadly through the silent giant trees. My friends woke up—with regret—my heartache, my sorrow, my life—my visions and my illusions. We started to sing a sad song, and my own heart whispered and trembled more strongly than my bedeviled monsters.

My companions burrowed into the leaves, and I sang, dreamed and prayed to my secret; oh, what sweet and painful moments in the beautiful time before the dawn, sweeter than sleep, more beautiful and ideal than any European poet has described it—this heavenly flash and blood-red-coral sun could only be described by a son of the glorious and imaginative east. Look at it and you will see it.

After a happy and pleasant halt at Mr. Setnik's, we continued our journey . . .

Bjelašnica Mountain, June 25, 1911.

GAVRILO PRINCIP,
Fifth grade,
The Sarajevo High School[94]

The schoolboy text, full of unfinished phrases and clichés, shows an important trait of Princip's character. He was an immensely sensitive boy, acutely aware of the things around him. He possessed the same trait that Tin Ujević recognized in Gaćinović's character—namely, that he carried to extremes a tendency to feel the sufferings of people around him as though they were his own.

Princip told Dr. Pappenheim the year 1911 had been critical in his life. He said that at that time he began to have ideals.[95] He actively joined the Young Bosnian secret groups. He fell in love. To Dr. Pappenheim he confessed that his love for the girl never vanished, but he never wrote her. He knew her in the fourth class and said that it was "ideal love, never kissed; in this connection will reveal no more of himself."[96]

In the spring of 1912, Princip decided to go to Belgrade. Because of his participation in public demonstrations against the Sarajevo authorities in February 1912, he was expelled from school; besides, he was ill and had received a bad mark in mathematics, the first one in his school career. This had caused him to lose the small stipend he had been getting from Prosvjeta, the student-aid group. Princip went to Belgrade on foot, informing no one about his departure. When he crossed the border, he kissed the soil of Serbia.[97]

At the beginning Princip lived under very difficult conditions in Belgrade; his brother refused to send him any money, because Gavrilo had left Sarajevo without his permission. He shared the life of the other Bosnian students, some of whom slept in dustbins or in empty dog kennels. When worse came to worst the Bosnian students would go to a monastery. With a letter of recommendation from a professor, the students were welcomed by the monks, who gave them good food and engaged them in debates most of the time.

Princip's roommate Bora Jevtić recorded that Princip spent most of his time reading books. "These were hard times—no money, no food, and we would often return from our walks at night through the Kalemegdan Park, and Princip would start to recite his favorite poet Milan Rakić. Sometimes we were obliged to sell even our books to procure money for bread, but Princip refused to part with his favorite books."[98]

Princip soon made peace with his brother, promising him that he would finish the fifth grade. Money came, and life became easier. Princip bought some new books and with his Bosnian friends visited again the cafés at Zeleni Venac, playing billiards with success.

In June 1912, Gavrilo went to the First Belgrade *gimnazija* to try to pass the fifth grade. A few days later he sent a postcard to a friend in Sarajevo with only three words: "I flunked, Gavro."[99]

At that time the atmosphere in Belgrade was becoming more and more exciting. The Balkan states were preparing for war against the Turkish Empire. Serbia ordered mobilization. The members of Young Bosnia were crossing the frontier in flocks, trying to enlist in the Serbian army. Vladimir Gaćinović was already a volunteer in the Montenegrin army, together with several of his friends. Gavrilo Princip and his friends in Belgrade tried to join the *komite,* the irregular Serbian units which had already been operating for some years against the Turkish troops. Their leader was Major Vojislav Tankosić, one of the members of the central committee of Ujedinjenje ili Smrt.

The peak of Princip's misery came in the first days of October in Belgrade. He tried first the Bosnian headquarters of the Tankosić unit, but was rejected there because of his small build. In despair he hurried to Prokuplje, a Serbian town, just north of the Turkish frontier, where Tankosić had concentrated all his units before crossing the frontier.

Gavrilo, with a friend from Belgrade, Simo Miljuš, wrote a postcard to Sarajevo to Dragutin Mras, who was a leading member of the Young Bosnians:

Look up on the map where Prokuplje is. We are now here, and where we shall go further we do not know. ("For freedom and fatherland.")

Regards from yours,
GAVRO

Miljuš added a postscript:

If we do not see each other, please accept this as our last greetings. Where we go I know, and if we survive we shall know where we have been. If you are pious, pray to God for us, but if you are not, ask the young ladies to pray for us.[100]

Dragutin Mras, as a volunteer in the Serbian army, was killed in the first battle in which he took part, in 1914, while Miljuš survived the First World War, becoming one of the top leaders of the Yugoslav Communist Party, and was purged by Stalin in the 1930's.

Major Tankosić was a brisk man. When he saw Princip he just waved his hand. "You are too small and too weak."[101] Princip left Prokuplje in complete despair.

He did not stay long in Belgrade, but decided to return to the village of Hadžići. In the meantime, the Serbian army won a victory over the Turks at Kumanovo; the Greeks and the Montenegrins advanced quickly also. Europe, especially Austria-Hungary, was surprised at the rapid advance of the Serbian troops.

Not only in Serbia, but throughout most of the South Slav lands in the Habsburg empire, the victories of the Serbian army were greeted with an explosion of enthusiasm. The pupils in Sarajevo went to their classes with ribbons on their caps with the names of the towns liberated by the Serbian army. Demonstrations broke out in many towns. Several high schools were closed. Even in faraway Slovenia, parents were giving the names of the main heroes in the Kosovo cycle of Serbian heroic folk poetry to their newly born.

Gavrilo Princip these days in the village Hadžići had to listen to the grumblings of his brother over his failure to pass the fifth grade in the *gimnazija*, while his friends in the Tankosić units, wearing their khaki uniforms with bandoleers over their chests and fur caps with the skull-and-crossbone insigne, were marching over the sacred Kosovo Polje, as the avengers of the defeat of 1389, when the Serbian medieval state was annihilated and the Turkish yoke was established over the Serbs, to last for more than five hundred years. Princip's failure to be enlisted in the *komite* because of his small build was one of the primary personal motives which pushed him to do something exceptionally brave in order to prove to others that he was their equal.

He continued to visit Belgrade for a few months each year, and in the summer of 1913 he passed the fifth and sixth grades of high school. But he did not forget the insult he had suffered at the hands of Major Tankosić. When he was already involved in the Sarajevo conspiracy and Tankosić asked to see him and two other assassins-to-be, Nedeljko Čabrinović and Trifko Grabež, Princip had his moment of revenge: he flatly refused to go and visit Tankosić, and at the Sarajevo trial he called him "a naïve man."[102] Princip's ego got its satisfaction after he had assassinated the Archduke Franz Ferdinand, when he stated in the first minutes of the interrogation, on June 28, 1914: "I had little to do with people at all. Wherever I went, people took me for a weakling— indeed, for a man who would be completely ruined by immoderate study of literature. And I pretended that I was a weak person, even though I was not."[103]

Nedeljko Čabrinović, the first conspirator to throw a bomb at the Archduke on June 28, 1914, was a young man with an even more complex character than Gavrilo Princip. He was born in Sarajevo on January 20, 1895. His father came from a village near Trebinje, in Hercegovina. After many difficulties, the elder Čabrinović opened a third-class café in Sarajevo. After a few years, he became prosperous even by Bosnian standards. Yet he had to pay a heavy price for it; in order to get permission to open the café, the elder Čabrinović had to perform services for the local police. He was, in fact, accused of being a regular informer.[104]

When the young Čabrinović grew up, this connection with the Austro-Hungarian police was one of the main causes of conflict between him and his father. The elder Čabrinović was a giant of a man, weighing more than 240 pounds. He had nine children, of whom Nedeljko was the oldest. He tried to educate them in a Spartan way; for the slightest mistake the children were exposed to beatings and curses. Young Nedeljko, who in 1907 was a pupil in the Merchants School in Trebinje and was staying with some relatives, received a letter from his eldest sister Vukosava, informing him how his father maltreated them all including their mother. Being very sensitive and dearly loving his two sisters Vukosava and Jovanka, Nedeljko wrote back saying that he had wept when he read Vukosava's lines. He denounced his father's behavior, using such strong expressions as "Let him be ashamed of what he did"; "let his bones be disturbed in his grave"; "my dear Mother, do not be angry and do not cry"; "if I were there I would sue him in the law court at once"; "I want to come there at once."[105]

Nedeljko left the school in Trebinje—it is not clear on whose advice —and came to Sarajevo Merchants School at the very end of the school year, 1907–8. Nedeljko was, judging from his letters, a good stylist and an intelligent boy for his age, but he failed to pass the final exam. He complained that the program in the Sarajevo school was different and that he had been ill. His father punished him brutally for this failure, and an open enmity erupted between them. Nedeljko was sent to learn a trade at a locksmith's, but an elderly journeyman for fun put a piece of red-hot iron on the boy's neck and Nedeljko fled home. His father apprenticed him to be a *dreher*, a lathe operator, but Nedeljko did not like that type of work either. The third trade the boy tried was typesetting. He worked for two years in the Serbian printing plant in Sarajevo, but the conflicts with his father intensified. Nedeljko was very sorry to have to leave school. He read a lot, and one night his father discovered him reading Chernishevsky's *What Is to Be Done?*; he struck the boy and took away the electric-light bulb.[106] At that time, Nedeljko, a boy of fourteen, was elected by his fellow apprentices to be the first president of the Printers' Apprentice Guild.

The notes of a speech which Čabrinović gave to a group of apprentices he drafted on a piece of paper, and this has been preserved in the Belgrade archives. He began his talk on the need for organizing the apprentices with the proverb: "It is easy to break one stick, but it is quite another thing to break a bunch of them." After this lead, he gave a peppery warning to those of his colleagues who were under the influence of the priests: "Due to the fact that among you there are some who have no idea what our organization means, and who know only of Church miracles, who are accustomed to listening only to the priests without questioning whether what they say is true or not, and due to the fact that you were brainwashed by these swindlers, it is necessary for you to learn about our organization, to know what it is, and why it is so urgent that we organize. . . ."[107]

After his talk, Čabrinović advised his friends about the literature that they should read. It included such pamphlets as *The Meaning of the First of May Celebration* and *The Program of the Social Democratic Party of Croatia and Slavonia*, and the Communist Manifesto.[108]

It happened at about that time that an older worker slapped Nedeljko during work, and the boy quit his job. For this his father kicked him out of the house, and the boy fled to Zagreb, where he tried to find work. He returned after a month, running into new troubles at home. Nedeljko was already a boy of fifteen, tall and strong for his age, and his father could not beat him as easily as before. After a quarrel between him and a servant girl, his father asked him to apologize to her. When Nedeljko refused, his father went to his friends in the local police and had Nedeljko arrested and kept in jail for three days. Soon afterward, Nedeljko completed his apprenticeship and became a journeyman.

After this incident, Nedeljko fled again from his home. He walked to Novi Sad, more than a hundred miles away from Sarajevo. He worked there for a time, and then in the monastery printing plant in nearby Karlovci. His revolt against his father became identified with his revolt against society. After Karlovci, for a time Nedeljko worked in Šid, in a printing plant owned by the Social Democratic party of Croatia. The boy came with high hopes of "seeing the red house, the banners," but in several letters written in the summer of 1911 he complained bitterly to his friend in Sarajevo, Andrija Ljubojević, a typesetter.[109] In a letter of June 1, Nedeljko wrote how he was unemployed in Novi Sad, how he had to sell all his belongings in order to pay back two workers the loans he had received for his food and lodgings, how he had to come on foot from Novi Sad to the Social Democratic printing plant in Šid. "What a disappointment," Nedeljko wrote. "This is not a Socialist printing press but a capitalist one. . . . I was struck to hear that the working hours in this Socialist printing plant are nine hours."[110] Nedeljko also complained that he missed his books; and he asked: "How are Kropotkin, Clara Zetkin, Masaryk and others?"[111]

Without a passport or any money, Nedeljko went from Šid to Belgrade, where he worked in a printing plant which was publishing anarchist literature. He met there the leader of the Serbian anarchosyndicalists, Krsto Cicvarić, who gave him books. Under the influence of the workers in this printing plant, Nedeljko became an anarchist. He returned at the beginning of 1912 to Sarajevo again, and having no money for the trip, a Bosnian friend advised him to go to Narodna Odbrana, the Serbian defense organization, and ask for help. Nedeljko went there and met Major Milan Vasić, the secretary of Narodna Odbrana. Seeing in the boy's pocket a book by Guy de Maupassant, Vasić advised him not to read such books, and gave him some pamphlets on Narodna Odbrana and a collection of Serbo-Croat folk poetry and a few dinars.[112] Nedeljko put all his books in a trunk and mailed them to Sarajevo, spending all the money on postage; he traveled back home on foot. The long journey without much food exhausted the boy, and he came home ill.

He was not received well by either of his parents. Finding the trunk with the anarchist books, his mother burned them all. Nedeljko found work in a local printing plant, but when a strike broke out, he again quarreled bitterly with his father, who ordered the boy not to take part in it. Nedeljko refused this, and his father kicked him out of the house again. Nedeljko found refuge in the home of Stevan Obilić, a printer with anarchist views. During the strike, in the summer of 1912, Nedeljko and Obilić went to Zenica, a town north of Sarajevo, meeting the incoming trains to Sarajevo to see if there were any printers. The two warned them that there was a strike going on and that they should not become strikebreakers. The police closely followed Nedeljko's activities, and he was accused of wishing to set fire to some printing shops which were working, particularly one owned by the Sarajevo Catholic Archbishop Stadler. Nedeljko was arrested, and he spent three days in jail. The police asked him particularly to reveal where Obilić was hiding. Nedeljko refused to give away the name of the leader of the strikers, and he was banished from Sarajevo for five years. In the meantime, Obilić succeeded in fleeing from Bosnia. He got on a ship in Dalmatia and sailed to the United States.

Nedeljko was exiled to Trebinje. An official lectured him on ethics and ordered policemen to escort the boy at once out of Sarajevo. This incident left a very bitter memory with Čabrinović. In the police investigation and at his trial in Sarajevo in October 1914, he said of his political and personal motives for the assassination of the Archduke: "A personal motive drove me to vengeance after I was banished from Sarajevo. I was suffering because a foreigner, who came to my country, banished me from my native town."[113] Remembering the incident with the official, Čabrinović said: "I was sorry that at that moment I had no weapon with me. I was prepared to shoot all six bullets into him."[114] After he was banished to Trebinje, Nedeljko wrote a postcard to Jovo Šmitran, a friend of Danilo Ilić's, and a socialist with an understanding of national problems, on July 9, 1912:

Perhaps you have already heard that I was arrested. I was in jail for three days because I refused to say where Obilić was, and I was banished for five years from Sarajevo. I beseech you, make a resolution of protest against this. Look at what kind of constitutional rights we have. Believe me that I would fare better in Siberia. While I was in jail I read the book *The Education of Will.*[115]

From Trebinje, Nedeljko fled to Belgrade, where he worked in different printing shops, but his father and the heads of the printers' union succeeded in getting the banishment lifted, and Nedeljko returned to Sarajevo. In December 1912, he was at last promoted to be a full member of the printers' union. Together with a few friends, he led a campaign against local Social Democratic leaders, criticizing them for the lack of democratic methods in their work. Čabrinović wrote an article in the local paper *Srpska Riječ*, but the Social Democratic *Glas Slobode* retorted with sharp counterattacks, accusing Nedeljko of being "a spy," and "an agent of the Serbian government." Insinuations were made also concerning the services his father had performed for the Sarajevo police. Nedeljko suffered from these attacks. This was perhaps the reason why he shouted proudly, when he was caught after he had thrown the bomb at the Archduke and the detectives asked him who he was: "I am a Serb hero!"[116]

Nedeljko again had difficulties at home, and his father ordered him not to write to his sister Vukosava, who was studying at the Teachers College in a town in Croatia, and who held similar views. Their father called them both "anarchists." Nedeljko kept writing to his younger sister, Jovanka. In one letter, dated merely July 17, he said: "You asked me if I am still a Socialist. Yes I am, but a little more intelligently, a little differently. You asked me if I am hungry. For the moment I am not, but I have been hungry many times. On our saint's day you ate steak and I had only dry bread."[117]

In 1912, Čabrinović met Princip in Sarajevo. They read together often, including William Morris's *News from Nowhere*. A copy of that book has been preserved with the autographs of both young men. They underlined many places in the book, particularly references to revolution and the need for the emancipation of women. At the end, Čabrinović added his own sad comment: "I have just finished reading this book at a time when I was both individually and socially in the darkest mood as compared with the optimism of this book."[118]

Having quarreled again with his father and the local Social Democrats, Nedeljko left Sarajevo in March 1913, hoping to go to work in Germany, but on his way there he stopped in Trieste, where he remained until October. From Trieste, Nedeljko went back to Belgrade, working there until the end of May 1914.

These few facts about the lives of some of the most prominent Young Bosnians are characteristic of the greater number of their colleagues and followers. The factors which led to the emergence of the Young Bosnians and which influenced its subsequent growth are complex. No doubt the deterioration of political and social conditions in Bosnia and Hercegovina in the 1900's was of primary importance for the action of the Young Bosnians.

The two provinces experienced two major social upheavals: the general strike in 1906, and the peasant uprising of 1910. With the industrialization of the country, the number of workers increased to fifty thousand, but they were denied their basic rights. A general strike broke out in the spring of 1906.[119] The workers asked for a nine-hour workday and complained that some factories did not pay them on time. On April 30, a strike broke out in the Sarajevo tobacco factory as well as in a brick factory. On May 3 the police fired on a workers' procession and killed and wounded several people. From Sarajevo the strike spread to seventeen other towns. Three workers were killed on May 14 in Zenica.[120] Vienna urged factory directors not to give any pay increases.[121] Army units were sent against the strikers, but at Vareš they did not succeed in breaking the workers' demonstrations. Free peasants and *kmets* in the Sarajevo district decided to join the workers and organize a strike in the villages to solve their own problems.[122] At Ljubuški over two thousand workers and *kmets* demonstrated asking for an increase in wages and obligatory liberation of *kmets*. Only after strong military measures were used did the strike end.

There were many other grievances in Bosnia and Hercegovina. Only about 26 per cent of all the civil servants in 1904 were natives of the country, and most of these were Roman Catholic Croats.[123]

The educational system was obsolete. Of all the school-age children only 17.48 per cent were able to attend classes.[124] For each thousand foreigners settled in Bosnia there was one school, while for the Bosnians there was one school for each six thousand people.[125] Compared to other Balkan states, there were many fewer high schools in Bosnia, and there were fewer primary schools than in Serbia.[126]

Vienna and Budapest had different opinions about how the two provinces should be governed. Count Stefan Burian de Rajec, who became Joint Minister of Finance after 1903, maintained that reforms in Bosnia should be made from above, not from below.[127] He initiated some concessions to the rising Serbian bourgeoisie and to the Moslem feudal lords. The Serbian Eastern Orthodox Church and Mohammedans were given more autonomy.

But reforms came too slowly, and when they were finally implemented, they did not produce the results which had been originally anticipated. This is clearly shown in the case of a constitution for Bosnia and Hercegovina, which was octroyed by the Emperor's letters patent of February 17, 1910. A parliament was envisaged, but it had no power to choose, supervise or control the executive, which was in the hands of an appointed governor and supervised by the Joint Minister of Finance in Vienna. The *Sabor* did not have its representatives in the Delegations. Only in a few matters of secondary importance could the *Sabor* have a right to express its opinion. The whole system of elections was undemocratic. Out of 92 members of the *Sabor*, twenty were appointed by the Emperor, who favored Roman Catholics over Eastern Orthodox Catholics.[128]

The Archduke Franz Ferdinand attacked Burian's policy in Bosnia and Hercegovina on the grounds that it favored the Magyars and was too liberal. At the same time, he believed that the Serb national movement was spread in Bosnia and Hercegovina under the protection of the Hungarian government. The Archduke said:

. . . we must put a stop to Burian's dangerous system and in his place put a man like Varešanin . . . Varešanin with full authority will achieve this in a glorious way. I would prefer to leave the annexation aside for a moment, to remove Burian, and replace him with Varešanin, who would end the Serbs' obstruction and pacify the country in two months.[129]

In 1909 the Archduke obtained General Marijan Varešanin's appointment as Bosnian governor, and the latter started to rule with an iron hand. Peasant rebellion broke out in northern Bosnia. *Kmets* stayed in servitude as in Turkish times: they could not obtain freedom unless the landlords agreed to it. The latter refused to do so because they received 12.4 per cent rent every year from the *kmets*.[130] In the summer of 1910 the discontent in the villages increased. That year more than 13,500 peasants and *kmets* were evicted by the authorities from the land they tilled, because they were accused of not paying the tribute to the feudal lords and taxes to the state, and some 56,000 judiciary investigations were opened.[131] The first open clash between the peasants and local authorities took place in Bosanska Krajina, in August 1910, when the *kmets* started the so-called peasants' strike. Refusing to pay taxes and tributes, the rebels burned down some feudal estates. The local gendarmerie was unable to deal with the rebellion, and General Varešanin in Sarajevo and Count Burian in Vienna were asked for emergency help. Burian ordered the military authorities to use any means at their disposal to put down the uprising.[132] General Varešanin sent troops from the 49th and 90th Regiments of Sarajevo to the north, as well as other military units from other parts of Bosnia. Around Doboj the army opened fire on *kmets*. The unrest, which spread to many other parts of Bosnia, was not finally put down until the autumn.

The Archduke had direct contacts with military commanders in Bosnia and Hercegovina who sent him regular reports about the political situation in the two provinces. General Moritz von Auffenberg, the commander of the 15th Corps in Sarajevo, used to prepare special memorandums for the Archduke. In August 1910, he suggested his plans for the colonization of Bosnia and Hercegovina "through the settlement of retired noncommissioned officers."[133]

In 1886 there were only 16,275 Austro-Hungarian subjects in the two provinces, but by 1910 there were 108,000.[134] This influx of foreigners provided one of the main sources of complaints for almost all political groups in Bosnia and Hercegovina in 1913. In Temesvár in southern Hungary [now Timişoara, Rumania] the Pester Komercialbank of Budapest opened a special bank for colonization in Bosnia and Hercegovina. Magyar peasants and small landholders received an offer to settle on the lands of the impoverished *kmets* and peasants which Pester Komercialbank bought in Bosnia and Hercegovina.[135]

The Archduke's *Militärkanzlei* participated in the program of Germanization of Bosnia and Hercegovina. On February 23, 1911, General Auffenberg suggested to the *Militärkanzlei* that the German schools be helped either by a captain of industry or by the state.[136] These matters were settled when General Oskar Potiorek became governor in 1911. Instead of only two German military schools, financed by the state in 1911, their number was increased to seven in April 1912. *Militärkanzlei* fully supported Potiorek's action.[137]

General Potiorek was also actively engaged in proselytizing. In a letter to *Militärkanzlei* on March 3, 1913, he advocated the policy of more direct help from the state to the Catholic Church and recommended the building of fifty more Catholic churches in Bosnia and Hercegovina.

"The Roman Catholic Church in Bosnia and Hercegovina," he wrote, "has to be helped extensively and quickly, as not merely religious but also political and dynastic interests are at stake."[138] He asked Bardolff to urge the Archduke to help. He suggested that Father Galen's Bonifaziusverein could help to fulfill this mission by finding money in Austria.[139] In another letter, Potiorek further suggested that "the Catholics of Bosnia and Hercegovina should be supported in building churches. The Bosnian Franciscans have achieved most in this respect. . . . The monasteries cannot do it all themselves; they are not so rich. About fifty churches and parsonages have to be built in Bosnia and Hercegovina. Most urgent is the provision of a new church for Sarajevo; also a cathedral for Mostar."[140]

This policy of Potiorek implemented many of the ideas which the Archduke Franz Ferdinand had expressed before on the necessity of proselytism. In his attitude toward the Eastern Orthodox Serbs, the Archduke was influenced primarily by dynastic and ecclesiastic reasons. Margutti once asked the Archduke about his view on the religious differences between Catholic Slovenes and Croats on one side and Eastern Orthodox Serbs on the other. The Archduke answered: "Of course, the Catholics must certainly have priority."[141] Kristoffy recorded also that the Archduke "wanted to prevent the spread of Orthodoxy by leading as many Serbs as possible back into the bosom of the Catholic Church."[142]

In his policy toward the non-Catholic nationalities in Bosnia and Hercegovina, the Archduke advised Brosch: "First of all, put all of them (Orthodox, Moslems and Catholics) into one pot, and then let the Catholics spread at the top."[143]

From a few remarks of the Archduke written on the documents dealing with political unrest in Bosnia and Hercegovina and other South Slav provinces one gets the impression that the Archduke always advocated strong measures and reprisals against the rebels and demonstrators. On February 2, 1913, the newspaper *Ostdeutsche Rundschau* published a pro-Serb pamphlet, which was distributed in Mostar. The Archduke received from his *Militärkanzlei* a short summary of this news item, and he added in longhand the following instructions to Colonel Bardolff, the chief of the *Militärkanzlei:* "Inquiries: Why is this pamphlet not immediately confiscated? It appears to me (if this is true) that the much-praised strictness in Bosnia is not so great after all. F.F."[144] The Archduke reacted on several more occasions in the same spirit.

On January 6, 1913, the liberal paper *Zeit* reported that the Serbian government had asked the Vienna cabinet for permission to establish consulates in Dubrovnik, Sarajevo, Mostar and Banja Luka. The next morning the Archduke instructed his *Militärkanzlei* to immediately get in touch with the Foreign Ministry with instructions that the consulates "must absolutely not be permitted because these are only patented seats for revolution and agitation."[145]

The headquarters of the 13th Corps from Zagreb informed the Ministry of War in Vienna on January 22, 1914, that the Sokol, organizations of Serbs in Croatia, were preparing to visit the Kosovo Polje on June 28, 1914, and to take part in a festival with the Sokols from Serbia and the Sokols "of the not yet liberated parts." This report was sent to the *Militärkanzlei*, and the Archduke wrote in his own hand on the margin: *"Sehr im Auge behalten"* ("They should be observed very carefully").[146]

In Bosnia and Hercegovina, General Potiorek followed the Archduke's advice strictly. Despite the Bosnian Constitution and the *Sabor*, he succeeded in strengthening the role of the governor. The function of the so-called *Civilian Adlatus* ceased to exist and was handed over to the governor. He became even more independent of the Joint Minister of Finance.

The Archduke finally influenced the Emperor to dismiss Burian as Joint Minister of Finance in 1912,[147] and in his place Leon von Bilinski, a Polish nobleman, was appointed. Bilinski quickly came into conflict with the Archduke and Governor Potiorek.

After the 1910 uprising of *kmets* in northern Bosnia, Emperor Franz Josef, at Bilinski's suggestion, decided to do something. On June 13, 1911, he issued an Imperial *Novelle*, proclaiming the principle of slow voluntary liberation of *kmets*. According to the calculations of Professor Karl Grünberg in Vienna, this system would have brought a definite liquidation of the feudal system in Bosnia and Hercegovina only in the year 2025.[148] Bilinski commented that the solution of the agrarian problem in Bosnia and Hercegovina was "moving at the pace of a tortoise."[149]

In a letter of May 28, 1913, General Potiorek opposed Bilinski's attitude and said that "the Serb agricultural population should also be maintained in the future in their lethargic state of mind."[150] Bilinski later recorded that Potiorek's "hatred toward the Serbs was both political and personal."[151]

Potiorek was particularly alarmed by the rapprochement between the Serbs and Croats and did his best to deepen the conflicts between them. In that respect he found strong support in the activities of Father Anton Puntigam, who was an expert in combating liberal and socialist influence among the youth. After the 1906 general strike Father Puntigam gave special sermons in the Sarajevo Cathedral in which he described socialists as atheists and enemies of the Emperor and the state, whose ranks no Catholic should join,[152] and he continued this kind of work up to 1914. Once a group of young anarchists was threatened by the followers of Father Puntigam. But the Father then invited two of the anarchists to his office, gave them coffee and discussed their ideology with them. One of these boys was Nedeljko Čabrinović.[153]

Puntigam was a constant visitor at Belvedere and Konopischt and tried to influence all the ruling circles in Vienna toward a tougher policy in Bosnia and Hercegovina. He wrote a letter on November 12, 1912, to Friedrich Funder, editor of *Reichspost*, asking that the leading paper of Catholic Austria should do everything possible to advise against unifying the Serbs and Croats.[154]

Bilinski and Potiorek differed on political tactics. Bilinski favored a rapprochement with Serb bourgeois groups in Bosnia, while Potiorek completely opposed such policies. Bilinski wanted to play the different national, religious and class groups against each other; Potiorek was for a firm hand against all Serb groups. Bilinski realized that between the Serbian bourgeoisie, particularly merchants and small bankers, and the vast peasant population there was a widening rift, which he wanted to use for his own political purposes. Although the Serb bourgeoisie was hampered in building up local industry, nevertheless they played an important role in Bosnian and Hercegovinian trade. Baernreither in his many journeys to Bosnia and Hercegovina had remarked that the Serbian bourgeoisie was much more dynamic than their Croat or Moslem counterparts.[155] The number of local banks with Serb capital was increased. In 1903 the first Serb bank was organized in Mostar and in 1914 there were twenty-six banks in all; their capital was raised from 180,000 florins to 5,000,000.[156]

With the advancement of capitalism in Bosnia and Hercegovina, social stratification among the Serbs deepened as well. A number of Serb merchants became landowners, while the position of the *kmets*, owing to the preservation of the feudal system in land ownership, deteriorated.

The Austro-Hungarian authorities succeeded in causing a definite split among the Serbian political groups within the *Sabor*. Vojislav Šola's group backed the government, particularly in economic and social questions.[157] Šola was against the mandatory liberation of the *kmets*. The banks behind which were Bosnian Serbs increased their dealings with the villages, pressing the peasants to pay a 12 per cent interest on their loans. According to the statistics of 1910, 6.5 per cent of all feudal lords in Bosnia and Hercegovina were Serbs. All this made the position of the *kmets* worse; "they gained the new burdens of capitalism, while they had not yet been able to save themselves from the yoke of feudalism." The *kmets* referred to their Christian brothers, the feudal lords and moneylenders, as *kmetoders*, people who skin the *kmets*.[158]

Such an attitude of the Serbian bourgeoisie provoked a strong reaction among the Young Bosnians. Many youths were personally involved in this painful struggle; in almost every family there was a revolt of the younger generation against the older. This was the case not only with Gavrilo Princip, who rebelled against the money-making passion of his brother Jovo, and with Nedeljko Čabrinović, but also with many other Young Bosnians. Even within some Serbian landlord families, the younger ones denounced the methods of their grandfathers and fathers and joined the Young Bosnians.

Gavrilo Princip expressed his hatred of the business section of Sarajevo, *čaršija*, by saying on the eve of June 28, 1914: "If I could force the whole of *čaršija* into a box of matches, I would set it alight."[159] The same feelings were expressed by Nedeljko Čabrinović, who confessed to the investigation judge on June 28: "I had been toying with the idea of entering the *Sabor* and from the galleries throwing a bomb among the legislators, because I was convinced that they were scoundrels and cowards, who do not work, and even if they try to work they produce nothing."[160]

Gaćinović denounced the older generation with these words: "Our fathers, our dictators, are real tyrants who want to drag us along with them and want to dictate to us how we should lead our own lives."[161] He attacked particularly what he described as their lack of patriotism during the annexation crisis, when all the leading Serbian political parties in Bosnia and Hercegovina accepted the unilateral act of Vienna. Only a few individuals demonstrated by resigning from the civil service,[162] and the only mass protest came from the youngest generation of Bosnians in the Sarajevo Eastern Orthodox Cathedral, where a special mass was held to celebrate the annexation. One of Bilinski's Chiefs of Section described the incident:

At the end of the mass, the Eastern Orthodox Metropolitan Letica in his gold-and-silver vestments, with both hands raised, asked all the worshipers to kneel down and pray for divine blessings for the Emperor Franz Josef and the Habsburg dynasty. All went down except a group of boys from the high school. They stood firmly upright among their kneeling elders.[163]

This was not only a demonstration of the Young Bosnians against Austro-Hungarian rule, but also an expression of the gulf that divided the different generations of Bosnian Serbs.

Talking to Dr. Pappenheim, Princip defined the line between the Serbian political groups and the Young Bosnians as separating those who were for revolution and those who were against it: "Our old generation was mostly conservative, but in the people as a whole there existed the wish for national liberation. The older generation was of a different opinion from the younger one as to how to bring it about. . . . The older generation wanted to secure liberty from Austria in a legal way; we do not believe in such liberty."[164]

These Young Bosnians believed that society could be transformed only by the influence of morally strong and socially developed persons, who by their own examples would create a new, better type of man. In this attitude there was the influence of Chernishevsky and other Russian Populists, and of Mazzini, but particularly of the founder of Serbian socialism, Svetozar Marković, whose socialist idealism Jovan Skerlić has summed up: "Particularly in small countries, ideas are worth only as much as the men who advocate them."[165]

Princip and his friends upheld the morality of the simple life and the virtues of mutual aid; in their private lives they tended to adopt revolutionary asceticism and puritanism. They did not drink; an expression of love toward a girl was regarded as a violation of her dignity; physiological life had little meaning. Gaćinović wrote to Trotsky: "In our organization there is a rule of obligatory abstinence from love-making and drinking, and you must believe me when I tell you that all of us remain true to this rule."[166] The hard core of the Young Bosnians kept to such standards. It was a personal reaction against the stark realities of Bosnia and Hercegovina, a wish to be different from their fathers, and a revival of the ethics of the idyllic days of the *zadruga*. Chastity was a strict rule among the Young Bosnians. Žerajić, although a man of twenty-five, never had sexual intercourse, as the Sarajevo police established after his death.[167] Princip confessed the same thing to Dr. Pappenheim.[168] They did not drink. Princip never tasted wine until the eve of June 28, 1914, when he purposely sat in cafés with a glass in front of him in order to put the police on the wrong track.

Dr. Vojislav Jovanović, who knew many of the Young Bosnians personally, described them as "living ascetics for whom physiological life had no meaning."[169] They firmly believed that the Habsburg authorities were deliberately fomenting the moral corruption of the population. They pointed, for instance, to the introduction of special military brothels, institutions unknown in the history of Bosnia and Hercegovina up to 1878. How deeply these measures of the Austro-Hungarian authorities offended the young people in Sarajevo has been recorded by Rebecca West in her book *Black Lamb and Grey Falcon*.[170]

Perhaps there was an element of exaggeration in the words of this intellectual, but Gavrilo Princip likewise had a firm opinion on this issue. As he said to a friend: "Syphilis and clericalism are an unhappy inheritance from the Middle Ages which the present civilization does not know how to cure."[171]

Gaćinović also criticized what he termed the exclusively materialistic outlook of the Bosnian students studying abroad, their "physical, intellectual and moral degeneration" evidenced by the empty hours they spent in cafés, saying that the younger generation was living generally "in a regime of desperation and alcoholism"; "these young men are losing the most striking features of the beauty of our race, absorbing in the gutters of Vienna, Berlin and Paris the ugliest side of Europe, which they later bring back among us."[172]

Svetozar Marković also influenced Gaćinović greatly on the question of the equality of men and women. This problem was particularly difficult in Bosnia and Hercegovina, where the patriarchalism of the *kmets* had been strengthened by the attitudes of the Turks. Gaćinović also followed the advice of Jovan Skerlić on the necessity of a struggle for women's rights. In his essay on Žerajić, Gaćinović criticized a few girl students from Bosnia because they had taken the same road as their fellow Serbian students in their "catastrophic way of life in cafés full of cynicism." In the spirit of Chernishevsky, he wished that the emancipated women of Bosnia should play the role of social reformers— "Let them remember the enlightened apostolic mission of Russian, French, Spanish and Italian women, who died on the gallows with the cry for liberty and greetings to their country and their people."[173] His idol was Sonya Perovskaya, one of the conspirators in the assassination of Tsar Alexander II, "who died like a character from fable and legend in the wet and heavy atmosphere of Russia."[174] Gaćinović firmly believed that women could be of vital importance in a revolutionary struggle. "When revolution broke down in Russia, it entered into a woman's heart, in order to burst into flames again and thus charge revolution with new energies and new force."[175]

On the other hand, it is a fact that among the conspirators of the June 26 plot there was no woman like the Russian Vera Zasulich or Sonya Perovskaya. This was due, primarily, to the fact that in Bosnia and Hercegovina there were few intellectuals, and among them only a very few women, coming mostly from the towns. In Russia many a revolutionary girl came from an aristocratic family. However, despite the small number of intellectual women in Bosnia, some of them were in the Young Bosnia secret societies. Jelena Borić from Sarajevo, a student at Vienna University, actively participated in the work of the Ljubljana *kruzhoks* as a link between Gaćinović and the Slovene revolutionaries and was once arrested in Ljubljana.[176] Several girls served as couriers, like Ljubica Stakić from Tuzla, or Jovanka Čubrilović, a teacher who came to Belgrade with secret messages from the Sarajevo *kruzhok*. She expressed a wish to take part in an assassination plot against Emperor Franz Josef.[177] Leposava Djurić, a printer, was also a courier for Gaćinović, who kept contact with several girl students (Rosa Šusić-Merćep, Leposava Gatalova, Persa Stojanović) and exchanged many letters, as Svetozar Marković used to do.

Gaćinović personally had close spiritual relations with several girls in the Russian revolutionary movement. One of them was called by clandestine names Marusya and Zhenya, and Gaćinović met her in Lausanne in 1911. Lebedev described her from a photo as "simple, but very pleasant in her simplicity, small head, rich hair around it, white neck, modest dress . . . typical example of a teacher revolutionary . . ."[178] After a meeting with her, Gaćinović returned flushed and worried, because she criticized him strongly for his nationalist outlook and similar prejudices.[179]

In 1916 when he was in the United States, Gaćinović dedicated to her a prose poem called "To the Comrade by the Volga," in which he symbolized his ideal woman revolutionary:

Now you are somewhere on the Volga, embroidering flaxen shirts with your companions from the village, teaching them hygiene, handwork and how to read and write. You are sowing without fatigue on the shores of the Mother River the seeds of freedom which will germinate and blossom from the little Kushiks, the children of your compassions of today.

You are like the sowers of souls and beauty, comrades whom one meets in life only for a moment, only to exchange a smile and press their hands, departing quickly, continuing preparations for some faraway happy harvests. These sowers are white, warm suns traveling the earth, from ocean to ocean, from town to town, flooding with the red-hot colors of dreams the ancient crust of earth.

Do sow, comrade from the Volga, do sow the red seeds of freedom.[180]

Gavrilo Princip, less sentimental than Gaćinović, and more reserved in the expression of his feelings, cherished a similar attitude toward women, believing that creative work is the primary goal of life. He was a friend of Nedeljko Čabrinović's sister, Vukosava, who was three years younger than himself. When she was twelve years old, Gavrilo found her reading a cheap novel called *The Secrets of the Istanbul Palace*. He took the book from her hands, bringing next time Oscar Wilde's stories and a novel by Uskoković, a Serbian writer.[181] They exchanged many letters afterward, and the girl once pawned her golden cross in order to send some money to her brother and Princip when they were in Belgrade in the winter of 1913–14. Vukosava remembered Gavrilo as a "reserved boy, sometimes witty, almost sarcastic, with deep eyes, handsome teeth and a very high forehead."[182] He tried to widen the girl's intellectual horizons, sending her books and reproductions of well-known paintings. He also wrote her poems and many letters. After June 28, 1914, Vukosava buried all his letters and poems in the village Duži in Hercegovina, and they disappeared during the war. After the war, Dobrosav Jevdjević published some of Princip's letters to Vukosava, but she said to this writer that he did not have the originals; Jevdjević reconstructed them on the basis of Vukosava's memory. She thinks that some of these letters expressed Princip's thoughts, particularly the one he sent on the eve of June 28. In Jevdjević's version the letter reads:

I feel a deep, sincere pain reading your letter, as if I were looking at the grief of a girl abandoned by everyone and forgotten. Do not suffer and do not let bloodshot eyes reveal your sorrow. Think and work. One needs a lot of strength in order to live, and action creates this. Physical labor also strengthens the character and firmness of will. Be individualistic, never altruistic. My life also is full of bitterness and gall, my wreath has more thorns than others. I go from nothingness to nothingness, from day to day, and in me there is less and less of myself. Do read, you must read; this is the best way to forget the tragic side of reality. How beautiful Wilde's *The Happy Prince* is. . . . Is the rose I gave you on our departure still alive? I know that it withered a long time ago, but perhaps the memory is enough to make it blush. I would like so much to be with you again in the first warm days of autumn somewhere under the leafy branches, and to hear you reciting to me:

In the black knot of the pine tree
The cricket chirps away

With the stifling trochee and strident black iambus.
It is noon. The sun's dithyramb is dispersed like the becalmed sea.[183]

Both Mitrinović and Gaćinović were anxious to work out an ethical system based on the moral conduct of the Young Bosnians. While Mitrinović was more interested in the relations between ethics and aesthetics, Gaćinović was influenced by Babeuf, Fourier and Saint-Simon. Mazzini's idea of a religion of humanity also had a strong impact on Gaćinović. One of the conspirators at the Sarajevo trial, Trifko Grabež, son of an Eastern Orthodox village priest, described this transition from the Christian faith to a faith in the nation. The following dialogue took place between young Grabež and the presiding judge:

"Are you a deist or an atheist?"
"I am a believer!"
"How could you reconcile your religion with the murder of a man made by God? From the religious point of view this is a sin."
"My religion does not go so far."
"Your father is a priest. What kind of education did he give you? Did he try to evoke religious feelings in you?"
"He gave me an education in the spirit of the Gospel."
"Did you follow the advice of your father?"
"As a child I listened to him, but when one comes into contact with other boys, then other influences prevail."
"Have these young men no faith?" finally asked the President.
"Not the faith you think; they have a national religion of a higher type," answered Grabež.[184]

On the other hand, Princip and Čabrinović were more doctrinaire atheists. Princip said to Dr. Pappenheim that "even as a child he was not particularly religious."[185] In the first year of the Merchants School in Sarajevo he protested against obligatory church attendance.[186] During his trial in 1914, when the presiding judge asked him whether Čabrinović's motives in the conspiracy were of a religious character (whether he was moved by hatred, as an Eastern Orthodox, against the Roman Catholic Archduke Franz Ferdinand), Princip answered that this was a comical question and that he was an atheist.[187] Čabrinović also confirmed that he was an atheist. The youngest conspirators were even more emphatic in the expression of their atheism. Vaso Čubrilović shocked his clerical-minded judges to such an extent that they added another three years to his ten-year sentence.

Princip and other conspirators, in addition to being influenced by Masaryk's rationalism and anticlericalism, reacted to the religious issue as it affected Bosnia and Hercegovina. Their efforts to unify the Bosnian youth were continually being frustrated by tension and strife among the three religious groups in Bosnia and Hercegovina, the Eastern Orthodox, the Moslems and the Roman Catholics.

Among the ethical systems which he studied, Gaćinović adopted many tenets from the teachings of Marie Jean Guyau, whom Kropotkin called "the founder of anarchist ethics." In his correspondence, Gaćinović called Guyau "our dear teacher"[188] and emphasized the highlights of Guyau's philosophy, such as that the condition of the maintenance of life is its expansion and that to feel within oneself that he is capable of acting is at the same time to become conscious of what it is one's duty to do.

It is true that at the very end of his life, when he moved to the position of Social Democracy, Gaćinović had second thoughts about Guyau's ethics. Taking his final examination in philosophy at Freiburg University, Gaćinović wrote an essay on Guyau in which he expressed his criticism.[189]

Much more than Guyau, Gaćinović paid attention to the problem of self-sacrifice. Like Mazzini, Gaćinović made a cult out of moral theology, preaching that life is a mission and that self-sacrifice is the greatest virtue. In his three essays on Žerajić, Gaćinović glorified self-sacrifice as the best means of arousing a new religious impulse among the Young Bosnians. He said: "These young people, not yet awakened, will be our apostles, the creators and cross-bearers of new religions and new hearts. They will awaken our dead gods, revive our fairies who had withered away because of sadness and love, they will bring a new empire of liberty and man, and save the Serbian soul from vice and decay."[190]

The most positive contribution of the Young Bosnians to the South Slav struggle for national liberation was that they tried to rise above the religious and national strife which raged among the inhabitants of Bosnia and Hercegovina, ethnically the purest South Slav province but divided into various religious and national groups by its historical development. Their task was even more difficult because the Habsburgs with their principle of divide and rule did their best to foment the existing differences. Indirectly, both pan-Serb and pan-Croat nationalists, with their claims to Bosnia and Hercegovina as "pure Serbian provinces" or "pure Croat provinces," abetted the policy of the Austro-Hungarian authorities. In Belgrade the Radical party and Colonel Apis wanted the incorporation of Bosnia and Hercegovina into Serbia. In Croatia the Mladohrvati asked for a kind of independent Croatia which would include Bosnia. The party of Dr. Frank and the clericals desired the formation of a third state unit within the Habsburg monarchy, comprising Croatia and Bosnia and Hercegovina. The Young Bosnians in the short period of their political activity, came out strongly in favor of the collaboration of Serbs, Croats and Moslems, and a federal solution for the future South Slav state, after the revolutionary destruction of Austria-Hungary.

Fighting for the principle of tolerance among Serbs, Croats and Moslems, the Young Bosnians had in their ranks young men of all three groups, although the Serbs were predominant, being the most numerous in the two provinces. The activities of Young Bosnia were influenced by political events in Serbia as well as in Croatia. The rapid rise of Serbia after 1903, the Serbian democratic way of life, the work of Slovenski Jug, a society which preached the unification of South Slavs through revolution, and particularly the successful Balkan wars, augmented the prestige of Serbia among the Young Bosnians; yet one should not underestimate the effects of the political struggle in Croatia on the youth of Bosnia and Hercegovina. The Croat-Serb Coalition of 1905 with its principle of cooperation between Croats and Serbs had a positive effect in Bosnia and Hercegovina. Although the Coalition did not in later years fulfill its role, some of its leaders like Fran Supilo continued to impress the Young Bosnians.[191]

It is significant that of all the Belgrade public figures, those who had the greatest influence over the Young Bosnians were those who preached the ideas of cooperation between Serbs and Croats, in the first place Jovan Skerlić and Jovan Cvijić. Although Skerlić was an enemy of modernism, pseudoaristocratism and pessimism in literature, preaching rationalism to writers and urging them to fulfill their patriotic tasks, he succeeded in exercising a remarkable moral power over Gaćinović and his followers. Skerlić was a convinced Yugoslav, and he advocated the elimination of all differences in the literary language and script of the Serbs and the Croats. His idea was that the Serbs should accept the Latin script and the Croats the eastern speech development of the *štokavski* dialect. In pure politics, Skerlić was an opponent of pan-Slavism, which he described "as a form of religious, political and national subjugation of the non-Russian and non-Eastern Orthodox peoples, and of the most enlightened elements of Russia."[192] He advocated neo-Slavism with autonomy and federation for all Slav peoples on an equal footing. Skerlić contributed to *Zora* and other reviews of the Young Bosnians. The Habsburg authorities banned Skerlić's writings in Bosnia and Hercegovina including his history of Serbian literature. When Skerlić died, Princip, in the name of the Young Bosnians, carried a wreath at his funeral in Belgrade on May 16, 1914, just a few days before he left for Sarajevo to kill the Archduke Franz Ferdinand.[193]

Jovan Cvijić, professor of geography and social anthropology in Belgrade held views similar to those of Skerlić. He believed in the cultural unity of the Serbs and Croats and held that, due to the constant movement of population in the Dinaric region, the basic differences between the Serbs and the Croats were much less significant than had been previously thought.

On the Croat side there was the influence of the followers of Bishop Strossmayer, who had preached the need for a unification of the South

Slavs. In Croatia in the first decade of our century, Fran Supilo propagated the same idea with even stronger vehemence. A majority of the South Slav students at Vienna and Prague universities were for the political unity of their peoples.

But the actual situation in Bosnia and Hercegovina, where there was marked fratricidal strife, did more than anything else to influence the Young Bosnians to adopt a Yugoslav orientation. Looking at the life around them, they came to the simple conclusion that unity of the Serbs, Croats and Moslems was the only way out. Ivo Andrić revealed something of this feeling in his "Story from 1920," which tells how obsessed the Young Bosnians were with the religious and national hatred which divided their compatriots:

Anyone who spends one night in Sarajevo sleepless on his bed, can hear the strange voices of the Sarajevo night. Heavy but steady strikes the clock on the Catholic Cathedral: it is 2 A.M. More than one minute will pass (exactly seventy-five seconds, I counted) and only then will the Serbian Eastern Orthodox Church announce itself. It strikes its 2 A.M. A while after, with hoarse faraway voice the Sahat Tower near Beg's Mosque, declares itself. It strikes eleven times, the eleven ghostly Turkish hours, according to some strange alien part of the world. The Jews have no clock of their own which strikes the hours, but only the good God would know what is their time, according to Sephardic and Ashkenazic calculations. And thus even during the night, when everybody is asleep, in this counting of the hours in the dead part of the night, the difference which divides these sleeping beings has been emphasized, beings who will, when they rise, rejoice and mourn, entertain and fast, according to their four different hostile calendars, and who will send all their wishes and prayers up to one heaven in four different church languages. And this difference, sometimes openly and visibly, sometimes invisibly and basely, appoaches hatred, often identifying with it.[194]

The Young Bosnians coming from a chauvinistic milieu had to fight hard for their new program of tolerance and brotherhood. Many of them carried within themselves what they had learned at home as children, but it needed a period of purification and inner struggle before they reached new positions. None of them escaped this process. Gaćinović in his first years of revolutionary activity said that "we should not pour Croat water in our pure Serbian wine." In 1912 he called Bosnia "a Serb's land"[195] and was behind the organization of Srpska Omladina, a weekly in Sarajevo published between September 1912 and June 1913 which preached the idea of Serbian nationalism. One of the chief contributors to this paper was Borivoje Jevtić, a writer from Sarajevo. But Srpska Omladina, under the influence of the feelings among Young Bosnians, left the positions of Serbian nationalism and joined the Yugoslav platform. At the same time Gaćinović underwent the same evolution. He became an ardent supporter of collab-oration with the Croats. In 1915, when he wrote an article for Trotsky about the work of youth organizations among South Slavs, he called *Srpska Omladina* just *Omladina*, cutting the adjective "Serbian," prov-ing that he had become an advocate of the Yugoslav idea.[196] The Croat poet Tin Ujević also regarded Gaćinović as a friend of federalism among the South Slavs.[197]

Princip went through a similar process. When he came from the Grahovo Valley to Sarajevo in 1907 with his father, he fled from a Moslem inn because he was afraid he might be killed. Until 1910 he was inclined to pan-Serb views in many respects; but a personal experience made him think about the other aspect of nationalist exclusiveness. He had just joined the high school and had trouble with several subjects, particularly Latin and Greek. The situation in the new school was tense; the Serb, Croat and Moslem boys were as bitterly divided as their elders. One day he was ill and did not attend classes. The next day a teacher asked him to repeat the lesson and Princip answered that he had been ill the previous day. The teacher did not accept this excuse and asked Princip if any of his school friends could confirm his statement. Princip's compatriots, the Serbian boys, giggled at his unpleasant posi-tion, but at that moment a Croat boy by the name of Kranjčević, got up and confirmed Princip's words. During the recess, Princip came to Kranjčević, who recorded this encounter as follows: "He thanked me for my friendly help, which surprised him, because I was a Croat and did not know him, while the Serbian boys were enjoying his misfor-tune and refused to help him."[198] After this day Princip and Kranjčević became good friends, often discussing politics and the relations be-tween Serbs and Croats in June 1914.

Up to that time the Serb and Croat schoolboys, even those of liberal tendencies, had their separate secret societies. Events in Croatia, how-ever, influenced the situation in Sarajevo. The Budapest authorities were applying unconstitutional methods of rule in Croatia. The Croat and Serbian students in Vienna and Prague came to the conclusion that they should form joint Serbo-Croat secret societies, in order to respond effectively to the new situation. This act influenced the radical Croat and Serb schoolboys in Sarajevo to organize Srpsko-Hrvatsku Na-prednu Organizaciju, a joint secret society in Sarajevo. This was achieved at the end of 1911. Ivo Andrić became their first president. This secret society had its secret badge, composed of both Serb and Croat flags. The new secret society, about whose work other school-boys soon heard, was attacked furiously by both pan-Serbs and pan-Croats. Its members were called "chameleons." "Both Serbs and Croats with unified force attacked them as traitors to their nations."[199] Gavrilo Princip was one of the first to join Andrić's secret society. In a letter to his student tutor Marko Maglov, written on April 7, 1912, Princip described the difficult atmosphere in which they had to work. Maglov had asked Princip about the situation among the schoolboys in Sarajevo, and Princip answered him in great detail. He described how the pan-Serb-oriented boys attacked them "with the worst expressions, objecting that we were not Serbs. This caused a deep breach and hatred between us."[200] Princip was not satisfied with the work of the new society and thought that it should have done much more.

Princip in this letter also mentioned that the new secret society accepted "the revolutionary program of Mitrinović," Gaćinović's friend from the Mostar Matica society.[201] Dimitrije Mitrinović worked out "The First Draft of a General Program for the Youth Club People's Unification," in Zagreb.[202] The main points of the program were:

1. To oppose everything national and antinational in the material and spiritual life of our peoples by means of

a. Radical anticlericalism

b. Radical elimination of destructive alien influence and promotion of Slavization of our culture against Germanization, Magyarization and Italianization

c. Fighting against attitudes of servility, sneaking and contemptibility and raising of national honor and pride

d. Expropriation of estates, liquidation of all prerogatives of aristocracy and all social privileges and the democratization of political consciousness and the political awakening of people.

2. A national defense against alien spiritual and material forces; national offensive to reawaken the subjugated and half-lost parts of our people by spiritual and material means.[203]

In many ways the Young Bosnians were a bridge linking the revolutionary youth groups of the different South Slav provinces, preaching the idea of Yugoslav federalism. In Belgrade they influenced a group around the paper *Preporod*, getting them to accept the idea of equality of all South Slavs. The *Preporod* group was composed primarily of enlightened youths who believed in republicanism and refused to join any political party. Their leading members were Vladimir and Stanoje Simić and Ljuba Radovanović. In the spring of 1912, Mitrinović came to Belgrade and read his program at a meeting attended by the members of the *Preporod* group. "All of us were profoundly taken by Mitrinović's intellectual brilliance, and we wholeheartedly accepted his ideas," Vladimir Simić stated.[204]

Mitrinović's program was also accepted as a basis for the work of revolutionary groups in Dalmatia. This South Slav province of the Habsburg empire was in many ways in a position similar to that of Bosnia and Hercegovina, one of economic backwardness. The obsolete *kolonat* agrarian system, dating from Roman times, laid a heavy burden on the peasants. Although there was more political freedom in Dalmatia than in Bosnia and Hercegovina, the Habsburg authorities tried to play one part of the Dalmatian population against the other. The small Italian minority in Dalmatia had much greater rights than the Slavs. Besides the Croats, who represented the majority of the Slavs, there were Serbs. Vienna sought to augment the differences between them. Dalmatia was the cradle of the medieval Croat state, but it was not united with Croatia, which belonged to the Hungarian part of the Habsburg empire. Many problems arose out of this state of affairs. For instance, if a Dalmatian youth went to study at Zagreb University, his diploma was not recognized in Dalmatia and other parts of the Habsburg empire belonging to Austria without additional examinations. For this reason, many Dalmatians, instead of going to Zagreb to study in their mother tongue, had to go to the universities in Vienna or Graz or Prague. The national divisions were intensified by religious strife between the Roman Catholics and the Eastern Orthodox.

It is no wonder that many young Dalmatians, like the Young Bosnians, adhered to the idea of Yugoslav federalism as the only solution to this painful dilemma. Yet this solution was a difficult one upon which to reach agreement. For several years Masaryk's ideas dominated in Dalmatia as well as in other South Slav lands. The paper *Hrvatski Djak* preached rationalism and the necessity for a national cultural revival as the best means of national liberations. In 1912, when Mitrinović's program was accepted by some groups in Dalmatia, a breach developed. While the followers of Masaryk wanted to continue to work through legal forms, the so-called "Nationalists" advocated illegal and revolutionary action. At the same time, this group linked itself to the anarchists in Italy.[205]

The leaders of this new force in Dalmatia were the students Tin Ujević, Oskar Tartalja, and Vladimir Čerina. Of the three of them, the nearest to the Young Bosnians was Čerina. He was not only a revolutionary, but a poet and literary critic of distinction. He used his publications *Val, Naš Val* and *Vihor* to express his revolutionary views. Although his papers were successively banned, in 1913 and 1914, Čerina became one of the best-known revolutionary leaders among the South Slav youth. The youngest generation of Young Bosnians esteemed him very highly and were better versed in his writings than in Gaćinović's works.

The Young Bosnians also cooperated with the Slovene revolutionary youth, gathered around the secret society Preporod (Rebirth). This was not accidental. Slovenia, farthest northwest of the Slav provinces, was endangered by the menace of Germanization.

Gaćinović was the first to write about these links between the Young Bosnians and the members of Preporod in his article on the Sarajevo assassination at the end of 1914. It must be borne in mind that the war was going on and that Gaćinović had to be very careful not to say too much, in order not to compromise his friends in Ljubljana. Gaćinović said that the Slovene Preporod was, of all the South Slav secret societies, "the most active and most methodical in their work."[206] He met the Slovene youth leaders in Vienna in 1911 and they declared themselves

in favor of a more active struggle and wished to establish links with Serbian and Croat youth. After two or three conversations in the Café Josephinum, we found a positive basis for our common action . . . That was the beginning of the Serbian-Slovene alliance for liberation. In the following years at our meetings we drafted our program and tactics. From this ideological laboratory came *Preporod* and *Zora*. The Slovenes are excellent organizers; the prolonged sufferings and struggle of their unhappy people have steeled their character. With their practical, sober views they were the perfect complement to us idealists and dreamers.[207]

Like Young Bosnians, Preporod was not ideologically completely defined, but expressed the restlessness of the youngest generation of Slovene intelligentsia in the hectic years before 1914. It was rationalistic and anticlerical, and was recruited mainly from the middle classes. It sprang, like Young Bosnia, from the *gimnazija* schoolboys, and when they grew up it took roots also among the Slovene students at Vienna and Prague universities.

In the past the Slovenes had contributed to the idea of South Slav unity as much as Croats and Serbs, although direct cultural relations between Ljubljana, Zagreb and Belgrade were not strong at the beginning of the twentieth century. The Slovenes followed much more closely the pulse of Prague and Moscow and St. Petersburg. At the same time, the Slovene clericals were propagating the idea of trialism, while the Social Democratic party in Ljubljana in 1909 came out with the idea of integral South Slav unity, that the South Slavs are culturally one people, but it remained, like the clericals, within legitimism. Under the influence of the Austrian Social Democratic party, the Slovene Socialists did not put forward a request for the unification of the South Slavs as a separate state outside the Habsburg monarchy.

Preporod was the first political group in Slovenia which *urbi et orbi* called for the revolutionary destruction of the Habsburg empire. It was organized under the initiative of France Fabjančič, the son of a village teacher, who preached, like the Young Bosnians, the need for the agnostic life. Fabjančič was a student of law in Vienna and was in contact with Gaćinović. "Between them there existed a strong feeling of friendship," Fabjančič's brother Vladislav, who was also a member of Preporod, has recorded.[208] France Fabjančič was by conviction a socialist, well versed in both socialist and anarchist literature, but he was against "the tendencies of German hegemonism among the Austrian

Socialists," and that was the reason why he had left the Socialist Youth Club. On that occasion he made a statement that the most important issues in Slovenia were the national problem and the danger of Germanization. Only when these questions are solved can one approach social problems.[209]

At the end of 1912 Preporod started to publish its journal, also called *Preporod*. The first issue appeared on November 1, 1912, and the twelfth and last on June 25, 1913, when it was banned by the Land Government in Ljubljana. The censors mutilated all twelve numbers of *Preporod;* yet the idea of the revolutionary liberation of the Slovenes, as well as the denunciation of the rapid Germanization of Slovene peasants, particularly in the northern parts of the country, was stated several times. *Preporod* published the text of Article 35 of the French Declaration on the Rights of Man and Citizen, which promulgated the right to revolution.

Within Preporod there were two trends of opinion on the question whether the South Slavs were a people, not only ethnically but also culturally. One group, known as the Integral Yugoslavs, maintained the existence of cultural as well as political unity among the South Slavs. For them the South Slavs were one people. The other group stood for political unity, but was of the opinion that the Slovenes had their own cultural traits, their own language, similar to Serbo-Croat but nevertheless a specific Slav language. They advocated the further development of the Slovene cultural personality. This position had been defended by the great Slovene poet Prešeren in the middle of the nineteenth century, and the second group was accordingly called Prešernovci. This dichotomy was expressed in the secret constitution of Preporod. Article 16 stated: "The organization is built on the basis of Yugoslav nationality, and in the spirit of full democraticism and spiritual freedom." The Prešernovci found a concession to their views in Article 18: "We want to approach other Slav, particularly South Slav, movements, and for that purpose we must study the Serbo-Croat language, South Slav culture, the national and political happenings, and the popularization of Serbo-Croat and Bulgarian literature among the Slovenes."[210]

The cultural unification of the South Slav people was advocated particularly by France Fabjančič. His idea of the cultural unity of the South Slavs was not shared by other leading members, particularly August Jenko, a poet, much influenced by Prešeren, and the brothers Kozak, Juš and Ferdo, both young men of marked literary talent.[211]

When Gaćinović left Vienna for Switzerland, contacts between Young Bosnia and Preporod were maintained through the Central South Slav Society in Vienna, and personally through two Slovene students, Juš Kozak and Anton Malik, while Ljubo Mijatović, from Mostar, and Jovan Zubović represented the Young Bosnians. Zubović recorded that some Slovene students wanted a unity of South Slavs not only in language but also in religion.[212] Juš Kozak did not share this view; he asked only for political unity. Zubović also said that besides Stepnyak, Kropotkin was read.[213] Gaćinović sent Juš Kozak four pamphlets of Bakunin. In the early summer of 1913 a secret conference took place in Ljubljana between the representatives of the two groups. The Young Bosnians were shadowed by the police, and several of them were arrested at Ljubljana railway station when they arrived from Vienna. Only Ljubo Mijatović and two girl students, Leposava Gatalova and Jelena Borić, evaded the detectives. Other members of Young Bosnia were released the same day and later took part in the second part of the conference, which lasted eight days. The meetings took place in various cafés outside Ljubljana, particularly in the café "Lev." Preporod was represented by France and Vladislav Fabjančič and Jenko and Juš Kozak. In the end a joint resolution was passed, with four points: (a) previous work was approved; (b) new plans for political actions were drawn up; (c) political rather than cultural union of the South Slavs was to be the primary task of both organizations (a victory for the Prešernovci, who advocated the preservation of the Slovene cultural identity); (d) a decision was reached that contacts should be made with political leaders and movements expressing similar ideas to those of Preporod and Young Bosnia.[214]

According to some reports it was decided that *Preporod* should become the joint journal of both the Young Bosnians and the Slovenes. But soon after this meeting *Preporod* was banned, France and Vladislav Fabjančič and Jenko went to Prague and organized a new journal, *Glas Juga*, which propagated ideas similar to *Preporod*'s. Its first issue was published in January 1914.

Following the decisions of the Ljubljana conference, Preporod contacted Fran Supilo, one of the most dynamic Croat leaders. Juš Kozak met Supilo in the office of his paper in Rijeka. The talk lasted an hour. Kozak reported that Supilo agreed that the revolutionary destruction of Austria was the only way out and that the new South Slav state should be built on democratic and federal principles.[215]

France Fabjančič met Ivan Cankar, the great Slovene poet and socialist, who was against the position of the Slovene Social Democratic party on the national question. Although Cankar was in favor only of the political unity of the South Slavs, he promised to support Preporod because of its revolutionary activity against Austria-Hungary.[216]

In 1913 and 1914 Preporod extended the scale of its activity. It numbered 100 members in Ljubljana, 40 in Novo Mesto, 50 in Kranj, and 20 in Gorica.[217] In the summer of 1913 Preporod decided to send Klemenčič to Russia to make contact with the Russian Social Revolutionaries. He went there and returned after a few months; his mission had had little success.[218]

At the same time, in order to attract Roman Catholic students, Preporod deleted from its program the anticlerical clause. On March 18, 1914, Preporod organized a protest strike in all Slovene *gimnazije;* it lasted three days. Many Roman Catholic schoolboys took part along with the rest. But the police were hard on the trail of Preporod leaders. In 1913 and 1914 a Slovene schoolboy from Rijeka, Ivan Endlicher, became very active in developing contacts with the Young Bosnians. He initiated a cover organization under the guise of a student holiday club, which arranged group tours of Slovene youth to Dalmatia and Bosnia and Hercegovina. Endlicher was several times in Bosnia and Hercegovina and maintained close contact with some of the leading members of the Young Bosnians, and his name was mentioned at the Sarajevo trial of Princip and his fellows.[219]

On several occasions, the paper *Preporod* publicly emphasized the strong links between Slovenia and Bosnia and Hercegovina. In its issue of January 1, 1913, it carried a prose poem from Bosnia entitled "Among Us Is the Powerful God, Perun," the head God of the Slavs. "We hear that the struggle has been waged in your part as well, that the voice of the God Perun is echoing. Do not be afraid, our friends. Do not waver, because we, from the Bosnian mountains, are with you, with our soul, hearts, and the devastating thunder of Perun's gift to us. Forward bravely for our joint deed, in the great struggle for Yugoslavia."

In its issue of March 1, 1913, *Preporod* said that

Austria as a state of free people is a Utopia because it is against the interests of its people. There exist two alternatives. Either Austria with a German-Magyar rule and the Slavs' slavery or real and full national liberty. . . . It is quite natural that a state which exists only because the people are not yet conscious, a state kept by militarism, centralism and terror, could exist only as long as the subjugated majority does not awake and become aware of itself. Austria is a state which is neither a geographical nor an ethnographic entity.

There is still no unanimity among historians as to the relative importance Young Bosnians gave to national and social problems of the two provinces. Did they wish to solve the national issue, and only then, in a nationally free Bosnia and Hercegovina, start tackling the social problems?

Even among themselves they did not have a clear conception of this choice, although most of them agreed that the agrarian problem, the liquidation of the feudal relations in the villages and the mandatory liberation of *kmets,* should be solved at once. Yet as they matured, on the very eve of June 28, 1914, Danilo Ilić entered into public polemics with Social Democrats in both Sarajevo and Belgrade over the issue of nationalism. The argument continued after the Sarajevo assassination among the members of the Young Bosnians who survived the ordeal, as well as between Gaćinović and Trotsky.

In an economically underdeveloped country with a large peasant population and with only about 5 per cent workers (of whom many were peasants—i.e., seasonal laborers), the Social Democratic party could not establish any firm roots. The Social Democrats themselves were responsible for their weakness in Bosnia and Hercegovina, because they completely neglected the national problem. The core of the membership of the Bosnian Social Democratic party consisted of skilled workers from other parts of the Habsburg empire, mostly Germans, Magyars and Poles. They had insufficient understanding of local problems in Bosnia and Hercegovina.

The Social Democratic party in Sarajevo was content to follow the political direction of their leadership in Vienna, where the Social Democrats, like the British Labourites, had no understanding of the struggle for the emancipation of colonial peoples. Dr. Karl Renner and Otto Bauer defended the preservation of a reformed Austria-Hungary. They did not recognize the principle of nationality as a starting point for the formation of separate states out of the body of the Habsburg empire.[220]

It is interesting that Svetozar Marković already in the 1870's had criticized the Austrian socialists because of their attitude toward the non-German nationalities in the empire.[221] The Serbian Social Democratic party in the first decade of the twentieth century made almost the same accusations against Austrian Social Democracy as Svetozar Marković did in the 1870's.[222]

The conflict between the Austrian and Serbian Social Democratic parties broke out also at the Congress of the Socialist International in Copenhagen on August 17, 1910. The Serbian leader Dimitrije Tucović openly criticized his Austrian comrades for their attitude during the annexation crisis.[223] The Socialist International did not accept Tucović's proposal in its original form, although a part of it was mentioned in the final resolution of the Congress.

The principal side of this issue was revived by Danilo Ilić in June 1914. When the first issue of *Zvono* appeared, *Radničke Novine*, the main paper of Serbian Social Democracy, criticized *Zvono* for "its nationalistic tendencies." Danilo Ilić wrote a long article on June 15, giving the position of the Young Bosnians on the complex issue of nationalism, under the title "Our Nationalism."

International capitalism created the internationalism of the proletariat and the Socialists. As the Socialists are attacking the capitalists—who are at the same time the official representatives of nationalism—so it might appear that Socialists are attacking nationalism; the word internationalism thus might be understood as antinational or at least anational. Among us at least it was understood in that way, because Socialism was brought to us by foreigners, who had no understanding of our nationalism.[224]

In order to establish its position, Ilić adduced several passages from Marx and commented as follows:

In our last issue we published Marx's opinion of the Balkan peoples. He was against the colonial policy of subjugation and he was for the autonomy of each people and its right to self-determination. His opinion has been assailed by the bosses of our Socialist movement to such an extent that they publicly declare that we Bosnians should be happy to be a colony. It is strange that the words of the Austrian foreign minister accord with the opinion of our "bosses" that Albania should receive autonomy, while they deny the same right to us South Slavs.[225]

After these explanations, Ilić answered *Radničke Novine*'s charge directly, reminding the Belgrade Social Democrats of the attitude of the Serbian Social Democratic leader Tucović at the Copenhagen Congress of the Socialist International when he objected to the German and Austro-Hungarian Social Democrats: "They were discredited in the eyes of the workers of Serbia, because they did not fight enough for the small Balkan nation-peoples, who are crushed by the paws of the great powers." Ilić added his own comment to it:

It is obvious that Socialism has to think first of all of the interests of the wide popular and working masses. In Serbia, where there is no danger that the local element will be pushed around by foreigners as is the case among us in Bosnia, this international solidarity should be even wider here than in our land, where foreigners actually impose on us their own national characteristics: their language, alphabet, etc.[226]

Ilić ended his article:

The consequences of such foolish Socialist leadership in Bosnia is a diminishing of Socialist consciousness . . . We are convinced that we have contributed to clear these issues, which were blurred by the not so intelligent work of the interpreters of Socialism to date. We hope that our healthy movement will be a strong wind which will clear the atmosphere of unhealthy bacilli.[227]

Besides criticizing Social Democracy for the lack of understanding of national problems of people-nations living under colonial conditions, Young Bosnia accused the Social Democratic parties of having what they termed a lack of inner democracy and a tendency toward bureaucratization. This criticism was expressed directly by Nedeljko Čabrinović in his letters about his experiences in the printing plant of the Social Democratic party of Croatia in Šid; he repeated them even more strongly in front of the investigating judge on June 28, 1914: "The paper *Glas Slobode* may be a Socialist paper, but its adherents have become the Socialist priests. They are thoroughly rotten, and I no longer trust them. In the same way, the Christians, as long as Christ taught them, were quite attractive, but later degenerated."[228]

The same criticism was expressed in a more sophisticated way by Danilo Ilić in the article entitled "Democracy Among Us" in *Zvono* of May 24, 1914. He first criticized all the existing political parties in Bosnia and Hercegovina, and then he turned his blast against the Social Democrats:

Even the most democratic party among us, the Social Democratic, by its internal life does not differ from other bourgeois parties (in our public life it does not yet play any role). According to its party rules, it is not organized from the bottom upward on a federalist basis, but on the contrary, from the top down on the principle of centralism and hierarchy like the Catholic Church. The central party leadership has absolute power over the members, who are obliged to submit without a word, so that even the slightest sign of criticism is completely excluded. We know how many dedicated members have been expelled because they did not see eye to eye with some member of the leadership; they were even thrown out of the trade-union organizations (although the party should not have this influence on them), with the sole object of curbing those workers who dared to say freely what they thought about some mean gesture of some of the "bosses." The party is ruled by a few big leaders according to their personal views and personal interests. Whoever does not wish to listen is expelled from the party, in the interest of party discipline. Therefore, this party is based also on undemocratic, conservative, and even autocratic principles. And when such practices, so dangerous to Socialist interests, have been criticized in pamphlets and papers, the leaders have defended themselves, naturally clumsily and without success. Socialism today in Bosnia is in a state of crisis, the best members are resigning from the party, and the working masses are falling into lethargy and discouragement; the flag of liberty, equality, and fraternity consists today of a few money-grabbing bosses.[229]

Ilić ended the article with the words:

Zvono sets itself the task of serving as an organ for the advancement of the principles and methods of real democracy. From this platform we shall subject to merciless criticism the whole of our public life to the extent that it violates democratic ideas. We shall unmask and denounce all manifestations of conservatism and reaction in the state and among the political parties. Thereby we shall do much for the democratic education of our people, particularly of the working masses. They must turn their back on the false leaders who are enriching themselves from their wages earned at the price of so much blood.[230]

Such a way of thinking no doubt reflected a dilemma which had already started in the European revolutionary movement in the 1850's, when debate began on the type of revolutionary parties, their goals and particularly on the problem of permanent revolution. Ilić's attitude reveals the influence of Proudhon and Bakunin and of the criticism of the Social Democratic parties by the Russian anarchists and the Russian left-wing Social Revolutionaries between 1900 and 1910.

The Young Bosnians were often described as anarchists by the Habsburg authorities.[231] There was no doubt a trace of anarchist philosophy among them and that they were acquainted with the leading anarchist philosophers—some of them called themselves "Socialist Anarchists"— but it would be historically incorrect to identify them completely with either the Individual Anarchists, Anarchosyndicalists, or Anarchocommunists. One must take into consideration that the main core of the Young Bosnians was recruited from *kmet* families, bringing from their villages instinctive feelings of rebellion, a concern for social justice, and a detestation of foreign rule leading to a suspicion of any kind of omnipotent or oppressive institutions, domestic or alien.

Nor could the Young Bosnians be identified with the Russian Populists. Gaćinović called himself a "Bakuninist."[232] The Young Bosnians shared many ideological and political views of the Russian Populists. First comes the idea of the role of the individual in history and the strategy of revolution from above, caused by direct action; in this respect, they followed Lavrov's belief in heroic individuals and the precious minority, and that "critically thinking individuals are the only instruments of human progress."[233] From the Populists, the Young Bosnians accepted the ideal of a new and better man as a prerequisite of revolution.

Gaćinović himself liked to stress the influence of the Russian Populists on the Young Bosnians, when he wrote to Trotsky:

You Russians know very little about us, much less than we know about you. There is nothing strange in that fact. Your country is big, you have great tasks in front of you and in many respects you have gone far ahead of us. In the sense of social development we are behind you by several decades. If you were to look closely into our Serbo-Croat and indeed the South Slav intelligentsia in general, you would find many features of your own movement as it was in the 1860's or 1870's. We know the history of your ideas and we like it; in many respects we are producing it in our own midst. Among our best teachers we count Chernishevsky, Herzen, Lavrov and Bakunin. We are, if you wish, your ideological colony. All colonies lag behind their metropolis.[234]

In his comparison with Russian Populists, Gaćinović neglected some aspects as Milovan Djilas pointed out in his essay on Gaćinović in 1937:

It would be a mistake to identify the situation in Bosnia and Hercegovina with Russia of the 1880's, when the Russian Populists and other dissatisfied elements organized conspiracies and secret societies. In the Russia of that period (especially in Great Russia) there was no national problem; besides, the Russian capitalism of that period was on a lower level than that of Austria at the time of the annexation of Bosnia and Hercegovina. The Populists maintained against the Marxists that Russia should not go through capitalism; the Young Bosnians were not clear on that issue. A similarity existed between the two intelligentsia: both were isolated from society, that is all.[235]

To Djilas's arguments one should add that one of the basic differences between the Russian and Bosnian intelligentsia was their different social backgrounds. The Russian Populists came to a large extent from aristocratic circles or from the bourgeoisie, while the Young Bosnians came primarily from villages in which, at the beginning of the twentieth century, there existed the social psychology of a tribal society.

What he meant by Populism Gaćinović expressed more clearly in an obituary written in 1916 for his friend Jovan Živanović, who was killed during the war:

He was a *narodnjak*, a Populist in the best sense of the word, on the pattern of the Russian and European Populists, whom he studied from books and at political meetings. . . . The first part of his stay abroad, he spent studying the works of these men, who could not tolerate passively the subjugation of whole nations by a few masters. Živanović was also of the purest rebel stock, the race whom deep feelings of justice and liberty led to the stake or the gallows; he was also the first who paved new roads and discovered new worlds. . . . I met him so often in the streets, in the gardens, in the fields of Switzerland, with a book of Kropotkin or Bakunin, submerged in reading and thought. In these moments his soul was enriched with new forces, which made of him a thinker, a martyr and a victor in life. . . . The work of Jovan Živanović was a joyous hymn to all freedoms, personal freedom, nationally and socially, freedom of intercourse, of thought and of conscience, freedom of forms and particularly freedom of content, freedom of the masses of the people, which, dark and poor, stand outside the ring of light, stooped over the hard black earth.[236]

As we have seen in Chapter IV, Svetozar Marković (in the 1870's) wrote that the Russian kind of socialism was much nearer to the predominantly peasant society of the Balkans than the Western European socialism with its doctrines pertaining primarily to urban labor populations. Thus, fifty years later, Gaćinović expressed basically the same thought. He sensed the evolution within Russian socialism from 1910, when Lenin began to adapt Marx's teachings to the overwhelmingly peasant societies. Without doubt, Gaćinović will be remembered in the history of Yugoslav socialism as the man who almost half a century after the days of Svetozar Marković, re-established strong links with all the variants of the Russian revolutionary thought.

It would be historically incorrect to pigeonhole the Young Bosnians as a mere projection of some outside ideology; they clung to traits of their own milieu. The fact is that the Young Bosnians were not only a revolutionary political movement, but at the same time they initiated new ideas among the South Slavs in ethics and aesthetics.

Literature and literary clubs played a primary role in the work of Young Bosnia, both in shaping ideas and in matters of organization. This cannot be explained by any single factor. Some writers on the subject give as a main reason the lack of political freedom which forced the Young Bosnians to find an outlet in literary activities, which would least arouse suspicion among political and school authorities. But this is an oversimplification which fails to take into account the role of literature among the South Slavs in the period of their national awakening. There is some similarity between the role of the writer in Russia—especially after Pushkin—and that of the writer in the Balkans: revolution in the spiritual life of individuals must precede all social and political changes; literature should be put at the disposal of progressive, rational and useful ideas; therefore writers are "the soldiers of thought." Chernishevsky with these ideas in the 1860's forged links between literature and progressive political thought. Svetozar Marković tried to do the same among the South Slavs. Yet for the South Slavs it had an even greater importance, for unlike Russia, which had its long traditions, its own aristocratic and ecclesiastical circles from which literature and the arts emanated, the South Slavs, with the continuity of their traditions broken by the Ottoman and Habsburg invasions, arrived at the beginning of the nineteenth century as a society of peasants, rich in folklore but lacking any educational institutions, and in conditions of national and social subjugation.

It is true that there was some literary tradition in Dubrovnik, Dalmatia, among the Slovene Protestants, and in the Croat Zagorje, but all this was peripheral and did not have any decisive influence on the mass of South Slavs. At the same time, the South Slav peasantry under the Habsburgs was exposed to a rapid process of Germanization owing to the rise of industrial towns. In these conditions literature represented a focal point for national feeling and also a means of national self-preservation. For example, the very fact that the leading Slovene poet of the Romantic period, Prešeren, could write his verses in the Slovene language, means that he gave the Slovene peasant a feeling of national consciousness and fixed for the future the high esteem accorded to the writer in Slovenia, one quite unparalleled in Britain, for instance, where the historical process was different. The nearest parallels are in Scandinavia and among the Czechs and Slovaks in Germany, where, although tradition existed, the Romantic movement played an important role in the national awakening. Here, under the influence of Slovene romanticism, which was derived as a literary movement from European romanticism (particularly German), Vuk Karadžić raised the common language of the Hercegovinian *kmets* to the rank of a literary language, but, following in some respects the Czechs and Slovaks, he introduced a simple and rational orthography.

Realism, which followed romanticism, did not lead to a diminution of the role of the writer in South Slav society. The influence here came mainly from Russia. It was the period of the renaissance of rationalism and materialism; the best Serbian realists were under the influence of Chernishevsky and believed that the writer's first duty was to be a social reformer. All the negative traits of the bureaucracy of the newly formed Serbian national state came under the fire of the realist writers.

The turn of the century saw a marked penetration of French symbolism, which was called *Moderna*, among the South Slavs. The Young Bosnians became the forerunners of modernistic individualism, and their review *Bosanska Vila* in Sarajevo was the most outspoken supporter of Moderna. A similar process took place among their colleagues in Slovenia and Dalmatia. Oton Župančič, the greatest modern Slovene poet, wrote as a motto for *Preporod*, in its first issue, his "Kovaška," the poem of smiths.[237] In 1913 Čerina published a book of literary criticism, more than three hundred pages long, about Janko Polić-Kamov, the Croat poet-rebel whose motto resembled Nadson's "let your poem ignite the flame of dissatisfaction."[238]

This at first glance strange contact between social rebels and pure poets, was not a trait peculiar to Bosnia and Hercegovina. Among the French "ascetic assassins" of the 1880's and 1890's there was many a poet. Émile Henry was a boy with considerable literary ability. As George Woodcock has stated, in France of that time "anarchism with its complex pattern of urges towards liberation from social, moral and artistic bonds was recognized by both intellectuals and artists."[239] Both Camille Pissarro and his son Lucien were intimately involved in the anarchist movement. Vlaminck and other Fauve painters found anarchism a congenial doctrine. Among the symbolist poets there was a similar trend: Stuart Merrill, Paul Valéry, Stéphane Mallarmé, and particularly Gaćinović's favorite poet, Émile Verhaeren, had connections with anarchism in its literary aspects.[240] In Prague both Franz Kafka and Jaroslav Hašek, the author of *The Good Soldier Schweik*, were sympathizers of the libertarian literary circle in Prague.[241]

A similar process took place in the Russian Revolution in 1917 and the years after, when symbolist and postsymbolist writers (like Blok and Mayakovsky) were in the vanguard of the revolutionary forces. But among the South Slavs in the years immediately prior to 1914, the posi-

tion was even more complex: the individual sought to express his rebellion against national subjugation and all strangleholds in every aspect of
social life, in education, in religion, in family relations, and above all in
the arts. Ivo Andrić understood this mentality of the rebellious Croat
intellectual when he wrote: "The whole of our society is snoring un-
gracefully; only the poets and revolutionaries are awake."[242]

To be a poet, as we have seen, was regarded in Princip's generation as
a special mark of distinction. Almost all of them tried their hand at
literary criticism, poetry or short-story writing. Some of them were
poets more in their way of life than in the texts they left behind. For
instance, this was the case of both Princip and Čabrinović. Their friend
Dragutin Mras wrote in vers libre as a sign of protest against the dog-
matic teachers who preferred classical verse. Miloš Vidaković at the
age of twenty was already known as a good literary critic and was the
author of several prose poems. Drago Radović and Jovo Varagić also
gained reputations as poets in their teens. The few who survived the
First World War included some who became well-known names in the
Yugoslav literary world: Borivoje Jevtić, the writer and dramatist,
Pero Slijepčević and Špiro Soldo, essayists and historians of literature.
In 1962 Ivo Andrić became the only Yugoslav to win the Nobel Prize in
literature.

In 1913 the Young Bosnians were so much engaged in literature that
Borivoje Jevtić identified them in an article in *Bosanska Vila* solely as
"a literary movement."[243] They translated Kierkegaard, Strindberg,
Ibsen and Edgar Allan Poe. The young Ivo Andrić translated Walt
Whitman's "Song of Myself." Whitman's directness and love of nature,
his struggle for the integrity of the individual, attracted the Young
Bosnians.[244] Danilo Ilić, despite his preoccupations in plotting assassinations against the Habsburg dignitaries, found time to translate Oscar
Wilde's *Thoughts About Art and Criticism*. The Young Bosnians
fought also for the purity of the Serbo-Croat language.[245] Vladimir
Gaćinović also had great literary ambitions. He tried his hand first at
literary criticism and then at poetical prose writing. Like Mazzini he
was torn between literature and politics, and several times he endeav-
ored to make the "great sacrifice" and wholly abandon literature for
the pursuit of political aims. But he never succeeded, and he remained a
poet—unhappily, never a great one—until his death, producing some of
his finest work toward the end of his life.

But the Young Bosnians as well as other modernists created a strange
situation in the South Slav literature. They were revolutionaries, but in
poetry they introduced a general trend toward pessimism. Jovan
Skerlić, the most widely recognized literary critic, commented sadly:

Under the influence of the difficult political conditions in which Serbia and
the Serbian people lived, as a reflection of the general mental depression,

literature also expressed a kind of fatigue, tiredness and desperation; the writers were in a dark and heavy mood. A wave of pessimism flooded the whole of Serbian literature, never were the graveyards so much the object of poets' attention, never had nirvana looked so far away, as in these somber and sad times.[246]

Even Gavrilo Princip, one of the least sophisticated of the Young Bosnians, preferred pessimistic poets. Among the Serb poets, his idol was Sima Pandurović.[247] When he was in Belgrade in 1912 and 1913, preparing for his exams in the First High School, Princip's sole friend among the local boys was Momčilo Nastasijević, who grew up to become the poet of sadness and pessimism.[248] Princip's experience was not accidental. When Dimitrije Mitrinović came to Sarajevo in 1907, he soon became the real editor of the literary review *Bosanska Vila*. He transformed *Bosanska Vila* into a mouthpiece of modernism. Two of the leading theoreticians of symbolism among Serb poets, Sima Pandurović and Svetislav Stefanović, got a permanent platform to express their views. Mitrinović braved the most established authorities and critics in Serb literature, like Skerlić, with whom he agreed on many other issues, particularly political. At the same time, Mitrinović worked as an art critic. Thanks to him, the South Slav intellectual world learned about Kandinsky and Picasso. Mitrinović also celebrated the works of the Croat sculptor Ivan Meštrović, who combined modern forms with motifs from Serbo-Croat folk poetry, particularly the Kosovo cycle. The preoccupation with literature drew Mitrinović away from active political work, although he kept personal contacts with his former colleagues. In 1918 he was in London and arranged the burial of his friend Dušan Popović, one of the leaders of the Serbian Social Democracy. He chose a grave just by Karl Marx's tomb at Highgate Cemetery.[249] After the First World War, Mitrinović returned from England to Munich, where he lived among futurist, cubist and expressionist artists and poets. This talented but unsteady man left literary and art criticism, occupied himself with theosophy, spiritual ecstasy, and even occultism, and ended his life in London, in 1953, far away from his Mostar.[250]

As far back as 1908 Mitrinović tried to give his own explanation of that strange fusion of symbolism with the revolutionary tasks of the Young Bosnians. In an article "The National Milieu and Modernism," he wrote: "If one wishes to be a real poet he must be first of all a human being in the fullest sense of the word," because "the utmost and eternal subject of art is the human being everywhere and eternal."[251] Mitrinović further stated that "an individual is not only a member of a national group but also a member of the human race. . . . To be a modern man means to feel today's chaos of the most controversial and paradoxical points of view and systems, to feel this nervous, unsettled and undefined atmosphere of our transitory and perhaps extremely important epoch. To detach oneself from today's problems of science and social problems, to be cold and unmoved as regards the new strivings of the liberated but puzzled human spirit, means not to be modern and present; it means even more: not to be worth living. It is not important which attitude a man takes as regards today's problems. One could be a Socialist, an individualist, a spiritist, a theosophist, a Buddhist metaphysic—whatever he likes—but the most important thing is to feel our pain and our efforts, to understand today's problems. The one who feels this agitation of our time, who is trying to find the remedy for today's calamities, is modern, despite his opinion as to what this remedy consists of. Modern man is the one who in this epoch of democracy and libertarianism, feels in our country the whole absurdity of an anachronistic system, who feels hunger and the lack of justice for our poor masses and who is fighting for bread and freedom for a naked and starved people."[252]

In the same article Mitrinović expressed the idea of individual anarchism so near to Ibsen: "To be modern and to be a man of today means the same thing. Modernism is not something stagnating and absolute, and one; it is a relative phenomenon exposed to constant changes."[253] Writing about Janko Polić-Kamov, Čerina expressed the same idea even more clearly: "The thought, the free thought, is the greatest and bravest ruler of the universe. It has huge, space wings of the freest and the most audacious bird, for which fear and danger do not exist. Its wild flight goes to infinity and eternity. It destroys today what was created yesterday. It destroys every dogma, every norm, every authority. It has no other faith, but the faith in its power. It creates critics, subversives, rebels, and wreckers . . ."[254]

No doubt Mitrinović and Čerina, two of the leading thinkers of the young South Slav revolutionary generation, expressed the elements of Ibsen's notion of permanent rebellion as the main law of life on the eve of 1914.

In his essay on Polić-Kamov, Čerina described Ibsen as "a poet-revolutionary of proud individuals and social reformers," a "poet of instinct."[255] It is significant that Ibsen was much discussed by Young Bosnians. They knew his plays well, and in *Zora*, Numbers 2 to 10 of 1910, they ran a long essay by Luka Smodlaka on Ibsen, starting with Catiline's conception of permanent revolt.

> *And is not life an everlasting fight*
> *Between the hostile forces of the soul?*
> *And this fight is the soul's own life.*

The two letters of Ibsen to Georg Brandes on December 20, 1870, and February 17, 1871, dealing with the idea of permanent revolution were well known among the Young Bosnians, particularly the second one, which ends with these words:

Equality and brotherhood are not what they used to be in the old days of the guillotine. Politicians do not wish to understand this and I hate them. They want only partial revolution, the revolution of the surface . . . What nonsense! The only thing that is worthwhile is the revolt of man's spirit. The notion of freedom consists of the fact that it should be enlarged all the time. . . . Do not be puzzled by the antiquity of the institutions . . . even greater ones will perish; there is no religion which will not be destroyed. Neither moral principles nor artistic expressions will last forever.[256]

Yet, the Young Bosnians could not be identified as Ibsenists in the proper sense of the word. As we shall see in the next chapter, their notions of permanent rebellion and tyrannicide were primarily influenced by the local folkloric philosophy as expressed in the heroic Serbo-Croat epics and in the poetry of the Montenegrin poet-bishop Njegoš (Petar II).

It is difficult to identify the Young Bosnians with any outside group or ideology in the Europe of their day. They were a kind of primitive rebel, whose restlessness was rooted in the realities of their own society. Most of them perished on the scaffolds and in the jails of the Habsburg monarchy between 1914 and 1918. Among the few who survived the ordeal was Ivo Andrić. Although he was not involved in the plot of June 28, 1914, he was arrested and spent most of the war in jail and internment. When he came out, he wrote two collections of poetical prose, *Ex Ponto* and *Nemiri*. In the second, he published a short story called "A Story From Japan," a kind of spiritual testament of the Young Bosnians, stating their notion of permanent rebellion.

Among the Three Hundred and Fifty conspirators banished under the rule of the Empress Au-Ung, was the poet Mori Ipo.

He spent three years on the smallest of the Seven Isles in a hut made of reeds. But when the Empress fell ill and her power started to fade, he, like the majority of the Three Hundred and Fifty, succeeded in returning to the capital city Jedo. He lived on the outskirts of the city in a wing of a temple.

The citizens, sickened with the bloodthirsty tyranny of the mad and cruel Empress, grew to love the poet more and more, and the Three Hundred and Fifty were his inseparable companions. His short verses about heroism and death were passed secretly from hand to hand, and his kind smile often settled the disputes of his comrades.

It happened that the Empress died unexpectedly from the poison of general hatred. Her corrupt chamberlains ran away, and she lay ugly and swollen in the deserted palace, and there was no one to bury her.

The Three Hundred and Fifty conspirators quickly assembled and took over power. Among themselves they divided the ranks and honors and began to rule over the unified Empire on the Seven Isles.

When the first ceremonial meeting was convened in the palace of the late Empress, after the count up of the Three Hundred and Fifty, it was discovered that one of them was missing. And when the list of conspirators was read aloud, it was found that the poet Mori Ipo was absent. They refused to deliberate without him and at once a slave with a rickshaw was dispatched for him. After a time the slave returned with the empty rickshaw; he was told that Mori Ipo had gone and that he had left a written message for the Council of the Three Hundred and Fifty. The oldest in the Council took the folded paper and handed it to the Chief of State Learned Ones, who began to read aloud:

"Mori Ipo extends his greetings to his comrade conspirators, at this hour of departure!

"Deep thanks from my heart, comrades of mine, for the common sufferings and for our common faith and victory. I beg you humbly to forgive me because I cannot share with you authority as I shared the struggle. Poets —unlike other men—are faithful only in the hour of calamity and leave those who are enjoying well-being. We poets are born for struggle; we are passionate hunters, but we do not eat the prey. A thin and almost invisible fence divides us; it is not as keen as the edge of the swords but nevertheless it is just as lethal. Without damage to my soul I could not cross this line, because we can endure everything but authority. This is the reason I am leaving you, my comrade conspirators, I am going to see if there is somewhere a thought which has not yet been realized or a cause unfulfilled, but if any calamity or danger should befall our Empire of the Seven Isles and the need comes for struggle and succor, then seek me out."

At that moment the chairman of the Council, who was a little deaf, interrupted the reading, and with the impatience of an old man and with disapproval in his voice, said:

"No calamity could befall the Empire during the just and enlightened rule of the Three Hundred and Fifty."

All the counselors nodded, and the older ones smiled with disdain and pity. What nonsense! The reading was discontinued and the bill on customs duty on imports was taken up instead.

Only the Chief of the State Learned Ones read the poet's message to the end, but to himself, and then he wrapped it up and deposited it in the Archives of the former Empress.[257]

CHAPTER XI

THE KOSOVO
TYRANNICIDE

*Among the Serbs every peasant soldier knows
what he is fighting for. When he was a baby,
his mother greeted him: "Hail, little avenger of
Kosovo!"*

—JOHN REED

A STUDY OF THE POLITICAL TACTICS of the Young Bosnians reveals strikingly that their conversion to the philosophy and practice of political assassination was a painful process. Among the Young Bosnians not all the groups were prepared to accept individual terrorism as the only means of struggle against Habsburg rule. Even in the hard core of the movement there was a constant evolution on this issue. Vladimir Gaćinović, under the influence of modern European thought, started to waver on the eve of June 28, 1914, on the wisdom of political assassination. The chief organizer of the Sarajevo plot, Danilo Ilić, in the fateful weeks before the Archduke's violent death, questioned the rightness of the philosophy of political homicide and even the necessity of the Archduke's murder.

But the younger elements among the Young Bosnians, headed by Gavrilo Princip, who never left their homes for the universities in the great capitals of Europe, had a different opinion. On the same day when Zora, the society of Serbian students in Vienna, publicly declared mass revolution preferable to individual terrorism, the shots of Gavrilo Princip in Sarajevo showed that a younger generation had won the day in a great controversy which divided the ranks of Bosnians.

Princip's act demonstrated that the influence of modern ideologies, which advocate mass resistance against tyrannical foreign rule, was not sufficiently strong to counteract the tradition of backward Bosnian society. It is a historic fact that nowhere in Europe in the twentieth century was the idea of tyrannicide so alive among broad masses of people as it was among the South Slav peasantry, particularly in Bosnia, Hercegovina, Montenegro and Lika. This was a result of the social and economic forms of patriarchal tribalism that had survived as if in a deep freeze through the centuries-long Ottoman occupation. It is true that under the influence of capitalism this burden of the past was starting to disintegrate, but the folklore of tribalism, in an impoverished and illiterate peasantry, remained alive even in our century. The historic circumstances under which the South Slavs lived, in an uninterrupted state of rebellion against foreign occupiers, facilitated the preservation of the ancient idea, expressed in the folklore epic of Kosovo, that the assassination of a tyrannical foreign ruler is one of the noblest aims of life.

What particularly attracted the Young Bosnians to the Kosovo legend was the sacrifice of one of the founders of their movement, Bogdan Žerajić, who, in despair over the annexation of Bosnia and Hercegovina, decided to kill the Emperor Franz Josef when he visited Mostar on June 3, 1910. Žerajić changed his mind at the last moment, although he had been only a few steps from the Habsburg Emperor with a revolver in his pocket. He returned to Sarajevo and on the day when the new Bosnian *Sabor* was opened, on June 15, 1910, fired five shots at the governor of the two provinces, General Marijan Varešanin, and then killed himself with the sixth bullet in the belief that his attempt had succeeded.

Žerajić's act has been compared with similar deeds in modern European history. Just as the attempted assassination in 1878 of the Governor of St. Petersburg, General Trepov, by Vera Ivanovna Zasulich, triggered the wave of terrorist acts by Narodnaya Volya which culminated in the murder of Tsar Alexander II in 1881, so Žerajić's attempt marked the beginning of a systematic use of political assassination against the leading figures of the Habsburg realm. After seven similar incidents and a dozen detected and undetected plots, the climax was reached with the violent death of Franz Ferdinand, on June 28, 1914, on the same street in Sarajevo and only one block away from where Žerajić fired his last shots. For others, Žerajić's act resembled even more closely the deed of Karl Ludwig Sand, the German student who in 1819 killed the Russian Emperor's spy among the German radicals, August von Kotzebue, and then drove his dagger through his own heart.

These comparisons are good only up to a point. Žerajić acted even more spontaneously than Sand, with a frenzied desperation and a kind of religious urge to sacrifice himself. Žerajić's suicide in the tradition of the Kosovo legend proved to be a powerful attraction to the martyr strain latent in the *kmet* character, and he was idolized by many a Young Bosnian; his shrine, hidden among the graves of suicides in the Sarajevo cemetery, became the object of pilgrimages. In 1912 Gavrilo Princip swore on it his oath to revenge Žerajić's death.

After finishing high school in Mostar in 1907, Žerajić entered Zagreb University as a student of law. Having no financial means, he left Zagreb the same year and went to Serbia to visit his uncle, Dr. Milan Žerajić, a Serbian Royal Medical Officer, who had been educated in Russia. Žerajić worked for a short time as a teacher in a primary school in the Kruševac district of Serbia. In 1908 he returned to his native village Miljevac in Hercegovina. Gaćinović wrote that Žerajić came back from Serbia with many books by Prince Kropotkin, saying that "Kropotkin has the soul of that handsome pure Jesus who for us comes from Russia."[1] According to Gaćinović, Žerajić was a well-read young man who knew by heart poems of Carducci, the poet of the *Risorgimento*, and of the young Russian Populist poet Nadson.

At the news of the annexation of Bosnia and Hercegovina, in October, 1908, Žerajić, like many Young Bosnians, fled to Serbia and joined the volunteer units of irregular troops called *komite*, organized by Narodna Odbrana in preparation for the war against Austria-Hungary, which seemed imminent. The declaration of the Serbian government accepting the act of annexation, and the passivity of the Bosnian Serbs were cruel blows to Žerajić. While he was undergoing military training in Serbia, he told a Serbian officer that "we must liberate ourselves or die." This was the main slogan under which the Hercegovinian insurgents fought in the great rebellion of 1875–78, which started at Nevesinje, Žerajić's home.[2]

On his return from Serbia, Žerajić proceeded to Zagreb, where he continued his studies. Pero Slijepčević has preserved his correspondence with Žerajić from that period. Žerajić was a very active Young Bosnian; he worked in Zagreb and also took part in the preparation of the first issue of *Zora* in Vienna. His letters are sensitive and sometimes sentimental. He urged his colleagues in Vienna to help some poor students who did not have stipends.[3] In another letter he expressed his sadness for not being together with his friends in Vienna, and he even reproached them for not writing often to him.[4] His mood was in a constant state of flux. From utter desperation he went into fits of gaiety and wit. Once he wrote a prose poem about the polemics between Pero Slijepčević and Luka Smodlaka in *Zora* on the role of Moderna literature and Ibsen among the Young Bosnians.[5] Božidar Zečević, a close friend of Žerajić from these days, wrote that Žerajić fell into complete depression, neglected his studies, living from day to day, spending most of his time at Zagreb cafés, listening and spreading unconfirmed political news, but spending most of his time alone, quiet, in a world of his own fantasies.[6]

During this period, Žerajić underwent deep changes as far as his theories on the methods of political struggle were concerned. As far back as the end of November 1909 he argued strongly for the application of Masaryk's methods of cultural revival among the Young Bosnians. In a letter to Slijepčević on November 2, 1909, he expounded his ideas in detail, stressing that the basis of the work should consist of "one's own education" and cultural work in the villages.[7] He was also interested in problems of sociology and ethics.[8] Yet only a short time afterward, Žerajić discarded Masaryk's program. Slijepčević formulated the disagreement with Masaryk thus: "We had hidden within our Balkan peasant tunics something which he did not possess: the idea of revolution."[9] Or as Borivoje Jevtić said, "Masaryk realism, good for the northern country and its inhabitants at a much higher level of civilization, was not applicable to Bosnia, which had no corresponding culture and which for its awakening needed the smell of blood more than the 'three R's.' "[10]

That Žerajić was thinking of applying new methods in the political struggle in Bosnia and Hercegovina is proved by a letter which he wrote to Gaćinović on January 12, 1910:

. . . I am suffering from tremendous emotional torments, my feelings are extremely gloomy and I do not have the strength to tell anyone but you.

I have become a skeptic, I do not trust in anything anymore, I only believe that I have bad luck, that people who are naturally unlucky do exist. I am one of them.

There is only one thing which satisfies me. I still have strength and it seems to me I shall have it until the end. I have deep understanding of all the difficulty of our situation. The position in which we find ourselves is distressing. The individual spirit is chained by the shackles of the general will. All that used to be great and sacred, just and true is completely quiet today.

This causes great pain to a man who feels sincerely. Added to this are personal sufferings, both physical and spiritual. This, my friend, is my mood.

Please send my regards to Joca Patriot and tell him he should not be angry with me. He doesn't need this little thing now, since the armistice has been proclaimed, and he can be assured that it will not be wasted.[11]

Žerajić's last sentence shows that he had made up his mind to take up political assassination; he referred to a revolver which he had borrowed from a Bosnian student of engineering, Jovo Gašić, who came from Bosanska Gradiška and studied at Belgrade University.[12] By the word "armistice" he meant the acceptance of annexation by Serbia.

In order to mark the annexation and the introduction of a new constitution, the Viennese government organized an official tour of the two provinces for the Emperor Franz Josef, the first he had made in this part of the Habsburg empire.[13] At the beginning of March 1910, the press published the details of his itinerary from May 30 to June 5.

This event moved Žerajić to a decisive action; he decided to assassinate the old Emperor. Whether he was alone in the conspiracy or not is a controversial question. Gaćinović described in detail his behavior during the days of preparation for the attempt. After Žerajić's death, Gaćinović published an essay on him in the November 1910 issue of *Zora*, under the title "To Those Who Are Coming." To avoid censorship Gaćinović wrote the whole essay in Aesopian style, without using Žerajić's name. Gaćinović described Žerajić's views on the Bosnian political scene, the mental climate and life in general as follows:

> Down among our people the whole of life is aimed at slavery; the whole of society is full of slavishness. After many generations of *kmets* who gave much in the struggle, the people of the present day are weak, petty and bent-backed. There is no healthy pulse; there are no great and noble gestures. Young Bosnians are without expression, petrified. They have none of the vital feelings which unite the different elements of a race and make them profoundly dependent on one another in great and tragic days. . . . We, the youngest, have to make a new history. Into our frozen society we have to bring sunshine, we have to awaken the dead and cheer up the resigned. We must wage a deadly war against pessimism, against fear and low spirits, we the messengers of new generations and new people. Having a belief stronger than life and a love which is capable of lifting people out of the grave, we shall win.[14]

Gaćinović also described Žerajić's departure for Bosnia. His story is full of sadness and pathos for his dead friend:

> One afternoon he came to our group. A great event was expected in a few days. He, serious and full of tears, said that he was going home because of personal affairs. In silence, which spoke for itself, we departed. In the evening I accompanied him to the station. He grabbed me in his arms, as if he were seeing me for the last time. He was silent, and when the bell rang for the departure of the train, he told me his last words, the message to all young ones and to all his friends: "Youth must prepare for sacrifices. Tell them." He departed, quiet, noble and unobserved. And with deeds he confirmed his words, his faith.[15]

The Emperor Franz Josef arrived in Bosnia on Monday, May 30. After listening to welcoming speeches at the border town of Bosanski Brod, he left half an hour later for Sarajevo in the new imperial coach of the Bosnian State Railways. The special train stopped at many stations, where masses of people were assembled. It arrived in Sarajevo at three o'clock on the afternoon of May 31.[16] After more speeches the Emperor proceeded in a four-horse *Daumontwagen* to the *Konak*, the Governor's residence, passing along the two-mile-long Appel Quay, where four years later his Heir Apparent, Franz Ferdinand, was to meet his death. Two lines of soldiers protected the imperial route. In the evening there was a torchlight procession. Everything went well the first day.

The second day was filled with receptions; the Emperor received the leaders of the five religious groups (the Moslems, Roman Catholics, Eastern Orthodox, Protestants and Jews) separately. The French ministry in Belgrade, in its report of Franz Josef's visit to Sarajevo, noted that he addressed the Serbian leaders in French.[17] At the end of the day, the Emperor said to General Varešanin: "I assure you this voyage has made me twenty years younger."[18]

After another day in Sarajevo, witnessing a military parade, the Emperor left the town without any incidents having occurred; he stopped in Mostar for four hours, visiting the ancient Neretva Bridge, and proceeded to Vienna. From Hofburg he sent a letter to General Varešanin on June 6, 1910, expressing his thanks for the reception and the success of the whole trip.[19]

Neither the Emperor nor the authorities knew what great danger he had faced. Only after Žerajić's attempt against Governor Varešanin, on June 15, was the whole story revealed. Žerajić had shadowed the old Emperor for most of his journey. On June 2 at Spa Ilidže and on June 3 at Mostar he succeeded in approaching him very closely. There have been several attempts by different authors to explain why Žerajić did not shoot at the Emperor when he had such good opportunities. Leo Pfeffer, the judge investigating the Sarajevo conspiracy, suggested that "the venerable old age of the Emperor, by which Žerajić was greatly struck, persuaded him not to carry out his attempt, or to turn it against some other personality."[20] Another Habsburg official, Božo Čerović, wrote in his reminiscences: "Neither was Žerajić an assassin . . . Žerajić was an adherent of the tactics of gradual, cultural progress, and it was his misfortune that he drew the lot to kill Franz Josef . . . When he saw the old Emperor, his hand could not draw his Browning from his pocket. . . ."[21]

The police found among Žerajić's belongings a letter which he wrote after June 3, when he missed shooting the Emperor. Although Žerajić was in an agitated state of mind and some words were left half finished and others missing, the content of it is nevertheless quite clear:

In a [s]tab of pain, in sorrow, in the anguish of a nightmare—in such a spirit should I write to you, if there was not a rule that one should not make a parody of one's own feelings; I would need a million of M. Tević's aphorisms in order to express what is in my heart.

When I rushed to the place, I thought I should be able to shout as Caesar did, but for me his words mean: V[ae], V[ae] v[ictus] sum.

Oh, my sorrow, my sorrow passing through Sarajevo, I was reciting your Ode to Dubrovnik of 1905 . . . How Sarajevo looked, as if it were damned. Everybody was bowing, everybody went to bow. And I spoke with pain: This is blasphemy against histo[ry], as you would say. . . .

During his arrival there were a lot of peop[le] . . . The bishops had ordered a[ll] priests and church commi[ttees] to send their representatives to welcome the sove[reign]. They all were sad and wor[ried]-looking. As he drove by, the king rema[rked] that there were no *kmets* to greet him.—The *kmets* did not wish to respond to the summons of the gen[darmes]. Our good old *kmet*, he does not like genda[rmes]. While he was still in Sara H.E.H. passed through. . . ."22

The police scribe seems to have lost patience and abandoned his efforts to decipher the letter further, merely ending, in German, *unleserlich*—"unreadable." It was never established to whom Žerajić addressed this letter.

How depressed Žerajić was at not having carried out the attempt against the Emperor is confirmed in a letter of June 4, 1910, in which he said: "Even those walking to the scaffold could feel no worse than I."23 At that moment he decided to try his hand against Governor Varešanin. This was recorded by several of his friends who met him between June 3 and June 15, 1910. One of the leaders of the older generation of Bosnian intellectuals, Vasilj Grdjić, a liberal member of *Sabor*, who kept contacts with the Young Bosnians and knew Žerajić well, described the feeling of depression among the Serbs during Franz Josef's visit to Bosnia:

Everyone was obsequious. Even the opposition press—at that time *Srpska Rijec*—had, it was said, to greet the new sovereign in its editorial. Although without much enthusiasm, although under duress, they mumbled old clichés of devotion and loyalty: "The old Emperor is a good man. How could he be otherwise? Only his counselors are bad. Now he is actually meeting the people. It will be better from now on." Something of that sort had to be said. About his journeys, acclamations, his visits, the welcoming speeches, about these things I read in the ordinary and extra editions of the official press. Our hearts were filled with bitterness against everything. We hated even our own life. . . .24

After this Grdjić described his sudden meeting with Žerajić:

It took place in the restaurant T. Katić, behind the new Catholic church, where I used to eat. One evening I came a little bit earlier. There, in one of the smaller rooms with three tables, I met Žerajić. He was eating. When I entered, we looked at each other and only exchanged greetings. I sat at the same table, but at the other end. While we were eating we did not speak, but looked at each other several times. I knew him well. That is to say, I believed in his patriotism. We looked at each other more often. Our glances reflected much pain, misery and almost horror. We had the same thoughts. Without finishing his dinner, Žerajić got up, approached me with wavering step, slowly, almost inaudibly. We were alone. He stopped by me and whispered: "He was so near me—I could almost have touched him," and with the right hand he made a gesture as if aiming a pistol. I understood everything, was thunderstruck and asked only: "Where?" "At the Mostar railway station," he answered. I cannot even today assess this event properly. The cup was full to overflowing. Only a drop was needed. My heart burst, words flowed. I almost shrieked: "Such men are not to be found among us." We agreed completely. We are slaves. Perhaps there is bravery among us. But collective. Let the heroes come forward. In crowds we rush on the enemy's naked sword. The tribes then are proud of the bravery of their members. But we have no individual bravery. For this a higher culture is needed, stronger national feelings than mere tribal pride. We have no heroes who could start great fights. We have no man, who, all alone, asking no one, could perform a memorable deed. Tribes have their own heroes, but the nation is waiting for its own—which up to now have not come forward. "They do not exist," I repeated several times sharply, agitatedly. We were in a kind of ecstasy. Žerajić, trembling, with his beautiful, deep, burning black eyes. When I said the last words, he looked at me speechless, and we departed almost without saying goodbye. I thought that he could do much, but I, miserable, did not believe that he could do everything. Before and since, many people had spoken like Žerajić. Perhaps this fact made me speak as abruptly as I did when I had my last conversation with this man, who, only hours later, was to become the first to perform such an exploit, unprecedented for us.[25]

Grdjić's feelings were shared by the leading Serbian review in Sarajevo, *Pregled*, in which Riste Radulović wrote on June 1, 1910, in an article entitled "Our Political Morality": "In our immediate past and in contemporary times we can boast no bright examples to prove we are a people fighting for our rights; there is not one single tragedy of the kind which are so often necessary to spur people on to action."[26] Pero Slijepčević, who also saw Žerajić on the eve of June 15, wrote that Žerajić read that article in front of him and said briskly: "But there will be tragedies."[27]

First Žerajić tried to enter the building in which the *Sabor* had its meetings, but couldn't obtain a ticket, even though he tried to bribe one of the pages.[28] He was seen in the company of another Young Bosnian, Jovan Starović, who was walking up and down in front of the *Sabor* building. Starović had met Žerajić on his return from Mostar, and Žerajić had confessed to him that he had intended to assassinate the old Emperor. They agreed that Žerajić should try his hand against

Varešanin. Žerajić started reading the Emperor's letter opening the *Sabor*. He informed Starović when he was unable to enter the *Sabor*. Seconds later Žerajić shot at Varešanin, who was leaving the *Sabor* session.[29]

In Franz Ferdinand's *Nachlass* there is a report which Governor Varešanin sent to the Archduke, describing Žerajić's attempt in detail, enclosing a sketch of the bridge over the Miljacka at the Appel Quay from which Žerajić fired at him. On June 15, 1910, at 11:20 A.M., after the opening of the *Sabor*, the Governor was returning to his residence, accompanied in his coach by his aide-de-camp, Major Wolfgang Heller. Žerajić fired five bullets at him from a short distance. The first hit the step of the driver's seat, the second went through the roof of the coach near the Governor's eyes. The third would have hit him in the heart if he had not in the meantime moved forward and if the driver had not accelerated. The fourth hit the back of the coach at the height of the Governor's head. The last bullet hit the back of the coach. So, all five bullets missed, but only just.[30] The Governor further reported that he ordered that the coach be stopped at once and he returned to the bridge, finding Žerajić, who in the meantime had committed suicide, "lying across the bridge in his death agony, thick blood flowing from his mouth."[31]

At the news of the attempt on Varešanin's life, the Archduke sent a telegram congratulating him on his escape. General Varešanin answered immediately: "Deeply moved by most gracious sympathy. Beg graciously to receive most submissive and most respectful thanks. Population regardless of religion indignant about accursed anarchist crime."[32]

In another dispatch, sent by the Bosnian government to Vienna, the following details were given about Žerajić:

The assassin, Bogdan Žerajić, was born in 1887 in the district of Nevesinje, of Serb-Orthodox creed, the son of a small free peasant, who had great difficulty in providing for his family of nine. Žerajić came to the high school in Mostar in 1900 and got a scholarship of 200 crowns from the government and a scholarship of 100 crowns from the Municipality of Nevesinje. In 1902 both scholarships were taken away from him, because of the unsatisfactory advance in his studies, and from this time on, he continued his studies at the high school with the support of his uncle Dr. Milan Žerajić, the Serbian Royal Medical Officer from Zaječar, and of the association Prosvjeta. Bogdan Žerajić was often in Belgrade and had frequent contact with two members of the *Sabor*, Vasilj Grdjić and Dr. Savo Ljubibratić, whom he had met recently. Among his closest friends were two students born in the district of Nevesinje, Božidar Zečević and Špiro Soldo, whom the police had started to observe. A house search in Nevesinje had been ordered at the homes of Veljko Simović, town councilor Cuprković, former gendarme

Soldo and Božidar's father Djuro Zečević, people with whom the assassin was known to be on intimate terms.[33]

The dispatches also mentioned that on Žerajić's body a badge was found

consisting of a red cardboard circle approximately 10 centimeters wide, bordered by a black rim, showing the portrait of a man without a beard, carrying a scythe and with passionately distorted countenance, open mouth and flying hair. The badge is reproduced here and will be sent for expert opinion to the headquarters of the police of the European capitals.[34]

The dispatch ended:

According to the police report the assassin came from Zagreb, and in the statements of all persons questioned here he is described as a closed, quiet and steady man. According to the police report, he left Zagreb for his home 16 days ago because of sickness and lack of money. The fact that among his possessions were found 110 crowns makes it probable that he had received material support, and investigations of this are now in progress. At the search of his house in Zagreb anarchistic books were found. According to a telegram of the district office Nevesinje which has just arrived, the police headquarters in Vienna were asked to search the house of the above-mentioned student Božidar Zečević while Špiro Soldo is said to live in Belgrade, Kralja Milutina 41.[35]

The Budapest police were the first to decipher the badge. "The headquarters of the Royal State Police in Budapest reported on July 26, 1910, that this badge was identical with the cover of the book *The History of the French Revolution*, written by Peter Kropotkin, published by Theodor Thomas, publishers, of Leipzig."[36]

As far as Žerajić's motives were concerned, the official version was that his attempt was a purely anarchist act. Varešanin in his report to the Archduke Franz Ferdinand said: "In all probability it is a well-prepared anarchist act; definite national political motives, or even more the assumption of a personal act of revenge, appear to be excluded."[37] The *Reichspost* on June 16, 1910, wrote that "Žerajić was an anarchist" and "a member of a Russian society," known in Belgrade as an anarchist, who together "with the anarchist leaders Krsto Cicvarić and Petar Minić edited the anarchist paper *Radnička Borba*. The *Reichspost* correspondent also claimed that Žerajić was the author of a leaflet with anarchist ideas signed with the pseudonym Kalojev, the assassin of the Russian statesman Plehve.[38] The story that Žerajić was an anarchist was accepted by all the press, and Belgrade's *Politika* wrote on June 16, 1910, that "according to the papers found on the assassin it seems that he had been in contact with anarchists."

The whole investigation of Žerajić's attempt was officially closed on October 13, 1910, with the verdict that he had no accomplices—as Governor Varešanin had reported to Vienna in June of the same year.[39] But on June 15, 1910, the Austro-Hungarian authorities had in their hands proof that Žerajić had intended to assassinate the Emperor Franz Josef. Obviously for political reasons, this matter had been hidden from the press and the general public. On the very day Žerajić tried to assassinate Varešanin an anonymous letter was sent from Zagreb to an official of the Bosnian Government:

YOUR EXCELLENCY,

We know very well Bogdan Žerajić, the second-year law student, who today tried to kill His Highness General Marijan Varešanin. But you should know that this attempt was intended for another person.[40]

The letter mentioned that behind Žerajić was Dimitrije Mitrinović, "son of a poor teacher," who gets "600 crowns a month from Belgrade" and pays "in advance to the Croat writers for their contributions to Serbian papers. . . ."[41] Besides Mitrinović, another Bosnian student was mentioned. The police searched Mitrinović's rooms and arrested him, but after a few days, he was released because there were no proofs that he had anything to do with the attempt.

The documents in the Austrian archives show that the Austro-Hungarian Foreign Office was warned from Paris, on May 18, 1910, and then from Sofia, on May 21, that there was a plot to assassinate the Emperor during his journey to Bosnia.[42] An Austro-Hungarian citizen had come to the Austrian Embassy in Paris describing himself as a student of philosophy, born in a town on the Hungarian-Croatian border, of non-South Slav parents, and giving his name as Brinkman. He said that in Paris he had attended several meetings of the "anarchist society called Association Jugo-Slav and that he had learned there that its members were dissatisfied because of the annexation of Bosnia and Hercegovina and that they intended to commit a "revolver *attentat*" against the Emperor Franz Josef during his stay in Mostar. Brinkman gave an exact description of the four members of the society who should already have left for Bosnia—Milivioj Radoičić and Lazar Djukić on May 16, and Jefta Popović and Ivo Carić on May 17.[43] The Vienna authorities informed the Paris police as well as the police of other European capitals about the plot. The Austrian Embassy in Paris was inclined to disbelieve Brinkman's information. He had visited the Embassy some weeks before, complaining that he was short of money and asking if his scholarship grant could be increased. He left the impression that he was suffering from "morbid lying mania," because he admitted that his real name was not Brinkman but Friedrich Eisenstadter (although later he used the name of Eisenstaedter) and that he was not a student of philosophy but a student of medicine.[44]

The Paris police were of a similar opinion. They submitted a report of their investigations to the Austrian Embassy. It said that the anarchist society Association Jugo-Slav held public meetings. It was composed mostly of Serbian students and workers, but there were among them a few Bulgars and Croats:

They have no patriotic feelings as was shown during the events in connection with the annexation of Bosnia. They held public meetings protesting against a war between Serbia and Bulgaria, stating that they were indifferent as to who was going to rule in Bosnia; whether a Habsburg or a Karadjordjević, it was just the same for them.

The police also found out that the description of Jefta Popović fitted a man named Branko Popović, a painter from Belgrade.[45]

The police in Sarajevo arrested a man called Jozo Carić, who said that he had a brother Ivo, but that he had gone to Hamburg some time ago; a Serbian citizen named Petar Daničić was also put in jail together with a Russian citizen, Josef Wiliamowski, and the printer Jozo Šimunović from Mostar. None of them had weapons and they denied any connection with Paris. The French papers carried news items about these arrests.

A denunciation from Sofia came from Ljube Harizanov, editor of the left-wing paper Balkanska Tribuna. He presumably had connections with members of the Belgrade society Slovenski Jug and he also worked as Sofia correspondent of the Belgrade Politika. Harizanov confidentially informed the Austrian Embassy in Sofia that an attempt was being organized against the Emperor. He had heard this from the vice-president of Slovenski Jug, Milorad Godjevac, a fifty-year-old physician from Belgrade, well known as the organizer of komite, Serbian guerrilla units which were fighting in Turkey. Harizanov promised that he would go to Belgrade and even to Bosnia to investigate the whole matter further and asked for money for that purpose.[46] To this telegram from Sofia, Aehrenthal added in his own longhand: "Strongly gives impression of forged swindles from last year, therefore meant to intimidate. Nevertheless the telegram should be communicated to the other offices so far instructed and to Belgrade . . ."[47]

Harizanov returned from Belgrade and on May 25, 1910, the Austrian Embassy in Sofia informed Aehrenthal that Harizanov named as involved in the conspiracy three leading Serbian politicians in Bosnia, Dr. Nikola Stojanović, Dr. Uroš Krulj and Vasilj Grdjić, whom he described as the chief supporters of Slovenski Jug. He said they were in personal correspondence with Prince Djordje, the eldest son of King Petar of Serbia. Harizanov also said that "a technician from the Serbian arsenal in Kragujevac and a Serb who is resident in Russia had gone to Mostar or Sarajevo and were hiding in the apartment of one of the three personalities mentioned above."[48] Harizanov gave further information that the Serbian journalist Milenović, junior editor of *Politika* and "a fervent supporter of Prince Djordje," was also involved in this plot and that he had already left for Bosnia. Harizanov again asked for money, but the Austrian ambassador in Sofia refused to give him any. He believed "that Harizanov is an *agent provocateur* of the Bulgarian King Ferdinand" and that *Balkanska Tribuna* dismissed him a "short time ago on the suspicion of being a spy for the Palace or the government." It is interesting that in his dispatches to *Politika* just before this affair Harizanov had denounced the Austrian government for organizing, on Bulgarian territory, attempts against the life of the Serbian King Petar through "the Russian anarchist Seromjatnikov." In *Politika* of April 5, 1910, he wrote that "Seromjatnikov and three of his accomplices are Austrian agents, who are trying in every way to compromise and to hamper the rapprochement among the Balkan states."

Aehrenthal issued instructions to his Belgrade Minister Forgach to visit the Serbian Foreign Minister Milovanović and investigate the reports of a conspiracy against the Emperor Franz Josef: "These reports, taken together with the article in *Politika*, give the impression that they want to start their old tricks again in Serbia, on the occasion of the Emperor's journey to Bosnia, and to begin with attempts at intimidation." Aehrenthal further stressed that his minister should, during the conversations with Milovanović, draw attention to the fact "that we see through these tactics and will not be deflected by them. But we expect from the Serbian government a correct neighborly attitude and a watchful eye regarding the revolutionary activities which apparently are going on and which seem to have their origin in Belgrade."[49]

Forgach answered that Milovanović assured him that "the Serbian government will take all necessary measures and will either prevent every departure of elements suspected in any way or inform the Austrian government immediately. Milovanović said that he had already spoken with the head of the Belgrade police, but the latter had informed him that they knew nothing which indicated any plans for an *attentat* on the occasion of the Emperor's journey to Bosnia."[50]

Between May 29 and June 2, 1910, Forgach inquired about Harizanov's report that Milenović of *Politika* was involved in the conspiracy. He was told by the police that Milenović on May 30 was still in Belgrade and that he did not intend to go to Bosnia. "The Serbian Foreign Minister," Forgach wired to Vienna, "thinks it impossible that Milenović would take active part in an *attentat*. But all politically or criminally suspect individuals are watched most strictly by the police and their departure would be prevented."[51]

But after Žerajić's attempt against Governor Varešanin and proof that Žerajić had intended to assassinate the Emperor, the confidential reports from Paris and Sofia were taken seriously. That the Emperor

Franz Josef knew he had escaped assassination by Žerajić is confirmed by Franz Ferdinand's son Maximilian Hohenberg, who wrote that his family was much disturbed at the news of Franz Ferdinand's trip to Sarajevo in 1914, "because the old Emperor had escaped an *attentat* in Sarajevo only by a miracle."[52]

In Paris the informer Eisenstadter appeared again at the Austrian Embassy. This time he was not rejected as a maniac. He was received attentively and was advised to address his request directly to Foreign Minister Aehrenthal. The Austro-Hungarian Ministry of Foreign Affairs directed that the informer on the planned *attentat* against His Imperial and Royal Apostolic Majesty should be compensated. Three hundred Austrian crowns were granted to him, with the suggestion to the Embassy "that since Eisenstaedter offers to give further information, one should accept his occasional information"; but the Embassy was warned to be reserved toward him and to give him not the slightest impression that he was in regular employment as a confidant.[53] On July 9, Count Nemes sent a report to the Foreign Minister "that Eisenstaedter was paid 315 francs and 10 centimes (300 crowns) for which he signed the enclosed receipt."[54]

In Sofia on the very morning that the local newspapers carried the news of Žerajić's attempt and death, the Bulgar Harizanov called on the Austrian minister, asking once more that his expenses in connection with his information should be met. Aehrenthal was informed the same day, June 16, that Harizanov "had received 100 francs for his first information about the presumably planned attempt against Emperor Franz Josef, then 200 francs for his traveling expenses to and from Belgrade, and 100 francs for the information he got there." On June 23, the Ministry of Foreign Affairs informed the Embassy in Sofia of its approval that the sum of 400 francs had been given to Harizanov.[55]

The question of whether Žerajić was alone in his attempt remains unanswered. Evidence is still lacking for exact confirmation of any of the possible explanations. As with many of the Fenian plots in Ireland, there will always be some aspects of this attempt which will never be fully explained. According to Dr. Werner Frauendienst of Berlin University, writing in 1941, Žerajić obtained his revolver from a major in the Serbian army, Božin Simić, a member of Apis's Ujedinjenje ili Smrt, who instructed him in the use of the weapon.[56] But Simić claimed that he had never met Žerajić.[57]

Žerajić's body was buried secretly by the police right at the end of Sarajevo's cemetery among the suicides and vagrants. There were rumors that the Sarajevo police, firmly believing in the theory of the Italian criminologist Lombroso that every criminal has some physiological defect, cut off Žerajić's head and kept it in the Museum of Criminology in Sarajevo. Stevan Žakula, who supervised the exhumation of Žerajić's body in 1919 after the fall of the Habsburg empire, stated that

Žerajić's skeleton had no skull. It was found later in the museum and placed with the rest of the body.[58]

Žerajić's attempt was described in the official press in Bosnia as well as in most of the papers in Belgrade as the act of a lunatic or a mixed-up young man. The older generation of Serbs in Sarajevo took a similar attitude. The Serbian banker and politician, Vojislav Šola, publicly expressed his "disgust for Bogdan Žerajić's base act" at the first meeting of the Bosnian *Sabor*.[59]

Among the younger generation Žerajić's case at first provoked bewilderment. Dragoslav Ljubibratić wrote:

I was then in the fourth class of the Sarajevo school. Up to that time we had only read about the terrorist exploits of the revolutionaries, which stirred our imagination, but we had never dreamed that something like that could happen in our own town. Josip Vrinjanin, at that time a pupil in the fifth grade of high school described the effect of Žerajić's deed among the schoolboys thus: "His act during such bleak times appeared to us something which could not be understood, something odd, and all the youths were struck by such an act of courage." This first reaction lasted only a few days. A change came very quickly. It seemed as if the eyes of the youth had suddenly been opened. Young men passing by the Emperor's Bridge, where Žerajić killed himself after the unsuccessful attempt on the life of the Governor, started to pay him homage by taking off their caps.[60]

Legends soon sprang up around Žerajić's name. It was said that his last words were: "I leave my revenge to Serbdom." Borivoje Jevtić wrote that Governor Varešanin "approached Žerajić, who was lying in blood and mud with his skull shattered by the bullet, and kicked him, saying 'You scum.' This 'You scum,'" Jevtić continued, "never died in the feelings of the Young Bosnians, hurting as the worst wound."[61] Božo Čerović asserted in his memoirs that the Governor pushed Žerajić's body and uttered words "which it is better not to repeat."[62] But Ljubibriatić denied that the Governor desecrated Žerajić's body.[63]

Although Žerajić was secretly buried, the Young Bosnians discovered his grave and decorated it. Gavrilo Princip told his mother how he stole flowers from other graves in order to put them on Žerajić's and how in the morning the police would remove them.[64] After his arrest, Princip in his statement said "that he had already in 1912 given his oath on Žerajić's grave that he would avenge him."[65] When Princip visited Serbia for the first time he brought back a handful of "the earth of free Serbia"[66] and put it on Žerajić's grave, and on the eve of June 28, Princip paid a final visit to the shrine. Ilić and Čabrinović did the same.

During the trial, on October 19, 1914, Gaćinović's pamphlet on Žerajić, "The Death of a Hero," was read out as literature which, according to the indictment, had influenced the act of the accused. The court minutes described this incident in the following way:

"The Death of a Hero" is being read.

The presiding judge: "Let only the introduction be read."

The Court clerk reading: "Despite all its enslavement, the Serbian people are showing signs of life. It is expressed by the young Serbians who are effecting a spiritual revolution. There exist many of these young men who sacrifice their own life for a common goal. They are preaching a revolution of changed, new notions, a new, bright ethic is being created, the ethic of dying for an idea, for freedom. For this enlightened idea the blood of Bogdan Žerajić was spilled on the streets of Sarajevo—"

The presiding judge, interrupting the clerk: "We should not read further. Princip, what do you have to say about this text?"

Princip, shouting: "Hail to Žerajić! Hail and nothing else!"

The presiding judge: "What, 'Hail to Žerajić'! Is that so? The session is adjourned. Let everybody wait for the decision of the court!"

The session is adjourned. The verdict of the court afterward. The presiding judge: "After its deliberation the court has decided to issue a strong warning to Princip. If he does the same thing again he will be excluded from the court, which will be continued without him."

Princip: "I accept the ruling and warning, but I retain my opinions."[67]

Of all Žerajić's friends Vladimir Gaćinović was most responsible for creating the legend of Žerajić as the first martyr and symbol of the Young Bosnians. At his insistence, Žerajić's name was kept on the list of contributors to *Zora*, and he wrote three essays on the meaning of Žerajić's sacrifice.[68]

Žerajić's death also initiated in *Zora* and other reviews to which the Young Bosnians contributed a discussion about individual terror and the right of resistance.

Neither Žerajić nor Princip can be fully understood without a detailed study of the Kosovo legend. The South Slav tradition of tyrannicide is centered around the battle at Kosovo Field (The Field of Blackbirds), where on June 28, 1389, an Ottoman army commanded by the Sultan Murad annihilated the Serbian feudal army led by Prince Lazar, while both warlords were killed. This defeat marked the end of the independence of the medieval Serbian state, and the beginning of more than four centuries of harsh rule by the Ottomans over the Serbs and other South Slavs.

Historical sources confirm the principal facts of this decisive battle, but they are less clear about the circumstances under which Sultan Murad lost his life. It is known only that on the eve of the battle a Serbian nobleman by the name of Miloš Obilić penetrated by ruse into the Turkish ranks and ripped the Sultan's stomach with his dagger. Whether this happened on the battlefield or in the Sultan's tent, and what Obilić's motives were, primary historical sources do not say or else they give contradictory evidence. Several historians, some of them in the fifteenth and sixteenth centuries, have commented on the Kosovo battle and Obilić's exploit. Two Byzantine writers, Ducas and Chalco-condylas, described Sultan Murad as a tyrant and hailed Obilić's deed as a great and heroic one.[69] Works of these two historians were translated into Latin and published in Paris; through them the events of Kosovo and Miloš's tyrannicide became widely known in Europe.[70] Knolles wrote in the seventeenth century: "The name of Miloš was worthy of eternal memory" because of his courage.[71] These writers were read by Gibbon, who commented in his *Foundation of the Ottoman Empire:* "It is a commentary on the Serbian character that this questionable act has been held up to posterity as the most saintly and heroic deed of national history."[72]

The subjugated South Slavs created an oral tradition of the Kosovo battle and Miloš's exploit. The Turks forced the Serbian aristocracy to accept their religion, and they destroyed the towns and other centers of medieval Serbian culture. A vast part of the population was either killed or taken into slavery and driven into other parts of the Ottoman Empire. The rest fled into the mountains, where the basic social forms of tribal life were rejuvenated, like the joint family (*zadruga*) and the tribe(*pleme*). Being illiterate, the vast peasant masses relied on oral folklore for their spiritual and cultural life. In this respect they were helped by the monks in a few monasteries which the Turks did not destroy or convert into mosques. As far back as the fifteenth century the first heroic folklore poems appeared describing the Kosovo battle, the death of Prince Lazar, and the deed of Miloš Obilić.

On the eve of June 28, 1389, the songs narrated, Prince Lazar gave a last dinner to his commanders, asking them to be faithful to him in tomorrow's battle:

> *When we swore our solemn oath before him,*
> *Then the Prince of Serbia adjured us,*
> *He adjured us, threatened us with curses:*
> *"He who is a Serb, with Serbian forebears,*
> *And of Serbian blood and Serbian nurture,*
> *And comes not to battle at Kosovo,*
> *He shall ne'er be blessed with descendants,*
> *With descendants, either male or female,*
> *And beneath his hand shall nothing flourish,*
> *Neither yellow wine nor waving cornfield:*
> *Let him rot, together with his children!"*

Prince Lazar afterward toasted each commander, but when the turn came for Miloš Obilić, the Prince accused him of treachery:

> *"But if hero's prowess decides my choice,*
> *Then I drain it to Miloš the Voivode:*
> *To no other it be pledged.*

To the health of Miloš Obilić!
Thy health, O Miloš, loyal and false—
First loyal to me—and at last to me false.
Tomorrow thou wilt in battle betray me,
Wilt pass over to Murad's army.
Thy health, O Miloš, and drain the beaker:
Drink, and keep it as a gift."

Deeply offended and enraged, Miloš answered.

Up to his feet sprang Miloš Obilić,
Then to the black earth down he bowed.
"Thanks to thee, most gracious Tsar Lazar,
My heartfelt thanks to thee for thy toast;
For thy toast and for thy present;
But no thanks for such a speech!
For—else may my faith undo me—
Never unfaithful have I been,
Ne'er have I been, and ne'er shall be.
But I am resolved on the field tomorrow
For the faith of Christ to give my life.
But faithless sits at thy very knee
And drinks the wine from his silk-draped glass,
He the accursed, the traitor Branković.
On the sacred Vitus Day tomorrow
We shall see on the Field of Blackbirds,
Who is faithful and who is faithless.
But by God the Almighty I swear it—
Tomorrow I'll go to the Field of Blackbirds,
And there I shall kill the Sultan Murad,
And plant my foot upon his throat."

Folklore poems initiated the legend of Kosovo among the South Slavs. The difficult conditions of the Ottoman occupation contributed to the development of the Kosovo myth. The element of martyrdom was emphasized. Miloš Obilić became the incarnation of the cult of heroic self-sacrifice. The battle of 1389 was described as the most vital event in the history of the people. The conflict between South Slavs and Turks, Christianity and Mohammedanism, the West and the East, became the main motif of folk poetry not only among the Serbs and Croats, but also among the Slovenes, who never fell under Turkish rule.

With the decline of the Ottoman empire and an increase in the uprisings of the subjugated people, the Kosovo legend took on the meaning of a powerful ideology of rebellion against foreign rule. This was particularly true in Montenegro, where a kind of semi-independent state existed through the centuries, defying the Ottoman authority. The Serbian uprising of 1804 emphasized the Kosovo legend as a symbol of the highest patriotism.

Oral heroic and lyric poetry at the turn of the eighteenth century was functional; it was the only means of spiritual communication for the illiterate peasant masses. When literary activities started again among the Serbs, some men of letters began to group together the heroic songs about Kosovo and in 1805 the first collection of them was published by Gavrilo Kovačević. Ten years later, under the influence of the Slovene scholar Jernej Kopitar, Vuk Karadžić published in Vienna a greater collection of the heroic folk songs, which he had recorded from the *guslars*, or popular ballad singers. European romantic poets, in their search for the exotic, for the heroic and mystic, found in Serbo-Croat poetry a new source of inspiration. The songs were translated into several European languages. "Between 1825 and 1827 in the *Kunst und Altertum* Goethe spoke about South Slav folklore poetry ten times. Byron highly esteemed the Bosnian poems; Walter Scott tried his hand at translating them into English, as did Pushkin into Russian and Mickiewicz into Polish."[73]

South Slav poets and writers took the folklore poetry and its philosophy as inspiration for their works. The major literary interpretation of folklore ethics was given by the Montenegrin Prince-Bishop Petar Petrović Njegoš (1793–1851). He played a powerful role among the South Slavs, particularly as the struggle against both the Ottomans and the Habsburgs was gaining momentum in the nineteenth century. In all of the three epics by Njegoš—*Mountain Wreath, The False Emperor Stefan,* and *The Ray of the Microcosm*—the symbol of heroism as one of the basic elements of folklore ethics was combined with the idea of patriotism. Njegoš was a self-educated man, who had taught himself Russian, French and German.

The problem of who influenced Njegoš most in his philosophical and literary development has been treated extensively by historians of literature. Through the Bible he inherited many ancient Hebrew motifs; he read much Milton, particularly his *Paradise Lost;* he began to translate the *Iliad* and read Pindar. But, as Anica Savić-Rebac stressed in the introduction to her English translation of *The Ray of the Microcosm,*[74] it was not through literary influence that Njegoš became a poet of themes belonging to Greek and Eastern antiquity, but through sympathy with the latent and often deeply hidden currents of his own nation. She maintained that Njegoš was the epitome of the ancient Balkans, heroic and mystic, the Balkans of fighting and *agones,* and the Balkans of Orphism and Bogomilism, complicated in the richness of its motifs and simple in its artistic expression, something of a folk poetry overladen with the wisdom of centuries, and for this very reason, less artistic than genuine folk poetry.[75] "Our patriotism," Anica Savić-Rebac said, "developed under different conditions, under the impact of the fall of our independent state and the cult of self-sacrifice; but its main feature is the Greek (and Roman) patriotic religiousness. Njegoš became the highest poet of his nation in the nineteenth century because he is the most typical singer of the heroic ideal and the glory which outlives the fallen hero, and because he conceived these elements as a high reality and the most precious of achievements."[76]

Njegoš did not find the source of right to resistance against a tyrant only in the divine, natural law; outside and above nature he sought its justification in nature, in human society as such, in the constant state of restlessness of the South Slav peasantry against the oppressive Ottoman rule. As in most of the peasant uprisings against feudal institutions, the ideology of unrest was expressed primarily in religious forms. Njegoš also followed this pattern, although he added to the element of divine determinism also the principle of voluntarism, that the outcome of a struggle depends also on the positive action of people themselves. This he stressed in the following verse:

> *What right has anyone of us to hope*
> *Except in God and in his own right arm.*

This dichotomy existed among Serb intellectuals, both ecclesiastical and lay, all through the process of emancipation from Ottoman rule. The radical Harvard graduate, John Reed, recorded in a rather drastic way in 1915, during his visit to Serbia, the opinion on that issue of the Hercegovinian bishop and poet Dučić. According to Reed, Bishop Dučić was engaged in a discussion with the Bishop of London, who said to Dučić: "You are fortunate in your people. I am told they are very devoted?"

"Yes," answered Dučić, "in Serbia we do not trust too much to God. We prayed God five centuries to free us from the Turks, and finally took guns and did it ourselves."[77]

Although one should not underestimate the outside influences on Njegoš, consideration must be given to the extent to which Njegoš's idea of permanent rebellion grew out of his own perception of similar ideas existing in the South Slav folklore philosophy.[78] Ideas of conflict and struggle were repeatedly expressed in forms such as the Neo-Manichaeanism of the medieval Bogomils in the South Slav tradition in which Njegoš was nourished. Even more important is the degree to which he was influenced by the conditions under which he and his restless Montenegrin peasant tribes were living in the first part of the nineteenth century. In Europe the atmosphere of the 1830 revolution prevailed. Nearer to Montenegro, the two Serbian uprisings of 1804 and 1815 occurred, bringing about the resurrection of the Serbian state, although not yet in a fully independent form. In nearby Bosnia and

Hercegovina there were several uprisings of the *kmets* and a mutiny of the local feudal lords against Istanbul. Montenegro itself was faced with several threats of invasion by Ottoman troops. The severed heads of Turks, hoisted on sticks, just outside Njegoš's monastery window, were a reminder for him of the cruel times through which he had been living.

Within Montenegro itself there was no peace either; its clans were not only attacking other clans under Ottoman sovereignty, stealing their cattle and sheep, but also fighting among themselves for the same reason. In Njegoš's time *Krvna osveta*, the blood feud, plagued Montenegro, and he had to use the harshest means to stop it and at the same time to put all the clans under his own authority and jurisdiction in a modern state. It seems to me that these turbulent times and conditions, and particularly the peasant restlessness and the spirit of rebellion shaped Njegoš's idea of permanent revolution; readings of Pindar, Heraclitus, Bruno and others only confirmed his own deeply felt feelings of the changeability of the world around him.

Njegoš's treatment of self-sacrifice should be compared with the *Kiddush ha-Shem*, the classical conception of martyrdom in Judaism— "that everything within man's power should be done to glorify the name of God before the world."[79] The South Slav heroic folklore poetry treated the defeat of Kosovo as an act of martyrdom. Prince Lazar chose the "kingdom of heaven" against the "kingdom of earth" and gave his life. What the West Wall of the destroyed holy temple Beth Hamikdash in Jerusalem became for the Jews, Kosovo became for the South Slavs in their folk poetry. Njegoš laments in the front of the Serbian Wailing Wall:

> *O Kosovo, thou Field of ever tragic name*
> *No heavier doom had Sodom in her flame!*
>
> *Our hope it was all buried long ago*
> *In one great grave on Kosovo's broad field.*
>
> *Except by way of death was never resurrection . . .*

As in Judaic conceptions of martyrdom, those of Njegoš contain both a religious and a national element. A martyr sacrifices his life both to glorify God and to help his people. But there are marked differences between the two. *Kiddush ha-Shem* contained the idea of nonviolent resistance—"Every Israelite is enjoined to surrender his life rather than by public transgression of the Law to desecrate the name of God"[80]— while Njegoš, like the Maccabeans, preached a fight to the very end against the superior forces and for the martyrdom of a warrior for the defense of both one's religion and one's people.

Living at the time when the South Slav struggle for liberation was emerging, Njegoš's saw in its final victory the realization of the goals of the whole nation. The Kosovo martyrdom had a new, more optimistic character; it became an anticipation of the future. The tragic element in the folk poetry became the most powerful incentive for the liberation of the South Slavs.

One should also assess Njegoš's influence in the nineteenth century in the light of the social psychology of the South Slav peasantry, particularly of those living in the highlands of the Dinaric Mountains (Montenegro, Hercegovina, Bosnia, Lika, and Kordun). Professor Jovan Cvijić spent several decades studying the social psychology and traditions of the Slavs in the Dinaric Highlands, as well as in the other parts of the Balkans. He was helped in his studies by a great number of assistants, who lived and worked in the villages. Cvijić based his theories principally on the influence of social conditions on the formation of personality. He was led to the conclusion that in the Dinaric Highlands and the surrounding regions a special type of personality was shaped, arising from the unique combination of geographical conditions, techniques of economic production, and traditions. Its cradle was the *zadruga*, which had survived from medieval days, through the period of Turkish rule, into modern times. The Turks were not able to impose as firm a feudal system and administrative control in the highlands as that which they imposed in the valleys, through which important communications passed, and this fact was an additional reason for specific traits in the social psychology of the Dinaric Slavs. Being mainly shepherds, they had much time for lesiure, brooding about the world and man's fate; their creative imagination was markedly developed. Among these men, feelings of honor, a desire for heroic deeds and a readiness for martyrdom were highly esteemed; in the last centuries of Turkish rule the general condition of the population deteriorated and this tended to strengthen these character traits among the Dinaric Slavs.[81]

Professor Cvijić emphasized the negative elements in the social psychology of the Dinaric Slavs. The shepherd's way of life was responsible for laziness and various other features, such as egotism, obsessional egocentricity, unlimited ambition, and pretentiousness. They were, according to his studies, particularly expressed in the so-called Violent Dinaric Type, which often feels underestimated, not understood by society, and persecuted by it; in some cases the delirium of greatness and the complex of persecution appear side by side. Professor Cvijić believed that the positive characteristics of the violent type were derived from the same dispositions as the negative ones: both show a marked concentration of attention, will and activity. They can be revolutionary in the realm of spiritual life, able to provoke events which could bring great practical consequences, often positive ones. They are conscious of the general trend of evolution and produce adequate channels for the ideas and movements which engulf masses. They are people extremely sensitive to injustice, they rebel against it, sweeping along with them the whole of the society in which they live, in which case they become the source of the greatest and noblest trends of social life.

Cvijić classified many a leader of the uprisings against the Turks as belonging to this psychological type, as well as *hajduci* and *uskoci*, individuals who took justice into their own hands, attacking the feudal lords and applying a kind of agrarian terrorism. All these types of men showed features of unselfishness and magnanimity and were ready for personal sacrifice. They could elevate themselves, forgetting their bodies, becoming purified and almost solely spiritual beings; they would subordinate their personal needs to the service of an idea or a great task in front of them. The national idea could become their deep faith and passion; national pride and the urge for national liberation with the use of force became their main characteristics. But, because of their extreme sensitiveness and misanthropy, the Violent Type could often become a destructive element in their environment and by their sudden arbitrary decisions could compromise the best cause which they had so well initiated. In addition, people in these regions were inclined toward Messianism and mysticism and had "an infinite capacity for enduring hardships of all kinds." Some of them were "as just as God, but others can hate with a consuming passion and a violence that reaches a white heat." It was the latter who were "the chief bearers of the Dinaric war cry of 'holy vengeance.' "[82]

Even Njegoš recognized that in the character of his idol Miloš Obilić there existed some of these traits of the Dinaric Violent Type. One of the Turks in the *Mountain Wreath* complains about Miloš Obilić: "Miloš is pushing men in a kind of unreasonability in a drunkenness without limits."

The theories of Cvijić have been criticized from several angles: that he inclined too much to geographical materialism; that the amount of data collected was not sufficient for scholarly deductions; and that the conclusions were too general.[83] But his Dinaric type theory is not derived from anthropological or racial grounds; it is rather a sociological and sociopsychological phenomenon.[84]

The problem of the role of heroic folklore poetry and Njegoš's work in the formation of the ideology of the South Slav peasantry has been discussed extensively among Yugoslav historians and political theoreticians. No doubt there existed several interpretations of folk poetry and Njegoš: the peasant one, the radical one, and the one formulated by the intellectual leaders of the pan-Serb movement. The last one was very precisely formulated by Bishop Nikolaj Velimirović in his essay on Njegoš in 1911, on the very eve of the Balkan War, when Serbia, Bulgaria, Greece and Montenegro finally pushed the Turks out of Europe. In Belgrade among the pan-Serbs the idea was growing that the Serbs should rule over the other South Slavs who up to that time had lived under Ottoman or Habsburg rule. Serbian supremacy over the Macedonians was justified on the basis of the "higher racial qualities" of the Serbs, which were inherited by them in accordance with a higher, divine law. Bishop Nikolaj Velimirović interpreted Njegoš's philosophy as if the Serbs and Montenegrins were predestined by Heaven for a special mission among the South Slavs; Miloš Obilić became a kind of deity.[85]

The radical thinkers gave quite an opposite interpretation to Njegoš's ideas. Svetozar Marković, a die-hard enemy of the pan-Serbs, when speaking about the role of the poet and intellectual in South Slav society, stressed that they have the quality of "feeling deeply all the sufferings of people and realizing them in an artistic form."[86] Marković wrote that "they are the real poets, they are the awakened part of the people, they are the people's consciousness of themselves and their sufferings. This awakened consciousness becomes the ray of light which enlightens the uphill road of a people's liberation. Among these poets were those who initiated heroic folklore poems; among them was the Montenegrin poet Njegoš."[87] In the present time Radovan Zogović in his essay on Njegoš has repeated this opinion of Marković, but Milovan Djilas has challenged him for exaggerating Njegoš's role to the point of ascribing a greater role to Njegoš than to Karl Marx in the revolutionary activities of the Yugoslavs in the twentieth century.[88]

One could argue about the merits of these ideological interpretations of Njegoš and folk ethics, but among the peasant masses it has been a fact of life. Despite the spread of modernization and the increase of the urban population, the bulk of the South Slavs have lived in villages, fostering the oral tradition of the Kosovo legend. It is interesting to compare eyewitness accounts from the middle of the nineteenth century up to the twentieth century on the extent to which folk ethics functioned among the South Slavs as the main means of spiritual communication among the people who were still 90 per cent illiterate. Roaming through the South Slav provinces in the 1870's, Arthur Evans recorded that "the memory of Kosovo, one of the greatest battles of the world, decisive even in its indecisiveness, remained alive up to contemporary times," as the philosophy of resistance among the *kmets* against foreign oppression.[89] In one of his articles for the *Manchester Guardian*, Evans wrote:

There is not a name in that heroic muster roll which is not a household word wherever the Serbian tongue is spoken. Epic lays of the fatal days of Kosovo are still sung every day to throngs of peasant listeners by minstrels of the people, whose rhapsodies, set to the dolorous strains of the *gusla*, resound in a great national dirge along the willowed banks of Sava and

Danube, through the beechwood glens of Bosnia, the dark recesses of the
Balkan, the mountain strongholds of the Czernagora, till, far away across the
Illyrian desert, they find an echo in the caverned waste of rock that frowns
above the blue waters of the Adriatic. The battle of Kosovo has grown on
the imagination of oppressed peoples who only realized its full significance
long afterwards. Tragic and romantic as were the actual incidents of that
great contest, they stand out against the disastrous twilight that succeeded, in
fantastic and supernatural relief, lit up by the lurid conflagrations of after
ravages. . . .[90]

The situation was the same in the first decade of the twentieth century, as the Austrian statesman Baernreither reported from Bosnia and
Hercegovina, where he had been sent by the Archduke Franz Ferdinand to explore conditions: "In the country there are minstrels with
their *guslas*, putting pictures of the glories of the Serbian past into
folks' heads."[91]

The Balkan Wars and the liberation of Kosovo Field invigorated the
Kosovo myth even more among the South Slavs. Observing the Serbian
Army at that time, Cvijić witnessed among officers and soldiers "a deep
and ethical feeling . . . for self-sacrifice without limits, to the point of
destruction of their own life, as Prince Lazar, Miloš Obilić and Saint
Sava did . . . I knew many of these officers and soldiers who asked to
be told what was the most useful way to die, because they were determined to die for truth and justice; they looked like mentally
unbalanced people to those who did not know the trait of our people
for self-sacrifice, an inheritance from many generations back."[92]

No doubt in the social psychology of the South Slavs there have
existed these elements of the mentality of persecuted groups, of martyrdom for a higher cause, as in the history of the Jews, the Irish and the
Poles. This irrational motive can become a reality in the process of
great political strife. A similar phenomenon was observed in the thinking and action of Padraic Pearse, a member of the Irish Republican
Brotherhood and an outstanding member of the Irish Volunteers, who
distinguished himself in the Dublin uprising in 1916. He urged the necessity of an uprising against all odds and against all military reasoning
in order to emphasize the importance of self-sacrifice for the cause of
Ireland. This irrational attitude produced a rational result in the fact
that only a few years after Pearse's execution, Ireland secured Home
Rule.

Many other observers too of the South Slavs' life in the Pre–World
War I years—for instance John Reed—were much puzzled by this survival of the Kosovo myth among the Serbs.[93]

The decision of the Archduke Franz Ferdinand to visit Sarajevo on
the very anniversary of the Kosovo battle, on June 28, 1914, was an
additional factor which stirred Princip, who knew Njegoš's *Mountain*

Wreath by heart. Vaso Čubrilović, at that time a boy of sixteen, described to Albertini the meaning of the Kosovo legend for the Bosnian rebels:

"The Serbs carry on a hero cult, and today with the name of Miloš Obilić they bracket that of Gavrilo Princip; the former stands for Serbian heroism in the tragedy of the Kosovo Field, the latter for Serbian heroism in the final liberation."[94]

CHAPTER XII

YOUNG BOSNIANS
IN ACTION

*Today Jukić made an attempt on Cuvaj's life.
How splendid it is when the secret threads of
conspiracy and revolt are drawing together!
How happy I am to get this presage of the days
of great works to come! Long live those who
are dying on the pavements, expressing so well
our common misfortune. Long live those who
secretly, with a few words, are scheming new
rebellions. But unfortunately, I am not one of
them. . . .*

—Ivo ANDRIĆ, in his diary,
June 8, 1912

PRINCIP AND HIS FELLOWS did not choose the Archduke Franz Ferdinand as the only target of their conspiracy; they were ready to kill any
Habsburg, as a protest against the conditions under which their country lived. They had plotted against the Emperor Franz Josef, his ministers Burian and Bilinski, and against all the Bosnian governors. Before
the Archduke Franz Ferdinand decided to visit Bosnia and Hercegovina, the Young Bosnians were involved in a dozen plots undertaken
either alone or in collaboration with secret societies among other South
Slavs in Dalmatia, Croatia and Serbia.

In evaluating the surviving records of this activity, one has to be
aware that the controversy over responsibility for the First World
War as well as internal political conflicts among the South Slavs have

affected the objectivity of the documentation. Also, some partisans of Young Bosnia in their description of the events failed to distinguish between mere talk about the plots and their actual execution.

The first big conspiracy involved Luka Jukić, a Croat student from Bosnia who tried to assassinate the Ban, the Governor of Croatia and the Royal Commissioner in Zagreb, Count Slavko Cuvaj, on June 8, 1912. In this plot students from Dalmatia and Zagreb, Young Bosnians, and the secret societies of Serbia were all involved. The motives for Jukić's attempt grew out of the general political situation in Croatia. At the elections in December 1911, the government parties in Croatia, backed by Budapest, were routed, and a Croat-Serb coalition won an absolute majority of seats in the Croat *Sabor*. But they were not allowed to form a new government. Count Cuvaj was nominated on January 21, 1912, as the Ban of Croatia, with instructions to govern with a firm hand; he ordered the adjournment of the *Sabor* and introduced an anticonstitutional regime, prohibiting all political gatherings. The Croat-Serb coalition reacted meekly to this violation of their political rights. This caused dissatisfaction among the young Croats, who wanted more energetic action. A meeting of protest was organized in front of the University of Zagreb on January 31. The police banned the meeting, and the students transferred it to the University Hall. In order to break it up, the police were instructed to charge with sabers drawn, and several students were seriously wounded. Nevertheless, the students beat off all attacks and barricaded themselves for thirty-six hours in the University Hall. At the same time, there were more demonstrations and fights with the police in several districts of the city; the students, reinforced by many workers, stoned the police. A black flag was hoisted at the university.

As a sign of solidarity the youth in many towns of Croatia, Dalmatia, Bosnia and Hercegovina and Slovenia staged street demonstrations, fighting the police and army units. The South Slav university students in Vienna held protest meetings against "the lawless system of terror in Croatia." Police dispersed the demonstrators, and several of them were arrested. At Graz University three hundred Croat, Serb and Slovene youths gathered on February 7 and passed a resolution against the methods of rule of Governor Cuvaj in Croatia.[1] The most violent demonstration took place in Sarajevo on February 18, when many students were injured, one of them seriously. This provoked a new chain of protests throughout Croatia. The police in Sušak, a suburb of Rijeka, banned the demonstrations, but the pupils of the local high school on March 3 proclaimed a protest strike, refusing to attend classes. This initiative was accepted by youth in other towns. On March 12 in Zagreb alone from five to six thousand pupils in secondary schools were on strike.[2] By March 15 the strike became general, both Croat and Serb youth participating in it, and the government was obliged to issue an order closing all schools indefinitely. At the news of the events in Croatia, academic youth in Belgrade organized a meeting on March 17, attended by five thousand people. One of the speakers was the Croat symbolist poet Tin Ujević, who said: "I greet you, my dear brothers, from free Serbia. I am deeply moved, seeing that our pain resounds in your hearts. We in Croatia have no greater and more generous encouragement than to know that you and your army are behind us."[3]

In Croatia the authorities tried to break up the demonstrations by all means at their disposal. The government press in Croatia made several appeals to schoolboys' parents to forbid their children to take part in political demonstrations. Police issued special orders that all house doors were to be closed after 7 P.M., and youths under eighteen were banned from the streets after this hour. A teacher, at the request of the authorities, wrote a pamphlet called "The Pupils' Strike," attacking the schoolboys for their preoccupation with politics.

The leadership of the schoolboys in Zagreb decided to answer these charges, and a special committee was formed to state the views of the students in a pamphlet.[4] It was composed predominantly of high-school pupils, headed by August Cesarec, a high-school senior, who wrote the pamphlet. Luka Jukić added a short preface, and the pamphlet was distributed all through the South Slav lands.

The pamphlet, called "Schoolboys' Movement," stated the two main reasons for the general strike of schoolboys of Croatia: the political situation in the country and the "outdated educational system in schools and the reactionary disciplinary methods applied against the pupils."[5] In the preface Jukić stressed the political motive:

The youngest generation of the Croat-Serb people has already been carefully watching for some time what goes on in Croatia under the pretext of enforcement of the law. Our country is being exploited, our people are driven from their own homes. If the voice of resistance is raised, it is suppressed at once by foreign brute force. Owing to the fact that we live in the century of enlightenment, we do not wish to degenerate. We rose up against our oppressors in order to convince them that they have not succeeded nor will they succeed with their method of occupation. The struggle is in the hands of the youngest fighters for liberty.[6]

Cesarec tried to explain why the schoolboys' strike took place:

We, Croats and Serbs, are unlucky people. Although we have enough means and strength we do not know how to organize ourselves in defense against foreign rule. That is the reason why our people is not yet free. This lack of freedom is the first reason for this youth movement. Young people—like youth in every country if they come from the ranks of the people—are the carriers of energy and the natural right of resistance, feeling all crimes ap-

plied to all sections of the population as if they were their own. Our comrades rose and left the schools, not out of a wish to evade classes, but in order
to fight as part of our people and for our people . . . Zagreb University was
closed and sprinkled with blood; the streets of Zagreb went through a sad
day when the authorities unleashed the beasts of the police, who fatally
wounded Šahinagić, provoked a revolt in the whole of Bosnia and Hercegovina; the armed gendarmes broke into the schools (Sušak, Sarajevo); the
individuals were arrested, although the whole people was united against
tyranny. And all this happened because people asked for their own rights.[7]

Among the members of the South Slav secret societies the groups
which preached individual terrorism got the upper hand. This mental
climate was described in the Jukić-Cesarec pamphlet which ended
with these threatening words: "Any terror against our comrades we
shall accept as terror against the whole of our society. We shall treat it
as if it were a bomb thrown amongst us, and our answer to such a bomb
attack sponsored by the government will be an explosion which will
destroy this bomb and its owner. Sooner or later we must win. It does
not matter how much one tries to constrain this. It will burst forth to
tear to pieces the bearer of evil. We do not threaten, we do not warn
anyone, we merely promise what they are going to get. . . ."[8]

Besides the group in Zagreb, the Dalmatians, as materials from the
Habsburg archives reveal, were particularly given to political assassination. Their leader Vladimir Čerina, editing his apper *Val* in Zagreb, was
in constant touch with secret clubs in Dalmatia and in Croatia. Among
the youth in Zagreb, the Bosnian law student Luka Jukić was the most
ardent defender of these tactics. The Austro-Hungarian authorities
kept an eye on Jukić and knew about his beliefs. The Bosnian government had a report that Jukić had deserted from the army. He was described as "a Socialist who publicly defends his views and is a bitter
enemy of absolutism." Before he fled from the army he told a friend
that "history will remember Jukić. . . . This country is doomed
under such a government, and no salvation will come unless we find
such revolutionary spirits as exist in Russia, and organize in Bosnia a
society whose role will be to put an end to brutal absolutist rule."[9]
Another dispatch said that Jukić had been dismissed from the army
because he was mentally unbalanced.[10]

In the midst of the 1912 crisis, a Dalmatian student, Oskar Tartalja,
and Luka Jukić came to Sarajevo to organize the demonstrations against
the Habsburg authority. Lazar Djukić, one of the chief organizers of
Young Bosnian secret clubs also helped Tartalja and Jukić to plan the
demonstrations in Sarajevo. They broke out on February 18. The demonstrators publicly burned a Hungarian flag. The police reacted vigorously, and a Moslem schoolboy, Salih Šahinagić, was wounded in the
head by a rifle bullet. Seventeen demonstrators were arrested. Gavrilo

Princip, Lazar Djukić and Marko Perin, who two years later took part
in the conspiracy against the Archduke Franz Ferdinand, and several
other Serb boys were at the head of the demonstration.[11] In the scuffle
with the police Princip was wounded by a saber stroke, and his clothes
were torn.[12] The next day a general strike was proclaimed in all schools;
in it, for the first time in Bosnian history, Croats, Serbs and Moslems
took part together. "Princip went from class to class, threatening with
his knuckle-duster all the boys who wavered in coming to the new
demonstrations,"[13] one of the boys recorded in his diary. The second
demonstration took place on February 19 and was dispersed by army
units.

L. Klofač, a student in Sarajevo, described in a letter to his family the
course of the demonstrations, stressing that even some shops in the
čaršija were attacked:

There were about 1,000 young men . . . We disarmed some policemen . . .
after dispersing them we started to destroy the shops and throw out goods
on the pavements. The Hungarian primary school was damaged as well.
When we started to destroy the Hungarian bank the police returned with
two squadrons of Hungarian hussars, but again they could not do anything
against us. We pushed them back, because the workers joined us and also
some soldiers of Czech nationality.[14]

One of Princip's intimate friends, Miloš Pjanić, wrote an article for
Zora, emphasizing the most important reasons why the Young Bosnians
joined the demonstration:

The demonstration brought us together (Serbs, Croats and Moslems),
bound us together, because we are one, despite all party squabbling. We felt
the need of harmony, unification, and strong and sincere joint work against
the third and fouth enemy [Aesopian terms used because of the censorship],
who are working against the life of all of us. Among the Serbs only the
Old Radicals refused to take part in the demonstrations.[15]

Luka Jukić himself had undergone a remarkable transformation. As
late as 1906 he led demonstrations against Serbian youth, but six years
later, after the increase of oppression in Croatia and Bosnia and Hercegovina, he came to the conclusion that an understanding between the
Croats and Serbs was the only guarantee for the future of the South
Slavs.

The Sarajevo police were particularly eager to arrest Jukić but
Djukić gave him his *pelerina*, a kind of cape, to make his escape easier.
Before leaving, Jukić attended a secret meeting of the Young Bosnians,
giving his solemn oath that he would assassinate the Governor of Croatia, Čuvaj, for the terror he was using against schoolboys.[16] By this time,

the Dalmatian youth had already expressed a similar idea.

In retaliation against the demonstrators, the school authorities expelled about twenty schoolboys, most of whom were Young Bosnians. Some of them, like Ivo Kranjčević, a participant in the 1914 Sarajevo plot, went to Croatia to continue their studies, and several others went to Serbia. Among the latter was also Djulaga Bukovac, a Moslem boy who in 1914 helped Gavrilo Princip in Belgrade to procure revolvers and bombs for the Sarajevo assassination.

Kranjčević and his group were met in Zagreb by Jukić and his followers. "All our conversations," Kranjčević recorded, "were concentrated on two issues: an assassination attempt against the life of Governor Cuvaj; and, second, the preparation of a revolution against Austria."[17] One day Jukić invited the Young Bosnians to a party given by the Zagreb University students. Jukić was a kind of poet, and his poem "Zlotvor" ("Evildoer"), was publicly recited for the first time. It spoke about a tyrant surrounded by scoundrels. A fool comes into the hall and places a time bomb, blowing up the tyrant and his aides.

On April 4, the Croat constitution was suspended, and Cuvaj, under the title of Royal Commissioner, started to rule by decree. At that time the Dalmatian secret society in Split decided at a meeting to assassinate Governor Cuvaj. The members drew lots, and Ivan Alfirević, a student from Split, was chosen to go to Zagreb. Prior to this, the Dalmatians had had in mind killing the Governor of Dalmatia, Count Mario Attems, but after the suspension of the Croat constitution, they decided to shift their plotting against Governor Cuvaj in Zagreb.[18] One of the students, Anton Filipić, had a revolver, which he gave to Alfirević, and the would-be assassin left for Zagreb.[19] Simultaneously, a group of 150 Croat students of all political affiliations, including the clericals, led by two university professors, paid a visit to Belgrade. They were greeted with enthusiasm. The streets through which they went were lined with masses of people; at the university they were greeted by Jovan Skerlić, and at the Officers' Club by Colonel Apis. At the outskirts of Belgrade they witnessed a specially arranged military parade. The reception in other Serbian towns was no less enthusiastic. At Smederevo, the Croat guests danced the kolo, a folk dance, through the streets of the town. The organ of Colonel Apis's organization, Pijemont, issued two pamphlets, Gaćinović's on Žerajić and Tin Ujević's (under a pseudonym) entitled "Croatia in the Struggle for Liberty." Ujević advocated individual terrorism—"In Croatia we have to answer the system by force, rebellion and terror, as Kvaternik did."[20]

Jukić too was in Belgrade, from April 19 to April 27. Before he left for Belgrade he had said at a meeting with his friends in Zagreb, as was later revealed at his trial: "This schoolboys' movement is not enough. It is too innocent. Other means must be applied, and Cuvaj should be removed at all costs and I am prepared to do it, either with poison following Hofritter's example, or with bombs and revolvers."[21] Two Bosnian schoolboys who shared the same hotel room with Jukić remembered how he would jump out of bed in the middle of the night and start to recite his poem "Evildoer."

Oskar Tartalja wrote in his memoirs that Jukić came to Belgrade to obtain weapons for his attempt. Tartalja recorded that he introduced Jukić to Colonel Apis, the leader of Ujedinjenje ili Smrt at a dinner in the small dining room of the Moskva Hotel in Belgrade. Apis accepted Jukić's suggestion and advised him to contact Major Vojin Tankosić, the leader of the *komite* units. According to Tartalja, Tankosić gave Jukić instructions on how to use the revolver and bomb. According to some sources, members of Ujedinjenje ili Smrt were divided about whether or not to give arms to Jukić.[22] Jukić took the revolver with him, while the bombs were transported to Croatia by other men.

On his return to Zagreb, Jukić wrote a poem called "My Motto," which expressed his feelings at that time. It reads:

> *I feel sorry for my folk,*
> *For my beloved kin,*
> *I feel sorry for my beautiful*
> *Fatherland.*
> *I feel sorry for the sweet hopes*
> *Of my young days,*
> *I am sorry for my golden one*
> *All in tears;*
> *I feel sorry for myself,*
> *But I have no other choice.*
>
> . . . .
> *For freedom and people,*
> *I will sacrifice everything!*

In Zagreb, Jukić found out that the Dalmatians were also plotting against Governor Cuvaj. He met Alfirević and insisted that he should try to assassinate the Governor. But Oskar Tartalja did not like the fact that so many young people were involved in the plot, and he ordered that the bombs which were brought from Belgrade be dropped in the River Sava. Some sources indicate that Narodna Odbrana issued urgent instructions from Belgrade to stop the attempt at once.[23] Alfirević gave his revolver to Jukić anyway and took him to the park, Zrinjevac, at the outskirts of town, where he gave him lessons in shooting.[24] Jukić was angry with Tartalja for keeping the weapons from Belgrade.

It is not clear whether Vladimir Čerina favored the attempt against the Governor's life or not. According to some sources, he shared Tartalja's views and insisted that the conspiracy be stopped,[25] yet other sources, as we shall see, say that he was all for the plot.

Alfirević got instructions from Split to urge Jukić to act.[26] Jukić wavered for a time, and the Dalmatians were quite angry with him. Some younger members of the conspiracy of the Zagreb group also urged Jukić to go on with his intentions. One of the youngest conspirators, Djuka Čvijić, said to Jukić that he would shoot the Governor instead.[27] Jukić promised that he would kill the Governor on June 6, during a religious procession, but he backed out again. His argument was that he could not shoot as he was afraid of wounding innocent children in the procession.[28] A quarrel ensued between them. Another of the younger conspirators, August Cesarec, accused him of being "a coward and a braggart" and said that "only Russians are capable of executing assassinations, because they have desperate men in their ranks."[29] In his rage, Cesarec spat on Jukić, who then became so furious that he said he would abandon the whole project and go home to Bosnia.[30]

But by the following day he had changed his mind. He struck on June 8, 1912, at one o'clock in the afternoon. Count Cuvaj was driving in his car with his wife and Ivo Hervojević, a member of his government. At the corner of Mesnicka and Lisinski Streets in Zagreb, Jukić rushed at the running car and, from a distance of three feet, fired a shot at Count Cuvaj, missing him but gravely wounding Hervojević in the neck. Jukić had no more chance to shoot, because the policemen were on him. With their sabers drawn, they chased him through the streets for more than twenty minutes, and with one bullet he wounded two policemen, Petar Borščak and Antun Šušić. When Borščak, despite his neck and shoulder wound, continued the pursuit, almost hitting Jukić with his saber, the youth fired a shot at his head and killed him instantly. Jukić fled to a nearby park, Tuskanac, but other policemen were behind him. A police official by the name of Antun Fuckar tried to corner him with his walking stick, but Jukić shot at him and wounded him in the shoulder. Jukić could have fled but was apprehended several minutes later by a passerby who noticed that he was carrying a gun. Jukić also shot at him, but missed.[31]

The same night the police arrested eleven other conspirators. The French minister in Belgrade reported that the authorities in Zagreb were also informed in advance of the *attentat*. "One student [later identified as Dragutin Bublić] told his uncle, a police officer of the plot. The police with their usual inefficiency did nothing, hoping for an excuse for reprisals against the South Slavs."[32] The information was correct, however.

The report which Governor Potiorek of Bosnia received from the Commander of the 16th Corps in Dubrovnik shows how widely it had been known among the South Slav youth that Jukić was going to kill Cuvaj:

In the evening of the day Jukić committed his *attentat*, a large number of young people demonstrated in Dubrovnik, shouting *"Živio* [Long live]

Jukić." But at this time neither the District Command nor the District Commander knew anything of the *attentat*. He received the information only the next morning.[33]

Arrests were made in Dalmatia too. The commander of the local corps in Dubrovnik informed the Archduke Franz Ferdinand's *Militärkanzlei* on June 26 of the discovery of a South Slav secret society and of the arrest of three youths, Filipić, Ćurin, and Alfirević. The organization had been founded seven years before, and since August 1911 it had clearly pursued "revolutionary antistate activities."[34] The authorities seized letters and other papers which indicated that the organization was connected with radical Slav youth in Prague, Vienna, Zagreb, Belgrade and Italy. In Zagreb its center was the paper *Val*, which filled "Croat, Serbian and Dalmatian youth with revolutionary, anarchist, anticlerical tendencies." Investigations at two schools in Zadar proved that two secret societies existed: one composed of pupils with radical-progressive tendencies, and the second one Catholic nationalist. Both secret societies had taken part in the schoolboy strike in March 1912. The report further stated that after Jukić's attempted assassination the secret societies staged new demonstrations for Jukić, singing the "Marseillaise" and shouting "Hail the Revolution!" Similar demonstrations took place in Split.

In connection with Jukić, the report continued, the police had found proofs of a secret revolutionary organization of South Slav youth of Dalmatia, which planned new attempts against officials in other Slav countries in the south of the empire. The official title of the organization was Srpsko-Hrvatska Napredna Omladina, with its center in Split and four other groups in Zadar, Šibenik, Dubrovnik and Kotor. It had been organized in 1904, according to the report, and its members were composed of schoolboys, students and writers. At the home of Anton Filipić, a pupil in the eighth form of the *gimnazija* in Zadar, "100 copies of the pamphlet with the title 'Sanjin [What Should We Do? What Should We Think?]' were found with a proclamation of the creation of a South Slav republic called Yugoslavia." In the proclamation it was stated: "Our key word is revolution of the South Slav nation, revolution in theory and practice, creation of Home Rule, which we South Slavs do not have under Austria. . . . Persecution, high treason . . . all this does not matter . . . go on, you South Slavs, only with blood can we solve our national question, morally and materially armed we have to await the dawn of our nation."[35] Filipić was named as the local leader in Zadar and his group was accused of reading "revolutionary, Socialistic, anarchist and Russian literature." Among the other members was Dušan Milaš, the nephew of the Eastern Orthodox Bishop of Zadar, Dr. Nikola Milaš. In Split a certain Nani was an active member, a friend of the writer Anton Čerina, who maintained connections with Rome.

At the end of this report it was stated that according to the information of the Zagreb police, "a short time before the attempt against the Royal Commissioner, a student, named 'Ivan,' from Zadar, had been in Zagreb, had met Jukić and had said that the attempt had to be carried out immediately. 'Čerina had said so.' Ivan Alfirević was accused of being that person."[36]

This 1912 document from the Habsburg archives should no doubt carry more historical weight than the memoirs of the participants ten or fifteen years later. It clearly proves the participation of Young Dalmatians in Jukić's conspiracy.

Jukić's trial was scheduled for the beginning of August 1912. Besides him there were eleven other schoolboys accused of conspiracy: Djuka Čvijić, August Cesarec, Dragutin Bublić, Granjo Neidhardt, Kamilo Horvatin, Roman Horvat, Vladimir Badalić, Dušan Narančić, Vatroslav Dolenc, Josip Sarinić and Stjepan Galogaza. The oldest was Jukić, then twenty-five years of age, and all the others were between fifteen and eighteen. The Dalmatian student Ivan Alfirević was tried separately.

Although one of the conspirators, Dragutin Bublić, betrayed his colleagues, all the others behaved courageously at the investigation. August Cesarec wrote a letter to Čerina the very day after the attempt giving the reasons for tyrannicide in Croatia. This letter has been preserved by Cesarec's relatives. Cesarec admitted that the "act of June 8 was desperate," but he called it "something healthy, great, rebellious and permanent." He underlined the importance of drawing world attention to the plight of Croatia, saying "that the act of June 8 brought Croatia into the focus of Europe."[37] Cesarec also stressed that Jukić's act unified the efforts of the Croat and Serb revolutionary youth. "Jukić completed Žerajić's deed. The Serb bullet was echoed by a Croat one—the goal is the same. . . . In this fact of harmonious completion I found the most beautiful expression of joint wishes of our peoples. Let us create thousands of Jukićs and Žerajićes, let us cultivate them, let them extend the left hand for mutual peace, and let them shoot with the right one. . . ."[38]

At the trial Jukić appeared in the courtroom dressed in a black suit with a red rose in his buttonhole. He was as defiant as ever. When the presiding judge asked if a revolutionary organization existed in Croatia, Jukić answered: "A revolutionary organization does not yet exist, but it will be organized if conditions are not changed . . ."[39]

The fifteen-year-old Djuro Čvijić reminded the court of the classic theory of tyrannicide: "With the attempt against the life of the Governor we wanted not only to remove him personally, but also to bring an end to his office, and in such a way as to stir our people to action. Jukić told me that 'we should kill Cuvaj, because it is not a crime but a good deed when a tyrant is killed.' "[40]

The sixteen-year-old Stjepan Galogaza, a schoolboy of Serb descent, stated: "There are only ten of us here but in ten years our number is going to increase to ten thousand."[41]

Jukić was sentenced to death by hanging. Of his accomplices, Horvat was sentenced to six years, Čvijić, Cesarec, Bublić, Neidhardt, Horvatin to five years, and Sarinić to six months. When the sentence was read, Jukić shouted: "You cannot judge me, my judge is my country, Croatia."[42]

At that moment, demonstrations broke out in the courtroom. A student from the visitor's gallery yelled: "They are persecuting us today and we will do the same to them tomorrow."[43] Before the courtroom was cleared of the demonstrators a girl threw Jukić a fresh rose, and he turned back with the shout: "Down with tyranny!"

The trial and the behavior of the accused made a deep impact on all the South Slav revolutionary youth at that time. The Dalmatian secret society in Zadar, the capital of Dalmatia, published a weekly called *Naprednjak* (Progressive). It had a subtitle: "In Spite of an Unheroic Epoch." On the front page of its issue of August 14, 1912, appeared a poem entitled "L.J." (meaning Luka Jukić), with a leading text: "Hail Twelve Apostles, Glorious Thoughts of the Nazarene. Glory to you, we take off our hats and bow down to the black earth before you."

Naprednjak was banned after this poem, but other papers and reviews under the influence of secret revolutionary societies similarly praised the events in Zagreb. *Zora* in Vienna issued a special number with the pictures of Jukić and the Dalmatian student Alfirević along with their poems.[44] *Sloboda* in Split, announcing the Zagreb sentence against Jukić and his friends, published its issue with blood-red letters and a commentary which ended with the words: "Let us rejoice, because blood and jail will bring freedom."[45] The Slovene *Preporod* also put Jukić's poem "Moje Geslo (My Motto)," on its front page.[46]

This was the first case in the modern political history of Croatia wherein an assassination attempt was made and most of the official and oppositional papers declared against it; nevertheless, in Dalmatia—as a member of the Austrian parliament, Baernreither, reported—the town council of Split had to be dissolved because it had voted a gift to Jukić.[47]

Also after Jukić's trial 270 students from Prague University sent a registered letter under their full names to Count Cuvaj threatening that they would settle accounts with him forever if he did not resign at once.[48] The Archduke Franz Ferdinand's *Militärkanzlei* received several reports about demonstrations, both in Zagreb and in Vienna, at which Jukić was hailed as a national hero.

Pester Lloyd on October 27 reported a demonstration in Zagreb's National Theater. There students in the gallery shouted "Long live the Balkan union" and started to sing the Slav anthem. The whole house joined in, standing up. Police intervened, and the gallery and balcony were cleared. Six students were arrested. This caused indignation among the audience, and shouts were heard: "Down with tyrants." "Down with Cuvaj." The orchestra also had to be cleared and demonstrations continued in the streets.

The Habsburg authorities intervened energetically; most of the youth papers and reviews were banned, and many arrests were made. During the first four months of 1913 two hundred high-treason trials were held, and as many police punishments were ordered.[49]

Under the pressure of public opinion, the sentences against Jukić and his colleagues had been commuted. Jukić got life imprisonment, and the sentences of the others were reduced. Jukić remained in jail until 1918, when he was released after the fall of the Habsburg empire. He spent the rest of his life in his village in Bosnia where he died a pauper in 1929, leaving to his wife and small children only a notebook of his poems.[50]

The Habsburg authorities were afraid to stage the trial of the Dalmatian youth Ivan Alfirević either in Dalmatia or Croatia, and transferred it to Klagenfurt, in Carinthia. Yet the jury acquitted Alfirević, for lack of evidence. The Slovene *Preporod* commented on this: "Alfirević, the student from Zadar, who was accused of taking part in the plot against Cuvaj, was acquitted by the jury in Celovec [Klagenfurt]. Our congratulations to Alfirević. . . . After this hard blow, let us proceed in our work for a free Yugoslavia."[51]

The secret revolutionary youth groups did not leave the Governor of Croatia in peace, and he was guarded day and night by police. On October 31, 1912, Ivan Planinščak, a student of law, climbed a telegraph pole, just opposite the Governor's residence at the Markov Trg in Zagreb, and when Cuvaj appeared at the window, Planinščak shot at him, but missed. Planinščak afterward committed suicide, in the tradition of Bogdan Žerajić. His attempt has not yet been fully described; with him died the secret of his conspiracy.

The political situation in Croatia caused a stir among the South Slav youth not only in Austria-Hungary but also among South Slav immigrants in the United States. The South Slavs, like the Irish Fenians, plotted wherever they lived, against oppression in their native land. Some of the Croats and Serbs in the United States, particularly those under the influence of Johann Most and his followers, formed secret clubs to fight against the Habsburg authorities in the old country. Already in 1903, before the Serbian secret societies like Slovenski Jug, Ujedinjenje ili Smrt and Narodna Odbrana had been started, Viennese police were warned about the activities of Croat immigrants in America. A dispatch of June 29, 1903, from the Austro-Hungarian Embassy in Washington, gave the information that at Manchester, Massachusetts, a conspiracy had been initiated to assassinate the Ban of Croatia. A certain Benčić and a certain Grčević were named as the main plotters.[52]

In 1908, when the annexation crisis broke out, Narodna Odbrana, of

Belgrade, organized clubs in the United States as well.[53] To what extent these Narodna Odbrana clubs were linked with the older, more anarchist societies among South Slav immigrants in the United States is not clear. Another open question is: Who was behind an attempt against Governor Cuvaj undertaken by Stjepan Dojčić, a Croat worker from Kenosha, Wisconsin, who returned to Croatia to carry out his plan?

Dojčić had been born in Ludbreg, Croatia, where he learned the trade of house painter, and in 1909, as a nineteen-year-old, he emigrated to America. In Chenoa lived his sister Marija, whose husband Ivan Draganić was a locksmith in a local automobile factory. Through his brother-in-law, Dojčić was employed at this factory. Dojčić worked for cooperation among the different Croat societies and clubs which existed in Chenoa. In 1909 he formed the Croat Workers Choir and a Balkan Club with a library attached to it. On May 5, 1912, he organized a lecture in the Germania Hall in Chenoa; the speakers were the brothers Stjepan and Mirko Seljan. Dojčić greeted them in the name of the club and, according to a newspaper report in Zagreb, "in a base way violated the esteem due to His Imperial Majesty the Emperor and Apostolic King, trying to provoke the audience to hatred and contempt against His Majesty, as well as against the system of government in Croatia."[54]

In October 1912, Dojčić came to the conclusion that he should return to Croatia and kill Count Cuvaj. Together with several friends, he decided this after "the sermon of the Roman Catholic priest Krmpotić, who described the sufferings of people at home."[55] By October 20, Dojčić was in Zagreb. It was very difficult for him to approach Count Cuvaj, whose whereabouts were kept secret, particularly after Planinščak's attempt. In a Zagreb paper, Dojčić read that Madame Cuvaj had built a special winter garden at her home. The news of such squandering of money so incensed him that he wrote words cursing Cuvaj on a hospital wall. The police caught him and he was sentenced to fifteen days in jail. The police were unable to learn anything about his intentions; the revolver, which he had bought in New York, he had hidden with his brother. As soon as Dojčić was out of jail, he continued his search for Cuvaj. He went to Budapest three times in his attempts to trace him, and while there he bought a new revolver of the "bulldog" type. His search in Budapest was in vain and he proceeded to Trieste, as he had heard that Cuvaj was recuperating there. From Trieste he went to Rijeka, and returned after six months to his native town, Ludbreg.

A letter was waiting for him there, written by one of his friends in Chenoa, informing him that people in Chenoa were making jokes about him for not doing what he had promised to do.[56] In desperation, Dojčić decided to shoot somebody else. In July 1913 he went to Zagreb and on August 18, the Emperor's birthday, waited in front of the Roman Catholic Cathedral for the new Ban, Baron Ivo Skerletz, to come out of the Thanksgiving service. When he recognized the new Ban in his full-dress uniform, he shot at him, wounding him in the arm.

At his trial on September 26, in Zagreb, Dojčić defended his act. Asked by the presiding judge why he had shot at the Governor, Dojčić answered:

"To kill him. To execute a deed of justice against those who are subjugating us and trampling on all the laws."

The Presiding judge: "Are you entitled to do so?"

"According to law no, but by the voice of my soul, yes."

"You are still immature. Do you think that it is just to kill a man?"

"In this case it is. It is the general opinion in America, and behind me are five hundred thousand American Croats. I am not the last among them. We cannot make a revolution here, because the army consists of different nationalities. If the Czechs mutiny, the Habsburgs send German soldiers against them. Therefore the attempts against the lives of dignitaries is our only weapon. . . ."

"Do you not feel sorry now for your deed?"

"No. Skerletz is not dead. If he were killed, I would feel sorry for him as a man, but not as a governor."

"Did you not think that you might have killed somebody else in the entourage of the Governor?"

"Yes, if that had happened I would have killed myself at once. I never fought as a boy. I cannot look at the blood of other people, the only blood I wanted to see was that of a traitor."[57]

In his final words Stjepan Dojčić spoke again about his motives:

In America there is full freedom in political affairs. Here, in Croatia and Slavonia, we are deprived even of the right to live. Even in China today things are better. Our crippled autonomy has been taken away from us. All public posts are filled by Magyars, and we are obliged to emigrate to America. Now we have neither franchise nor the right to hold meetings. We have no freedom of the press. . . ."[58]

The prosecutor described Dojčić as a tool of a conspiracy engineered in Chenoa, Illinois. He accused "unscrupulous American newspapers which use freedom of the press in order to spread sinful ideas." His special target were Croat societies in America "which were in the lead in anti-Austrian politics, spreading the idea of unification of the South Slavs."[59]

At the very end of the trial Dojčić paid tribute to his organization in the United States, the Hrvatski Savez.[60] Again, as in Jukić's case, demonstrations broke out in court during the reading of the sentence. Dojčić was sentenced to sixteen years at hard labor. He hailed Croatia and her freedom once more, and a few youths in the gallery acknowledged his shouts. Before the gendarmes dragged him away he called to his followers: "I am convinced that after me will come others."[61]

After Dojčić's attempt against Baron Skerletz, Austro-Hungarian authorities increased their surveillance of South Slav immigrants in the United States. (At the end of the First World War, when Dojčić left jail, he stated in a letter to the Yugoslav King Alexander, that he had tried to kill Governor Skerletz after receiving permission of the leaders of the Croat immigrants in the United States.[62]) Several reports in the Archduke Franz Ferdinand's *Militärkanzlei* recorded their activity. On October 30, 1913, Trieste police informed Vienna of a conspiracy extending from Austria-Hungary to the United States. From its agents in Trieste, the police learned that "anti-Austrian and anarchist agitation among the Slavs in Chicago, especially among Serbs and Montenegrins, is steadily increasing" and that "the assassins Jukić and Dojčić, have virtually been trained for their mission by these groups. Of late, increasing agitation has been observed among the Slavs of Chicago; three months ago they gave a farewell banquet to a certain Dušan Trbuhović in the Hotel La Salle in Chicago. This was connected with an attempt which was being planned against the life of the Archduke Franz Ferdinand."[63] The Trieste police concluded that their agents' report seemed reliable. The Ministry of the Interior in Vienna circulated the report throughout Austria-Hungary. From Zagreb came the information that Trbuhović had been mixed up in a treason trial there in 1909 involving a pro-Yugoslav group of Serbs and Croats. In another report, Trbuhović was described as an anarchist. Police headquarters in Vienna, Prague, Trieste and in all German ports were alerted by instructions, concerning Trbuhović and a certain friend of his named Bornemisa.[64]

One of the reports described Trbuhović as a "pupil of Michael Pupin,"[65] the well-known professor of electromechanics at Columbia University and the head of the Organization of Americans of Serbian Descent. The Habsburg intelligence service in the United States watched Pupin's work closely, and their consul in Cleveland reported in April 1914 that the Serbian society "Srpska Slega has a membership of 9,000 headed by Michael Pupin and that his organization decided to bring an Eastern Orthodox bishop from Serbia."[66] The consul urged that the bishop should come from Austria-Hungary, because most of the Serb emigrees in the United States came from Austria-Hungary. This report was forwarded by Berchtold to the *Militärkanzlei* on May 18, 1914, with his answer, saying that he should "welcome the initiative," but before making a final decision, he needed more reports on the subject.[67] The Archduke read this document and on its margin expressed his disapproval of Berchtold's decision to ask for more details: "Then nothing will be done at all. Therefore appeal to the Ministry of Foreign Affairs on my behalf so that they really do something."[68] The morning after June 28, 1914, Professor Pupin gave a long interview to *The New York Times*, giving his explanation of the causes of the assassination, stressing particularly the difficult situation in Bosnia and Hercegovina and the persecution of the Serbs. He also said that he had been falsely accused of being behind the acts of Dojčić and Jukić.

In the meantime, the situation in Croatia and Dalmatia deteriorated. The Budapest government opened new schools in the Magyar language in Croatia. Zagreb University was denied the right to reciprocity with other universities in Austria-Hungary, and a new law was prepared forbidding the Croats to build homes on the shores of the Adriatic Littoral.

Although some of the leading members of secret groups in Dalmatia were arrested, those remaining continued to plot against the Habsburg authorities. In the autumn of 1912, an attempt had been organized against the Governor of Dalmatia, Count Mario Attems. A young barber by the name of Ante Marjanović was sent from Split to Zadar, where he was met by Ivo Svetec and other members of the secret society. Marjanović brought a letter from Vladimir Čerina. It was decided that Marjanović was to shoot at the Governor on November 23, 1912, as he was leaving the local cathedral. But on the eve of that day, Marjanović was arrested and a revolver with four bullets was found on him.[69] He refused to tell why he had come to Zadar and what his intentions were there. Marjanović was brought to trial along with Ivo Svetec and Anton Filipić, but they were released because of the lack of evidence.

The Young Dalmatians continued their conspiracies and in the summer of 1913 the Zagreb police arrested Lujo Aljinović, a student in his third year at the Teachers College in Zadar. An informer tipped off the police that Aljinović had bought a revolver and that he intended to go to Vienna to assassinate the Archduke Franz Ferdinand. When interrogated, Aljinović confirmed the story. He said that he had been a volunteer in Serbia during the first Balkan War in 1912. On his return to Zagreb, he had heard "that the Archduke and General Conrad were preparing for the occupation of Serbia and Montenegro." He at once bought a revolver and decided to go to Vienna to accomplish the assassination. The police officer asked Aljinović how he returned from Serbia and who paid the traveling expenses. Aljinović answered that "a rich Serb gave me 100 dinars," but that "for 100 dinars no one could make me sacrifice my life. Franz Ferdinand is the enemy of the unification of the South Slavs and I wished to eliminate this rubbish which is hampering our national aspiration."[70]

There is no evidence to show that Aljinović was ever brought to trial. His brother told Vojislav Bogićević that Aljinović was proclaimed insane, and as soon as he had left the jail, the family put the maverick on the first ship from Split for South America.[71]

The attempts of Luka Jukić, Planinščak, Dojčić and Aljinović had a considerable influence on the Young Bosnians, particularly on Gavrilo Princip. When Franz Ferdinand was killed there was some truth in the statement in *Pester Lloyd*'s editorial that "Jukić's attempt was just a dress rehearsal for Princip's shots."[72]

It is significant that it was after the schoolboys' demonstrations in Sarajevo in February 1912 that Gavrilo Princip first thought of assassinating a Habsburg dignitary, as he himself stated at his investigation.[73] Within the secret club he belonged to was a group which held its meetings at the home of two Moslem boys, Ibrahim Fazlinović and Sadija Nikšić in Logavina Street in Sarajevo.[74] Fazlinović declared that he was ready to make an attempt against a police officer, some other higher official, or against Governor Potiorek. At first it was decided that an attempt should be made against the Joint Minister of Finance, Bilinski, and that somebody should go to Belgrade to procure weapons. It was also decided that lots should be drawn in order to ascertain who would be the assassin, but the poet Mras, Vladeta Bilbija, Princip's cousin, and Vrinjanin declared that they would like to try their hand against Bilinski.[75] Miloš Pjanić, a member of the group, went to Belgrade but could not get weapons, because Luka Jukić was there and all interest was in him.[76]

Some held that the old Emperor Franz Josef should be killed. This idea was advanced by Djulaga Bukovac, a student of the Teachers College, who had been expelled from school after the February 1912 demonstrations. He maintained that the attempt should be made by a Moslem boy. He went to Belgrade to continue his studies, but at the end of May or the beginning of June he was back in Sarajevo, advocating an attempt against the Emperor among the Moslem members of the Young Bosnians.[77] It was decided that lots should be drawn to decide who would be the assassin but Fazlinović declared that he wanted to volunteer. His argument was that he was an orphan and there would be no one to feel bereaved by his death. Bukovac and Fazlinović left immediately afterward for Belgrade.

But the Serb members of this group were against this attempt against the old Emperor. Lazar Djukić was sent immediately to Belgrade to stop Fazlinović and Bukovac. But he could not find them. Princip, who was in Belgrade preparing for his exams, told him that the two Moslem boys had gone to southern Serbia and joined a *komite* unit in order to learn how to use arms.

In the meantime the first Balkan War had broken out and this slowed plans for an attempt against the Emperor. Only in 1916 did the Austro-Hungarian authorities hear something about this plot and open an investigation. They searched Bukovac's lodgings in Belgrade and found a postcard written by a Young Bosnian to Bukovac on May 10, 1912, on which was written: "I think that Cuvaj is doomed."[78] This is another proof that the Young Bosnians knew in advance about Luka Jukić's conspiracy against Governor Cuvaj. The investigation was stopped because Fazlinović was dead by 1916. He had been recruited in 1914 and sent to the Carpathian front, where he was killed. The Habsburg authorities also heard about this conspiracy against the Emperor from Lazar Djukić on April 29, 1916. Djukić was in jail and ill. He thought that an investigation would give him a chance to leave the jail and attend the trial. Djukić told how the plot had been planned and how he had gone to Belgrade to bring back Fazlinović.[79] After Djukić's revelations, several Young Bosnians were questioned, among them Ivo Kranjčević, but they declared that Djukić was insane and his talk was just pure fantasy.[80]

The Balkan War, in which so many of the Young Bosnians participated as volunteers, delayed conspiratorial activities against the Habsburgs for a time. But events in Bosnia and Hercegovina in the spring of 1913 soon drove the Young Bosnians who remained in Sarajevo to action. Relations between Austria-Hungary and Serbia became very tense in the spring of 1913, and there was danger of an immediate attack on Serbia. To control the Bosnian Serbs, Governor Potiorek proclaimed the imposition of *Iznimne Mjere*, a state of emergency, on May 2, 1913, in Bosnia and Hercegovina. The real initiator of this measure was the Austro-Hungarian Foreign Minister Berchtold.

Governor Potiorek used this emergency measure for a general onslaught against all Serbian public, cultural and educational societies, as well as against trade unions and Socialist organizations. The civil courts were suspended, and military courts were introduced. All newspapers from Serbia were confiscated at the Bosnian borders. The 1910 Constitution of Bosnia and Hercegovina was suspended in some of its most important points and a military rule was established.[81] Potiorek also took the administration of all schools in Bosnia and Hercegovina directly into his own hands. He ordered that the Mostar High School should be closed for one year. The leader of the Serbian opposition in the *Sabor*, Vasilj Grdjić, Žerajić's friend, shouted to General Potiorek lines from a Serbo-Croat folk-poem which cursed the tyranny of the Disdar of Udbina, a Turkish commander who plundered Christian districts:

> *Burn and destroy us, oh, Disdar of Udbina,*
> *But keep in mind that one day shall come the turn of*
> *your own Tower.*[82]

In the meantime, two of the most active members of Princip's group, Miloš Pjanić and Dragoslav Ljubibratić, were arrested for fomenting revolutionary feelings in the countryside among the *kmets*, and for organizing secret societies. The group was exposed through a tip to the police that Dragutin Mras had a revolver at his home.[83] The revolver was found, and also a list of members of the secret club. In the investigation all the leading members were questioned: Princip on February 1, Djulaga Bukovac on February 13 and Fazlinović on February 14. On April 22 and 23, the District Court in Sarajevo sentenced Pjanić to three months in jail.

In these conditions, Princip's group was paralyzed, but Danilo Ilić decided that he would make an attempt against Governor Potiorek as a protest against the extraordinary measures in Bosnia and Hercegovina. He already had a revolver and started to learn the movements of the governor, but one of his friends stole the revolver.[84] The reason was that an attempt at such a time might have compromised some of the leading members of the Serbian political parties in the *Sabor*.[85] According to another source, Ilić himself decided that the attempt against Governor Potiorek should be postponed.

A short time after this, Ilić went to Switzerland with a passport which belonged to a worker who looked like Ilić. The purpose of Ilić's journey is not clear. At the trial he testified that he had gone to Switzerland to explore the possibilities of studying pedagogy at Zurich University. Obviously this was an excuse. According to other versions he met Gaćinović in Switzerland. Ljubibratić and other writers who are inclined to exaggerate the role of Gaćinović in the Sarajevo conspiracy say that Ilić informed Gaćinović of his plans against Potiorek and of the reasons why he had changed his plans at the last moment.[86] Ljubibratić said also that Ilić returned to Sarajevo with Gaćinović's message "that the heads of some of the leading dignitaries of the Empire must fall."[87] It is not clear whether Gaćinović meant Potiorek or someone else, perhaps the Archduke. But as Mirko Maksimović recorded a conversation with him, Ilić did not say anything on his return from Switzerland about the plot against Potiorek or the Archduke, but spoke in detail about his meetings with a group of Russian Social Revolutionaries and the literature he brought back.[88] Although Ilić still adhered to the idea of individual terrorism, he started to advocate in Sarajevo the idea of first building a political party and only then instigating revolutions through political assassinations. As we shall see later, Gaćinović had the same ideas.

Ilić did not stay long in Sarajevo, because the second Balkan War broke out and he volunteered for the Serbian army. But in September 1913 he was back in Sarajevo again. The idea of an attempt against Potiorek was not discarded, as Princip confirmed to Dr. Pappenheim:

Thought first of an attempt on Potiorek. Had come from Belgrade to Sarajevo, to his brother's. Was always in company of Ilić . . . His best friend. Resolved that one of them should make an attempt on Potiorek. That was in October or November, 1913. He [Ilić] was in hospital. Ilić was a little lightheaded, spoke of pan-Slavist ideas, said that they should first create an organization. In all Bosnia and Croatia. Then, when all was ready, they should make the attempt. Therefore the plan was given up. Wanted first to study further himself, at Belgrade in a library. Thought he was not yet ripe and independent enough to be able to think about it.[89]

The idea that an attempt had to be made against some official in Bosnia and Hercegovina was tormenting Nedeljko Čabrinović as well, who in the autumn of 1913 was working in the Slovene printing plant of *Edinost* in Trieste. He had been particularly stirred by the attempt of Stjepan Dojčić to assassinate Baron Skerletz. In a letter to Borivoje Jevtić on August 31, 1913, Čabrinović complained that his suggestions for doing something had not been accepted. Čabrinović said explicitly that he had informed Jevtić some time ago that he had bought a revolver, "but you did not answer anything, while that member of the proletariat, Dojčić, demonstrates."[90]

Čabrinović's whereabouts in Trieste, his contacts in that area, and the extent to which he was connected with the local anarchist groups have not yet been explored by historians. The former chief of the printing plant in Trieste, M. Ambrozić, has explained that he donated his revolver to Čabrinović.[91] One day Ambrozić was cleaning his Browning, when Čabrinović asked if he could have it. Ambrozić said that Čabrinović did not speak of his life in Sarajevo, nor did he say that he had been banished from Sarajevo because of his activities in the printers' strike. Ambrozić recorded, however, that Čabrinović told some workers that "they will hear about something great in connection with him."[92] At the beginning of October 1913, Čabrinović left Trieste and said, on his farewell, to Ambrozić: "I am going now, but you will hear about me." Ambrozić asked him what was the meaning of these words, and Čabrinović allegedly answered: "You will see what will happen when men with red striped trousers and high caps come to Sarajevo."[93] Ambrozić concluded that Čabrinović had in mind the arrival of some generals in Sarajevo.

This part of Ambrozić's statement is of dubious historical value, because it would have been impossible for Čabrinović at that time to know about the arrival of the Archduke Franz Ferdinand in Sarajevo. The decision for the journey to Bosnia and Hercegovina was made only a few weeks before it took place. Ambrozić wrote his memoirs in 1938, twenty-five years after Čabrinović left Trieste, and this is perhaps a reason for his imprecision.

There is no other source for details about Čabrinović's life in Trieste. In the morning of June 28, 1914, Čabrinović had a picture taken with his friend Tomo Vučinović and ordered six prints to be made, asking that one should be sent to Trieste to a certain Vušin Runić.[94] A man worked once under this name at Čabrinović's father's café, and Čabrinović had met him in Trieste.[95] It seems also that Čabrinović was reading Mazzini's works in Trieste,[96] and he sent Jevtić a portrait of Carducci.

From Trieste Čabrinović stopped at Opatija near Rijeka, where he met two local South Slav revolutionaries, Dr. Ivo Orlić and the Slovene Ivo Endlicher. In his memoirs, Orlić recorded that Čabrinović asked him if he could help him to obtain a passport for Serbia.[97] Orlić took Čabrinović's workers' book and got the passport. Čabrinović told Orlić about his plans for an attempt against a Habsburg dignitary, even mentioning the Archduke Franz Ferdinand.[98] Čabrinović continued to keep in touch with Orlić from Belgrade and Sarajevo. Čabrinović sent Orlić and his wife a postcard which read:

DEAR FRIENDS,
On the eve of my death, deadly ill, I wish you and your wife all possible happiness in our new and free fatherland.[99]

Dr. Orlić was arrested after June 28, 1914, and his family destroyed this postcard.[100]

From Rijeka, Čabrinović went to Karlovac to visit his sister, Vukosava, and then continued through Zagreb to Belgrade. It seems that Čabrinović tried to obtain a passport from a certain Cedomir Sandalj, from Banja Luka. In the Lebedev papers there is a postcard which Čabrinović wrote to Sandalj in October 1913 from Karlovac. It reads:

DEAR FRIEND,
Be in good health. I am sick of waiting and with the help of some money I received from the Croat printers and Dr. Orlić I arrived in Karlovac, and tomorrow will go to Zagreb. As far as the passport is concerned do not worry. May God grant that we meet in Belgrade.[101]

According to some sources Vladimir Gaćinović and the Young Bosnians who were in Switzerland and France were also making plans for attempts on the life of Habsburg dignitaries. About Gaćinović's activities at the end of 1913 and at the very beginning of 1914 there is little authentic documentation. He wrote a letter to Špiro Soldo on July 24, 1913, saying that he was in Paris and urging that Soldo "not tell nor write anyone that I am here."[102]

After the First World War rumors appeared that in the middle of January 1914 Gaćinović held a meeting in Toulouse, France, with several Young Bosnians, at which it was decided to make preparations against both Potiorek and the Archduke. The Toulouse meeting has been treated by historians in various ways. As Sidney Fay has stated, "there is disagreement as to the details in the accounts left by his fellow conspirators."[103]

The first to write about the Toulouse meeting was Leopold Mandl, a strong defender of Berchtold's policy, on June 27 and 28, 1924, in *Neues Acht Uhr Blatt* in Vienna. The *Arbeiter Zeitung* in an article during the First World War, on February 12, 1918, written by H. Wendel had called Mandl "a paid semiofficial scribe." It is not clear where Mandl got his information about the Toulouse meeting, but it seems he was in contact with Mustafa Golubić, who was then living as a political emigree in Vienna, embittered against King Alexander and his prime minister, Nikola Pašić, for the judicial murder of Colonel Apis in Salonika in 1917.[104]

Gaćinović himself never mentioned the Toulouse meeting either in his articles or in his letters. The meeting must have taken place between January 7 and February 3, because Gaćinović was away from Switzerland at that time.[105] The meeting took place in Toulouse because Golubić, still one of the leading Young Bosnians, was enrolled in Toulouse University in the school year 1913–14.[106] Gaćinović wrote a letter to a friend on January 7, 1914, saying that he did "not yet know Golubić's address." The conclusion could be drawn that he was asking for Golubić's address.

The meeting took place at the Hotel St. Jerome, Rue St. Jerome. It is not clear how many people attended the meeting. Slijepčević recorded that besides the Young Bosnians, "a Pole was present as well, who later was killed as a volunteer in the Serbian army."[107] Also present was Mehmed Mehmedbašić, son of an impoverished Moslem feudal lord in Stolac in Hercegovina, who had learned the carpenter's trade. He had received a summons from Mustafa Golubić (they were born in the same town) to come to Toulouse. Mehmedbašić had met Gaćinović in 1912 in Belgrade, where Mehmedbašić was on an excursion with a group of Moslem youth. Mehmedbašić had a very high esteem for Golubić, who introduced him to Gaćinović.

In order to obtain financial means for his trip, Mehmedbašić granted liberation to the last two *kmets* his family owned.[108] They paid him a sum of money and became free. This money covered Mehmedbašić's trip to France and back, and Mehmedbašić sent the balance to Gaćinović, to enable him to come to Toulouse from Switzerland.

There are differences of opinion as to whom the participants of the Toulouse meeting decided to assassinate.[109] Mandl, Golubić and Miloš Bogićević have stated that the decision was that it should be directed primarily against the Archduke Franz Ferdinand, while Seton-Watson has stated that Potiorek was chosen as the main target of the attack.[110]

Mehmedbašić told his story to four people: D. Tvrdoreka, N. Trišić, L. Albertini and H. Ćurić.[111] Albertini wrote that various possibilities were discussed, among them the idea of an attempt on the life of the Archduke, "but above all, stress was laid on the importance of an attack on Potiorek for the effect that it would produce. Gaćinović thought it urgently necessary. So the others were dropped in favor of the attack on Potiorek."[112] According to Albertini, Mehmedbašić told the rest of the story:

> I was entrusted with the task of carrying out the attempt against Potiorek. A dagger was chosen as the surest weapon, especially if poisoned beforehand. Gaćinović gave me a little bottle of poison with which I was to moisten the blade of the dagger before doing the deed. From Toulouse I went to Marseilles and there embarked for Ragusa [Dubrovnik]. At Ragusa I took the train, but I noticed that gendarmes were searching the compartments for something. Fearing I was the man they wanted I threw away the dagger and poison in the lavatory. I afterward found that it was a petty thief they were after. When I reached Stolac I wrote Gaćinović and, pending his reply, did nothing more about carrying out the outrage.[113]

Trišić, a lifelong friend of Mehmedbašić, confirmed Albertini's story on this point, but he went further, including what Albertini failed to record. According to this version, Mehmedbašić found a revolver in Stolac and came to Sarajevo on March 26, when the Governor should have attended the installation of a new Moslem religious chief for Bosnia and Hercegovina.[114] Mehmedbašić met Danilo Ilić, who advised him to postpone the attempt against Potiorek, because it was already known that Franz Ferdinand would visit Sarajevo and preparations for his murder were in full swing. Mehmedbašić returned to Hercegovina, and Ilić promised that he would contact him in time.[115]

Some authors suggest that a discussion was going on in Toulouse of an attempt against the Archduke. A local paper, *La Depêche de Toulouse*, reported at the beginning of January 1914 that the Archduke might visit France in connection with the conclusion of an Austrian state loan. The conspirators at that time did not yet know that the Archduke would visit Sarajevo.

Ilić and Princip, at the time of the Toulouse meeting, were in Sarajevo. They were still thinking of an attempt against Potiorek. In November 1913 Ilić had gone to Serbia and in Užice had visited Captain Čeda Popović, a member of the Central Committee of the secret society of Colonel Apis, telling him

that the youth of Bosnia was in a ferment and something had to be done. Popović replied that the thing to do was to strengthen the revolutionary organization and await a favorable moment. Ilić seemed not to be convinced, pressing his demand and asking what Popović would think of his going to Belgrade to talk things over with Apis, whom he knew personally. Popović thought it an excellent idea and provided him with the necessary money and papers for crossing into Serbia, asking to be told by Ilić on his return what had been decided by Dimitrijević. He did not see Ilić again, because Ilić returned by another route; but it is probable that, with Apis, Ilić talked over the question of an attempt on the life of Potiorek.[116]

According to Ljubibratić, Gaćinović thought that an attempt should be made during Franz Ferdinand's intended visit to France. Since Mehmedbašić had gone in the meantime, Gaćinović wrote a letter from France to Princip inviting him to come to Switzerland to prepare for the attempt.[117] The letter was sent through Switzerland because Gaćinović did not have Princip's address with him in France.[118] Princip at once informed Ilić about Gaćinović's suggestion. They wrote together to Gaćinović that Princip would come to Switzerland, but that he would first go to Belgrade to find some more friends and weapons.[119] But this hypothesis has not been confirmed by any other source and it seems doubtful.

Recently discovered documents in the archives of the Serbian Ministry of Foreign Affairs show that the Serbian Minister to Montenegro informed his government that Mehmedbašić had fled from Hercegovina to Montenegro, and that he had stated that the conspiracy originated in Tours, France. The French Minister to Montenegro confirmed this in his report to Paris on July 23, 1914, stating that the Montenegrin Minister of Foreign Affairs had said this about Mehmedbašić. But the French Minister told the Montenegrin Minister that he did not believe Mehmedbašić's statement was true.

It is true that Princip left Sarajevo at the end of January for Belgrade, but many sources confirm that he went there to pass the exams in the high school. On his way to Belgrade he stopped in his village to see his parents. His brother paid his fare to Grahovo. Princip spent some two weeks at his parents' place. Lebedev has recorded a talk with Princip's mother Nana about his last stay in the Grahovo Valley. It was a harsh winter, the snow was as high as the house roof, and Princip was brooding, even more silent than usual. His mother remembered that he spent all the time in the company of his relative Vladeta Bilbija.[120] They left at the end of February via Dalmatia, Rijeka and Zagreb for Belgrade, where Princip registered his arrival with the police on March 13, 1914.

CHAPTER XIII

THE CONSPIRATORS
UNIFY THEIR EFFORTS

A sacred burden is this life ye bear:
Look on it, lift it, bear it solemnly,
Stand up and walk beneath it steadfastly.
Fail not for sorrow, falter not for sin,
But onward, upward, till the goal ye win.
—FRANCES ANNE KEMBLE (FANNY KEMBLE)

THE ARCHDUKE FRANZ FERDINAND'S DECISION to visit Bosnia and Hercegovina in June 1914 was based on military, political and personal considerations. Great summer maneuvers were planned in the two provinces. As Inspector General of the Armed Forces of the Empire since 1913, the Archduke was expected to attend them. It was customary for the Emperor himself to take part in such maneuvers but, because of his advanced age, he had asked the Archduke in the preceding autumn to represent him at the maneuvers which took place in Bohemia. This time the Emperor himself commanded the Archduke to represent him in Bosnia.

General Conrad, chief of the Austro-Hungarian General Staff, has left his own description of the events which led to the arrival of the Archduke at Sarajevo in 1914. During the maneuvers of 1913, Conrad had learned from the Archduke personally that he intended to go to Bosnia to attend the maneuvers of the 15th and 16th Army Corps, which were to have been directed by General Potiorek.[1] Conrad wrote further that "on whose initiative the decision for the Heir Apparent's visit originated, and who fixed the measures for it, I do not know. But that an imperial prince should at least visit Bosnia again, like Crown Prince Rudolf in earlier days, seemed only natural in the interests of the dynasty, especially when it was the heir to the throne himself who should undertake this visit."[2] Conrad also wrote that on September 29, 1913, Potiorek had come to see him:

> We discussed the possibility of an action against Serbia. Potiorek thought that we could count on the Moslems and Croats. Then he raised questions of prime importance, which had been freely discussed since 1907. Finally he told me that the Heir Apparent, the Archduke Franz Ferdinand, wanted the maneuvers of the 15th and 16th Army Corps under Potiorek's command to take place in North Bosnia in 1914. He wished to be present at these maneuvers and had said that the Duchess also desired to accompany him on this occasion.[3]

From the point of view of Austria-Hungary's foreign policy, too, it was desirable that the Archduke be present in Sarajevo—as a gesture against Serbia and her increased role in the Balkans after her victories in the 1912 and 1913 wars. An internal political reason influenced the Archduke. He had been advised that the Serbs, after their military success, were gaining the upper hand in the two provinces. The steps which General Potiorek had taken against them in 1913 had not brought significant results and had only made the Serbs more defiant. What worried Potiorek was a marked decline of support among the Croats for the policies of Vienna. This was admitted by the Archduke in his *Thronwechsel* instructions, definitely drafted just before he left for Sarajevo.[4]

Personal motives influenced the Archduke's decision as well. The question of his hurt pride was involved. Ever since his unhappy visit to Hercegovina and Dubrovnik in 1906, when he was humiliated by the populace, the Archduke had wished to return to the two provinces and be received with acclamation. The Archduke also desired to take his wife on such an official visit. Margutti wrote that the journey to Bosnia in June 1914 was an unexpectedly favorable opportunity for her to present herself as the wife of the heir, an opportunity at which she eagerly snatched: "Here at last was a chance for the Duchess of Hohenberg to step into the full limelight at her husband's side within the domains of the Emperor Franz Josef."[5] The same idea was expressed by Count Carlo Collas,[6] and a similar explanation has been given by A. J. P. Taylor.[7] Dr. Eisenmenger, however, has denied this, saying that "as a matter of fact, the opposite is true."[8] The Duchess was a dutiful wife who was afraid for the safety of her husband and wished to share his fate. Max Hohenberg has confirmed most convincingly that the main reason why his mother accompanied the Archduke was her fear for his safety.[9]

The Archduke's decision to visit Sarajevo in 1914 was, therefore, based on military, political and personal reasons. As Wegerer summarized it:

The reason for the journey was to emphasize once more that the House of Habsburg, after the change in the balance of power following the Balkan Wars, still attributed importance to the possession of Bosnia and Hercegovina. Through the Heir Apparent's visit, the Croat and Moslem population of Bosnia would be strengthened in their loyalty. Besides, this was an occasion to give to the morganatic wife of the Heir Apparent an opportunity to be received with imperial honors in Bosnia. Also the understandable wish of Governor Potiorek was to give the Archduke, in his capacity of Inspector General of the Armed Forces, a chance of convincing himself how well trained were his troops and of gaining an impression of conditions in Bosnia. Since the Emperor Franz Josef's journey in the summer of 1910, no prince had visited Bosnia. The Archduke's visit thus did not represent anything unusual.[10]

In the meantime the news of the Archduke Franz Ferdinand's visit was made public; an announcement appeared in the press in the middle of March 1914.

It stirred the Young Bosnians and other South Slav secret societies which had been planning an attempt against the Archduke's life in Vienna. Now the Archduke was coming to Bosnia and Hercegovina. Some of the Young Bosnians regarded this visit as a prelude to a war against Serbia.

Princip and Čabrinović were in Belgrade in the middle of March. Princip was preparing for his sixth-class examinations in the First Belgrade High School and at the same time was trying to find more conspirators and weapons for the assassination of the Archduke. Princip lived in Carigradska Street, at Number 23, sharing a room with other friends, for a time with Trifko Grabež. In the same flat lived other students from Bosnia and Hercegovina, Ratko Parežanin, Risto Milićević, Vladeta Bilbija and Dobrosav Jevdjević. The last-named remembered that Princip read much during these days. His favorite poets were the modernist Sima Pandurović, who described in his poetry his grief for his dead love, his helplessness and his general disgust with life, and Vladimir Vidrić, a poet of visions, cynical toward his own self-delusion in love, but at the same time a critic of the sad state of affairs in Croatia.

How hard Princip tried to reconcile his social optimism with his personal pessimism is shown by a copy of Pandurović's poems *Days and Nights*, published in 1912, in which Princip underlined the following lines in the poem "Our Today":

Even if we have not created anything ourselves,
We shall at least have put an end to the misery of our time.
Our grave will yet be the foundation
Of the new life without the flaws of today
Of the better life which at least leads somewhere,
If not to an honorable peace, then to war,
If not to happiness, then to liberty.[11]

Princip knew by heart many verses of his favorite poets. Jevdjević recorded that he often recited Nietzsche's verses:

I know whence I arrive,
Unsatisfied like the flame.
I glow and writhe.
Everything that I embrace becomes light,
Everything that I leave becomes coal,
Flame am I, surely.[12]

Princip had no contact with local students. When he received money from home, he would go to one of the two cafés, Acorn Garland and Golden Sturgeon, on one of the main Belgrade market places called the Green Wreath, not far from the house in which he lived. Princip frequented these two cafés because they were meeting places of the youth of Bosnia and Hercegovina who studied in Belgrade or were during the Balkan Wars members of the volunteer irregulars called *komite*. For the latter, life was hard. War was over, most of them were afraid to go back to their native country, and it was very difficult to find a job in Belgrade. Čabrinović too was in one of these two cafés almost every day.

Among the former *komite*, Princip had particularly close relations with two of his compatriots. The first was Djulaga Bukovac, a Moslem boy from Ljubuški in Hercegovina, who had been expelled from the Sarajevo High School after the demonstrations of February 1912 and had to continue his studies in Belgrade. Bukovac was a very active Young Bosnian. Bukovac, as we have seen, in 1912 initiated a conspiracy against the Emperor which did not materialize because the First Balkan War broke out. Bukovac joined the *komite* and was on the battlefield until the end of the Second Balkan War; he was once wounded. Bukovac was of Princip's age and they had been good friends in Sarajevo.

The second man, Djuro Šarac, from the village of Cujluk in Bosnia, was four years older than Princip and Bukovac. In 1909 he was a pupil in the sixth grade of Sarajevo High School. Of the annexation of Bosnia and Hercegovina, he said in his class: "The annexation of Bosnia and Hercegovina is sheer theft of somebody else's property." Somebody reported him, and the boy was arrested and sentenced to two months' imprisonment. When he was released he fled to Serbia to continue his schooling. He got a stipend at the Serbian Eastern Orthodox Seminary at Prizren, which at that time was under Turkish rule. Šarac graduated from the seminary with honors, but he did not wish to become a priest. The plight of the population in Prizren led him to join the *komite*. He excelled in the fighting and became the personal bodyguard of Major Vojin Tankosić, the commander of all *komite* units. Tankosić himself was of Bosnian descent (his village was near those of Princip and Šarac) and almost all of his *komite* were volunteers from Bosnia and Hercegovina. Tankosić would often test the courage of his men, both in battle and when they were resting. Once in Belgrade he ordered Mustafa Golubić and some other Hercegovinians to dive into the river Sava from the railway bridge, some forty-five feet high, "just to see whether you are going to fulfill all my orders."[13] Šarac was always at the side of Tankosić, as John Reed recorded during one of his visits to Belgrade during the Balkan Wars. But when the war was over, Šarac lost his job and spent most of his time hanging around the cafés at the Green Wreath, often telling the other Bosnian students about his exploits in the *komite* units during the war.

When and how Princip decided to take part in the Sarajevo conspiracy is very difficult to ascertain, because there has been very little authentic documentation. Only recently some documents have been found which throw more light on this issue, adding to what Princip and his fellows decided to say during their trial in Sarajevo.

The news of the Archduke Franz Ferdinand's visit to Bosnia and Hercegovina was widely reported in newspapers in Austria-Hungary and abroad. The poet Jovan Varagić read the news in Sarajevo, discussed it with other Young Bosnians and decided that their members in Belgrade should be informed about it. The news item was cut out of the paper, pasted on a piece of paper, and put in an envelope without any enclosed note. Somebody suggested that it should be sent to Nedeljko Čabrinović in Belgrade, because he had already informed his friend Borivoje Jevtić from Opatija that he was in possession of a revolver. Mihajlo Pušara, one of the Young Bosnians, took the envelope with him to his office in the City Hall where he was employed as a clerk. He typed Čabrinović's name and the address of the Golden Sturgeon café in Belgrade, and mailed the letter from Zenica, a nearby town, to evade the censorship of the Sarajevo police.

At the Sarajevo trial Čabrinović revealed that he had received this letter. Princip added that he had read about the Archduke's arrival in the Viennese newspaper *Zeit*. The letter from Sarajevo reached Čabrinović in Belgrade at the end of March. He opened it, went to his work, and forgot about its substance while working.[14] During lunch at the Acorn Garland he showed the letter to Princip, who read it but said nothing. That evening they met again in another café and Princip asked him to join him for a walk in the nearby park next to the present-day Hotel Palace in Belgrade. There they sat on a bench, and Princip invited Čabrinović to join him in assassinating Franz Ferdinand. "After a short moment's hesitation, I accepted this offer. We gave each other our word of honor, shook hands and departed."[15] This was Čabrinović's description of the moment when the decision for the assassination was made in Sarajevo. They needed a third man in the plot, and Princip suggested his roommate, Grabež. He asked him if he was willing to participate, and Grabež accepted the offer wholeheartedly.

It was decided that Princip should find the weapons, because Čabrinović had left his revolver in Opatija. Princip remembered that another Bosnian youth, a member of the *komite*, Milan Ciganović, had at his lodgings a collection of bombs which he had kept for himself when the war was over. Ciganović, six years older than Princip, had been born in a village near Grahovo. He had been a student in the Merchants School, but in 1909 had fled to Serbia, fought as a *komita* and won a gold medal for bravery, which added to his prestige among the Young Bosnians. Princip had known Ciganović from the days when he first came to Belgrade in 1912; he had even lived in the same house with Ciganović and had seen the bombs, which Ciganović kept in a wooden box. However, Bukovac and Šarac were chosen to approach Ciganović. Afterward, Čabrinović acquainted him with the decisions that he and Princip and Grabež had made. Ciganović gave an evasive answer as far as the weapons were concerned, telling him that he had first to consult a *gospodin* (gentleman).[16] Some days later Ciganović brought a definite answer to Čabrinović, telling him that they would get six bombs and four revolvers. Princip, Čabrinović and Grabež were also trained in the use of weapons; their teachers were Šarac, Ciganović and another member of the *komite*, called Milan Mojić. The name of the "gentleman" was revealed in the investigation and at the trial; he was Major Vojin Tankosić.[17]

When the trial was over, an investigation was opened on October 27, 1914, of Danilo Ilić and Nedeljko Čabrinović on the basis of an anonymous denunciation which, as was later ascertained, had been sent by Čabrinović's lawyer, Konstantin Premužić. Čabrinović was an open young man, and Premužić talked much with him. According to Premužić's denunciation, Čabrinović told him that there existed a "terrorist organization" with headquarters in Belgrade and branches in Sarajevo, Mostar, Bosanski Brod, Tuzla, then in Zagreb, Voloska, and Sušak in Croatia, and in Zadar, Split and Dubrovnik in Dalmatia. Čabrinović had given his solemn oath a year or eighteen months before, that he would take part in a conspiracy against the Archduke Franz Ferdinand and other Habsburg officials.[18] Djuro Šarac, together with Ciganović and the seminarian Radovan Kazimirović, were the leading figures, and they established contacts with Major Tankosić and other people who were also preparing an attempt against the Archduke's life. On the basis of this denunciation, Ilić was questioned on October 28, 1914, and he denied the existence of this organization:

> I told everything that I knew . . . The atmosphere in which we live, the assassination attempts in Zagreb and in the monarchy, the students' nationalist newspapers beginning with *Zora*, which was published in Prague, agitating for a revolution, revolutionary books like *Underground Russia*, the glorification of the assassins in poems—all this developed such revolutionary spirit among the students that if I needed fifteen students to take part in a plot, I would find all of them ready. . . .[19]

Čabrinović also vehemently denied that he said anything of this kind to his lawyer. After these two statements the investigation was closed.

One biographer of Gaćinović and Princip, Dr. Drago Ljubibratić, himself a Young Bosnian, discovered in 1961 in the archives of *Matica Srpska* in Novi Sad a biography of Djuro Šarac, written by his close friend Dušan Slavić in 1928 and deposited the same year in the archives with instructions that it was not to be opened during Slavić's lifetime. Although Šarac's biography is a document written some fourteen years after the event took place, it still has some elements which suggest that there may have been some truth in the anonymous denunciation of October 1914.

Dušan Slavić was himself a Hercegovinian, who at the time of the assassination owned a bookshop in Belgrade. Slavić wrote that Šarac proposed on the night of March 31 to Ciganović and another friend that an attempt be organized against the Archduke. Ciganović answered that such an attempt could not be carried out, but a few days later, when the newspapers published the news about the Archduke's visit to Sarajevo, Ciganović changed his mind. In order to carry out the conspiracy, Šarac founded in the first days of April a secret society under the name of Smrt ili Život (Death or Life).

Djuro Šarac established special rules for Smrt ili Život which had many elements of the Carbonari and of Colonel Apis's Ujedinjenje ili Smrt in its organization. The central council consisted of seven members, who called each other *duhovi* (spirits) of the Avengers of Kosovo. After a member expressed a wish to join the secret organization, he had to give an oath of allegiance with all the usual Carbonari ritual, swearing that he would not reveal the secret of the organization to anyone, neither to his father or mother, or brother or sister, or his sweetheart or anybody else, and that all the orders of the council would be carried out to the end. At the same time, each member had to write in his own hand a letter to the Council of Spirits, giving his word of honor that he would commit suicide, if need be, after the fulfillment of his tasks for Smrt ili Život.[20]

It is interesting that the Montenegrin youth organized a similar secret society in Belgrade in 1909 for the purpose of assassinating all persons in Montenegro who were against the major goals of the Montenegro People's Party. Only Montenegrins living in Belgrade could become members and its constitution explicitly stated that each member was to commit suicide to protect the secrecy of the society and its work.[21]

The rules of Smrt ili Život explicitly stated that the members could only be Serbs from Bosnia and Hercegovina, who were of honest behavior and did not drink alcohol. Djuro Šarac was the leader of the organization, and two other leading members were Dušan Slavić and Milan Ciganović.

The Council of Spirits held its first two meetings in the big park Košutnjak, a few miles outside Belgrade, at the place where in 1868, the Serbian Prince Mihailo Obrenović, who was much concerned at that time with his plans for Serbian uprisings within the Ottoman and Habsburg empires, was murdered. The Council of Spirits purposely held those meetings on the site of Prince Mihailo's assassination, in order to emphasize the element of vengeance against the Habsburgs, since there had been rumors that the assassins of the Prince had received support from Austria-Hungary. At these meetings a list of possible assassins of Franz Ferdinand was drawn up; it consisted of nineteen youths, among whom was Djordje Lakić, a shoemaker from Mostar, who had strong links with the Nihilists in Moscow. Also on the list were the names of Princip, Čabrinović, and Grabež.

Dr. Drago Ljubibratić, who at that time was a student in Belgrade and a friend of Princip's, believes that there is much that is true in Slavić's story. Dr. Ljubibratić remembers vividly that he saw Slavić several times at the cafés in Green Wreath square, with Šarac, Ciganović, Princip, and Grabež. Slavić describes in his manuscript how Čabrinović and Princip were sworn in at midnight in the cellar of a house in Kraljica Natalija Street.

The procuring of arms was one of the greatest difficulties faced by the conspirators. They said at their trial that Milan Ciganović had found them. In his story Slavić said that at first they thought of sending someone to Macedonia, where some *komite* units were still operating against Bulgarian guerrillas from across the frontier, to try to obtain a few bombs from the Bosnians among the *komite*.

This was rejected for two reasons, Slavić said. In the first place, they were afraid that the bombs might be too old and might not function properly; secondly, they feared that Serbian civil authorities might find out about the conspiracy through some of the *komite*. So it was decided that Ciganović should approach Major Vojin Tankosić personally, after asking for his word of honor that he would not reveal the plot. Besides Ciganović, Slavić went along to see the leader of the *komite* units. When Ciganović explained the purpose of his visit, Major Tankosić, according to Slavić, answered:

If a similar request came from anyone else, I would reject it outright, but I cannot do this to you. And I want to tell you why. Up to now, for similar purposes, I have given many weapons, and not only has nothing been done but even the firing of the weapons has not been heard. This time the whole plot seems serious and I am ready to give not only the weapons but myself also for this cause.

Both Ciganović and Slavić shouted with one voice: "Long live Vojveda!"[22] Tankosić then gave the first revolver, which had no trademark on it, and which he said he had received from the armament factory as a gift when he was in France as a member of the Serbian Army's commission for supervision of armaments bought in France.

The next day, Ciganović met Čabrinović and told him that the weapons were in his hands: four revolvers and six bombs. The bombs were the so-called offensive type made at the Kragujevac arsenal. The ones Princip and his friends obtained were used by *komite*. They resembled a rectangular cake of soap and had a cap on the top of the detonator. One had to snap off the cap and hit the detonator which caused the bomb to explode after approximately twelve seconds. When Princip heard that the weapons had been obtained, he immediately wrote to inform Ilić. The letter was written in code and it asked Ilić to find a few more conspirators. Just at that time Grabež had finished the eighth class of high school and returned to his home in Bosnia for a visit. Princip instructed him to see Ilić and inform him about the technicalities of the plot. Grabež soon came back bringing Ilić's answer that everything was all right.

In the meantime the conspirators in Belgrade had to solve three problems: to train themselves in the use of arms; to procure money for the trip to Bosnia; and to work out a plan of how best to cover the two hundred miles from Belgrade to Sarajevo, crossing the Austro-Hungarian frontier, while at the same time safely carrying the six bombs and four revolvers.

Ciganović, Šarac and Milan Mojić took care of the first task. According to Slavić's story, Princip satisfactorily passed the test after six days of practice in the almost empty Košutnjak park. As a target he used the trunk of an old oak tree which had the shape of a man's body. The first series of shots were fired from a standing position. At a distance of 200 meters, with ten shots he scored six hits, and from a distance of 60 meters, eight perfect hits. The second series was while running. This time at 200 meters Princip scored two hits, and from 60 meters distance, three hits.

There are several accounts of how they obtained money. According to Slavić, they organized a collection among rich Belgrade merchants of Bosnian and Hercegovinian descent, under the pretext of building a school in Hercegovina. They even made a special seal and counterfeited a request from a board of school governors in Hercegovina for the charity. Djuro Šarac visited the merchants and collected more than one thousand dinars. On the other hand, at the Sarajevo trial, the conspirators confessed that the money had been obtained on an I.O.U.

The Russian Minister Hartvig telegraphed to Petrograd after June 28, 1914, that the police in Belgrade established that Princip pawned his winter coat for eight dinars before he left for Sarajevo.[23]

During Princip's trial it was recorded that the police found in Ilić's house about one thousand Austrian crowns. Ilić claimed that this money belonged to his mother, but later Božin Simić said that Ujedinjenje ili Smrt had sent this money to Princip. It seems that Ilić spoke the truth, because according to a document in the *Nachlass* the money was found in many different places within the house and it was all in different kinds of currency: paper, gold, silver, and even some Turkish coins. This money must have been the savings of the old lady, who had been hiding it through the years in different places in her home.

As to the problem of travel to Sarajevo and the transport of the weapons, it was obvious that the conspirators had to hide themselves and their weapons not only from the Austro-Hungarian authorities but also from the civil authorities of the Kingdom of Serbia. Slavić says in his history that Major Tankosić promised at the first meeting that he would give them his help through his *kanal*, the underground route from Belgrade to Sarajevo;[24] the weapons would be sent through trusted agents to the spot the conspirators selected. They at first did not know what the word *kanal* meant; Čabrinović interpreted it in its literal sense, thinking that some underground tunnel to Bosnia and Hercegovina existed.

At last all the preparations were completed, and Princip, Čabrinović and Grabež left Belgrade on May 28, after a farewell dinner, as Slavić has reported, with the Council of Spirits. It is interesting that Princip stated at the investigation that Šarac and Mojić were the only men of those who accompanied the conspirators to get the boat for Šabac. Together with the weapons and money, all three conspirators received some cyanide, which was to be taken after the assassination of Franz Ferdinand. Princip told Ciganović that he intended to kill himself immediately after the attempt.

Before their departure Tankosić expressed a wish to meet the conspirators. Princip, Grabež and Čabrinović discussed who should go to see him. Princip was against sending Čabrinović, on the ground that he was too talkative and might make a bad impression. Princip, as the leader of the group, decided that Grabež should go. Princip himself refused to see Tankosić; even at this date he did not forgive the major's humiliating words in Prokuplje in 1912, when he rejected Princip's application to join the *komite* units because of his small build.[25]

Other sources describe Princip's behavior on the eve of his departure for Sarajevo as usual. He was much with his books, from time to time making a joke with friends. Once he was reading a paper and shouted all of a sudden: "The Russian Emperor has been killed." Looking his friends straight in the face, he added: "I am joking, I just wanted to see what kind of revolutionaries you are and how you would react."[26]

One cannot reconstruct precisely how the conspirators traveled from Belgrade to Sarajevo. They told a story at the investigation and at the trial, but several facts have to be taken into consideration. Each of them tried his best to take all the blame on himself, particularly as far as their peasant guides through Bosnia were concerned. Both Princip and Grabež said at the trial that they threatened the peasants with the use of force if they did not obey and lead them through the Bosnian forests. In addition, it was not clear whether the conspirators carried the weapons through Serbia themselves or whether somebody else brought them to the Bosnian border.[27]

According to what was revealed at the investigation and at the trial, it took eight days and nights for Princip, Grabež, and Čabrinović to reach Sarajevo, covering the most dangerous parts of the journey on foot. They left Belgrade in the morning of May 28 by boat for Šabac, a town some forty miles west of Belgrade on the river Sava. On the eve of their departure, Grabež discussed with Ciganović the route to Sarajevo. Grabež studied a map of Bosnia and marked a path which would evade all the gendarmes and police posts.[28] According to Grabež, Ciganović also told him that in case they could not carry the weapons from Tuzla to Sarajevo, they should rely on a merchant in that town by the name of Mihailo "Miško" Jovanović.[29] Princip denied that Ciganović told them this.[30] The conspirators said at the trial that they carried the weapons through Serbia with them; each had two bombs tied around his waist and in his pockets revolvers, ammunition and a bottle of cyanide.

Ciganović warned them that they should at all costs evade the Serbian gendarmes and police.[31] Before the group left Belgrade, Princip told both Grabež and Čabrinović that they should not speak a word to anyone on their way about where they were going and what they were carrying. At the end of this talk, all three gave their word of honor that they would stick to this decision.[32] To Princip's and Grabež's annoyance, Čabrinović engaged in conversation with a Serbian gendarme on the boat, but luckily for the conspirators the gendarme did not respond to the talkative Čabrinović. His partners felt that Čabrinović had no feeling for conspiratorial work.

In Šabac, Princip went to find their first contact, a captain of the Frontier Guard units, Rade Popović, who had a special intelligence assignment on the Austro-Hungarian frontier. His superior commander was Major Ljubomir Vulović, a member of the Central Committee of

Ujedinjenje ili Smrt and by virtue of his military function in direct contact with the head of the Intelligence Department of the General Staff of the Serbian Army, who happened to be Colonel Apis.

Captain Popović was not in his office; he was playing cards in the Amerika café. Princip approached and asked him to come to a corner as he wished to speak to him. The captain asked him to wait for a moment, until he finished the last game. Princip waited for a while and, when the captain came, showed him a note in a small open envelope on which there were only the two initials, M.C. The captain nodded, recognizing the initials of Milan Ciganović. He took Princip and his companions to his office. Princip explained that they wanted to cross the frontier unobserved. Captain Popović offered him a route through Klenak village, but Princip declined it. Then Popović advised him that the best place would be some forty miles southwest of Šabac, near the town of Loznica, on the river Drina, which separates Serbia and Bosnia. Popović gave them a pass and wrote a note for his colleague Captain Jovan Prvanović: "Take care of these men and take them over wherever you think is best."[33] Princip asked whether he could help them to get a reduction on the train fare from Šabac to Loznica. The captain looked at a list of names of Customs employees and wrote three names on a form. Thus Princip traveled as a Customs sergeant with his two companions.

The conspirators spent the night in a local hotel in Šabac. They hid the bombs and revolvers in a stove. The next morning they took the first train for Loznica and went to see Captain Prvanović. Princip told him that they wanted to cross the frontier in such a way that even the Serbian gendarmes should not know anything about their journey. Prvanović telephoned three different Customs posts asking for his contacts, three sergeants, to come to his office the following morning. The conspirators had a full day in front of them. They went to the Koviljača Spa nearby. But again Čabrinović ran into trouble. He met a former member of the *komite* who saw that Čabrinović was carrying bombs, and asked him where he was going. Princip only after some difficulty succeeded in stopping Čabrinović from talking, but this incident set off a quarrel among the conspirators.

In Koviljača Spa they bought several postcards. Princip wanted to cover their traces completely and wrote to his cousin Vladeta Bilbija in Belgrade that he was traveling to a monastery in order to prepare himself for an examination.[34] Čabrinović wrote a postcard to his sister Vukosava, and both Princip and Grabež added their greetings. The postcard was later found by the Austro-Hungarian police, and the conspirators were questioned about it during the trial.

Čabrinović at that stage became very sentimental and wrote another five or six postcards to various friends, both male and female, in Sarajevo, Trieste and other cities of the Habsburg empire in which he had worked. Seeing the pure green hills of his beloved Bosnia rising just over the river Drina, Čabrinović wanted some outlet for his feelings, and on one postcard he wrote lines from the Serbian heroic folk poem of the days of the first Serbian uprising against the Turks in 1804, "The Rebellion against Dahijas":

> *Oh you Drina river, noble frontier,*
> *Between Bosnia and Serbia,*
> *But the time will soon arrive,*
> *And I will cross over you,*
> *And visit my dear Bosnia.*

On another one he wrote: "A good horse and a hero will always find the best way to break through." This caused a new argument with Princip and Grabež. Princip and Grabež took Čabrinović out of the café and warned him to control himself as he had promised to do. Čabrinović said at the investigation that Princip had told him: "What your enemy should not know, do not tell even to your own friend."[35] Čabrinović retorted sharply, and the conspirators quarreled again. After this incident Princip and Grabež refused to speak to Čabrinović for the rest of the day, although at the trial Princip called it "just a friendly argument which quickly disappeared."[36]

But Princip and Grabež did not take any risks, particularly on the second part of the journey through Bosnia, and decided that Čabrinović should leave them and travel to Tuzla in Bosnia on his own. Čabrinović consented, although he was much hurt. Princip said that he should cross the frontier near Zvornik, a town just a few miles south of Loznica, with Grabež's school registration card. At that time a convention existed between Austria-Hungary and Serbia that a passport was not necessary for crossing the frontier; any kind of identification card was sufficient. Besides, Čabrinović and Grabež looked very much alike and were almost the same age. Before Čabrinović left them, Princip asked him to leave his bombs behind. He and Grabež intended to take them with the other weapons by the secret way over the frontier to Tuzla.

Captain Prvanović was informed by the Customs sergeants that the safest way to cross the frontier was at Sergeant Rade Grbić's sector. When the conspirators went to the captain's office at noon on May 30, Grbić, a giant of a man with a big red nose, took care of them. On their way to his post, they stopped to rest in a café. The schoolboys marched with difficulty, as each of them now had three bombs around his waist and a revolver in his pocket. Being in a separate room with the sergeant, they removed the weapons in order to breathe more easily. They spent the rest of the day with the sergeant at his post in the country. Princip, thinking he had not had enough practice, tried his revolver and shot a hawk on a tree. They spent the night of May 30 at Grbić's post.

In the meantime, Sergeant Grbić was arranging further contacts. In the middle of the swift river Drina there was an island, Isakovića Ada, covered with willows, which belonged to Serbia. Sergeant Grbić's duty was not only to fight smugglers; on this island he had a post where all the intelligence reports from Bosnia arrived. To cover up this secret work, the Sergeant had permitted a peasant by the name of Milan Čula to open an illegal bar, selling *rakija*, plum brandy, much cheaper than in Bosnia. Near the island there was a ford which could be crossed with little difficulty, and many peasants from Bosnia, despite strict controls, came to the island for cheap, good drink.

Sergeant Grbić took Princip and Grabež on May 31 to Isakovića Ada. There he met a pleasant youth from Bosnia named Mićo Mićić, who worked in a bakery but preferred the lazy life of the island. Mićić was on his way to a Serbian village, where he had a girl whom he intended to take to a dance. But he had no luck that day. Sergeant Grbić ordered him to return to Bosnia and bring back a peasant, Jakov Milović, who lived in a village not far away. Milović was known as a fisherman and occasional smuggler, but at the same time he was a secret courier for Sergeant Grbić, taking messages deep into Bosnian territory. Princip and Grabež practiced their shooting most of the day, firing at a tree through the open window of the bar.

When Mićić returned with Milović, a Hercegovinian peasant in his late forties with a weather-beaten face, they still had the revolvers in their hands. Sergeant Grbić gave instructions to Milović, while Princip and Grabež prepared for the long march over the border. The sergeant also thought it wise to warn the young Mićić, who had seen the school-boys shooting their revolvers—"These young men are preparing something great. Just keep your mouth shut."[37]

Before they reached the next contact, deep in Bosnian territory, the party had to march for a full twenty-one hours with only a short rest. Their journey, which began in the night between June 1 and June 2, was hampered by a storm. Milović had to lead them through plowed fields and forests to evade the Austrian gendarmes and soldiers. Both Princip and Grabež were soaked by rain and could hardly move with their heavy load of bombs and revolvers. They asked Milović to stop at a peasant hut and see if they could find someone to help them carry the weapons. Milović had a friend in a village nearby by the name of Obren Milošević. He served them Turkish coffee, and the schoolboys asked for a bag in which to put the bombs. In the meantime, the younger peasant Mićić had disappeared, and Princip asked Milošević to come along and help them.

The next contact was Veljko Čubrilović, a teacher in Priboj village several hours' walk from Milošević's hut. The night was dark and the short cuts through the fields were very slippery. The peasants carried the weapons, Milović four revolvers and Milošević the six bombs and ammunition. The party arrived in the morning not far from

Čubrilović's village. Princip and Grabež hid in a bush while the peasants went to find the teacher. He was out riding his horse, just on the outskirts of the village, expecting Milović.

Čubrilović was a strong man with a black mustache, well known throughout the district. He told Milović and Milošević to return at once and gave them five crowns each. Princip added another word of warning to Milošević not to tell anyone what had happened that night.[38] He also gave each peasant a few crowns. Princip explained to Čubrilović that they had to continue to Tuzla and they needed a horse and wagon. Čubrilović took them to the house of Kerović, a *zadruga* headed by the old peasant Mitar. Before they started Princip and Grabež brought the bag containing the weapons. Čubrilović looked at it and asked Princip: "Please do tell me, are these weapons for the arrival of the Heir Apparent?" After a short moment, Princip answered tersely: "If you want to know, they are. We are going to Sarajevo to assassinate the Heir Apparent. Now you know about it, you have to keep it quiet."[39]

The old peasant Mitar greeted the teacher with respect; Čubrilović was the godfather of his grandchildren. He at once brought out his best plum brandy to serve the guests. Princip and Grabež, tired after so many hours of walking, lay down on the bed and fell asleep. Some hours later, half-asleep, Princip heard the teacher explaining to old Mitar and his sons what a bomb is and how one uses it. He pointed to the schoolboys, saying: "They are sacrificing their lives and therefore we have to keep their secret."[40]

Princip did not want to lower Čubrilović's prestige in front of the peasants. He got up and showed them how to throw the bomb. Old Mitar invited Princip and Grabež to take dinner with him and his eldest son. At one point Princip spoke of relations between Serbia and Bosnia: "Bosnia is a tear in the eye of Serbia." Late at night, the son of old Mitar, Jovo, and a neighbor, Cvijan Stjepanović, prepared a wagon with two horses to take the conspirators to Tuzla. When they departed one of Kerović's family said, "Brave hearts these schoolboys have. They will murder the Heir Apparent." Not long after, in an Austrian dungeon, old Mitar and his son Nedjo had to pay with their lives for the secret of this night.

The contact man in Tuzla was Miško Jovanović, a man in his late forties with a sharp nose and upturned mustache, married only six months before. Jovanović was one of the most distinguished citizens of Tuzla, the president of several Serbian clubs, a member of the Eastern Orthodox Lay Church Council, and of the Board of Directors of the Serbian Bank, a businessman and owner of the first cinema in Tuzla. His estate had an estimated value between 300,000 and 400,000 crowns.

When the peasants woke him early in the morning and placed six bombs and four revolvers on the kitchen table, he needed some time to recover. They gave him a short note from the teacher Čubrilović, informing him also that he should be in the Serbian reading room at nine o'clock to meet the two schoolboys.

Princip and Grabež had got off the wagon a few miles before Tuzla and washed their clothes in a brook, but they were still very dirty when they came into the town, in which both of them were well known, since they had studied for a year in the local high school. They bought new trousers, and before nine o'clock they went to the Serbian reading room, which was in the same house where Jovanović lived. Some school friends recognized Princip, and one of them, Božidar Tomić, shouted: "Look how Gavrilo has grown up!" Another retorted: "No, he is still small."[41]

Jovanović, still nervous from the morning's strange encounter, waited for Princip and Grabež. One of the peasants was also in the reading room, and he winked at Jovanović when the schoolboys entered. Jovanović took them to a separate room, and they asked him if he could take the weapons to Sarajevo. Jovanović wavered. Princip then asked if he could keep them until he or somebody else came to fetch them. Jovanović agreed to this and asked that in case Princip could not come, the courier should show him a box of Štefanija cigarettes. Jovanović returned home, packed the weapons in a black cardboard box, and hid it in the wide base of the dining table; this act led him a few months later to the gallows.

The third conspirator, Nedeljko Čabrinović, had arrived in Tuzla two days before Princip and Grabež, after many adventures.[42] They met in a café and proceeded the same evening by train for Sarajevo. But Čabrinović was soon in trouble again. In a café in Tuzla he met a police agent—a man from Sarajevo by the name of Ivan Vila. The agent had escorted to Tuzla prison a Young Bosnian who had been arrested in a demonstration in Mostar against an Austrian theatrical group which performed an anti-Polish play.

The detective Vila knew Čabrinović's father well and said to the boy that he had seen his father only the day before. In the conversation, the detective asked Čabrinović where he had been, and Čabrinović answered that he had been in Dalmatia and Serbia. They met again on the train to Sarajevo. This time they talked at great length about Serbia and about the arrival in Sarajevo of the Heir Apparent. Čabrinović asked the detective when the Archduke was expected to arrive in Sarajevo and the police agent answered: "On June 28."[43]

Princip and Grabež were in the same carriage, but in a different compartment. At one point the detective asked Čabrinović what was the name of the fellow with the dark eyes, energetic chin and long hair in the first carriage. Čabrinović answered calmly: "Gavrilo Princip."[44] A few months later, at the trial, Detective Vila had to go through the ordeal of describing how he had talked with Franz Ferdinand's assassins and failed to notice anything suspicious.

In the morning, Čabrinović went to Princip and told him that he had heard from Detective Vila that Franz Ferdinand would arrive in Sarajevo on June 28. Up to that moment the conspirators had not known the exact day of his visit to the Bosnian capital. Princip, Grabež and Čabrinović arrived in Sarajevo in the morning of June 4.

As Franz Ferdinand and Gavrilo Princip approached the day at the end of June when their paths were to cross, both were under great strain. The Archduke, as the eighty-year-old Emperor Franz Josef was ill again, was making last-minute changes in the detailed plans for his accession to the throne. He left Austria against the advice of many people, and despite his own forebodings about the journey. Because of his medieval upbringing, the Archduke was very superstitious. His political adviser and late foreign minister, Count Ottokar Czernin, recorded in his book *In the World War* that the Archduke told him "how a fortune teller once predicted that 'he would one day let loose a world war.' Although to a certain extent this prophecy flattered him, containing as it did the unspoken recognition that the world would have to reckon with him as a powerful factor, still he emphatically pointed out how mad such a prophecy was."[45]

Despite all forebodings and warnings, the Archduke throughout his journey demonstrated his sense of humor. He departed with the Duchess from their estate Chlumetz on June 23, leaving their children there. The couple should have traveled in Franz Ferdinand's private car, but the axles were not in order and they had to take a first-class compartment on the Vienna express. The Archduke's remark was: "Well, our journey starts with an extremely promising omen. Here our car burns and down there they will throw bombs on us."[46] The Archduke stayed in Vienna for only a very short time, just to accompany his wife to Belvedere, and then he returned to the *Sudbahnhof* to take the train for Trieste. The Duchess was supposed to go straight from Vienna to Bosnia via Budapest. The Archduke's secretary accompanied him to the station and recorded further morbid comments made by Franz Ferdinand concerning the journey. The special parlor car was ready, but this time the electric light did not function. The Archduke was sitting at the table with several candles around him as he smilingly said goodbye to his secretary: "Another premonitory sign. . . . How do you find this way of illumination? Is it not like in a grave?"[47]

The next morning, June 24, the Archduke, wearing his Admiral's uniform, arrived in Trieste, where the battleship *Viribus Unitis* waited to take him to the harbor of Metković. After a smooth twenty-four-hour passage he came to the border of Hercegovina on the morning of June 25, to be greeted by the Governor, General Potiorek. He proceeded by special train to Mostar, where he was received at 8:30 A.M. by the Lord Mayor and other local dignitaries. In the afternoon of the same day he met his wife at the Ildiže Spa, a few miles south of Sarajevo. The 15th and 16th Army Corps were ready for the maneuvers, which were to start next morning, June 26.

Historical sources on the daily life of the conspirators from the time they arrived in Sarajevo until June 28 must be treated with reserve. They themselves left few accounts except for what they stated at the investigation and the trial. As with many other clandestine, revolutionary groups, their history was written often either by members who survived the ordeal or by observers on the fringe of events. This is particularly true of the Young Bosnians. The writer Jevtić had almost a monopoly after 1918 on descriptions of Princip's life in the weeks before the Sarajevo assassination. Being a fiction writer first and only afterward an objective witness of a historical process, Jevtić did not take much care with his facts, and in addition he introduced a personal element to his description of the whole conspiracy and the character of its main participants. He was the author of accusations against Čabrinović's[48] and to a certain extent Danilo Ilić's "bad behavior" at the investigation.[49] Jevdjević went further and described Ilić as almost a traitor. Many historians, especially outside Yugoslavia, have taken these descriptions for granted. But Jevtić's own behavior was caused by a guilty conscience. He was for a time very close to Princip and other leading Young Bosnians, but as June 28 approached, he became less and less inclined to do anything.

As the recently discovered minutes of Jevtić's interrogation in Sarajevo after June 28, 1914, reveal, Jevtić tried to dissociate himself from Princip and the Young Bosnians. He said that Princip "never told him about his revolutionary ideas," that he did not know anything about the plot and that if he had known, "he would have dissuaded him, for the assassination of individuals cannot eliminate a system."[50] Jevtić also attacked Princip personally, saying that he had been in his company "because we are poets and futurists, eager to live, but Princip tried to hide behind us, and now all of us are suffering because of him."[51] Although the police found Jevtić's correspondence with Čabrinović, Gaćinović, and other Young Bosnians, the judge at the investigation ruled that there was no basis for prosecuting Jevtić.

As we shall see later, Princip himself at the investigation gave an opinion of Jevtić and the group of people around him. Surviving the war and the death of his former comrades, Jevtić became thoroughly bitter and disregarded historical facts. Jevdjević suffered even more from this same complex.

The main Jevtić thesis was that Princip was a hero and Ilić and Čabrinović were cowards, the latter close to being a traitor. After the downfall of the Habsburg empire and the formation of Yugoslavia, a kind of idolatry was built up around Princip's memory, and Jevtić contributed to it more than anybody else. Other, weaker characters joined him for various personal reasons. Bilinski's former Chef de Cabinet, Božo Čerović, in his memoirs, portrayed Princip in glorifying terms and accused Čabrinović of being a police spy.[52] The investigation judge, Leo Pfeffer, a faithful Habsburg civil servant, wanted to prove his allegiance to the new regime in 1930, when he published his book on the Sarajevo affair. As we shall see later, he falsified the minutes of the investigation in order to portray Ilić and Čabrinović according to the fashion of the day.

On the arrival of Princip, Čabrinović and Grabež at Sarajevo on June 4, each of them went his own way. Princip first saw Ilić and then went to the village of Hadžici to greet his brother and his family. In order to make his brother happy, he told him that he had passed the examinations for eighth class of high school and that he would take the matriculation examination in the autumn,[53] although this was not true. Princip was back in Sarajevo on June 6 when he attended a *selo*, a kind of public evening party, organized by Srpsko-Hrvatska Napredna Omladina, a youth organization preaching the unity of Serbs and Croats. Some money was collected at this party for Croat schools in Istria.

Princip decided to stay in Sarajevo in the house of Danilo Ilić's mother, at 3 Oprkanj Street. Although Princip himself described the street as "a safe one" and Ilić as "a quiet young man about whom no one had any suspicion," nevertheless he made a grave blunder as far as the conspiracy was concerned. The leader of the group of assassins took a room at the home of the chief technical organizer of the assassination, and—what was worse—Princip registered at the police station, filling out the form as a lodger of Stoja Ilić.[54]

Before the arrival of the first *troika*, the three men from Belgrade (Princip, Grabež and Čabrinović), Danilo Ilić had prepared a second *troika*. Its first member was Mehmed Mehmedbašić, the Moslem carpenter from Stolac who had attended the Toulouse meeting with Gaćinović in January 1914. Ilić, as we have seen, had got in touch with him in March and had told him to hold off on his plans against Governor Potiorek as preparations were already under way for an attempt against the Archduke. Mehmedbašić returned to Stolac and in the middle of May he met Ilić in Mostar. It was not clear who provided the initiative for this meeting, but Mehmedbašić accepted Ilić's invitation to come to Sarajevo and try his hand against the Archduke whenever Ilić would tell him to come.[55]

The two other members of the second *troika* Ilić recruited from the youngest generation of Young Bosnians, schoolboys between sixteen and eighteen. This group was even more radical than Princip and his fellows; they were completely oriented as Yugoslavs, preaching destruction of the Habsburg empire and cultural and political unity for the South Slavs. The main political organizer of this group was Lazar Djukić, an eighteen-year-old student in his second year of Teachers

College. These schoolboys, independently of Ilić, Gaćinović and Princip, were discussing the necessity of an attempt against Franz Ferdinand during his visit to Sarajevo.

Once Djukić raised this matter with Vaso Čubrilović, a seventeen-year-old student of the sixth class in Sarajevo High School. Čubrilović was from a well-known family in Bosanska Krajina; one of his relatives was Vaso Vidović, the leader of the uprising of 1875–78, who had attended the Congress of Berlin. Vaso's brother, the teacher Veljko Čubrilović, had helped Princip's group on their way through Bosnia. Vaso studied in the Tuzla High School, one of the strongholds of the Young Bosnians, but was expelled from school when he ostentatiously walked out on the celebrations for the Serbian patron saint, Sava, as the Habsburg anthem was being played. Afterward Vaso enrolled in the Sarajevo High School.

In the middle of May, Čubrilović said to Djukić that Ferdinand was coming and that they should ambush him. Djukić answered: "If there are men for it." And Čubrilović said: "I would do it, only I have no weapons."[56] Djukić had previously been in contact with Ilić and knew something about the conspiracy. So Djukić answered Čubrilović: "I will introduce you to a man who will give you weapons."[57] A few days later at the Appel Quay, the same street where the Archduke was killed, Čubrilović met Ilić.

Other members of Djukić's group also discussed an attempt against the Archduke. Once Čubrilović, after his contacts with Ilić, spoke about it with Cvetko Popović, a sixteen-year-old student in third year of Teachers College. It was around May 20, and Cvetko Popović expressed willingness to take part in the plot.[58] A third schoolboy, a Croat named Ivo Kranjčević, who knew about the plot, said he was ready to hide Čubrilović's arms if the need arose.

When Princip came to Sarajevo, Ilić informed him that the second *troika* was ready, but did not tell him the names of its members. At the same time, Ilić made preparations to bring weapons from Tuzla. He personally went to Tuzla on June 14, found Miško Jovanović and showed him a box of Štefanija cigarettes, as had been agreed upon with Princip. Ilić asked Jovanović to take the weapons to a railway station a few stops from Tuzla and only then to give them to him. Jovanović packed the bombs and revolvers in a black box of sugar, wrapped it in newspaper and tied it with string, and traveled to the junction of Doboj. He did not see Ilić there and left the box for a time in the waiting room of the railway station, covered with his coat, while he was looking for Ilić.[59] Ilić had not yet arrived at Doboj, and Jovanović left the box in the shop of a friend, Vuko Jakšić, a local tailor. At last Ilić turned up and Jovanović delivered the box.

Ilić also succeeded in avoiding police control in Sarajevo by getting out of the train at Alipaša Most Station, a few miles from Sarajevo.

Here he took a local train for Ilidže and got out at Mariendvor Station inside Sarajevo; the police did not watch the local trains carefully. Arriving safely, Ilić took a streetcar to the Roman Catholic cathedral and from there he carried the box with bombs and revolvers to his home. He deposited the weapons in a small wooden box under the bed in which Princip slept. It happened that on that very day, June 15, Princip registered his residence with the police.

The two weeks before June 28 were spent differently by each of the conspirators. The youngest among them, Cvetko Popović, recorded his feelings during these days:

> After I gave my word to join the plot I spent the whole night thinking and dreaming about the assassination. In the morning I was quite a different man. Convinced that I had only until June 28 to live, Vidovdan—St. Vitus Day—I looked upon everything from a new angle. I left my school books, I hardly glanced at the newspapers which up to that day I read with interest. I almost failed to react to the jokes of my friends at which the day before I would have exploded. I tried to make jokes. Only one thought tormented me: that we might not succeed and thus make fools of ourselves.[60]

On his arrival at Sarajevo, Čabrinović went first to his grandmother's house and only later in the day visited his father's home at 69 Franz Josef Street. He was afraid of how his father would receive him. When Čabrinović's father registered the arrival of his son with the police on June 4, to the question on the police form where Nedeljko had lived before, he answered: "All around the world."[61] The first encounter was not stormy and Čabrinović stayed with his parents and found work in a local printing plant, bringing his earnings home. In his free time, Čabrinović made excursions around Sarajevo. On three occasions he visited the Ilidže, where preparations were being made for the arrival of the Archduke.[62] The last time he was there, with his mother on Saturday, June 20, he was told that the baths were closed to the public, because of the Archduke's arrival. Being a talkative young man, Čabrinović spoke to the members of his father's household about his journey from Belgrade. To the servant Marija Talanga he said that he had spent seven days journeying with two friends from Belgrade to Sarajevo.[63] He told his younger sister similar things and his friend Tomo Vučinović.[64] Čabrinović's relations with Princip were still strained after the quarrel at Koviljača Spa in Serbia. They would meet occasionally on the streets, but Princip did not tell him that the weapons had arrived or that there were other conspirators in the plot.

Grabež was living in the village Pale, some fifteen miles southeast of Sarajevo. He came to Sarajevo several times, and Ilić and Princip kept him informed about the preparations. Grabež spent much time with a local teacher, a girl by the name of Leposava Lalić.

There is little authentic documentation on Princip's life in these days. He did not have enough money to cover his expenses. He had to pay Ilić's mother fourteen crowns for his bed and he also needed money for his meals. He borrowed twenty crowns from Ilić. In the last week before June 28 he found work at Prosvjeta, through its Secretary General Vasilj Grdjić. Princip's job was to copy the minutes of Prosvjeta's meetings and for that he got ten or fifteen crowns.[65] Presumably, Princip wanted to pay all his debts before June 28.[66]

In order not to be detected by the police, Princip spent most of the evenings in the company of Borivoje Jevtić and his friends, who used to meet at the Semiz wine shop in a street which had just been named for the Archduke. Jevtić was a Bohemian who liked wine, and Princip had a glass or two for the first time in his life. At the investigation Princip described this incident: "I went around in the last month in Sarajevo with fellows who liked to drink, and this was only in order not to arouse suspicion. These fellows were for the most part people incapable of a great idea."[67]

Of all the conspirators, Danilo Ilić was passing through the most complex crisis. Although the chief technical organizer of the attempt, during these fateful weeks he had started to question not only the wisdom of murdering the Archduke but also the whole idea of individual terror as the best means for political activity. Yet it was not a conflict with clear-cut issues. Ilić was not sure of his views; they were changing from day to day, and all the while he was hounded by the problem of deciding whether to go on with the plot or not. The whole matter was complicated by strong emotional factors; Ilić was a good friend and did not in any way wish to let down the other conspirators, particularly Princip, who until his last breath regarded Ilić as "his best friend."[68]

Ilić's new orientation on the question of "direct action" had begun during his trip to Switzerland in the early summer of 1913, when he met Gaćinović and some Russian Social Revolutionaries. As we have seen, Gaćinović's idea was that a political party should be formed first, which would spread among all the South Slavs, including the Bulgars, and only after this organization became firmly established should political assassinations be carried out to provoke a revolution.[69] Gaćinović continued to work toward this goal in Switzerland and even, with his friend Jovan Živanović, prepared a proclamation for the new political party.[70]

On his return to Bosnia, Ilić was hampered in his work for Gaćinović's new program by the outbreak of the Second Balkan War. He had gone to Serbia and volunteered to fight. On his return he fell ill and spent a month and a half in a hospital. About his days in Switzerland and his contacts with the Social Revolutionaries, Ilić told his good friend the priest Mirko Maksimović that he had met in Zurich a *kruzhok*, consisting of three men and two women who were without any financial means and lived for months on bread and tea; but they refused to give him any advice, when Ilić asked them for it, as to the best methods of work in his own country.[71]

Already in October and November of 1913, Ilić and Princip had had an argument over the new line the Young Bosnians were taking when they planned an attempt against Potiorek's life. To Dr. Pappenheim, Princip said about this: "Ilić was a little lightheaded; spoke of pan-Slav ideas, said that they should first form an organization. In all Bosnia and Croatia. Then, when all was ready, they should make the attempt. Therefore the plan was given up."[72]

Ilić had continued his preparations for the creation of a political party. Together with Jovo Smitran, he started to publish a weekly paper Zvono (The Bell), and an edition of political pamphlets, most of them translations of Engels, Kautsky, W. Morris, Kropotkin, Bakunin, Ramus and other writers of similar trends. The first issue of Zvono appeared on May 15 and, despite all preparations for the assassination, Ilić kept writing articles for the paper and translating materials for the political series. On the very day when he returned from Tuzla with six bombs and four revolvers, a satire by him appeared in Zvono under the headline "Oh These Poor Birds":

To the great joy of the whole people in Bosnia and Hercegovina, the Provincial government has issued an important announcement that the number of singing birds in Sarajevo has increased. For this extraordinary step forward in the cultural life of our fatherland, we must be grateful to the industrious sacrifices of the municipal authorities who have painstakingly constructed, in gardens and parks, shelters where the poor magpies and sparrows are fed in winter. And you poor, suffering people who bear on your bowed backs the whole weight of the social edifice, in vain you have waited for years for somebody to take care of you and to build proper houses with sweated tax money so that you do not have to die a miserable death in filthy hovels.

Why are we not birds too?

In the same issue Zvono published under Ilić's full name an essay on the Russian writer Leonid Andreyev. In this essay Ilić showed how profoundly he was obsessed by the question of the meaning of life in general, trying to reconcile a revolutionary goal with the philosophical question of man in time and space.

Leonid Andreyev, himself a revolutionary and one of the best Russian writers of the period, had presented this very issue in 1908 in his story The Seven Who Were Hanged, expressing the dilemma of the Russian revolutionaries after the unsuccessful revolution of 1905. This was not only a humanitarian protest against the brutality of Emperor Nicholas II and against capital punishment, but also a philosophical study of the meaning of death. His heroes, from the moment they were arrested after their attempt upon the life of a member of the government and while they are waiting for execution, do not reflect upon their deed; their minds are engaged in a strange mystical game of awaiting death.

The Seven Who Were Hanged was translated into Serbian in 1910 and the story was much read among the Young Bosnians. Danilo Ilić, a sensitive and thoughtful man, was deeply influenced by Andreyev's story. His own hard personal life and his inclination toward individual pessimism led him to find in Andreyev's study an emotional and intellectual stimulus on the very eve of June 28.

Ilić argued hour after hour with Princip about the desirability of the Archduke's assassination. It was not just a coincidence that Ilić, so deeply absorbed in his argument with Princip and in his own inner struggle, found time to write the essay on Andreyev, which amounted to a statement of his own inner controversy. The censors, obtuse as ever, never dreamed what it was about, and being unable to penetrate Ilić's Aesopian language gave their imprimatur to this public polemic between the two future chief assassins of the Heir Apparent.

Andreyev, [wrote Ilić] has made a break in his later works with his earlier literary moralism; he looks at life through an aesthetical-philosophical prism, based on certain philosophical principles. His description of man's darkest feelings places Andreyev above all other Russian writers. This deep spiritual analysis, the specific notion of life and a kind of mysticism, of fatalism, which run like a red thread through all his writings, his modern, impressionistic style—all this has contributed to the high place of Andreyev in world literature.

In his works he often treats subjects connected with political and social questions. The story *The Red Laugh* is an attack upon the futile Russo-Japanese War; *The Seven Who Were Hanged* is an important contribution to the argument against capital punishment, and *The Human Son* deals with the problem of conscience. Most of his stories help toward the solution of social and philosophical problems. His love for humanity, his enlightened and libertarian views, his protest against the tyranny which reigns in his own country—these are the main reasons for his great literary success in Russia.

He likes especially to portray the heroes of the "period of liberation," revolutionaries with whom he himself actively participated in the revolution. The deep spiritual crises, the tremors and breaks which are going on in the souls of these great idealists and apostles of liberty, Andreyev described with especial love, with great realism and artistic force.

Ilić ended his review with the words:

His best work is *The Seven Who Were Hanged*, in which Andreyev has tried to solve the problem of the conquest of death, of its subjugation in the name of a higher goal. In one of his letters Andreyev says: "It is my intention with this story to point out the horror and impermissibility of capital punishment. The death penalty confuses the conscience even of resolute men; it results in much greater havoc among the weak. Werner can pit his intelligence and will power, Musya her purity and innocence, against this last instinctive horror of inevitable death; what is left for the weak and sinful, how can they face it, unless at the cost of their rational consciousness, ravaged to the depths of their souls?"

At the investigation and at the trial, Ilić and Princip spoke openly about their disagreement over whether the attempt against the Archduke should be made or not. Princip said to Judge Pfeffer on July 3:

In any case Ilić had in the last ten days repeatedly expressed the opinion that we should not attempt this assassination because the present time was not favorably chosen and we would have no profit from this assassination. But I was not in agreement with the postponement of the assassination because a certain morbid yearning for it had been awakened in me.[73]

Grabež also confirmed that Ilić urged him to put off the attempt.[74] Ilić, both at the investigation and at the trial, stated resolutely that he was against the assassination of the Archduke.[75]

Ilić's attitude presumably was strengthened by the fact (according to some sources) that Colonel Apis's secret society in Belgrade, which through Major Vojin Tankosić had given technical assistance to the conspirators, also changed its attitude toward the attempt. On the orders of Colonel Apis, the main go-between for Princip and Major Tankosić in Belgrade, Djuro Šarac, the president of the secret society Smrt ili Život, was sent to Bosnia to stop the plot. He could not come to Sarajevo, because he was known there. He chose Bosanski Brod as a meeting place with Ilić, who came from Sarajevo on June 16. During the trial Ilić stated that he was in Brod "in order to stop the plot,"[76] but obviously he did not mention his meeting with Šarac.

On his return, Ilić tried once more to convince Princip, saying that the reaction of the authorities after the attempt would be disastrous and the people would suffer greatly, particularly the Serbs, but all this was in vain. Princip gave evasive answers, but stuck to his first decision that the Archduke must be killed. Ljubibratić believed that Ilić made his decision for the postponement of the attempt after receiving orders from Belgrade.[77] But this writer maintains that Ilić's attitude was influenced basically by his own philosophical and political considerations. In this respect he shared the views of Gaćinović, who also had second thoughts about the political wisdom of the assassination in Sarajevo. In the article written for Trotsky in 1915, Gaćinović claimed that Ilić and Princip had written to him about their disagreement:

The last time Ilić wrote to me was together with Princip, a few days before the assassination. They informed me about the internal differences in our former Sarajevo group which had been caused by some new developments; they spoke about it indirectly and in Aesopian language. Perhaps some comrades were against the event of June 28 and tried to put moral pressure on the group, which had been determined to act at all costs. I felt uneasy reading this disturbing letter, written by Princip with a few sentences added by Ilić. . . .[78]

That Gaćinović, under the influence of modern doctrines in Switzerland and far away from the conditions of Bosnian feudalism, was changing his mind about individual terror as the sole means of social revolution may be connected with the conference held in Vienna on June 28, 1914, on the occasion of the sixteenth anniversary of Zora. Some of Gaćinović's closest friends were present. Špiro Soldo, the president of Zora, presided over the conference. Among the others, Pero Slijepčević attended the meeting as did the leaders of Preporod, Fabjančić, Jenko, and Juš Kozak.[79] There were two kinds of meetings during the celebration, public ones attended by representatives of Belgrade University and other cultural South Slav institutions, and secret ones. At the secret ones it was decided that a unified organization of all South Slav youth should be formed. Due to the fact that in 1917 a revision of the Compromise between Austria and Hungary was to come about and that this event would provoke a crisis between these two powers, the South Slav youth were preparing to exploit the unrest and lead a revolution for liberation from Austria-Hungary. The secret conference was presided over by Ljubo Mijatović, Gaćinović's right-hand man. The conference brought a resolution against the use of individual terror. While a special committee was drafting a resolution against the use of political assassination, news arrived concerning Princip's act in Sarajevo.[80]

It is interesting to note that also among the Slovene youth gathered around Preporod there was a division between the older generation, which preached revolution through mass movements, and the younger one, which favored political assassination. While Fabjančič, Jenko and Kozak advocated the first program, Ivan Endlicher favored the second. Endlicher was the man who advised the younger generation of Young Bosnians to reorganize their secret societies, as Lazar Djukić stated at the interrogation.[81] The exact relationship between Endlicher and the conspirators of June 28, 1914, is not yet clear. According to one source he informed the Young Bosnians that he could obtain weapons from anarchists in Trieste.[82] After 1918, Jurković wrote that he had met Endlicher in Zadar a few weeks before June 28 and had been told by him that an attempt would be made against the Archduke.[83] To a schoolboy he pointed to a portrait of the Archduke saying: "This one will not last long."[84] After the war, Cvetko Popović, one of the Sarajevo assassins, wrote about Endlicher: "If Princip had not succeeded, I am certain that Endlicher would have tried his hand against the Archduke."[85] Immediately after the Sarajevo assassination Endlicher was arrested. He took his secret with him to his grave when he died in jail in 1915.

The younger Croat generations were also for the use of terrorist action, despite the fact that some of their leaders had attended the meeting in Vienna which denounced the use of individual terror as the best means of political struggle. On May 15, 1914, a student by the name of Jakov Šefer, from a commercial college, tried to kill the Archduke Salvator and the Ban Skerletz when they were leaving a theater in Zagreb. Šefer pulled his gun, but before he could shoot, a detective jumped on him. During the investigation of Šefer, another student by the name of Rudolf Hercigonja was accused of being the real instigator. Several young men accused him of trying to talk them into killing either the Archduke Franz Ferdinand or the Hungarian Prime Minister Tisza, or some other high dignitaries.[86]

Hercigonja had some connections with Gaćinović in 1912,[87] but not in 1914. It is interesting that a few weeks before the Sarajevo assassination, Špiro Soldo and other leading members of Zora sent one of their important members, Bogoljub Konstantinović to Sarajevo to speak to the younger generation of the Young Bosnians about the need for broad political action, but against the use of individual terror. Vaso Čubrilović attended one of these lectures and did not like it.[88]

Gaćinović himself wrote in an article for Trotsky that he had had no chance to answer Ilić and Princip as to who was right and who was wrong. In the article for Trotsky he also wrote: "I was preparing to answer them, advising them to cool off, but Princip's deed echoed through the whole world."[89] In a letter to a Hercegovinian girl, Gaćinović wrote immediately after June 28: "Five or six days before the assassination, I received from them two comradely letters. I saw that they were nervous, impatient, and that there was a kind of quarreling between them. But being completely submerged these days with the studies of philosophical and social problems, I did not know nor did I feel that we were on the eve of a catastrophe."[90]

Gaćinović's opinion, if it had been sent, could not have reached Princip in time. Princip was determined to go on with the preparations. At this point, Ilić gave up his opposition, although he was still convinced that the attempt should not be made. He was a man of complex character. He was a devoted comrade of Princip; he was afraid that somebody might reproach him for intending to betray his friends. Princip never doubted Ilić's honesty, but he said to Čabrinović that Ilić had socialist ideas and that he was afraid that Ilić might become a socialist.[91] Besides, Princip had much stronger will power than Ilić. To Dr. Pappenheim he said that Ilić "had no energy. Reading had—he confessed—made him quite slack. Ilić was under his influence, though he was five years older and already a teacher."[92]

In the meantime, great preparations were made in Sarajevo for the

Archduke's arrival. The streets were repaired and, as a Belgrade paper remarked, "many parts of the town which have been neglected ever since Sarajevo was built, got a new face for this occasion."[93] The Lord Mayor of Sarajevo issued a proclamation to all citizens to decorate their houses; the police issued an order that throwing flowers on the imperial procession would not be allowed.[94]

The local press, with the exception of the Serbian paper *Narod*, published editorials welcoming the Heir Apparent. The Jesuit-controlled *Hrvatski Dnevnik* in its issue of June 25 carried the headline: "Hail, Our Hope" and the editorial read as follows:

He is coming to Bosnia as the Commander in Chief of all the armed forces of our Monarchy. This is his first official visit to this country. We feel that he is sending to us and all our enemies the following clear message: Never will Bosnia leave the Habsburg Monarchy. The whole armed forces of the Monarchy will defend the Bosnian possessions to the last ounce of strength. He came here in order to stand up at the head of two Army corps of 50,000 men, showing us what he intends to do in the event of a reality of bloodshed.

On the other hand *Narod* had no news of the arrival of Franz Ferdinand on its front page. Only on one of the back pages, among the local news, was a short item informing its readers that 40,000 golden crowns had been spent merely for the adaptation of a chapel in the Hotel Bosna at Ilidže so that a mass could be celebrated for the Heir Apparent. Just above this news item there was another one, stating quite simply that before Franz Ferdinand arrived in Ilidže, all the Serbian and Croat national flags were put down by order of the authorities, and only Austrian black-and-yellow ones were left.[95]

Before going to attend the next morning's maneuvers in the mountains southwest of Sarajevo, the Archduke suddenly had an impulse to visit the town, on the evening of June 25. Together with his wife he drove to Baš Čaršija, the most picturesque street of Sarajevo, full of artisans' shops where exotic handicrafts were made and sold at the same time.

Jevtić wrote that by pure coincidence Princip was in the crowd watching the imperial party as it entered the Kabiljo carpet shop. The same evening he told Jevtić's group assembled at the Semiz wineshop about this incident, saying that he could not do anything, because a policeman was just behind him.[96] One of the officials of the Bosnian government wrote that Princip stated at his first interrogation on June 28, 1914, that he did not wish to fire in the small shop because he might have hit the Duchess of Hohenberg.[97] But in the *Nachlass* collection of the investigation papers, there is nothing about Princip's alleged meeting with the Archduke on June 25.

Having at last been persuaded by Princip to participate in the plot, Ilić continued with all the technical preparations. On June 26 he telegraphed Mehmedbašić to come to Sarajevo. Mehmedbašić declared to the police in Stolac that he intended to go to Mostar to a dentist, and he received a proper pass. From Mostar he continued straight to Sarajevo. Having a proper pass, Mehmedbašić stayed in the Hotel Sarajevo. Ilić and some friends spent the whole night until 3 A.M. with Mehmedbašić. Ilić was telling stories about the life of Russian revolutionaries.

Ilić had worked out where the conspirators should wait for the Archduke.[98] In the local paper *Bosnische Post* they learned the exact route of the imperial party. The authorities were eager to publish it beforehand in order to inform the population in which streets it should gather to greet the Heir Apparent.

The most appropriate place for Ilić to wait for the Archduke was the Appel Quay, the long street alongside the river Miljacka, leading from the railway station to the town hall. He chose this street because the imperial party had to pass through it twice. The six conspirators were divided into three pairs, with instructions that the first pair should strike with bombs simultaneously. If they failed, then it would be the turn of the next ambushers. The conspirators were to stand at intervals along a three-hundred-yard stretch of the Appel Quay, between the Čumurija, Lateiner, and Emperor bridges. The first was Mehmedbašić, the oldest, who had to wait in front of the garden of the Mostar Café, while next to him was the youngest conspirator, Vaso Čubrilović. On the other side of the street by the river Miljacka, Nedeljko Čabrinović was stationed. Just opposite the Čumurija Bridge was the position assigned to Popović, and Ilić chose to be near him. Princip's place was some two hundred yards farther down, near the Lateiner Bridge on the river side, and Grabež was still further on down the Quay, which was thirteen yards wide with pavements on both sides, each seven feet wide.

The weapons were distributed to the youngest conspirators, Čubrilović and Cvetko Popović, between three and four o'clock in the afternoon of June 27 at Bembaša, on the outskirts of Sarajevo. Ilić gave Čubrilović and Popović one bomb and one revolver each. He explained how to use the weapons and fired a revolver shot into a tunnel, saying: "Where this one hits, no medicine can help."[99] In the garden of the Mostar Café, late in the evening of the same day, he met Mehmedbašić and accompanied him to the hotel where Mehmedbašić was staying. On the way he gave him a bomb, with brief instructions on how to handle it. Princip met Čabrinović the same evening and told him to be at the pastry shop of Djuro Vlajnić in Čumurija Street, at eight o'clock the following morning. Grabež was expected to be there at the same time. The same night Ilić walked to the Kosovo Cemetery and spent a few moments at Žerajić's shrine. Čabrinović did the same a few hours before. Princip sat in the Semiz Café with Jevtić's group until 11 P.M. On his way home he too visited Žerajić's grave, depositing some flowers on it. At home he read Kropotkin and dreamed about the world federation of the free communes.

CHAPTER XIV

PRINCIP'S LUCK

There is no armor against fate,
Death lays his icy hands on kings.
Scepter and crown
Must tumble down,
And in the dust be equal made
With the poor crooked scythes and spade.
—JAMES SHIRLEY

ALL SEVEN CONSPIRATORS were at their places in the morning of June 28. Ilić left his home before eight o'clock and went straight to the Vlajnić cake shop to meet Grabež and Čabrinović. Princip came some time later. Čabrinović left his house that morning with a heavy heart; he had quarreled with his father the day before, because the elder Čabrinović had wanted to hoist the Habsburg imperial flag in honor of the Archduke's arrival. At his interrogation, Čabrinović described the incident:

I was rather at loggerheads with my father and mother. I was annoyed with my parents because Father wanted to hoist the Serbian and the imperial flags on our house, but could not find the flagpoles, although they had searched the whole house; I did not wish to tell him where the poles were. When my father started to curse my mother because of this, I thought it would be better for my father to hoist the imperial flag as well. At least I would not be suspected, and so I told him that the flagpoles were in the closet. At last my father put out the flags. When I reproached him for hoisting the imperial flag as well as the Serbian, he told me that he lived under this Emperor, that he esteemed him, that he was enjoying a good life, and if this house did not suit me I should look for a better place.[1]

The elder Čabrinović was angry at his son because Nedeljko had said on Friday night to Marija Talanga, the servant: "I bet Franz Ferdinand will not be the sovereign in one year's time. King Petar of Serbia will rule here, instead."[2]

The young Čabrinović distributed all his belongings and a few crowns he had, either on the eve or on the morning of June 28. Although his mother was angry with him because of the incident with the flags, he gave her his pocket knife and his watch. From the wages he had earned during the previous week, he gave his grandmother twenty crowns and his sister Jovanka five crowns. Čabrinović was fond of his grandmother—"I gave her money because I love her and I had promised her that I would help her. On her side, she always gave me money when I had no work. I told my sister Jovanka that I was going away and that we should never see each other again. . . . She went and I stood alone, crying." Thus Čabrinović described their departure to the investigation judge. With his last few crowns, Čabrinović bought a bouquet of flowers and sent it to a girl by the name of Jela Uljarević.[3] Leaving his paternal house, Čabrinović was followed by the family dog, a lively animal. When he saw that the dog had been following him all the time, he took the dog home and left him there.

At 8:15 A.M. Čabrinović was in the Vlajnić cake shop, where he found Grabež and Danilo Ilić. The latter was making jokes with a girl by the name of Erna, who served them. "Here Grabež asked me," Čabrinović said to the investigation judge, "if Princip had told me where to stand, to which I replied that I knew. I said nothing to Ilić. After I had eaten three cakes, Princip came to us in the rear room and quickly gave me the bomb, which I stuck in my belt."[4] Čabrinović also received some cyanide poison wrapped in pieces of paper.

From the cake shop, Čabrinović went for a walk to the Appel Quay, where he met his friend Tomo Vučinović. He asked him to go with him to be photographed. The first photographer was closed, so they proceeded to the Circus Square, where the photographer Josef Schrei took photos, which were ready in an hour's time. Vučinović met two girls he knew, and Čabrinović made a few jokes with them. Čabrinović asked for six pictures and told Vučinović that he was leaving for Zagreb and asked him to give one to his grandmother, one to his sister, one to a friend in Belgrade, another to a friend in Trieste, and to send the rest to Zagreb, to Mitar Mitrović, at Ilica 16.[5] The pictures were ready the same morning and Vučinović sent them to the given addresses. At the investigation, this gesture of Čabrinović was a matter of great concern to the investigating judge. Čabrinović explained at the trial: "I thought that posterity should have my picture taken on that day"; and he was right. His features, trimmed mustache, stiff white collar, dark necktie and dark suit, and the hand of his friend Tomo Vučinović resting on his shoulder photographed that morning have been reproduced in many books since 1914.

This photo shows that in the pocket of his coat Čabrinović had that morning's issue of the Serbian paper *Narod*. Its editor, Riste Radulović, had splashed on the front page a long editorial on the anniversary of the Kosovo battle with many poems; there was no news about Franz Ferdinand's visit. A day later the Joint Minister of Finance Bilinski informed Governor Potiorek: "I am resolutely and firmly demanding that *Narod* should disappear from the eyes of Bosnia and Hercegovina because of its openly hostile way of writing in connection with the visit of the late lamented Heir Apparent."[6] The editor of *Narod* died in the Nezider detention camp in Hungary during the First World War.

While Ilić took Grabež to his house to give him a bomb and a revolver, Princip was at the Appel Quay from 9 A.M., with his bomb and revolver hidden at his waist. He was in the company of his former school friend Maxim, the son of the Attorney General of Sarajevo, Franjo Švara, and another schoolboy Špirić. A few weeks later Maxim's father was to write the official indictment against Princip. But this walk with the young Švara helped Princip to divert the attention of the detectives. Švara soon went to mass at the Roman Catholic cathedral, and Princip remained alone.

Vaso Čubrilović and Cvetko Popović were also at their places on the Quay. Čubrilović had had arguments with some school friends about the attempt. He had hinted to Branko Zagorac ten days before June 28 that he was going to make an attempt against the Archduke. But Zagorac answered that he did not believe that he would dare to do it. On June 27, just after he had received from Ilić his revolver and his bomb, Čubrilović met his two friends Dragan Kalember and Marko Perin in a cake shop. To them also Čubrilović had confessed his intentions, but they also thought he was joking. This time Čubrilović offered to let them feel the weapons in his pocket, in order to prove to them that he was not lying. They had just finished their ice cream and had to leave the shop.

All seven conspirators mingled freely with the crowds along the Appel Quay for more than an hour and fifteen minutes without being detected by the police. Princip and his fellows had lots of luck. One of the reasons for this was the almost complete lack of security measures set up by the authorities in Bosnia and Hercegovina, despite many warnings from all sides that there was a danger to the Archduke's life in Sarajevo. Bosnia and Hercegovina had a first-class system of political intelligence, yet the conspirators were able to travel slowly from one village to another, laden with bombs and revolvers, and involving more than a dozen different people. More than two weeks before June 28, both Princip and Čabrinović had registered with the Sarajevo police, according to regulations, giving their correct addresses, and no one bothered to keep an eye on them. When the Emperor Franz Josef visited Sarajevo in 1910, all newcomers were obliged to register within six hours of their arrival; Žerajić from the start had two detectives shadowing every step he made. Princip and Čabrinović walked freely through

Sarajevo, and Čabrinović actually went three times to Ilidže, where the Archduke and his wife were stopping.[7] On the Sarajevo streets through which the imperial party had to pass, there were no lines of soldiers, as there had been during the Emperor's visit in 1910. All together, 150 police agents were at the disposal of the Sarajevo chief of police.

When the imperial party of six cars came through the section of the Appel Quay where the conspirators were waiting, five of them did not react. The first conspirator, Mehmedbašić, explained later to a friend that Ilić had told him he should toss the bomb only if he really recognized the Archduke, in order not to miss him; if unsure, he was to wait until the car came back from the town hall and aim carefully.[8] On the other hand, when Albertini interviewed Mehmedbašić years later, he was told that Mehmedbašić had done nothing "because at the moment when the procession was approaching, a gendarme happened, as if by chance, to stand behind him. He feared that if he brought out the bomb which he carried at his belt, the gendarme would seize him by the arm and this would have revealed the plot and prevented the other conspirators from doing anything. While he revolved these thoughts in his mind the Archduke's car went by and he had lost his opportunity."[9] The youngest conspirator, Vaso Čubrilović, said to the investigation judge that "he did not shoot because he had pity for the Duchess."[10] At the trial he said: "I did not pull out the revolver, because the Duchess was there; I did not wish to shoot."[11] Čubrilović complained after the war to Albertini that the conspirators had been poorly placed along the long straight main road, and that a street with corners and curves would have been necessary for a successful attempt.[12]

Popović told a friend that he did not see the Archduke in the first car because he was nearsighted, and while he was hesitating Čabrinović threw his bomb. At the trial Popović confessed: "I had no courage. I do not know what happened to me."[13] But he defended the assassination and the motives of the conspirators at the trial. Princip had a first-class opportunity to shoot at the Archduke's car when it stopped for a brief moment, but he did not. Princip at his first interrogation said simply: "In my excitement I did not recognize the Heir Apparent, but only saw the cars going quickly by."[14] On Grabež's failure there exist five different versions. At the investigation of July 16, he said that he "did not have enough strength to carry out such a thing."[15] At the trial he mentioned that "two detectives were behind him."[16] Pfeffer, the investigating judge, said in his book that Grabež did not shoot because of the Duchess.[17] Grabež's friend Jevdjević, who saw Grabež immediately after the assassination, wrote in his book that Grabež saw many old women and children on the street and was afraid to throw the bomb among them.[18] Perhaps the most important reason why Grabež did not act can be found in his wavering between Ilić and Princip as to whether the assassination should be carried out or not. Also, at the trial, where Grabež behaved with great moral courage, he mentioned that someone was standing at his side at that very moment and might have been involved if he had acted.[19]

Although the imperial cortege of six open cars passed through a "regular avenue of assassins," as the Roman Catholic Archbishop Stadler, of Sarajevo, later described it, none of the six shot at the Archduke except the one suspected by his companions of being unreliable and a joker, whose bomb had been taken away and returned only on the very morning of the attempt—Nedeljko Čabrinović. He had left his post and approached the one assigned to Mehmedbašić and Čubrilović in order to have the first opportunity to throw the bomb. A few minutes before the Archduke's car passed him, he was in the company of a mute boy, Moritz Alkalaj, with whom the jokers of Sarajevo liked to pass their time. In order to be sure which was the Archduke's car, Čabrinović asked a police agent who was walking up and down the pavement, and who, when the imperial procession approached, stopped to look at it instead of keeping an eye on the onlookers as all the security officers had been instructed to do that morning. At Čabrinović's question, "In which car is His Majesty?" the excited detective replied that it was the third.[20] Čabrinović took the bomb from his waist and knocked the detonator off against the lamppost. He could not wait twelve seconds as he had been advised by the *komite* in Belgrade, because the car would have passed by. He threw the bomb at the green feathers of the Archduke's ceremonial hat. These few seconds saved Franz Ferdinand's life. The bomb fell exactly behind him on the car's folded roof, but did not explode at that moment. It fell to the street and burst under the next oncoming car, wounding a dozen people.[21]

Nedeljko Čabrinović recalled at the trial: "At that very second I saw Ferdinand turning his cold and piercing glance at me . . . I threw myself on the ground, put the poison in my mouth, and then jumped over the embankment into the river Miljacka."[22]

The fact that Čabrinović was the first of the conspirators to dare to throw his bomb at the Archduke Franz Ferdinand boosted his wounded ego very much. When he was caught, seconds after his attempt, in the river Miljacka and was asked who he was, he answered proudly, "I am a Serbian hero."[23]

The idea that he had to show Princip and his other friends that he was capable of brave deeds had tormented him. On the eve of June 28, he wrote to a friend of his: "Tomorrow is Vidovdan and we shall see who is faithful and who is unfaithful. Do you remember the great oath of Miloš Obilić?"[24]

At the investigation, Čabrinović said that when he read in the papers that the Archduke would make an official visit to Sarajevo on Vidov-dan (St. Vitus Day)—

for us, Serbs, the greatest national day—this fact fired me with zeal to carry out the attempt. Our folklore tradition tells how the hero Miloš Obilić was accused before Vidovdan that he was a traitor, and how he answered: "On Vidovdan we shall see who is and who is not a traitor." And Obilić became the first assassin who went into the enemy camp and murdered Sultan Murad. The local Socialists have called me a spy like my father . . .[25]

Čabrinović's case clearly shows how personal and political motives can be deeply interwoven. From the moment he threw the bomb he became a new man. At the investigation and at the trial, he always tried to show Princip that they were equals.

At the trial Princip described what happened after Čabrinović's abortive attempt in the following words:

The car approached and I heard the detonation of the bomb. I knew that it was one of ours, but I did not know which one. The crowd pushed forward and I followed it. The cars were stopped. I thought all was over and I saw Čabrinović being escorted away. The thought flashed through my mind to kill him in order to keep the secret of the conspiracy, and afterward to kill myself. The cars proceeded and that moment I changed my mind. I did not see the Archduke. I went to the Lateiner Bridge and only then I heard that the attempt had failed. I reflected for a second where to wait in ambush, because I knew from the newspapers where he should pass again. . . .[26]

Princip also missed the chance to shoot at the Archduke while his car was standing still. A moment later it sped swiftly past Princip and he did not recognize the Archduke. In the meantime the police started to clear the Appel Quay, and Princip left his place by the embankment, crossed the Appel Quay and stood at the corner of the Quay and Franz Josef Street in front of the delicatessen of Moritz Schiller. According to the program, the Archduke should have passed from the Appel Quay through the narrow Franz Josef Street. But at the town hall he changed his route. He wanted to drive straight through the Appel Quay to the military hospital to visit one of the wounded officers.

But none of the Archduke's entourage or the police informed the driver that he should not turn into Franz Josef Street. He followed the first two cars, which kept to the original schedule and entered Franz Josef Street. Realizing the mistake, Governor Potiorek shouted at him to stop and go back.

The driver stopped the car and started to back up, just a few steps from the place where Princip was standing. Forty-five minutes later Princip said to the investigation judge, Pfeffer:

When the second car arrived, I recognized the Heir Apparent. But as I saw that a lady was sitting next to him I reflected for a moment whether I should shoot or not. At the same moment I was filled with a peculiar feeling and I aimed at the Heir Apparent from the pavement—which was made easier because the car was proceeding slower at that moment. Where I aimed I do not know. But I know that I aimed at the Heir Apparent. I believe that I fired twice, perhaps more, because I was so excited. Whether I hit the victims or not, I cannot tell, because instantly people started to hit me.[27]

At the investigation of July 3, Princip described why he did not use the bomb, but only the revolver:

At the first moment I intended to throw the bomb, which I had in my belt on the left side. But because the bomb was screwed closed it would not have been easy for me to open. Also, in so great a crowd it would have been difficult to take it out and throw it. Therefore I drew the revolver instead and raised it against the automobile without aiming. I even turned my head as I shot. I let go two shots one after the other, but I am not certain whether I shot twice or more often, because I was very excited. That is also why I did not want to throw the bomb, because the strength for this failed me. Thereupon the people began to lynch me. Somebody took the revolver away from me, and the bomb fell out of my belt.[28]

Besides the mistake of the driver of Franz Ferdinand's car, the second element whch enabled Princip to succeed was the intervention at the decisive moment of Mihajlo Pušara. "At the instant when Princip raised his gun at the Archduke, a detective tried to intercept him, but Mihajlo Pušara kicked the policeman in the knee, so that he lost his balance and missed the opportunity to prevent the assassination of the Heir Apparent."[29]

Pušara was a tall, handsome young man, an employee in the town hall, and a gifted actor and singer who played juvenile leads and excelled in romantic roles. The Belgrade National Theater had offered him an engagement, but he refused it: he preferred to stay in Sarajevo. Mihajlo Pušara not only pushed aside the detective who wanted to intercept Princip, but he even charged at Lieutenant Dr. Andreas Freiherr von Morsey, who jumped from one of the cars from the imperial cortege and attacked Princip with his saber. Lieutenant Morsey described this scene thus:

As I hit him twice two civilians were standing to my right and left sides. One of them shouted, in German, "Do not touch him," then continued with some Serbian words which I did not understand, as I cannot speak the language. I delivered some strong strokes with my saber and shouted: "Anyone who touches me will die." My helmet was dented, because I was hit several times with powerful blows. I called to somebody standing near me whom I thought to be a police lieutenant, "Arrest him"; and pointed him out with my saber. I think that I also hurt this man with my saber, but I am not sure of it. The one who shouted "Do not touch him" was arrested as well, I think. He was a young man between eighteen and twenty, quite tall, and as far as I can recall he wore a soft black hat and had a lean face. The second civilian was also a young man. But I do not remember his face. Also I heard several shouts from the crowd: "See that you clear out of here"—and this in the German language! Then I returned to my car and went to the Governor's residence, where the death of their Majesties was ascertained.[30]

Besides Pušara, another young man, Ferdinand Behr, tried to help Princip. He too was arrested, and while he was being taken to the police, a photographer took his picture. He looked very much like Gavrilo Princip, and his picture later appeared in many newspapers and books, some of them years after the assassination.[31]

At the trial, Detective Smail Spahović described the scene:

I stood about ten steps from the assassin. I had instructions not to look at the car, but to watch the crowd. Standing like this and doing my duty, I heard a revolver shot. I turned my head to the left; there was nothing; I looked to the right; a second shot was echoing. I plunged through the crowd, overtaking everybody else, and charged at the assassin, grabbing him by the arm; then somebody ambushed me and landed a fist in my stomach. I was even hit on my head by Princip himself with a revolver. I saw Pušara. I grabbed Princip's hand. At that moment the officers started charging Princip with sabers, and I was not able to drag him away until my chief came and helped me to grab Princip.[32]

The detective also said that he did not see who attacked the officers: "I did not see anything, I had such pains in my stomach from the blow somebody delivered. Pušara was the nearest, and he should know who hit me."

Princip said in evidence that he succeeded in putting the poison in his mouth while the officers were beating him, but at that moment his bomb fell down on the pavement.[33] Another witness, Ante Velić, said that he saw Princip raising his revolver to his temple, but at that very moment Velić struck his hand. Princip agreed that this was true and said that he had intended to commit suicide.[34]

While Princip was being dragged to the police station, Pušara succeeded in mingling with the crowd and getting away. He went to the Sloga society, where he joined a choir which was taking part in a religious service for Vidovdan. But somebody had recognized him in the crowd and told the detectives. He was soon arrested, apologizing to his friends in the choir as he was taken away: "I shall not be long."[35]

Princip wanted to save Pušara, and he described the incident to the investigation judge in this way:

After Čabrinović was caught, I went to the corner of the Appel Quay and Franz Josef Street, just at Schiller's shop, when Mihajlo Pušara came to me, saying: "Look what has happened!" I replied: "I have seen it. What nonsense to commit such a thing at this time!" He then said that this had not been a good thing to do, and he invited me to go to the Sloga society, because there was a celebration. I was very much afraid of Mihajlo Pušara, because he was often in our company. I thought he was a spy, because he used to dine at his relative Simon Pušara's, who is an innkeeper and a detective, and therefore I thought that when Pušara took me by the arm he wanted to take me somewhere and search me. Therefore, I did not let myself be taken by the arm and when a moment later "Long Live" was heard, I succeeded in getting through the crowd to the corner of Schiller's shop.[36]

Čabrinović also, when asked by the investigation judge whether he knew Pušara, answered that he regarded him as a spy.[37]

Each of them repeated his statement at the trial and the court believed them. Yet Pušara was one of the most active Young Bosnians. He had been the man who had mailed the letter to Belgrade, at the suggestion of the Sarajevo group, with the newspaper clipping about the arrival of Franz Ferdinand.[38]

On the morning of June 28, Pušara had attended mass at the Serbian Eastern Orthodox Church and had sung in the choir during the Service of Remembrance for the Serbian heroes fallen in the battle of Kosovo on June 28, 1389.[39] Immediately afterward he ran to the Appel Quay to join his friends when Franz Ferdinand was scheduled to arrive.

According to Jevtić, Pušara was assigned another duty. In the event of all the attempts in Sarajevo failing that morning, his duty would have been to go to the nearby town of Visoko and wait for the Archduke to pass by on the evening of June 28.[40] But no other source confirms this.

This narrative of the Sarajevo assassination shows that it was one of the most amateurish regicides of modern times. Despite their number, their single-mindedness of purpose, and the coolheadedness of their leader Princip in the most decisive minute of the day, the success of the conspiracy was due mainly to sheer luck.

CHAPTER XV

THE TRIAL

*Sons of Yugoslavia, do you not feel that our
life lies in blood, that* attentat *is the supreme
god of all the gods of the nation, because it
proves that Young Bosnia is alive, that there
exists an element which is prepared to be martyred? The life of a nation consists in blood,
blood is the god of a nation, death superseded
the Insurrection, and the assassination is the Insurrection of the nation.*
—From the diary of Todor Ilić,
schoolboy from Tuzla, June 28, 1914.

Despite its many weaknesses Austria-Hungary had an established legal system, and the assassins had a fair chance to state their
political and personal motives, both at the initial interrogation by the
investigation judge and at their trial. Luckily for the historians, most of
these minutes have been preserved,[1] and they provide a clear picture of
the behavior of the young conspirators faced by their judges and give
considerable insight into the general principles on which they claimed
to have acted. These documents represent the fullest and most accurate
exposition of the Young Bosnians' beliefs as to how their country
should be liberated and how Bosnian society should be changed.

The preliminary hearing was conducted by Leo Pfeffer, investigation judge of the Sarajevo District Court, a man of thirty-seven years at
that time, born in Karlovac, in Croatia. Pfeffer was a short, fat man
with a pale, puffy face and yellow, irregular teeth. On the morning of
June 28 he was walking with his little daughter through the Appel
Quay when Čabrinović's bomb exploded. He directed the child to go

home and hurried to his office, which was in the town hall. He had to wait until the imperial party had left the building, before he could get in. Meanwhile, police officers were dragging Čabrinović toward the town hall; a crowd was following the would-be assassin, shouting at him. Pfeffer followed him into the police medical-aid room, which was just opposite his office. Čabrinović's face was streaming blood from the many blows he had received. When Pfeffer saw him, he was sitting on a bench waiting for the physician to attend him. "With his alert, lively black eyes he looked around defiantly, and on his lips there was a provocative grin. He had a very white complexion and rosy cheeks, and a short black mustache. He was a tall, strong young man. He was wearing a sports cap, and my first impression was that he had committed the assassination because of anarchist principles."[2]

The head of the district court informed Pfeffer a few minutes later that he, Pfeffer, was to conduct the investigation. While they were talking, a police detective rushed into the town hall, shouting that the Heir Apparent was wounded. Pfeffer ran out of the building and saw a group of detectives leading a short young man whose head was bleeding. A crowd followed them, and some members of it were trying to hit the man with their walking sticks. Princip was led into the medical-aid room, and after his wounds were dressed Pfeffer conducted the first interrogation in his office, at 11:15 A.M. in the presence of his secretary Mitrović.

Pfeffer described Gavrilo Princip in this way:

The young assassin, exhausted by his beating, was unable to utter a word. He was undersized, emaciated, sallow, sharp-featured. It was difficult to imagine that so frail-looking an individual could have committed so serious a deed. Even his clear blue eyes, burning and piercing but serene, had nothing cruel or criminal in their expression. Then spoke of innate intelligence, of steady and harmonious energy. When I told him I was the investigating judge and asked if he had strength to speak he answered my questions with perfect clearness in a voice that grew steadily stronger and more assured.[3]

Neither the investigation judge nor Princip knew at that time that Princip's shots had been fatal. At that instant both the Archduke and the Duchess were dying. The same day at seven o'clock in the evening the judge was again in Princip's cell. He announced the opening of the preliminary investigation and charged him with the assassination of the Heir Apparent and his wife. In the *Franz Ferdinand Nachlass* a copy of the minutes of this event was recorded as follows:

I open against you the preliminary judicial investigation of the crime of murder which you committed today through shooting treacherously from the closest distance with a Browning pistol at the Heir Apparent and his wife, the Duchess of Hohenberg, with the intention to kill them, and hitting them both, which caused their death a short time afterward. At the same time I put you in preliminary imprisonment according to Paragraph 184, points 1, 2, 3, 189, of the Penal Code.

Princip's answer was recorded: "I acknowledge it and do not complain, but I am sorry that I have killed the Duchess of Hohenberg, because I had no intention of killing her."[4]

Čabrinović, questioned at 2 P.M. by Judge Marčec, declared that he did not feel guilty and that he had carried the idea of an attempt at assassination in his head for two years.[5] About his general motives he stated:

I am an adherent of the radical anarchist idea, which aims at destroying the present system through terrorism in order to bring in the liberal system in its place. Therefore I hate all representatives of the constitutional system —of course, not this or that person as such but as the bearer of power which oppresses the people. I have educated myself in this spirit through the reading of socialist and anarchist writings and I can say that I have read through almost all the literature of this type that I could get in the Serbo-Croatian language.[6]

He said further:

I aimed specifically at the Archduke, in order to kill him, because he—as far as I know from periodicals—is an enemy of the Slavs in general but especially of the Serbs.[7]

Here Čabrinović added that the Archduke and Governor Potiorek were responsible for the introduction in 1913 of the Extraordinary Measures against the Serbs and that he "therefore does not regret his deed in any way."[8]

Čabrinović stated that he was the only conspirator: "No one but me in Sarajevo knew about this bomb, because I mentioned to no one that I would carry out this assassination attempt. For I had such great trust in no one."[9]

To the judge's question whether he knew Gavrilo Princip, Čabrinović answered that he had known him for the last three or four years, but that he "did not observe that Gavro had the same anarchist ideals as himself, and that he was a very reserved man."[10] Čabrinović added that in his encounters with Princip they discussed general things, but that they never talked about the realization of anarchist ideas through terror: "I do not know whether Princip tried something today against the Archduke for the same reasons as I did. But if he has done this, it was without my knowledge, and I cannot conclude on the basis of this that the same ideas led us."[11]

In the evening of June 28 Čabrinović was questioned again by Judge Pfeffer. Here Čabrinović heard definitely that Princip had succeeded in assassinating the Archduke. Pfeffer also said that a preliminary judicial investigation had been opened against him and that he was charged with an attempt against the lives of the Archduke Franz Ferdinand, the Duchess of Hohenberg and Governor Potiorek, as well as with being an accomplice of Princip in the actual assassination.[12]

After the first interrogations, Princip and Čabrinović were escorted into the military prison, which was within the Military Camp. They were immediately put in chains, as was the rule in military prisons of Austria-Hungary.

The question is whether they had planned between themselves before the assassination what they would say if they were caught alive. All the evidence is to the contrary. Princip stated at his interrogation on August 1:

I had the firm intention to kill myself and therefore had the opinion that no one would know after the completed assassination why it was done. My thought was therefore only on the success of the assassination; of some unfavorable consequence or other I had not thought at all.[13]

We have already seen how Princip, the moment after he fired the fatal shots, tried to kill himself, first by raising his revolver to his head and then, when he was blocked by others from shooting himself, by putting into his mouth the poison he had brought from Belgrade; the dose was not sufficient.

Čabrinović too had tried to commit suicide. He took a double dose of poison when he jumped into the river Miljacka, and for a few days after June 28 was unable to eat anything because his mouth and throat were injured. At the trial Čabrinović stated that he tried to commit suicide because he "could not live a day like a slave."[14] Also Grabež, Vaso Čubrilović and Popović said that they had been ready to kill themselves after the attempt.[15]

There is no doubt that in this attitude there was a strong desire to sacrifice their lives for the goals in which they believed, a kind of martyrdom based on the example of Žerajić, who had killed himself with his last shot. This martyrdom is also a part of the whole Kosovo legend.

Not having agreed previously on what to say to the police or investigation judge, Princip and Čabrinović in their first interrogations mentioned a few things which helped the interrogators in their search for other members of the conspiracy.

Princip made the initial mistake of stating that he lived in the house of Ilić's mother. He further said that he had lived there when he came to Sarajevo in 1907. This fact led to the arrest of Ilić on the afternoon of June 28. It seems that Princip became aware of his initial mistake and tried to correct himself in the second hearing, stating that he had not lived in Ilić's home in 1907, but it was too late. Ilić had already been arrested.

The whole of Čabrinović's family was put in jail as well, together with the servants and maids working in the café. From them the investigators found out that Čabrinović had said to them that he arrived from Belgrade with two friends. This fact suggested to Pfeffer that Princip and Čabrinović had not operated independently of each other and that there were other conspirators in their group.

After the assassination all other conspirators—Mehmedbašić, Čubrilović, Popović and Grabež—succeeded in escaping arrest and left Sarajevo. Grabež made a fatal mistake by dropping his high-school certificate into a toilet, and the police found it on June 30. On the same day he tried to travel from his native village, Pale, to Višegrad, a town on the Serbian border, but was arrested because he did not have a special permit for traveling. On him was found a passport in which it was written that he had come from Serbia on May 30. He was arrested and escorted to Sarajevo under the suspicion that he might be the third man with whom Princip and Čabrinović had arrived in Sarajevo.

There was another element which placed Princip and Čabrinović in a difficult position during the investigation. The assassination of the Archduke had triggered pogroms against the Serbs in Bosnia and Hercegovina. Some writers believe that they were organized by the Austro-Hungarian authorities and by Archbishop Stadler.[16] The first demonstrations started in the evening of June 28, but the next day they spread all over town. Many Serbian shops and houses were sacked and burned down. The home and the café of Čabrinović's father were plundered. The correspondent of the *Frankfurter Zeitung* described the demonstrations:

I was a witness when the mob destroyed the Serbian shops, one after the other. The police appeared only when the whole business was over and when the mob started to plunder a different place. . . . The scum of the streets broke into private flats, destroying everything they could lay their hands on and grabbing all the valuables.

At the same time the police arrested many leading Serbian merchants, intellectuals and priests as a reprisal for the assassination of the Archduke, even though the Serbian *čaršija* was outraged by Princip's act. The Serbian Eastern Orthodox Bishop of Sarajevo, in his sermon after the *Te Deum* service for the Archduke, called Princip and Čabrinović "antichrists."[17] When, a few weeks later, war broke out, a large group of leading Serbs from Bosnia and Hercegovina presented a petition asking that they be sent to the front at once to prove by their "own deeds that they had nothing to do with the assassination."[18] Some cousins of Čabrinović and Princip even changed their family names in order to express their disgust with the assassination.[19] But all these measures did not help the Serbs much. In the first forty-eight hours after the assassination more than two hundred leading Serbs were arrested in Sarajevo alone. The police treated them harshly. All of them were taken to the same military prison where Princip and Čabrinović were being held, and were ordered to stay in the courtyards and to look at the sun for a whole hot summer day, without water.[20] Soon Serbian peasants from the Sarajevo neighborhood were brought as well. Police beat some of them, and Princip and Čabrinović heard their screaming and groaning. When the investigation was over, gallows were erected and several peasants from the Sarajevo district were hanged in the courtyard of the military prison just below Princip and Čabrinović's window.[21] The prisoners were warned not to come to the window to look at what was going on, but Čabrinović did not obey this order and a soldier fired at his window, barely missing him.[22]

There is controversy among historians whether the conspirators were physically tortured in jail. Princip did not say anything about it, while Vaso Čubrilović[23] and Branko Zagorac[24] stated explicitly that they had not been tortured. On the other hand, Grabež at his trial complained that he had been tortured.[25] In a letter which he succeeded in sending to his father after the trial, he described in great detail the way he was tortured.

This writer is of the opinion that the conspirators were not tortured with the knowledge of the investigation judge, but that some of them, particularly Grabež, were tortured by the police under the instructions of the officer Viktor Ivasjuk, a lean man, with a hooked nose and close-set eyes. Grabež said that Ivasjuk immersed him in water and applied many other kinds of torture. During the first few days after the assassination, both the police and the investigation judge were interrogating the conspirators. Pfeffer heard that during the night the police had taken the conspirators out of the jail without his knowledge.[26] He complained to the president of the district court, Ilnitsky, who told him that he knew about the tortures, and that "the police officials were interrogating Princip and Čabrinović during the night, burning their wounds with lapis."[27] Ilnitsky instructed Pfeffer to complain to the chief of the Bosnian government's Judiciary Department, which issued an order to the effect that the police must have no contact with the arrested assassins without Pfeffer's permission.[28] Pfeffer's statement should be treated with reserve. In the trial documents, it is recorded that Bela Geza Kaczvinsky, the secretary of the District Court of Sarajevo, stated that he had been "a representative of the court in the police headquarters during the interrogation of the accused" and that "after the police interrogation, I had to question the accused separately."[29] From this it is obvious that there existed a close collaboration between the police and the court, a practice no doubt against the then existing laws in Austria-Hungary.

One of the conspirators who survived this ordeal told this writer that the president of the district court visited them every fourteen days, asking if they had any complaints against the jail.[30] The conspirators received the same food as other prisoners in the military jail and had the right to get new linen and underwear.

Seeing that many innocent people were being arrested because of him, Princip began to have second thoughts about whether he should name the other conspirators. If the Young Bosnians had not prepared themselves for what they would say at the investigation, still they had discussed how they should behave in the hands of the Habsburg police and law courts, and whether they should admit their activities or not.

Danilo Ilić's trusted friend, the Eastern Orthodox priest Mirko Maksimović, described in great detail the controversy over this question:

In the Sarajevo revolutionary groups besides the studies of revolutionary literature in general, there were discussions about the question of revolutionary actions. Danilo Ilić who was for direct action opened up the problem of confession to the authorities after the revolutionary act was accomplished. There were different opinions in the groups. Ilić was for unconditional confession. His reasons were the following: The Russian revolutionaries did not have on this issue a meritorious solution. Everything depended on the conditions under which the acts were performed and the men who did them. The refusal to confess anything had quite a different meaning among the Russians. Their action had its specific traits and, according to Ilić's opinion, the whole world knew well of their methods of struggle. In order to popularize their action, the trials, confessions and statements were not necessary, because the people were acquainted with the whole work of the organization, which had its flags as old as those of the Decembrists. "We are," Ilić argued, "a small people with a small radius of action, and therefore we have to build strong personalities, which cannot express themselves by keeping quiet and denying at the many trials their own activities. . . . To us the mission is designated to educate the new generation with our martyrdom and our full public confession about our deeds."[31]

The authenticity of Mirko Maksimović's statement was confirmed by the behavior of Princip on July 2. According to the minutes of his investigation in front of Pfeffer, as they are preserved in the *Nachlass*, Princip was led from the jail and he stated:

I will explain everything in detail and name the guilty, but only so that innocent people do not suffer. For we guilty ones were in any case ready to go to our deaths. I nevertheless request that you confront me briefly before the hearing with Danilo Ilić and Trifko Grabež, to whom I want to say only two or three words. Then I will tell everything. Otherwise I will confess nothing at all, even if you beat me to death.

The minutes continued:

Because it is useless to try to cause the suspect to testify before meeting his demand and because Grabež has not yet been sent to prison, the hearing was interrupted until the delivery of Grabež.[32]

Up to that moment Grabež, despite police torture, had refused to admit anything. In his interrogation by Pfeffer he stated:

I denied everything before the police, because I was of the opinion that Princip and Čabrinović had betrayed nothing, and I was arrested only because I was a Belgrade student. Then I was handed over to the detectives, who tortured me terribly, but I wanted to tell them nothing either.[33]

On July 2 at 2 P.M. Princip was confronted with both Grabež and Ilić. The minutes read:

Gavro Princip is led from confinement and, at a distance of eight steps from Trifko Grabež, says:

"Confess everything, how we got the bombs, how we traveled and in what society we were, so that just people do not come to harm."

Danilo Ilić is now led from confinement, and after Trifko Grabež is led away is confronted with Princip, at which the latter explains:

"Since the court has already learned much and so that we can save the innocent it is necessary that you tell everything, among whom you divided the weapons and where the weapons are."

Thereupon Danilo Ilić was led away to confinement and also he said, as had Grabež before, that he would confess all.[34]

Princip's lawyer, Dr. Max Feldbauer, in his defense at the trial, on October 22, said about this confrontation: "I want to stress, Most Honorable Court, that Princip was the one who admitted his deed to the investigation judge. I want to stress that he has good qualities, as well. In this way he made the whole investigation much easier and the culprits were detected. Only after this was Ilić detected."[35]

This document from the *Nachlass* about the confrontation on July 2 throws full light on the controversy initiated by Jevtić, Jevdjević and Pfeffer about the behavior of the conspirators after they were arrested. Jevtić put the blame on Čabrinović as the one who betrayed his comrades, and to a certain extent on Ilić,[36] while Jevdjević proclaimed that Ilić was simply a traitor. Jevdjević described Ilić as a "cynical man with the physiognomy of a fish . . . aloof from others . . . a man who liked the good life."[37] Jevdjević in his book in 1934 described the confrontation of Princip and Grabež and Ilić, and he falsified a letter of Grabež, adding a sentence claiming that Princip had said to Grabež: " 'Trišo, it is a pity, everything has been betrayed; you should not permit yourself to be tortured,' and afterward Princip spat in the face of Danilo Ilić, who was present in the room."[38]

When Pfeffer wrote his book in 1938, he too hid the basic facts about the confrontation of July 2. First, he did not mention it at all; second, he claimed that he made a deal with Ilić, who had asked him to promise him that his life would be spared, and Ilić then would confess everything,[39] although in the minutes of the interrogation, as preserved in the *Nachlass*, there is nothing about this.

The motives of Pfeffer were obvious. By 1938 the most chauvinistic elements in Yugoslavia were glorifying Princip, and Pfeffer, a conformist by nature, wanted to contribute to this attitude. Besides, he wished to deepen the controversy raised by Jevtić and Jevdjević. There are several proofs that Pfeffer operated with malicious intentions against Ilić. For instance, when he described his first interrogation of Princip, he deliberately omitted Princip's statement that he was living at the home of Danilo Ilić; and it was on the basis of this statement that Ilić was at once arrested.[40]

He also did not mention that Ilić was interrogated twice, on June 29 and June 30, as the *Nachlass* documentation shows, denying that he knew anything about the plot. He admitted that he knew Princip and that they had had discussions on various topics. One has to keep in mind that in Ilić's pocket the police had found poison wrapped in paper which he should have given to Grabež.

Despite the fact that Princip was the first to mention, at the confrontation of July 2, that innocent men should not suffer, he and Ilić did not have the same attitude on how far they should reveal the conspiracy. Princip wanted to reveal the names of only six Sarajevo conspirators, and not Miško Jovanović, Veljko Čubrilović and the peasants who led Princip and his group through Bosnia and who had helped to carry the weapons.[41] On the other hand, Ilić went further and in his interrogation of July 4 gave the names of both groups of assassins, as well as the name of Miško Jovanović.

So all the assassins and their main accomplices were arrested, except the Moslem carpenter Mehmed Mehmedbašić, who spent the first night after the assassination with some Moslem youths who were preparing to become imams. Mehmedbašić knew them from the *medresa*, the Moslem religious school, where he had spent seven and a half years of his childhood.[42] Having a travel permit and with a fez on his head, he left Sarajevo by train for Hercegovina on June 30. He succeeded in fleeing to Montenegro and crossed the border on Friday, July 3. Several people helped him in Hercegovina, including his former *kmets*.

Vaso Čubrilović was arrested in Dubica, a town in western Bosnia, on

July 3. Cvetko Popović was arrested on the same day. From Sarajevo he had slipped away to Semlin (Zemun), where his parents lived. On July 3, the Semlin police sent him a summons. Popović thought that this was a routine checkup, because if he had been named as an assassin by someone in Sarajevo, the police would have seized him at once. Popović reported to a police official who read him the accusations from Sarajevo regarding his part in the events on June 28. The policeman himself hardly believed it, but to his horror Popović answered simply: "Yes, everything is true."[43] Ivo Kranjčević, the Croat boy who had helped Čubrilović to hide his arms, was arrested on July 6. The next day all his relatives who knew about the weapons were put in jail: Ivan Momčinović, Franjo and Angela Sadilo. Neither Miško Jovanović nor Veljko Čubrilović tried to flee. They were arrested and brought to Sarajevo, but Čubrilović refused for several days to reveal the names of the peasants. Jakov Milović, the courier who had brought Princip and Grabež from Serbia to Bosnia, was arrested only on August 11, after Pfeffer, who knew only Milović's first name, had brought five peasants named Jakov from the village in which Milović lived.

The preliminary investigation lasted until September 19, 1914. After the first week, Princip and his companions established contact between themselves by the so-called "Russian letter," which they had learned from Stepnyak's *Underground Russia*. It was a special system of knocking on the walls of their cells on the basis of an alphabetic code:

	1	2	3	4	5
1	A	B	C	D	E
2	F	G	H	I	J
3	K	L	M	N	O
4	P	R	S	T	U
5	V	W	X	Y	Z

Sharp knocks meant the vertical column of letters, and deliberate knocks indicated the horizontal.

They exchanged information about the newly arrested men, although they did not have a chance to use the code in the first few vital days of the investigation. This code was also a means of spreading the news they learned about Austria-Hungary's declaration of war on Serbia on July 28, in which the Sarajevo assassination was used as a pretext.

Čabrinović originated another means of communication among the prisoners. On the bottom of his metal plate he would scratch a few words with his spoon. The jailers would take away the plates and without realizing anything would give them, with the next meal, to other conspirators. The others adopted this device, and soon each of them had his "newspaper." Čabrinović named his *The Bowl*, Grabež's was *The Bomb* and Princip's *The Woodpecker*.[44] Princip even used his *Woodpecker* to publish his poems. One of them reads:

Time goes slowly and
There is nothing new—
Today everything is like yesterday,
And tomorrow will bring the same—
But I will always remember
The just words of the fallen falcon Žerajić:

"He who wants to live, has to die.
He who is ready to die, will live for ever."

In another poem Princip deplored their being in jail while the soldiers were fighting on the battlefields:

Instead of being on the battlefields,
Where the war trumpets are blown;
Here we are in the dungeons,
Listening to the jingling of chains.[45]

Čabrinović too tried his hand at poetry; most of his works were satiric ones.

Two of the youngest conspirators, Lazar Djukić and Cvetko Popović, played ticktacktoe by knocking on the walls through the nights when they could not sleep.[46]

An anecdote told to this writer by Vaso Čubrilović throws some light on the relations between Princip and Ilić during these weeks. Čabrinović was knocking on Ilić's wall, but Ilić did not answer, because he was asleep. Čabrinović concluded that Ilić had hanged himself and spread the news to Princip and the others. Princip answered: "He was such a good friend." But a few hours later, when Ilić awoke, Čabrinović's mistake was established. Princip was pleased, and he made one of his typical jokes, tapping on the wall to Ilić: "O.K. If you did not hang yourself *Švabe* [the Serbian nickname for Austrians and Germans] will hang you."[47]

On September 28 the indictment was handed to the accused. For the first time since June 28 they met together. Cvetko Popović said that no one paid any attention to Pfeffer while he was reading it. Pfeffer was disturbed by their attitude, saying that they were "behaving like children," while their fate was at stake. Princip answered: "Please do understand us, sir. We see each other after such a long time. What you are reading is well known to us, and we also know what we have to expect."[48] Pfeffer informed them that they had a legal right of appeal from the indictment, although this might only delay the trial. Čabrinović wanted to use right: "War goes on and nobody knows what shall come tomorrow." Pfeffer answered him: "Do you expect to be acquitted? Even before the war is over, fourteen Čabrinovićes will be hanged."[49] "This will make the position of the hangmen even worse," retorted Čabrinović. But at the insistence of the others Čabrinović agreed to withdraw his appeal, because most of the accused wished to have the trial as soon as possible.

Princip used this first joint encounter of the accused to tell them how he intended to behave at the trial. Kranjčević recorded this incident:

The younger conspirators agreed to behave calmly, not to use any sharp expressions, in order not to make the situation of the older conspirators, who were faced with the death penalty, more difficult. The only exception was Gavrilo Princip, who said that he would not be submissive and that he would speak his mind openly. He was the only one aware that one day public opinion would judge their statements and therefore he regarded it as his duty to behave bravely.[50]

All the accused had lawyers. Dr. Max Feldbauer was appointed by the court to defend Princip and three other conspirators. When he came to Princip and informed him that he was going to defend him, Princip answered him abruptly:

Do not pay any attention to my defense, concentrate all your efforts on the defense of the other three; try to save their necks and study their cases more thoroughly. If you waste your time on my defense, this will be at the expense of the other three. You could help them, because they are innocent, while I, in any case, am ready to face the worst.[51]

At his first meeting with his accomplices, Princip had informed them that he intended to try to shield the *kmets* who had helped them to carry the weapons: the Kerovićes, Milović, Stjepanović and Milošević. He said he would claim that he had used violence and the threat of violence against them.

Kranjčević recorded that each accused had received one printed copy of the indictment, but that later all the copies were withdrawn, because the prosecutor had decided to delete some passages. In the first version, it was said of Čabrinovic's attempt that "the Almighty saved His Imperial and Royal Highness the Archduke Franz Ferdinand, by not permitting the bomb to explode in the car," while the description of Princip's assassination said that "with the Almighty's will the bullets hit their target."[52] When Princip and his accomplices returned to their cells, they read these passages and in their atheistic orientation joked about them in their "newspapers." Kranjčević recorded that in one of the "newspapers" was written: "The chief accused ought to be the Almighty, and we should all be released at once, because we are innocent according to the indictment."[53] Kranjčević claimed that shortly afterward all copies of the first version of the indictment were withdrawn and a new printed copy was delivered instead, which omitted the references to God. But this incident brought the end of *Bomb*,

Woodpecker and the other "newspapers." Thereafter, the metal plates were checked, and if there were any marks on them they were withdrawn from circulation.

For a time Bilinski and Potiorek thought of postponing the trial until after the end of the war, but then they changed their minds.[54] Foreign Minister Count Berchtold intervened with a letter to Bilinski, dated October 1, in which he asked indirectly that pressure be brought to bear on the judges in Sarajevo. Berchtold made two points: 1) The sentence should take into account its international implications, since otherwise it could have the most adverse effect on domestic and foreign policy, especially in the light of official statements on conditions in Bosnia and Hercegovina and of the action against Serbia; 2) the sentence should be given before the conflict was resolved on the battlefield, since otherwise, if Austria won, others would say that she had not dared to render justice before she was sure of the outcome of the war, and if Austria lost, she would be subject to undesirable pressure—however just the sentence, it would seem to be an act of revenge, and it would subject Austria to even more pressure from the victors.[55]

The trial opened on October 12 and lasted until October 23. Altogether twenty-five persons were brought to trial. All six assassins were boys under twenty years of age at the time of the assassination, except Mehmedbašić, who was twenty-seven. Gavrilo Princip was nineteen years and eleven months; Čabrinović nineteen years and five months; Grabež eighteen years and ten months; Vaso Čubrilović seventeen years and six months; Popović eighteen years and three months. Danilo Ilić was just twenty-four. Among the accomplices too there were many young ones: Kranjčević, nineteen years and one month; Marko Perin sixteen years and ten months; and Dragan Kalember, sixteen years and one month.

The trial took place in a large room of the military prison. The presiding judge was Luigi von Curinaldi. There were also two other judges, Bogdan Naumović and Mayer Hofmann, the first one of Ukrainian nationality and the second a German. The trial was not completely public; only people with special invitations could attend. Of all the Bosnian Serbs only the brothers Jakšić, the leaders of the Social Democratic party, were admitted.[56] The head of the Jesuits, Father Anton Puntigam, was present all through the trial. He was a frail man, and at the end of a session, whenever the accused would pass by him, he would pull himself back so that they could not touch him.[57] Under his influence the president of the court, Luigi von Curinaldi, went to a monastery and became a friar at the end of the trial. There were six journalists, three from Sarajevo, two from Budapest and one from Vienna. The state's attorney charged twenty-two of the accused with high treason and first-degree murder and three with complicity in the murder.

On the whole, Princip, Grabež and Ilić behaved as they had during the investigation, while Čubrilović, Popović, Kranjčević and Zagorac were bolder in stating why they had taken part in the conspiracy. All of them claimed the right of resistance, to the point of assassinating a bad ruler, as the main motive for their deed; they admitted that the initiative had been solely theirs and that they had obtained from Ciganović and Tankosić only the weapons.

The most concise statement of the classical right to resistance was made by Branko Zagorac, who was accused of knowing about the preparations for the assassination from his friend Vaso Čubrilović and of not informing the authorities. Between Judge Curinaldi and Zagorac the following dialogue took place:

"Therefore you are of the opinion that there are cases when assassination is necessary?"

"Yes, there are."

"In which cases?"

"When the man is a tyrant."

"In that case everybody is entitled to assassinate him?"

"Not everybody, just the one who wants to do it."[58]

The same concept was expressed by Princip, when he stated: "I do not feel like a criminal because I put away the one who was doing evil." And again: "Austria represents the evil for our people, as it is, and therefore it should not exist."[59]

The sharp-tongued Čabrinović had the most colorful exchanges with the judges and the state's attorney. He stated that vengeance is a moral duty for men and therefore he had resolved to sacrifice himself.[60] He quoted from two articles that had appeared in Zora, on the classical concept of tyrannicide.

Even Ilić, although still claiming that he had been against the attempt, stated that in principle the assassination was justified as the best means of protest against a bad ruler.[61]

As concrete grievances, Princip,[62] Grabež,[63] Čabrinović,[64] and Vaso Čubrilović[65] mentioned the extraordinary measures in Bosnia and Hercegovina in March 1913, when all the Serbian cultural societies were banned. Cvetko Popović stated explicitly that he joined the conspiracy for "vengeance against persecution of the Slavs in the whole of the monarchy."

The plight of the kmets was stressed by Princip and Čabrinović. The presiding judge asked him to define what he meant by the "sufferings of the people," and Princip answered: "The people have been impoverished, they are treated like cattle. I am the son of a kmet, and I know what life is like in the villages."[66]

The revolutionary destruction of Austria-Hungary and the liberation of the South Slavs were mentioned by all the chief conspirators. Princip stated several times that he was a revolutionary, that he hated Austria, and that it should be destroyed.[67] Grabež stated that the Slavs should be recognized as equal with other peoples in the monarchy and that they should get the most elementary political rights.[68] The presiding judge had an argument over that question and said to Grabež that "there are many Slavs who are fighting for Austria" and Grabež retorted: "When Slav soldiers fight for Austria, then they are just an unconscious mass."[69] The state's attorney declared at once that he would prosecute Grabež for this statement.

Čabrinović said that "Austria is rotten within," and when the presiding judge asked him to elaborate on this, he answered: "A state which is not built on the nationality principle, which subjugates other states, could not be regarded as a stable state; nothing links its parts except sheer discipline. Its whole strength lies in bayonets."[70]

Vaso Čubrilović defined the goal of nationalism as "to fight so that your own people raises itself to the level of other peoples." When the presiding judge asked him what he thought was the basis of the Austro-Hungarian Empire, Čabrinović answered: "I can state that the monarchy is ruled by the Germans and the Magyars, while the Slavs are oppressed."[71] Kranjčević said that he wanted to protest against "the German influence, which is killing us."[72] He described Austria as a pawn of Germany, where all directives against the Slavs are initiated.[73]

Grabež called the Sarajevo assassination "the greatest revolutionary act in history."[74] He said that the moment he learned that Franz Ferdinand would come to Bosnia, he and Princip came to the conclusion that it was time that Austria "and Franz Ferdinand in particular" should pay for everything that was going on in Bosnia and Hercegovina and for "all evil things there."

Grabež further insisted that the Slavs did not enjoy equal rights with other people, and that their free cultural development was hampered, that they did not have enough primary schools, high schools or universities. Curinaldi challenged this statement, but Grabež retorted: "Why do you deny what every honest man thinks?"[75]

The presiding judge had a long argument with Čabrinović over the question of individual terror and revolution. He read him first his statement at the July 12 investigation: "It is, for example, my conviction that such an assassination is the predecessor of revolution. For, as in Poland the assassinations were the predecessors of the revolution, so also Russia, which is a rotten state, will only be saved by a revolution and then will become one of the leading states, and for Austria a revolution will suffice to destroy it completely." After he asked Čabrinović whether he still thought like this, Čabrinović answered: ". . . I have asked myself why there are no assassinations in France, Germany and England, and why they happen in Austria."

The presiding judge interrupted him: "There were no assassinations in Austria."

"But what about Sychinsky in Poland, Žerajić in Sarajevo, then Jukić, Dojčić, Njegoš? I know five or six of them," answered Čabrinović.

"King Umberto was killed in Italy," retorted the presiding judge.

"These are rare occurrences. The King of Greece was also killed. That was one assassination, and here there are six of them among all peoples. I compared Austria with Poland. In Poland before the revolution there were assassinations . . ."[76]

It is is interesting that the assassins did not emphasize that they wanted to kill only the Archduke Franz Ferdinand and not the other Habsburgs. Princip at his first interrogation had stated that for two years he had had the idea of killing any high person in Austria who represented its power.[77] Grabež stated also "that the personality of the Archduke did not play any role; the main thing was the feeling of the people."[78]

To specific questions of the judges about their grievances against the Archduke, Princip mentioned that he had been the instigator of the Extraordinary Measures in Bosnia and the high-treason trials in Croatia.[79]

Čabrinović had a different opinion. He stated that he would never have carried out an attempt against the life of Emperor Franz Josef, even though he had been ready to kill the Archduke:

An anarchist does not recognize any laws and regards himself as entitled to vengeance. I know from papers and from discussions that at Ballhausplatz [Ministry of Foreign Affairs in Vienna] there is a clique called the war party and that the deceased Franz Ferdinand was the chief of that group, which has aspirations for the conquest of Serbia and other Slav countries. I thought in pursuing my vengeance against him I had the feeling that I revenged myself on all others also.[80]

About the old Emperor, Čabrinović said:

I hated the Heir Apparent because he was an enemy of Serbia. I knew that the Emperor Franz Josef was a good friend of the Serbian people, as was the case with the Crown Prince Rudolf. Our Emperor was on good terms with King Milan. In Serbia I heard a good report on their relations . . . Although I have anarchist ideas, although I hated everything, I had nothing against His Apostolic Majesty Franz Josef. The only thing I object to about him is that he is getting 60,000 crowns a day . . .[81]

The conspirators from time to time expressed derogatory opinions about čaršija and the Serbian bourgeoisie in Bosnia and Hercegovina.

Čabrinović said that he was struck by the servile attitude of some Serbs, whom he described as the government's mamelukes. His lawyer asked him if his remark was aimed against the political group of loyal Serbs headed by Dr. Danilo Dimović, and Čabrinović retorted: "It is not clear to me and I do not understand that. I have read only revolutionary literature, and I cannot grasp how Serbs could publish a progovernment paper and, what is worse, call it *Istina* [Truth]. We made jokes about that in our printing shop."[82]

At the trial there was a marked difference between the behavior of the younger and that of the older conspirators. Princip, Čabrinović, Grabež, Ilić, and the other assassins knew in advance what was going to happen to them. They were revolutionaries in their ideals, always ready to die for them. The accused peasants, Milović, the Kerovićes, Mićić and Milošević, were not men of doctrine. They regarded themselves as good Serbs, they were connected with Narodna Odbrana and they had helped the conspirators to go through Bosnia. In a way, their sacrifice was much greater than that of the Young Bosnians. Old Kerović was a relatively rich peasant; he owned more than three thousand plum trees. He was the head of a *zadruga*, and all the men from it were arrested because he had received Princip and Grabež under his roof. Jakov Milović was a poor peasant, leaving four small children all alone at home, as he was a widower.

All the peasants were reluctant in their defense. They behaved humbly, in order to get as mild a sentence as possible. Still, deep in their hearts, they supported Princip and his friends. One of the younger Kerovićes was acquitted at the end of the trial and sent immediately to the front line in the Carpathians. Only a few days later, in its first encounter with the Russian army, he fled from the Habsburg army and joined the so-called Dobrovoljačka Vojska, an army composed of volunteers, former Habsburg soldiers now under the Serbian flag, fighting against the Germans and the Austrians. Less than a year after he was acquitted, young Kerović was killed in action while fighting against the Habsburgs and their allies.[83]

In a similar situation were Veljko Čubrilović, the teacher from Priboj, and his friend the rich merchant Miško Jovanović from Tuzla. Both of them were members of Narodna Odbrana, working in the Serbian cultural society and sending secret information to Serbia about the movements of the Austro-Hungarian army. Still, they did not believe in individual terror as the best means of political struggle. Both Čubrilović and Jovanović stated that plainly. They admitted that they had helped the Young Bosnians, but they declared that they did not favor the revolutionary destruction of the Habsburg empire, desiring instead autonomy for Bosnia and Hercegovina. Both Jovanović and Čubrilović could have fled after June 28—they were not arrested until several weeks later—but, they remained at home. "What would my peasants have said if I had fled and left them alone in these trying days," said Veljko Čubrilović to one of the conspirators.[84]

Veljko's younger brother, Vaso Čubrilović, defended himself differently during the trial, illustrating the basic differences between the two generations of Bosnian intellectuals. Vaso openly stated that he desired the revolutionary destruction of the Habsburg empire and that he was an atheist, while his brother prayed until his last breath and read the Gospel of Saint John. In addition to his thirteen-year sentence, Vaso received an additional sentence of three years because at the question of the presiding judge as to whether he felt guilty taking part in the conspiracy which ended in the killing of the Archduke he answered: "And who is responsible for the war which takes the lives of hundreds of thousands of men?"[85]

The brothers also disagreed on the problem of relations between the Serbs and Croats. Veljko was basically concerned with the liberation of the Serbs and when the presiding judge asked Vaso whether he were a Serb, or a Serbo-Croat, he answered: "I am a Serbo-Croat." At the question, "What does this mean?" he answered: "It means that I do not consider myself only as a Serb and that I would work not only for Serbia, but also for Croatia."

Princip, Grabež, and Čabrinović also were for Yugoslav unity. Princip made many statements along this line both at the investigation and at the trial. On August 15 he stated to Pfeffer:

The political union of the Yugoslavs was always before my eyes, and that was my basic idea. Therefore it was necessary in the first place to free the Yugoslavs from the *Švabe* and from Austria; for every misfortune which hits the Yugoslavs stems from Austria.

This spirit was especially developed among the youth in the Yugoslav lands and was a consequence of the embitterment of the people.

This and all the rest moved me to carry out the assassination of the Heir Apparent, for I considered him, in regard to his activity, as very dangerous for Yugoslavia.[86]

"I am a Yugoslav nationalist, aiming for the unification of all Yugoslavs, and I do not care what form of state, but it must be free from Austria," Princip told the court.[87] He stated that Ilić was a Yugoslav nationalist like himself, dedicated to the unification of all South Slavs, but at that point the presiding judge interrupted him:

"A unification under Austria?"

Princip retorted: "God save us from that. I do not like dynasties. We did not go so far; we thought of unification, as conditions permit."[88]

Among the younger accused the only one who declared against unification of South Slavs was Nikola Forkapić, a student in his fourth year at the Teachers College. He was accused of knowing from Čubrilović about the preparations for the attempt and not reporting it to the police. He said that he was a member of the Old Radical party and that he did not wish for a political union of Serbs and Croats, that he regarded Bosnia and Hercegovina as countries in which Serbs lived, but he was against unification with Serbia and thought that the two lands were Austrian lands.[89]

The Austro-Hungarian authorities tried to conceal the fact that there were Croats and Moslems among the conspirators, because they wished to present the whole plot as of Serbian origin and executed solely by Serbs. For that purpose Kranjčević's name Ivo, a typical Croat name, was changed in the press reports to Milan, both before the trial and during it.[90] The Jesuit paper *Hrvatski Dnevnik* published a short article on July 8, denying that Kranjčević was a Catholic, claiming that this had been invented by the Serbs.

From the first hour of the investigation the Austro-Hungarian authorities had tried to prove that the assassination was initiated in Belgrade, and that Princip and his fellows were just young men led astray by pan-Serb propaganda. The Sarajevo police were particularly eager to prove that point. The police officer Ivasjuk took Čabrinović out of jail on July 2, pressing him to admit that they had received their weapons from Narodna Odbrana in Belgrade through its Secretary Milan Pribićević. Ivasjuk claimed that Čabrinović admitted that Princip had told him he would get the weapons for the assassination from Narodna Odbrana.[91]

When Pfeffer asked Čabrinović if this were true, Čabrinović denied it vehemently. On July 4, Pfeffer organized a confrontation between Čabrinović and Ivasjuk, and the former flatly stated that Ivasjuk's statement was not true.[92]

The conspirators' main point was that the idea for the assassination had been their own, that they had not been influenced by anyone in Belgrade to take part in the conspiracy, except that they had asked for weapons from the Bosnia *komite* in Belgrade, and had taken their help also in crossing the border. Čabrinović complained of how people in Belgrade ridiculed the Young Bosnians for being able to tolerate a system of tyranny in their own home and not do anything about it.[93]

Grabež stated flatly: "I was led not by Serbia but solely by Bosnia."[94] Princip stated that in Belgrade he had no friends, except the Bosnian students and *komite* whom he had known from Sarajevo.[95] It is also a fact that in the conspiracy no student from Belgrade took part; only Bosnians and Hercegovinians were involved.

Princip even said that he could have crossed from Serbia to Bosnia without anybody's help—"I have crossed so many times from Serbia to Bosnia and vice versa, and this time I could have done the same, but I wished to make a crossing this time as safe as possible."[96]

Ilić, Čubrilović Čabrinović, Princip and Grabež independently of one another claimed that in Serbia there was a conflict between the government and the military people, as well as between Narodna Odbrana and the military people, and that the military people advised them to be watchful of the civil authorities during the crossing of the frontier.[97]

Vaso Čubrilović said on July 5 to the investigation judge Pfeffer that he once asked Ilić if the weapons had arrived and Ilić answered that the weapons would come, although they were difficult to obtain, because official Serbia was keeping an eye on weapons and bombs, and also because the official circles in Belgrade were afraid of some foolish act in general, and particularly that somebody would attempt to kill the Archduke Franz Ferdinand. For that reason they had to get the weapons from unofficial circles in Serbia.[98]

At the trial both Čubrilović and Ilić confirmed this.[99] Čabrinović said explicitly that they had to be very careful traveling through Serbia, so that the Minister of Interior Stojan Protić did not hear about their journey.[100] Grabež stated that Major Vojin Tankosić was an enemy of Narodna Odbrana,[101] and Princip expressed a similar opinion. Ilić stated that "in Serbia there is freedom, and everyone can obtain weapons."

After all twenty-five accused had given their statements, and after the documentary evidence had been read, the state's attorney, Dr. Franjo Švara, took the floor again on October 22. His main point was that Princip and the other conspirators were the victims of pan-Serb propaganda from Belgrade. He also raised the question of Princip's age, claiming that he has been born on June 13, 1894, that he was over twenty years old at the time of the assassination, and that he should be punished with the death penalty.[102]

Princip's lawyer Max Feldbauer challenged the state's attorney's assertion as to Princip's birth date and brought evidence that his date of birth was July 13, 1894.[103] On the other hand, Feldbauer accepted the state's attorney's thesis that Princip was not the initiator of the assassination and that he was a victim of pan-Serb propaganda.

Other lawyers followed Feldbauer's thesis, and some of them behaved as if they were the accusers and not the defenders of their clients. That was particularly true of Čabrinović's lawyer, Dr. Premužić, and of Grabež's lawyer, Štrupl. The latter's defense consisted of only fifty-six words.[104]

The only exception was the defense presented by Rudolf Cistler, who was the lawyer for Veljko and Vaso Čubrilović, Ivo Kranjčević and Nedjo Kerović. He argued that from the strictly legal point of view his defendants could not be accused of high treason, because Bosnia and Hercegovina were not within the territorial integrity of the monarchy but represented a separate entity under the Habsburg crown.[105] Basically, Cistler defended the right to self-determination of the South Slavs. The presiding judge ordered him to stop giving his defense and the state's attorney began proceedings against Cistler and he was banished from Sarajevo after the trial.[106]

In addition to defense of their motives for the assassination, Princip and his accomplices were concerned with their own personal problems, which no doubt helped to determine how they finally acted. In this respect there was even a degree of rivalry among some of the conspirators, especially between Princip and Čabrinović.

Both during the investigation and at the trial each of them gave new information about the character of their divergences. Although Princip himself wished to prove by the assassination that he was equal to others who did not think him capable of bravery, he himself behaved toward Čabrinović with a show of superiority. There are several reasons for Princip's behavior. Like the other Young Bosnians, he was self-consciously an intellectual; Čabrinović was the only one who had not gone to school and who was a worker by trade. Princip said to Dr. Pappenheim that Čabrinović "was a typesetter, of insufficient intelligence."[107] Besides, there were slight political differences between the two. To Dr. Pappenheim, Princip said that he "thought that Čabrinović was not sufficiently nationalistic," because he had been previously "an anarchist and socialist."[108] Ilić said that both Princip and Grabež regarded Čabrinović "as a naïve man, not capable of executing an assassination."[109]

Čabrinović was well aware of Princip's opinion of him. He had had an argument with the Young Bosnian group to which both of them belonged in Sarajevo in 1912, and he was expelled from it. During the journey from Belgrade to Sarajevo they had quarreled, and Princip had taken the bomb away from Čabrinović.

All these humiliations Čabrinović could not forget. The fact that he was the first one who threw a bomb at the Archduke, and that all the other conspirators failed to shoot or to throw their bombs during the first passage of the Archduke through the Appel Quay, gave him such strength that he openly challenged Princip several times during the investigation and the trial. Čabrinović complained to Pfeffer that Princip was "a real dictator and was not honest with me," and that "Princip is a very reserved man."[110]

Čabrinović was a very emotional boy who could not hide his feelings, often going from one extreme to the other. During the trial he forgave his father for all he had suffered from him. A letter from Čabrinović's father was read in which he complained that his children were ungrateful toward him, and he wished that their children should in turn pay them for this ingratitude with the same behavior. When the presiding judge said to Čabrinović: "You see what an ungrateful son you are," he retorted: "I do not wish to denounce my own father, but if his pedagogy had been better I would not be sitting on this bench."[111] But on another occasion, when a political opinion of his father was mentioned, Čabrinović jumped to his feet and shouted to the presiding judge: "He was your spy."[112]

The difference in temperament between Princip and Čabrinović was clearly expressed at the very end of the trial. When the presiding judge asked Princip if he had anything to add in his own defense, Princip said just a few words: "As far as suggestions are concerned that somebody talked us into committing the assassination, that is not true. The idea for the assassination grew among us, and we realized it. We loved our people. In my own defense I have nothing to say."[113]

Čabrinović's nature led him to emotional outbursts, even to tears in front of the judges, in contrast to the cool, self-controlled Princip, who answered as if it were beneath his dignity to defend himself in front of an enemy law court. Čabrinović wished to convince the judges that he and his colleagues were innocent. His last speech is full of the contradictions caused by his emotions. It ended with the words:

> We did not hate Austria, but Austria after thirty-three years of occupying Bosnia did not solve our conditions, did not solve the agrarian problem. These are the motives which led us to the assassination. . . .
>
> I want to add a few words. Although Princip likes to show that he is brave, although all of us like to do the same, all of us nevertheless feel sorry, because we did not know that the late Franz Ferdinand was the father of a family. We were extremely impressed by the words which he uttered to his wife before he died: "Soferl, Soferl, don't die. Live for our children." We are everything you wish, but we are not criminals. In my name and in the name of all my comrades, I am humbly submitting my apologies to the children of the Heir Apparent asking them to forgive us, and you can punish us as you wish. We are not criminals, we are honest and noble, we are idealists. We wanted to do good. We loved our people, we are dying for our ideals.[114]

After this, as one of the lawyers recorded, Čabrinović sat on the bench with his head bowed, barely controlling his feelings, while "Princip's giant nature, his enormous vitality, would not let him accept Čabrinović's words unchallenged. . . . Princip jumped up and said briefly that Čabrinović had not been authorized to speak in his name."[115]

The proceedings were interrupted for five minutes; one of the lawyers came up to Princip and asked him what he thought about Franz Ferdinand's words. Princip answered: "What do you think I am, a beast?"[116]

After sentence had been passed, as Ivo Kranjčević recorded in his book, the head of the Jesuits in Sarajevo, the former father-confessor of the Archduke, Father Anton Puntigam, who had attended the whole trial, came personally to Čabrinović's cell.

He brought along a letter written to him by Franz Ferdinand's children asking him to inform Čabrinović that they had forgiven him everything, because he had recanted and expressed his regrets for the death of their parents. Father Puntigam took this opportunity to deliver a long sermon. Čabrinović was surprised and bewildered by the children's forgiveness and remained silent all the time.[117]

The investigation judge, Pfeffer, described the final scene of the trial:

When the proceedings were finished, the presiding judge asked all the accused to stand up if they felt sorry for their act. All stood except Princip. When the presiding judge asked him why he did not get up, Princip answered that he felt sorry for the children who had lost their father and mother; he felt especially sorry for assassinating the Duchess Sophie because she was a Czech. He had had no intention of killing her—the bullet was designed for General Potiorek. But he did not feel sorry for murdering the Austrian Heir Apparent, because he wanted to kill him. After the other conspirators, who were sitting while Princip spoke, heard what Princip had said, Čabrinović jumped up, completely excited, shouting: "I do not feel sorry, either."[118]

The trial ended on October 23, and the sentence was read five days later, on October 28. While the judges, dressed entirely in black—a sign that death sentences would be passed—read the verdict, the convicted men stood chained in pairs.

Princip was sentenced to twenty years at hard labor, with a fast once a month and on each June 28 during his jail term a hard bed in a darkened cell. Nedeljko Čabrinović and Trifko Grabež got the same kind of sentence. Vaso Čubrilović was sentenced to sixteen years in jail, Cvetko Popović to thirteen, and Lazar Djukić to ten.

Danilo Ilić, Veljko Čubrilović, Nedjo Kerović, Miško Jovanović and Jakov Milović were sentenced to be hanged.

Mitar Kerović got life imprisonment. Ivo Kranjčević ten years in jail, Cvijan Stjepanović seven, Branko Zagorac and Marko Perin three years.

Nine of the accused were set free: Nikola Forkapić, Dragan Kalember, Ivan Momčinović, Franjo and Angela Sadilo, as well as four of the peasants, Mićo Mićić, Obren Milošević, and Jovo and Blagoje Kerović. It seems that the judges believed the testimony of Princip and Grabež that they had forced the peasants by threats of violence to show them the road.

The state's attorney filed a protest against the verdict, asking that Princip should be sentenced to death because he was over twenty on the day of the assassination. He also asked that the two peasants who first helped Princip in Bosnia, Obren Milošević and Mićo Mićić, should be sentenced to death instead of being acquitted.

While Princip and his accomplices were being tried, one after another secret organization of Young Bosnians was discovered by the police not only in Sarajevo but in all the towns of Bosnia and Hercegovina. The police discovered the secret groups often by sheer chance. When headmasters and teachers were searching for pupils who were missing after the assassination, they checked the students' books and papers and desks and benches in the classrooms. On the bench of a Moslem schoolboy by the name of Mehmed Zvono was written: "For all people's rights. Hail Bogdan Žerajić. Hail Lazar Djukić. Let us rebel. Long live revolution. Hail Luka Jukić. Hail Yugoslavia." Besides these slogans there were two skulls and crossbones inscribed with the words: "Death to tyrants. Long live Yugoslavia." This provided a clue for the police and led to further arrests.[119]

A similar discovery in Trebinje prompted the arrest of a group of schoolboys there. Arrests were made in all the other towns of Bosnia and Hercegovina.

At Tuzla the diary of Todor Ilić was found at his home. At the news of Franz Ferdinand's assassination, Ilić had entered the following words:

Sons of Yugoslavia do you not feel that our life lies in blood, that *attentat* is the supreme god of all the gods of the nation, because it proves that Young Bosnia is alive, that there exists an element which is prepared to be martyred? The life of a nation consists in blood, blood is the god of a nation, death superseded the Insurrection, and the assassination is the Insurrection of the nation. Žerajić as the first one did not succeed in a formal sense, but in fact he was successful, because after four years of silence he returned in the explosion of bombs and revolver shots at the Quay. The first success in eliminating a branch, by chance the main branch, of the infamous reigning house of Austria. . . . For this first successful assassination which brought much great result . . . I acclaim you, great purified sons of the prophets of Yugoslavia.[120]

Together with the other arrested members of Young Bosnia from Tuzla, Todor Ilić was tried in Bihac and sentenced to death on September 13, 1915. His sentence was later commuted to life imprisonment. Altogether forty schoolboys from Tuzla were sentenced, six of them were given from ten to sixteen years' imprisonment, and others received shorter terms. Also four teachers were sentenced for not reporting their pupils.

Sixty-five members of the Sarajevo groups were tried in Travnik on June 14, 1915. Djukić, Vaso Čubrilović, Cvetko Popović, Ivo Kranjčević and Branko Zagorac again were tried and were sentenced to several years' more imprisonment.

At the same time, persecution of the Serbs in Bosnia and in Hercegovina was intensified, particularly after the outbreak of the war. Special auxiliary units called *Schutzcorps* were formed, composed of all the local Moslems and Croats with full powers to deal with the Serbian population. All together, five thousand Serbs were in jail by the end of July 1914. In the first few months of the war about one hundred fifty Serbs were hanged, among them thirty-seven at Trebinje, the town which demonstrated against the Archduke during his first visit to Bosnia and Hercegovina, in 1906.[121] Most of these executions followed sentences passed by extraordinary military courts. But in several cases the *Schutzcorps* carried out their own vengeance. On the Drina bridge in Foča they hanged the archpriest Josif Kočević, Vasilije Kandić, another priest, and three other Serbs.[122] Cyrillic script was officially banned in Bosnia and Hercegovina, the Serbian confessional schools were closed, and special laws were passed on the basis of which the property of all Serbs was confiscated if members of their families had fled from their residence. In Petrovaradin, Arad and Nezider, concentration camps were opened and tens of thousands of Serbs were herded into them. Few of the prisoners survived, owing to malnutrition—they were given only 100 grams of bread a day—and typhus and typhoid epidemics. At a trial in Banja Luka on November 3, 1915, almost half of the Serbian intellectuals of Bosnia were tried, 156 persons all together, among them 7 members of the *Sabor*, 24 professors and teachers, 21 priests and 8 students. On April 22, 1916, the trial was concluded and fifteen of the accused were sentenced to death. In the meantime the Emperor Franz Josef had died and his successor, the Emperor Karl, commuted the death sentences to life imprisonment.[123]

Danilo Ilić, Miško Jovanović and Veljko Čubrilović were executed on February 3, 1915, and the Bosnian government tersely informed the Joint Minister of Finance in Vienna on the same day: "Execution of the participants in the trial for *attentat*, Veljko Čubrilović, Miško Jovanović and Danilo Ilić, took place today between 9 and 10 A.M. without incident."[124]

Franz Josef himself, with his own hand, had sealed their fate on January 25.[125] The condemned men were informed on the eve of the execution that their sentences had been confirmed and that they would be hanged next morning. Nedjo Kerović and Jakov Milović, who were also sentenced to death on October 28, 1914, were reprieved by imperial grace, and their sentences were commuted to life imprisonment and twenty years' imprisonment respectively.[126]

The available material suggests that the three condemned men died with dignity. The statement of Jevdjević that "Ilić displayed cowardice during the execution"[127] has not been confirmed by any other source. Jevdjević, moreover, does not quote the source of his information and his unsupported statement on this subject should be treated with reserve.

The executioner, Alois Seifried, an Austrian, has left the following description of the last minutes of Ilić, Čubrilović, and Jovanović:

The chains of the doomed men had already been removed from them in their cells and they walked to the gallows preceded by a priest reciting prayers. They were quite composed and fully aware of what was going on. They listened quietly to the reading of the verdict; then the first one, a short man, stepped forward. His name was Veljko Čubrilović. He took his place under the gallows, trying to unbutton his shirt and loosen his tie. I tried to help him, because his fingers worked clumsily, but he refused my offer: "I'll do it," he said calmly. The second was a lean man [Jovanović]. He was also calm. The third, who had the greatest guilt on his soul, was serene. One of them, I do not remember which, said to me: "Please don't torment me for long." And I answered him: "Don't worry, I am a master in my trade; it will all be over in a second."[128]

When the executioner was asked whether they shouted anything against Austria-Hungary, he answered:

Indeed they did. I heard that better than anybody else, because the drums were rolling all the time. They expressed themselves very strongly against Austria. As an Austrian loyal to my own Sovereign, I can assure you that I never met such brave, calm delinquents in all my experience.[129]

The description left by the priest, an Orthodox chaplain by the name of Milan Mratinković, although given after the end of the First World War and the destruction of Austria-Hungary, confirms the impressions of the executioner.[130] He described the scene in the courtyard of the Sarajevo garrison, in which the gallows were erected. It was a bright Bosnian winter morning; snow covered all the mountain peaks around Sarajevo, and a platoon of soldiers with fixed bayonets was drawn up in a square.

They were commanded by an officer in white gloves, who gave an order to start beating drums immediately the executioner began his business. Because of the drums the priest did not hear all the words they said in their last moments, but he commented: "All three went to their death with dignity, acclaiming fatherland and freedom."[131]

Afraid that the graves of Ilić and his friends might become like Žerajić's tomb a new place of pilgrimage, the authorities took steps to have them buried in a secret place. At first, the president of the district court, Ilnitsky, proposed to give the bodies to their families for burial, according to Austro-Hungarian law, but Ivasjuk protested. He wrote a letter to the Bosnian government "stressing that if the assassins were to be buried at the Orthodox cemetery the same thing would happen as with the grave of Žerajić; their graves will be decorated with flowers every night as if they were martyrs and heroes."[132]

The policeman won his point against the legal-minded president of the district court, and Ilić and his friends were secretly buried on the night of February 3.

The whereabouts of their grave was unknown until Ilić's painting instructor at the Teachers College, Mane Krnić, found it by chance.[133] The old professor liked to walk around Sarajevo choosing subjects for his landscape paintings. Once, near the village of Nahorevo, the peasants told him that in the night of February 3, 1915, one of their boys was watching from a mill and saw policemen from Sarajevo digging graves. Krnić at once realized that this must be the grave of his pupil Ilić and his two friends. When the war was over he informed the new authorities. The graves of Ilić, Jovanović, and Čubrilović were opened and their remains were reburied in Sarajevo.

CHAPTER XVI

THE END OF PRINCIP
AND HIS ACCOMPLICES

If he will not other wayes confesse, gentler torturs are to be first usid unto him et sic per gradus ad ima tenditur *and so God speede your goode worke.*

—KING JAMES's letter of instructions to the interrogators of Guy Fawkes.

OF THE THIRTEEN CONSPIRATORS sentenced to jail terms by the Sarajevo court on October 28, 1914, only five of the youngest (Vaso Čubrilović, Kranjčević, Cvetko Popović, Stjepanović and Zagorac) came out alive. Of the other eight, Perin died before the end of 1914, and Čabrinović, Kerović father and son, Milović and Grabež perished of tuberculosis and malnutrition in 1916, and hunger drove Djukić mad in 1917. Princip struggled longest and survived to within a few months of the downfall of the Habsburg empire, but passed away on April 28, 1918, one arm amputated and his body decaying from the ravages of tuberculosis.

The three chief assassins, Princip, Čabrinović, and Grabež, were sent to serve their sentences outside Bosnia and Hercegovina, in the military prison of Theresienstadt in Bohemia, while the other ten conspirators were transported to Zenica, the largest prison in the two provinces.

Princip, Čabrinović and Grabež left Sarajevo on December 2, 1914. Escorting them was a gendarme from Bosnia, a Serb by nationality, who after the war described the journey.[1] Although some parts of his story can be questioned, it conveys the atmosphere of the transportation. There were four gendarmes in the party, and the assassins were chained to their seats in a special coach with drawn blinds. The chief guard was a German petty officer named Hunter. News had just reached Sarajevo that General Potiorek's new offensive against Serbia was at last proving successful; his Fifth Army entered Belgrade at the same time as Princip and his two accomplices were being sent to Theresienstadt. Hunter told the assassins the news and, according to the Bosnian Serb's story, Princip answered, "Serbia may be invaded but not conquered; Serbia will one day create Yugoslavia, mother of all South Slavs."[2] Hunter did not like this answer and asked Princip whether he felt sorry that he was going to leave his bones in jail. The Bosnian Serb recounts that Princip just smiled and waved his hand, saying that he had counted on that. Hunter also asked Princip why he killed the Duchess, who was the mother of three children. He was told: "I did not wish to kill a mother. It simply happened that I killed her. A bullet does not go precisely where one wishes and I struck her first. They were sitting close to one another. It was the Archduke's mistake, for he wanted to subjugate and destroy the whole of our people and all Slavs."[3]

On the evening of December 4, the party reached Vienna on their way to Bohemia. An army unit and numerous police blocked the entire station. A crowd was waiting for the assassins. "When we took them out of the train, people railed against the Serbs as thieves, and against Serbia, and called on us to shoot all three of them at once. We had considerable difficulty in bringing them to the station, where we spent the night. The next morning we continued our journey to Theresienstadt."[4]

Theresienstadt was an old fortress converted into a military prison, a few miles from the town of the same name. The fortress was of stone and brick, and in front was a deep moat full of water from the surrounding marshes, which received the fortress sewage. The outside wall was over four feet thick; the inner ones were of normal thickness. All the cells were built within walls. The casemates were large rooms in each of which were from twelve to fifteen men, and the solitary cells were between the casemates.

There are no records concerning the first months of Princip's sojourn in Theresienstadt, but after March 1915 they are numerous. Already on February 8, 1915, the Bosnian *Landesregierung* proposed to the Joint Ministry of Finance that the remaining nine conspirators (Perin died in December 1914) should be transferred outside Bosnia and Hercegovina. The *Landesregierung* gave several reasons for this measure. The first was "the consequences of the war."[5] General Potiorek had suffered a shattering defeat in Serbia, losing 150,000 men altogether. On December 15, 1914, the Serbian cavalry galloped into Belgrade. A communiqué from Vienna stated that the troops of the Habsburg empire had been withdrawn from Serbia "owing to difficulties of provisioning"; it added that the Emperor Franz Josef had deigned to relieve Potiorek of his command, "at the latter's request, for reasons of health." Some Serbian units crossed into Bosnia and the *Landesregierung* thought it would be safer to transfer all the Sarajevo conspirators outside the two provinces.

The *Landesregierung* also complained that guarding the prisoners had become very difficult—"the number of the guards is not complete, because in winter in the rough and unfavorable weather many are sick every day."[6]

A further reason was the political unreliability of the guards. The *Landesregierung* reported that "the extent and the intensity of treasonable activity in Bosnia and Hercegovina require the greatest caution, and among the guards there is a large number of fellow countrymen of the convicts, and the trustworthiness of each individual guard cannot be assured."[7] The *Landesregierung* stressed that the transfer from Bosnia should last "until the return of normal circumstances."

The Joint Ministry of Finance agreed with this proposal, and on March 2 Kranjčević, Djukić and Stjepanović arrived in Theresienstadt, while Vaso Čubrilović, Kerović father and son, Milović and Popović were sent to Möllersdorf, a military prison near Vienna, and Perin to Pilsen (Plzeň in Bohemia).

At the same time, the Joint Ministry of Finance issued special instructions to the prison commanders regarding the treatment of the prisoners: solitary confinement, heavy guard and surveillance. The prisoners should be kept apart from each other and from other prisoners and their relations with the outside world closely watched. Appropriate measures were to be taken to this end and certain of them, such as the increase in the number of guards, were to be requested from the military command.[8] The Ministry of Finance empowered the prison commanders to take extraordinary measures to carry out these orders.

The first direct news of Princip, Čabrinović and Grabež came through Kranjčević and Cedo Jandrić, an Austrian officer of Serb nationality, who was sentenced to two years in Theresienstadt for "treasonable activities against the state." Jandrić wrote that the jailers' behavior was strictly according to rule. There was no physical torture, but the regulations themselves were inhuman and brutal, and their application was enough to break down the healthiest prisoner.[9] According to the provisions of Habsburg military prisons, each prisoner had to be chained with shackles weighing ten kilograms (about twenty-two pounds). Although the Ministry of War ordered that chaining be abolished during the war because of lack of proper nourishment for the prisoners, the practice was still employed against Princip and his accomplices. Jandrić stressed that the food was completely inadequate. Princip was permitted to walk alone in the courtyard, after all other prisoners, for half an hour daily.

Kranjčević also recorded that there was no physical terror, but he complained that the food grew worse every day, fresh laundry was issued only once a month, and soap rations were completely stopped. The cells were unheated, and every night the water in the jugs froze. Kranjčevič described his conditions:

Although for want of sufficient food, all other prisoners had their chains removed at the beginning of the war, ours were left on. . . . I got rheumatism because of them. . . . At first I did not know how to protect myself from them. The first winter I left the shackles outside my bed. The chain thus sucked the warmth from my body, and in the morning I was frozen stiff and had great difficulty standing up. . . . The second winter I realized that I should bring the chain into bed and warm it with my hands, so that it remained warm all night and did not lead my heat away. But I realized this rather late. . . .[10]

Čabrinović was the first of the conspirators to be stricken by hunger, cold and solitary confinement. During both the trial and preceding interrogation, he had been very tense and strained; but then he could at least argue and defend himself, while in Theresienstadt came long days and nights of complete isolation, which he found quite unbearable. Čabrinović's health had not been robust even before June 28, 1914.

At the very end of 1915 Čabrinović's health deteriorated so much that he was transferred to the closed section of Hospital Number 13 in the nearby town of Theresienstadt. The doctors found his condition to be incurable, and the prison authorities ordered that Čabrinović should be returned to jail to die there. That same day Čabrinović was seen by Franz Werfel, well-known Austrian writer and author of *The Forty Days of Musa Dagh*. He recorded this encounter in his war diary, and immediately after the war he wrote a letter to Čabrinović's sister, Vukosava, telling her about his meeting with her brother.[11] Werfel published this part of his diary in 1924.[12]

There is no eyewitness account of Čabrinović's death on January 23, 1916. But in the *Kriegsarchiv* in Vienna there are several documents in connection with the request of the Criminal Department of the Sarajevo police that Čabrinović's skull should be cut off, preserved and sent to Sarajevo.[13] This extraordinary correspondence was begun by the Sarajevo police on February 13, 1916, when a telegram was sent to the military command in Leitmeritz, whose jurisdiction included the Theresienstadt military prison. It was ordered that Čabrinović's body be exhumed and his skull cut off and dispatched to Sarajevo "in order to be displayed in the museum."[14] The Sarajevo police also said it would pay all expenses. The Leitmeritz command sent this telegram to the Ministry of War in Vienna, which examined the request and decided it did not fall under its competence, because the Joint Ministry of Finance had previously decided on the transfer of Čabrinović to Theresienstadt.

So all the documents were sent from the Ministry of War to the Joint Ministry of Finance which made a decision on April 13, 1916, informing the Ministry of War that the request of the Criminal Department of the Sarajevo police was not granted.[15]

It seems that there the matter ended, because when Čabrinović's body was exhumed in 1920, to be transported to Sarajevo, the skull was with the skeleton. Yet there is evidence that the Sarajevo police succeeded in obtaining the skulls of some of the dead members of the Bosnian revolutionary societies. In 1920 the grave of Bogdan Žerajić was opened and his skull was missing.[16] It had been exhibited in the Criminal Museum, and in 1919 was removed from there and put with Žerajić's remains. The chief police investigator of the Sarajevo conspiracy, Viktor Ivasjuk, used Žerajić's skull for other purposes. Questioning one of the younger assassins, Ivasjuk ordered Žerajić's skull to be brought into his office, and then put some ink into it, threatening the accused, "If you do not admit everything, I shall make ink pots out of your heads as I did with Žerajić's."[17] The fact that Žerajić's skull was missing from his body in the grave, proves the accuracy of the story. There were also rumors that Ivasjuk had succeeded in obtaining Djukić's skull,[18] but Djukić's grave was never found, and there was no way of checking the accuracy of this story.

Princip fell ill at the same time as Čabrinović. There is no accurate report about him during the first year of his jail term. Both Jandrić and Kranjčević speak generally, without mentioning specific dates. Kranjčević described how his chains were taken off on the anniversary of Franz Josef's accession to the throne, but that Princip had continued to carry his own. It seems that despite great surveillance, Princip managed from time to time to get news from the front. Jandrić mentioned a Polish barber by the name of Spak who smuggled in news written by Jandrić for Princip, in the handle of his shaving brush.[19] On the other hand, one must assume that the authorities themselves saw to it that Princip was informed of Serbia's disaster in the autumn of 1915, when Austro-Hungarian troops, reinforced by eleven German divisions, attacked Serbia. At the same time, the entire Bulgarian army attacked Serbia from the rear, and King Petar and the army had to evacuate Serbian territory through the mountains of Albania.

On February 27, 1916, the Sarajevo *Hrvatski Dnevnik* quoted an Austrian official as saying that "Princip is very ill and suffering from consumption (tuberculosis of the bones). He is a finished man; his chest is sunken, his eyes are deep in their sockets, he has wasted away completely and is now in the prison hospital. The news that Serbia has been conquered and that King Petar has fled profoundly distressed him. When he learned that Čabrinović was dead he was quite overwhelmed."

The inaccuracy of this news item on at least one point can be established. According to Princip's official death certificate, he entered hospital not in February, but only on April 7, 1916. There does exist, however, one authentic document about Princip's health and mental disposition at this time. From October 1915 until June 1916, Dr. Martin Pappenheim, well-known psychiatrist, at that time a lecturer and later a professor at Vienna University, was at Theresienstadt studying cases of shell shock and various abnormal types. Dr. Pappenheim succeeded in convincing Princip that he was not a spy, and he talked four times with Princip; on February 19, 1916, when Princip was still in his cell, and on May 12, May 18 and June 5, of the same year in Hospital Number 13 in Theresienstadt. Princip spoke broken German, and Dr. Pappenheim jotted down stenographic notes on their conversation. Eleven years later they were deciphered, when Dr. Pappenheim decided to publish them. He did not elaborate but merely presented the notes in the rough form in which he had made them. At the same time, Dr. Pappenheim asked Princip to write two texts for him. Princip carried out Dr. Pappenheim's request, and these two documents confirm the fact of his talks with Dr. Pappenheim.

In his first conversation, Princip said that he had been in solitary confinement the whole time and that his chains had been taken off three days earlier. Then Princip answered questions about his childhood, his parents, his health: "Always been healthy. Knew nothing of serious injuries before the assassination. At that time injuries on the head and all over. At that time senseless."[20] Then he described his mood:

It is very hard in solitary confinement, without books, with absolutely nothing to read and intercourse with nobody. Always accustomed to read, suffering most from not having anything to read. Sleeps usually only four hours in the night. Dreams a great deal. Beautiful dreams. About life, about love, not uneasy. Thinks about everything, particularly about conditions in his country. He had heard something about the war. Had heard a tragic thing, that Serbia no longer exists. His life in general is painful, now that Serbia does not exist. It goes hard with my people. The World War would not have failed to come, independent of it. Was a man of ideals, wanted to revenge the people. The motives—revenge and love. All the young men were in the same sort of revolutionary temper. Spoke of anarchistic pamphlets which incited to murder.

Thinks differently today, thinks a social revolution is possible in all Europe, as things are changing. Will say no more in the presence of the guard. Is not badly treated. All behave properly toward him.[21]

Princip told Dr. Pappenheim that he had tried to commit suicide in January 1916, without mentioning specifically why.

Admits suicide attempt a month ago. Wanted to hang himself with the towel. It would be stupid to have a hope. Has a wound on the breast and on the arms, *fungus*. A life like mine, that's impossible. At that time, about 12 o'clock, he could not eat, was in bad spirits, and on a sudden came the idea to hang himself. If he had the opportunity he would do it. Thinks of his parents and all, but hears nothing of them. Confesses longing. That must exist in everybody.[22]

Dr. Pappenheim saw Princip again on May 12, 1916, when he was transferred to hospital:

He recognizes me immediately and shows pleasure at seeing me. Since 7 IV here in hospital. Always nervous. Is hungry, does not get enough. Loneliness. Gets no air and sun here; in the fortress took walks. Has no longer any hope for his life. There is nothing for him to hope for. Life is lost. Everything that was bound up with his ideals is all destroyed. My Serbian people. Hopes that something may turn for the better, but is skeptical. The ideal of the young people was the unity of the South Slav peoples, Serbs, Croats and Slovenes, but not under Austria. In a kind of state, republic or something of the sort. Thought if Austria were thrown into difficulties that revolution will come. But for such revolution one must prepare the ground, work up feeling. Nothing happened. By assassination this spirit might be prepared. There already had been attempts at assassinations before. The perpetrators were like heroes to our young people. He had no thought of becoming a hero. He wanted merely to die for his idea. Before the assassination he had read an article of Kropotkin about what we can do in case of world-wide social revolution. Studied, talked about it. Was convinced it was possible.

For two months has heard nothing more of events. But it is all indifferent to him, on account of his illness and misfortune of his people. Has sacrificed his life for the people. Could not believe that such a World War could break out as the result of an act like this. They did indeed think that such a World War might break out, but not at that moment.

On being requested to write, something on the social revolution, he writes on sheet of paper the following, saying that for two years he has not had the pen in his hand. Translates: "On certain occasion we spoke among comrades on a question which Kropotkin had put in *Welfare for All*—what the anarchists will do in the case of a social revolution? We all took this more for a phrase of an old revolutionist than that he had seriously thought such revolution possible at this time. But we nevertheless all debated over this revolution, and nearly all admitted that such a revolution is possible, but according to our conviction that previously in all Europe there must be created between peoples . . ."

Broke off here, feeling ill. My thoughts are already— I am very nervous.

(*Do you believe that (assassination was) a service?*) Cannot believe that the World War was a consequence of the assassination; cannot feel himself responsible for the catastrophe; therefore, cannot say if it was a service. But fears he did it in vain. Thought that Serbia and Montenegro should help in case of a revolution of the national states in Austria.

(*Illegible question.*) Our old generation was mostly conservative, but in the people as a whole existed the wish for national liberation. The older generation was of a different opinion from the younger as to how to bring it about. In the year 1878 many Serb leaders and generals prayed for liberation from the Turks. The older generation wanted to secure liberty from Austria in a legal way; we do not believe in such a liberty.

It naturally goes hard with our co-nationals in Austria. Also does not believe it goes well with the Czechs and Poles. Has heard and read that the Slav peoples in Austria are badly off, are persecuted. In Bosnia high treason trials and *Iznimne mjere*—exceptional law. That often existed in Bosnia. In Bosnia too few schools. In Serbia, more, ten times more. In Belgrade six gymnasia, in all Bosnia four. One million nine hundred thousand people of all faiths.

The time before, he wrote ten lines and one word. Now after this talk he continued writing again. Stops often and reflects. Complains himself that it is difficult for him. Ceases writing again after fifteen lines. Again translates; ". . . there must be created relations where all differences equalize, (adds) are equalized, between European peoples. But we as nationalists, although we had read socialist and anarchist writings, did not occupy ourselves much with this question. Thinking that each of us had another duty—a national duty." (*He is adding the last words now.*)[23]

During the third visit, on May 18, 1916, Dr. Pappenheim recorded:

Wound worse, discharging very freely. Looking miserable. Suicide by any sure means is impossible. "Wait to the end." Resigned, but not really very sad.

(*What do you think about?*) Sometimes in a philosophical mood, sometimes poetical, sometimes quite prosaic. Thinks about the human soul. What is the essential in human life, instinct, or will, or spirit—what moves man?

Many who have spoken with him think he was inspired by others, only because he cannot express himself sufficiently, is not in general gifted as a talker. Always a reader and always alone, not often engaging in debates.[24]

Princip continued to speak about the history of the plot, the roles of Ilić, Grabež and Čabrinović, repeating the main points as during the investigation and at his trial, and ending up with the problems of revolution, but this time more reserved toward Dr. Pappenheim:

Thought that as a result of repeated attempts at assassination there could be built up an organization such as Ilić desired, and that then there would be general revolution among the people. Now comprehends that a revolution especially in the military state of Austria, is of no use. What he now thinks the right thing he would not say. Has no desire to speak on the matter. It makes him unquiet to speak about it. When he thinks by himself, then everything is clear, but when he speaks with anybody, then he becomes uncertain.

If he had something to read for only 2-3 days, he could then think more clearly and express himself better. Does not speak to anybody for a month. Then when I come he wants to speak about ideas, about dominating thoughts. He considered that if he prepared the atmosphere the idea of revolution and liberation would spread among men of intelligence and then later in the masses. Thought that thereby attention of intelligentsia would be directed upon it. As for instance what Mazzini did in Italy at the time of the Italian liberation. Thought that the kingdom of Serbia and Montenegro should be united.[25]

Dr. Pappenheim saw Princip for the last time on June 5, 1916. His minutes were very brief:

When permission has come, arm is to be amputated. His usual resigned disposition.[26]

It is not clear whether Princip spent all of the last two years of his life, from April 7, 1916, until April 28, 1918, in the hospital or whether he was transferred back to his prison cell from time to time. Kranjčević, who had been in Theresienstadt prison from March 1915 until mid-1917, narrated that Princip had not been in the hospital all the time.[27] Kranjčević also stressed that the treatment of Princip and the other conspirators depended much on the prison commander. He complained about the first commander, "an old lieutenant colonel," and praised the second commander, "a captain, a German by nationality, who behaved like a man towards us, who did not consider it his duty to make the conditions prescribed by the law courts worse for us."[28] Kranjčević tells us how he succeeded in getting into direct contact with Princip, thanks to several guards, particularly a Czech called Karl Hrouška, who had been a restaurant owner in Prague in peacetime. Kranjčević describes this encounter as follows:

Gavro was ill, losing strength more and more, but spiritually he remained alert. He was very pleased that he had been put in the same cell where Hadži Lojo [leader of the insurgents against the Habsburgs in Bosnia in 1878] served his term, because "it is a special privilege that he, the last Austrian prisoner from Bosnia, is put in the cell of the first prisoner."
Once when his pains seemed unbearable, he said to me, "While I was at liberty I was ill, and I even spat blood. And here in these miserable conditions, without food and without air, I live and cannot relieve myself of this slavery." He was convinced that he would not live long enough to see the end of the war, but he was sure that the end of Austria was certain, and that he had opened the road to her doom and it was all the same to him whether or not he lived to see the end of the war itself.

Kranjčević says also that Princip was much cheered by the news that Rumania had entered the war, at the end of August 1916.[29]

With the approach of winter in 1916, the prisoners' condition again deteriorated, particularly because of the cold. Princip had once again been transferred to the hospital, and Grabež was moved into his cell, where Kranjčević once managed to see him:

Grabež was lying weak and exhausted. Nevertheless, his face did not give the impression that he was dying. He told me that his stomach was weakened and that he could not take any food. He could not stand or sit. I told him that he did not look badly and that he would recover; that I also suffered from stomach troubles . . . I said goodbye, expressing the wish that we should see each other again, if we could find good guards who would allow us. . . . But the next morning Grabež was found dead in his cell. He died of general exhaustion caused by chronic starvation.[30]

In 1916 three conspirators also died in Möllersdorf, (Jakov Milović on April 16, Nedjo Kerović on April 22, and his father, Mitar, on October 1), although Cvetko Popović recorded that the conditions in this prison were not as bad as those in Theresienstadt. Thanks to a Czech chaplain by the name of Vilko Drabek, Popović received books to read from the prison library and he also communicated with other prisoners.[31]

Vaso Čubrilović described the last days of old Kerović, his son, and Milović. Old Kerović asked him to write a letter every three months to his *zadruga,* giving detailed instructions on seasonal activities. His death came suddenly. Milović was continually ill. When he was arrested, the Habsburg gendarmes beat him with the butts of their rifles and injured his kidneys. An Eastern Orthodox priest was allowed to visit Milović before he died. Vaso Čubrilović asked the priest, who was a Serb, to tell him about his conversations with Milović. "He only asked if it was true that Serbia had been conquered," answered the priest.[32]

Zagorac in Pilsen had a very hard time; for two years he was not allowed to take walks in the courtyard.[33]

Then Lazar Djukić's turn came. After he had been sentenced in Sarajevo with Princip, he was tried again on charges of participation in the organization of *kruzhoks* in the interior of Bosnia, and his sentence was increased. Afterward Djukić was returned to Theresienstadt, where his condition worsened. One day he started to talk to his guard about an attempt in 1912 to kill the Emperor Franz Josef. He mentional several individuals, among them Kranjčević, who was immediately summoned to the investigation judge to answer these charges. Kranjčević denied the accusation but was brought face to face with Djukić. Kranjčević described this meeting with his old friend:

"He was pale, just skin and bone. His right eye was a big open wound. It was painful to look at him. The interrogation judge said that Djukić admitted that he was in a conspiracy to kill the old Emperor, and he asked me to admit the same."[34] Kranjčević denied any knowledge of it, and when he was faced with Djukić, the latter also denied that he had said anything about it.

Soon afterward Djukić was sent to Prague, where he died on March 19, 1917. He was buried secretly and his grave has never been found.

The death of Emperor Franz Josef on November 21, 1916, and the accession of the Archduke Karl, nephew of Franz Ferdinand, resulted in some mitigation of the hardships suffered by the political prisoners. The new Emperor and his wife were aware that the situation of Austria-Hungary was deteriorating, and they were anxious to make peace. Through Empress Zita's brother, Prince Sixtus of Bourbon-Parma, an officer in the French army, they contacted the French government.

While negotiations proceeded, the Viennese authorities were eager to ingratiate themselves with the Allies and in this atmosphere Danilo Dimović, a Serb from Bosnia, Vice-President of the *Sabor*, took the opportunity to obtain an audience with the Emperor Karl on June 19, 1917, to ask for better conditions for political prisoners in Zenica.[35] Before this step, several South Slav members of the Vienna parliament had asked questions about the treatment of imprisoned Serb political leaders from Bosnia and Hercegovina. The Social Democratic paper in Vienna, *Arbeiter Zeitung*, in its issue of August 2, 1917, also raised the question, stating that political prisoners in Theresienstadt and Möllersdorf were strictly isolated from the other inmates and kept in solitary confinement, and that until the opening of the last session of parliament, they had not been allowed to receive visitors, not even their closest relatives. On one occasion, it reported, the brother of one of the condemned men had come from Bosnia, but had to return without having seen his brother.

In the *Kriegsarchiv* in Vienna there are several documents from this period which throw more light on the conditions of imprisonment in Theresienstadt and Möllersdorf. The Ministry of War ordered an inspection in 1917, in January. There were then 866 prisoners in Theresienstadt prison and 21 of these were ill in jail and 24 in the town hospital. Thirty-seven prisoners died during 1916.[36] The Ministry of War discussed the question of ending the solitary confinement of Princip and his accomplices (Kranjčević, Stjepanović, Čubrilović, Popović and Zagorac), who had survived up to that time. The Ministry had also received a petition by Petar Stjepanović, a second lieutenant of the Medical Corps, who asked to be transferred to the cell of his brother, Cvijan Stjepanović, in Theresienstadt, because he wanted to save his brother in view of his declining health.

On September 13, 1917, it was decided to have the survivors from both military prisons (Princip, Kranjčević, Stjepanović, Popović, Čubrilović, and Zagorac) sent back to the Zenica prison in Bosnia. This was duly carried out, and all the prisoners were moved except Princip. He remained in the hospital in Theresienstadt. It is not clear what the reason was for this, whether he was too ill to travel or had been expressly exempted from the order. When his colleagues were being transported to Zenica an incident occurred. They were escorted by eight soldiers of German nationality from Vienna. The soldiers fraternized with the prisoners, and one of them wrote home about the experience. The soldiers were arrested and tried by a military court.[37]

There is very controversial evidence about the details of Princip's physical and mental condition after he talked to Dr. Pappenheim and Kranjčević in the middle of 1916. The secretary of Archduke Franz Ferdinand, Paul Nikitsch-Boulles, narrates in his memoirs how he was told after the war of a meeting between Princip and an Austrian officer from high aristocratic circles in Vienna. The officer told Nikitsch-Boulles that

throughout his stay in Theresienstadt Princip had to stay in solitary confinement and, moreover, in a constantly darkened cell. . . . Nobody can imagine what this means. Minutes become hours, hours become days, and days weeks, all the more as through lack of light every possibility was removed of shortening the time by work or by some writing or reading. Moreover, during the day hours Princip was chained with both hands to the cell wall. Under the severest penalty, nobody was allowed to address a single word to the captive. Under these conditions it is understandable that Princip contracted tuberculosis so soon. This illness made such progress in the last weeks of his life that Princip was hanging half-conscious in his chains.[38]

Nikitsch-Boulles added that this officer told him "how Princip was tortured by extreme repentance and cried and asked to be forgiven."

The officer said that "the unfortunate man told him, sobbing and in broken words, how he was forced to do the deed and how the act had been described to him as glorious but idiotic, and how he had been put into such a literally fanatical state of intoxication that he himself came to the conviction in the end that the elimination of the Austro-Hungarian successor to the throne would ease the oppression of the fatherland and free it from the yoke of subjugation."[39]

The Nikitsch-Boulles story has been challenged by several witnesses. First of all, Princip died in a hospital and not in prison, and his chains had already been removed in 1916. An Austrian officer of Serb nationality, Svetislav Gavrilović, was in the hospital with Princip in April 1918, and he recalled an incident at that time between Princip and General von Ruprecht, the leader of a team of inspectors looking at conditions in the hospital. According to Gavrilović, General von Ruprecht tried to argue with Princip about the motives for the assassination, and Princip answered that Austria-Hungary was doomed and would lose the war.[40]

The doctors who attended Princip from April 1916 until April 1918 left more reliable information. Besides Dr. Pappenheim, four other physicians were named. Kranjčević mentions a Jewish doctor who was sentenced to twenty years in prison for helping Czechs evade military service by issuing falsified health certificates. "He would visit Princip and secretly give him a piece of chocolate or some other delicacy brought from home. But one day the doctor heard that his fiancée was dead, and he at once committed suicide. Thus Princip lost a great comforter."[41] The name of this doctor may have been Levin. He and a Dr. Mosel amputated Princip's arm. They "tended Princip with fatherly care."[42] There were two other doctors in Theresienstadt hospital who treated Princip, Drs. Spatni and Marsch. The latter in 1936, with the aid of documentary materials from the hospital, published his recollections of Princip:

Already in the summer of 1916 Princip was a candidate for death, a living corpse with his meager body wasted to the bone with several tuberculosis ulcers as large as a hand. Princip certainly had been carrying the tuberculosis germ in his body before his arrest. But the two years of imprisonment in the dungeons of Theresienstadt were enough to cause the outbreak of the illness, so that the death of the patient was to be expected before long. It must be credited to the military departments of the Theresienstadt, who were responsible for Princip, that they let him be brought into the garrison hospital at the moment when the first serious symptoms of tuberculosis were seen. Here he had the same treatment and feeding as sick or wounded soldiers, but was very strictly guarded. One soldier with fixed bayonet stood in his room, and two outside his door, while two walked to and fro under the windows of his room, although any attempt by the patient to escape was highly unlikely, as he could not walk more than two hundred meters.

In spite of strict orders not to speak to him, I occasionally found an opportunity during the treatment to talk with him for a short while. It was for him—since he was not allowed to write, to read, or to talk to anybody—like a great release, if he could just communicate with anybody. . . . In my presence he never uttered any repentance for his deed; on the contrary he stated that he would have still done it even if he had known about the terrible consequences of the *attentat*, including the outbreak of the war. On the lines of his face there was an almost solemn earnestness, the eyes sunken in their sockets, had lost their brightness and the fire of youth. Except when he was speaking about the liberation of his people, then they would brighten up for a moment. Patiently he had surrendered to his fate, as far as he was concerned earthly life for him was finished and his early end he expected with stoical serenity. . . . In good German he talked to me about his family and about his short life, but he never mentioned the man from the Black

Hand, who, in the opinion of the Austro-Hungarian secret police, had provoked him to doing what he did.

During the two years' imprisonment he had grown a long beard, so that he
looked ten years older. When this beard had been shaved off, I saw an intelligent, young face, full of expression. The slim frail body showed the typical
tubercular appearance. As already mentioned, his chest was covered with
tuberculosis ulcers of hand size and full of pus. The disease had destroyed
the elbow joint of his left arm to such an extent that the lower part of this
limb had to be connected with the upper part by a silver wire. Why the
doctors were forbidden to amputate the lower part of the arm, which had
become completely useless, I am unable to explain to this day.

Usually Princip came to me every second day, to the operations hall for
dressings. As it was necessary to dress the whole upper part of the body, I
had to use more bandages on him than was needed for five wounded soldiers.
The process of tuberculosis rapidly advanced. The days of Princip were
numbered. . . .[43]

There is no eyewitness of Princip's last days. But his death certificate
has been preserved. It says that Princip died on April 28, 1918, at 6:30
P.M. in Room 33 of the closed part of Theresienstadt Hospital Number
13. Tuberculosis of the bones was given as the cause of his death.[44]

Princip was buried secretly, during the night, on April 28. At the end
of the war no one knew, not even Dr. Spatni nor Dr. Mosel, where
Princip was buried. But an Austrian soldier of Czech nationality, called
František Löbl, found Princip's grave. Together with four other soldiers he had been ordered to bury Princip in the local Roman Catholic
cemetery, with instructions not to reveal the whereabouts of the grave.
When the soldiers came to the graveyard they found the grave already
dug in the middle of a path. After lowering the coffin they filled in the
hole, removing all traces of the burial to prevent the grave from ever
being discovered. But František Löbl that same night sketched a map of
the graveyard and Princip's grave. He sent it to his father to keep in
case he should be sent to the front and killed there. František Löbl
survived the war and on his return immediately went to Theresienstadt
and placed a Czech flag on Princip's grave.[45]

On June 9, 1920, Princip's remains were exhumed. Among those
present was Dr. Mosel, who had amputated Princip's arm. When the
grave was opened, the skeleton was found to have only one arm—proof
that František Löbl had made an accurate sketch.

Princip's remains, together with those of Čabrinović, Grabež and the
other conspirators who died in Theresienstadt and Möllersdorf, were
transported to Sarajevo, where they were buried in one common grave.
Also buried in the same common grave were the remains of Ilić, the
elder Čubrilović, Jovanović and Žerajić.

The man in charge of removing Princip's remains to Sarajevo found the following lines in Princip's handwriting on the cell wall—his last attempt at poetry, written in the first months of his imprisonment in Theresienstadt:

> *Our ghosts will walk through Vienna*
> *And roam through the Palace, frightening the lords.*[46]

CHAPTER XVII

SERBIA AND SARAJEVO

I know that history at all times draws the
strangest consequences from the remotest cause.
—T. S. Eliot

THE BEHAVIOR OF THE CONSPIRATORS during their interrogation, at their trial and in prison left no doubt about their motive for killing the Archduke Franz Ferdinand: they regarded him as a tyrant, the symbol of a regime of oppression over their native land. Yet Princip and his accomplices did not live in a vacuum, but in the conditions of the great crisis which gripped Europe on the eve of the First World War. The Balkans, and particularly Bosnia and Hercegovina, were a bone of contention among the great powers.

Did the idealism of the Young Bosnians coincide with less idealistic schemes of other parties, concerned with eliminating the heir to the Habsburg throne for reasons of their own? Was there in fact a coincidence of interests behind the Archduke's assassination?

Historians have fixed on six main groups of possible instigators, and variously claim that each of them or several of them together were behind the young assassins in Sarajevo: Serbia—the Serbian Government, the Regent Alexander and the powerful secret society of Colonel Apis; Tsarist Russia—the Russian General Staff, the secret police Okhrana, or the Russian revolutionaries and left-wing Social Revolutionaries; Hungary—Prime Minister Count Stephen Tisza; Germany—pan-German, anti-Habsburg elements; France and Britain—through Continental Freemasonry or through their intelligence services.

This issue of who may have instigated the deed remains the most puzzling part of the Sarajevo story, but recently opened historical documents reveal more than was previously known. The Austrian,[1] the

German[2] and the Yugoslav[3] archives, now available to scholars, have clarified part of the picture; it remains to be seen what Russian, British and French documents will reveal.

The role of the Prime Minister of Serbia, Nikola Pašić, Regent Alexander and Colonel Apis in the Sarajevo plot cannot be assessed without an analysis of their political and personal relations in the years prior to 1914 and of their influence on Serbia's foreign policy over the preceding decade.

From the 1903 *coup d'état*, when the absolutist rule of King Alexander Obrenović was overthrown, until the 1908–9 crisis caused by the Austro-Hungarian annexation of Bosnia and Hercegovina, a balance of power existed between civilian and military authorities in Serbia. The new king, Prince Petar Karadjordjević, let the political parties rule, while the military conspirators who had toppled Alexander Obrenović had the final word in all army matters.

The first decade of the twentieth century saw Serbia flourishing economically and politically; there was a rapid industrial expansion, achieved mostly through foreign investments. Reorganization of the army, and its rearmament with modern quick-firing weapons, was proceeding efficiently. Several state loans were concluded in France for that purpose. A new bourgeoisie was emerging, bringing with it dynamism and corruption.

Under King Petar, himself a liberal at heart, Serbia enjoyed a system of constitutional monarchy. The regicides who had killed his predecessor did not impose their dictatorship after 1903. Political liberties were granted, and the press criticized, sometimes bitterly, the new king, his two young sons, Djordje and Alexander, and the government. Some of the newspapers were subsidized by the great powers and defended the policies of those powers. The franchise was greatly enlarged, and Serbia's peasant population was granted more generous voting rights than the people of many Western countries enjoyed.[4] The workers were permitted to organize trade unions, and various political parties functioned, such as the Social Democrats and, to a lesser extent, the Anarchosyndicalists, while republicanism established strong roots in this period. Of all political parties, the biggest was the Old Radical party, whose leading man was Nikola Pašić. In his younger days, Pašić had been a follower of Bakunin and Svetozar Marković, but he had moved gradually to the right, representing the interests of merchants, new entrepreneur groups and rich peasants. The main opposition to Pašić's party came from the Young Radicals, a more liberal political group.

Yet Serbia remained basically a peasant country; only a little over 10 per cent of the whole population lived in towns. The middle class was small and the number of intellectuals not great, although Belgrade University gained a European reputation for the quality of its scholars.

In the first years of King Petar's reign, basic changes occurred in the relations between the great European powers. France and Russia had already in 1897 established closer links; in 1904 the Entente Cordiale was concluded between England and France, and in 1907 the century-long enmity between Russia and England was ended. In the same period Germany and Austria-Hungary cemented their alliance.

Serbia's foreign policy up to 1903 had been firmly oriented in an Austro-Hungarian direction; King Petar's accession brought a marked change. In the first decade of the twentieth century, the leading statesmen of Serbia sought to rely more on the Western powers, in order to evade the domination of Vienna. The Old Radicals looked to Russia as the main protector of Serbia.

On the other hand, Austria-Hungary increased its open political and economic pressure to secure through Serbia its penetration into the Balkans. A sharp fight was in progress between the Austrian Škoda, the German Krupp and Erhard, the French Schneider-Creusot and Société Française des Munitions de Guerre, of St.-Chamond, and the British Armstrong interests, over Serbia's armament purchases. The competition was strong, and all the big powers put pressure on Serbian political parties and on different groups in the army and even in the palace to secure orders for their munitions firms.

The Austro-Hungarian minister in Belgrade, Dumba, wrote in his memoirs that the highest authorities in Vienna insisted strongly that Škoda should receive the contract for Serbian cannon. Škoda was in financial difficulties and owed four million crowns to the Kreditanstalt bank. It could not get new credits, and orders from Austria-Hungary were not sufficient for its expanded production. Therefore, Serbia was regarded as the best market for Škoda's products. Dumba wrote that at a palace ball in Vienna the Emperor Franz Josef himself asked him to see the contract through and that the same desire was expressed by the Archduke Franz Ferdinand and Foreign Minister Goluchowski.[5] The Serbian minister in Vienna reported that the pressure for the Serbian contract was explained by the fact that the Archduke had shares in Škoda. He also learned that the Emperor had personally promised Škoda that it would receive at least part of the Serbian contracts.[6] The German military attaché in Belgrade, in a dispatch on October 5, 1906, informed Berlin that the Archduke had a personal interest in the Škoda contract.[7]

The Austrian authorities threatened to apply a tariff against Serbian cattle if the artillery order were not given to Škoda. The Belgrade government, despite pressure from some of the regicides around King Petar, rejected Vienna's demand. Their first argument was that the guns obtained from Škoda in 1903 had not proved efficient. The Serbian government had organized a test of the guns of different manufacturers and Škoda's had fared poorly and were not recommended. Belgrade's new regime also had no wish to rely on Austria-Hungary for armament; they feared a change of policy in Vienna and considered it un-wise to depend on a potential enemy to supply defensive weapons. When the Serbian government announced that it would buy French guns, Vienna regarded this act as a blow to the Habsburg empire's pres-tige. An economic blockade of Serbia for political purposes was applied and the ensuing "Pig War" (so called because the export of pigs was a major item in Serbia's foreign trade) lasted until 1911, with only a few interruptions.

At that time Serbia's foreign trade was virtually monopolized by Austria-Hungary, which handled 66 per cent of all her imports and 93 per cent of all her exports. Consequently, Serbia found herself in an extremely dangerous position. Having no outlet to the sea, she de-pended for her foreign trade on the good will of Austria-Hungary and the Ottoman Empire. Being denied the route through Austria, Serbia turned to the south to Salonika in the Ottoman Empire and opened new markets in Italy, Egypt, France, Sweden, Russia and particularly in Germany. Thus the Habsburgs' economic sanctions against Serbia mis-fired and intensified the tension between the two states.

It is significant that although at that time relations between Austria-Hungary and Germany were growing closer, there were differences in their policies toward Serbia. Without a doubt the economic factor was of vital importance. From 1905 to 1907 Serbian exports to Germany increased from 2.1 to 32 million dinars, while Serbian exports to Austria-Hungary fell from 64.7 to 12 million dinars. This economic competi-tion in Serbia between Germany and Austria-Hungary lasted to the very eve of the First World War.

The annexation of Bosnia and Hercegovina in 1908 marked a divid-ing line in Britain's relations with Serbia and the other South Slavs in the Balkans. For more than a century a kind of Disraelian attitude had been taken toward the South Slavs; any effort of the South Slavs to liberate themselves from the Ottoman yoke was interpreted in London as strengthening Russia's position in the Balkans. Gladstone's argument that this was not a necessary consequence had never gained official ac-ceptance in Britain. Now the Gladstonian attitude on the Balkans at last prevailed, mainly because of the increased threat of Germany to British imperial interests. British diplomacy still had to overcome the opposi-tion of King Edward VII, who in 1903 broke off diplomatic relations with Serbia. The French ambassador in St. Petersburg ascribed this atti-tude of King Edward to his legitimist principles; by boycotting King Petar "Edward VII thinks he is supporting the general cause of mon-archy as an institution."[8] There were rumors in London that the Eng-lish Prince Arthur, Duke of Connaught, might come to the Serbian throne. But the interests of the British Empire prevailed in the end. In 1906 diplomatic relations with Serbia were re-established, after the Ser-bian government agreed to pension off some of the older leading regicides; this gave the leadership of the surviving regicides to Colonel Apis.

Public opinion in Serbia was much aroused by the annexation of Bosnia and Hercegovina. Demonstrations broke out against the Habsburgs, and their flag was publicly burned. The Serbian heir apparent, Prince Djordje, personally took part in the demonstrations. The leading Serbian scholar, Jovan Cvijić wrote a pamphlet on the importance of Bosnia and Hercegovina for the South Slavs.[9] The two provinces have always had a central position, both ethnically and geographically, among the ten million South Slavs who people the Balkans from Trieste to Salonika. The finest folklore comes from this area. The language of Hercegovina was made by Vuk Karadžić the literary language of all the Serbian people, and in the early nineteenth century the Croats also accepted it for their literature.

Professor Cvijić emphasized the crucial role of Bosnia and Hercegovina in the solution of the problem of Yugoslav unity, the need to reconcile Serbs and Croats, whose differences are merely the result of historical accident. Living closely together, the two groups had felt themselves an entity up to 1878, when Austria-Hungary occupied the provinces. The aim of the Austrian occupation was to aggravate the historical differences between Serb and Croat, and play one off against the other for political reasons.[10]

On March 19, 1909, Austria-Hungary presented an ultimatum demanding not only that Serbia accept the act of annexation, but also that she demobilize her armies and give assurances of a good-neighbor policy toward Austria-Hungary. In a dispatch to Robert Bacon, Secretary of State in Washington, Norman Hutchinson, the American chargé d'affaires in Bucharest (the American ministry accredited to Belgrade had its seat at Bucharest), described the situation in Belgrade:

There is something tragic in the present position of Serbia. The entire nation declares itself ready to die or to triumph in its national ideal . . . Surrounded on every side by enemies, lying directly between the hostility of the Bulgarians and the enmity of the Austrians, having no outlet for her economic life, save through the great power which seems to crush them, it is perhaps not strange that the Serbians have arrived at the point of believing that it will be much more consoling to risk a desperate war than to die slowly from the strangulation which unfortunate circumstances impose upon them.[11]

Abandoned by Russia, and under pressure from the other great powers, the Serbian government, despite great opposition in Belgrade, was forced to give way. On March 31, 1909, the Serbian minister in Vienna made the following statement:

Serbia recognizes that her rights have not been endangered by the *fait accompli* in connection with Bosnia and Hercegovina, and will accordingly adapt herself to the ruling of the great powers concerning Article 25 of the Treaty of Berlin. Yielding to the advice of the great powers, Serbia binds herself, as from now on, to relinquish the opposition and end the protests over the annexation, which she has maintained since last autumn, and further binds herself to change the course of her policy toward Austria-Hungary in order to live with her in a good-neighbor relationship. In accordance with this statement and with confidence in the peace-loving intentions of Austria-Hungary, Serbia will reduce her army to the level of the spring of 1908, as far as its organization, location and effectives are concerned. She will disarm and disband the volunteers and their companies and will not permit the formation of irregular units on her territory.[12]

During the peak of the crisis, the intense concern roused by the annexation of Bosnia and Hercegovina had united the whole Serbian nation and reconciled the political parties. But once the magnitude of the national humiliation had been recognized, an emotional reaction, particularly among military circles and the restless younger generation, produced profound resentment, not only against the Habsburg empire but also against the Serbian politicians responsible for what was regarded as capitulation to the dictate of the great powers.

A direct product of the climate of despair provoked in Belgrade by the annexation of Bosnia and Hercegovina was the formation by Colonel Apis of the secret organization called Ujedinjenje ili Smrt. Up to that time the regicides, particularly the younger ones headed by Apis, had been concerned primarily with military affairs, leaving foreign and internal political issues to the political parties. It is true that they participated in the action in Macedonia, but under the control of and with the approval of the Serbian government.[13] After the 1908–9 crisis they turned toward a so-called "national propaganda" and through that to the realm of foreign policy, in which they no longer saw eye to eye with the political parties.

This change in Colonel Apis's political course coincided with the growing importance of the army in both the external and internal relations of Serbia. This same phenomenon was present in all European states, which were expanding their arms and reorganizing their forces. Even in England and France, military men were becoming more independent of the civil authorities; the British and French general staffs were holding secret conversations about which most of the members of their respective governments knew nothing. In Germany and Austria-Hungary the role of the generals became even stronger; they combined forces with armament manufacturers and preached the need for foreign expansion. In such a way *Militarismus nach aussen* produced the phenomenon of *Militarismus nach innen*.

Yet militarism in Serbia cannot be completely identified with the militarism of Germany, Austria-Hungary and the other great powers. A study of Serbia in the first decade of the twentieth century affords an illustration of the role of the army in the national liberation period in an economically underdeveloped country lacking major industry, with a predominantly peasant population, and without a powerful bourgeoisie, middle class or proletariat. Bureaucracy and the army were able to perform those functions which in Western Europe were carried out by the spontaneous economic drive of a fully developed bourgeois society. In this respect Serbian militarism has more similarities with militarism as an instrument of social drive in many other poor countries in the later decades of the twentieth century.

Colonel Apis was the initiator of this kind of militarism in Serbia. Although he was regarded after the 1903 *coup d'état* as the real minister of war of Serbia, a kind of *éminence grise* of Serbian political life, he himself held a rather modest position; in 1909 he was only the chief of staff of the Drina division. At that time the first steps were made for the organization of his secret society Ujedinjenje ili Smrt.

Besides the hard core of the 1903 regicides, headed by Colonel Apis, there were two strong groups of civilians among the initiators of the society. The more important of the two was led by Ljuba Jovanović, nicknamed Čupa ("Bushy One"). He came from a poor family in Užice and had to work as a servant during his schooling in the *gimnazija*. He entered the Belgrade Law School and took part in the organization of Slovenski Jug, a society which preached unification of the South Slavs through revolution. Jovanović took an active part in the demonstrations of April 1903 in Belgrade and was forced to leave the country for a while. He was in Vienna during the 1903 *coup d'état* and he returned to play an important role in the activities of Slovenski Jug. He also joined the *komite* and took part in several armed conflicts with the Turkish army in Macedonia. In 1908 he took his law degree at Belgrade University and received a government scholarship for advanced studies abroad. He spent several years in Brussels and other western capitals, but kept contact with events at home. Besides studying law, Jovanović made a detailed survey of the history of European secret societies, beginning with the Carbonari, Freemasons, the German patriotic clubs, and in particular the Buonarrotti societies. From all available evidence, Jovanović became at that time a Freemason.

Jovanović played a more important role in the organization of Colonel Apis's Ujedinjenje ili Smrt than has been supposed up to now. He was strongly backed in his work by Bogdan Radenković, a clerical Serb from Kosovo, the president of the organization of the Serbs in the Ottoman empire, who had been sentenced to life imprisonment for his activities against Ottoman rule. When he was released from jail, he established close contacts with the Young Turks, a secret society which played an important role in the 1908 revolution in Turkey. Radenković was a pan-Serb, and followed the philosophy of Eastern Orthodox clericalism. In 1910 he became an official of the Serbian Ministry of Foreign Affairs, dealing with affairs in Macedonia.

The only primary source discovered up to now which speaks about the organization of Ujedinjenje ili Smrt is the private diary of Major Velimir Vemić, himself a prominent regicide. This writer has read the original of Vemić's diary in the Belgrade Archives.[14] Vemić recorded that between March 22 and October 23, 1909, there were several meetings attended by Jovanović, Radenković, Vojin Tankosić, Petar Živković, Milan Pribićević and several other persons. During these sessions they discussed the need to organize a patriotic secret society.[15] On April 14, 1909, Jovanović went to Brussels. He played a prominent role in all preparatory meetings. But the work was interrupted several times for various reasons. On February 24, 1910, Radenković suggested to Vemić that the group stop its action. Nevertheless, preparations were revived at the end of 1910, Jovanović again being the most active. On November 22, 1910, he gave the initiative when he advised Vemić on how to acquire money for paper; on December 1, 1910, he went to Berlin to get the printing press; and he chose the name of the future paper *Pijemont* on February 21, 1911.[16]

Vemić's diary mentioned Apis several times, particularly concerning Apis's talks with King Petar and his sons Alexander and Djordje. According to Vemić's diary, only on March 6, 1911, in connection with the organization of a secret society did they contact him. Writing about his meeting with Apis at the Grand Hotel in Belgrade, he said: "I expounded to him our ideas and invited him to join us. He accepted in principle at once and with no hesitation."[17] Yet, it seems that Apis had been informed about their work from the very beginning. He was a born conspirator, and because of his taciturn nature many of his most trusted friends did not know all that was going through his mind. The noted Serbian historian Slobodan Jovanović, who knew Apis personally, described very vividly his character and method of work:

Apis did not correspond to the image that existed in the general public about him. He was neither temperamental nor highhanded; he was what one calls "a good friend." But not only that. Through conversations with his friends I learned to know him better. He worked hard for the advancement of his followers; he was always pushing them ahead. For himself personally he did not move a finger. Although he was a soldier with ambitions, he was indifferent to his career. He never spoke about his own personal merits and successes; he was not boastful nor a big talker. When he would recall the *coup d'état* of 1903, he would tell everything except his own role. [Apis led the regicides and was gravely wounded during the attack on the palace.] He was one of those leaders who accomplishes more than they speak. As all fanatics, he esteemed more the success of a cause than the lives of men. He sent his own nephew [Apis like most revolutionaries never married] into the *komite*, and the boy was killed the moment he crossed the Turkish border. Friends for Apis were at the same time very dear and very cheap. His friendship had a dangerous quality; but this made his personality very attractive. When he wanted to draw his friends into a conspiracy or into some other adventure, he behaved like a seducer.[18]

What the relations were between Apis and Jovanović-Čupa is hard to tell, because primary sources are not yet available. But from several facts one may conclude that they were rather close. In May 1911 all the preparations for the organization of Ujedinjenje ili Smrt had been made. It was arranged that the society should have its clandestine and its public work. In that sense, two programs were elaborated, and it was decided that Jovanović-Čupa become the first editor in chief of the daily *Pijemont*.

The secret part of the program of Ujedinjenje ili Smrt was contained in two documents: the constitution of the organization and the bylaws. The constitution had 37 articles divided into five parts and the bylaws had 28 articles.[19]

The first section of the constitution spoke about the goals of the society:

Article 1: This organization is formed in order to achieve the ideal of unification of Serbdom; all Serbs, regardless of sex, religion or place of birth, can become members, and anyone else who is prepared to serve this ideal faithfully.

Article 2: This organization chooses revolutionary action rather than cultural, and is, therefore, kept secret from the general public.

Article 3: The name of the organization is Ujedinjenje ili Smrt.

Article 4 detailed the aims of Ujedinjenje ili Smrt, stating that the society

1. in accordance with its essential nature, will influence Serbia, at official levels and throughout all classes of society, to become a Piedmont;

2. undertakes the organization of revolutionary activities in all territories inhabited by Serbs;

3. will fight with all the means available to it those outside the frontiers who are enemies of the ideal;

4. will maintain contact with all states, organizations and individuals who are friendly toward Serbia and the Serbs;

5. offers help to all peoples and organizations who are likewise struggling for liberation and unification.[20]

From other parts of the constitution and bylaws it is obvious that Jovanović-Čupa relied heavily on Buonarroti and the experience and ritual of the secret societies in Italy and Germany. M. Milenković, a member of Ujedinjenje ili Smrt, said that Jovanović's draft program was based on the "pattern of similar German secret nationalist organizations and Italian Carbonari societies."[21] V. Vemić shared this opinion.[22] Like the Carbonari, Ujedinjenje ili Smrt possessed a seal, engraved with the skull-and-crossbones flag, a dagger, bomb and poison. According to Article 35 of its constitution the following oath of allegiance had to be taken:

I [so and so] becoming a member of the organization Ujedinjenje ili Smrt, swear by the sun which is shining on me, by the earth which is feeding me, by God, by the blood of my ancestors, by my honor and my life, that from this moment until my death, I will serve faithfully the cause of this organization and will always be ready to undergo any sacrifices for it. I swear by God, by honor and my life, that I will carry out all orders and commands unconditionally. I swear by God, honor and life, that I shall take to the grave all secrets of this organization. May God and my comrades in this organization judge me, if intentionally or unintentionally, I break or fail to observe this oath of allegiance.[23]

Oskar Tartalja has described how he was received in 1912 into the secret society, after Ljuba Jovanović-Čupa had convinced him that he should join. Tartalja was led to a darkened room by a member of the editorial board of *Pijemont*. The man lit a small candle, and Tartalja saw lying on a table with a black cloth a cross, a dagger and a revolver. After the goals of the secret society were explained once more to Tartalja, the door silently opened and into the darkened room came a man dressed in a long black domino with a hood on his head and a black mask over his face. He was a member of the central committee of Ujedinjenje ili Smrt.

He did not say a word, but stood motionless in front of us. I started to repeat the oath of allegiance. When I was through, the man who brought me in hugged me, but the black mask shook hands with me and walked out. After that the light was put on and the man who brought me in read to me the constitution and the bylaws of Ujedinjenje ili Smrt, and I had to sign my name under the text of the oath of allegiance.[24]

The organization was controlled by a central committee of eleven members, each of whom had signed their full names on the constitution. Its first president was Colonel Ilija Radivojević, at that time chief of the Serbian gendarmerie, who together with another member of this body, Velimir Vemić, had carried out the actual murder of King Alexander and Queen Draga.[25]

According to Article 26, members of the organization, with the exception of the central committee, did not use their real names when communicating with one another, but were referred to by number. Each member belonged to a cell and was obliged to report anything he might learn in his official capacity in civilian life or as a member of the organization, to higher ranks within the society. The advertisement section of a local Belgrade daily, *Trgovinski Glasnik*, was used for establishing contacts between the different groups. If a group lost contact with the higher body, Article 19 of the bylaws advised that it should place an ad with the words: "One seeks a link with a rich person for the purpose of a big deal," signed with the number of the group. It would appear that Jovanović had consulted Nechayev's *Revolutionary Catechism* in framing the constitution of Ujedinjenje ili Smrt. Some formulations from paragraphs 1 and 5 of the *Catechism* are reproduced in several articles of the Serbian society's constitution, particularly in Article 30:

Each member must realize that in becoming a member of this organization the individual loses his personality; he can expect no glory, no personal benefits, material or moral. Any member, therefore, who attempts to misuse the organization for his personal, class or party interests will be punished. If the organization suffers any damage because of him, he will be punished by death.

The public part of the program, its political postulates, was published in the first issue of *Pijemont*, on September 3, 1911. It proclaimed "opposition to the government as well as to the opposition," and claimed "that all political parties have showed in practice their immorality, their lack of patriotism and understanding of culture."

Ujedinjenje ili Smrt, through *Pijemont*, did not state its opposition to the ruling Radicals and other political groups, but came out against the whole political system existing at that time in Serbia; it preached antiparliamentarianism, advocating a curtailment of political rights and a widening of the role of the state in the life of the nation. *Pijemont* expressed this clearly in its program:

Instead of the political parties of today, which are neither statist, nor nationalist, nor militarist, nor even cultural in the modern sense of the word, we must organize a party with pure statist principles. . . . Only this kind of movement . . . strong in statism, nationalism and militarism, will succeed in bringing happiness to the Serbian people.

Pijemont, emphasizing the role of the army and of the youth of the country, urged that the whole educational system be placed in the hands of the state, and pleaded for "the racial regeneration of the Serbian people if Serbia wants to become the Piedmont of the Serbs."

Pijemont represented the only political movement in Serbia before 1914 which tried to implement active Eastern Orthodox clericalism. The program asserted that the people of Serbia are undergoing the most profound religious crisis experienced since the acceptance of Christianity. This is understandable, since in modern Serbia no party or government has had a definite religious policy. Because religion is the philosophy of the mass of the people, because it is the necessary condition of their life's happiness, morality and order, the friend of the state and the national idea, it is essential to raise the prestige of religion by establishing a modern type of priest.

The Socialists were a particular target for criticism in *Pijemont*, which advocated the "economic welfare of all classes" but emphasized that the state "should draw its financial resources from that part of the nation which is economically strong." Every year on the first of May the paper carried special articles greeting the workers of Serbia, but warning them that the world was far removed from the gates of heaven. On May 1, 1913, *Pijemont* warned: "Our whole planet lives under the sign of capitalism and militarism, such as the world has never before witnessed." After drawing attention to its program for the racial regeneration of the Serbian people, *Pijemont* acknowledged the right of the proletariat to fight against exploitation, but asked that it should lend its help to the Serbian people in their struggle for equality with other peoples and for liberation and unification. "Our people must not lay aside its military shield before the idyllic society is realized. Before we see the arrival of heaven on earth, our people must fight and work in order to secure for themselves a place in Europe and under the sun."

Apis's men tried to penetrate not only governmental agencies but also many other societies and clubs. For the subject of this book, the relations of Ujedinjenje ili Smrt with Narodna Odbrana, a public society which worked behind Serbia's frontiers, is of great importance, particularly because the Austro-Hungarian government in its ultimatum to Serbia on July 23, 1914, did not accuse Ujedinjenje ili Smrt of being the main instigator of Princip's deed, but put the whole blame on Narodna Odbrana.

In the midst of the annexation crisis, in December 1908, a group of prominent citizens, believing that the national feeling roused by the annexation could be usefully canalized, organized Narodna Odbrana for the purpose of strengthening Serbian defenses and preparing adequate forcible means (revolutionary action, guerrilla volunteer units, etc.) to prevent the Habsburgs from carrying out the annexation of Bosnia and Hercegovina. The society published ordinances and organized auxiliary units of volunteers. In a short time it had more than 220 local committees in Serbia, and others among the Serbs in Bosnia and Hercegovina, and even among those living in the United States. Many young men from Bosnia and Hercegovina fled across the frontier into Serbia and joined Narodna Odbrana auxiliary units for military training.[26] But after the Serbian government's statement of March 1909 indicating Serbia's formal acceptance of Austria-Hungary's ultimatum, Narodna Odbrana had to modify its organization and conform to the change in policy. Instead of being a paramilitary society, an auxiliary force promoting revolutionary activity among the South Slavs under Habsburg rule in preparation for a defensive war, Narodna Odbrana henceforth concerned itself with cultural matters. It did, however, use its contacts among the subject South Slavs to establish a network of confidential agents who obtained information on any Austro-Hungarian military preparations which threatened Serbia.

Colonel Apis's Ujedinjenje ili Smrt, on the other hand, was organized as a protest against what it described as "the treason of the government" in connection with the capitulation of 1909. The difference between Ujedinjenje ili Smrt and Narodna Odbrana (in the second period of its work after March 1909) is emphasized by Article 2 of the former's constitution: "This organization prefers revolutionary action to cultural."

But Colonel Apis permitted some of the leading members of his secret society to operate as undercover agents within Narodna Odbrana. This was the case not only with the central organization of Narodna Odbrana (one of its general secretaries was Captain Milan Vasić, a member of the central committee of Ujedinjenje ili Smrt) but also with some of the local units. After Captain Vasić was killed in 1913, Colonel Apis had no direct contact with the work of the central body of Narodna Odbrana; relations between the two societies even became strained. The president of Narodna Odbrana, General Boža Janković, was a conservative, strongly on the side of Prime Minister Nikola Pašić. But in some of the local organizations of Narodna Odbrana there were agents of Ujedinjenje ili Smrt. Colonel Apis had another means of penetrating Narodna Odbrana. In 1913 he was appointed Chief of the Intelligence Department of the Serbian General Staff. Since Serbian Intelligence was using the *kanali*, the links of communications of Narodna Odbrana through trusted agents between Serbia and Bosnia, Ujedinjenje ili Smrt used them also. This was the situation when Princip and his two accomplices had to cross with their weapons from Serbia into Bosnia; some of the men who led them through the *kanali* of Ujedinjenje ili Smrt happened to be at the same time old Narodna Odbrana men.

Of particular interest are the relations between Ujedinjenje ili Smrt and the Young Bosnians and the extent to which Colonel Apis's men succeeded in penetrating into Princip's secret group in Sarajevo, and the nature of their relationship. Miloš Bogićević claimed that both Danilo Ilić and Princip were members of Ujedinjenje ili Smrt[27] but does not quote any source for his statement. As to the number and names of the membership of the secret society, there are differences of opinion. It seems that complete lists were made, but they were probably destroyed by Colonel Apis himself before he left Belgrade in 1915[28] or by some other member of the central committee.[29] In 1916 in Salonika three lists were detected: Vemić's list contained 517 names, Radoje Lazić's 19, and Kosta Tucaković's two. The question is: How many members were in Ujedinjenje ili Smrt? Stanoje Stanojević estimated 300,[30] which is obviously incorrect; Velimir Vemić mentioned the number 2,000 in his diary on September 23, 1911.[31] But the society continued to enroll new members after that time. In a report on November 20, 1911, the French minister in Belgrade spoke of 2,500 members.[32] Miloš Bogićević claimed that Ujedinjenje ili Smrt had 150,000 members, which is obviously an exaggeration.[33]

In one published list of the members of Colonel Apis's secret society the name of Vladimir Gaćinović, the ideological leader of the Young Bosnians, was mentioned in Group 203, holding the membership number 217.[34] On July 3, 1911, Vemić made an entry in his diary stating that at a meeting at his home it was decided that "groups from Bosnia which were already organized should be incorporated in order to undertake the work there."[35] No doubt, Vemić had in mind the secret groups of Young Bosnians organized at the end of 1908 in Vienna. But from that group neither Božidar Zečević nor Pero Slipjepčević joined Ujedinjenje ili Smrt. Zečević was a member of Narodna Odbrana, while Gaćinović was for a time a member of both these organizations. In his talks with Trotsky, Gaćinović explained that he had very high esteem for Ljuba Jovanović-Čupa, with whom he was in constant contact; he called him "the Mazzini of young Serbia," a man who fulfills his tasks "with apostolic fervor," but it is significant to note that Gaćinović joined Ujedinjenje ili Smrt as an ideologically formed man, as a "Bakuninist," as he called himself, for the sake of cooperation in national revolutionary work against the Habsburgs. He also joined Narodna Odbrana and regularly sent it reports about the political and military situation in Bosnia and Hercegovina.[36] The fact that there was equality in the relations between the Young Bosnians and Ujedinjenje ili Smrt was recognized by Ljuba Jovanović-Čupa, as Gaćinović wrote for Trotsky:

He was sitting alone, stooped over the table. He was writing an article for tomorrow's issue of the paper. "This is the answer! You are a Bakuninist . . . Our thoughts touch each other. But look at the reality and you will agree with me: the movement for the national idea must be strengthened, otherwise it will collapse. We must sound the alarm bell, to change one's own soul, to steel oneself." I used to see him often at seven in the evening, when he left his office, all submerged in his own thoughts, like a mysterious shadow. When I think of Serbia I always see, over the Serbian horizon, his apostolic figure.[37]

The common goal of the Young Bosnians and Ujedinjenje ili Smrt was national liberation; but they differed in their philosophy and in their approach to the internal problems of South Slav society. Colonel Apis was for a pan-Serb solution, with Serbia's leadership over other South Slav states, not so much on the pattern of Piedmont, but rather on that of Prussia. In Article 1 of its constitution, Ujedinjenje ili Smrt speaks about the "unification of Serbdom"; in Article 7 it lists Bosnia and Hercegovina, Montenegro, Macedonia, Croatia and the Dalmatian Littoral as Serbian lands, a pan-Serb thesis expressed up to that time only by the most chauvinistic elements in Belgrade.

On the other hand, Princip and his groups were against chauvinism and religious and national intolerance; they were for a South Slav federation in the fullest sense of the word. *Pijemont*, on October 19, 1914, even falsified the words of Princip at his trial in Sarajevo, claiming that he said that he had killed the Archduke Franz Ferdinand "in order to reestablish the Serbian Empire," a statement which Princip never made, according to the official minutes of the trial.

They differed over several other issues. The Young Bosnians were for tyrannicide in its classical sense—an act executed for "the common good"; for Colonel Apis it was just a matter of tactics, as the third point of Article 4 of the constitution of Ujedinjenje ili Smrt states, that the members should fight their enemies "with all means available."

Closer contacts were established between the Young Bosnians and Ujedinjenje ili Smrt especially after the wars of 1912–1913, when the prestige of Serbia, the Serbian army and the *komite* units led by Tankosić increased sharply among the South Slav revolutionary youth in the Habsburg empire. Colonel Apis also kept links with some of the leading South Slav politicians in Croatia and Bosnia and Hercegovina.[38]

To what extent Ujedinjenje ili Smrt succeeded in penetrating the ruling circles, Skupština, and the governmental departments of Serbia is a controversial issue. Vemić claimed that a cousin of Nikola Pašić, Milutin Jovanović, on two occasions in January 1910 promised to talk to Pašić about Colonel Apis.[39] During his trial Apis once mentioned Pašić's name, but the presiding judge stopped him.[40] There were rumors that Milorad Drašković, the strong man of the Young Radicals, was a member of Colonel Apis's secret society.[41]

Colonel Apis did not have much success with the Old Radicals, except with Milovan Milovanović, a newcomer among the Radicals, who succeeded in becoming not only foreign minister but for a time even prime minister of Serbia, from 1909 until his death in 1912. Milovanović was first exposed to open threats by Ujedinjenje ili Smrt. Major Vojin Tankosić was the man in charge of such pressure tactics against many leading men of Serbia. As far back as 1909, while Milovanović's cab was going through the streets of Belgrade, Tankosić jumped into it and threatened him with his *komite* toughs.[42] After this incident, Milovanović had two bodyguards always with him. It seems that Tankosić did not have much success, because in 1911 *Pijemont* made Milovanović the primary target of its attacks against what they described as Serbia's lenient policy toward Austria-Hungary.

"His foreign policy has no firm hand," the paper claimed on September 12, 1911; he is an "Austrophile," it said on September 24, "a man without beliefs or ideals, who is poisoning our national life, and who ought to be banished from his post, where he is sitting as the symbol of our disaster." On October 3 an editorial, "Milovanović or Serbia," demanded his resignation "in order to save Serbia from the annexation which has befallen Bosnia." The Prime Minister sued the editor Jovanović for these attacks, and a trial took place in March 1912. Despite this, *Pijemont* continued to abuse Milovanović for his attitude toward annexation, until his death in June 1912, and even in his obituary the infamous note of the Serbian government of March 1909 was not forgotten.

At his trial in 1917, Colonel Apis claimed that he had established contacts with Prime Minister Milovanović and informed him about the aims of Ujedinjenje ili Smrt. According to Apis, Milovanović asked him to permit him to use Ujedinjenje ili Smrt for good purposes.[43] It happened that at the end of 1911, when this meeting took place, Milovanović and Colonel Apis saw eye to eye at least on one point of Serbian foreign policy: the relations with Bulgaria on the eve of the 1912 alliance between the two countries. Besides, one has to take into consideration that Milovanović was a Freemason and that the meeting between him and Apis was arranged perhaps at the suggestion of Ljuba Jovanović-Čupa.[44]

The hard core of the Old Radical party headed by Nikola Pašić and Stojan Protić were die-hard enemies of Colonel Apis. They looked upon his group as pretorians who were threatening the whole political system of Serbia. *Pijemont* particularly attacked the Old Radicals for their corruption. In many cases the name of Prime Minister Pašić was mentioned openly. On their side the Old Radicals answered with accusations of militarism. From Radical circles Ujedinjenje ili Smrt received its nickname, Black Hand, and this became the familiar name for Colonel Apis's secret society not only in Serbia but also abroad.

The success of the Serbian Army in the First Balkan War, of 1912, against the Ottoman empire, which few military experts in Europe had expected, boosted the prestige of Colonel Apis and increased suspicion of him among the politicians, particularly the Old Radicals. At this stage a third factor in this tug of war for power in Serbia came onto the scene—the sons of King Petar, Djordje and Alexander.

King Petar Karadjordjević was sixty-two when he came to the throne in 1903 with the help of the regicides. During his long exile in Switzerland, he had learned to lead a life of chastity and frugality. The Russian Tsar Nicholas II asked Petar in 1899 to send his two sons,

Djordje and Alexander, and his nephew Paul to school at the Imperial Corps des Pages in St. Petersburg. Although a democrat by conviction, Petar accepted this offer because of the state of his finances. Alexander, at that time a boy of eleven, went to St. Petersburg and returned to Serbia for good only in 1909.

The private diary of King Petar from the time when he came to the throne is full of entries about his illness, his finances and his troubles with his children.[45] Being a king-democrat in a real sense, he declined to identify the state purse with his own. He also felt obliged to the regicides, who had brought him to the throne, and besides giving them occasional gifts, he listened to their political advice. Many old followers of the Karadjordjević dynasty were always hanging around the palace asking for favors.

The heir apparent, Prince Djordje, was a wild youth, sharp-minded, with a rare gift for mathematics. His tutor, Levasseur, described the prince to the French minister in Belgrade as "a simple *petit pupille*, the friend of the best assassins of Belgrade, quite intelligent, but has unformed character and no moral education."[46] The prince did not like his French tutor much. Once he offended him so much that King Petar ordered Djordje to be shut in the Kalemegdan dungeons for several days. Djordje was a riotous youth in many ways, but he had a feeling for justice. He was for a time a pal of Major Vojin Tankosić, but they quarreled and Tankosić boxed the ears of the heir apparent. Djordje mixed freely with people, like his father, attacking bureaucratic officials for their corruption. In the 1908–9 annexation crisis, Djordje took a most active part. He was one of the leading demonstrators when the Habsburg flag was publicly burned down. As the French minister reported from Belgrade on January 16, 1909, Prince Djordje picked a quarrel with the Austrian military attaché in the streets of Belgrade, and the Austrian Minister Forgach ostentatiously refused to attend a reception of Prince Djordje.[47] In the Austrian parliament a deputy denounced Prince Djordje and the whole Serbian royal family. Rumors of Prince Djordje's abdication had already got around at the beginning of the annexation crisis. The French ambassador in Vienna learned on October 18, 1908, that there was "a movement in Serbia to depose King Petar and pass over Prince Djordje for Prince Alexander, who is rumored to be an Austrophile."[48]

The pretext for Djordje's abdication was the death of his butler, Kolaković. According to press reports in Belgrade, the Prince kicked him in the stomach and he died later. There were rumors that the butler had been caught reading Djordje's mail. On March 25, 1909, Prince Djordje sent a letter of resignation to the Prime Minister Stojan Novaković. He mentioned the rumors "about the murder of a man in my palace"[49] as a cause for this action.

The regicides, particularly Colonel Apis, played an important role in this change. Some of them did not like Prince Djordje much, particularly after the defeat over the annexation; among them there was hostility toward all the members of the Karadjordjević dynasty. According to Vemić's diary, as far back as October 18, 1907, the regicides had discussed the possibility of poisoning Prince Djordje. Vemić noted that on that day, at a meeting attended by Apis and five other younger regicides, it was decided that "the poison should be given to the madman," and that "Apis had five bottles of it."[50] Milan Živanović, Apis's nephew, confirmed the fact that there was such a meeting at which the fate of Prince Djordje was discussed, but that the conspirators did not act at all and the whole affair came to an end with this talk.[51]

Živanović also claims that "Colonel Apis was the initiator of the action for Djordje's abdication."[52] He even says that Apis and Alexander cooperated in this task long before the whole matter had been raised in public and before it came before King Petar and the government,[53] and that Alexander expressed his gratitude by establishing "personal relations" with Apis and his colleagues and by giving them gifts of "rings, gold watches and cigarette cases."[54]

In 1910 the relations between Colonel Apis and Prince Alexander were tolerant on both sides. Colonel Apis greatly underestimated the new heir apparent, who was much more agile than his brother had been. He brought from the Imperial Corps des Pages of St. Petersburg a general dislike for the regicides as elements of disorder bordering on republicanism. Unlike his father, who wanted only to reign, Alexander wished to rule, to be the sole factor in the political life of Serbia. The Russian Tsar Nicholas II had advised King Petar year after year to get rid of the regicides; what he was unable or unwilling to do, his son Alexander at once tackled, using a remarkable talent for political maneuvering in this difficult task. At first he sided with the regicides in order to improve his position at the court at the expense of his own father and brother; having achieved this and having become the heir apparent, he joined the regicides in their dislike of civil authorities. At the end he provoked a split among the regicides and joined hands with the Old Radicals and Nikola Pašić in order to wipe out Colonel Apis once and for all and to seize control not only of the army, but of the whole political life of Serbia. As will be seen, Alexander executed Colonel Apis in 1917 and following the First World War he proclaimed an absolute dictatorship.

It took Alexander many years of cunning moves to achieve this goal. In 1910 the prince was a young man of twenty-two, but he proved the equal of Colonel Apis. Alexander knew about Apis's preparations for the organization of Ujedinjenje ili Smrt. According to Živanović, the leading members of the secret society decided that Alexander should be informed about the aims of the society.[55] Apis at the same time influenced Alexander to give 20,000 dinars in gold for *Pijemont*, a remarkable gesture from Alexander, who was known to be as stingy as his father. The marked antiparliamentarian points in *Pijemont's* program no doubt pleased Alexander. During these honeymoon days between Apis and Alexander, as Živanović recorded, Colonel Apis went to King Petar on February 5, 1911, with Alexander's consent and "asked him to abdicate in favor of Alexander, but this action did not have any results."[56] Vemić in his diary for January 23, 1911, confirmed this.[57] Immediately afterward the French minister in Belgrade informed Paris that the Skupština ratified an act giving King Petar special powers over his family in order to control "their bad behavior with the force of law."[58] He did not mention Alexander in this report, but only Prince Djordje, saying that he was still misbehaving.

Djordje at that time was leading a campaign for the annulment of his abdication of March 1909. Alexander was much alarmed by it. According to some reports he tried to poison Djordje with the help of some of the regicides. Alexander approached Petar Živković, an officer who had played a rather important role in the 1903 *coup d'état*. On the eve of the fatal night of June 12, 1903, Živković had been on duty in the palace, and he had opened the main gate from the inside to the conspirators headed by Apis.

There is no primary source for this affair,[59] but Aca Blagojević, an officer and regicide himself, in his unpublished memoirs gave Apis's version of the event as he told it to him in 1916. Živković formed a group of five people to help him in the plot, but before he started to operate he succeeded in getting a letter from Alexander saying that he was the one who had initiated the idea of Djordje's assassination. The letter was to have been used only as a cover for Živković in case Djordje discovered the plot beforehand. Živković tried to persuade Apis to take part in the plot, and he brought him Alexander's letter. Apis, according to Blagojević, rejected it with the words: "Leave these Gypsies alone. It is not right that all Europe should be cursing us because of them. They are not good people."[60] Apis here used the expression "Gypsies" because of the dark complexion of the Karadjordjević family. They came originally from a Montenegrin clan, the Vasojevići. Miloš Bogićević claimed that they were of Gypsy origin.[61] It is interesting that the Archduke Franz Ferdinand, when he met Prince Alexander Karadjordjević for the first and last time in London in 1910 at the funeral of King Edward VII, described him as "a bad copy of a Gypsy."[62]

Despite this rejection from Apis, Živković continued his preparations. He pumped poison through the cork of a bottle of mineral water which Djordje's aide-de-camp, Stojan Popović, whom Živković had succeeded in bringing into the plot, was to serve to Djordje during a boating excursion on the river Sava. But Popović consulted Apis on what to do, and Apis ordered him not to proceed with the plot. Popović kicked the bottle with his spur, pretending to have done it accidentally, and Djordje was saved.[63] Immediately after the death of King Petar, Alexander put Djordje into solitary confinement, where he was kept for two decades.[64]

Although the attempt to poison Djordje needs more documentation to be fully confirmed, this period represents an important stage in the relations between Alexander and Apis. With the help of Živković, Alexander influenced a group of regicides to come over to his side. They formed the so-called Bela Ruka (White Hand) and became the die-hard enemies of Apis.[65] Živković's political career advanced rapidly and he became in the 1920's the first prime minister of Alexander's epoch of dictatorial rule.

The break between Apis and Pašić was open. *Pijemont* asked King Petar to be resolute, warning him that his ministers "are ready to ruin all the results we gained with our weapons." Apis was suspicious of Pašić's vacillation in the relations with Bulgaria over the division of Macedonia. He knew that Pašić had been a political emigree in Bulgaria in 1880 and that he had been very lenient toward Bulgaria's pretension over Macedonia. Apis advocated that Serbia should not wait for the verdict of the Russian Tsar on how Serbia and Bulgaria should divide Macedonia, but that the Serbian Army should attack Bulgaria at once and settle the dispute by the force of arms. While these exchanges between Apis and Pašić were going on, the Bulgarian army attacked Serbian troops unexpectedly in June 1913, inflicting heavy losses. Some of Apis's most devoted friends were killed in action in the war against the Bulgars, among them three members of the central committee of Ujedinjenje ili Smrt: Jovanović-Čupa, Milan Vasić and Ilija Radiovojević. Some of the surviving members of Apis's society were scheming to assassinate Pašić at that time.

Slobodan Jovanović spent some time in 1914 with Apis and has left a portrait of that strange man:

He met me in a polite way as he used to do with everybody. He expressed himself in an ambiguous way, never finishing his sentences, as if he remembered all of a sudden that it would be better not to say everything that he had on his mind. He had not yet recovered from his grave illness; there were still traces of poison in his body. He did not stand firmly on his legs, which, wrapped in the military bindings, looked giantlike. He was gaining weight because he did not move about enough. He had an unhealthy pale color and his head was completely bald. Sitting by the table, with his huge body and bald head, he looked, as a foreign correspondent described him, like a giant Mongolian.[66]

Jovanović noted that Apis's political strength was waning. Before Alexander began interfering in military affairs, everybody who sought a better position crowded around Apis. Now these people slowly but steadily were going from Apis to Alexander. The circle around Apis became smaller, consisting of his real friends. The war, which did not cease to mow down officers, at the same time decreased the number of Apis's followers. Apis told Jovanović about his feelings toward Alexander:

He is a Karadjordjević, and Karadjordjevićes do not know how to make friends. He does not care about anybody's friendship. . . . From men he does not ask fidelity, but subservience, and I am not a lackey. I have given to the dynasty enough proofs of my own faithfulness. But if one asks from me that I should take off the jack boots of the heir apparent, well, I will not do that thing and I shall not do it. He has his orderlies. . . .[67]

Apis, Jovanović continued,

started to get excited; his enormous chest was trembling. For a moment, instead of an everyday Apis, I saw a temperamental and proud man, conscious of his value and his might. Looking at him, so big and so heavy, I realized that for him any kind of bowing in front of somebody was an impossible act, from both the moral and the physical point of view.[68]

Jovanović also had occasion to talk about Apis with Alexander, who told him that he received reports that some people were calling Apis "the real heir apparent," without whom the first heir apparent is not allowed to do anything. "I had no impression," Jovanović recorded,

that Alexander was offended because Apis was not a type of man who wished to bow. There was, also, something of that, but it was not the main cause. What offended Alexander more than anything else was the fact that Apis had among the officers a popularity which decreased Alexander's role even as a future king. Instead of being thankful for his position to Alexander, the case was just the reverse. With this feeling of debasement, there was also in Alexander some kind of uneasiness and fear. In his past Apis had on his conscience the murder of a king and an heir apparent. Alexander did not know what might happen to him if he himself did not get rid of Apis in time. In any case, Alexander's hesitation toward Apis was much more complex than Apis had thought. . . . Alexander was not a coward, but he had weak nerves. He could not tolerate in his presence people he did not like. The reports against Apis were coming constantly; the joint dinners and lunches of Apis and his friends in his office seemed suspicious to Alexander. The thought that Apis was near him, in the same town, in the same headquarters, became for Alexander at last unbearable.[69]

The climax of the struggle between Apis, Pašić and Alexander was reached in the fateful weeks before June 28, 1914. The immediate cause was the so-called Priority Question—who was going to have the upper hand in the affairs of Macedonia, the civil or the military authorities.

In the Macedonian provinces occupied by Serbia in 1912–13, the Old Radical appointed as civil servants many of their followers from Serbia, among whom were many with stained records, particularly as far as corruption was concerned. The Serbian constitution was not applied in Macedonia at that time. Between these authorities and the Macedonian population relations became strained. On the other hand, the army could not regard passively the deterioration of political conditions in such a strategically important province as Macedonia.

Pijemont criticized conditions in Macedonia, and Minister of Interior Stojan Protić, the most energetic Radical leader, banned *Pijemont* in Macedonia. Relations between the army and the government became even worse when in December 1913, during a festival in the Russian consulate in Bitolj, attended by both the local military and civil authorities, the chief of the district, Marko Novaković, stood up first to drink a toast to the health of the Russian Tsar Nicholas II. But he was abruptly interrupted by the commander of the 16th Regiment, Colonel Voja Živanović, who stated that he, as a colonel, had priority over a civilian, who during the war could not hold a rank higher than a petty officer.[70] After this incident the government issued the so-called Priority Ordinance, giving precedence to civil servants over military personnel in all public functions.

This measure aroused the protests of almost all officers, even those who did not follow Colonel Apis. But Pašić and Protić were determined not to give up. At the beginning of January 1914 they struck at the minister of war, General Miloš Božanović, Colonel Apis's man. In 1913 Major Vemić had been sentenced to eight months in jail for killing a soldier who refused to obey an order during a military action in the 1912 war. Božanović granted an amnesty to Vemić without the approval of the other members of the government and as a result had to give up his ministerial post.

Pijemont on May 6, 1914, vehemently criticized the Radicals "as a gang of men without conscience, who are attacking not only the purse of the people and state funds, but also our army." Protić was attacked particularly because of the situation in Macedonia: "His police officers, under his mighty protection, are simply brigands and crooks . . . This government cannot be tolerated for a moment, or rebellion and anarchy will break out in the country . . . Other factors in Serbia have to say their word." In the meantime, Colonel Apis succeeded in establishing a common political platform with the leaders of the opposition against the Radicals. Pressure was brought to bear on King Petar through General Radomir Putnik, the chief of the General Staff, to dismiss the Radical government. It seems that King Petar gave Putnik his word of honor that he would do as he was advised.[71] On the other hand, Protić put the gendarmerie on alert; day and night vigil was introduced, and the gendarmes got orders to shoot to kill at the first move of army units. The Radicals also prepared an act to pension off Apis, Tankosić and several other leading officers of Ujedinjenje ili Smrt, but King Petar refused to sign it.

On June 2 Pašić had to resign. *Pijemont* declared triumphantly: "The white-haired heads with long beards [an allusion to Pašić] have now to be forgotten forever. The Negroes have finished their jobs and they can go."

Yet the situation changed overnight, through the intervention of the Russian government and Alexander, although Apis had warned Alexander to stand aside on the Priority issue. They backed Pašić all the way. Colonel Apis called an urgent meeting of Ujedinjenje ili Smrt, and Tankosić proposed that he should threaten Pašić and Protić physically.[72] Apis had other ideas. He decided to organize a *coup d'état* in Macedonia through his men among the commanders of the army units. On June 7, 1914, he wrote instructions to that effect and sent oral orders as well.[73] But his request was rejected by his best friends; they did not wish to move army units against civil authorities, despite their devotion to Apis. Thus Apis lost his fight and from that day his star started to fall rapidly, although he continued to put pressure on the Radicals and tried to organize an alliance with the civilian opposition in Belgrade.

On June 24, 1914, Pašić got a mandate to dissolve the Skupština and he announced new elections for August 1. King Petar, as a man of honor, drew adequate conclusions. On the same date he resigned, giving an official explanation of bad health, and appointed Alexander as Prince Regent and Commander in Chief of the Army.

Jakov Milović, the Bosnian peasant from Obriježje, who took Princip and Grabež over the river Drina to Bosnia, not only was used as a link by Serbian Military Intelligence—at the same time he was a trusted agent of Narodna Odbrana. Immediately after he had helped Princip and Grabež, he informed Boža Milanović, the head of Narodna Odbrana in the Serbian border town of Šabac. Milanović forwarded the information at once to the president of Narodna Odbrana in Belgrade, General Boža Janković, who in turn sent the message through Minister of Interior Stojan Protić to Prime Minister Nikola Pašić.

These facts were confirmed by a Serbian government document of paramount importance to understanding the full background of the Sarajevo assassination. Jakov Milović's report appears as follows:

I

On the 19th instant in the evening Miloš Milošević from Janja received two high-school students, one of whom was called Triša. I don't know where the students were from, but they were Bosnians by birth.

Miloš sent the students to Jakov Milović from Obriježje.

Jakov led the students to the teacher V. Čubrilović in Priboj, by Tuzla, and the teacher had to bring them to the trusted agent in Tuzla, whose name is M.J., and M.J. had to take them to Sarajevo.

Jakov told Boža all this after he escorted the students to Čubrilović.

The students carried six hand grenades and four revolvers.

The students' purpose he did not know.

The students were sent by the captain of the border guards in Šabac, Rade Popović, and Major Kosta Todorović, and as the students said, they met in Belgrade where they received hand grenades and pistols.

The students crossed the border at the Island of Mladen Isaković, and they were brought by the Sergeant of the Border Guards, Grbić.

Boža has informed all the agents that they should not receive anyone, unless he produces the password given by Boža.

II

Fourteen days ago Captain Rade met Rade Malobabić [a man sentenced at the high-treason trial in Croatia] and the agent, Milan Vračarić, from Badovince, while they were traveling; they told Miloš that a box of hand grenades would come to him and that he was to give them to the agents in Bosnia. Their duty is to hide the grenades and weapons and use them only when they receive orders to do so. Milan informed Boža of all this. Boža told him to receive the grenades and weapons, but not to carry them over to Bosnia, but only inform him when they came. The weapons have not yet been received.

III

Major Dimitrije Pavlović sent across before the war six boxes of hand grenades to Bosnia. Fourteen of these grenades were found in the river Sava near Brcko. The rest are still over there among the agents. Four hand grenades are with Moja Bikicki in Mitrovica. The rest are in Croatia and they were distributed by Rade Malobabić.[74]

The decisive proof of the authenticity of this document, besides the details given in Note 74, is the fact that Prime Minister Pašić summarized in his own hand the first part of it.[75]

The most important aspect of this document is the fact that it does not say anything about the plot against Franz Ferdinand, but mentions only the crossing of the two pupils who went to Bosnia with six hand grenades and four revolvers. The vital question, in relation to the responsibility of the Serbian government, is what measures Prime Minister Pašić took when he received this information.

The fact that he made a summary of the document suggests that he took the information seriously. Although the name of the Archduke was not mentioned in the document, Pašić no doubt concluded that the crossing of the boys with lethal weapons at the time of the Archduke's visit to Bosnia was a thing which should be investigated at once. On the other hand, Parts II and III of the document say that the weapons were transported for use by the trusted agents of Narodna Odbrana at a given time.

From all the available sources, it seems that Pašić undertook several measures:

1. He discussed the matter with some of the cabinet ministers.

2. He ordered an investigation by civilian authorities at the border, and the Minister of the Interior issued adequate orders against illegal traffic of weapons across the border.[76]

3. He ordered an investigation of Colonel Apis by military authorities at the same time the Minister of War issued an order against illegal traffic of armed men over the frontier.

4. Measures were taken through other channels to stop the group which had already crossed the border.

5. It is not yet clear what measures Pašić took to warn the Viennese government about armed men crossing into Bosnia.

Between the two world wars a heated debate was going on among the contemporaries and historians about whether the Serbian government knew of the preparations for the Sarajevo assassination.[77] There are some primary historical sources which confirm, at least, that Prime Minister Pašić ordered an investigation through both civil and military authorities as soon as he was informed that some armed young men had crossed from Serbia into Bosnia.

Several sources confirm that the civilian investigation took place. In 1914 the Austrian army captured in Serbia a copy of an order of the Chief of Podrinje District, Kosta Jezdić, to the commander of the Fifth Company of the Border Guards on June 16, 1914, in which it was said:

I have learned that customs sentinels on the Bosnian border, through our men and men in Bosnia, are transporting from Serbia into Bosnia armaments, ammunition and other explosives. After an investigation I found out through Rajko Stepanović, the sergeant of the Guard troops, that about ten days ago four revolvers and 400 bullets were transported from our territory to Bosnia; at the same time the mentioned Stepanović and Milan Aničić brought a suitcase from Badovince in which there were weapons and hand grenades, in order to be transported to Bosnia and delivered there to Rade Malobabić . . . On that occasion Sergeant Stepanović showed Vračarić your written order about it. It is not necessary to explain to you what could happen and how bad the consequences could be if the Austro-Hungarian authorities learn about the transport of arms, and this could happen not only by the way the arms are transported but also at the time when it took place and particularly which persons were doing this. Informing you about this, I am advising you to stop your business immediately and to hamper any attempt to transport arms and ammunition from Serbia to Bosnia; if you don't do this I shall make you responsible to the Minister in charge. You should inform me at once that you have taken notice of this act and in particular whether you have done the above-mentioned things and if so under whose orders and knowledge you did them, and also what was in the suitcase? At the same time you will send Sergeant Rajko Stepanović for the necessary investigation in connection with this thing.

The Chief of District, KOSTA JEZDIĆ[78]

The great struggle of Pašić and Stojan Protić against Colonel Apis was conducted also on the district level, but Colonel Apis's men refused to be investigated by the civil authorities. It happened that the commander in chief of all the Border Guard units on the Austrian frontier was Major Ljubomir Vulović, one of the most active members of the central committee of Ujedinjenje ili Smrt.

Under these conditions Stojan Protić relieved the district chief, Kosta Jezdić, and appointed in his place Kosta Tucaković, an energetic police officer from Belgrade. But even Tucaković could not make Major Vulović budge. At the investigation before the trial of Colonel Apis in 1917, Tucaković said:

I went personally to search the log cabin of Milan Vračarić in Badovince, but I did not search the pill-boxes of the frontier guards. I sent a telegram to Major Vulović, the Commander in Chief of the frontier guards, to stop certain things and to either send Sergeant Stepanović to me or to proceed with his interrogation. I did not get an answer to this telegram, nor did Stepanović turn up. I complained to the Minister of War, but when I did not get an answer from him either, I submitted a long report to the Minister of Interior. Mr. Malobabić was mixed up in this affair as well, and my impression is that he followed somebody's advice, while Colonel Dimitrijević [Apis] and Major Vulović denied that they had anything to do with this thing, as Colonel Stanko Cvetković told me.[79]

In this situation Pašić contacted the Chief of the General Staff, General Putnik, under whose jurisdiction Colonel Apis ran the Military Intelligence Department. It is significant that M. Bogićević, in no way a friend of Pašić and one of the strongest accusers of the Serbian government as responsible for the Sarajevo assassination, mentioned in his book on Colonel Apis that Pašić approached Putnik with a request to investigate Apis.[80]

In the Serbian archives there exists a text written in Apis's hand in which he gives his answer to the charges made in Tucaković's report.[81] One should note that Apis first answered Tucaković's hint that Malobabić might have been an Austrian spy. Apis at great length described the qualities of Malobabić as a good Serb patriot and as an excellent intelligence agent.

Concerning the transport of arms to Bosnia, Apis said that he had permitted Malobabić to arm his secret agents in Austrian territory so that they could defend themselves in case of danger; for that purpose he gave Malobabić four revolvers and adequate ammunition. Due to the fact that Major Vulović was appointed just at that time to his new post, Apis said that he had brought him into contact with Malobabić so that they could cooperate in their intelligence work. Apis wrote that he advised both of them not to reveal their activities to anyone except the General Staff of the Army. Apis here spoke explicitly about the conflict between Narodna Odbrana and his men:

I gave such instruction to both of them and underlined them particularly because Mr. Malobabić mentioned that Narodna Odbrana is expressing a certain interest in his work and that they have even asked him openly with whom he is going to work—with Narodna Odbrana or with the General Staff. Giving such instructions to Malobabić, I advised him that he should continue to be at the disposal of Narodna Odbrana and its tasks as far as is consistent with the tasks he has to do for the General Staff.[82]

Further, Apis complained that the police authorities and Narodna Odbrana people were pressing his confidants who were also members of Narodna Odbrana not to accept any orders from the military and that they should inform the civilian authorities about everything.[83]

Apis denied that he had issued any hand grenades to Malobabić. In connection with the suitcase, mentioned in Tucaković's report, Apis said that Malobabić might have asked someone to bring it to the border.

The text of Apis's statement was passed on to Prime Minister Pašić who was not satisfied with it. He ordered the Minister of War, Dušan Stefanović, to open an investigation. The Minister sent for Colonel Stanko Cvetković, the head of the Judiciary Department, and told him that with the government's consent he should proceed with the matter, giving him all the documents concerned. He was told to go to the border and investigate there; for the sake of efficiency and secrecy he was ordered to go in mufti. Colonel Cvetković questioned Tucaković and Vulović and several other persons. All the acts from this investigation, which had not been included in the official books of his department, he handed to the Minister of War, who in turn sent them to Pašić.[84]

These documents of Cvetković's investigation have not yet been found, and so it is not known when Cvetković's work started and when it ended. According to statements he made in 1953 when he was eighty-three, Cvetković said that Apis admitted to him that from the whole affair he knew only that Tankosić trained some Bosnian youths to use the arms.[85] From this, one can infer that this part of the investigation took place after June 28, 1914.

Although Colonel Apis and Major Vulović denied that they had known anything about the crossing of armed men into Bosnia, admitting only that they had armed their secret agents with revolvers, we must discover what measures the Serbian government had undertaken through the underground channels of communication of Narodna Odbrana and other available means to stop the possible action of "the two armed boys" who crossed into Bosnia on the night of June 1 and 2.

At the trial, Princip's disagreement with Ilić and to a certain extent with Grabež was made manifest. Ilić claimed that he was against the attempt to assassinate the Archduke. When the presiding judge asked Princip if what Ilić said were true, Princip answered: "He advised me several times not to do it, explaining that the act has no sense and that the Serbian people will suffer."[86] Grabež also affirmed that Ilić had tried to talk him out of killing the Archduke.[87]

From all available sources, Ilić does not seem to have been a man of weak nerves who was suddenly frightened and decided to quit the plot. Obviously he changed his attitude under the influence of other people.

According to Čeda Popović, a member of the central committee of Ujedinjenje ili Smrt, the central committee was informed by Apis and Tankosić on June 15 that they had given arms to a group of young Bosnians to go to Sarajevo and try to assassinate the Archduke. All the other members of the central committee rejected this decision outright.[88] Probably after this, and with knowledge of Pašić's investigation of him, Apis sent a message through Tankosić to Sarajevo saying that the plot had to be stopped. Slobodan Jovanović, who had more opportunity to consult the relevant Serbian documents than any other historian, confirmed in his memoirs the facts mentioned by Čeda Popović.[89]

According to Čeda Popović, Tankosić dispatched Šarac to get in contact with Ilić.[90] It seems that this information is true, since it helps to explain the behavior of Ilić in Sarajevo. On June 15 he went personally to Tuzla and brought the bombs and revolvers to Sarajevo. It is obvious that he was then determined to go on with the plot. Yet, after June 15 his attitude changed. He left Sarajevo again a few days later and went to the border town of Šabac. At the trial Ilić had trouble explaining what he was doing there. He refused to give any adequate answer. He kept the secret for himself. In Šabac, he met Šarac, who brought him Tankosić's message, after which he returned to Sarajevo and tried to convince Princip that the whole conspiracy had to be stopped. But Princip firmly refused to obey.

There were other attempts from Belgrade to stop the assassination. According to a Bosnian lawyer by the name of Predrag Kašiković, who lived in Sarajevo in 1914 and who was one of the confidants of Boža Milanović from Narodna Odbrana in Šabac, Milanović sent a special courier to ask him to come urgently to Šabac, but Kašiković could not come, because he had to pass his lawyer's exam. After the war, Milanović told him that he had wanted to ask his help in stopping the assassination, "because it was the deed of individuals who had no relations with Narodna Odbrana."[91]

Kosta Krajšumović has recorded that two local secret agents of Narodna Odbrana from Srebrenica and Bijeljina in Bosnia were warned by Boža Milanović and Kosta Tucaković "not to lose their heads and not to accept anyone without their permission."[92] Jakov Milović, who led Princip and Grabež to Bosnia, fled after June 28 to Serbia, but Boža Milanović ordered him back: "You never told me what you were at, and now you can go back and take the rap."[93] Milović returned and was sentenced to death, the sentence being commuted to twenty years in prison. Before he died in Möllersdorf he confessed his secret to Vaso Čubrilović.[94]

There is evidence also that Pašić and Stojan Protić, through Belgrade's Chief of Police Manojlo Lazarević, tried to warn Vasilj Grdjić, the most militant Serb leader in the Bosnian *Sabor*. Prior to the Sarajevo assassination, the leader of the right-wing Bosnian Serbs, Dr. Dušan Jeftanović, was in Belgrade, and Lazarević told him that there were rumors that some people intended to cross to Bosnia "with evil intentions to assassinate somebody, perhaps the Archduke." Lazarević appealed to Jeftanović to get into contact with Vasilj Grdjić and to ask him to try to dissuade maverick local elements from doing anything.[95] Jeftanović did not take this warning seriously, believing that security measures would be as strong as in 1910, when the Emperor Franz Josef was in Sarajevo.

It is possible that Ilić might have stopped Princip, in spite of the latter's stubbornness, which at one point impelled him to say to Ilić: "After me the deluge; I do not care." But, as Ljubibratić claims, Rade Malobabić, Colonel Apis's chief intelligence man in Austria-Hungary, appeared in Sarajevo on the eve of June 28.[96]

During the trial several school friends of Grabež testified that they had seen him in Tuzla a few days before June 28. Grabež denied vehemently that he had been there, because, he said, he had never left his village Pale near Sarajevo. But in a letter to his father after the verdict of the court, Grabež said he was happy in one thing—"that he had saved a very important person." According to Ljubibratić, that person was Malobabić, who was standing by the *beledija*, or town hall, in Sarajevo on the morning of June 28. Ilić's mother said that on the eve of June 28, a man with "big feet" had been at her home to see her son, and Malobabić truly had very long feet.[97]

Here comes one of the crucial points of the whole mystery of Archduke Franz Ferdinand's assassination. If Malobabić brought word that the attempt should not be postponed, thus supporting Princip, under whose instructions did he do it—Colonel Apis's, Major Tankosić's or somebody else's? And if it was under Colonel Apis's order, what were his motives in changing his mind after the investigation of him had been started and after the decision of June 15?

There is a possibility that the power struggle between Pašić and Apis led Apis to approve Tankosić's delivery of the arms to the Sarajevo assassins. It seems that Apis did not expect that Princip and his accomplices would succeed in killing the Archduke, although he did think their efforts might provoke a greater strain in relations between Pašić and the Austro-Hungarian government and that such complications would further weaken Pašić's position in relation to Apis. This thesis is strengthened by Tankosić's statement when he was arrested after the delivery of the Austrian ultimatum to Serbia. A general present at the arrest asked: "Why have you done this?" Tankosić answered: "To spite Pašić."[98]

Finally the question remains: Did the Serbian government warn the Austro-Hungarian government that armed men had crossed from Serbia into Bosnia? If it did, when was the warning dispatched to Vienna, to whom was it delivered, and in what form was the warning?

On this issue there exists a vast literature of the most controversial character. At least ten sources mentioned, either immediately after June 28, 1914, or between the two world wars, that the Serbian government had warned Vienna.[99] Some of these sources claimed that Pašić himself stated that the warning was sent to the Austro-Hungarian government; but Pašić denied this on two occasions.[100] The Austrian government on three different occasions denied that the warning was delivered.[101]

This writer believes that the Serbian government did not officially inform Vienna of the results of its investigations before June 28, as the archives of the Serbian Ministry of Foreign Affairs confirm.[102] It is not clear whether or not the Serbian minister in Vienna, Jovan Jovanović-Pižon, on his own initiative, expressed his fears about the Archduke's visit to Sarajevo. There are several different versions of this issue, but it seems safe to say that Jovanović-Pižon went to Count Bilinski and mentioned vaguely the dangers for the Archduke during his trip to Bosnia and Hercegovina.[103]

The outbreak of war on July 28, after the Serbian government rejected the Austro-Hungarian ultimatum, postponed an open clash between the warring factions in Serbian political life—Alexander, Pašić and Apis. But the differences aroused by the assassination did not settle down. On July 25, Rade Malobabić went back to Belgrade, and Colonel Apis told him that the Belgrade police wanted to see him.[104] Malobabić went to the police and was immediately arrested. On August 1, *Politika* carried a news item sent via St. Petersburg from Niš, where the seat of the Serbian government was, charging that Malobabić, "an Austrian reserve officer, was in the service of Austrian espionage and that he was closely connected with the assassination of Franz Ferdinand and his wife." Colonel Apis tried to get in touch with Malobabić, but without success. While Malobabić was being transported from Belgrade to Niš, he jumped off the moving express train, without his shoes, but was soon caught again.[105] He was kept in chains in prison until November 1915, when the Serbian Army had to leave its national territory under the pressure of the German, Bulgarian and Austrian troops. Apis by chance met Malobabić, who was very ill after maltreatment in jail. Apis took care of him, keeping him constantly at his side.

The defeat of Serbia at the end of 1915 brought the struggle between Alexander, Apis and Pašić again to the fore. Apis accused Pašić of being responsible for the defeat, because the Serbian Army command had wanted to occupy Bulgaria in the summer of 1915 so that it would not be exposed to the Bulgars' attack in the autumn of the same year, when the Germans attacked from the north.

Alexander wavered at that time over whom to strike first, Apis or Pašić. Already in the summer of 1915, Apis had been dismissed as chief of Military Intelligence. Many of his best friends had been killed in action. Major Vojin Tankosić was gravely wounded on October 18, 1915, and died a few days later. He was buried by his faithful soldier Djuro Šarac. The remnants of the Young Bosnians who survived the fighting were gathered together by Colonel Apis; among them were Mehmed Mehmedbašić and Mustafa Golubić. The number of Apis's enemies was increasing. Alexander was getting long daily reports about threats from Apis's side. Slobodan Jovanović, who saw Alexander at that time, recorded that the Regent "was obsessed with the idea that Apis was plotting against his head. The whole of Apis's past as a regicide, the cocky behavior of his followers, daily denunciations of Apis by the police—all this kept Alexander in such a frantic state of mind that he did not distinguish between fear based on his imagination and fear based on the truth. . . . Listening to all these things, Alexander came to the conclusion that it was dangerous to let Apis be free. . . ."[106]

One of the accusations against Apis was that he had been negotiating secretly with the Germans for a separate peace treaty—an accusation for which this writer has not been able to find documentation in the German archives—and on December 15, 1916, Apis was arrested, together with the leading members of Ujedinjenje ili Smrt, on the charge that he was planning to assassinate Alexander and Pašić and to incite a mutiny in the army in order to cross over to the enemy side. The original text of the constitution and the bylaws of Ujedinjenje ili Smrt was found in his room, and among the belongings of two of his followers were lists of the members of the organization.

At that time Serbia's situation was serious. The whole country was overrun by the enemy and an army of only 125,000, who had survived the retreat through the Albanian mountains, was assembled on the Salonika front. The prospects for a quick Allied victory were also grim.

The investigation of Apis lasted three and a half months. In the meantime, the new Habsburg Emperor, Karl, opened secret negotiations with French Premier Clemenceau for a separate peace treaty, without Germany's knowledge. Through his brother-in-law, Prince Sixtus of Bourbon-Parma, the first meeting took place in February 1917, when the Habsburgs presented their proposals. One of their demands was that all those responsible for the Sarajevo assassination should be punished. Emperor Karl accepted the idea that Serbia should remain an independent state, but under the condition that all secret societies and organizations which had been working against the Habsburg empire should be dissolved. He also asked that the great powers should guarantee Austria-Hungary that Serbia would keep this promise.[107]

In the meantime the revolution had taken place in Russia, and Alexander and the Old Radicals had lost their faithful ally, Tsar Nicholas II. At that period of the First World War it seemed clear that both England and France intended to preserve the Austro-Hungarian empire. Alexander and Pašić learned the details of the secret talks and became much alarmed over what to do and how to prove that they had not been involved in any way with the Sarajevo conspiracy.

Under these conditions, the trial of Colonel Apis and his followers was opened in Salonika on April 2, 1917. Among the judges were some of the personal enemies of Colonel Apis. But on April 9, the trial was interrupted and two new accused came to the court. The first was Rade Malobabić and the second Mehmed Mehmedbašić, the only assassin of Sarajevo who had succeeded in escaping after June 28, 1914. He had been a volunteer in the Serbian army. Rade Malobabić was accused of being the chief culprit and perpetrator, and Mehmed Mehmedbašić of being his accomplice, in an attempt upon the life of Alexander on September 11, 1916, about 5 P.M., when the Regent was returning from the front line. Colonel Apis was accused of being the initiator and organizer of the alleged attempt.

All evidence proves that there was no attempt by Colonel Apis against Alexander on September 11 and that the charges were false.[108] But the Serbian police had succeeded in breaking Malobabić, and he accused Apis of the plot. They tried to do the same with Mehmed Mehmedbašić, but he was very stubborn; despite torture and threats, he denied the accusations, saying simply: "There was no idea behind this so-called attempt, and therefore I could not take part in it."[109] The police tortured Mustafa Golubić also, but he did not give in and refused to say anything against Colonel Apis.

Slobodan Jovanović has reported that Apis did not defend himself cleverly in Salonika. It was hard for Apis to believe that his enemies would use such low methods; besides, he counted heavily on the intervention of his friends in England, France and particularly Russia, where his position had been strengthened with the downfall of Tsarism.

At this time, Alexander made another move through his main political adviser, General Petar Živković, the leader of the Bela Ruka. Through a jailer, Živković established contact with Apis, sending him messages that he should not worry, that everything would be all right in the end. After the indictments had been extended to include Malobabić and Mehmedbašić, Živković hinted that the whole trial could be ended at once if Apis would give the full story of the Sarajevo assassination and describe his, Malobabić's and Vulović's roles in it. At the beginning of the investigation in Salonika, before Malobabić and Mehmedbašić were brought in, Apis had been questioned again about the Sarajevo assassination; he had denied any connection with it, repeating the main points which he had made at the 1914 investigation, and adding a new technical detail: the four revolvers that he gave Malobabić were of the "Nagan" type, he now said, and he even kept the invoice to prove it.[110]

But now the situation was different, and on April 11, Apis handed the president of the court a new report on the Sarajevo conspiracy, as he had been advised to do by Petar Živković. This report among other points attempted to explain his connection with Malobabić and Mehmedbašić as a logical result of their joint participation in the planning of the Sarajevo assassination:

As the Chief of the Intelligence Department of the General Staff, I engaged Rade Malobabić to organize the information service in Austria-Hungary. I took this step in agreement with the Russian Military Attaché Artamonov, who had a meeting with Rade in my presence. Feeling that Austria was planning a war with us, I thought that the disappearance of the Austrian Heir Apparent would weaken the power of the military clique he headed, and thus the danger of war would be removed or postponed for a while. I engaged Malobabić to organize the assassination on the occasion of the announced arrival of Franz Ferdinand to Sarajevo. I made up my mind about this only when Artamonov assured me that Russia would not leave us without protection if we were attacked by Austria. On this occasion I did not mention my intention for the assassination, and my motive for asking his opinion about Russia's attitude was the possibility that Austria might become aware of our activities, and use this as a pretext to attack us. Malobabić executed my order, organized and performed the assassination. His chief accomplices were in my service and received small payments from me. Some of their receipts are in the hands of the Russians, since I got money for this purpose from Mr. Artamonov, as the General Staff did not have funds available for this increased activity.[111]

Without a doubt, Colonel Apis in this report exaggerated Malobabić's role in the Sarajevo assassination. This can be explained by his mental condition at the time he wrote it. He was convinced that this new confession would produce a straight withdrawal of the Salonika charges. In the same report Apis spoke about his own role, contrary to his habit of not boasting about his work. In the report he went to the other extreme.

All the accused at the Salonika trial were asked what they knew about the Sarajevo plot, including Vulović, Mehmedbašić, and Malobabić. It is interesting that their testimonies were not preserved in the archives of the Salonika trial. One of the reasons for this could be that they did not confirm Apis's story. Before his death, Malobabić confessed to a priest in the Salonika prison: "They [meaning obviously Apis and Vulović] ordered me to go to Sarajevo when that assassination was to take place, and when everything was over, they ordered me to come back and fulfill other missions, and then there was the outbreak of the war."[112] This last statement of Malobabić does not speak about the organization of the Archduke's assassination, but only says that Malobabić was ordered to go to Sarajevo. Why he went remains a controversy—to stop the assassination or to approve it.

On this occasion Colonel Apis revealed again his lack of political tactics, his weakness in underestimating his political opponents' cunning tricks, and his loss of nerve. On April 12, he wrote a personal letter to Alexander in which he again pleaded for Malobabić and Mehmedbašić, and at the same time capitulated entirely to Alexander, asking his clemency and mercy in the most shameless manner. He sent a similar letter to King Petar, saying that he was guilty of what he had been accused of.[113]

With both of Apis's letters on his table, Alexander proceeded with his schemes. On June 5, 1917, the military court sentenced Apis, Milovanović, Lazić, Čedomir Popović, Tucaković, Vemić, Radenković, Vulović and Malobabić to death. Mehmedbašić was sentenced to fifteen years' penal servitude and Damjan Popović to ten years'. A higher military court on June 18 altered these sentences by commuting the capital punishment of Čedomir Popović and Radenković to twenty years, and increasing Damjan Popović's sentence from ten to twenty years.

The British and Russian governments advised Alexander to grant an amnesty. Particularly strong pressure was brought to bear by Tereshchenko, the Minister of Foreign Affairs of the Russian Provisional Government.[114] The attitude of the French government on this issue is not clear. Apis had been arrested only after the commander of the Allied forces on the Salonika front, the French General Sarrail, gave his consent.[115] Dragiša Stojadinović claims that Clemenceau personally insisted that Apis should be executed and sent a telegram to that effect.[116]

Alexander waved aside all the interventions for Apis. The sentence was executed in the early morning of June 26, in a ditch near Salonika. It was purposely arranged to torment Apis as much as possible. The reading of the sentence lasted more than two hours, while Apis, Vulović and Malobabić stood by the open graves. At last at 4:47 A.M. the reading was over. Fifteen gendarmes were waiting with their rifles. Several times at some movement around him during the reading of the sentence, Apis raised his head as if he were expecting a reprieve at the last moment. It never came. The commanding officer lowered his saber. Malobabić fell from the first round of five bullets. Apis shouted: "Long live Serbia! Long live Yugoslavia!"[117] The gendarmes had to fire three times at him before life left his giant body.

CHAPTER XVIII

VIENNA AND SARAJEVO

*Rejoice, rejoice, enemies of Austria, rejoice
and cheer. Because you are witnessing a very
happy event: you have destroyed the most
valuable life of New Austria. You have destroyed the hope of our future. You have
broken the highest branch of our hopes—you,
dirty dogs, knew better than many an Austrian
that Franz Ferdinand was the man who would
settle accounts with you, who would make you
feel a respect for Austria again. This is the reason you murdered him.*

Danzers Armee Zeitung,
Vienna, July 2, 1914

CHARGES OF AUSTRO-HUNGARIAN RESPONSIBILITY for the Sarajevo
assassination have been made on two chief counts: first, negligence in
not taking seriously the warnings of danger in the Archduke's visit to
Sarajevo and the lack of adequate security measures; second, instigation
of the assassination by circles in Vienna and Budapest who had their
agents in the South Slav secret societies. Some writers have believed
that Austria-Hungary provoked the Sarajevo assassination in order to
have an excuse for an attack on Serbia, while others have charged that
the real man behind the whole conspiracy was the Hungarian Prime
Minister Count Stephen Tisza, who wanted to get rid of the Archduke
because of his marked anti-Magyar feelings and his designs to crush
Hungary with arms the moment he came to the throne.

The Archduke himself was well aware that he had many enemies. He
had been receiving threats for almost fifteen years before his death, not

only from South Slavs but also from Italians and pan-Germans; very few were from Hungary. Here one must distinguish between the rumors, which were numerous, and the actual plots detected by the security forces. Some sources indicate that before 1914 there were three actual attempts against the Archduke's life.

The first took place in 1902. The Archduke visited Italy in February of that year and on his return complained to Foreign Minister Goluchowski about the "excessive zeal of the Italian security organs responsible for his protection."[1] On March 2, Goluchowski instructed the Austro-Hungarian ambassador in Rome to make a representation at the Italian Foreign Office in connection with the Archduke's complaint. The answer came from Rome on March 3: "The Italian security police have been worried on account of the shots fired at the special train of the Archduke near Regensburg."[2]

The second one, according to a report of the French ambassador in Vienna, apparently took place in Slovenia in 1906, when a coach of his train was blown up and three shots were fired at him.[3] In the *Nachlass* and in the *Militärkanzlei* records there is no document pertaining to this incident. But Oscar Jászi, quoting an article in the *Neue Freie Presse* of July 25, 1926, confirmed the report of the French ambassador in Vienna. According to Jászi the plot "was organized by Slovene and Italian Irredentists on the occasion of the opening of the second railway communication between Vienna and Trieste. The Archduke was charged with the representation of the Emperor at the festival, because, considering the vehement Slovenian and Italian Irredentist agitations in these parts of the country, the Council of Ministers vetoed the original plan for the Emperor personally to assist in the solemn opening. A special court train went through the stations . . . but it was occupied only by some police officials . . . a bomb exploded in a great tunnel which the empty special train passed through, and killed four gendarmes."[4]

The third attempt is said to have taken place on August 14, 1910, while the Archduke attended maneuvers near Mährisch-Ostrau (Moravská Ostrava). The attempt was allegedly made by three Bosnian recruits: Sergeants Stančić and Nogo and Corporal Golić. The information about this attempt comes from Bosnia, but it has not been confirmed by other sources.[5]

In the Viennese archives, on the other hand, there are documents which show that from 1902 until 1914 the police were alerted at least a dozen times by rumors of conspiracies against the Archduke. The tips came from Serbia, Croatia, Trieste, Italy, the United States, Egypt and Turkey. On the margins of the reports, the Archduke added his own comments and instructions on how the police should work against the conspirators. Some of the reports proved to be wrong, but in several cases the suspects were arrested and brought to trial.

When the Archduke was visiting Egypt, in March 1903, the Cairo police informed Vienna that they were shadowing a certain Pietro Rainer, of Trieste, because there were reasons to believe that he had come to Egypt in connection with the visit of the Archduke.[6]

The Austro-Hungarian consul in Venice received an anonymous postcard on November 10, 1906, which said that Italian Irredentists, with the support of the Italian government, were preparing the assassination of the Archduke, and that five assassins (two Montenegrins, two Italians and one Serb) were already on their way to Austria. The consul rejected this warning as unfounded.[7]

On November 20, 1907, the Austro-Hungarian ambassador in Constantinople, Markgraf Pallavicini, telegraphed Vienna that "the anarchists were planning an assassination of the Archduke" and that a certain Grujker had left Bucharest for Vienna.[8]

On two occasions, in 1909 and 1911, some Austrian and German papers wrote that the Serbian Prince Djordje was plotting to kill the Archduke. Stanoje Stanojević wrote that Vojin Tankosić sent a certain Živa Jovanović to Vienna to kill either the Emperor Franz Josef or the Archduke Franz Ferdinand.[9] Vemić in his diary on September 1, 1911, confirmed this. And Major Milan Vasić, another member of Ujedinjenje ili Smrt, was plotting against the Archduke in the summer of 1913, as his diary revealed.[10] The German paper *Vossische Zeitung* in early 1911 published the story that Prince Djordje was behind a conspiracy against the Archduke. The Archduke's *Militärkanzlei* asked the Ministry of Foreign Affairs and the General Staff to find out what lay behind the rumors. On February 5, 1911, the Ministry of Foreign Affairs sent a negative answer: "One does not know how the rumors came about in the spring of 1909 that Prince Djordje was preparing to kill the Archduke. . . . The source of the information given by the Austrian papers was the secretary of the Serbian legation, Dobra Arnautović. . . . A certain Jeftović also reported to the Ministry of Foreign Affairs that he had been asked to take part in an assassination planned by Prince Djordje. When he was asked to give written proof, he failed to turn up." The report concluded that the *Vossische Zeitung* was a "known anti-Austrian paper" and that "it had warmed up these stories on the initiative of Serbian groups connected with these two men."[11]

To this document, the Archduke added in his own hand the following information for Colonel Brosch:

"I have asked the Ministry of Foreign Affairs about the many reports concerning the assassination and I received this answer. What do you think about the whole affair? Is there not after all some truth in it? The Minister of Foreign Affairs, in his love for the Serbs, will not admit the truth."[12]

From the General Staff came confirmation of the views already expressed by the Foreign Ministry and a statement to the effect that it "does not possess the slightest evidence for the rumors about the assassination."[13]

Despite these two denials, the suspicions of the Archduke that his life was in danger increased. In June 1912 the Austrian intelligence service in Belgrade reported that assassins connected with Narodna Odbrana and the Serbian government had been sent from Serbia to kill the Archduke, and that they had received instructions to contact the president of Zora, the club for Serbian students in Vienna, to help them in their attempt. The name of the first assassin was given as Lazar Antić. Should he not succeed, a student by the name of Jovan Puljo had been instructed to take over. Puljo intended to disguise himself as a girl, under the false name of Zorka Veljićeva, and ask for an audience with the Heir Apparent with the intention of killing him.[14] These documents were published in the official collection of Austro-Hungarian documents connected with the outbreak of the First World War.[15]

On January 25, 1913, Miloš Stanković, a medical student, was arrested in Innsbruck because he told a waitress in a café that he belonged to a secret society and that he had given an oath that he would go to Vienna, in the event of Austria-Hungary's attacking Serbia, and kill "the one nearest to the Emperor."[16] The police handed the talkative youth to the country court in Innsbruck and he was tried for high treason. The court did not take his statement seriously; it discarded it as the boasting of a young man under the influence of drink in the presence of a girl. Stanković was acquitted and the verdict was confirmed by the Court of Cassation in Vienna. He was subsequently expelled from Austria-Hungary.[17]

A month after Stanković's arrest, a twenty-year-old Italian boy, Mario Belutta, was arrested in Trieste on his admission that he had been assigned by lot to make an attempt on the Archduke's life. He said that he belonged to a secret Milanese society called Circolo Indipendente Internazionale. The police were alerted, and Berchtold, foreign minister at the time, instructed the embassy in Rome to inform the Italian government as to the results of the investigation. Meanwhile, two friends of Belutta were arrested, both painters, Vittorio Margonari, from Trient (Trento), and Giovanni Carlini from Caldonazzo. Both were under twenty years of age.[18]

On March 16, 1913, the Ministry of Interior informed the *Militär-kanzlei* that Belutta had denied his earlier statements, claiming that everything had been arranged by Circolo Indipendente Internazionale in order "to try out the methods of the Austrian official institutions."[19] Belutta was sent for a medical checkup. The first group of psychiatrists claimed that he was insane and should be sent to an insane asylum. The second group declared that he was fully responsible for his actions. In the end Belutta was sentenced to ten months' imprisonment for slander.

At his final trial Belutta adhered to his statement that he was a member of the anarchist society Circolo Indipendente Internazionale of Milan, and that he had acted on orders to explore the reactions of the authorities in view of any future attempt that might be made on the Archduke's life.[20]

Even some non-German officers of the Austro-Hungarian Army plotted against the Archduke. In the papers of the late Adam Pribićević, a Serbian political leader from Croatia, there is a summary of a talk with his brother, Milan Pribićević, a former officer in the Habsburg Army. Milan stated that among non-German officers of Count Kovenhiller's regiment in Graz there had been discussions about a plot against the Archduke when he attended maneuvers in Styria in 1905.

Warnings on the Archduke's visit to Sarajevo were even more numerous; they came from all sides, from Vienna, Budapest, Berlin, the United States (in connection with the accusations against Michael Pupin of Columbia University)[21] and Belgrade. It is interesting to note that the Archduke planned a journey to Bosnia as early as 1911, but he postponed it because he was warned by some of his most trusted advisers in Bosnia not to face the danger of an attempted assassination. Immediately after Franz Josef's journey to Bosnia and Hercegovina in 1910, the Archduke had the idea of making a similar journey. It seems that the Jesuit Father Puntigam advised him that such a visit was desirable. One of the Archduke's most trusted advisers, Father Augustin Count Galen of the Prague Benedictine Abbey, was sent confidentially to Sarajevo in 1911 to discover, as a nonpolitical observer, the city's potential reaction to a visit from the Heir Apparent. Friedrich Funder, one of the members of the inner circle at Belvedere, describing the aim of Galen's trip, said that he was "concerned to dissolve the stupid stories which were spread about the Archduke and his so-called inimical attitudes toward the South Slavs."[22] Archbishop Stadler and his Jesuit advisers were in favor of the Archduke's visit. General Potiorek had the same feeling. But Galen found a different atmosphere when he approached the leader of the Bosnian Croats and the Vice President of the *Sabor*, Josip Sunarić, behind whom stood the Franciscans. Sunarić was strongly against the Archduke's visit. Funder recorded Sunarić's answer to Galen: "I know the Serbs. I know that they will wait for him in ambush as murderers."[23] Sunarić persistently advised against the journey, and Galen wondered how it was possible that Archbishop Stadler and Potiorek held exactly opposite views. On his return to Belvedere, Galen reported unfavorably on what he had heard in Sarajevo. Major Brosch was on his side, and the Archduke decided to postpone the journey, to the great regret of the Jesuits and of Potiorek. It is interesting to note that Sunarić was equally opposed to the visit in 1914 and that he sent a telegram to Joint Minister of Finance Bilinski, warning him of the dangers which the Archduke and his wife would face in

Sarajevo. For this Sunarić was personally rebuked in public, at a dinner on the eve of June 28, 1914, by the Duchess of Hohenberg.[24]

The chief of the Department of the Interior of the Bosnian government, Tošo Zurunić, wrote that on the eve of June 28 he received many warnings that the Archduke should not come to Sarajevo and all of them were forwarded in time to Vienna and to the military committee for the reception of the Archduke in Sarajevo.[25]

Bilinski also confirms the existence of the warnings.[26] Some came from Berlin. German State Secretary Gottlieb von Jagow wrote in 1919 that the Archduke had been warned by many persons, but that General Potiorek had guaranteed his safety.[27]

Even Minister of Foreign Affairs Berchtold was warned about the danger of the Archduke's journey to Sarajevo, in connection with the strike of the students at the Teachers College in Pakrac in Croatia. This college was one of the oldest Serbian educational institutions in Croatia; the students followed political affairs in Croatia and Serbia with great interest and publicly expressed their views. At the end of 1913 they declared a strike, and in March 1914 eighteen of them were barred from all schools in the Habsburg monarchy forever, and eight of them were demoted to a lower class for a year.[28] The Austrian police watched them, and on March 19 Berchtold informed Bilinski that his ministry had learned from a confidential source that a few weeks previously a group of students from the college had given up their studies and fled to Serbia, some of them having been expelled after disagreements with their tutors and others leaving voluntarily. They had passed through Semlin (Zemun) or, according to a second report, had gone via Zvornik in Bosnia. One of the students by the name of Janko Pokrajac had apparently been heard to say that "if something were to happen in the monarchy" he would "at once start blowing up bridges and throwing bombs." According to the report, he had gone on to say that he and his companions would prove that Bosnia was a Serbian land on the very day that the Archduke was scheduled to travel through the country. He had ended with the provocative words: "The time for empty boasting is over, and now we must start work in earnest. Bombs and not merely loose tongues must go into action. . . . If they catch you, just swallow a little poison. A dead mouth cannot talk."[29] The chief of police in Semlin had received information about Pokrajac's statement but he had not taken it very seriously although he had agreed that special measures of precaution would be taken for the Archduke's journey and he had suggested that the Mitrovica-Bosanski-Brod Railway line should be especially protected, "because Serbian youth is ready for anything."[30]

Austro-Hungarian military authorities also received many warnings about the danger. August Urbanski von Ostrymiecz, Chief of the Intelligence Department of the Austro-Hungarian General Staff, wrote that "the Archduke's visit to Sarajevo should have been postponed absolutely," because he had received reports from Serbia that "indignation exploded at the news of the Archduke's visit to Sarajevo."[31]

The questions which have to be answered are, first, why the Archduke's journey was not postponed; and second, how the Austro-Hungarian authorities attempted to protect his life in Bosnia and Hercegovina.

At one point there was discussion in the Archduke's family about the advisability of going to Sarajevo. The Archduke's physician, Dr. Eisenmenger, recorded that "the mission was a rather unpleasant one for the Archduke after his experiences at the maneuvers at Dubrovnik [in 1906]. He remarked to me that he would have preferred it if the Emperor had entrusted the mission to someone else."[32] Dr. Eisenmenger also mentioned that "the Duchess was in great fear for his life on this trip,"[33] and that she expressed "doubts on the necessity of the visit in a long telephone conversation with Dr. Eisenmenger's wife."[34]

The Archduke actually took positive steps to explore the possibilities for the postponement of his journey. He asked the Controller of the Archducal Household, Rumerskirch, to contact the right-hand man of Emperor Franz Josef, Prince Montenuovo, the Controller of the Imperial Household, and to discuss the whole issue with him, taking into account the illness of the Emperor. On May 21, Prince Montenuovo declared himself against the Archduke's visit. The letter reads:

. . . Concerning the Bosnian trip I informed the Prince about Your Imperial Highness's doubts. Detailing his point of view, Montenuovo would like to leave out His Majesty's illness completely, because the recuperation has progressed so far that in a few days His Majesty will be able to go out and, if everything develops normally, by the end of June will be completely recovered again, so that the state of His Majesty's health at this time will not require further consideration. But for the other reasons Montenuovo not only has full understanding, but shares your Imperial Highness's point of view completely, that with regard to these Oriental peoples especially, it would perhaps not be apt if your Imperial Highness were to visit the country for the first time merely as an inspecting general and not with great pomp and ceremonies. Since the latter, after the recent official trip of His Majesty to Bosnia, is hardly possible, he would, in his most private opinion and without considering the military or political factors involved, think that it would perhaps be better to cancel this trip. . . .[35]

Torn between a sense of duty and his personal feelings about the visit to Sarajevo, the Archduke obtained an audience with the Emperor at the beginning of June. Both Conrad and the Archduke's son Dr. Max Hohenberg have given their versions of what transpired at this meeting. Conrad said that he was received by the Emperor on June 4 and on that occasion Prince Montenuovo told him that the Archduke saw the

Emperor and complained that "he would not like to attend the Bosnian maneuvers because of bad health and because he cannot support high temperatures. The Emperor answered him: 'Do as you wish.' The Archduke then asked if his wife, the Duchess of Hohenberg, could go with him to Spa Ilidže, and the Emperor agreed to this."[36] Max Hohenberg's version differs. According to him, the Emperor tried to convince the Archduke not to go to Bosnia:

The High Command decided that the great maneuvers should take place that year in Bosnia. The choice of this country, recently annexed by Austria, where a muffled rebellion persisted, was deplorable. We were distressed to learn that the old Emperor Franz Josef—who only escaped an attempt on his life during the visit to Sarajevo by a miracle—advised our father against going to the great maneuvers. Would we thus be deprived of this treat? Our joy returned when we learned that our father had scoffed at the Emperor's prudent advice. One evening he said at the table: "I am Inspector General of the Austro-Hungarian Armed Forces. I must go to Sarajevo. The soldiers would never be able to explain my absence."[37]

The security measures for the Archduke's journey to Bosnia and Hercegovina were not impressive. The Archduke himself sometimes had a fatalistic attitude toward the warnings he had been receiving. Two months before his death, while discussing with his legal adviser Eichhoff the points of *Thronwechsel* at Miramare, near Trieste, he decided to take a short excursion. Somebody mentioned the question of security, and the Archduke said: "Preparations? Security measures? Measures of the head of the Trieste police? . . . I do not care the tiniest bit about this. Everywhere one is in God's hands. Look, out of this bush, here at the right, some chap could jump at me. . . . Fears and precautions paralyze your life. To fear is always a dangerous business."[38] The Archduke expressed a similar opinion to Bardolff: "I am sure your warning is justified, but I do not let myself be kept under a glass cover. Our life is constantly in danger. One has to rely upon God."[39] In such a frame of mind, it was not strange that the Archduke came into conflict over the question of security measures with Austrian, Italian and French police forces.[40]

Responsibility for security was in the hands of General Potiorek, the Governor of Bosnia and Hercegovina. In Potiorek's letter to Bardolff from Sarajevo on February 22, he explicitly stated that he would undertake full responsibility: "Concerning your remark that a nonofficial visit to the parts of Bosnia and Hercegovina which are the most interesting for his Imperial and Royal Highness could be undertaken at some other time of the year, I kindly ask you to inform His Highness that in these times under existing circumstances I can well undertake full responsibility for such a trip by His Imperial and Royal Highness which would take place according to a program known a reasonably long time ahead, thus enabling security measures to be taken in time, but not for a more or less sudden nonofficial visit to the country."[41]

For the purpose of organizing the Archduke's visit a special military committee was formed, composed of officers of the *Militärkanzlei* and officers of the General Inspectorate of the Armed Forces. Another member was Dr. Edmund Gerde, the chief of police of Sarajevo. He was a Magyar by nationality, and he had at his disposal 120 policemen, among whom were six detectives in civilian clothes. In the central police office there were also five higher officials and eight administrative officials, and one detective-inspector, Peter Maksimević, a Serb by nationality.

After the assassination, security measures in Sarajevo were criticized from all sides as inadequate. General Michael Appel, the commander of the 15th Corps and commanding general in Sarajevo, immediately after the assassination accused General Potiorek, in a letter to Brosch, of inefficiency in organizing security measures.[42] Margutti wrote that the inadequacy of the precautions baffled every description.[43] Bilinski expressed his indignation to Potiorek in a letter of July 3,[44] and Count Tisza raised the matter in the Hungarian parliament.[45]

That there were many loopholes in the security measures is obvious, since the conspiracy was not detected, particularly when the assassins came to Sarajevo almost a month before June 28, and since adequate measures were not taken on the very day of the Archduke's death. The following points demonstrate the neglect of the authorities:

1. When the students from Pakrac Teachers College fled to Serbia and on their way were talking of what might happen to the Archduke, Berchtold informed Bilinski, who issued directives to Potiorek about the danger. On May 27, the Bosnian government issued a warning to all Border Guards to keep an eye out for all persons coming from Serbia. The authorities at Zvornik, where Čabrinović crossed the frontier, received this order on the very day when he came to town, but did not follow it.[46]

2. Čabrinović came to Tuzla with Grabež's papers and spent a night in the hotel, registering under Grabež's name. The police did not intervene, although Grabež was known to be a rebellious youth who had been expelled from the *gimnazija*.

3. On June 10 the Bosnian government issued an order to the police for the strict application of passport rules and obligatory registration of all newcomers to Sarajevo between June 15 and 28.[47] On June 15 Princip filled out his form, stating that he had a room at the home of Danilo Ilić's mother. The police paid no attention to it, although Princip was known to the authorities for his "anti-state activities." Danilo Ilić too was on the black list, because of his trip to Switzerland. Čabrinović was registered by his father and he too was well known to the police as a

maverick who had been sentenced to five years' banishment from Sarajevo because of political activities.

4. Čabrinović was spotted by police agents in Tuzla, on the train between Doboj and Sarajevo and he even visited Ilidže, where the Archduke stayed before going to Sarajevo.[48] On several occasions he spoke with police agents, and from one of them he even learned the exact day of the Archduke's arrival in Sarajevo.[49]

5. When so many people knew about the conspiracy in Sarajevo, it is strange that the police did not detect it in time.

6. The security precautions on the day of the assassination were almost nonexistent, particularly if one compares them with the police protection for the Emperor Franz Josef on his visit to Sarajevo in June 1910. For the Emperor's visit the route through which he was passing had been lined with a double cordon of soldiers, while for the Archduke there were no soldiers on the streets, although 70,000 of them were just outside Sarajevo. When the Emperor came, hundreds of suspicious citizens were ordered not to leave their homes, while no such measure was applied for the Archduke.

7. After Čabrinović's attempt, the most fateful decision was that the Archduke continue with his program. At that stage, Potiorek lost his head and not only issued new orders for security on the streets, but to the explicit question of the Archduke, "What about these bombs, and will it happen again?" answered as Rumerskirch recorded, "Your Imperial Highness, you can travel quite happily, I take the responsibility."[50]

The police officials of Sarajevo defended themselves and put the blame on Potiorek, the *Militärkanzlei* and especially on the military committee for the reception of the Archduke. Wladislaw Glück, a high official of the Sarajevo police, has given his side of the story. His first point is that Potiorek had been warned about the tense atmosphere among the Serbian youth long before June 28, by Count Carlo Collas, the chief of the Political Department of the Bosnian government, who prepared a special report on the activities of the Young Bosnians in 1913 but was rebuked "for having a fear of children."[51]

As June 28 was approaching, the Chief of the Sarajevo police, Dr. Gerde, again tried to warn both General Potiorek and the military committee about the dangerous atmosphere. Gerde first approached his superior in the administration, Tošo Zurunić, the chief of the Department of Internal Affairs of the government, explaining that the Archduke should not visit Sarajevo on St. Vitus Day, the great holiday of the Serbs. Zurunić advised him that he should express his anxiety to the military committee, whose meetings Gerde attended. But the officers, members of the committee, ridiculed Gerde, commenting: "Do not worry. These lesser breeds would not dare to do anything."[52] The chief of the committee said ironically to Gerde, "You see ghosts everywhere."[53] Gerde insisted that his warnings should be entered in the official minutes, and while this was done the officers continued to make their remarks.

The Sarajevo police believed that if the Archduke had made a private visit to Sarajevo, security measures would have been adequate. But the Archduke and Potiorek insisted on making a triumphal march through Sarajevo. The Lord Mayor of Sarajevo had to issue a proclamation on June 23 calling the population into the streets to express their feelings toward the Archduke, giving the exact route of the imperial procession on June 28. Gerde insisted that the route should not be disclosed before June 27, but the military committee rejected this request.[54] Gerde also twice urged his superior Zurunić to pay a visit to Potiorek and inform him about the state of things. On the first occasion, Potiorek answered: "The Archduke is coming here as a general and it is none of your business to take care of this visit."[55] After Gerde bombarded his superior with more information about the lack of personnel for the protection of the Archduke, Zurunić dared to visit Potiorek a second time. He was received with marked arrogance and got the same answer.[56] The military committee also rejected the request that a cordon of soldiers be on the streets on June 28. Glück in despair commented that "security measures on June 28 were in the hands of Providence."[57] On their own initiative the police issued orders to their 120 men, reinforced by a few detectives from Budapest and Trieste who did not know the local language, to turn their faces toward the crowd during the passage of the imperial party. But 120 men could not do much on a route of about four miles. The police also obtained an order that all schools were to finish their work by June 15 and that all students who did not reside in Sarajevo had to leave town at once. Yet the police, according to Glück, felt that this was not adequate.

This writer had an opportunity to study the *Nachlass* and *Militärkanzlei* papers as well as the many telegrams and letters exchanged between Potiorek and Bardolff in connection with the work of this committee. The problem of security was neglected. On the other hand, trivia were discussed at great length—the menus of official dinners, what kind of wines the Archduke preferred, whether they should be sweet or dry (the Archduke's preference was for dry), whether they should be chilled or served at room temperature. Many telegrams were exchanged as to which Bosnian politicians should attend the official receptions, and where they should be seated at the table. Even the details of the stirrup length for the horse on which the Archduke should ride during the maneuvers was not forgotten. Colonel Bardolff answered that it should be 72 centimeters long.[58] The nearer the date of the Archduke's visit, the more the bureaucrats were concerned with questions of protocol and pomp. On June 8, Colonel Bardolff received a message from Sarajevo: "Would you be so kind as to inform me whether His Imperial Highness wants some music to be played during the *dejeuner* in the *Konak*, that is to say, whether he would enjoy it? With best regards, most submissively . . ."[59] The answer came back: "In reply to your inquiry of June 8, I inform you that for the lunch in the *Konak* on June 28 a small string quartet . . . should be chosen, whose program should be restricted to light Viennese music. . . ."[60]

It is interesting that one of the surviving conspirators, Ivo Kranjčević, expressed in his memoirs the view that the Sarajevo police took strong security measures.[61] He mentioned particularly the order that all schoolboys had to leave town and that Vaso Čubrilović and Cvetko Popović had difficulty staying in Sarajevo until June 28. Kranjčević also said that Ilić brought the weapons to Sarajevo on June 15 with great risk and difficulty. The police had already blocked the main Sarajevo railway station, checking all the passengers and their belongings. He knew this and got out of the train a station before Sarajevo.[62]

The lack of police protection for the Archduke has been interpreted in two ways: for some, the measures were inadequate because of *Schlamperei*, or simple carelessness; for others, the inadequate protection was deliberate and the Austro-Hungarian authorities intended to get rid of the Archduke. The advocates of the latter view have come out with several theories.

Henry Wickham Steed published a story that at the second Konopischt meeting on June 12–14, 1914, Kaiser Wilhelm and the Archduke made a plan for the postwar reorganization of Europe, envisaging the formation of several federative states united in a joint German and Austrian empire. In one of these units, a kingdom comprising Bohemia, Croatia, Hungary and Serbia, the eldest son of the Archduke, Max Hohenberg, was to be king. When the news of this decision leaked out in Vienna, the Archduke was proclaimed a traitor, and his execution through hired assassins in Sarajevo was prepared.[63] This version is not based on any documentation. Princip and his accomplices were in Sarajevo ten days before the Konopischt meeting. Also, the Archduke firmly believed in the Habsburg realm; his intentions were to revive its past glories, not to assist in its decomposition. Lastly, both the Emperor Franz Josef and Montenuovo expressed anxiety over the Archduke's journey to Sarajevo.

A French writer, Jules Chopin, produced another theory of the Konopischt meeting. According to him, Wilhelm and Franz Ferdinand decided to attack Serbia. In order to find a good pretext, a provocation had to be devised which would shake the whole world and give Austria-Hungary a morally justifiable cause for aggressive war. For Chopin, Nedeljko Čabrinović was an *agent-provocateur* of the Austrian police, and his task was to make a faked attack on the Archduke. But the whole conspiracy failed because Princip, a real patriot, intervened and killed the Archduke. This version seems even more ridiculous than Wickham Steed's. It is highly improbable that the Archduke would risk his own life by a faked attempt against himself and his own wife. Furthermore, the theory that Nedeljko Čabrinović was an agent of the Austrian police has no historical foundation. It was planted by circles around Regent Alexander as a kind of revenge against Čabrinović because he had mentioned in Sarajevo that he had met the Regent in Belgrade a few months before the Sarajevo assassination, when Alexander was visiting the State Printing Office, in which Čabrinović worked. Semiofficial Serbian circles fomented this accusation, as well as such writers as Bora Jevtić.[64]

Among these theories of a secret relationship between Austro-Hungarian authorities and the conspirators, one connected Apis's secret society with Vienna and Budapest. This thesis was expressed in general terms in the verdict of the Salonika trial, when Colonel Apis was sentenced to death. Its main protagonist was D. Stojadinović, who accused Hungarian Prime Minister Tisza of being secretly in league with Colonel Apis in a plot to liquidate the Archduke Franz Ferdinand. D. Stojadinović claimed that Tisza was the man who gave Apis special assurances that Austria-Hungary would not wage war against Serbia after the Archduke's death. This charge involves the relations of Colonel Apis's secret society and the Austro-Hungarian authorities.

Some of the regicides who killed King Alexander Obrenović in 1903 had had some contacts with Austro-Hungarian officials at that time. Svetozar Pribićević has described these relations as "a necessity, because one had to ask the opinion of the Austrian government in Vienna in order to know how it would react to the newly created situation in Serbia."[65] These tasks were assigned to Jakov Nenadović, a cousin of Petar Karadjordjević and one of the chief civilian conspirators, and Vukašin Petrović, who did not play such a prominent role in the conspiracy but served as a go-between in Vienna. Wickham Steed expressed the opinion that the whole 1903 conspiracy was organized under Russian auspices, but that the Austro-Hungarian government knew about it as well[66] and was informed about the meetings of conspirators in Vienna. Steed quoted his conversation in early March of 1903 with Benjamin von Kallay, Austro-Hungarian Minister of Finance and an expert on South Slav affairs: "King Alexander was in a perilous position and might not have many weeks to live."[67]

Miloš Bogićević has given his version of the relations between the 1903 regicides and the Austro-Hungarian authorities. He wrote that both Petrović and Nenadović were assigned to obtain tacit approval from the Austro-Hungarian government for the removal of King Alexander Obrenović, to ensure that Serbia would not be threatened after the *coup d'état* by an Austro-Hungarian invasion. Müller von Rohoj, chief of the Information Department of the Ministry of Foreign

Affairs, entered into discussion with the representatives of the regicides.[68] Bogićević stressed that "one should not assume that the Austrian government knew about the preparations for the assassination of the royal couple" in Serbia, but he added the comment "that the Minister of Foreign Affairs in Vienna, Count Goluchowski spoke in very unfavorable terms about King Alexander, and, secondly, that the Austrian Government gave the Serbian emigrants all kinds of help while they stayed in Austria-Hungary." He claimed that Austro-Hungarian authorities helped the regicides by safeguarding their secret communications from Vienna to Belgrade from the watchful eye of the Serbian political police, and that on the night of the assassination, June 12, 1903, all the telegrams of Nenadović were sent to Belgrade through the official channels of the Austrian government, and after the success of the assassination, Nenadović gave a dinner in honor of Müller von Rohoj.[69] Bogićević contradicted himself, because on the very pages on which he claimed that the Austro-Hungarian government did not know about the preparations of the assassination, he gave details which allow the opposite to be deduced. Bogićević also said that during his talks with Müller von Rohoj Nenadović sent him a letter written by Petar Karadjordjević in which he said that in the event of his gaining the throne he would maintain loyal and amicable relations with Austria-Hungary.[70]

Although King Petar tried to conduct a foreign policy which relied on France and Russia, some of the older regicides in his immediate entourage were inclined, in some specific issues of Serbia's internal relations, to rely on Austria-Hungary rather than on the other great powers. This was the case especially with the so-called "old regicides": Colonels Alexander Mašin and Damjan Popović and Lieutenant Colonel Petar Mišić. Both Austrian and French archives confirm this impression.[71]

Despite the relations of the "old regicides" with Vienna, the younger regicides headed by Colonel Apis regarded the Habsburg empire as their deadliest enemy. Viennese authorities were well informed all the time about their activities, particularly when they discussed the possibility of replacing the Karadjordjević dynasty with a foreign one in 1909.[72] How Conrad obtained that information is not clear, but the fact is that some of the older regicides, like Colonel Damjan Popović, retained good relations with Colonel Apis; Popović was accused together with Colonel Apis at the Salonika trial in 1917 and was sentenced to twenty years in jail. These strange relations between Austro-Hungarian authorities and the older regicides might explain why the Austro-Hungarian government in its ultimatum to Serbia on July 23, 1914, accused only Narodna Odbrana as being involved in the Sarajevo plot. Ujedinjenje ili Smrt was not mentioned at all, although Major Vojin Tankosić, the right-hand man of Colonel Apis, was personally accused of providing weapons and training Princip and his accomplices. From the Austrian archives it is obvious that the Vienna authorities were well informed from the first day of the organization of the Ujedinjenje ili Smrt about its activities. In the Austrian archives there exists a special dossier on Ujedinjenje ili Smrt.[73]

At the same time, Colonel Apis's *Pijemont* was the bitterest critic of Austria-Hungary. In its first issue in 1911, *Pijemont* announced that "for Serbia, a defensive war against this new aggressor is inevitable. Serbia cannot evade this unless it intends to lay down its arms in the face of this infamous opponent, whose armies have always turned tail in the face of peoples who were fighting for their liberation. We are convinced that these known deserters will flee at the decisive moment when faced by the Serbian people." In many later editorials, the same feeling was expressed.

The Austro-Hungarian authorities had banned the distribution of *Pijemont* by the end of 1912, but as relations between the two countries deteriorated the paper kept up its criticism of the Habsburg state. On May 25, 1912, an editorial headed "The War between Serbia and Austria" said:

We do not say this war is declared yet, but we believe that it is inevitable. If Serbia wants to live in honor, she can do so only by this war. This war is determined by our obligation to our traditions and the world of culture. This war derives from the duty of our race which will not permit itself to be assimilated. This war must bring about the eternal freedom of Serbia, of the South Slavs, of the Balkan peoples. Our whole race must stand together to halt the onslaught of these aliens from the north.

Pijemont especially attacked the Archduke. On his fiftieth birthday, January 2, 1914, it published an article by Stefan Grossmann from the German review *März:*

Austria is not an organic entity. She keeps her parts joined with the help of old glue which might not survive a sharper crisis . . . We have translated this article so that our readers can see who the future Austro-Hungarian ruler is, what kind of a man he is. After these lines, which are clear enough, we can only add the comment that our sacrifices in preparations and armaments should not prove too expensive, because His Future Imperial and Apostolic Majesty, taking his life in his hands, will himself pay for them on his fated day.

There is no documentary evidence that Colonel Apis had relations with Vienna authorities; on the contrary he regarded them as the chief enemies of Serbia's independence. But was this the case with people around Colonel Apis, and particularly with Malobabić, who brought the final directive that the conspirators in Sarajevo should go on with their preparation of the plot, despite the fact that Colonel Apis in the middle of June had issued orders for the cancellation of the conspiracy?

On Malobabić, opinions differ. Stojan Protić firmly believed that Malobabić was an Austrian spy. On the other hand, Svetozar Pribićević[74] and Slobodan Jovanović[75] regarded Malobabić as a patriot. Austrian counterintelligence often succeeded in penetrating deeply into the inner core of the secret societies in Serbia. In 1907 one of their agents, Djordje Nastić, fooled even Jovanović-Čupa and brought to an end the revolutionary activities of Slovenski Jug. The French minister in Belgrade carefully watched the work of the Austrian secret agents and informed Paris on several occasions how Austrian spies found their way into the entourage of Prince Djordje, even after his abdication.[76] But this writer has not found in the Austrian archives any document proving that Malobabić was in Vienna's service.

One question remains to be answered in connection with Colonel Apis and the Sarajevo conspiracy. It is obvious that he did not wish to push Serbia into a war with Austria-Hungary at a time when his own country was not prepared for it. But the assassination of the Heir Apparent of the Habsburg empire would greatly increase this danger. What influenced Colonel Apis to conclude that Austria-Hungary would not make a *casus belli* out of the Archduke's murder?

Some historians, defending the point of view of the Regent Alexander, have suggested collusion between Colonel Apis and Count Tisza. D. Stojadinović, for instance, expressed the opinion that Colonel Apis and Count Tisza had made an agreement for the assassination of the Archduke; on his part, Tisza gave Apis a guarantee that Austria-Hungary would not wage war against Serbia, asking in return only a guarantee of future good neighbor relations, and the expulsion of the Karadjordjević dynasty and the Old Radicals from political power in Serbia.[77]

Stojadinović even named two merchants, Jovan Dada and Djordje Slavković, who served as go-betweens for Apis and Tisza;[78] and in the Yugoslav parliament on July 21, 1935, he accused the leader of the Serbs in Croatia, Svetozar Pribićević, of having been the main political link between Apis and Tisza.[79]

The behavior of Tisza and his party after the assassination has been cited as support for Stojadinović's charge. When news came to Budapest of Franz Ferdinand's death, "Tisza's party made no attempt to conceal their joy," wrote Prince Ludwig Windischgraetz.[80] Other sources confirmed Tisza's attitude.[81] In his letter to Bilinski on July 3, 1914, he came out against a war with Serbia:

. . . In view of revelations contained in Your Excellency's telegram of June 30 regarding the situation in Bosnia-Hercegovina, the local administration can scarcely have the right to lay the blame on Serbia, when they themselves passively watched the agitation spread in their own land and allowed it to grow unchecked until awakened from their optimism by the horrible deed of the 28th.

If facts are produced which justify us in making a *démarche* in Serbia, then whatever is necessary must be done. Serbia will hardly give us grounds for warlike measures, and without them it would be an inexcusable mistake to enter upon such a war.[82]

At the July 7 Ministerial Council, Tisza strongly opposed military action against Serbia.[83] After war broke out between Austria-Hungary and Serbia, Tisza took an active part in secret negotiations for a separate peace treaty between Serbia and the Central Powers in 1915.

All these facts no doubt speak for Stojadinović's thesis, but the main accusation that there were secret links between Apis and Tisza is not proved by any historical facts. The main weakness of Stojadinović's theory is its context in terms of Serbian internal politics. Apis and Alexander were in a deadly political battle, which ended with the judicial murder of Apis, and all means had to be used by Stojadinović, as the Regent's man, to portray Apis as a foreign agent. Tisza's conflict with the Archduke and his other political moves in June and July 1914 gave Stojadinović a chance to elaborate his thesis. It was nothing more than a by-product of the Salonika verdict which brought about the physical death of Colonel Apis; Stojadinović's work was intended to kill Apis's reputation.

Yet if there is no proof of Vienna's or Budapest's complicity in the Sarajevo conspiracy, the fact is that for the Viennese war party the tragic event "was a godsend, or rather a gift from Mars."[84] Finally, the long-sought excuse for the settling of accounts with Serbia was found. Conrad wrote: "This is not the crime of a single fanatic; assassination represents Serbia's declaration of war on Austria-Hungary. . . . If we miss this occasion, the Monarchy will be exposed to new explosions of South Slav, Czech, Russian, Rumanian and Italian aspirations. . . . Austria-Hungary must wage war for political reasons."[85] In his report read at the Ministerial Council at Vienna, General Potiorek stressed that for two years he had shared the view that Austria-Hungary must wage war against Serbia if she wished to remain in the Balkans.[86] The Austrian Minister Giesl, in Belgrade, informed Berchtold that the assassination "has . . . created for us a fortunate moral position."[87]

Berchtold at first had the idea of attacking Serbia without any warning. Tisza's attitude forced him to send Serbia an ultimatum, which was purely a formality because the decision to wage war against Serbia was already made. This was done despite the fact that the investigation in Sarajevo did not provide any proof of the responsibility of the Serbian government. A special emissary of the Viennese Foreign Ministry,

Friedrich von Wiesner, went to Sarajevo on July 10, 1914, to study the investigation material and find out whether the Serbian government had any responsibility for the assassination. On July 13 Wiesner telegraphed:

There is nothing to show the complicity of the Serbian government in the direction of the assassination or in its preparations or in the supplying of weapons. Nor is there anything to lead one even to conjecture such a thing. On the contrary, there is evidence that would appear to show such complicity is out of the question. . . . If the intentions prevailing at my departure still exist, demands might be extended for

a. suppression of complicity of Serbian government officials in smuggling persons and material across the frontier;

b. dismissal of Serbian frontier officers at Šabac and Loznica and implicated customs officials;

c. criminal proceedings against Ciganović and Tankosić.[88]

It is interesting that German authorities came to a similar conclusion. The former Chancellor von Bülow wrote in his memoirs:

Although the horrible murder was the work of a Serbian society with branches all over the country, many details prove that the Serbian government had neither instigated it nor desired it. The Serbs were exhausted by two wars. The most hotheaded among them might have paused at the thought of war with Austria-Hungary, so overwhelmingly superior especially since, in her rear, Serbians had Bulgarians full of rancor and knew that the Rumanians were untrustworthy. Thus at least did Herr von Griesinger, our minister in Belgrade, sum up the position, as did also the Belgrade correspondents of every important German newspaper.[89]

Nevertheless, in its note and ultimatum to Serbia on July 23, 1914, the Austro-Hungarian government chose to draw quite different conclusions and asserted that the Serbian government had

tolerated the machinations of various societies and associations directed against the monarchy, unrestrained language on the part of the press, glorification of the perpetrators of outrages, participation of officers and officials in subversive agitation, unwholesome propaganda in public education—in short, tolerated all manifestations of a nature to inculcate in the Serbian population hatred of the monarchy and contempt for its institutions . . . the culpable tolerance on the part of the Royal Government of Serbia had not ceased at the moment when the events of June 28 revealed its disastrous consequences for the whole world.[90]

The Austro-Hungarian government asked the Serbian government to undertake specifically these ten points:

1. To suppress all publications inciting to hatred of Austria-Hungary and directed against her territorial integrity;
2. To dissolve forthwith the Narodna Odbrana, and "to confiscate all its means of propaganda"; to treat similarly all societies engaged in propaganda against Austria-Hungary, and to prevent their revival in some other form;
3. To eliminate from the Serbian educational system anything which might foment such propaganda;
4. To dismiss all officers or officials guilty of such propaganda, whose names might be subsequently communicated by Vienna;
5. To accept "the collaboration in Serbia" of Austro-Hungarian officials in suppressing "this subversive movement against the monarchy's territorial integrity";
6. To open a judicial inquiry against those implicated in the murder, and to allow delegates of Austria-Hungary to take part in this;
7. To arrest without delay Major Tankosić and Milan Ciganović, implicated by the Sarajevo inquiry;
8. To put an effectual stop to Serbian frontier officials sharing in "the illicit traffic in arms and explosives," and to dismiss certain officials at Šabac and Loznica who had helped the murderers to cross over;
9. To give explanations regarding the "unjustifiable" language used by high Serbian officials after the murder;
10. To notify Vienna without delay of the execution of all the above measures.[91]

The Serbian government accepted all the demands, except Point 6—"as regards participation in this inquiry of Austro-Hungarian agents, we cannot accept such an arrangement, as it would be a violation of the Constitution and of the Law of Criminal Procedure." The Serbian government stressed also that if the Austro-Hungarian government was not satisfied with the reply, it was "ready, as always, to accept a peaceful agreement, by referring this question either to the decision of the International Tribunal at The Hague, or to the great powers which took part in drawing up the declaration made by the Serbian government on March 31, 1909."[92]

Although even in Berlin the Serbian answer was regarded as favorable, Austria-Hungary declared war on Serbia on July 28, and in a week's time all the European powers were involved in hostilities.

CHAPTER XIX

COLONEL APIS AND GERMANY

*The blame, in the common cry, shall follow the
injured side, as always, but the vengeance shall
be testimony to the truth that dispenses it.*
— DANTE ALIGHIERI, *The Divine Comedy*

THE CHARGE OF GERMAN COMPLICITY in the Sarajevo assassination
comes from two separate sources: the Archduke Franz Ferdinand's
eldest son, Dr. Max Hohenberg, and a group of Serbian historians and
politicians defending the verdict of the Salonika trial of 1917.

Dr. Hohenberg elaborated his accusation in two interviews he gave
to Maurice Verne in Vienna on June 28, 1937, which were published in
Paris-Soir-Dimanche. Dr. Hohenberg stated that on the basis of what
he knew and from his study of his father's papers, the Archduke

envisaged forming a federal entente of all the national groups comprising the
Austro-Hungarian Empire, and of settling in the best interest of each people
the troublesome Danubian problem. . . . But this union of national groups,
simply administered from Vienna, threatened the interests of certain powers
which harbored projects of annexation and conquest. My father's plans em-
barrassed them, and it was in order to stop his fulfilling them that they
armed in Sarajevo the wretches whose crime was to unleash on the world
the most frightful of slaughters.[1]

Dr. Hohenberg concluded that the death of his father had relieved
Kaiser Wilhelm of many worries, notably of this project for a federation of Eastern European states envisaged by the Archduke. "This

project worried Berlin very much and it has been established that the German secret police worked hand in hand with the *komite* in the preparation of the Sarajevo assassination."[2]

Except for this, Dr. Hohenberg did not elaborate in detail on his accusation and did not offer any documentary evidence. There are several theories as to what influenced him to take such a stand. In his father's *Nachlass* there is a clipping from the paper *Vaterland* of April 22, 1901, which warned the Archduke that his life was in danger because of the strong anti-Prussian and anti-Protestant statements he had made in connection with the Katholischer Schulverein incident.[3] Dr. Hohenberg, also a Habsburg legitimist by political conviction, was always suspicious of Germany's hopes for *Anschluss* with Austria. Another possibility is that he heard something about the relations of Colonel Apis and some German military circles.

The historians and politicians (Stanoje Stanojević, Djordje Jelenić, Dragiša Stojadinović and others) who have upheld the verdict of the Salonika trial of Apis in 1917 have maintained that his gravest mistake was envisioning a solution of the South Slav problem by relying on Germany, and counting on her victory in the struggle against Russia, France and England; the elimination of the Archduke served both Serbia and Germany well. This group makes several points:

1. Relations did exist between Colonel Apis and Dr. Miloš Bogićević.[4] This man was a complex personality, a former Serbian diplomat who defected to the German side during the First World War and later became one of the strongest defenders of Germany and Austria-Hungary in the debate over war guilt.

Bogićević came from a well-known Serbian family; one of his ancestors was one of the leaders of the first Serbian uprising in 1804, and the family strongly backed the Obrenović dynasty until 1900, when King Alexander Obrenović dismissed Bogićević's father, Milan Bogićević, at that time Serbian minister in Berlin and a former Foreign Minister of Serbia.[5] The elder Bogićević had arranged a marriage for Alexander with a princess from the Schaumburg-Lippe family, but Alexander chose Draga Mašin as his queen. This conflict led the young Bogićević to join the anti-Alexander ranks in 1903. Bogićević was a well-educated man, was graduated from the Theresianum Public School in Vienna and had a Ph.D. from Vienna University; he was elected associate professor of international law at Belgrade University, but in 1904 he chose to be a diplomat. He served first in Paris and then in Berlin, where he had the rank of chargé d'affaires from 1907 to 1914. Because of his father's connections and his own, he was well received in Berlin; he was admitted to the Eilenburg Club, where the immediate entourage of the German Kaiser used to meet.[6]

In 1907 Bogićević met Apis, who had come to Berlin to improve his German. Two years earlier Apis had been in Germany on a private

visit and had attended the maneuvers at Breslau as an unofficial observer.[7] Apis visited Berlin again in the spring of 1913. *Pijemont*, in its
issue of April 14, 1913, said Colonel Apis had gone to recuperate in a
Berlin sanatorium after six months of illness. He stayed there until July
18, when he returned to Serbia. Bogićević wrote that he "introduced
Apis to many leading personalities of the German army and helped him
to write articles for German papers about the problems of Serbia."[8]
Bogićević concluded "that Apis impressed higher German officers."[9]
Bogićević called Apis his "great friend";[10] other writers mention that
Apis was Bogićević's *pobratim*, closer than a blood brother. After the
outbreak of the war, Bogićević came to Serbia and spent several weeks
with Apis in his office in the Supreme Command of the Serbian Army;[11]
only a few months later Bogićević defected to the German side.

2. German help for *Pijemont* has been alleged. In his diary Vemić
wrote on January 25, 1911, that Ljuba Jovanović-Čupa, the editor of
Pijemont, was to leave "tomorrow for Berlin for the printing press."[12]
This entry has been interpreted by Apis's opponents as meaning that
some German circles had bought a printing press for *Pijemont*.

3. Slovenia, in the program of Ujedinjenje ili Smrt, is the only South
Slav country which was not mentioned as part of the union with Serbia
at the end of the war. With the advance of industrialization, the Slovenes had been exposed to Germanization. Stojadinović believed that
Bogićević influenced Apis to exclude Slovenia from the organization's
program because Germany regarded Slovenia as a crownland of the
German Empire and therefore outside the aspirations of Serbia.[13] Stojadinović also believed that Bogićević was one of the most influential
members of Ujedinjenje ili Smrt.

4. Apis's links with the Young Turks have been cited as evidence of
a pro-German line. The Young Turks tried to make Turkey a vassal of
German imperialism in order to gain territorial compensations, and
Apis was in touch with the Young Turks, particularly through Bogdan
Radenković.[14] Since most of the members of the Young Turks were
young officers, an additional line of contact between them and their
military friends in Berlin was established.[15] On March 2, 1920, *Samouprava*, the paper of the Old Radicals, wrote that in 1907 Apis met in
Berlin one of the leaders of the Young Turks, Enver Bey, who was at
that time the Turkish military attaché.

5. *Pijemont's* praise of the German army and German military and
paramilitary societies was strong and consistent. *Pijemont* had a correspondent in Germany, using the pseudonym Davison, who continually
praised the part played by the German army in what he called "the
regeneration of the German nation," and indicated that this should be
taken as a useful example for Serbia to follow. Davison paid particular
attention to the Jung Deutschland Bund, a youth society initiated by
General von der Goltz who had been responsible for the reorganization

of the Turkish army and who had strong links with the Young Turks. In the May 6, 1912, issue of *Pijemont*, Davison praised Goltz's organization, ending with the following eulogy:

It is wonderful to observe a great company of Young Germans, with their badges, drummers and military equipment, as they set out, every holiday, for the wide and beautiful countryside of Grünenwald in order to spend a few hours in training, running and jumping, military exercises and war games. These young men seemed to me to be concentrating so deeply on the goal of their movement, to be so very thorough, that we can easily imagine how strong an army composed of such well-drilled, and physically and morally powerful new generations will be. I shall never forget this moment. I am forced to admire this great state and the work it is doing, but I feel some anxiety in admitting this. Up to now we Serbs do not have any comparable movements. We cannot work for our state and our people if we are divided among ourselves, undermining our Piedmont, our Serbia. "Here there are no parties" is a basic premise of this society, but among us they exist everywhere. Here people are working day and night on patriotic tasks, while we Serbs work at everything else but these. Here there is not a single citizen who would not spend his free time in one of the organizations which exist for the purpose of strengthening the state. And all, I stress, all without exception, are so devoted to these tasks, that they could serve as a useful example.

6. Stojadinović maintains that through the Sarajevo assassination Apis wanted to compromise the Karadjordjević dynasty and the pro-Russian Old Radicals in the eyes of Europe, to take power in Serbia, and to lead the country into German waters.[16] German military circles gave their approval through Bogićević and confirmed that Serbia would not be attacked by Austria-Hungary.

7. Apis is charged with having had secret talks with the Germans and Count Tisza about a separate peace treaty between Serbia and Germany. According to this charge, even before the outbreak of the war Bogićević had approached the leaders of the Croat-Serbian Coalition in Croatia (Svetozar Pribićević and Damjan Popović), offering them his links with German military circles in order to realize a solution of the South Slav problem, relying on Germany. Pašić heard about this step of Bogićević and at once issued an order that Bogićević should be transferred from Berlin to Cairo, as a consul of third grade.[17]

Bogićević left the Serbian diplomatic service without informing his superiors, and he went to Switzerland, where he established contacts with Jules Cambon, former French ambassador in Berlin, whom he knew personally, and with the German Under Secretary for Foreign Affairs, Arthur Zimmermann, proposing to them the conclusion of a separate peace treaty between Germany and France.[18] Bogićević also had a list of Serbian military and political personalities who wished a separate peace treaty, headed by Colonel Apis.[19]

At the beginning of 1915 Bogićević gave the signal to German political and military circles to open negotiations with Colonel Apis and a part of the Serbian opposition for a separate peace treaty between Serbia and Germany.[20] At the same time, Apis was to have started action within Serbia for a government take-over and the liquidation of the Old Radicals and Alexander, as the strongest pro-Russian representatives.

These accusations against Apis can be refuted with the following facts:

1. Relations between Serbia and Germany were not the same as relations between Serbia and Austria-Hungary in the decade before the First World War. Germany had helped Serbia to survive the Austro-Hungarian economic blockade during the "Pig War," becoming Serbia's biggest trade partner. Germany on several occasions between 1908 and 1913 advised Vienna to proceed with more caution in her relations with Serbia. Therefore there was strong support in Serbian public opinion for closer relations with Germany, particularly to drive a wedge between Germany and Austria-Hungary. If Colonel Apis also favored this policy, he had in mind primarily the interests of Serbia. As we have seen, Colonel Apis did not favor in general a rapprochement between Serbia and any of the great powers; he was a defender of the rights of small nations and was critical of both Russia and France, as well as of Germany, particularly after the summer of 1913, when it became clear that Germany was yielding to Vienna's pressure for a free hand against Serbia.

2. Looking for primary sources dealing with the relations of Colonel Apis and German diplomatic and military representatives in Belgrade or in Berlin, this writer went through the reports of the German diplomatic representatives in Belgrade from 1903 to 1914. Not one confirmed the theories of Stojadinović and other writers of the same school. Unfortunately, the papers of the German Supreme Command from the 1903–14 period are not available, a part of them having been destroyed in Berlin in 1945.

Vemić's diary is not clear in connection with Ljuba Jovanović-Čupa's going to Berlin to get a printing press for *Pijemont*. Had Jovanović gone to buy a printing press or to receive it as a gift from somebody? Also, omission of the liberation of Slovenia as one of the war aims should not be given the interpretation which Stojadinović has implied. Among pan-Serbs, Slovenia was often regarded as a non-Serb province, because the Slovenes speak a language which differs somewhat from Serbo-Croatian. Some of the leading personalities in Belgrade had little interest in the Slovenes. In 1913 when Pašić received a group of Slovene youths, he greeted their leader with the words: "You are a Slovak?" The puzzled young Slovene answered: "No, I am not a Slovak but a Slovene." Pašić muttered: "I know. Slovenes and Slovaks are almost the same thing."[21]

3. Bogićević could not be described simply as a paid German agent; he was a man of independent financial means. After his disillusionment with Alexander Obrenović, he turned quickly back to his hatred for the Karadjordjević dynasty and its policies. He believed in a German orientation of Serbian foreign policy, no doubt, as did several other public figures in Serbia of his day.

It is difficult to write of his relations with Apis without his own papers. Bogićević was found dead in a hotel in Berlin in July 1938, a few months after he had asked the Serbian embassy in Berlin to permit him to come back to his own country. According to one version he committed suicide; others speak of assassination by the Nazis.[22] Bogićević's papers, as well as the papers of his father, were in his flat in Vienna at the time of his death. In the archives of the German Ministry of Foreign Affairs there are a few documents on Bogićević's activity. Apis's nephew, Milan Živanović, in his voluminous work on his uncle devoted only a few words to Bogićević, saying simply that he was a political emigree.[23]

If Bogićević was Apis's friend, he kept at the same time close contacts with King Petar and Alexander. The secretary of the Serbian Legation in Berlin from 1911 to 1914, Milutin Jovanović, Pašić's nephew, in a letter to this writer confirmed the fact that Bogićević "enjoyed great benevolence from King Petar and was in constant correspondence with Alexander."[24]

4. Bogićević's role in the preparation of the Sarajevo assassination has not been confirmed by any documentation. Any collaboration of Apis with Kaiser Wilhelm for this purpose seems ridiculous. From several sources it has been confirmed that Apis was working on the organization of a plot to assassinate Kaiser Wilhelm.[25] Mustafa Golubić and another Bosnian youth came to Apis in 1916 with the idea that they should go to Switzerland and try to cross to Germany and kill the German ruler.[26] Apis's arrest in Salonika ended this plan. In the spring of 1916 Apis accepted the offer of the Young Bosnians "to sacrifice their lives for the Entente cause" and to kill Kaiser Wilhelm's two most faithful allies in the Balkans, the Greek King Constantine and the Bulgarian Tsar Ferdinand. Mehmedbašić and Arežina volunteered to go to Athens and assassinate Constantine. Vulović was in charge of the technical side of the plot and the two assassins went to the Greek capital. Mehmedbašić waited for the Greek king in a theater, but his victim had a cold that day and missed the performance. It seems that the Serbian police heard about the plot and both Mehmedbašić and Arežina had to leave Athens. Mehmedbašić was ill and went to a hospital, while

Arežina was killed by a Greek officer in Salonika under obscure circumstances.[27] The Serbian police accused Vulović of organizing this murder to punish Arežina for not fulfilling the given order, according to the secret rules of Ujedinjenje ili Smrt. Colonel Apis's men hinted that the Serbian police were behind Arežina's murder.[28]

Colonel Apis was plotting in 1911 and in February 1914 against the Bulgarian Tsar Ferdinand. He made a deal with a secret revolutionary group in Bulgaria for that purpose, but the Bulgars changed their mind at the last moment.[29] Apis renewed his efforts against Ferdinand in 1916, but his arrest stopped all activity in this direction.

5. Regarding Bogićević's support of a separate treaty between Serbia and Germany and the accusation that Colonel Apis was involved in it, several points must be emphasized. During the First World War proposals for a cessation of hostilities by all belligerents or by some of them were numerous; the go-betweens were the Scandinavian kings, the Pope, statesmen in Washington, and others.

Serbia found herself at the beginning of 1915 in a difficult situation despite her three great victories over Potiorek and the army under his command. The Allies negotiated secretly with Italy and, in the London Pact of May 1915, gave her the right to occupy the greater part of the South Slav lands. At the same time, the Allies were pressing Serbia to cede parts of Macedonia to Bulgaria in order to bring this state over to the Allied side. Under these conditions Serbia started to explore the possibilities of a separate peace treaty with Germany and Austria-Hungary.

Stojadinović accuses Bogićević and Apis of being the only ones who made such overtures. Of Bogićević's action there are proofs in the German archives, but this writer has not found anything connecting Apis with this. Separate talks were going on with Tisza, and his two men Dada and Slavković were at Niš negotiating for a separate peace treaty.[30]

The initiative for these separate peace talks is not clear. Stojadinović pointed to Bogićević as the originator of the idea. Yet this writer is of the opinion that Bogićević made his move with at least the tacit agreement of Pašić. Although Bogićević left his post in March 1915, Pašić pensioned him off only in September 1915. A Serbian civil servant who left his working post without permission was automatically dismissed after ten days. In the Serbian archives there is no proof that Pašić used Bogićević as a go-between, but his delay in pensioning Bogićević off requires explanation. Only after the First World War, when the opposition pressed Pašić with questions about his attitude toward Bogićević, did Pašić order the opening of a criminal investigation of Bogićević in 1921. The investigation died down, and the state's attorney never asked for a trial.[31]

At the same time, in the archives of the German Ministry of Foreign

Affairs there are documents showing that Pašić negotiated directly through his diplomatic representatives in Bucharest and Athens for a separate peace treaty with Germany. The purpose of these negotiations is not clear: Did Pašić really intend to get Serbia out of the war, or did he want only to threaten the Allies?

In the archives of Tsarist Russia it was recorded that the Serbian minister in Petrograd, Spalajković, stated that Serbia would rather give itself to Austria-Hungary than permit Bulgaria to take a piece of Macedonia.[32]

This action of Pašić was known in Serbia. Slobodan Jovanović wrote that Alexander feared that Pašić might collapse and accept a separate peace treaty.[33] At the same time that Pašić was negotiating with Berlin, offering Macedonia to Bulgaria, Colonel Apis and his men in the Supreme Command advocated a sudden attack on Bulgaria, to clear Serbia's rear in case of a combined offensive of German and Austro-Hungarian divisions from the north.[34] Pašić rejected this suggestion of Colonel Apis, and only a few weeks later disaster fell on Serbia as she was attacked from the rear by the Bulgars and from the north by the Germans and Austro-Hungarians.

This writer believes that both Dr. Hohenberg's and Stojadinović's views about the involvement of Germany in the organization of the Sarajevo assassination are based on inadequate historical documentation. Dr. Hohenberg is the victim of his upbringing and his legitimist obsession; Stojadinović takes as his starting point the verdict of the Salonika trial, a typical *Justizmord*, trying desperately by bits and pieces to prove his thesis. In 1922 he was unable to find, with Zimmermann's permission, any documents in the German Foreign Office archives which could support this thesis.[35] This writer forty years later, when all the German archives, with the exception of the Supreme Command archives, have been opened to historians, has not found any proof of Dr. Hohenberg's or Stojadinović's accusation.

CHAPTER XX

THE OKHRANA, THE BOLSHEVIKS AND THE FREEMASONS

For neither Man nor Angel can discern
Hypocrisy, the only evil that walks
Invisible, except to God alone
By his permissive will through Heav'n and Earth.
                    —JOHN MILTON, *Paradise Lost*

THERE ARE almost no reliable historical sources with which to check the frequent charges that Russia, either official or revolutionary, or the anarchists, or Freemasonry and through it France and Britain, were involved, directly or indirectly, in the instigation of the Sarajevo assassination.

Among historians there has been no agreement on which factors in Russia, if any, were involved in the Sarajevo conspiracy. The Russian General Staff and its two representatives in Belgrade, Colonel Viktor Alexeyevich Artamonov and his assistant Alexander Ivanovich Verkhovsky, as well as the Russian minister in Belgrade, Nikolai Hartvig, and even the Russian Foreign Minister Sazonov, have all been mentioned.[1] But before going into the problem of direct contacts between Artamonov, Verkhovsky or Hartvig and either Colonel Apis or Malobabić or Princip's immediate group, an assessment of the political attitude of Colonel Apis toward the Russian government and its foreign policy is necessary.

Unlike Pašić and the Old Radicals, who had a special relationship with the Russian government, Colonel Apis adopted a complex approach to the problem of relations with Russia. Beginning with his general principle that Serbia should be independent of all the great powers, Colonel Apis made a comparative evaluation of the forces within Russia on which he could rely; and the court and the Tsarist government were at the bottom of his list. Both in the constitution of Ujedinjenje ili Smrt and in *Pijemont*'s declaration on foreign policy, reliance on Russia through Slavophilism—the basis of Pašić's policy—was not mentioned; instead, the self-reliance of the Balkan peoples was advocated: "In the national question, in order to achieve full success, one must formally adopt the policy that favors the brotherhood and alliance of all Balkan peoples, and in particular, the South Slavs. In this way Serbia can fulfill her role as the Piedmont of the Balkans."[2]

Colonel Apis went further and proclaimed the principle of solidarity of small nations against big ones, a remarkable foresight for the period in which he lived. In the issue of September 11, 1911, criticizing the Old Radicals' paper *Samouprava* for its attitude toward the Moroccan crisis, *Pijemont* attacked all the great powers and their methods of "surprise pitfalls, blackmail and plunder," comparing Serbia's position with Morocco and Korea:

> Korea was the victim of the Russo-Japanese War, the Serbian people the victims of Austria-Hungary's annexation of Bosnia and Hercegovina, and Morocco the victim of the expedition to El-Ksavi and Agadir. We cannot, therefore, rejoice at this solution to the Franco-German conflict, and we shall do our best to see that Serbia does not fall into the kind of trap to which Morocco was led by *Samouprava*.

Colonel Apis bitterly criticized both Tsarist Russia and the Habsburgs for their secret treaties dividing the Balkans into spheres of influence. In the first year of its publication, *Pijemont* attacked in eight different articles the methods of secret diplomacy. In a review of Gornjakov's book *The Bosporus and the Dardanelles*, which the paper carried on December 13, 1911, an open question was put to the Russian government: "When is Russian diplomacy finally going to realize that all the agreements with Austria over the Balkans were made at the expense of Russia and the Slavs in general? Russia will discover shortly that her Balkan brothers are her most natural and trusted allies." This question was put after *Pijemont* in its issue of October 26, 1911, had called Russia a "Brotherly Judas," identifying it with the domestic Judases, Pašić and Milovanović: "One should not expect much help from our brothers in the north because they, like our own Serbian people, are under the rule of Judas."

But the strongest attacks on official Russia were made for its share in the responsibility for the annexation of Bosnia and Hercegovina. On several occasions *Pijemont* attributed the annexation to the secret dealings of the Austrian and Russian diplomats. In an article headed "Whither Russia?" of October 3, 1911, *Pijemont* referred to the secret treaty between Russia and Austria-Hungary, concerned with the demarcation of their spheres of influence in the Balkans, which was signed in 1898, and claimed that the annexation of Bosnia was its logical outcome. This accusation was repeated on February 20, 1912. On May 4 of the same year *Pijemont*, fearing that a new deal might be made between Russia and Austria-Hungary, published the anxious comment: "We are still inclined to believe in the good intentions of Russia and in her sincere desire to help the Balkan Slavs. Nevertheless we take the liberty of expressing our anxiety lest a new agreement be reached between our protector and our gravest enemy. The Balkan states would feel much safer under the shield of Russia if they knew the horrid black-and-yellow bird would never land on it."

The Russian minister in Belgrade, Hartvig, wished to counter these views and declared in an interview that "Serbia is the incarnation of the Slav ideal in the Balkans, and I personally think it impossible that Russia could betray Serbia or that she could forget her historic role in the Balkans for the sake of her interests in Persia and the Far East."

In the issue of July 9, 1912, *Pijemont* published the text of the interview with Hartvig, but followed it with a devastating criticism of Russian diplomacy. *Pijemont* began by saying that its fear and anxiety had not been abated by the interview. "We believe in the goodness of the Russian soul, of the Russian people, but we do not trust Russian diplomacy." The article continued by enumerating all the secret treaties concluded between Russia and Austria-Hungary concerning their spheres of influence in the Balkans.

The Russian court and the Russian government, on their side, were suspicious of the regicides and Colonel Apis from the beginning, partly because of the close contacts of some older regicides (Popović and Mašin) with Vienna, and even more because they suspected the regicides of being republicans and rebels. The French ambassador in St. Petersburg informed Paris on April 3, 1910, that St. Petersburg was afraid of the growing republican movement in Serbia, that King Petar would get rid of the regicides little by little, and that the French government should not be impatient.[3] The Russian government seven years later was still insisting that King Petar put the regicides away. From Vienna, the French ambassador learned on April 30, 1910, that Tsar Nicholas II had advised King Petar, when he visited St. Petersburg, to eliminate the influence of the regicide officers. According to the same source, King Petar promised to do this when he returned to Serbia.[4] The French ambassador in Constantinople also confirmed this news on April 10, 1910. He might have heard this from Serbia's minister in Turkey, Dr. Jakov Nenadović, one of the chief civil conspirators in the 1903 plot, who later came into conflict with Colonel Apis. According to Milan Zivanović, Nenadović was the first one to urge Alexander "to rid himself of his obligations to the regicides and their influence by simply sending their leaders, particularly Colonel Apis, to Karaburma,"[5] the execution ground on the outskirts of Belgrade. When King Petar visited St. Petersburg again, in September 1911, the regicides became alarmed. The French minister informed Paris that the regicides were afraid that their "crowned accomplice" might be "seduced by pomp of monarchy," and that the regicides reminded King Petar of "his bloody origins."[6] It is significant that in May 1914, when the conflict between the Old Radicals and Colonel Apis broke out in violent form, the Russian government stepped in on Pašić's side. *Pijemont* had already (September 28, 1912) accused the Russian minister, Hartvig, of being the real ruler of Serbia.

Only after the first Konopischt meeting between Kaiser Wilhelm and the Archduke, when it became obvious that Austria-Hungary would attack Serbia, did Colonel Apis come out in full praise of Russia. "Oh, do gather us all round yourself, why should we wander to the West? Our bayonets will serve you and your allies. Oh, You, Great Sister, have deeply marked our future paths."[7] On March 14, 1914, *Pijemont* praised the rearmament and the readiness of the Russian Army:

> We Slavs have to be the shield against the invasion of the Germans to the East . . . The German regiments, and the comic-opera troops of Austria and Italy will tremble. The rearmament of Russia is the main security of the Slav peoples. As Slavs, as the most faithful and grateful brothers of the Russians, we Serbs must rejoice and greet these hopes of a great Slav future.

One of the fields for any historian's further study of the story of Colonel Apis would be Apis's relations with unofficial Russia, particularly with revolutionary circles. When more authentic documentation becomes available, more light will be thrown on Apis's contacts with the Russian Social Revolutionaries. The fact is that of all members of the Entente, the Russian government intervened most emphatically, through the Foreign Minister Tereshchenko in the summer of 1917, trying to dissuade the Regent Alexander from carrying out Apis's death sentence.[8] At that time the minister of war in the Kerensky government was Alexander Ivanovich Verkhovsky, who had been in Belgrade in 1914 as the assistant of Colonel Artamonov, the military attaché.

People who knew Colonel Apis described him as an antagonist of pan-Slavism and its teachings that Tsarist Russia should be the leader of all the Slavs. He adhered more to a neo-Slav concept of the equality of all

Slavs and the regulation of their relations on a federative basis. In *Pije-mont* on April 3, 1915, Dr. Jevto Dedijer elaborated in detail the future relations between Russia and South Slavs, in an article entitled "On the Eve of a Great Future." He wrote:

The day is not far off when all the Serbs and Croats, and perhaps the Slovenes too, will be joined together in a large and independent state . . . we shall come into contact with the great Slav Empire and with the states of the Roman peoples in the West . . . Fate has granted the Russian people the task of the spiritual refreshment and moral reformation of Europe, of the awakening of the deep and mighty Orient which went to sleep so many centuries ago, of achieving the cultural unification of Europe and Asia, perhaps even of creating a new culture. . . . In this great creative work embarked on by the Russian people, we, being the nearest and most closely related people, will be drawn in as helpers and collaborators. We shall be the link between the refined and complicated European West and the keen and vigorous Slav-Asian East. Such a position is undoubtedly a favorable one, but at the same time it is delicately balanced, full of honor and great responsibility to history and to humanity. We should not be afraid of our small numbers; small peoples can yet do great things if they are determined and gifted. We have examples in classical Greece and, among contemporaries, in Scandinavia . . .

From the summer of 1913, when Colonel Apis became chief of Military Intelligence of the Serbian General Staff, he came into contact with the Russian military attaché in Belgrade, Colonel Artamonov, and his assistant Verkhovsky. He handed them the information he received on military matters from his trusted agents in Austria-Hungary. Artamonov from time to time gave a sum of money for the expenses of Apis's agents incurred in connection with their work.

During the First World War and immediately afterward, accusations were made that Colonel Apis had organized the Sarajevo assassination with the knowledge and approval of the Russian General Staff and of the Russian government. *Neue Freie Presse*, of July 29, 1916, and *Hrvatski Dnevnik*, of August 1, 1916, reported that Bulgarian authorities, after the capture of Niš, found in the archives of the Serbian Ministry of Foreign Affairs a report of the Russian minister in Belgrade, Nikolai Hartvig, that "official circles in St. Petersburg expected the news of the Archduke's assassination, because they knew well that the assassination was going to take place."[9]

It is obvious that this news item was not correct, since neither the Bulgarian nor the German nor the Austrian authorities ever published this document, which would have supported their main thesis on the responsibility for the Sarajevo assassination. After the war, Victor Serge and *Fédération Balkanique*, a review in Vienna run by a group of left-wing Balkan emigrees under the patronage of the Third International, came out with the accusation that Artamonov and Hartvig had known about the plot and had even encouraged it. Mustafa Golubić, the member of Ujedinjenje ili Smrt who was arrested in 1917 during the Salonika trial, claimed that Colonel Apis had organized and financed the assassination in Sarajevo with the knowledge of Artamonov, Hartvig, Pašić, and Alexander.[10] Serge, who wrote on the basis of his talks with Golubić and two of his friends, stated that the Sarajevo assassination had been provoked and later authorized by the Russian General Staff. When Apis informed Artamonov, the latter allegedly answered him: "Go on. If they attack you, you are not going to be alone."[11] It is interesting to note that Leopold Mandl, a protégé of Berchtold who defended the official Austro-Hungarian thesis on Sarajevo during the First World War, also published an article of the same character, obviously getting the information from Golubić.[12] Božin Simić, one of the leaders of the Ujedinjenje ili Smrt, also claimed that Hartvig and Artamonov knew about the plot, but later changed his statement by saying that only Artamonov, and not Hartvig, was involved in the conspiracy.[13]

In Soviet historiography similar opinions were expressed by Professor M. N. Pokrovsky,[14] who vehemently challenged an opposite thesis of Eugene V. Tarle.[15] N. V. Poletika, a pupil of Pokrovsky, in two of his books emphatically claimed that the Russian General Staff was behind the plot, adding that Britain and France also knew about it, although in 1964 he changed his mind.[16] When the Soviet government published the archives of the Tsarist government, despite many revealing facts about the secret diplomacy of the Tsarist regime no document confirmed any of these allegations.[17]

Colonel Apis himself, in his secret report about the Sarajevo conspiracy to the Salonika court on April 11, 1917, said emphatically that he did not inform Artamonov about the steps taken against the Archduke Franz Ferdinand.[18] Golubić's version, therefore, is completely unreliable.

The question is why did Golubić and Simić claim that Artamonov, Hartvig, Pašić and Alexander knew about the plot? A major reason might be that being in political conflict with Pašić and Alexander, having to leave their own country, and embittered because of the execution of Colonel Apis, they made these accusations in a spirit of revenge.

The problem of the roles of Artamonov and Verkhovsky in the Sarajevo plot cannot yet be closed. There remain some questions to be answered. Louis de Trywdar-Burzynski, a former member of the Archaeological Institute in St. Petersburg, claimed in his memoirs, which were published in 1926, that the Sarajevo assassination was organized by Russian military agents in Belgrade. He said he had this information directly from Verkhovsky, whom he knew personally.[19] This writer could not find out whether Verkhovsky ever answered these charges. Verkhovsky was a rather well-known personality in Russia. In 1917 he commanded the armies of the Moscow military district, and in the autumn of the same year he became minister of war in the Kerensky government, but he resigned on the eve of the October Revolution.[20] The *Little Soviet Encyclopaedia*, in its 1930 edition, records that after the October Revolution, Verkhovsky "was in the camp of the enemy," even though he was "working in scientific and academic organizations of the Red Army."[21]

Apis said he had engaged Malobabić to organize an information service in Austria-Hungary in agreement with Artamonov, who had a meeting with Malobabić in his presence.[22] It is not clear whether Malobabić knew Artamonov before, or had been in his service before he came to work for Colonel Apis. The minutes of the Salonika trial confirm that Malobabić had direct contacts with Artamonov. When Malobabić was arrested in Belgrade on his return from Austria-Hungary on July 25, he was escorted to Niš by train. During this trip he tried to escape from the police agents, and running through the cars he ran into the secretary of the Russian legation in Belgrade, Strandman, whom he had met through Artamonov. But Strandman pretended he did not know Malobabić, who had to jump from the moving express in order to avoid the policemen, although they caught him soon afterwards.[23]

Malobabić's relations with Artamonov are important for our study, particularly because of different theories about Malobabić's role in the Sarajevo assassination. If Malobabić was sent to Sarajevo, on whose orders did he act—Colonel Apis's, Artamonov's, or somebody else's? This question can be answered only after further study.

Another point which should be clarified is the number of assassins who were in Sarajevo. Ilić had six of them under his control, but was Malobabić on the very spot of the assassination on the fateful day? Kiszling expressed the opinion that there were more than six assassins.[24] According to a story in Belgrade's *Vreme* on May 9, 1937, Andra Djordjević, a former member of the *komite*, was invited to Bucharest by an old friend of his, who was in contact with "some Russians who tried to escape from the Russian legation." Djordjević was sent to Sarajevo to contact Čabrinović, who gave him a bomb and a Russian Nagan pistol. Djordjević was instructed to shoot the Archduke at the station from which the Archduke was to leave Sarajevo. After Princip's shots, Djordjević threw the weapons away, but was arrested because he had a Rumanian passport. After twenty-seven days he was released and he returned to Bucharest, where he got 20,000 leys. Djordjević said that there were about ten different groups of assassins in Sarajevo and that they did not know each other.

The accuracy of this story is hard to assess. Djordjević did not tell it to *Vreme* directly; but a friend of his, a cook in a monastery at Matka,

near Skoplje, gave the details to the press. Čabrinović did not mention
this version. Yet two things must be taken into consideration. The Russian paper *Russkiye Vedomosti* wrote on June 30, 1914, that a "third
attempt had been prepared against the Archduke."[25] Secondly, in his
account at the investigation in Salonika, when Colonel Apis was asked
about an invoice covering payment for the four Russian Nagans he had
bought in Belgrade in 1914, he answered that he had given the guns to
Malobabić for the protection of his trusted agents in Austria-Hungary.
Princip and his accomplices had Browning revolvers, while Djordjević
mentioned that he had had a Nagan.

Next must be considered the extent to which the Young Bosnians
had contact with the Tsarist secret police Okhrana, either directly or
indirectly. According to some people who knew Golubić as a schoolboy, he was already an Okhrana agent.[26] In the Hoover Institution on
War, Revolution and Peace, in the Paris Okhrana operational files, this
writer checked the names of all the leading Young Bosnians, with negative results. Up to 1904 the headquarters of the Balkan Okhrana were in
Vienna, but after it was proved that its chief, Alexander Weissman, was
a foreign agent, the so-called Balkanska Agentura was dissolved.
Among the leading figures in Serbia on the list of the Okhrana agents
were Jovan Djaja, one of the leading Old Radicals, and the vice-mayor
of Belgrade, Gnjidić. After 1904 the headquarters of the Balkan
Okhrana were in Paris, where they operated in the disguise of a private
detective agency formally headed by two retired French policemen. It
seems that this center was much more interested in Macedonia than in
Bosnia and Hercegovina. The names on the list of its agents in Bosnia
and Hercegovina have no connection with the Young Bosnians or the
Sarajevo conspiracy.

Relations between the Young Bosnians, particularly Gaćinović and
Ilić, and the Russian left-wing Social Revolutionaries were close. There
is a possibility that the Okhrana operated through some of the leaders
of the Social Revolutionaries. But Evno Fiselevich Azef, the Okhrana
agent who penetrated into the top ranks of Social Revolutionaries in
1901 and headed its Terrorist Brigade, had been exposed in 1908. On
the party commission which proved Azef's crime was Natanson-
Bobrov, the friend of Gaćinović.

It is, of course, possible that Natanson-Bobrov or some of his friends
directly advised Gaćinović to organize an attempt against the life of the
Archduke Franz Ferdinand, but there is no proof of this theory. One
piece of information, however, proves that Natanson-Bobrov knew
something about the preparation of the plot. Gaćinović wrote that
after the Sarajevo assassination his Russian friends advised him to leave
Switzerland at once, because the Austro-Hungarian authorities might
demand his extradition from the Swiss, and the chances were that this
request would have been granted.[27] Also Milovan Prodanović,

Gaćinović's friend, wrote in a letter that one day before June 28, 1914, "Gaćinović returned from the Alps with his hands all burned because he was practicing throwing bombs with his Russian friends."[28]

Danilo Ilić's confidential conversation with Father Mirko Maksimović in Sarajevo, after he returned from Switzerland in late summer 1913, shows that the Social Revolutionaries whom he had met in Switzerland had refused to give him any concrete advice about possible action in Bosnia and Hercegovina, leaving this matter entirely in the hands of the local revolutionaries.[29] It is interesting to note that the Social Revolutionary Lebedev, who after 1919 worked on a book on Princip, does not mention either in his manuscripts or in the notes for his book anything which might suggest that the Social Revolutionaries had anything to do with the Sarajevo assassination. He only mentions that Gaćinović went to Paris early in 1914 to obtain weapons for an attempt against Governor Potiorek. He tried to contact former Russian Social Revolutionary Vladimir Lvovich Burchev, but without success.

Since 1937 attempts have been made in several quarters, both Yugoslav and German, to connect the Russian Bolsheviks with the Sarajevo assassination.[30] The pretext for this was Karl Radek's statement at his trial in Moscow in the morning of January 29, 1937, when, according to the official minutes of the trial, he said in his final plea:

. . . And we must also tell the world what Lenin—I tremble to mention his name from this dock—said in the letter, in the directions he gave to the delegation that was about to leave for The Hague, about the secret of war. A fragment of this secret was in the possession of the young Serbian nationalist, Gabriel Princip, who could die in a fortress without revealing it. He was a Serbian nationalist and felt the justice of his cause when fighting for the secret which was kept by the Serbian national movement. I cannot conceal this secret and carry it with me to the grave, because while in view of what I have confessed here, I have not the right to speak as a repentant Communist, nevertheless the 35 years I worked in the labor movement despite all the errors and crimes with which they ended, entitle me to ask you to believe one thing—that, after all, the masses of the people with whom I marched do mean something to me. And if I concealed this truth and departed this life with it, as Zinoviev did and as Mrachkovsky did, then when I thought over these things, I would have heard in my hour of death the execrations of those people who will be slaughtered in the future war, and whom, by my testimony, I could have furnished with a weapon against the war that is being fomented. . . .[31]

Radek had been interested in the problem of the responsibility for the Sarajevo assassination. In *Izvestia*, June 28, 1934, he criticized Russian historian Poletika for his thesis that the Serbian government was behind the plot. But Radek's statement at the trial is a complete mystery. What were his motives for mentioning Princip? What was his "secret war"? What did Lenin and the directives "he gave to the delegation that was about to leave for The Hague" have to do with Princip's secret? Which Hague conference did he have in mind? In August 1914 the Bolsheviks were planning to hold a conference in The Hague, and there were two postwar Hague conferences which Bolshevik delegates attended: a June–July 1922 conference on the question of war debts and a pacifist conference in December 1922, which was attended by ten delegates from Moscow.

Čeda Popović, a member of the central committee of the Ujedinjenje ili Smrt, wrote an article for *Nova Evropa* of November 26, 1937, denying categorically that either the Bolsheviks or Trotsky had anything to do with the Sarajevo plot.

The January 1938 issue of *Berliner Monatshefte*, edited by Wegerer, commented on Radek's statement as well as the polemics it started in Yugoslavia, stressing the point that in discussing the problem of responsibility for the Sarajevo assassination one should not omit the role of the revolutionary societies. Wegerer rejected the theory of the complicity of the Bolsheviks. However, in a book published in 1939, Wegerer took a contrary view, stating that Gaćinović, who had attended the Toulouse meeting in January 1914, when a plot against Potiorek or the Archduke was discussed, "was an intellectual revolutionary in contact with the leading Bolsheviks, such as Trotsky, Lunacharsky, and others."[32]

During the Second World War, when Ribbentrop gave directives to renew the accusation that the Russians had been responsible for the Sarajevo assassination, Hans Übersberger revived this allegation in *Auswärtige Politik*.[33]

D. Ljubibratić in his book on Princip in 1960 denied any links between Princip's group and the Bolsheviks, although he admitted that Radek, who had been in Switzerland during the war, might have heard through Gaćinović something about "Princip's secret."[34]

This writer has carefully explored the Trotsky papers in Houghton Library at Harvard University to learn about his relations with Gaćinović. The Trotsky archives begin only with his activities in 1919. He did not find any clue which might have suggested the meaning of Radek's statement.

Just as Radek's statement provoked controversy over the Bolsheviks' links with the Sarajevo conspiracy, so an interview in *The New York Times* of June 29, 1914, with the American anarchist Alexander Berkman (1870–1936) opened the question of whether the anarchists were involved in the assassination. An emigree from Russia, where he had taken part in anarchist activities, Berkman came to the United States and on July 23, 1892, tried to kill Henry Clay Frick, head of the Carnegie Steel Company at Homestead, Pennsylvania, because the Carnegie

Company had hired sluggers to terrorize its workers with the aid of the Pinkerton Detective Agency. Berkman was sentenced to twenty-two years' hard labor and was released only in 1906. In the tradition of Johan Most, he defended "action by deed . . . to remove a tyrant in the struggle against the capitalists" and edited his paper *Blast* in San Francisco until 1914. Berkman, together with Emma Goldman, was a leading protagonist of anarchism in the United States.

Berkman's interview in *The New York Times* on the morning after the Sarajevo assassination reads:

CALLS IT ANARCHIST PLOT
Berkman Says Revolutionists Killed the Crown Prince

The assassination of Franz Ferdinand was a plot of the anarchists and revolutionaries, according to Alexander Berkman, the anarchist, who asserted last night that it was the plan of the revolutionists to strike down the only man strong enough to continue the iron rule of Emperor Francis Joseph.

It was pointed out by Berkman that the present Emperor had been able to meet every move of the revolutionists, who thought the time was opportune to put the Crown Prince beyond the reach of the throne "in the only logical way," now that the Emperor was on the verge of the grave.

"Austria-Hungary is a hotbed of revolution," said Berkman, "and the country has been torn. Francis Joseph has ruled the country with a strong rein, but with great tact. The rule of the present Emperor would have been continued by the Crown Prince had he succeeded to the throne.

"The anarchists, the revolutionists, and the strong republican factor knew this, and they have tried to make complications which would bring on a civil war. There is no successor of the blood royal strong enough to deal with them."

Berkman did not deny the authenticity of the interview, although in his book *Now and After: The ABC of Communist Anarchism*, published in New York in 1929, he said that Gavrilo Princip was a "Serbian patriot," who "had never heard of anarchism."[35]

Berkman's interview in *The New York Times* is still a puzzle for historians; on the basis of it one cannot conclude that he or his anarchist group were connected with the Sarajevo plot, although there is a possibility that Berkman had heard something either through his European links or through South Slav emigree organizations in the United States.

Finally, there is a theory that the real instigators of the Sarajevo crime were the Freemasons. At the trial, in the morning session of October 12, 1914, Čabrinović was asked whether Tankosić was a Freemason and whether Čabrinović had read any of his Freemasonry books. Čabrinović answered that Tankosić was a Freemason, as was Ciganović, but he declined to answer whether he himself was a Freemason.[36] In the afternoon session the presiding judge continued to ask Čabrinović about Freemasonry; he confirmed again that Tankosić and Ciganović were Freemasons, but he denied that he had been instructed by the Freemasons to kill the Archduke. To the explicit question of the presiding judge whether the fact that Tankosić and Ciganović were Freemasons had anything to do with the assassination, Čabrinović answered:

"Yes, as far as we are the followers of Freemasonry ideas."

"Do these ideas as far as you know recommend that assassination should be committed against sovereigns?" the presiding judge asked.

"It recommends this. I was personally told by Ciganović that the late Ferdinand was sentenced to death by Freemasons. He told me this after I had made my decision to take part in the assassination."[37]

Princip confirmed Čabrinović's statement during his interrogation on October 13, 1914. After stating that both Tankosić and Ciganović were Freemasons, he stated: "Once, while we were talking about the plot at the Café Sturgeon, Ciganović told us that on such and such a year the Freemasons sentenced Franz Ferdinand to death."

The presiding judge commented: "But that was after you had already committed yourself to the plot?"

Princip confirmed this and denied that he was a Freemason, but added that Čabrinović had wanted to join a Freemason lodge, but he did not know whether Čabrinović had ever done so.

To the presiding judge's comment, "It is of primary importance that the issue of Freemasons did not in any way influence your decision," Princip answered: "As far as I am concerned, Ciganović did not wish to give us weapons when we asked him the first time; he did this only at our second meeting. He said that he wanted to talk about the whole thing in detail with one man."[38]

Grabež also denied that he was a Freemason, on October 13, 1914, stating that that organization did not give him instructions for the assassination.[39]

But on October 17 Čabrinović was again questioned about the Freemasons, and he stated that besides Ciganović, Tankosić, Šarac, and Bukovac, there was another person, "a friend of Tankosić's," who knew about the plot. He refused to name him, saying only that he was a "mysterious person," but at that moment Princip interrupted: "His name was Kazimirović and he graduated from a theology academy in Russia."[40]

After Princip's intervention, Čabrinović became more talkative and described Kazimirović in greater detail, saying that he graduated in Kiev but had refused to be ordained. He also said that the conspirators did not have the means for an assassination and that Ciganović talked to Tankosić and Tankosić to "the other person," and afterward "that person" went abroad. Only after his return did Ciganović tell them that they would get the weapons.

Princip added that Ciganović had told him about that man and the Freemasons, but Princip insisted that he should not be informed about the plot. Ciganović stressed that the man could be trusted. Princip said that he would not take part in the conspiracy if anybody else knew about it, but Ciganović again insisted that this man could be trusted, that he was a good friend and that his name was Kazimirović.[41]

On October 19 Čabrinović was more explicit. He described Kazimirović as Tankosić's chief in their Freemason lodge and said that he had gone abroad immediately after they asked for arms, traveling through the whole continent.

He was in Budapest, in France, in Russia . . . When I asked Ciganović what is new, he always answered, "Wait until he returns." Ciganović told me on that occasion that two years before, the Freemasons had sentenced the late Heir Apparent but they did not have the men to kill him. Later, when he gave me the Browning and ammunition, he told me that the man had just come back from Budapest. I knew that he had traveled abroad in connection with the plot and that he had held some conferences.[42]

Čabrinović added that Princip was annoyed by the whole affair. Princip confirmed this, stating that he had said to Ciganović that he had no wish to meet Kazimirović and that "it is ridiculous that people from abroad should be mixed up in this."[43]

The first accusation that the Freemasons had been involved in the plot was published by a certain Horatio Bottomley in a London paper called *John Bull*, under the headline "To Hell with Serbia," on July 11, 1914. He claimed that Princip had been in Paris before the assassination and that the French Freemasonry lodge Grand Orient was involved in the plot. It seems that the Austro-Hungarian secret police supplied Bottomley with materials.[44] The same accusation was repeated by C. H. Norman in his book *A Searchlight on the European War*, published in London in 1924, as well as in E. Durham's *The Sarajevo Crime*, which appeared in London in 1925.

But the full-scale attack against the Freemasons was launched by Father Anton Puntigam, S.J., when in 1918, under the pseudonym Professor Pharos, he published his version of the minutes of the Sarajevo trial. According to Albert Mousset[45] and even more Vojislav Bogićević,[46] who gave their own versions of the proceedings of the trial, Puntigam deliberately falsified them in several places in order to accuse the Freemasons of being the real instigators of the Sarajevo crime. In a preface to Puntigam's book, Professor Josef Kohler, of Berlin University, claimed that French Freemasonry provided Tankosić with the weapons and the money for the crime.

Puntigam tried to stir up old prejudices against the Freemasons and Jews as instigators of the French Revolution of 1789 and all the other revolutions in Europe. Puntigam's thesis was revived after the war, in 1919, by Father Herman Gruber, S.J., who had written a special three-volume work for the Archduke Franz Ferdinand on the role of Free-masonry in modern revolutions.[47] But the strongest accuser of the Freemasons was the former German Chief of Staff, General Erich Ludendorff, in two books published in 1928 and 1934.[48] He claimed that Colonel Apis was a Freemason who had connections "with a certain Major Susley, the head of a secret office in London."[49] For Ludendorff, Princip was a Jew, and the proof for this allegation was that Princip's first name was Gavrilo, or Gabriel in English.[50] Ludendorff also accused German, Austrian, and Hungarian Freemasons of being in secret league with Colonel Apis. The chancellery of Emperor Franz Josef in Vienna received reports about these links, but Prince Montenuovo ordered that the matter should not be further investigated.[51] The Freemasons of Germany sued General Ludendorff for libel, and in 1931 he was fined 500 marks.[52] Nevertheless, he continued his attacks. In his writings, Ludendorff mentioned the Grand Master of the Serbian Freemason lodge *Pobratim*, Svetomir Nikolajević, as the man most responsible for linking Belgrade with French and other European lodges. Nikolajević's son, Dušan Nikolajević, answered these charges against his father in 1928.[53] He said that in 1908 his father had initiated a movement among European Freemasons to help Serbia during the annexation crisis. Also, in July 1914, his father had advised Pašić that he should place the conflict with Austria-Hungary before the International Tribunal in The Hague. But he denied categorically that the Freemasons or his father had anything to do with the Sarajevo plot. He reminded General Ludendorff that after the occupation of Serbia in 1915, Germany offered his father, through General Westarp, the post of Civil Governor of Serbia, but he declined it.[54]

Besides Ludendorff, E. Reventlow kept up the attacks on Freemasonry, particularly against the German lodges.[55] But the strongest accusations came from the Nazis. They claimed that the French Masonic lodges had decided in 1912 or 1913 that the Archduke Franz Ferdinand, as the die-hard enemy of Freemasonry, should be killed. The Sarajevo assassins were only the executioners of this verdict. Tankosić, a Freemason himself, organized the assassination, Freemasonry financed the plot, and some of the assassins, Čabrinović certainly and Grabež probably, were Freemasons.[56] Princip was accused of being a Jew. The *Völkischer Beobachter*, in an article on January 8, 1936, called him "a Jew and a Freemason." After the downfall of France, Nazi attacks concentrated on Britain. The stories of the activities of the British Major Susley in London were revived. In his proclamation to the German people on April 6, 1941, when Germany and her satellites attacked Yugoslavia, Hitler stated that the Sarajevo assassination had been organized by the British Intelligence Service.[57]

Two of the members of Princip's conspiracy who survived the First World War, Vaso Čubrilović and Ivo Kranjčević, have given their versions of Čabrinović's statement at the trial about Freemasons. Vaso Čubrilović told Luigi Albertini that the accusation was initiated by Father Puntigam and Čabrinović's counsel, Dr. Konstantin Premužić, and it happened in this way:

After the first days of their arrest the defendants began to communicate among themselves by an alphabetical system made up of long and short knocks on the wall in a method they had all learned from Stepnyak's *Underground Russia,* thus keeping one another informed of the proceeding of the preliminary investigation. One day Čabrinović signaled:

"Advocate Premužić [who was a Clerical under the influence of Archduke Franz Ferdinand's confessor, Father Puntigam] tells me that the Freemasons must have had a hand in the outrage and that it would be for the good of Serbia and myself if I made the confession that I am a Mason and that Freemasonry made me perpetrate the outrage. What shall I do?"

The advice came back:

"Let him believe it; it can't do us any harm and will draw off attention from Serbia."

This was the origin of the legend, which the accused, especially Čabrinović, in vain tried to substantiate in their evidence.[58]

Ivo Kranjčević confirmed this story in his memoirs, written after the Second World War.

Freemason lodges operated among the South Slavs all through the nineteenth century, although they never identified themselves with any regime or any political group. Under the reign of King Alexander Obrenović, some of the Freemasons backed the king, as Svetomir Nikolajević did; while others were among the regicides, for instance Djordje Vajfert, the leading Serbian industrialist of his day, who gave substantial financial help to the families of the regicides killed during the *coup d'état.*

There is no evidence that Colonel Apis was a Freemason, but Ljuba Jovanović-Čupa, the editor of *Pijemont,* was definitely a Freemason. The Masonic periodical *Neimar* (Architect) in its issue of January–February 1925, included Ljuba Jovanović-Čupa in a list of dead Freemasons. *Pijemont* on four occasions in 1912 had articles praising the work of the Freemasons in France, Belgium and Hungary, and attacking the Austrian authorities for banning Masonic activities. At his trial Apis confirmed that Ljuba Jovanović-Čupa had been a Freemason.

As far as Tankosić was concerned, opinions are divided whether he had been a Freemason. The periodical *Sestar* (Compass), the organ of the great lodge Yugoslavia, emphatically denied it, in its issue of April–May 1930. Tankosić, with his character and his escapades, would hardly fit into a Masonic lodge. Some writers say that both Ljuba Jovanović-Čupa and Tankosić left the ranks of Freemasonry quickly.[59]

Radovan Kazimirović, whom Princip mentioned, was a professor in a high school in Belgrade, where he had met Princip during his examinations. In an article in 1932, Kazimirović explained his relations with Princip.[60] He said he had traveled to Prague in 1913 for private reasons; he denied going to Russia or France. Kazimirović was a known contributor to *Pijemont*, a fact which the Austro-Hungarian authorities could not miss.[61]

The links of the South Slav Freemasons with other Freemason lodges abroad were numerous. Contacts were kept with French, Belgian, Italian and also German and Hungarian lodges. Among the Russian Populists were many Freemasons. Bakunin himself was a member of a Freemason lodge. In 1905, Freemason lodges gained influence in Russia, particularly among the liberals, Social Revolutionaries, and a few Social Democrats. Marx never liked Freemasonry, and perhaps this was one of the reasons why, at the time of the formation of the Third International, Bolsheviks introduced the principle that no Freemason could be a member. German Freemasonry kept contacts with the Serbian lodges, as the French minister in Belgrade reported in the decade after 1910.[62] But these reports have nothing in them to suggest that Colonel Apis and his men were involved in these relations.

On the other hand, the Archduke himself believed that Freemasons had sentenced him to death, as he told Czernin.[63] In 1908, Aehrenthal had exchanged many reports with his ambassadors in Paris, Lisbon and Berlin about alleged links between anarchists and Freemasons for the purpose of carrying out assassinations of the crowned heads of Europe.[64]

CONCLUSION

Today, half a century after Sarajevo, extensive historical research and the perspective afforded by the turbulent experience of mankind since then make possible a more detached and balanced view of the characters involved, their complex motives, and the relation of the Sarajevo assassination to the outbreak of the First World War.

To describe the Sarajevo assassination as either an underlying or an immediate cause of the 1914–18 war is to commit an enormity. It was an incident which under more normal international circumstances could not have provoked such momentous consequences. At the same time it was truly an unexpected gift from Mars to the Viennese war party, which had sought, ever since the annexation crisis of 1908–9, a pretext for attacking Serbia, pacifying the South Slavs, and extending Habsburg power to the very gates of Salonika. Only in this sense were the South Slav national aspirations and the colonial conditions of Bosnia and Hercegovina among the causes of the First World War. To this extent there is much truth in the conclusion of the Bosnian historian and economist Veselin Masleša that Princip "challenged with his gun the *Drang nach Osten*."[1]

The story of the instigators of the Sarajevo assassination is also simpler than it was believed to be. The debate over war guilt which followed 1918 blurred this problem badly. In order to prove that this or that belligerent state provoked the war by instigating the murder of the Heir Apparent, the smallest details of the Sarajevo event have been chosen and often distorted to fit the needs of a particular thesis. The social and political aspects of the assassination have been neglected, particularly the milieu in which it occurred and the conditions, both domestic and international, under which Bosnia and Hercegovina lived.

The hypotheses according to which the Sarajevo assassination was instigated by the secret agencies of Russia, France and Britain, or similar bodies in Germany, Hungary and Austria, either directly or indirectly through cover organizations, have not been confirmed by historical research, although even at this late date not all the archives have yet been opened.

Young Bosnians were a part of the revolutionary movement of the South Slavs within the Habsburg monarchy. Because of the retarded development of their own society and the colonial conditions prevailing in Bosnia and Hercegovina, they were primitive rebels, and as such, unable to adapt themselves to the modern ideologies of mass movements against systems of oppression.

For them the assassination of the Archduke Franz Ferdinand was a clear case of tyrannicide, committed for the common good, on the basis of the teaching of natural law—that all men are born equal and are entitled to rebel against obsolete institutions which hamper them in the realization of their basic human rights and to use terror against indecent conditions imposed by a system of terror. The Archduke was killed by the Young Bosnians, in cooperation with other revolutionary societies among the South Slavs, as a protest against the colonial status of Bosnia and Hercegovina, and as an integral part of the intensified struggle of the South Slavs for national self-determination.

The leading statesmen and historians of the pre-1914 world, as well as the defenders of legitimism afterward, greatly underestimated the nationality question, particularly the long history of South Slav yearning for independence against the feudal institutions of the Habsburgs, the Venetians and the Ottomans. On the eve of 1914 the South Slavs, who lived in four different states under eight different systems of government, were striving for liberation and unification, as the Germans, the Italians and the Magyars, to a large degree, had striven some sixty years before. From the history of the emancipation of these once subject peoples, the Habsburgs learned nothing. The Archduke Franz Ferdinand, though conscious of the problem, looked for a solution in the past. His proposed revival of monarchical absolutism was incompatible with the demand of rising nationalities in an era of modernization.

Princip's shots heralded not only the Archduke's death, but also, the destruction, four years later, of the multinational Habsburg empire and its anachronistic institutions, including the medieval *kmet* system in Bosnia and Hercegovina. While Princip was suffering through his dying hours in Theresienstadt in April 1918 the Bosnian horizons were lighted every night by the burning of feudal landlords' *konaks*, announcing the end of the bondage which had lasted for so many centuries. It is true that the South Slavs had to pay a tremendous price in blood for their liberation. "The combined loss of population, as a result of the wars between 1912 and 1918, suffered by all South Slav provinces which since 1918 have formed the state of Yugoslavia, amounted to the staggering figure of about 1,900,000."[2] This represents about 16 per cent of the South Slav population.

The Young Bosnians were not isolated from outside ideologies, but they could not be identified with Mazzini's Young Italy, or with the German student clubs in the period of the unification of Germany, or with Russian Populists, although there are certain characteristics common to all of them. They were, in fact, the peculiar product of Bosnian conditions, deeply influenced by the Kosovo legend, in the era of sharp imperialist conflict which shook the world at the beginning of the twentieth century.

Despite their primitive theories of direct action, the Young Bosnians and their counterparts among the Slovene Preporod and Croat revolutionary youth movement had a firmer grasp of historical perspective than most of their contemporaries among the South Slavs. They recognized, first, the inevitability of the revolutionary destruction of the Habsburg empire and, second, the need to form a federal South Slav state and to establish tolerance among different South Slav nationpeoples of the same ethnic origin but divided by historical development.

This situation among the South Slavs bears remarkable similarities to the organization and function of secret terrorist societies among oppressed peoples in other countries—particularly Ireland and India—on the eve of World War I, although the Slav societies had no direct contact with India and Ireland, separated as they were by geography and culture.[3] The Bosnian experiences also bear similarities to processes of self-determination going on today in many economically underdeveloped parts of the world. Although their movement was short-lived and developed without a strictly defined ideology, Young Bosnians anticipated the historical content of struggles for national liberation in our own day. For they understood the dynamic character of relations between metropolitan and colonial peoples; the effect of war on obsolete institutions and the disintegration of imperial states; the interrelations of national and social elements in revolutionary movements in the unindustrialized parts of the world; and the significance of the ethical element in the conception of socialism.

One can deplore and disagree with the methods of political struggle used by Gavrilo Princip and his friends, but as individuals the men of Sarajevo—for patriotism, courage and selflessness—belong securely among that lofty group of primitive rebels which includes Sand and Orsini, Zasulich and Perovskaya, Connolly and Pearse.

MAJOR POLITICAL ASSASSINATIONS

1792-1914

1792 Gustavus III, King of Sweden
1793 Jean-Paul Marat, French Revolutionary leader
1793 Archbishop of Arles
1801 Paul I, Tsar of Russia
1804 Charles Pichegru, French general
1808 Selim III, Sultan of Turkey
1810 Count Axel Fersen, Swedish marshal
1812 Spencer Perceval, Prime Minister of Great Britain
1815 Guillaume Brune, French marshal
1817 Karadjorje, Serbian leader
1819 August Friedrich von Kotzebue, German dramatist, agent of Russian Tsar
1820 Charles Ferdinand, Duke de Berry, son of the French Heir Apparent
1829 Alexander Sergeyevich Griboyedov, Russian poet and ambassador to Persia
1829 Don Manuel Dorego, Governor of Buenos Aires
1841 Count Ioannes Antonios Kapodistrias, Greek statesman
1848 Count Pellegrino Luigi Rossi, Italian political leader
1854 Carlo III, Duke of Parma
1860 Danilo I, Prince of Montenegro
1865 Abraham Lincoln, President of the United States
1868 Thomas D'Arcy McGee, Canadian M. P.
1868 Mihailo Obrenović, Prince of Serbia
1869 S. Gutiérrez de Castro, Governor of Burgos
1870 Marshal Juan Prim, Prime Minister of Spain
1870 Victor Noir, French journalist
1872 Richard Southwell Bourke, Earl of Mayo, Viceroy of India
1875 Dr. Gabriel García Moreno, President of Ecuador
1876 Abdul Aziz, Sultan of Turkey

1876 Hussein Avni, Grand Vizier of Turkey
1878 N. V. Mezentsov, Russian general
1879 Prince D. N. Kropotkin, Governor of Kharkov
1881 Alexander II, Tsar of Russia
1881 James A. Garfield, President of the United States
1882 Lord Frederick Cavendish, British Chief Secretary for Ireland, and
      Thomas Henry Burke, Under Secretary
1882 Mehemet Ali Pasha, German-born Turkish general
1883 Colonel Grigori Porfirevich Sudeikin, Inspector of the Okhrana
1885 Bishop James Hannington
1886 French Deputy-Director Watrin
1890 Russian General Seliverstov
1891 James Wallace Quinton, British Commissioner in Assam
1892 Dr. Vucović, Bulgarian diplomat
1893 Carter Harrison, Mayor of Chicago
1894 Sadi Carnot, President of France
1895 Stefan Stambolov, Bulgarian statesman
1896 Nasr-ed-din, Shah of Persia
1896 Idiarte Borda, President of Uruguay
1897 Antonio Canovas del Castillo, Prime Minister of Spain
1898 José María Reina Barrios, President of Guatemala
1898 Empress Elisabeth of Austria
1899 Ulises Heureaux, President of Dominican Republic
1899 Notarbartolo of Palermo, member of the Italian Parliament
1900 James Lyall, British deputy consul in Bolivia
1900 Umberto, King of Italy
1901 Nikolai Pavlovich Bogolepov, Russian Minister of Education
1901 William McKinley, President of the United States
1902 Dmitri Sergeevich Sipiagin, Russian Minister of the Interior
1903 Alexander Obrenović, King of Serbia, and his wife, Queen Draga
1903 M. Bogdanovich, Russian governor
1904 General N. I. Bobrikov, Governor of Finland
1904 Viacheslav Konstantinovich Plehve, Russian Minister of the Interior
1904 Bogoslavsky, Governor of the Caucasus
1905 M. Johnson, Procurator of the Finnish Senate
1905 Grand Duke Sergei of Russia
1905 Theodoros Delyannis, Prime Minister of Greece
1905 Count I. E. Shuvalov, Prefect of the Moscow Police
1905 August von Hennings, Assistant Chief of Courland
1906 Professor Mikhail Yakovlevich Herzenstein, Jewish member of the Russian
      Duma
1906 Count Alexei Ignatiev of Moscow
1906 General Liarpiarski, Military Governor of Warsaw
1907 General von der Launitz, Prefect of the St. Petersburg Police
1907 Nikola Petkov, Prime Minister of Bulgaria
1907 Amin-es-Sultan, Prime Minister of Persia
1908 Carlos I, King of Portugal, and Luis Felipe, Crown Prince
1908 Count Potocky, Governor of Galicia
1908 Scott-Moncrieff, British Deputy Inspector of the Blue Nile Province
1909 Asutosh Bisuas, Public Prosecutor of Bengal
1909 Prince Dizhavakov of Transcaucasia
1909 Fehmi Effendi, Albanian politician
1909 Marquis Hirobumi Ito, Japanese statesman
1910 Butrus Pasha Gali, Prime Minister of Egypt
1911 Robert Ashe, District Magistrate at Tinnevelly, India
1911 Pyotr Arkadyevich Stolypin, Prime Minister of Russia
1911 Ramón Cáceres, President of the Dominican Republic
1912 José Canalejas y Méndez, Prime Minister of Spain

1912   Kopassis Effendi, Turkish Governor of Samos
1913   Francisco I. Madero, President of Mexico
1913   Franz Schuhmeier, Austrian Socialist leader
1913   George, King of Greece
1913   Nazim Pasha, Commander in Chief of the Turkish Army

ACKNOWLEDGMENTS

The author is indebted to the following archives, institutes and libraries for allowing him access to their collections:

The Archives of the Secretariat of Foreign Affairs of Yugoslavia for the Archives of Serbia, 1914–1917;

The State Archives of Bosnia and Hercegovina in Sarajevo;

The Archives of the City of Sarajevo;

The University Library Svetozar Marković, Belgrade;

The Haus-Hoff-Staatsarchiv in Vienna;

The Österreichisches Staatsarchiv Kriegsarchiv, Vienna;

The Auswärtiges Amt Archives in Bonn;

The Archives of the Ministère des Affaires Étrangères in Paris for the files on Serbia;

The National Archives of the United States of America for the papers of the American representatives in Serbia, 1903–1918.

Widener Library, Harvard University;

Houghton Library, also at Harvard, for permission to consult the papers of Leon Trotsky and John Reed;

The Hoover Institute for War, Peace and Revolution, Stanford, California, for information about the Okhrana files and Serbia, 1903–1917;

The Archives of the Utrikes Ministerium, Stockholm;

The Institute of Social History, Amsterdam;

St. Antony Library, Oxford, for the papers of Dragiša Stojadinović.

Professor E. Boltin of Moscow shared with me his knowledge of the Soviet bibliography relevant to the Sarajevo assassination.

I want particularly to record my gratitude to the late Dr. Max Hohenberg for opening the papers of his father, the Archduke Franz Ferdinand, to my inquiries. I thank Dr. Stoyan Pribićević for permission to quote from the archives of his late uncle, Adam Pribićević.

My understanding of the subject has been much enriched by conversation and correspondence with these contemporaries of the Sarajevo event: the late Ljubica Jovanović, Mrs. Jovanka Čubrilović, Dr. Vukosava Branisavljević-Čabrinović, Professor Vojislav Jovanović, Professor Božidar Zečević, Dr. Drago Ljubibratić, Professor Pero Slijepčević, Vojislav Gaćinović, Dr. Vid Gaković, Professor Juš Kozak, Dr. Srdjan Bjudisavljević, Professor Viktor Novak, and Professor Božidar Tomić, the last-named an important principal in the case and one of my earliest teachers, who deserves much of the ultimate credit and none of the blame for this work.

Miss Johanna Broda eased the burden of my work by unraveling the intricacies of the Austrian archives and by the sheer joy she brought to the task. My thanks also to Miss H. Pogats for her help in Vienna. Mrs. Pamela Bisdee was unusually helpful in the French archives as were Miss Slavica Fran, Mrs. Dušanka Barović and Miss Vuka Bugarčić in the Belgrade archives; Dr. Jovanka and Aco Djuričić and Miss B. Milević in the Sarajevo archives and Mrs. Lidija Subotin and Mrs. Vera Šuktić at University Library in Belgrade.

The author extends his thanks to his editor, Joseph Barnes, and to Jean Highland for her editorial assistance.

A word of appreciation is also due to many others who helped clear my literary conscience by turning fledgling English to somewhat more graceful prose, particularly Miss Muriel Brown in England and Miss Joan Reischauer in the United States. Mr. D. Ziegler was helpful in checking the footnotes. My deep thanks to Miss Imelda Lucas for her help in Manchester.

Much of my research was done while I was a research fellow at St. Antony's College, Oxford, from January 1961 through October 1963; I want to acknowledge the hospitality of its Warden, W. H. Deakin, and the eager assistance of its Librarian, Miss Anne Abbey.

The Sarajevo legend has tormented me from my early childhood. One of my uncles, Konstantin Babić, was a Young Bosnian who was killed at the age of nineteen. My late father, Professor Jevto Dedijer, was a close friend of Colonel Dragutin Dimitrijević-Apis, the leader of the Serbian secret society, Ujedinjenje ili Smrt (Unification or Death). My emotional interest turned to systematic thinking in 1937, when I edited together with a group of young Hercegovinians a *Festschrift* on the occasion of the twentieth anniversary of the death of Vladimir Gaćinović, the ideological leader of the Young Bosnians. Unfortunately, the book was banned at once by the government in Yugoslavia of that day. My pleasure was great when I found a volume of this rare and for me cherished book in the stacks of Widener Library.

I continued studying and discussing the Young Bosnians during the Second World War, particularly in long conversations with Veselin Masleša, a leading Bosnian economist and philosopher, during the night marches of our Partisan brigades through the mountains of Bosnia.

In 1953 I wrote two essays in the review *Nova Misao* in Belgrade, criticizing belief in the progressiveness of Colonel Apis and his followers, a notion cherished by my father. This theme was later developed in two articles in the review *Heute* in Vienna in 1959 and in the *Historical Journal* of Lund University in Sweden the following year.

In the course of discussing the outline of this book I turned again and again to Marijan Stilinović for the kind of rigorous criticism only an old and loyal friend can proffer. The dedication of this volume to his memory is hardly commensurate with my sense of obligation to him.

I want to take this opportunity to express my warmest appreciation for the friendship of the late D. P. Costello and of his wife, Bela, both of whom rendered my translations of Serbo-Croat poetry into the elegant prosody on these pages. His deep understanding of the tragic in life and his great knowledge of the elevated history of his native Ireland helped me to grasp the endless sadness of my own Bosnia and Hercegovina. I am also grateful to Mary Gluckman for her help in translating Ivo Andrić's "A Story from Japan."

I have also profited, as my work progressed, from queries and comments by students and faculty in the following universities where I have been privileged to lecture or teach: City College of New York, 1960 (On the Causes and Responsibility for the First World War); Oxford University, 1961 (a seminar on Serbian Government, Colonel Apis and the Young Bosnians); Stanford University, 1961 (a course on Yugoslav Primary Sources for the Outbreak of the First World War); Copenhagen University, 1961 (Ivo Andrić and the Young Bosnians); Lund University, Sweden, 1962 (Primitive Rebels of Bosnia); Studentersamfund, Oslo, 1963 (Ibsen and the Idea of Permanent Revolution— His Influence on the Young Bosnia Movement); Uppsala University, 1963 (*Widerstandsrecht* in Scandinavian Constitutional Law); Columbia University, 1964 (On Permanent Revolution).

The last pages and finishing touches of this book were written as the sun came up over the Charles River in Cambridge, Massachusetts. I am anxious to note my appreciation for the opportunity to write freely in the congenial community of disciplined minds that is Harvard University. For over three centuries Harvard has been a citadel of academic freedom, and with no less courage and dedication during the postwar ordeal of American liberty. And I am delighted to take this opportunity to thank Master John H. Finley for welcoming me and my family to Eliot House, over which he presides with special personal grace and intellectual authority.

—VLADIMIR DEDIJER

Widener Library, June 9, 1964

NOTES

CHAPTER I   (*pages 9–16*)

1. Militärkanzlei Erzherzog Franz Ferdinand Österreichisches Staatsarchiv-Kriegsarchiv (MKEFF), 1914, *Separatfascikel 50—Programm III für die Reise Seiner k. und k. Hoheit des durchlauchtigsten Herrn Generalinspektors der gesamten bewaffneten Macht Erzherzogs Franz Ferdinand nach Bosnien und der Hercegovina, vom 23–30 Juni 1914. Sonntag.* There is a special program for the Duchess of Hohenberg. She arrived before her husband, and because of her morganatic status, the Court Protocol did not allow her to attend some functions of her husband (e.g. the reception of the Bosnian government). In connection with this see Chapters XII, XIV, XVIII.

2. MKEFF, *loc. cit.*

3. Friedrich Funder, *Vom Gestern ins Heute*, p. 484.

4. A. Morsey, "Konopischt und Sarajevo," *Berliner Monatshefte*, June 1934, pp. 486–99.

5. *Narod*, Sarajevo, June 24, 1914.

6. L. Bilinski, *Wspomnienia i dokumenty 1846–1922*, p. 282.

7. B. Jevtić, *Sarajevski atentat*, p. 37.

8. *Ibid.*; V. Ćorović, *Odnosi izmedju Srbije i Austro-Ugarske u XX veku*, p. 595; D. Jevdjević, *Sarajevski atentatori*, p. 107.

9. Haus-Hof-Staatsarchiv (HHSTA); Nachlass Erzherzog Franz Ferdinand (NEFF), *Prozess in Sarajevo.*

10. *Neue Freie Presse*, June 29, 1914.

11. *Ibid.; Reichspost*, June 29, 1914.

12. *Neue Freie Presse*, June 29, 1914. Reuter's version, as published in *The Times* and the *Manchester Guardian* on June 29, 1914: "Herr Bürgermeister, we come here to pay a visit and bombs are thrown at us. Altogether this is an amazing indignity."

13. *Neue Freie Presse*, June 29, 1914.

14. *Ibid.*

15. P. Nikitsch-Boulles, *Vor dem Sturm*, p. 215.

16. P. Höger, "Erinnerungen an die Todesfahrt," *Österreichische Wehrzeitung*, June 27 and July 4, 1924.

17. NEFF, *Prozess in Sarajevo.* Potiorek's statement to the investigation judge on June 28, 1914.

18. *Ibid.*

19. Bilinski, p. 282.

20. Max Hohenberg in an interview by Maurice Verne, in *Paris-Soir-Dimanche*, July 4, 1937.

21. NEFF, *Prozess in Sarajevo.* Potiorek's statement to the investigation judge on June 28, 1914.

22. Max Hohenberg in an interview by Maurice Verne, *loc. cit.*

23. See Chapters XIV, XV and XVIII.

24. NEFF, *Prozess in Sarajevo.* Potiorek's statement to the investigation judge on June 28, 1914.

25. See Chapter XIV.

26. NEFF, *Prozess in Sarajevo.* Count Franz Harrach's statement

to the investigation judge on June 28, 1914.

27. Anonymous, *Sarajevska tragedija* (Djakovo, 1914), cited by N. Trišić, *Sarajevski atentat*, p. 39, and W. Glück, *Sarajewo*, p. 157.

28. This is the opinion of V. Ćorović (*Odnosi*, p. 595). The autopsy on the Archduke and the Duchess was carried out by Dr. Karl Wolfgang and Dr. Richard Pollak in the presence of Dr. Ferdinand Fischer, a physician in the imperial party, and two members of the Archduke's *Militärkanzlei* (NEFF, *Prozess in Sarajevo*). In the official minutes of the autopsy it was found that the Archduke's fatal wound was on the right side of the neck, 4 cm. from the chin and 2 cm. from the larynx, an irregular opening of 5 mm. The Duchess's wound was in the right groin, 4 cm. above the haunch bone (ilium), an opening of 6 cm. in the skin. It was stated that the wounds were entry wounds. The physicians concluded: "In both cases, the cause of death was internal bleeding. The wounds appear to be fatal ones, caused by a small-caliber weapon at close range; even immediate attention by a doctor would not have prevented death." (NEFF, *Prozess in Sarajevo*.)

29. The sculptress Ludmila Valić and her husband, painter Rudolf Valić, both from Sarajevo, were awakened in the night of June 28 and taken into the *Konak* to make death masks of the Archduke and his wife. Ludmila Valić described her experience and what she saw around the neck of the Archduke and his wife in an interview in *Vreme*, March 13, 1938.

CHAPTER II   *pages 17–26*

1. Viscount Grey of Fallodon, *Twenty-Five Years*, Vol. II, p. 308.

2. The estimate of Jovan Jo-

vanović, Serbian expert on 1914, quoted by Veselin Masleša, *Mlada Bosna*, p. 17.

3. Auswärtiges Amt 1939/41, Nr. 7, *Dokumente zum Konflikt mit Jugoslawien und Griechenland* (Berlin, 1941), p. 3; also Dr. Werner Frauendienst, *Jugoslawiens Weg zum Abgrund* (Berlin, 1941), pp. 11–25.

4. Professor Pharos (Father Anton Puntigam) stated this thesis in *Der Prozess gegen die Attentäter von Sarajevo*. Dr. Alfred von Wegerer expressed it several times in the review *Kriegsschuldfrage* and in the *Berliner Monatshefte*, which he edited until December 31, 1936; and he summarized the thesis in *Der Ausbruch des Weltkrieges*, Chapters I, II, V, VI, VII, IX, XIII, XX, XXI, XXIV, XXVIII and XIX. Also among the writers who upheld this idea are Dr. Hans Übersberger ("Das Sarajewoer Attentat und der Saloniki Prozess," *Neues Wiener Tageblatt*, May 31, 1927; *Der Saloniki Prozess*; "Dragutin Dimitrijevitsch und der Prozess von Saloniki," *Berliner Monatshefte*, October 1933, pp. 904–1004; "Das entscheidende Aktenstück zur Kriegsschuldfrage 1914," *Auswärtige Politik*, July 1943, pp. 429–38; *Österreich zwischen Russland und Serbien*, pp. 239–305) and Miloš Bogićević (*Causes of War; Le Procès de Salonique, Juin 1917; Le Colonel Dragoutine Dimitriewitch-Apis; Die auswärtige Politik Serbiens*); also Edith Durham (*The Sarajevo Crime*) and Harry Elmer Barnes (*The Genesis of the World War*). M. N. Pokrovsky, in the introduction to his *Imperiyalistecheskaya Voina* (Moscow, 1928), p. 8, stated that "Pašić and his ministers knew that the Archduke would be killed." The same thesis was expressed by N. P. Poletika in his *Sarayevsko Ubiistvo* (1930); but some thirty years later, after new

documents were found, Poletika adopted a different view in his *Vozniknovenie Pervoi Mirovoi Voini* (1964), pp. 236–37.

5. Sidney B. Fay, *The Origins of the World War*, 2d ed., Vol. II, p. 550. Of the antirevisionist historians in the Anglo-Saxon world the best known were Professor R. W. Seton-Watson, *Sarajevo*, and Professor Bernadotte Schmitt, *The Coming of the War*. A. J. P. Taylor has a similar thesis. He can be described as a revisionist of the revisionists, seeing their blind spots as they saw the blind spots of the original apologists for the war. In Yugoslavia the most complete defense of the Serbian government was given by Vladimir Ćorović, *Odnosi izmedju Srbije i Austro-Ugarske u XX veku*, in France by Ernest Denis, *La Grande Serbie* (Paris, 1917), and in the U.S.S.R. by E. V. Tarle, *Evropa v Epoku Imperiyalizma 1871–1919* (Moscow, 1928).

6. A group of Serbian left-wing political emigrees writing in *La Fédération Balkanique* in 1924 and 1925 denounced the heir apparent to the throne of Serbia in 1914, Prince Alexander Karadjordjević, as responsible for the assassination of the Archduke Franz Ferdinand. This accusation was repeated by Alfred von Wegerer in "König Alexander und die Attentäter von Sarajevo," *Kriegsschuldfrage*, July 1926, pp. 485–89.

7. This theory has been held by many writers from D. Lazarević, *Die Schwarze Hand*, (1914) until the present day, among them L. Albertini, *The Origins of the War of 1914*, Vol. II (1953); also Dragiša Stojadinović, "Srbija i Nemačka u Svetskom ratu," MS. written in 1935 and deposited in St. Antony's College Library, Oxford.

8. Professor Josef Kohler and Anton Puntigam, S.J., as early as 1918 hinted that Russia was to blame. They were followed by Nikola Nenadović ("Tajna beogradske kamarile," *La Fédération Balkanique*, December 1, 1924) and Victor Serge ("La Vérité sur l'attentat de Sarajevo—la complicité de l'état major russe," *Clarté*, May 1925), who alleged that the Russian General Staff was the driving force behind Colonel Dimitrijević-Apis. Hans Übersberger ("Das entscheidende Aktenstück zur Kriegsschuldfrage 1914," *loc. cit.*, and *Österreich zwischen Russland und Serbien*, pp. 239–305) expressed a similar view, as did H. E. Barnes (*op. cit.*, p. 12).

9. A. von Wegerer, "Das Attentat von Sarajevo und die Bolschewisten," *Berliner Monatshefte* XVI (January 1938), pp. 74–78, and *Der Ausbruch des Weltkrieges*, p. 82.

10. *The Official Shorthand Minutes of the Trial of the Trotskyite Center*, p. 594.

11. Count Ottokar Czernin, *In the World War* (London, 1919), p. 46. General Erich Ludendorff was a strong supporter of this theory, although at the same time he accused the Jesuits too of having a share in the plot. He was followed by Ernest Reventlow, H. Gruber and others. The story was that not only Serbian Freemasons, but also French, Hungarian, German and Scottish Freemasons took part in the conspiracy. Barnes (p. 96) claimed that the assassination was instigated by French President Poincaré and the Russian ambassador in Paris, Izvolsky. Poletika in his 1930 book said that it was not impossible that the French and British governments knew about the plot beforehand.

12. *Völkischer Beobachter*, January 29, 1936.

13. Auswärtiges Amt 1939/41, Nr. 7, *Dokumente*, p. 3.

14. Wickham Steed, article in *The Nineteenth Century*, October 1915; *Through Thirty Years*, pp. 400, 401, 403.

15. J. A. Žibert, *Der Mord von Sarajevo und Tiszas Schuld an dem Weltkriege;* also Stojadinović, *op. cit.* Czernin himself helped to give these theories currency by writing in 1919 that the Archduke Franz Ferdinand had complained to him about the plot against his life and "mentioned the names of several Austrian and Hungarian politicians who must have been in the secret." (Czernin, *op. cit.*, p. 46.) A. Debidour, *Histoire diplomatique de l'Europe* (Paris, 1916–17), Vol. I, p. 61, stated that Austrian authorities had organized the plot.

16. Max Hohenberg in an interview by Maurice Verne, *Paris-Soir-Dimanche*, July 4, 1937.

17. See William Bancroft, *McKinley, Garfield and Lincoln* (Chicago, 1901); John Coulter, *Our Martyr Presidents* (Chicago, 1901); Murat Halstead, *The Illustrious Life of William McKinley, Our Martyred President* (Chicago, 1901); Henry Neil, *Complete Life of William McKinley* (Chicago, 1901); George Washington Townsend, *Our Martyred President* (Philadelphia, 1901); R. Donovan, *The Assassins* (New York, 1952); and Margaret Leech, *In the Days of McKinley* (New York, 1959).

18. Lytton Strachey, *Queen Victoria* (London, 1931), pp. 239–42. In a report to the Home Secretary the Criminal Law Revision Committee recommended in 1963 that the verdict "guilty but insane" should be changed to one of "not guilty by reason of insanity."

19. Book of Judges 3:12–30; *ibid.* 4:18–24; Second Book of Kings, chapters 9 and 10.

20. Praise of tyrannicide is found as far back as the ancient Greek ode to Harmodius and Aristogei-ton (*Oxford Book of Greek Verse in Translation*, pp. 243 ff.). Among the more analytic Greek thinkers, Plato condemned tyranny in strong terms (*Republic*, Books IX and X) and Aristotle, though less severe, did not oppose tyrannicide (*Nicomachean Ethics*, VII, 10). Roman attitudes are indicated both by Cicero's praise for Caesar's assassins (*De Officiis*, III, 4) and by Tacitus' often quoted dictum, "*Nec regibus infinita aut libera potestas* —Neither is the power of kings free and unlimited" (*Germania*, 7).

21. *The Catholic Encyclopedia*, Vol. XV (New York, 1912), p. 108; *Enciclopedia cattolica*, Vol. XII (Rome, 1954), pp. 131–34. As for the attitude of the Roman Catholic Church today on the right to resistance and tyrannicide, the following account is given by the *Enciclopedia Cattolica:*

> A. The private citizen has no right to raise a murderous hand against the legitimate sovereign who has become a tyrant;
> B. People taken as an entity, as a political body, have the right to defend themselves against a government which is tyrannical; and in extreme cases, when oppression has reached a special degree of intensity and individual rights and personal safety are at stake, they have the right to resist actively, if there is no other way to shake off the yoke of tyranny.
>
> Pius XI recognized the positive value of this principle in the case of the oppressive regime in Mexico against the Catholics.

22. *Annual Register* (London, 1874), p. 225.

23. *The Times*, London, October 11, 1962.

24. This positive right of resistance is evident in such early medieval charters as the Golden Bull (1222), the *Joyeuse Entrée* of Brabant (1356), the Bavarian *Freiheitsbriefe* (c. 1301 and after), and the charters of many cities, which were given the express right to resist their princes and choose others if the reigning princes betrayed their trust by acting against the interest of the cities. (Wolzendorff, *Staatsrecht und Naturrecht in der Lehre vom Widerstandsrecht*, 1916, pp. 23–36.) This right derives from the dualistic constitution of the medieval corporate state, in which sovereignty is divided, part being located on one side in the ruler, part on the other in the estates, each side being self-sufficient and independent. The right of resistance was included as a means by which the lower orders could correct injustices and malfeasance by the sovereign. (Wolzendorff, p. 71.)

The idea originated in the practice by which a vassal could leave a lord who did not protect him, if he first declared his intention in a *diffidatio*. The right of resistance was then transferred from the individual vassal to the collective estate (*Stand*). It is an expression of the medieval principle that force not used in accordance with law may be resisted by force. (Wolzendorff, pp. 63–68.)

This grounding of the right of resistance in positive law extended to the "Monarchomachs," among whom the possibility of tyrannicide as a form of resistance was emphasized in opposition to the doctrine of the sovereignty of the prince then being strengthened by Roman law. These writers include many who opposed the absolute sovereignty of the prince for religious reasons: François Hotman, *Francogallia* (1573), Philippe du Plessis Mornay, *Vindiciae contra Tyrannos* (1574); Lambertus Danaeus, *Politices Christianae libri septem* (1596); J. Althusius, *Politica* (1603); and Juan de Mariana *De Rege et Regis Institutione* (1611).

25. *Milton's Prose Writing* (London, 1958), p. 186.

26. John Locke, *Of Civil Government*, Book II, Chapter 19.

27. John Stanhope, *The Cato Street Conspiracy* (London, 1962).

28. *Encyclopaedia Britannica* (1950), Vol. IX, p. 160.

29. Jean Maitron, *Histoire du mouvement anarchiste en France 1880–1914*, p. 236.

30. Boris Savinkov, *Memoirs of a Terrorist* (New York, 1931).

31. For instance, Woodcock (*Anarchism*, pp. 438–39) wrote the following about Czolgosz: "He claimed at his trial to be an anarchist, and bore himself with the same stoicism as Ravachol and Henry. But he belonged to no anarchist group and had only recently been denounced as a spy by a libertarian paper, *Free Society*, in Chicago."

32. Bernard Lewis, *Origins of Ismailism* (Cambridge, 1940); Vladimir Ivanow, *The Alleged Founder of Ismailism* (Bombay, 1946); and *Brief Survey of the Evolution of Ismailism* (Leiden, 1952).

33. *Annual Register* (1958), p. 34.

34. *Ibid.*

35. The Swedish professor Stig Jägerskjöld in 1962, after thorough research in the archives of the time of the Anckarström trial, published an essay in which he proved that the most important parts of Anckarström's confession were purposely excluded from the publition in 1792 of the written proceedings of the case; and that after the outrage derogatory rumors about Anckarström were ini-

tiated by persons in close proximity to the government and were passed on, in a crude form, as political propaganda. (Stig Jägerskjöld, *Tyrannmord och motståndsrätt 1792–1809.*)

Anckarström's defense was that he had put into practice the theory of resistance, that a subject possessed a legal right to resistance and regicide if the sovereign violated the constitutional rights of the people. Professor Jägerskjöld states that the doctrine of tyrannicide was energetically developed by the French Encyclopedists, whose teachings were widespread in Europe and well known to educated people in Sweden. It occurs in Swedish writings on constitutional law during the seventeeth and eighteenth centuries, which were strongly influenced by Milton, Locke, Montesquieu and Rousseau. The right of resistance to a usurping king was also implied in the Swedish Constitution of 1720, as well as in that of 1772. (Stig Jägerskjöld, *op. cit.*)

Professor Alfred Ross explains also in *Ever for demokrati* (Copenhagen, 1946), pp. 39–42, how much tyrannicide in Scandinavia was based on the constitutional tradition from early feudal times. He describes how kings in medieval Scandinavian countries were bound by positive law as well as by the very principles of law to accept the principle that the law was superior to them.

CHAPTER III   *pages 27–41*

1. The main works on Bogomilism are D. Kniewald, "The Veracity of the Latin Sources Regarding the Bosnian Christians," *Rad*, CCLXX, Yugoslav Academy of Science and Art; D. Obolensky, *The Bogomils* (Cambridge, 1948); B. Petranović, *Bogomili: Crkva bo-sanska i krstjani*, 1879; F. Rački, "The Bogomils and Patarini," *Rad*, VII, 84–179; VIII, 121–87; X, 160–263; J. Šidak, "The Problem of the 'Bosnian Church' in Our Historiography from Petranović to Glu-šac," *Rad*, CCLIX, 37–182; A. Solovjev, "The Disappearance of Bogomilism and the Islamization of Bosnia," *Godišnjak istoriskog društva Bosne i Hercegovine*, Vol. I, 42–79.

2. *Historija naroda Jugoslavije*, Vol. I (Zagreb, 1953), p. 586.

3. On the old Princips, B. Tomić wrote in *Nova Evropa, Narodna odbrana* and *Politika* several articles in 1939 and 1940. In letters to this writer he elaborated in greater detail some of the aspects of his research as published in 1939 and 1940. Wladyslaw Glück in *Sarajewo*, Chapter X, gives a thorough study of the life of the Princip family. Besides Tomić and Glück, G. Božović, D. Ljubibratić and particularly V. Lebedev contributed further details about the life of Princip's ancestors. The details about Princip's *zadruga* are from B. Tomić, "Rod i dom Gavrila Principa," *Narodna odbrana*, December 1, 1939.

4. B. Tomić, "Poreklo i detinjstvo Gavrila Principa," *Nova Evropa*, XXXII (1939); also G. Božović, "Rodni prag Gavrila Principa," *Politika*, July 21, 1939.

5. B. Tomić, "Poreklo i detinjstvo Gavrila Principa."

6. *Ibid.*

7. *Ibid.*

8. *Ibid.*

9. Glück, p. 197. The Montenegrin Prince-Bishop Petar Petrović Njegoš in his epic *The Mountain Wreath* also mentioned the word *princip*, in verse 1624.

10. T. Kruševac, *Petar Kočić*, p. 372. About the agrarian conditions before 1875 see K. Grünberg, *Die Agrarverfassung und die Grundent-*

lastungsprobleme in Bosnien und der Herzegowina, Chapters II and III; and V. Bogićević, "Stanje raje u Bosni i Hercegovini pred ustanak 1875-1878," *Godišnjak istoriskog društva Bosne i Hercegovine*, Vol. II, pp. 143-84.

11. In the Yugoslav historiography the two recent works on the 1875 uprising are V. Čubrilović, *Bosansko-hercegovački ustanak* (Belgrade, 1939), and M. Ekmečić, "Početak Bosanskog ustanak 1875 g.," *Godišnjak istoriskog društva Bosne i Hercegovine*, VI (1954), pp. 267-305, and *Ustanak u Bosni 1875-1878* (Sarajevo, 1960). Ekmečić treats the 1875-78 uprising primarily as an agrarian rebellion, while Professor Čubrilović sees also the national elements in it.

12. *Annual Register* (1875), p. 275.

13. *Ibid.*, p. 277.

14. V. Čubrilović, *Bosansko-hercegovački ustanak*, pp. 41-42. See also M. Ekmečić, "Uloga Don Ivana Mušića u Hercegovačkom ustanku 1875-1878," *Godišnjak istoriskog društva Bosne i Hercegovine*, VII (1955), pp. 141-69.

15. A. Evans, *Through Bosnia and Herzegovina on Foot;* and *Illyrian Letters*.

16. Evans, *Through Bosnia and Herzegovina on Foot*, p. 331.

17. *Ibid.*, p. 258.

18. V. Masleša, *Mlada Bosna*, p. 22.

19. Evans, *Through Bosnia and Herzegovina on Foot*, p. 336.

20. Evans, *Illyrian Letters*, pp. 18-19.

21. B. Tomić, "Poreklo i detinjstvo Gavrila Principa," *loc. cit.*

22. D. Ljubibratić, *Gavrilo Princip*, p. 24.

23. Evans, *Illyrian Letters*, pp. 15-16.

24. *Ibid.*, pp. 16-17.

25. *Ibid.*, pp. 41, 42.

26. *Ibid.*, pp. 33-34.

27. *Ibid.*, pp. 122-23.

28. Evans, *Through Bosnia*, p. 265.

29. *Ibid.*, p. 266.

30. A. Evans, article in the *Manchester Guardian*, February 8, 1877.

31. Evans, *Illyrian Letters*, p. 104-5.

32. Evans, *Through Bosnia*, p. 277.

33. B. Tomić, "Poreklo i detinjstvo Gavrila Principa," *loc. cit.*

34. Evans (*Illyrian Letters*, p. 218) estimated that 115,000 refugees fled to Dalmatia and Lika, 90,000 to Montenegro, and 40,000 to Serbia. G. Jakšić (*Bosna i Hercegovina na Berlinskom kongresu*, Belgrade 1955, p. 22) thought that the number of the refugees was 230,000.

CHAPTER IV   *pages 42-67*

1. B. H. Sumner, *Russia and the Balkans 1870-1880* (London, 1937), p. 100.

2. A. Fournier, *Wie wir zu Bosnien kamen* (Vienna, 1909), p. 4.

3. *Annual Register* (1878), p. 307.

4. *Ibid.*

5. Sumner, p. 102.

6. W. F. Monypenny and G. E. Buckle, *Life of Benjamin Disraeli*, Vol. VI, (London, 1920), p. 13.

7. R. W. Seton-Watson, *The Role of Bosnia in International Politics—1875-1914* (London, 1931), p. 17.

8. Monypenny and Buckle, Vol. VI, p. 35.

9. *Annual Register* (1876), p. 114.

10. Vaso Cubrilović, *Istorija političke misli u Srbiji XIX veka* (Belgrade, 1958), p. 160.

11. D. Stranjaković, "Kako je postalo Garašaninovo 'Načertanije,' " *Spomenik SAN*, XCI (Belgrade, 1939), p. 115.

12. *Ibid.*, p. 118.

13. *Ibid.*, p. 114.

14. *Ibid.*, p. 116.

15. The text of *Načertanije* was for the first time published by Milenko Vesnić in *Delo* in 1906, although the Austro-Hungarian authorities already in 1883 had a copy of this document. Hungarian historian J. Tim published the Magyar translation of *Načertanije* in 1931. See also: D. Stranjaković, *Vlada ustavobranitelja 1842–1853* (1932); "Jugoslovenski nacionalni državni program kneževine Srbije iz 1844," *Glasnik istoriskog društva*, IV (Novi Sad, 1931), pp. 392–418; and "Kako je postalo Garašaninovo 'Načertanije,'" *Spomenik SAN* (1939), pp. 63–113. Also M. Handelsmann, "La Question d'Orient et la politique Yougoslave du prince Czartoryski après 1840," *Séances et travaux de l'Académie des sciences morales et politiques* (Paris, 1929), pp. 19–26; V. Čubrilović, *Istorija političke misli*, pp. 156–95; V. J. Vučković, "Knez Miloš i osnovna politička misao sadržana-u Garašaninovom 'Načertanija,'" *Jugoslovenska revija za medjunarodno pravo*, Vol. I (Belgrade, 1957), pp. 35–44.

16. V. J. Vučković, "Nacionalno-revolucionarne akcije Srbije u Vojnoj Granici," *Zbornik Matice Srpske*, IX (Novi Sad, 1954), p. 4.

17. M. Ekmečić, "Nacionalna politika Srbije prema Bosni i Hercegovini i agrarno pitanje 1844–1875," *Godišnjak istoriskog društva Bosne i Hercegovine*, X (1959), pp. 197–219.

18. S. Jovanović, *Vlada Milana Obrenovića* (Belgrade, 1934), Vol. I, p. 81.

19. *Ibid.*, pp. 79–81.

20. *Annual Register* (1876), p. 114.

21. S. Jovanović, *Druga vlada Miloša i Mihaila* (Belgrade, 1933), p. 394.

22. *Ibid.*, p. 383.

23. V. Ćorović, "Hercegovački ustanak," *Enciklopedija Srba, Hrvata i Slovenaca*, Vol. I, pp. 240, 434.

24. Wilhelm E. Mallmann, "Giuseppe Mazzini und seine Epigonen," *Neues Abendland*, 4 (Munich, 1956), p. 338.

25. S. Jovanović, *Druga vlada*, p. 386. See also H. Wendel, *Bismarck und Serbien in Jahre 1866* (Berlin, 1927).

26. J. Skerlić, *Svetozar Marković*, (Belgrade, 1909), p. 27. In the Soviet Union several works have been published about Marković's early activities. E. Koseva, "Iz Russkoserbski Revolutsioni Svyazi 1870–h godov," *A.N. SSSR, Učbenie zapiski Slavjanovedenija*, I (Moscow, 1949). See also A. S. Pulinetz, "N. G. Chernishevsky and S. Marković," *Scientific Proceedings of Chernovitzki University*, Vol. XXX, Philological Series, No. VI (1958); J. D. Belayeva, "The Struggle of Marković for Realism in Serbian Literature," *Slav People's Literature*, No. III (Moscow, 1958).

27. Skerlić, *Marković*, p. 34.

28. Marković, "Ruski revolucionari i Nečajev," *Radenik* (Belgrade, 1871), No. 3, quoted by Skerlić, *Marković*, pp. 128–29.

29. *Ibid.*

30. Marković, "Slovenska Austrija i srpsko jedinstvo," *Radenik* (1881), No. 24, quoted from Skerlić, *Marković*, p. 183.

31. Vučković, "Nacionalno-revolucionarne," *Zbornik Matice Srpske*, IX (1954), p. 4.

32. Čubrilović, *Istorija političke misli*, p. 337.

33. *Ibid.*, p. 297.

34. Skerlić, *Marković*, p. 180.

35. *Ibid.* Skerlić cites as sources: *Sobranie sočinenia;* M. N. Dragomanova, *K. Biografii A. I. Zelyabova*, II (Paris), pp. 433–34.

36. Skerlić, "Ruski revolucionari i srpski ratovi 1875–1876" (a review of V. Bogucharski, *Russkoye Osvoboditelnoye Dvizhenie i Voina za Osvobozhdenie Bolgarii*), in *Srpski književni glasnik*, July 1911, pp. 74–78.

37. *Ibid.*

38. *Ibid.*

39. Skerlić, *Marković*, p. 180.

40. F. Venturi, *Roots of Revolution* (London, 1960), pp. 559–61.

41. Skerlić, "Ruski revolucionari," *loc. cit.*

42. Venturi, p. 561.

43. "Program Vase Pelagića iz 1874 o oslobodjenju Bosne i Hercegovine," *Pregled*, I (1959), p. 455.

44. V. Pelagić, *Borba za oslobodjenje—Istorija Bosansko-hercegovačke bune u svezi srpsko-vlaško-bugarsko i rusko-turksim ratom*, 3d ed. (Belgrade, 1882), pp. 131, 143.

45. *Ibid.*, pp. 149–50.

46. *Ibid.*, p. 181.

47. "*Zastava*" o Bosni i Hercegovini, *1874–1876*, III, (Sarajevo, 1954), p. 312. The name of Barbanti Brodano's book is *Su la Drina*, a part of *Ricordi a studi slavi* (Milan, 1878), p. 193.

48. R. Petković, "Djelovanje Dubrovačkog odbora za pomaganje hercegovačkih ustanika 1875–1878 godine," *Godišnjak istoriskog društva Bosne i Hercegovine* (1959), 10, pp. 221, 245.

49. Medlicott, *The Congress of Berlin and After* (London, 1938), p. 25.

50. G. Jakšić, *Bosna i Hercegovina na Berlinskom kongresu* (Belgrade, 1955), p. 38.

51. Monypenny and Buckle, *op. cit.*, Vol. VI, pp. 328–29.

52. *Annual Register* (1878), p. 292.

53. *Ibid.*

54. HHSTA, PA III, *Berliner Kongress*: Josef Freiherr von Schwegel, "Vom Berliner Kongress 1878 (Auszüge aus einer vertraulichen Korrespondenz)."

55. *Annual Register* (1874), p. 225.

56. Sumner, *op. cit.*, p. 507.

57. Monypenny and Buckle, Vol. VI, p. 328.

58. HHSTA, PA III, *Berliner Kongress*, 116, Protokoll 8.

59. *Ibid.*

60. *Ibid.*

61. Sumner, p. 506.

62. HHSTA, PA III, *Berliner Kongress*, 116, Protokoll 8.

63. *Ibid.*

64. Sumner, pp. 506–7.

65. HHSTA, PA III, *Berliner Kongress*, 116 Protokoll 8.

66. Monypenny and Buckle, Vol. VI, p. 320.

67. HHSTA, PA III, *Berliner Kongress*, 116, Protokoll 8.

68. *Ibid.*

69. *Ibid.*, 115.

70. *Ibid.*

71. Fournier, *op. cit.*, pp. 81–82; cf. Čubrilović, *Istorija političke misli*, pp. 379–83.

72. HHSTA, PA III, *Berliner Kongress*, 115.

73. *Annual Register* (1878), p. 312.

74. *Ibid.*, p. 321.

75. *Ibid.*

76. Monypenny and Buckle, Vol. VI, pp. 317–18.

77. HHSTA, PA III, *Berliner Kongress*, 116, Protokoll No. 32, June 27.

78. *Ibid.*, Protokoll No. 12, March 2.

79. Sumner, p. 513.

80. Skerlić, *Istorija nove srpske književnosti*, 3d ed. (Belgrade, 1953), p. 289.

81. *Ibid.*, p. 287.

82. *Ibid.*, p. 295.

83. J. Jovanović-Zmaj, "Posle rata—Konferencija," *Ilustrovna ratna kronika* (Novi Sad, 1877–78), 6, pp. 377–78.

84. *Annual Register* (1878), p. 313.

85. *Ibid.*

86. *Ibid.*, p. 316.

87. *Ibid.*, p. 131.

88. *Ibid.*, p. 318.

89. *Die Okkupation Bosnien und der Hercegovina durch K.K. Truppen im Jahre 1878. Nach authentischen Quellen dargestellt in der Abteilung für Kriegsgeschichte des K. K. Kriegs-Archivs. Verluste bei den Okkupationskämpfen, I–X, in Österr. militär. Zeitschrift 1878, 2* vols.

90. B. Tomić, "Rod i dom Gavrila Principa," *Narodna odbrana*, December 1, 1939; and "Poreklo i detinjstvo Gavrila Principa, *Nova Evropa*, XXXII (1939).

91. D. Jevdjević, *Sarajevski atentatori*, p. 99.

CHAPTER V   *pages 68–87*

1. NEFF, I—B, C, D.

2. F. Vaniček, *Spezialgeschichte der Militärgrenze* (Vienna, 1875), Vol. I, pp. 151, 182, 231, 254; Vol. II, p. 44; Vol. III, p. 296.

3. J. Cvijić, *Balkansko Poluostrvo i jugoslovenske zemlje*, Vol. II, p. 68.

4. Vaniček, Vol. I, p. 288.

5. *Ibid.*, p. 292.

6. *Ibid.*, p. 299.

7. *Ibid.*, p. 344.

8. *Ibid.*, Vol. II, p. 327.

9. *Ibid.*, p. 349.

10. *Ibid.*, p. 487.

11. *Ibid.*, Vol. IV, p. 103.

12. *Ibid.*, p. 141.

13. *Ibid.*

14. Metternich, *Mémoires*, Vol. V (Paris, 1880), p. 393.

15. B. King, *A History of Italian Unity*, Vol. I (London, 1889), p. 79.

16. Vaniček, Vol. IV, p. 174.

17. *Ibid.*, p. 179.

18. *Ibid.*, p. 211.

19. Vučković, "Nacionalno-revolucionarne akcije," *Zbornik Matice Srpske*, IX (1954), special print, p. 4.

20. Petar Petrović Njegoš, letter of November 20, 1848, *Pisma*, (Belgrade, 1955).

21. G. Schwarzenberger, *Power Politics* (London, 1953), p. 53.

22. O. Jászi, *The Dissolution of the Habsburg Monarchy*, p. 101.

23. O. Ernst, *Franz Joseph as Revealed by His Letters* (London, 1927), pp. 96–97.

24. *Ibid.*, p. 95.

25. *Ibid.*, p. 99.

26. *Ibid.*, p. 101.

27. *K. u. K. Statistische Zentralkommission, Census 1867.*

28. About Strossmayer's activity see F. Šišić, *Letters Rački–Strossmayer*, 4 vols. (Zagreb, 1928–31); Tade Smičiklas, *Nacrt života i rada biskupa J. J. Strossmayera* (Zagreb, 1926); Andrija Špiletak, *Biskup J. J. Strossmayer u vatikanskom koncilu* (Zagreb, 1929).

29. V. Dedijer, *Prilozi za biografiju J. B. Tita* (Belgrade, 1953), pp. 46–47.

30. R. Kann, *The Multinational Empire*, Vol. I (New York, 1950), p. 110.

31. J. Horvat, *Politička povijest Hrvatske* (Zagreb, 1936), p. 336.

32. For more details see F. Zwitter, Jaroslav Šidak, 2nd Vasa Bogdanov, *Les Problèmes nationaux dans la monarchie des Habsburg* (Belgrade, 1960).

33. HHSTA, PA III, *Berliner Kongress*, 116, Protokoll 8.

34. J. Baernreither, *Fragments of a Political Diary*, (London, 1930), p. 66.

35. *Ibid.*

36. T. Kruševac, *Petar Kočić*, p. 330.

37. *Die Ergebnisse der Volkszahlung in Bosnien und der Hercegovina vom 10 Oktober 1910* (Sarajevo, 1912), pp. 14–43. Of 1,898,-044 inhabitants only 177,168 were

literate. The number of children up
to seven years of age was 414,973.

38. See Chapter XII.

39. *Enciklopedija Srba, Hrvata i
Slovenaca*, Vol. II, p. 386.

40. S. Jovanović, *Vlada Milana
Obrenovića*, Vol. II, pp. 218–19.

41. HHSTA, PA III, *Berliner
Kongress*, 116, Protokoll 32–27/6.

42. G. Jakšić, "Istorija tajne kon-
vencije," *Arhiv za pravne i druš-
vene nauke* (Belgrade, 1924).

43. *Ibid.*

44. S. Jovanović, *Vlada Milana
Obrenovića*, Vol. II, p. 348.

45. J. Ristić, *Diplomatska istorija
Srbije*, Vol. II (Belgrade, 1893),
p. 250.

46. For the details of the plot see
D. Vasić, *Devetsto treća* (Belgrade,
1925).

47. Pavel Šatev, *V Makedonii
pod Robstvo* (Sofia, 1934), pp. 45–
46.

48. Ljuben Lapev, *Kratak pregled makedonske istorije*, (Belgrade, 1955), p. 20.

CHAPTER VI   *pages 88–117*

1. There exist several biographies
of the Archduke Franz Ferdinand.
Three of them were written during his lifetime. The first two—
Falkenegg, *Erzherzog Franz Ferdinand von Österreich-Este;* and H.
Heller, *Franz Ferdinand*—are of no
particular importance. This is not
the case with the third one, *Erzherzog Franz Ferdinand unser Thronfolger*, published as a special illus-
trated issue of *Österreichische
Rundschau*, December 18, 1913, on
the occasion of the Archduke's
fiftieth birthday. The Archduke
himself gave his approval for the
selection of the contributors (Sosnosky, *Franz Ferdinand, der Erzherzog-Thronfolger: Ein Lebensbild.* p. v). Leopold Count von
Chlumecky wrote the introduction.
He was the editor of *Österreichi-*

sche Rundschau, often regarded as
one of the mouthpieces of Belvedere. (G. Franz, *Erzherzog Franz
Ferdinand und die Pläne zur Reform der Habsburger Monarchie*,
p. 70.)

After the Archduke's death several biographies were published.
The first two in book form were
written by two of his former closest collaborators, Chlumecky (*Erzherzog Franz Ferdinands Wirken
und Wollen*) and Sosnosky (*Franz
Ferdinand der Erzherzog-Thronfolger*). Both Chlumecky and Sosnosky published a number of the
Archduke's letters. However, their
choice of letters and their portrait
of the Archduke were rather arbitrary; they tried to represent the
Archduke in such a light as to support the views of the Revisionists
in the great debate over the responsibility for the outbreak of the First
World War. Before them Edmund
Glaise-Horstenau published in
1926, in *Neue Österreichische Bibliographie*, a short biography of
the Archduke. Maurice Muret's
L'Archiduc François Ferdinand is
an anti-Revisionist book with lots
of material collected from the contemporaries of the Archduke, but
one of the weaknesses of this book
is its lack of source citations.

Of the books written by men
around the Archduke, the most revealing book was that of his private
physician Victor Eisenmenger,
Erzherzog Franz Ferdinand. The
Archduke's private secretary Paul
Nikitsch-Boulles published his recollections of the Archduke in *Vor
dem Sturm* (Berlin, 1925). The first
chief of the Archduke's *Militärkanzlei*, Colonel Alexander Brosch
von Aarenau wrote in 1913 a personal letter to General Woinovich
in which he described the Archduke's character. The letter is of
great historical importance, and
Chlumecky published it in his book

(pp. 354–62). The second chief of the *Militärkanzlei*, Colonel Dr. Karl Bardolff, in his *Soldat im alten Österreich* spoke in the third chapter (pp. 107–87) about the Archduke. Bardolff also published several articles about the Archduke and his plans for the reform of the Habsburg Empire (see Chapter VII). Several other people who either worked with the Archduke or knew him have written about him. Among these the most important are Albert Freiherr von Margutti, *Vom alten Kaiser* (English edition, *The Emperor Francis Joseph and His Times;* French edition, *La Tragédie des Habsbourgs*); Czernin, *Im Weltkriege* (English edition, *In the World War*); Moritz von Auffenberg-Komarow, *Aus Österreichs Höhe und Niedergang;* General Franz Conrad von Hötzendorf, *Aus meiner Dienstzeit 1906–1918* in five volumes. Rudolf Sieghardt (*Die letzten Jahrzehnte einer Grossmacht*), Alexander Spitzmüller-Harmersbach (. . . *und hat auch Ursach, es zu leben*) and Milan Hodža (*Federation in Central Europe*) wrote about their contacts with the Archduke. The former Austro-Hungarian Joint Minister of Finance, Leon von Bilinski in his memoirs (*Wspomnienia i dokumenty 1846–1922*) mentioned rather briefly his relations with the Archduke. J. Redlich's *Kaiser Franz Josef von Österreich* has a chapter on the Archduke.

There are several books on the Archduke in Hungarian. The most important was written by his close collaborator Josef von Kristoffy, *Magyarország kalváriája*. Others are Gyozo Bruckner, *Ferenc Ferdinand tronorokos magyarorszagi politikai* (Miskolc, 1929) and Oliver Eottevenyi, *Ferenc Ferdinand* (Budapest, 1942).

In 1943 Georg Franz published his valuable book *Erzherzog Franz Ferdinand und die Pläne zur Reform der Habsburger Monarchie.* Of similar historical value are Johann Christoph Allmayer-Beck's *Erzherzog Franz Ferdinand und Baron Max von Beck* (Vienna, 1948) and *Ministerpräsident Baron Beck* (Munich, 1956), both written on the basis of much previously unpublished historical evidence. Although Rudolf Kiszling was the first historian with access to the *Nachlass* to write a biography of the Archduke (*Erzherzog Franz Ferdinand von Österreich-Este*), his work is lacking in historical objectivity. In his choice of documents and in his interpretation, he defended the Habsburg legitimistic attitudes. Robert Kann's contribution is more objective. In his two-volume *The Multinational Empire* he describes the Archduke's plans for the reform of the Habsburg monarchy (Vol. II, pp. 187–97). After his research in the *Nachlass,* Kann wrote "Emperor William II and the Archduke Francis Ferdinand in Their Correspondence" (*American Historical Review,* LVII, January 1952) and "Count Ottokar Czernin and Archduke Francis Ferdinand" (*Journal of Central European Affairs,* July 1956).

2. The *Nachlass Erzherzog Franz Ferdinand* (NEFF) is deposited in the *Haus-Hoff-Staatsarchiv* (HHSTA) in Vienna. It consists of seven parts: (1) personal documents and papers; (2) letters (23 boxes and 3 fascicles); (3) *Obershofmeisteramtsaken* (14 fascicles); (4) the acts of the *Militärkanzlei* (24 fascicles); (5) memorandums and pamphlets (6 fascicles); (6) collection of clippings from the press (41 volumes and 4 fascicles); (7) the trial in Sarajevo (one volume).

3. The archives of the *Militärkanzlei* (MKEFF) are deposited in

the *Österreichisches Staatsarchiv-Kriegsarchiv* (KA) in Vienna, and they consist of 200 boxes and 40 bound volumes, covering the period of 1898–1914.

4. O. Ernst, *Franz Joseph as Revealed by His Letters*, p. 190.

5. J. Redlich, *Emperor Francis Joseph of Austria*, pp. 199–200.

6. O. Forst, *Ahnentafel Seiner Kaiserlichen und Königlichen Hoheit, Des Durchlauchtigsten Herrn Erzherzogs Franz Ferdinand von Österreich-Este* (Vienna and Leipzig, 1910), p. 16.

7. *Annual Register* (1856), p. 237.

8. Dr. Wiard Klopp, *Onno Klopp* (Osnabrück, 1907), p. 126.

9. Kiszling, *Erzherzog*, p. 11.

10. Muret, *L'Archiduc François Ferdinand*, p. 18.

11. Kiszling, *Erzherzog*, p. 11.

12. *Ibid.*

13. *Erzherzog Franz Ferdinand unser Thronfolger* (Vienna, 1913), p. 12.

14. Allmayer-Beck, *Ministerpräsident*, 26ff.

15. Eisenmenger, *Erzherzog Franz Ferdinand*, p. 210.

16. NEFF, Box 5. In the NEFF are a great number of letters, official and private, telegrams, memorandums and similar documents exchanged between the Emperor and his nephew, which throw more light on their relations. Their correspondence, containing mainly the letters of the Emperor to Franz Ferdinand is deposited in three boxes (1,2,23). There are, all together, 231 letters and telegrams. The first Franz Josef letter is dated April 13, 1878, and the last one April 25, 1914. Franz Ferdinand's first letter is dated May 15, 1893, and the last one October 25, 1913.

17. Sumner, *Russia and the Balkans 1870–1880*, p. 154; also D. Kosary, *A History of Hungary* (New York, 1941), p. 300.

18. Archduke Albrecht to Franz Ferdinand, October 18, 1889, NEFF, Box 2.

19. Margutti, *The Emperor Francis Joseph and His Times*, p. 106.

20. NEFF, Letters, Box 5.

21. *Ibid.*

22. *Ibid.*

23. *Ibid.*

24. NEFF, Letters, Box 2.

25. *Ibid.*

26. *Ibid.*

27. Eisenmenger, *Erzherzog Franz Ferdinand*, p. 215.

28. Adam Müller-Guttenbrunn, *Franz Ferdinands Lebensroman* (Stuttgart, 1919), p. 17.

29. Kiszling, *Erzherzog*, p. 19.

30. Glaise-Horstenau, *Franz Josefs Weggefährte* (Vienna, 1920), p. 476.

31. Jászi (*Dissolution of the Habsburg Monarchy*, p. 237) mentions the incident without giving the name of the British ambassador; Muret (*L'Archiduc*, p. 20) gives the name.

32. Redlich, *Emperor Francis Joseph*, p. 477; also Jászi p. 237.

33. Erzherzog Franz Ferdinand, *Tagebuch meiner Reise um die Erde*. Vol. I, Introduction.

34. NEFF, Letters, Box 1.

35. V. Eisenmenger, *Erzherzog Franz Ferdinand*, p. 279.

36. NEFF, Letters, Box 1.

37. *Documents diplomatiques français, 1871–1914* (DDF), Vol. VI, p. 570, the report of May 20, 1913, and Vol. X, p. 247.

38. Czernin, *In the World War*, p. 41.

39. Conrad, *Aus meiner Dienstzeit*, Vol. I, p. 158.

40. Seton-Watson, *Sarajevo*, pp. 90–91.

41. V. Eisenmenger, *Erzherzog Franz Ferdinand*, p. 277. A contrary opinion was expressed by Professor H. Kantorowicz in *Das Tagebuch* (Berlin), October 13,

1928; see also E. Bagger, *Francis Joseph* (New York, 1927), p. 52.

42. Chlumecky, pp. 356–57.

43. Eisenmenger, *Erzherzog*, p. 71.

44. *Ibid.*, pp. 202–3.

45. NEFF, Letters, Box 1.

46. Eisenmenger, *Erzherzog*, p. 186.

47. NEFF, Letters, Box 1.

48. Franz Ferdinand's letter to Major Brosch, April 18, 1909, published in Chlumecky, *Erzherzog Franz Ferdinand*, p. 327.

49. Eisenmenger, *Erzherzog*, p. 197.

50. Archives of the French Ministry of Foreign Affairs (AFR), FA, I, 90. VA–MAE, January 18, 1901.

51. Eisenmenger, *Erzherzog*, pp. 355–56.

52. *Ibid.*, p. 209.

53. Czernin, *In the World War*, p. 35.

54. S. Grossman, *März* (Munich), quoted in *Pijemont*, December 2, 1913.

55. Nikitsch-Boulles, *Vor dem Sturm*, p. 19.

56. Allmayer-Beck, *Ministerpräsident*, p. 48; also Sosnosky, *Franz Ferdinand der Erzherzog-Thronfolger*, p. 23.

57. K. Renner, quoted in *Arbeiter Zeitung*, March 16, 1910.

58. Allmayer-Beck, *Ministerpräsident*, p. 39; Sieghardt, *Die letzten Jahrzehnte*, p. 64.

59. Sosnosky, p. 35.

60. NEFF, Letters, Box 1.

61. *Ibid.*

62. *Ibid.*

63. NEFF, 15 2/5, 45.

64. Sforza, *Makers of Modern Europe* (London, 1932), p. 132.

65. Allmayer-Beck, *Ministerpräsident*, p. 48.

66. Eisenmenger, *Erzherzog*, p. 211.

67. Margutti *The Emperor Francis Joseph*, p. 129.

68. Kiszling, *Erzherzog*, p. 175.

69. Allmayer-Beck, *Ministerpräsident*, p. 54.

70. *Politika*, June 29, 1914.

71. Nikitsch-Boulles, *Vor dem Sturm*, pp. 52-56.

72. *Ibid.*

73. *Ibid.*

74. Spitzmüller-Harmersbach, *. . . und hat auch Ursach*, p. 99.

75. See Chapter VIII.

76. G. Salvemini, *Mussolini diplomatico* (Bari, 1946), pp. 269–70.

77. Kiszling, *Erzherzog*, p. 245.

78. Spitzmüller-Harmersbach p. 74.

79. Jenks, *Vienna and the Young Hitler* (New York, 1960), p. 49.

80. *Ibid.*, p. 50.

81. Hitler, *Mein Kampf* (New York, 1940), p. 72.

82. Bardolff, *Soldat im alten Österreich*, p. 123.

83. Kiszling, *Erzherzog*, p. 245.

84. *Annual Register* (1906), p. 310.

85. H. Heller, *Franz Ferdinand* (Vienna, 1911), p. 22.

86. NEFF, Letters, Box 1.

87. Kiszling, *Erzherzog*, p. 61.

88. Conrad, *Aus meiner Dienstzeit*, Vol. I, p. 328.

89. Bardolff, p. 133.

90. NEFF, Letters, Box 14.

91. *Ibid.*

92. *Ibid.*

93. *Ibid.*

94. *Ibid.*

95. *Ibid.*

96. Spitzmüller-Harmersbach, *. . . und hat auch Ursach*, p. 181.

97. NEFF, Letters, Box 5.

98. *Ibid.*

99. *Ibid.*

100. Margutti, *The Emperor Francis Joseph*, p. 124.

101. NEFF, Letters, Box 6

102. Czernin, *In the World War*, p. 65.

103. Kann, *Multinational Empire*, Vol. II, p. 223.

104. Kiszling, *Erzherzog*, p. 100.

105. *Ibid.*, p. 114.
106. NEFF, Archduke Albrecht to Franz Ferdinand, July 28, 1892.
107. Allmayer-Beck, *Ministerpräsident*, p. 101.
108. Brosch wrote about the role of the Archduke in the reorganization of the army in his letter to General Woinovich in 1913, as quoted by Chlumecky (p. 354–62): "Maybe nobody in the monarchy is so concerned as he that dynasty and army belong together, that they are both the basic pillars on which the state rises and falls. A reliable army, responsible only to the Emperor, indifferent to the nationalities, seemed to him absolutely necessary for the empire and for the existence of the dynasty." Both Bardolff (p. 140) and Sosnosky (p. 106) shared Brosch's opinion.
109. Redlich, *Emperor Francis Joseph of Austria*, p. 492.
110. MKEFF, Pa 17/10 res
111. *Arbeiter Zeitung*, March 16, 1910. A similar opinion was expressed by the Austrian Prime Minister E. Koerber: "We have not only two parliaments, but also two emperors" (Franz, *Erzherzog*, p. 33; Muret, *L'Archiduc*, p. 172).
112. MKEFF Po/74–1911: attacks of Deputy Dr. Alder on the Archduke Franz Ferdinand and the reply of Deputies Dr. Korošec, Sten. Prot., 39th sitting of the Reichsratt, XXI session.

CHAPTER VII   *pages 118–141*

1. This file consists of several parts: the Archduke's draft proclamation to the people as the new sovereign, an order of the day to the army, his internal political instructions on how the change-over should proceed, the texts of specific orders to civil and military authorities for execution of the provisions of his proclamation to the people, and similar acts. In the course of years, these documents were revised several times, because the old Emperor survived more than one bronchial attack. A group of the Archduke's close political collaborators and legal experts worked on these papers for the take-over. Their special *aide-mémoire* and memorandums represent an important section of the *Thronwechsel* documentation.

After the First World War, part of this documentation was published: Colonel Brosch's version of the *Thronwechsel* instructions and two other principal documents—the proclamation to the people and the order of the day to the army. (*Neues Wiener Journal*, December 31, 1923, and January 1, 1924; also reprinted in T. Sosnosky, *Franz Ferdinand, der Erzherzog-Thronfolger*, pp. 78–105, and G. Franz, *Erzherzog Franz Ferdinand und die Pläne*, pp. 123–49.)

Some political and legal advisers to Franz Ferdinand in the preparations for the take-over gave their comments on Brosch's documents, or wrote about their own contributions to the *Thronwechsel*, or published additional materials from the *Thronwechsel* collections:

Johan Andreas von Eichhoff, in the *Reichspost*, March 28, 1926, and in the *Berliner Tageblatt*, March 31, 1926; Colonel Bardolff, the second chief of the *Militärkanzlei*, added his remarks on Eichhoff's documents in the *Reichspost*, April 4, 1926, as well as in his other writings, particularly in his *Soldat im alten Österreich* (1938); Josef von Kristoffy, the Archduke's main expert on Magyar problems and Minister of Interior in the Fejervary cabinet in 1906, made his contributions to the *Thronwechsel* issue in 1928 in his two-volume *Magyarország kalváriája;* Sosnosky

(p. 78) gave his comments on the character of the *Thronwechsel* documentation published after the First World War; G. Franz in 1943 undertook the most extensive study of the Archduke's reform plans; R. Kiszling dealt with this issue in his biography of the Archduke and in his article "Erzherzog Franz Ferdinands Pläne für den Umbau der Donaumonarchie," published in *Neues Abendland* (1956), 11 (4), pp. 362–67; and so did Jacques Hannak in "Franz Ferdinand," *Die Zukunft*, 1954 (6/7), pp. 173–76; and Robert A. Kann in "Erzherzog Franz Ferdinand und das Österreichische Deutschtum (Dokumente aus den Nachlässen Erzherzog Franz Ferdinands? Baernreither und Schiessl)," *Mitteilungen des Österreichischen Staatsarchivs* (1960, 13: 392–403).

Publication of this partial documentation of the *Thronwechsel* came at a time of bitter controversy over the question of war guilt. The Archduke's plan for reform has not always been evaluated in terms of the social and political realities of the Habsburg empire, and not as part of the overall question of responsibility for the outbreak of the First World War. One must also consider the extent to which these experts' opinions were shared by the Archduke himself. Further, one must take into consideration the fact that some of the Archduke's advisers—for instance, Kristoffy—tried after the Archduke's death to justify their own roles at Belvedere in view of sharp criticism especially in Hungary. Kristoffy even speaks about a political testament of the Archduke, while his biographer, Rudolf Kiszling, challenged its very existence. (Kristoffy, Vol. I, p. 439 ff; Kiszling, *Erzherzog*, pp. 258–59.)

Nevertheless, the collection of documents called *Program für den Thronwechsel,* as it exists in the *Nachlass,* gives one a useful picture of the Archduke's reform plans and his personal contribution to them. But it is not the only source for his plans for the reorganization of the empire. His correspondence with the Emperor Franz Josef, with Kaiser Wilhelm, and with other political figures of his day has to be taken into consideration. Also Section V of the *Nachlass (Denkschriften und Broschuren),* as well as Section IV (*Militärkanzleiakten*) and the Archives of the *Militärkanzlei,* give additional material about this fateful issue.

Although this vast documentation now gives a greater possibility for study of the Archduke's reform plans than was the case immediately after the dissolution of the Habsburg empire, it is still not complete. While most of Kaiser Wilhelm's letters to the Archduke are available, the *Nachlass* does not have copies of all the Archduke's letters to the Kaiser. A similar problem exists with the correspondence between the Archduke and political and legal experts who helped him in the *Thronwechsel* preparations; most of their letters and papers are there, while the Archduke's answers are less numerous.

2. Jászi, *Dissolution of the Habsburg Monarchy,* p. 144.

3. Conrad, *Aus meiner Dienstzeit,* Vol. I, pp. 564–65; Pethö Sándor, *Andrássy és Ferenc Ferdinand,* in *Magyar Szemle,* Vol. 20 (Budapest, 1914), pp. 388–96.

4. NEFF, Letters, Box 2.

5. NEFF, *Thronwechsel.*

6. *Ibid.*

7. NEFF, Letters, Box 2.

8. *Ibid.*

9. *Ibid.*

10. Brosch's letter to General

Woinowich published in Chlumecky, *Erzherzog Franz Ferdinands
Wirken und Wollen*, p. 361.

11. Conrad, I, pp. 503-4.

12. Kiszling, *Erzherzog*, p. 251.

13. *Ibid.*

14. NEFF, Letters, Box 2.

15. See also the Archduke's letters
to Emperor Franz Josef of December 18, 1908, August 17, 1909, and
November 15, 1909.

16. O. Czernin, *Österreichs
Wahlrecht und Parlament* (Prague,
1905).

17. NEFF, Memoranda.

18. *Ibid.*

19. *Ibid.*

20. Kann's statement that Czernin attempted to persuade the
Archduke to moderate his attitude
toward the Magyars and grant an
audience to Count Tisza in August
1913 ("Czernin and Francis Ferdinand," *Journal of Central European Affairs*, July 1956, p. 126)
actually happened for the first
time in June 1912. After he saw
the Archduke on June 14, 1912, he
sent a memorandum to Bardolff on
June 15, 1912, proposing Tisza's
audience (MKEFF, 1912-Pu 22).
Bardolff gave a contrary opinion,
quoting Czernin's own opinion that
"Tisza is our greatest enemy."

21. NEFF, Memoranda.

22. Kiszling, *Erzherzog*, pp.
251-52.

23. NEFF, Letters, Box 10.

24. Some of the departures from
the Brosch text in the *Nachlass*
may be attributed to stylistic
changes or typographical errors—
for example, the substitution of
"common central authorities" for
"common institutions" on page 90
of Sosnosky's version of Brosch,
or "Sonnenberg" rather than "Samenberg" on page 102. Other differences change the emphasis in
certain passages. The most significant of these is a passage which in
the Brosch text (p. 103) reads: "We

want to hold fast to the proven
alliances, to remain on good terms
with all foreign states, and, in so
far as it is not a question of the
honor and existence of the Monarchy, to exert ourselves for the idea
of peace, so that the peoples of the
Monarchy can devote themselves
without disturbance to the cultural
and economic tasks for which we
will always be found the warmest
supporters." In the *Nachlass*, aside
from a few stylistic changes, the
phrase "in so far as it is not a question of the honor and existence of
the Monarchy" is replaced by "in
so far as the honor and existence
of the Monarchy are not attacked."
The phrase "to exert ourselves for
the idea of peace" is replaced by
"to exert ourselves for the preservation of peace."

Several changes occur in the
order in which items appear, the
most important being in the "Program for the Thronwechsel" (p.
79). In the *Nachlass* the first item,
"Preservation of the Unity of the
Empire," is the seventh item in
Brosch. The second and third
items, "Preservation of the Unity
of the Army" and "Preservation of
the '67 Compromise," are eighth
and ninth in Brosch. It is only in
fourth place that the item first in
Brosch appears, "Governance in accordance with the Constitution."
In fifth place is the tenth point in
Brosch, "Foreign Policy—Guarantee of Peace." The sixth item in the
Nachlass combines the third and
fourth items in Brosch, "Language
Conflict in Bohemia and Austria;
Equal Rights for All Nations in
Hungary." Only in ninth place
appears the item which is second
in the Brosch text, "Suffrage for
Hungary."

Of the changes in substance,
most significant is that concerning
the position of Serbia. On page 93
of the Brosch text, Section b reads,

"the title 'King of Serbia and Bulgaria' can be renounced, because Serbia and Bulgaria possess a sovereignty recognized in international law." The *Nachlass* reads, "the title 'King of Bulgaria' can be renounced, because Bulgaria possesses a sovereignty recognized in international law."

In a minor change in substance, the *Nachlass* adds "Danube shipping" and "air transport" to the "merchant marine" of the Brosch text (p. 58, part c). Another addition to the Brosch text is in the section on page 103, where the *Nachlass* includes an additional compliment on his "indefatigable ability to work," inserted between "his devotion to duty" and "his benevolence." Also, a sentence which appears in Brosch on page 96—"Until then, therefore, the greater public must not be informed of the postponement of the coronation"—is crossed out in the *Nachlass*. Underneath appears a sentence that is mostly illegible, parts of which seem to read, "Is in the . . . already indicated."

25. NEFF, *Thronwechsel.*
26. *Ibid.*
27. *Ibid.*
28. *Ibid.*
29. *Ibid.*
30. *Ibid.*
31. Kiszling, *Erzherzog*, p. 253.
32. *Ibid.*
33. NEFF, *Thronwechsel.*
34. *Ibid.*
35. Funder, *Vom Gestern ins Heute*, p. 504. Margutti, *The Emperor Francis Joseph and His Times* (London ed.), pp. 118–19, claims that the Archduke told him as far back as 1895 that he intended to use military force against the Magyars. Also Conrad, Vol. I, pp. 564–65; Sandor, pp. 388–96; and the Archduke's letter to Emperor Franz Josef from early summer, 1908.

36. NEFF, *Thronwechsel.*
37. *Die Grosse Politik der europäischen Kabinette (1871–1914). Sammlung der diplomatischen Akten des Auswärtigen Amtes* (GP) Vol. XXXIX, p. 367.
38. *Ibid.*, pp. 367–68.
39. Archduke Franz Ferdinand to Prime Minister Koerber, a letter published in *Neues Wiener Tageblatt*, October 31, 1926. See Franz, p. 54.
40. Muret, *L'Archiduc*, p. 125.
41. D. Dimović, "Poslednja večera," *Pogledi na savremena pitanja*, May 1934; also Glück, *Sarajewo*, p. 144.
42. A letter from Archduke Franz Ferdinand to Aehrenthal, August 6, 1908, published in Chlumecky, p. 98.
43. NEFF, Letters, Box 16a.
44. Bilinski, *Wspomnienia*, p. 264. See also F. Hauptman, "Borba za bosansko željezo pred prvi svetski rat," *Godišnjak istoriskog društva Bosne i Hercegovine*, X (1959), pp. 167–95.
45. Bilinski, p. 264.
46. MKEFF, 18–3/6 1913.
47. Bilinski, p. 248.
48. *Ibid.*
49. NEFF, *Thronwechsel.*
50. *Ibid.*
51. *Ibid.*
52. *Ibid.*
53. *Ibid.*
54. *Ibid.*
55. NEFF, Box 2.
56. Kann (*Multinational Empire*, Vol. II, p. 303), described Kopitar's program as political, not cultural.
57. Franz, *Erzherzog Franz Ferdinand und die Pläne*, p. 78.
58. *British Documents on the Origins of the War 1898–1914* (BD), Vol. IX, p. 548.
59. Kiszling, *Erzherzog*, p. 122.
60. HHSTA, MA, IB, 1906/2600–4.
61. Eisenmenger, *Archduke Fran-*

cis Ferdinand (London, 1931), pp. 232–33.

62. *Ibid.*, p. 234.

63. *Ibid.*, p. 233.

64. Archduke Franz Ferdinand to Brosch, July 16, 1917, quoted by Chlumecky, pp. 44–45.

65. NEFF, Letters, Box 11.

66. Bardolff, p. 153; Kiszling, pp. 250–51; Sosnosky, pp. 67, 75, 250.

67. NEFF, *Thronwechsel.*

68. NEFF, Letters, Box 6.

69. *Ibid.*

70. NEFF, *Thronwechsel.*

71. *Ibid.*

72. Jászi, *Dissolution of the Habsburg Monarchy*, pp. 220–26.

73. *Ibid.*

74. Franz, p. 62.

75. J. Tomašević, *Peasants, Politics and Economic Change in Yugoslavia* (Stanford, 1955), p. 147.

76. *Ibid.*

77. *Ibid.*, pp. 148–49.

78. NEFF, *Thronwechsel.*

79. W. Schüssler, *Österreich und das deutsche Schicksal* (Leipzig, 1925), p. 70—cited by Franz, p. 22.

80. Fay, *Origins of the World War*, Vol. II, pp. 21–22.

81. *Ibid.*, p. 22.

82. John Burgess, *Political Science and Comparative Constitutional Law*, Vol. I (Boston, London, 1890), p. 37.

83. *Ibid.*, p. 44.

84. *Ibid.*, pp. 45, 48.

85. Kautsky, *The Guilt of William Hohenzollern* (London, 1922), p. 31.

CHAPTER VIII   *pages 142–159*

1. W. M. Calgren, in *Iswolsky und Aehrenthal vor der bosnischen Annexionkrise* (Uppsala, 1955), p. 35, expressed the opinion that the Archduke Franz Ferdinand had little influence on the foreign policy of the empire. The same opinion was stated by Kiszling, although one has to differentiate between the Archduke's position when Aehrenthal was foreign minister and when Berchtold was foreign minister. In the 1913–14 period the Archduke no doubt augmented his influence.

2. Conrad, *Aus meiner Dienstzeit*, Vol. I, p. 536.

3. *Ibid.*, p. 35.

4. Fay, *The Origins of the World War*, Vol. II, p. 224.

5. H. Kanner, *Der Schlüssel zur Kriegsschuldfrage*, pp. 15–16.

6. Fay, I, p. 343.

7. Conrad, III, p. 601.

8. J. C. Allmayer-Beck, *Ministerpräsident Baron Beck*, p. 101.

9. Glaise-Horstenau, "Erzherzog Franz Ferdinand und der Krieg," *Kriegsschuldfrage* (1926), pp. 565 ff.

10. Eisenmenger, *Archduke Francis Ferdinand* (London, 1931), p. 170.

11. Spitzmüller-Harmersbach, *. . . und hat auch Ursach*, p. 103.

12. Margutti, *La Tragédie des Habsbourgs*, p. 70.

13. Muret, *L'Archiduc*, p. 226.

14. Conrad, III, p. 138.

15. Sosnosky, *Franz Ferdinand der Erzherzog-Thronfolger*, p. 142.

16. Margutti, *La Tragédie*, p. 115.

17. AA Film 1564 JX Ser. I, reel 101, Doc. Dept. 224/II; *St. Petersburg Zeitung*, 19/7 February 1891.

18. *Ibid.*

19. Margutti, *La Tragédie*, p. 115.

20. BD, IX; the report of the British Ambassador in St. Petersburg of February 24, 1912.

21. NEFF, Letters, Box 7.

22. DDF, 3 Series I, the report of the French chargé d'affaires from St. Petersburg, December 28, 1911.

23. Glaise-Horstenau, *op. cit.*, p. 566 (cited by Franz, p. 107).

24. *Deutsche Dokumente zum*

Kriegsausbruch (DD), (Berlin, 1926), Vol. I, p. 156.

25. Margutti, *La Tragédie*, p. 71.

26. NEFF, letter of the Heir Apparent Gustav of Sweden to the Archduke Franz Ferdinand, March 17, 1891.

27. Kiszling, *Erzherzog*, p. 147.

28. AA Film 1546 JX Ser. I, reel 101, Doc. Dept.

29. *Ibid.*

30. *Ibid.*

31. *Ibid.*

32. *Ibid.*

33. *Ibid.*

34. *Ibid.*

35. *Ibid.*

36. *Ibid.*

37. *Ibid.*

38. Kiszling, *Erzherzog*, pp. 246-47.

39. Max Hohenberg in interview by M. Verne, in *Paris-Soir-Dimanche*, July 4, 1937.

40. Franz Ferdinand's letter to Brosch on Bosnia, October 1908.

41. NEFF, Letters, Box 6.

42. *Ibid.*

43. K. Skalnik, *Dr. Karl Lueger*, p. 134.

44. Margutti, *La Tragédie*, pp. 125-26.

45. Albertini, *Origins of the War of 1914*, Vol. II, p. 13.

46. *Ibid.*

47. Kristoffy, *Magyarország kalváriája*, Vol. I, pp. 439-40.

48. Kiszling, *Erzherzog*, pp. 258-59.

49. Chlumecky, *Erzherzog Franz Ferdinands Wirken und Wollen*, p. 362.

50. See Fay, *Origins of the World War*, Vol. I pp. 346, 386; Gooch, *Before the War*, pp. 247, 248, 409, 415; E. C. Helmreich, "The Conflict between Germany and Austria over Balkan Policy 1913-1914," *McKay Essays in the History of Modern Europe* (New York, 1936).

51. G. P. Gooch, *Before the War* (London, 1938), Vol. II, p. 255; also Conrad, III, pp. 469-70; *Österreich-Ungarns Aussenpolitik von der Bosnischen Krise 1908 bis zum Kriegsausbruch 1914* (Oe-U) (Vienna, 1930), Vol. VII, p. 8934.

52. AA, Film 1546 JX Ser. I, reel 101, Doc. Dept.

53. *Ibid.*

54. NEFF, Letters, Box 6.

55. AA Film 1546 JX Ser. I, reel 101, Doc. Dept.

56. Gooch, II, pp. 424-25. See Hugo Hantsch's interpretation in his *Leopold Graf Berchtold*, 2 vols.

57. NEFF, Letters, Box 6.

58. On Miramare meeting, GP, XXXIX, 15717, 15720, 15721. Prince Bülow, in his *Memoirs*, p. 155, said that at the meeting the German Kaiser discussed "many plans for the future with the coming Emperor of Austria."

59. Albertini, II, p. 17.

60. Conrad, IV, p. 36.

61. *Ibid.*, pp. 38-39.

62. Albertini, II, p. 17.

63. NEFF, *Thronwechsel*.

64. *Ibid.*

65. *Ibid.*

66. *Ibid.*

67. *Ibid.*

CHAPTER IX   *pages 160-174*

1. As translated by D. P. Costello.

2. From the 1838 translation of *Wilhelm Tell* into English, published in Providence, Rhode Island.

3. *Ibid.*

4. *Ibid.*

5. *Ibid.*

6. *Ibid.*

7. *Ibid.*

8. *Annual Register* (1819), p. 186.

9. O. Jászi and J. D. Lewis, *Against the Tyrant*, pp. 35-36.

10. *Ibid.*, pp. 119-20.

11. *Ibid.*, p. 120.

12. *Ibid.*

13. V. Valdenberg, *Drevnie Russkie Ucheniya o Predelakh Tsarskoi Vlasti* (Moscow, 1910).
14. Jászi and Lewis, pp. 125–26.
15. *Ibid.*, p. 126.
16. *Ibid.*, p. 125.
17. *Ibid.*, p. 156.
18. *Ibid.*
19. *Ibid.*, p. 123.
20. *Ibid.*, p. 124.
21. Redlich (German edition), p. 195.
22. *Annual Register* (1853), p. 227.
23. Redlich (German edition), p. 126.
24. *Ibid.*, p. 195.
25. I. Kranjčević, *Uspomene jednog učesnika u sarajevskom atentatu*, p. 7.
26. *Annual Register* (1878), p. 265.
27. *Ibid.*
28. Woodcock, *Anarchism*, p. 406.
29. *Ibid.*, pp. 415–16.
30. *Annual Register* (1884), p. 305.
31. Woodcock, p. 407.
32. *Annual Register* (1893), pp. 62, 363.
33. J. Maitron, *Histoire du mouvement anarchiste en France 1880–1914*, p. 236.
34. "Anarchism and Outrage," unsigned article by Kropotkin in *Freedom*, December 1893.
35. Woodcock, p. 317.
36. *Enciclopedia italiana*, Vol. XIII; see also G. Bourgin, "La Mort de Guglielmo Oberdan," *Revue politique et parlamentaire*, 1955, pp. 61–66.
37. Ćorović, *Odnosi izmedju Srbije i Austre-Ugarske*, p. 575.
38. Woodcock, p. 436.
39. *Ibid.*
40. *Ibid.*, p. 326.
41. HHSTA, IB, 2519/4.
42. HHSTA, IB, 2213/4.
43. HHSTA, IB, 2496/4.
44. HHSTA, IB, 1939/4.
45. *Ibid.*
46. HHSTA, IB, 374/4.
47. *Ibid.*
48. HHSTA, IB, 1843/4.
49. HHSTA, IB, 1516/4.
50. HHSTA, IB, 1959/4.
51. HHSTA, IB, 2482/4.
52. Ljubibratić, *Gavrilo Princip*, p. 16.

CHAPTER X   *pages 175–234*

1. B. Zečević in a letter to the author on February 15, 1959, and in a special paper on the subject claims that the name "Young Bosnia" was used for the first time in P. Kočić's paper, *Otadžbina*, in 1907. Gaćinović, one of the leaders of the Young Bosnians, wrote an article with the title "Young Bosnia" in the almanac *Prosvjeta* for 1911, published in Sarajevo at the end of 1910. Also B. Jevtić used the title "Mlada Bosna" for an article in *Bosanska Vila*, December 1913. B. Purić in an obituary for V. Gaćinović in *Srpske novine*, Corfu, August 16, 1917, also used the term "Young Bosnia." However, it was only after 1918 that Princip and his group were described as "Young Bosnians," and that the collective name was accepted by the general public in Yugoslavia, although there was never a club or organization under such a title.

The primary sources on the basis of which one could make assessments of the work of the Young Bosnians are not numerous. The correspondence between their members, including Princip's letters to Vukosava Čabrinović, has, to a great extent, been lost. The correspondence between Pero Slijepčević and Vladimir Gaćinović was destroyed in 1941. Ljubica Jovanović, the wife of Miško Jovanović who was executed for taking part in the plot, told this writer

that all of her husband's correspondence was stolen from her in
the 1930's.

Something has been preserved
by the surviving Young Bosnians.
A few letters of Nedeljko Čabrinović survived both world wars;
Father Josip Markusić, a Franciscan friar and family friend, kept
them in his prayer book during the
Second World War. But more numerous are the letters which fell
into the hands of the Austro-Hungarian police. Some of this correspondence has been published by
Dr. Božo Ćerović in *Bosanski omladinci i Sarajevski atentat* and by
Vojislav Bogićević in *Mlada Bosna*,
a collection of letters of the Young
Bosnians published in Sarajevo in
1954. The correspondence of individual members of Young Bosnia
was published in various commem-
orative publications: *Spomenica
Vladimira Gaćinovića* (1921); *Današnjica i Mlada Bosna—Uloga
i značaj Vladimira Gaćinovića*
(1937); Vladimir Gaćinović, *Ogledi i pisma* (1956), edited by
Todor Kruševac. Several letters
of Danilo Ilić were published in
Spomenica Danila Ilića (1922). In
the archives and the libraries of
Belgrade and Sarajevo a certain
amount of the correspondence of
the Young Bosnians was assembled.

In their short lives some of the
Young Bosnians even published
their writings in the review *Zora*
in Vienna, and later in Prague, and
in *Zvono* in Sarajevo, and other
periodicals.

About the conspiratorial activities of the Young Bosnians very
little was recorded, due to the
character of their work. The only
exceptions are the archives of the
Slovene secret society Preporod,
which kept regular minutes of its
work, in cooperation with the
Young Bosnians.

During several of the trials of
the Young Bosnians in 1914 and
1915, the prosecution presented as
evidence diaries and letters seized
from the Young Bosnians. This
represents a valuable contribution
to the activities of Bosnian revolutionary societies. The text of their
interrogation is also first-class evidence, although one has to take
into consideration that some of the
accused either did not wish to reveal their secret activities or gave
false information in order to cover
up for their friends.

The Young Bosnians who survived the First World War have
published their memoirs about the
1914 events. An assessment of this
documentation will be given as
each of the works is mentioned.

2. N. Stojanović, "O zadacima
Bosne," *Letopis Matice Srpske*
(Novi Sad, 1929.)

3. *Državni arhiv Sarajevo*, DAS,
IV-4-2, dnevn, 157 (quoted by
V. Bogićević, *Mlada Bosna*, pp.
259–60.)

4. C. Popović, "Prilog Istoriji
Sarajevskog Atentata," *Politika*,
March 31, 1928.

5. V. Ćorović, *Odnosi izmedju
Srbije i Austro-Ugarske*, p. 549.

6. The most complete bibliography of Gaćinović's literary and
political writings, as well as of
essays and articles written about
Gaćinović, was published in *Ogledi
i Pisma* (pp. 333–36). Also one
should take into consideration Ljubibratić's biography of Gaćinović,
published in 1961.

7. T. Ujević, "Vladimir Gaćinović," *Jugoslavenska njiva*, November 1921.

8. *Ogledi i pisma*, pp. 82–83.

9. R. Parežanin, "Nekoliko reći
o Žerajić-Principovom naraštaju,"
Književni sever, February 1, May
1, and June 1, 1927.

10. *Ibid.*

11. V. Gaćinović in his letter to

M. Karanović, June 1908, published in *Ogledi i pisma* p. 185, also Ljubibratić, *Gaćinović*, p. 69.

12. V. Popović, "Vaskrs Italije," *Zora* (Vienna), Nos. 6, 7, 8, 9, 10.

13. Mazzini's revolutionary oath was published in *Zora* (1912), 4–5, p. 145. In the same issue, M. Deanović wrote an article on Italian nationalism. Gaćinović's article written for L. Trotsky, *Ogledi i pisma*, pp. 80–96.

14. V. Bogićević, *Sarajevski atentat*, pp. 32, 63, 84.

15. DAS, IV–4, dnevn. 713 (Original), quoted by V. Bogićević, *Mlada Bosna*, p. 391.

16. P. Slijepčević, *Napor Bosne i Hercegovine za oslobodjenje i ujedinjenje*, p. 202.

17. P. Slijepčević published in *Srpski književni glasnik*, March 16, 1930, an article on Masaryk's influence on the South Slav youth prior to the World War. J. Kršić wrote in *Pregled*, October 1937, on Masaryk and Bosnia.

18. T. Tadić, "Masarik," *Zora*, January 1, 1910. *Zora* also published an article on Masaryk's conceptions of nationalism (May 1912) as well as several essays on Masaryk. Dr. Anrost Blaha, "Massarikove filozofske i socioloske teorije," *Zora*, January-February 1911, and in writings of other authors.

19. *Ogledi i pisma*, pp. 303–4. See also Chapter XI.

20. In a letter to M. Karanović, Gaćinović complained that he had had to endure all kinds of hardships "in one of our Piedmonts" (V. Bogićević, *Mlada Bosna*, pp. 190–91). After crossing the Montenegrin frontier, Gaćinović was arrested on October 20, 1908 because he had begun to write leaflets against the Austro-Hungarian rule. (N. S. Martinović, "Bjekstvo Vladimira Gaćinovića iz Hercegovine preko Crne Gore za Srbiju," *Istoriski Zapisi*, 1954, pp.

240–43; see also I. Kećmanović, "Jedna epizoda iz života Vladimira Gaćinovića," *Život*, July–August 1955, pp. 425–29.)

21. P. Slijepčević, "Mlada Bosna," in *Napor Bosne i Hercegovine za oslobodjenje i ujedinjenje*, pp. 203–4. B. Zečević has described this action to the author both orally and in a special paper on the subject and a letter of February 15, 1959.

22. B. Zečević's letter of February 15, 1959.

23. *Ibid.*

24. See Chapter XVII.

25. B. Zečević, special paper and letter of February 15, 1959.

26. *Ibid.*

27. *Ibid.*

28. *Ibid.*

29. B. Zečević in his letter of September 15, 1964, said to the author that he decided to go to Russia when the Vienna court began an investigation of him, after one member of the Young Bosnians was arrested in Croatia. Zečević had a regular passport and went first to St. Petersburg and then to Moscow. His trip was financed from a secret fund which was collected in Bosnia and sent to him by Professor Sćepan Grdjić, of Tuzla. In St. Petersburg Zečević had contacts with official Slavophile circles, but at Moscow University, where he studied for a time, he was "in contact with students from Armenia, Georgia, and students of Jewish descent, who were hostile to the regime and spoke about the imminent revolution in Russia."

30. B. Zečević, special paper and letter of February 15, 1959.

31. *Ibid.*

32. From the autumn of 1910 to the summer of 1912, Gaćinović was registered in Vienna University as a student of philosophy. In the first semester Gaćinović heard the lec-

tures of Professor M. Rešetar on the grammar of the South Slav languages and the history of the Serbo-Croat literature in the eighteenth century and attended a seminar on Slavonic philology. He also took a course with Professor Becker on sixteenth-century French literature. In the second semester, he took courses in the French language and the history of the French novel. In the third semester he took a course in the history of South Slav literature to the fifteenth century, the historical grammar of the Serbo-Croat language and the history of the new French written language. In the last semester in Vienna, besides the above-mentioned courses of the third semester, he took French meter. (Archives of Vienna University.)

33. See Chapter XVII.

34. P. Slijepčević, *Napor*, p. 193.

35. *Zora*, October 1910, pp. 465–66.

36. According to V. Lebedev, "Vlado Gaćinović i ruski revolucionari," *Pregled*, July–August 1934, Gaćinović entered Lausanne University in the summer semester of 1913 and remained there until the summer semester of 1917.

37. *Ogledi i pisma*, pp. 191–92.

38. T. Ujević, "Vladimir Gaćinović," *Jugoslavenska njiva*, November 1921.

39. Ljubibratić, *Gaćinović*, p. 107. Soviet historian Pisarov, (*Osvoboditelnoye Dvizhenie*, p. 308) confirmed that Gaćinović met Lunacharsky in Switzerland.

40. T. Ujević, "Vladimir Gaćinović," *loc. cit.*

41. *Ogledi i pisma*, p. 82.

42. T. Ujević, "Vladimir Gaćinović," *loc. cit.*

43. *Ogledi i pisma*, pp. 81–82.

44. Vojislav Gaćinović, "Ognjista revolucije," *Pregled*, October 1953. See also Ljubibratić, *Gaćinović*, pp. 201–4.

45. P. Slijepčević in *Današnjica i Mlada Bosna*, p. 33.

46. *Ibid.*

47. *Ogledi i pisma*, p. 288. Vojislav Gaćinović in a letter to the author, June 27, 1961, stated that Natanson kept Gaćinović's correspondence dealing with the Sarajevo assassination for a time. It is not known whether Gaćinović on his return from the United States in 1916 took it from Natanson and burned it or hid it somewhere.

48. See Ljubibratić, *Gaćinović*, the chapter on Gaćinović's death, pp. 205–28.

49. See Chapter XVII.

50. According to a statement of Vaso Čubrilović on the participants of the June 28, 1914, conspiracy, his organization had no contacts with Gaćinović. This statement of V. Čubrilović has been authenticated by the fact that in the minutes of several trials of the Young Bosnians in 1914 and 1915, the name of Gaćinović has never been mentioned.

51. N. Trišić, "Danilo Ilić, čovjek i borac," *Pregled*, December 1940, p. 595.

52. *Ibid.*

53. *Ibid.*

54. Gradski muzej Sarajevo (GMS), Lebedev Papers.

55. *Ogledi i pisma*, p. 94.

56. B. Tomić, "Poreklo i detinjstvo Gavrila Principa," *Nova Evropa*, October 26, 1939; and "Rod i dom Gavrila Principa," *Narodna odbrana*, November 18, 1939.

57. Glück, *Sarajewo*, pp. 195–96.

58. B. Tomić, "Rod i dom Gavrila Principa," *Narodna odbrana*, November 18, 1939, p. 726.

59. V. Lebedev, "Rodjenje Gavrila Principa," *Politika*, September 28, 1936.

60. G. Božović, "Rodni prag Gavrila Principa," *Politika*, July 21, 1939.

61. Martin Pappenheim, "Dr. Pappenheim's Conversations with Princip," translated with an introduction by Hamilton Fish Armstrong, *Current History*, August 1927, pp. 669–707.

62. B. Tomić, "Poreklo i detinjstvo Gavrila Principa," *Nova Evropa*, October 26, 1939.

63. *Ibid.*

64. *Ibid.*

65. *Ibid.*

66. Lebedev, "Rodjenje Gavrila Principa," *Politika*, September 28, 1936.

67. *Ibid.*

68. *Ibid.*

69. *Ibid.*

70. M. Pappenheim, p. 703.

71. *Ibid.*, p. 702.

72. B. Tomić, "Umro je Petar Princip," *Politika*, January 28, 1940.

73. B. Tomić, "Poreklo i detinjstvo Gavrila Principa," *Nova Evropa*, October 26, 1939.

74. Pappenheim, p. 702.

75. G. Božović, "Rodni prag Gavrila Principa," *Politika*, July 21, 1939.

76. B. Tomić, "Poreklo i detinjstvo Gavrila Principa," *Nova Evropa*, October 26, 1939.

77. Pappenheim, p. 702.

78. Jevdjević, *Sarajevski atentatori*, p. 29.

79. B. Tomić, "Poreklo i detinjstvo Gavrila Principa," *Nova Evropa*, October 26, 1939.

80. *Ibid.*

81. Ljubibratić, *Princip*, pp. 42–43.

82. *Ibid.*

83. *Ibid.*

84. Radovan Jovanović, "Iz djaćkih dana Gavrila Principa," *Književni sever* (March–April 1928), pp. 173–74. Also letter of Dr. Vid Gaković to the author, December 24, 1960.

85. Ljubibratić, *Princip*, p. 35.

86. Pappenheim, p. 702.

87. Jevdjević, p. 27.

88. B. Tomić's letter to the author, February 3, 1960.

89. Ljubibratić, *Princip*, p. 66, quoting Pfeffer, *Istraga u Sarajevskom atentatu*, p. 79.

90. V. Bogićević, *Sarajevski atentat*, p. 288—statement of D. Jevdjević.

91. Pappenheim, pp. 702–6.

92. Jevdjević, p. 63.

93. Ljubibratić, *Princip*, p. 132.

94. Reprinted from *Srpska riječ*, June 17, 1920.

95. Pappenheim, p. 702.

96. *Ibid.*

97. Glück, *Sarajewo*, p. 211.

98. B. Jevtić, "Milan Rakić u duši 'Mlada Bosna,'" *Srpski književni glasnik*, July 16 and August 1, 1938.

99. V. Bogićević, *Mlada Bosna*, p. 143.

100. *Ibid.*, p. 138.

101. N. Trišić, "Bosanci i Hercegovci u komitskoj akciji," lecture given in Sarajevo on November 10, 1940; also *Politika*, June 30, 1914. At the investigation in Sarajevo (NEFF, *Prozess in Sarajevo*, Princip's statement of July 19, 1914), at the trial and to Dr. Pappenheim, Princip also mentioned his conflict with Tankosić. Ljubibratić (*Princip*, p. 58) is of a different opinion.

102. Princip described Tankosić in such a way at his investigation on July 7, then again on July 19, 1914. (NEFF, *Prozess in Sarajevo*.)

103. NEFF, *Prozess in Sarajevo*, Princip's statement on June 28, 1914.

104. This is the opinion of the investigation judge Pfeffer (*Istraga u Sarajevskom atentatu* pp. 183–84), Ćorović (*Odnosi*, p. 379) and several other writers. On June 23, 1925, old Čabrinović tried to commit suicide in Sarajevo. B. Jevtić commented in *Politika*, June 26, 1925, that old Cabrinović was an Austrian informer. On July 4, 1925, Čabrinović's daughter, Dr. Vukosava Branisavljević-Čabrinović de-

fended her father, and on July 6, 1925, in *Balkan* (Belgrade), the old man himself published a letter saying that he had tried to kill himself "because of injustice done to him and because of the rumors that he had been an Austrian spy."

105. Gradski muzej Sarajevo (GMS), Nedeljko Čabrinović's letter to his mother from 1907.

106. As told to this writer by Dr. Vukosava Branisavljević-Čabrinović, sister of Nedeljko Čabrinović.

107. DSIP, Tvrdoreka Papers.

108. *Ibid.*

109. Letters of May 20, June 1, 1911, and postcards of March 13 and June 4, 1911, are in the possession of Dr. Vukosava Branisavljević-Čabrinović.

110. *Ibid.*

111. *Ibid.*

112. N. Čabrinović's statement at the trial, October 12, 1914, in V. Bogićević, *Sarajevski atentat*, p. 30.

113. NEFF, *Prozess in Sarajevo*, V. Bogićević, *Sarajevski atentat*, p. 41.

114. *Ibid.*

115. J. Smitran, "Istorija jedne dopisnice Nedeljko, Čabrinovića," *Zvono*, February 2, 1921.

116. Statement of Jozef Mitro, a witness at the Sarajevo trial (Bogićević, *Sarajevski atentat*, p. 298).

117. DSIP, Tvrdoreka Papers.

118. J. Kršić, "Lektira sarajevskih atentatora," *Pregled*, February 1935, pp. 115–19.

119. K. Ivović, *Generalni štrajk u Bosni i Hercegovini 1906* (Sarajevo, 1963), consists of a collection of the documents from the archives of the Bosnian government and the Joint Ministry of Finance about the 1906 general strike. See also S. Elaković, *Generalni štrajk u 1906 u Bosni i Hercegovini* (Belgrade, 1951).

120. Ivović, p. 194.

121. *Ibid.*, p. 248.

122. *Ibid.*

123. A. Barre, *La Bosnie Herzegovine* (Paris, 1906), p. 221.

124. *Pregled*, 1912–1913, pp. 11, 292.

125. S. Grdjić, "Kolonizacija u Bosni i Hercegovini," *Pregled*, October 1, 1912, pp. 377–78.

126. Dj. Pejanović, "Srednje, stručne, vjerske i druge škole," *Pregled*, April 1, 1913.

127. Quoted from J. Pisarov, *Osvoboditelnoye Dvizhenie Yugoslavyanskikh Narodov Avstro-Vengrii*, p. 122.

128. The text of the new Constitution was published in *Glasnik zakona i naredaba za Bosnu i Hercegovinu*, II, Sarajevo, 1910.

129. Chlumecky, *Erzherzog Franz Ferdinands Wirken und Wollen*, p. 98.

130. Glück, *Sarajewo*, p. 64.

131. Dr. Perin, "Ekonomski razvitak sela od 1878–1928," in P. Slijepčević, *Napor*, p. 288.

132. V. Bogićević, "Seljački, pokret u Bosanskoj Krajini i Posavini 1910," *Godišnjak istoriskog društva Bosne i Hercegovine*, 1950, p. 236.

133. NEFF, Memoire über die politische Situation in Bosnien-Herzegovina nach Schluss der ersten Sabor-Session, von G.D.I. von Auffenberg (August, 1910).

134. N. Stojanovitch, *Bosnie-Herzégovine* (Geneva, 1917), p. 43.

135. Pisarov, p. 202.

136. KA, MKEFF, p. 8, 1911.

137. *Ibid.*, Ma 34a 1911 and Pb30 1912.

138. *Ibid.*, 8–13/1913

139. *Ibid.*

140. *Ibid.*

141. Margutti, *The Emperor Francis Joseph* (London ed.), p. 126.

142. Kristoffy, *Magyarország kalvariája*, Vol. II, p. 413.

143. Chlumecky, p. 187.

144. KA, MKEFF 59-15/1913.

145. *Ibid.*, 26-3-1913.

146. *Ibid.*, 14 6/2 1914

147. Kiszling, *Erzherzog*, p. 165;

Chlumecky, p. 98.

148. K. Grünberg, *Die Agrarverfassung und die Grundentlastungsprobleme in Bosnien und der Herzegowina* (Leipzig, 1911), p. 67.

149. Bilinski, *Wspomnienia*, p. 223.

150. Quoted from O. Jaszi, *Dissolution of the Habsburg Monarchy*, p. 226.

151. Bilinski, p. 264.

152. Kranjčević, *Uspomene*, pp. 8–9.

153. *Ibid.*, p. 16.

154. Funder, *Vom Gestern ins Heute*, pp. 475–76.

155. Baernreither, *Fragments of a Political Diary*, p. 128.

156. J. Dedijer, "Srpski novčani zavodi u Bosni i Hercegovini," *Pregled*, February 1, 1910.

157. Brosch informed the Archduke Franz Ferdinand on January 5, 1911 that Vojislav Šola was willing to back the government's plans for the railway line in Banja Luka–Jajce–Rama. In the report of February 5, 1911, Brosch reported that "Šola is completely loyal." In his plans for the reorganization of the empire, the Archduke had the idea of offering to Šola a government post. (*NEFF, Thronwechsel.*)

158. Masleša, *Mlada Bosna*, p. 69.

159. Jevtić, *Sarajevski atentat*, p. 35.

160. NEFF, *Prozess in Sarajevo.*

161. *Ogledi i pisma*, pp. 189–90.

162. V. Gaćinović wrote in *Ogledi i pisma* (p. 128) that "as an individual protest against the annexation, Vukan Krulj gave his demission as a civil servant. Together with the demission of the geographer Dedijer, that was the only gesture of a free individual during the whole annexation crisis."

163. Čerović, *Bosanski omladinci*, p. 47.

164. Pappenheim, pp. 704–5.

165. Skerlić, *Svetozar Marković* (Belgrade, 1909), p. 126.

166. *Ogledi i pisma*, p. 91.

167. V. Bogićević, "Atentat Bogdana Žerajića," *Godišnjak istoriskog društva Bosne i Hercegovine*," 1954, pp. 87–102.

168. Pappenheim, p. 702.

169. As told to this writer by Dr. Vojislav Jovanović.

170. Rebecca West, *Black Lamb and Grey Falcon* (New York, 1941), Vol. I, p. 443.

171. Jevdjević, *Sarajevski atentatori*, p. 34.

172. *Ogledi i pisma*, p. 74.

173. *Ibid.*, p. 125.

174. *Ibid.*, p. 127.

175. *Ibid.*

176. Letter of Juš Kozak to the author, February 2, 1959.

177. As told by Mrs. Jovanka Čubrilović to this writer.

178. V. Lebedev, "Vlada Gaćinović i ruski revolucionari," *Pregled*, July–August 1934.

179. *Ibid.*

180. *Ogledi i pisma*, p. 151.

181. As told to this writer by Dr. Vukosava Branisavljević-Čabrinović.

182. *Ibid.*

183. Jevdjević, p. 99.

184. V. Bogićević, *Sarajevski atentat*, pp. 91–92.

185. Pappenheim, "Conversations with Princip," p. 702.

186. Jevdjević, p. 27.

187. Mousset, *Un Drame historique*, p. 134.

188. *Ogledi i pisma*, p. 262.

189. *Ibid.*, p. 180.

190. *Ibid.*, p. 76.

191. F. Supilo wrote an article under the title "Omladina i narod" in *Zora* (June–July 1910), warning the young South Slavs to fight against chauvinism and clericalism, stating that the policy of people's unification could be achieved only through free thought and democracy. He advised the young South Slavs not to be afraid of new ideas, which should be implemented with

determination. At the end of the article he emphasized that Italy was unified with a similar program.

192. J. Skerlić, "Nedslavizam i Jugoslovenstvo," *Zora*, January 1910.

193. As told to the author by Božidar Tomić.

194. I. Andrić, "Story from 1920," *Nemiri* (Zagreb, 1920).

195. *Ogledi i pisma*, p. 70.

196. *Ibid.*, p. 91.

197. T. Ujević, "Vladimir Gaćinović," *Jugoslavenska njiva*, November 1921.

198. Kranjčević, *Uspomene*, pp. 29-30.

199. C. Popović, "Prilog istoriji Sarajevskog atentata," *Politika*, March 31, 1928.

200. V. Bogićević, *Mlada Bosna*, pp. 130-33.

201. *Ibid.*

202. D. Ljubibratić, *Princip*, p. 48.

203. This program was seized by the Austro-Hungarian authorities in June 1912, when Luka Jukić was arrested, and it was read at his trial as the document of the prosecution. It was reprinted by O. Tartalja in *Sloboda*, August 7, 1912, and by *Pijemont*, August 18, 1912. Here it is reproduced from Ljubibratić, *Princip*, p. 101.

204. As told to the author by Vladimir Simić.

205. As told by the author by Dr. Ljubo Jurković.

206. *Ogledi i pisma*, p. 89.

207. *Ibid.*

208. V. Fabjančič, "Ob 25 letnici veleizdajniskega procesa proti Preporodovcem," *Slovenski narod* (Ljubljana), December 23, 1939.

209. *Ibid.*

210. I. J. Kolar, *Preporodovci 1912-1914, 1914-1918*, p. 24.

211. Letter of Juš Kozak to the author, February 2, 1959.

212. As told to this writer by J. Zubović.

213. *Ibid.*

214. Letters of Professor Juš Kozak to the author on January 22 and February 2, 1959.

215. Kozak's letter of February 2, 1959.

216. *Ibid.*; also letter of March 21, 1959.

217. Kolar, p. 51.

218. Kozak's letter of February 2, 1959.

219. See Chapter XV.

220. Springer (Renner, Vienna, 1906), *Grundlagen*, pp. 28, ff; O. Bauer in his *Die Nationalitätenfrage und die Sozialdemokratie* (Vienna, 1907) shared basically Renner's view that the nationality principle is not a state-forming principle.

221. Skerlić, *Svetozar Marković*, p. 183.

222. *Istoriski arhiv KPJ*, III (Belgrade, 1947), pp. 127-29.

223. *Ibid.*

224. *Spomenica Danila Ilića.*

225. *Ibid.*

226. *Ibid.*

227. *Ibid.*

228. *Ibid.*

229. *Ibid.*

230. *Ibid.*

231. Pisarov, p. 136; Bogdan Žerajić was described by the Habsburg officials and press as an anarchist. (See Chapter XI.)

232. *Ogledi i pisma*, p. 185.

233. P. Lavrov, *Istoricheskiye Pisma* (Geneva, 1891), p. 79.

234. *Ogledi i pisma*, p. 81.

235. *Današnjica i Mlada Bosna*, p. 12.

236. *Ogledi i pisma*, p. 133.

237. Juš Kozak in his letter to the author on March 4, 1959, stressed the moral and ethical influence of Moderna on Slovene youth. The chief representatives of Moderna had the view that the Slovene people were oppressed and without freedom and called upon them to be aware of their strength and their

social role." Oton Župančič's poem at the head of the first issue of *Preporod*, November 1, 1912, reads as follows:

We are all of us smiths, we are forging,
forging our hearts, hammering out our strength,
and as our souls echo, we shall listen—why:
Perhaps one day will resound beneath this hammer
that heart, forged of the purest bronze,
which will sing like a bell and call us,
all together around it. . . .

For this we smiths will hammer,
will hammer hard, listening intensely,
to ensure that there are no false notes among us,
when the time comes,
when the day is here,
the master smith, the mighty master smith,
will rise and burst forth from our ranks.

It seems that *Pheporod* did not publish the whole poem, which contained a part with clear Socialist tendencies; this was published in Župančič's *Complete Works* in 1959.

238. V. Čerina, *Janko Polić-Kamov* (Rijeka, 1913), p. 73.

239. Woodcock, *Anarchism*, pp. 285–86.

240. *Ibid.*, See also Eugenia W. Herbert, *The Artist and Social Reform—France and Belgium, 1885–1898* (New Haven, 1961), pp. 208–213.

241. Woodcock, *Anarchism*, p. 431.

242. Ivo Andrić in *Vihor*, quoted by Vice Zaninović, "Mlada Hrvatska uoči i svjetskog rata," *Historijski Zbornik*, 1958–1959, p. 100.

243. B. Jevtić, "Mlada Bosna," *Bosanska Vila*, December 30, 1913, p. 337.

244. *Bosanska Vila*, June 30, 1912.

245. From their village the Young Bosnians brought their own rich language, which became the literary language of the Serbs and Croats, only to find that in the towns the new authorities were desecrating it. The linguistic purity which they demanded had definite political significance. Kočić, the leader of the *kmets* in the *Sabor* protested, for example, against the practice of the Austrian authorities in forming a so-called Bosnian language under the direction of Baron Kallay, the minister in Vienna. The Austrian officials, the greater part of whom came from other parts of the empire, did not speak Serbo-Croat, or spoke it imperfectly; they introduced into Serbo-Croat a foreign syntax and employed many words based on German. "In this dismemberment of our beautiful, free language we can feel our general servitude and subjugation," said Kočić in the *Sabor*.

246. J. Skerlić, *Istorija nove srpske književnosti*, Belgrade, 1953, p. 424.

247. I. Dimitrijević, "Sima Pandurović i Gavrilo Princip," *Spomenica Sime Pandurovića* (Belgrade, 1928), pp. 67–74.

248. Muharem Perović, *Momčilo Nastasijević* (Belgrade, 1963), pp. 158–59.

249. Mitrinović published at his own expense an obituary note for Dušan Popović on November 8, 1918, in which he called him "my venerable friend." It is preserved by Čedomir Mitrinović, his brother.

250. A study of Dimitrije Mitrinović's life and work is not yet written. Slavko Leovac wrote an essay on Mitrinović in *Život*, October 1953. B. Jevtić, V. Gligorić

and P. Palavestra mentioned Mitrinović's work in their writings.

251. D. Mitrinović, "Nacionalno
tlo i modernost," *Bosanska Vila*,
July 20, 1908, p. 306.

252. *Ibid*.

253. *Ibid*.

254. *Ibid*.

255. V. Cerina, *Janko Polić-
Kamov*, pp. 50, 83.

256. M. Grol, "Ibsen na Beograd-
skoj Pozornici," *Srpski književni
glasnik*. May, 1921.

257. I. Andrić, *Nemiri* (Zagreb,
1920), pp. 28–30.

CHAPTER XI   *pages 235–260*

1. *Ogledi i pisma*, pp. 68–69.

2. Božidar Zečević in his letter to
the author, May 12, 1963.

3. In a letter without a date, Žerajić asked Pero Slijepčević to help
Špiro Soldo to get a stipend.

4. Žerajić's letter to Slijepčević,
October 15, 1909.

5. Žerajić's letter to Slijepčević,
February 25, 1910.

6. Zečević's letter to the author,
May 12, 1963.

7. Žerajić's letter to Slijepčević,
November 2, 1909.

8. *Ibid*.

9. Slijepčević, "Masarik i pre-
dratna omladina," *Srpski književni
glasnik*, March 16, 1930, pp. 466–69.

10. Borivoje Jevtić, "Sarajevski
atentat," *Politika*, June 28, 1925.

11. Letter deposited in Univerzitetska Biblioteka (UB), Belgrade,
Ibr. 3183.

12. V. Bogićević, *Mlada Bosna*,
p. 44.

13. With only a few exceptions
the Belgrade papers reacted sharply
against the Austrian Emperor's trip.
It was described as rubbing salt
into a painful wound. In the polemics with the Viennese press the
leading Belgrade paper, *Politika*, on
May 23, 1910, called the visit "illegal" and "immoral."

14. *Ogledi i pisma*, p. 67.

15. *Ibid*., p. 69.

16. *Neue Freie Presse*, June 1,
1910.

17. AFR, FA III—194, FMB-
MAE, June 8, 1910.

18. *Reichspost*, June 1, 1910.

19. *Ibid*., June 6, 1910.

20. Pfeffer, *Istraga u Sarajevskom atentatu*, p. 176.

21. Čerović, *Bosanski Omladinci
i Sarajevski Atentat*, p. 46.

22. V. Bogićević, "Atentat Bogdana Žerajića," *Godišnjak istoriskog društva Bosne i Hercegovine*
(1954), pp. 87–102.

23. UB, Ibr. 3184.

24. V. Grdjić, "Iz mojih uspo-
mena, Posjeta Franje Josipa Bosni,
Zadnji moj razgovor sa Žerajićem,"
Pregled, January 1927. See also S.
Moljević, "Žerajićev atentat," *Raz-
vitak*, Feb. 1 and March 1, 1936.

25. V. Grdjić, "Iz mojih uspo-
mena, Posjeta Franje Josipa Bosni."

26. R. Radulović, *Naš politički
moral* (Belgrade, 1933).

27. Introduction by Pero Slijepčević in R. Radulović, *Naš politički
moral*.

28. V. Bogićević, "Atentat Bogdana Žerajića," *Godišnjak istoriskog*, p. 101.

29. Jovan Starović was still alive
in 1964. He lived in Belgrade as a
retired judge. He described the
events of June 15, 1910, to B. Zečević, who then conveyed them to
the author on March 22, 1963.

30. MKEFF, Mf/94 res/1910.

31. *Ibid*.

32. NEFF, Letters, Box 29.

33. HHSTA, II/h–3/56, June 16,
1910.

34. *Ibid*.

35. *Ibid*.

36. *Ibid*., Sar., August 5, 1910.

37. MKEFF, Mf/94 res/1910.

38. *Reichspost*, June 16, 1910.

39. *Ibid*.

40. Cited by V. Bogićević, "At-

entat Bogdana Žerajića," *Go-dišnjak istoriskog društva Bosne i Hercegovine* (1954), p. 98.

41. *Ibid.*

42. HHSTA Politisches Archiv, XL, Interna, Liasse XLVII/7, Box 226; also MKEFF, Pc 5 res/1910.

43. *Ibid.*
44. *Ibid.*
45. *Ibid.*
46. *Ibid.*
47. *Ibid.*
48. *Ibid.*
49. *Ibid.*
50. *Ibid.*
51. *Ibid.*

52. Max Hohenberg, in interview, *Paris-Soir-Dimanche*, July 4, 1937.

53. HHSTA Politisches Archiv, XL, Interna, Liasse XLVII/7, Box 226.

54. *Ibid.*
55. *Ibid.*

56. Dr. Werner Frauendienst, *Jugoslawiens Weg zum Abgrund* (Berlin, 1941).

57. N. Trišić, *Sarajevski atentat u Svjetlu Bibliografskih Podataka*, pp. 474-75.

58. Ljubibratić, *Gaćinović*, p. 64. See also Chapter XV on how the Sarajevo police wanted to cut off the head of Nedeljko Čabrinović after his death.

59. B. Jevtić, *Sarajevski atentat*, p. 20. It is interesting that *Slovenski jug* in its issue of June 25 (Serbian date, June 12), 1910, bitterly attacked public opinion in Serbia for the way it treated Žerajić's attempt against Governor Varešanin.

60. Ljubibratić, *Gaćinović*, pp. 63-64; also J. Vrinjanin, "Omladinske organizacije i sarajevski atentat," *Novosti*, July 15, 16 and 17, 1926.

61. B. Jevtić, *op. cit.*, p. 20.

62. B. Čerović, *Bosanski omladinci*, p. 50.

63. Ljubibratić, *Gaćinović*, p. 62.

64. *Gradski muzej Sarajevo*, Lebedev papers.

65. NEFF, *Prozess in Sarajevo*; also Pfeffer, p. 60.

66. Jevdjević, *Sarajevski atentatori*, p. 37.

67. A. Mousset, *Un Drame historique: l'attentat de Sarajevo*, pp. 511-12.

68. The first of Gaćinović's essays on Žerajić was published in *Zora* (Vienna), November 1910, under the title "To Those Who Are Coming," signed with the pseudonym Vladimir Ivanov; the second one was in the *Prosvjeta* yearbook for 1912 with the title "The Shriek of a Desperate Man," and the third in pamphlet form under the title "Death of a Hero," published by *Pijemont* (Belgrade, 1912).

69. Quoted from D. Subotić, *Yugoslav Popular Ballads* (Cambridge, Eng., 1932), p. 81.

70. *Ibid.*
71. *Ibid.*
72. *Ibid.*

73. Skerlić, *Istorija nove srpske književnosti* (Belgrade, 1953), p. 221.

74. *Harvard Slavic Studies*, Vol. III, *The Ray of the Microcosm*, trans. by A. Savić-Rebac (Cambridge, 1957), pp. 116-17.

75. *Ibid.*

76. *Ibid.*, p. 117.

77. John Reed, *The War in Eastern Europe*" (New York, 1916), p. 59.

78. V. Pelagić in the chapter "Why Revolutions Take Place," of his *Istorija Bosansko-hercegovačke bune*, traced the elements of permanent revolution in the Serbo-Croat folklore heroic poetry, particularly in the poem "Knez Bogosav i Starina Novak" (pp. 32-33) and in the poem "Buna na dahije" (p. 36), which described the Serbian uprisings of 1804.

79. *The Jewish Encyclopedia*,

Vol. VII (New York, London, 1904), pp. 484–85.
80. Ibid.
81. J. Cvijić, *Balkansko Poluostrvo i jugoslovenske zemlje.*
82. J. Cvijić, "O violentnon tipu dinarskih Srba," *Pregled,* March 1912; also J. Cvijić, *Govori i clanci* (Belgrade, 1921), Vol. I, pp. 237–243; Cvijić, *Balkansko Poluostrvo,* Vol. II, pp. 53–140; Cvijić, *Jedinstvo i psihicki tipovi dinarskih Juznih Slovena* (Niš, 1914); Cvijić, "Studies in Yugoslav Psychology," *Slavonic Review,* December 1930, pp. 368–84.
83. See criticism of Cvijić by D. Tomasić in *National Communism and Soviet Strategy,* pp. 57–58; M. Nedeljković, "Prilozi proučavanju violentnog tipa," *Srpski knjiźevni glasnik,* September 1912.
84. V. Milić, "Socioloska koncepcija Jovana Cvijića," *Knjiźevnost,* 1956, Nos. 9, 10, 11, 12.
85. Dr. N. Velimirović, *Religija Njegośeva* (Belgrade, 1911).
86. Quoted from the Introduction, by Radovan Zogović, in *Gorski Vijenac* (Belgrade, 1947), p. 36.
87. Ibid.
88. Djilas, *Legenda o Njegośu* (Belgrade, 1952), p. 71.
89. Evans, *Through Bosnia and Hercegovina on Foot.*
90. Evans, "Serbia's Greatest Battle," *London Times,* June 28, 1916.
91. Baernreither, p. 65.
92. J. Cvijić, *Balkansko Poluostrvo,* Vol. II, p. 54.
93. J. Reed, *The War in Eastern Europe,* p. 65.
94. Albertini, *The Origins of the War of 1914,* Vol. II, p. 47.

CHAPTER XII   *pages 261–284*

1. M. Durman, "Djački štrajk 1912," *Knjiźevnik,* February 1939, p. 72.

2. Ibid., p. 75.
3. *Pijemont,* March 18, 1912.
4. M. Durman, Djački štrajk," p. 75.
5. Ibid., p. 76.
6. Ibid.
7. Ibid., pp. 76–77.
8. Ibid., p. 78.
9. I. Kecmanović, "Jedna borbena omladinska organizacija," *Pregled,* January 1958, pp. 245–57, citing a confidential report of the Bosnian government, dated January 25, 1912.
10. Ibid.
11. Ljubibratić, *Princip,* p. 45. Also Pappenheim, "Conversations with Princip," p. 702.
12. Ljubibratić, *Princip,* p. 45.
13. As told by Djulaga Bukovac (Pero Slijepčević's papers).
14. V. Bogićević, *Mlada Bosna,* p. 124.
15. Miloš Pjanić published his article under the pseudonym Mica Julčin in *Zora,* March 1912.
16. Ljubibratić, *Princip,* p. 106; Vrinjanin, "Omladinske organizacije i sarajevski atentat," *Novosti,* July 15, 16 and 17, 1926; O. Tartalja, *Veleizdajnik,* p. 55.
17. Kranjčević, *Uspomene jednog učesnika,* pp. 44–46.
18. MKEFF, Ps/37, 1912; also A. Filipić's letter to Dr. Ljubo Jurković, May 26, 1962.
19. Ibid.
20. Ljubibratić, *Princip,* p. 106.
21. V. Zaninović, "Mlada Hrvatska uoči I. Svjetskoga rata," *Historijski zbornik* (1958–1959), p. 93.
22. Tartalja, pp. 55–56.
23. Ibid.
24. A. Filipić's letter to Dr. Ljubo Jurković, May 26, 1962.
25. Durman, "Djački štrajk," p. 81.
26. A. Filipić's letter to Dr. Ljubo Jurković, May 26, 1962.
27. *Obtożnica proti Luki Jukiću i Drugovima prilog Narodnih novina broj, 168,* Zagreb, 1912.

28. V. Zaninović, "Mlada Hrvatska uoči I. Svjetskoga rata," p. 89.
29. *Obtožnica proti Luki Jukiću i Drugovima prilog Narodnih novina broj 168*, Zagreb, 1912; and also V. Zaninović, "Mlada Hrvatska uoči I. Svjetskoga rata," p. 93.
30. *Ibid.*
31. *Obtožnica proti Luki Jukiću i Drugovima prilog Narodnih novina broj 168*, Zagreb, 1912.
32. AFR, FA III, 269, FMB–MAE, June 14, 1912. Also, *Riječki novi list*, August 1, 1912. A. Cesarec, Dj. Cvijić and K. Horvatin, "Jukićev atentat i Dragan Bublić u osvetljenje svog 'Atentata,'" *Književna Republika*, April 1927.
33. MKEFF Po/96 1912
34. MKEFF, Ps/37 1912.
35. *Ibid.*
36. *Ibid.*
37. V. Zaninović, "Mlada Hrvatska uoči I. Svjetskoga rata," pp. 93–94.
38. *Ibid.*
39. M. Durman, "Historijski značaj Jukićevog atentata," *Književnik*, June 1937, p. 227.
40. *Ibid.*, p. 228.
41. *Pijemont*, August 13, 1912.
42. *Ibid.*
43. *Ibid.*
44. *Zora*, 1912, Numbers 6, 7, 8.
45. Quoted from V. Zaninović, "Mlada Hrvatska uoči I. Svjetskoga rata," p. 93.
46. *Preporod*, February 1, 1913.
47. Baernreither (English edition), p. 162.
48. Ljubibratić, *Princip*, p. 109.
49. F. Šišić, "Kako su hrvati mislili u prvoj polovici 1913," *Riječ*, January 15, 1930.
50. P. Slijepčević, *Napor*, p. 207.
51. *Preporod*, January 1, 1913.
52. HHSTA 1653/4, J. B. 903.
53. *Narodna odbrana*, 1911; also A. Pribićević "Revolucionarni statut Milana Pribićevića," *Nova Evropa*, November 26, 1940, p. 374.

54. *Srbobran*, September 23, 1913.
55. *Ibid.*
56. *Ibid.*
57. *Pijemont*, September 27, 1913.
58. *Ibid.*
59. *Ibid.*
60. *Ibid.*
61. *Ibid.*
62. *DSIP, Zbirka Vojislava Jovanovića*, Dojčić's letter to King Alexander, November 29, 1919.
63. KA 45–18.
64. *Ibid.*
65. *Ibid.*
66. KA 45–18/1.
67. *Ibid.*
68. *Ibid.*
69. Ivo Svetec's letter to Dr. Ljubo Jurković of May 8, 1962, and the indictment of the state's attorney in Split of April 21, 1915, against O. Tartalja and others (deposited in the archives of Split).
70. V. Bogićević, "Austriske vlasti i sarajevski atentat," *Nova Evropa*, July 26, 1934. See also Bogićević, *Sarajevski atentat*, pp. 430–31.
71. V. Bogićević, "Lujo Aljinović namjeravao je pri je Gavrila Principa ubiti Franju Ferdinanda," *Glas Zadra*, June 28, 1952.
72. *Pester Lloyd*, June 29, 1914.
73. NEFF, *Prozess in Sarajevo*.
74. Ljubibratić, *Princip*, p. 45.
75. *Ibid.*
76. *Ibid.*, p. 137.
77. *Ibid.*, p. 139.
78. D. Šurmin, "Navodno spreman atentat na cara Franju Josipa 1912 godine," *Narodna odbrana*, May 31, 1938.
79. V. Bogićević, *Mlada Bosna*, p. 301.
80. *Ibid.* See also Kranjčević, pp. 138–39.
81. V. Bogićević, "Iznimne mjere u Bosni i Hercegovini u maju 1913," *Godišnjak istoriskog društva*

Bosne i Hercegovine, 1956, pp. 209–18.

82. B. Jevtić, "Vasilj Grdjić i 'Mlada Bosna,'" *Jugoslovenska pošta,* October 27, 1934.

83. Ljubibratić, *Princip,* p. 144.

84. N. Trišić, "Danilo Ilić, čovjek i borac," *Pregled,* December 1940, p. 596.

85. *Ibid.*

86. Ljubibratić, *Gaćinović,* p. 112.

87. *Ibid.*

88. Gradski muzej, Sarajevo (GMS), Lebedev papers.

89. Pappenheim, p. 706.

90. Čerović, *Bosanski omladinci,* p. 104.

91. M. Ambrožić, "Nedeljko Čabrinović u Trstu," *Nova Evropa,* February 26, 1938.

92. *Ibid.*

93. *Ibid.*

94. NEFF, *Prozess in Sarajevo.*

95. *Ibid.*

96. Čerović, p. 104; also Čabrinović's statement at the trial, V. Bogićević, *Sarajevski atentat,* p. 332.

97. I. Orlić, "Jugoslovenska secanja," *Riječ,* July 10, 1937.

98. *Ibid.*

99. *Ibid.*

100. *Ibid.*

101. GMS, Lebedev papers.

102. *Ogledi i pisma,* p. 201.

103. Fay, *Origins of the World War,* Vol. II, p. 103. The French minister in Montenegro informed Paris in early July, 1914, that Mehmedbašić had gone into Montenegro and that he had stated at a police investigation that the plot had originated in Tours, France. (DDF, X, 537.) His statement was never confirmed by the investigation conducted by French authorities in Tours. (DDF, X, 537 and 766fn.) See also *Serbiens Aussenpolitik,* Documents 11–14.

104. Golubić gave more information about the Toulouse meeting to Victor Serge-Kibalchich, who published an article, "La Verité sur l'attentat de Sarajevo," in *Clarté,* May 1925. But, as we shall see later, Golubić's story differs sharply from that of other participants at the meeting. R. Seton-Watson (*Sarajevo,* p. 74), M. Bogićević (*Le Procès de Salonique,* pp. 151–63), Golubić himself, under the pseudonym M. Vladirirom ("Seton Watson sur le mouvement révolutionnaire Yougoslave d'avant guerre," *La Fédération Balkanique,* December 1, 1925), D. Tvrdoreka (in *Novosti,* September 23 and 25, 1926), N. Trišić ("Danilo Ilić, čovjek i borac," *Pregled,* December 1940), Albertini (*Origins of the War of 1914,* Vol. II, pp. 76–77) and others published the materials they gathered on the Toulouse meeting.

105. From Gaćinović's letters in *Ogledi i pisma* (p. 203), he was in Lausanne on February 7, 1914, and in Geneva on February 3, 1914.

106. *Ibid.*

107. *Ibid.*

108. N. Trišić, "Oko Sarajevskog atentata," *Pregled,* January 1929, and "Slučaj Mehmeda Mehmedbašića," *Pregled,* February 1935.

109. Tvrdoreka, in *Novosti,* September 23, 1926.

110. Mandl, "Ein dusterer Gedenktag," *Neues acht Uhr Blatt,* June 28 and 29, 1924; V. Nikolić (M. Golubić), "Das Attentat von Sarajewo und die Kriegsschuldfrage," *La Fédération Balkanique,* May 31, 1925; M. Bogićević, *Le Procès de Salonique,* p. 160; Seton-Watson, *Sarajevo,* p. 74.

111. Tvrdoreka, in *Novosti,* September 23, 1926; Trišić, "Oko Sarajevskog atentata, *loc. cit.,* and "Slučaj Mehmeda Mehmedhašića," *loc. cit.;* Albertini, II, p. 78; H. Ču-

rić, "Jedan nacionalni revolucionar iz Hercegovine," *Kalendar Gajreta,* 1939, pp. 253–363.

112. Albertini, II, p. 78.

113. Trišić, "Oko Sarajevskog atentata," *loc. cit.,* and "Slučaj Mehmeda Mehmedbašića," *loc. cit.*

114. *Ibid.*

115. *Ibid.*

116. Albertini, II, p. 79.

117. Ljubibratić, *Gaćinović,* pp. 118–19.

118. *Ibid.*

119. *Ibid.,* p. 121.

120. GMS, Lebedev papers.

CHAPTER XIII   *pages 285–314*

1. Conrad, *Aus meiner Dienstzeit,* Vol. III, p. 445.

2. *Ibid.,* p. 702.

3. *Ibid.,* p. 445.

4. NEFF, *Thronwechsel.*

5. Margutti, *The Emperor Francis Joseph* (London ed.), pp. 126–27.

6. C. Collas, "Auf den Bosnischen Wegspuren der Kreigsschuldfrage," *Kriegsschuldfrage,* January 1927, pp. 11–27.

7. A. J. P. Taylor, in *The Observer* (London), November 16, 1958.

8. Eisenmenger (English edition), p. 264.

9. Max Hohenberg, in interview, *Paris-Soir-Dimanche,* July 4, 1937.

10. Wegerer, *Der Ausbruch des Weltkrieges,* p. 101.

11. I. Dimitrijević, "Sima Pandurović i Gavrilo Princip," *Spomenica Sime Pandurovića* (Belgrade, 1928), pp. 67–74.

12. Jevdjević, *Sarajevski atentatori,* p. 18.

13. As told by Mustafa Golubić to Stevan Dedijer.

14. According to Jevtić (*Sarajevski atentat,* p. 25), Mihailo Pušara sent a clipping from the Zagreb paper *Novi Srbobran* about the intended visit of Archduke Franz Ferdinand to Sarajevo. At the trial Čabrinović stated that the clipping was in Latin characters, while *Novi Srbobran* was published in Cyrillic. V. Bogićević ("Poreklo isečka iz novina," *Pregled,* November 1935) came out with the thesis that the clipping was not from *Novi Srbobran,* which carried the news of the Archduke's visit only on May 18, 1914, but from Sarajevo's *Hrvatski dnevnik* of March 17, 1914. At the investigation Princip stated that he had heard about the Archduke's visit to Sarajevo from the Viennese paper *Die Zeit.* The same opinion was expressed by B. Tomić ("Oduženje narodnog duga Gavrilu Principu," *Narodna odbrana,* September 3, 1939). On the other hand, Grabež claimed that he had read about the Archduke's visit in the Sarajevo paper *Istina.*

15. V. Bogićević, *Sarajevski atentat,* p. 35.

16. Pfeffer, *Istraga u Sarajevskom atentatu,* p. 61.

17. NEFF, *Prozess in Sarajevo.*

18. Pfeffer, *Istraga,* p. 142.

19. *Ibid.,* pp. 143–44.

20. Arhiv Matice Srpske (MS), Manuscript Collection, Inv. No. M.255.

21. Nikola Škerović, *Crna Gora na osvitku 20 vijeka* (Belgrade, 1963), pp. 486–87.

22. MS, *loc. cit.*

23. MO, Third Series, IV, 91.

24. *Ibid.*

25. Jevtić, *Sarajevski atentat,* p. 13; Pappenheim, "Conversations with Princip," *Current History,* August 1927, p. 702.

26. Jevdjević, p. 44.

27. See Chapter XVII.

28. V. Bogićević, *Sarajevski atentat,* p. 106.

29. NEFF, *Prozess in Sarajevo.*

30. V. Bogićević, *Sarajevski atentat,* p. 66.

31. *Ibid.,* pp. 66, 144.

32. NEFF, *Prozess in Sarajevo.*

33. V. Bogićević, *Sarajevski aten-tat*, p. 66.

34. NEFF, *Prozess in Sarajevo.*

35. *Ibid.* A book which once be-longed to Princip, is preserved in the Belgrade Archives (DSIP, *Zbirka Vojislava Jovanovića*). On the back page of it Princip trans-lated the following sentences from German into Serbo-Croatian: "What your enemy should not know, do not tell your friend. If I keep a secret, it is my slave. If I reveal it, it is my master. On the tree of silence hangs its fruit . . . Nothing to say, nothing to trust."

36. V. Bogićević, *Sarajevski aten-tat*, p. 66.

37. NEFF, *Prozess in Sarajevo.*

38. V. Bogićević, *Sarajevski aten-tat*, p. 67.

39. *Ibid.*, p. 148.

40. *Ibid.*, p. 234.

41. DSIP, *Zbirka Vojislava Jo-vanovića.*

42. Bogićević, *Sarajevski atentat*, pp. 301–2.

43. The police agent Ivan Vila denied at the trial this statement of Čabrinović. (Bogićević, *Sarajev-ski atentat*, p. 302.)

44. *Ibid.*

45. Czernin, *In the World War*, p. 44.

46. R. Kellerhoff, *Erinnerungen und die letzte Fahrt des Erzherzog Franz Ferdinand* (Prague, 1915), p. 83.

47. P. Nikitsch-Boulles, *Vor dem Sturm*, p. 212.

48. Jevtić, *Sarajevski atentat*, pp. 30, 46, 58.

49. *Ibid.*, p. 56.

50. DSIP, *Zbirka Vojislava Jova-novića*, Jevtić's interrogation of July 7 and August 28 and 29, 1914.

51. *Ibid.*

52. B. Čerović, *Bosanski omla-dinci i Sarajevski atentat*, pp. 68–70.

53. NEFF, *Prozess in Sarajevo.*

54. V. Bogićević, *Sarajevski aten-tat*, Annex.

55. *Ibid.*, p. 111; Pfeffer, *Istraga u Sarajevskom atentatu*, p. 62; NEFF, *Prozess in Sarajevo.*

56. NEFF, *Prozess in Sarajevo;* Pfeffer, p. 74; V. Bogićević, *Sara-jevski atentat*, p. 347.

57. NEFF, *Prozess in Sarajevo.*

58. *Ibid.*

59. *Ibid.*

60. Cvetko Popović, "Prilog is-toriji Sarajevskog atentata," *Pol-itika*, April 3, 1928.

61. V. Bogićević, *Sarajevski aten-tat*, Annex.

62. NEFF, *Prozess in Sarajevo.*

63. *Ibid.*

64. *Ibid.*

65. S. Djokić, "Poslednja zarada Gavrila Principa," *Vreme*, June 28, 1929.

66. *Ibid.*

67. NEFF, *Prozess in Sarajevo.*

68. Pappenheim, "Conversations with Princip," p. 705.

69. *Ogledi i pisma*, pp. 212–13.

70. *Ibid.*

71. GMS, Lebedev papers.

72. Pappenheim, p. 705.

73. NEFF, *Prozess in Sarajevo.*

74. V. Bogićević, *Sarajevski aten-tat*, pp. 100, 103, 364.

75. *Ibid.*, pp. 115, 118, 120.

76. *Ibid.*, p. 120.

77. Ljubibratić, *Princip*, p. 215.

78. *Ogledi i pisma*, p. 95.

79. Juš Kozak's letter to the au-thor, January 14, 1959.

80. Slijepčević, *Napor Bosne i Hercegovine*, pp. 191–92; Čorović, *Odnosi*, p. 562; Niko Bartulović, *Od revolucionarne omladine do Orjune* (Split 1925), p. 40.

81. V. Bogićević, *Mlada Bosna*, p. 424.

82. Todor Vujasinović, "Uz 40-godisnjicu Sarajevskog atentata," *Pregled*, June 1954.

83. Dr. Ljubo Jurković, *Orjuna.*

84. As told by Dr. Jurković to the author.

85. Cvetko Popović, "Prilog istoriji Sarajevskog atentata," *Politika*, April 1, 1928.

86. DSIP, *Zbirka Vojislava Jovanovića*.

87. Ljubibratić, *Gaćinović*, p. 96.

88. As told by Dr. Vaso Čubrilović to the author.

89. *Ogledi i pisma*, pp. 95–96.

90. *Ibid.*, pp. 212–13.

91. NEFF, *Prozess in Sarajevo*.

92. Pappenheim, p. 706.

93. *Politika*, June 28, 1914.

94. *Hrvatski dnevnik*, June 25, 1914; *Politika*, June 28, 1914.

95. *Narod*, June 24, 1914; *Hrvatski dnevnik*, June 24, 1914; Glück, *Sarajewo*, p. 146.

96. Jevtić, *Sarajevski atentat*, p. 33.

97. T. Žurunić, "Vidovdanski atentat 1914," *Vrbaske novine*, June 26, 27, 28, 1934.

98. NEFF, *Prozess in Sarajevo*.

99. *Ibid.*

CHAPTER XIV   *pages 315–323*

1. NEFF, *Prozess in Sarajevo*.

2. V. Bogićević, *Sarajevski atentat*, p. 267.

3. *Ibid.*, p. 274.

4. NEFF, *Prozess in Sarajevo*.

5. *Ibid.*

6. N. Trišić, *Sarajevski atentat*, p. 18.

7. NEFF, *Prozess in Sarajevo*.

8. N. Trišić, "Traganje austrougarskih vlasti za Muhamedom Mehmedbašićem," *Pregled*, January–February 1940.

9. L. Albertini, *Origins of the War of 1914*, Vol. II, pp. 46–47.

10. NEFF, *Prozess in Sarajevo*.

11. V. Bogićević, *Sarajevski atentat*, p. 127.

12. Albertini, II, p. 46.

13. V. Bogićević, *Sarajevski atentat*, p. 135.

14. NEFF, *Prozess in Sarajevo*.

15. *Ibid.*

16. V. Bogićević, *Sarajevski atentat*, pp. 100–1.

17. L. Pfeffer, *Istraga u Sarajevskom atentatu*, p. 71.

18. D. Jevdjević, *Sarajevski atentatori*, p. 50.

19. See Chapter XVII.

20. Jevdjević, p. 107; Jevtić, *Sarajevski atentat*, p. 37; Čorović, *Odnosi*, p. 595.

21. Reuters report in the *Manchester Guardian*, June 29, 1914, estimated that twenty people were wounded. At the trial seven wounded asked for damages (V. Bogićević, *Sarajevski atentat*, p. 269). Also three persons from the Archduke's party were wounded by Čabrinović's bomb.

22. V. Bogićević, *Sarajevski atentat*, pp. 49–50.

23. *Ibid.*, pp. 298–99.

24. NEFF, *Prozess in Sarajevo*.

25. *Ibid.*

26. V. Bogićević, *Sarajevski atentat*, p. 71.

27. NEFF, *Prozess in Sarajevo*.

28. *Ibid.*

29. Jevtić, *Sarajevski atentat*, p. 39; also Glück, *Sarajewo*, p. 158.

30. A. Morsey, "Konopischt und Sarajevo," *Berliner Monatshefte*, June 1934, pp. 486–99.

31. F. Behr, "Oko Sarajevskog atentat," *Pregled*, September, 1930, pp. 607–11.

32. V. Bogićević, *Sarajevski atentat*, pp. 277–78.

33. NEFF, *Prozess in Sarajevo*.

34. V. Bogićević, *Sarajevski atentat*, p. 288.

35. B. Jevtić, "Mihailo Pušara," *Politika*, December 21, 1923.

36. NEFF, *Prozess in Sarajevo*.

37. *Ibid.*

38. B. Jevtić, "Mihailo Pušara," *loc. cit.*

39. *Ibid.*

40. *Ibid.*

CHAPTER XV   *pages 324–350*

1. The investigation of Princip and his accomplices was conducted in the first few days after June 28, 1914, by both the police and the investigating judge, Leo Pfeffer, although the latter was the only official investigator. The minutes of the police investigation are missing, but most of their content was summarized in the reports of Governor Potiorek to Vienna; these reports are published in Volume 8 of the *Österreich-Ungarns Aussenpolitik* (Oe-U). A complete account of the investigations was made on September 19, 1914, and was handed over to the state's attorney in Sarajevo as the basis for the act of accusation. The statements of the accused were translated into German and sent to Vienna. One set of these acts and some other materials from Princip's trial are preserved in the NEFF; they represent a documentation of great historical value. Leo Pfeffer published his version of the investigation of Gavrilo Princip and his accomplices under the title *Istraga u Sarajevskom atentatu* (Investigation of the Sarajevo Assassination). But at the time of writing, Pfeffer did not have all the available documentation. It seems that he did not have, in particular, the statements of the main accused. He also used private notes he made during the investigation. We shall speak later about the historical value of Pfeffer's book. Pfeffer also published several articles on the subject, of which two are most important, "Kako sam vodio istragu u Sarajevskom atentatu" (How I Conducted the Investigation of the Sarajevo Assassination), *Nova Evropa*, March 1938, and "Aleksander Karadjordjević sukrivac Sarajevskog atentata" (Alexander Karadjordjević,

Accomplice in the Sarajevo Assassination), in *Hrvatski narod*, June 28, 1941.

The whole investigation material after the state's attorney used it was handed over to the District Court of Sarajevo and together with the minutes of the trial was sent by the Bosnian government at the request of Joint Ministry of Finance to the Haus-Hof-Staatsarchiv in Vienna, in June 1915. They remained there until the Second World War, when a group of Austrian and German historians, acting on a suggestion of the German Ministry of Foreign Affairs, used them for their publications about the responsibility of the Serbian and Russian governments for the outbreak of the First World War. Some documents dealing with the Sarajevo assassination which were in the Archives of the Joint Ministry of Finance were returned to Yugoslavia after 1918. Božo Čerović, chief of a section of the Joint Ministry, brought its archives dealing with Bosnia and Hercegovina, the so-called "Bosnian Acts," to Sarajevo. They were there until 1941, when they were returned to Vienna, but at the end of the Second World War a part of them came back to Sarajevo. The accusation act and the verdict against Princip and his accomplices were published by the State Publishing House in Sarajevo: *Obtužnica i obrazlozenje protiv Gavrila Principa i drugova radi atentata*, and *Osuda Okružnog suda u Sarajevu po zavrsenoj raspravi protiv Gavrila Principa i drugova.*

The official minutes of the trial have not yet been found. It is presumed that they are in Vienna. The German and Austrian historians who worked on the problem of the responsibility of the Serbian government during the Second

World War used the documents for their work. Vladimir Kesterčanek, a teacher in the technical school in Sarajevo, and Milan (or Pavo) Prpić, a student and stenographer of the *Sabor*, were the official stenographers at the trial. The paper of the Archbishop Stadler, *Hrvatski dnevnik*, had its own stenographer, Badalić, throughout the trial.

Kesterčanek and Prpić handed over their texts to Ladislav Chmielewsky, the Chief of the Justice Department of the Bosnian government, who organized the translation of the text into German.

After the trial several versions of these shorthand minutes were published, the first one in 1918 by Pharos (Anton Puntigam) and Kohler. It seems that they used Badalić's text. F. Wyss published in Bern in 1919 a book with the title *La Conspiration Serbe contre la Monarchie Austro-Hongroise* in which the proceedings of the trial were reported. V. Bogićević (*Sarajevski atentat*, p. 4) presumed that this book used the same shorthand materials as Puntigam's.

After the war Kesterčanek reconstructed the trial proceedings on the basis of his original shorthand notes and those of Prpić. The Sarajevo paper *Večernja pošta* in its April 6, 1925, issue, announced the publication of these notes, but due to the intervention of the Yugoslav government the publication was stopped and the notes were not published except those which had been printed on the first day, April 6, 1925.

In 1925, copies of the shorthand proceedings made in 1914 were found. Pero Slijepčević published in *Nova Evropa* (June 1, 1925) an article about the attitude of Princip and his followers on the national problem of the South Slavs, on the basis of shorthand minutes which he had received from Aco Poljanić, a bank clerk from Sarajevo. It is not clear whether this text was made by Kesterčanek or by Badalić.

It seems that a full text of the 1914 shorthand minutes was found in Sarajevo, in the archives of the Joint Ministry of Finance. One copy of it was given to Albert Mousset, who published it in Paris in 1930 under the title *Un Drame historique: l'attentat de Sarajevo*.

In Vienna during World War II Frau Übersberger worked on a new version of the Sarajevo trial minutes. She came into contact with Kesterčanek and Mousset and prepared a text of the minutes, but the end of the war hampered its publication.

Vojislav Bogićević published a Serbo-Croat version of the same text in Sarajevo in 1954 titled *Sarajevski atentat*. Bogićević revealed all the changes in the original text that Mousset made for political reasons. When France was occupied, Mousset was questioned by the German authorities about how he obtained the shorthand minutes. ("Sarajevo, ou la fausse enigme," *Le Monde*, June 28, 1953.)

In the NEFF there is no German translation of the shorthand minutes of 1914.

One has to consider additional sources for a fuller picture of what happened at the trial. A few newspapermen were allowed to attend the trial, but as V. Bogićević pointed out (*Sarajevski atentat*, p. 2), all the newsmen's reports were censored by the authorities in Sarajevo. At the same time, the Bosnian government sent the daily report about the trial proceedings to the Joint Ministry of Finance, presumably for the use of the Viennese press. The texts were published in Bogićević's *Sarajevski atentat*, pp. 407–43.

The last source about the investigation and trials is the reminiscences of the contemporaries. This writer gained the impression talking with Vaso Čubrilović that none of the published shorthand versions of the trial has given a complete picture of what happened. Other participants in the conspiracy have written valuable contributions, particularly I. Kranjčević (*Uspomene*, pp. 67–116), C. Popović and B. Zagorac. Although B. Jevtić was not a direct participant in the plot, he wrote about the life of Princip and his accomplices in jail and during the trail, in his *Sarajevski atentat*, but his material is biased for personal reasons.

Also several lawyers who defended the accused have left their own memoirs about their defense. Rudolf Cistler published his memoirs in *Narodno jedinstvo*, March 6, to 13, 1919; they have been reprinted several times. A lecture of Cistler on the same subject was published in Ljubljana in 1937 under the title *Kako sam branio Principa i drugove 1914 godine*. Princip's lawyer, Dr. Max Feldbauer, in *Večernja pošta*, June 27, 1929, published his reminiscences together with the copies of some original documents from the investigation and trial.

2. Pfeffer, *Istraga u Sarajevskom atentatu*, p. 27.

3. *Ibid.*, p. 29.

4. NEFF, *Sarajevo Prozess.*

5. *Ibid.*

6. *Ibid.*

7. *Ibid.*

8. *Ibid.*

9. *Ibid.*

10. *Ibid.*

11. *Ibid.*

12. *Ibid.*

13. *Ibid.*

14. *Ibid.*

15. *Ibid.*

16. B. Jevtić, *Sarajevski atentat*, pp. 42–43. Milan Toplica (Pero Slijepčević) *Rat protiv svojih podanika u Austro-Ugarskoj* (New York, 1914), pp. 9–12. Glück (*Sarajewo*, p. 164) was of the opinion that the police could not do anything against the demonstrators, but he believed that military authorities initiated the demonstrations.

17. Jevtić, *Sarajevski atentat*, p. 45.

18. *Ibid.*, p. 75.

19. Čerović, *Bosanski omladinci*, p. 95.

20. V. G. Maneli (pseudonym of Velimir Mandić), *Bosna u lancima ili povodom atentata Gavrila Principa* (Sarajevo, 1919), Introduction.

21. As told to the writer by Dr. Vaso Čubrilović.

22. *Ibid.*

23. Albertini, *Origins of the War of 1914*, Vol. II, p. 45 fn.

24. B. Zagorac, "Povodom Pfefferove knjige o sarajevskom atentatu," *Razvitak*, July 1, 1938, pp. 204–12.

25. V. Bogićević, *Sarajevski atentat*, p. 102.

26. Pfeffer, *Istraga*, p. 63. Tereza Lazi, a secretary in the Criminal Department of the Sarajevo police, confirmed also that the conspirators were beaten up by the police officials during the investigation. (P. Stojanović, in *Borba*, July 9, 1964.)

27. *Ibid.*, p. 67.

28. *Ibid.*

29. DSIP, *Zbirka Vojislava Jovanovića.*

30. As told to the writer by Vaso Čubrilović.

31. GMS, Lebedev papers.

32. NEFF, *Sarajevo Prozess.*

33. *Ibid.*

34. *Ibid.*

35. V. Bogićević, *Sarajevski atentat*, p. 347.

36. B. Jevtić, *Sarajevski atentat,* p. 30.

37. D. Jevdjević, *Sarajevski atentatori,* p. 77.

38. *Ibid.,* p. 77, 84, 154.

39. Pfeffer, *Istraga,* p. 57.

40. *Ibid.,* pp. 29–30.

41. V. Bogićević, *Sarajevski atentat,* p. 82.

42. H. Djurić, *Jedan nacionalni Revolucionar iz Hercegovine* (Sarajevo, 1938), p. 11.

43. C. Popović, "Prilog Istoriji Sarajevskog atentata," *Politika,* April 4, 1928.

44. *Ibid.*

45. *Zvono,* March 8, 1919.

46. Popović, "Prilog Istoriji Sarajevskog atentata," *loc. cit.*

47. As told by Vaso Čubrilović. See also Popović, "Prilog Istoriji Sarajevskog atentata," *loc. cit.*

48. *Ibid.*

49. *Ibid.*

50. I. Kranjčević, *Uspomene,* pp. 92–93.

51. M. Feldbauer, "Sa Gavrilom Principom u tamnickoj celiji," *Večernja pošta,* June 27, 1929.

52. I. Kranjčević, p. 92.

53. *Ibid.*

54. HHSTA.

55. Mousset, *Un Drame historique,* Introduction.

56. DSIP, *Solunski proces,* statement of Dušan Glumac.

57. As told to this writer by Dr. Vaso Čubrilović.

58. V. Bogićević, *Sarajevski atentat,* p. 193.

59. *Ibid.,* p. 61, 62.

60. *Ibid.,* p. 41.

61. *Ibid.,* p. 110.

62. *Ibid.,* p. 72.

63. *Ibid.,* p. 91.

64. *Ibid.,* p. 34.

65. *Ibid.,* p. 122.

66. *Ibid.,* p. 72.

67. *Ibid.,* pp. 64, 313, 336.

68. *Ibid.,* p. 90.

69. *Ibid.*

70. *Ibid.,* p. 38.

71. *Ibid.,* pp. 122, 131.

72. *Ibid.,* p. 182.

73. *Ibid.,* p. 186.

74. *Ibid.,* p. 106.

75. *Ibid.,* pp. 89, 91.

76. *Ibid.,* p. 51.

77. NEFF, *Prozess in Sarajevo.*

78. *Ibid.*

79. *Ibid.,* p. 72.

80. *Ibid.,* p. 41.

81. *Ibid.,* p. 37.

82. *Ibid.,* p. 138.

83. As told to the writer by Dr. Vaso Čubrilović.

84. N. Trišić, "Borba Mlade Bosne," *Glasnik Jugoslovenskog profesorskog društva,* November–December, 1939.

85. As told to the writer by Dr. Vaso Čubrilović.

86. NEFF, *Sarajevo Prozess.*

87. V. Bogićević, *Sarajevski atentat,* p. 62.

88. *Ibid.,* p. 70.

89. *Ibid.,* p. 199.

90. Trišić, *Sarajevski atentat,* p. 40.

91. NEFF, *Sarajevo Prozess.*

92. *Ibid.*

93. V. Bogićević, *Sarajevski atentat,* p. 38.

94. *Ibid.,* p. 90.

95. *Ibid.,* p. 73.

96. *Ibid.,* p. 75.

97. *Ibid.,* pp. 87–88, 103, 140, 141.

98. *Ibid.,* p. 123. The same statement Čubrilović made during the investigation (NEFF, *Prozess in Sarajevo*).

99. NEFF, *Prozess in Sarajevo.*

100. V. Bogićević, *Sarajevski atentat,* p. 140.

101. *Ibid.,* p. 103.

102. *Ibid.,* p. 343.

103. *Ibid.,* p. 347.

104. *Ibid.,* p. 364.

105. *Ibid.,* pp. 369–70.

106. *Ibid.,* p. 372.

107. Pappenheim, "Conversations with Princip," p. 706

108. *Ibid.*

109. V. Bogićević, *Sarajevski atentat*, p. 116.

110. NEFF, *Sarajevo Prozess.*

111. V. Bogićević, *Sarajevski atentat*, p. 328.

112. As told to the author by Dr. Vaso Čubrilović.

113. V. Bogićević, *Sarajevski atentat*, p. 399.

114. *Ibid.*, pp. 398–99.

115. R. Cistler, *Kako sam branio Principa i drugove 1914 godine.*

116. V. Bogićević, *Sarajevski atentat*, p. 348.

117. Kranjčević, *Uspomene*, p. 114.

118. Pfeffer, *Istraga u Sarajevskom atentatu*, p. 141.

119. V. Bogićević, "Kako je stradala 'Srpsko-hrvatska nacionalisticka omladina,'" *Prosvjeta*, June 1937, pp. 423–26.

120. D. Šurmin, "Dokumenta za Vidovdan 1914," *Letopis Matice Srpske*, February 1929, pp. 210–25.

121. V. Popović, *Patnje i zrtve Srba sreza Trebinjskog od 1914–1918* (Sarajevo, 1921); V. Čorović, *Crna Knjiga.*

122. *Ibid.*

123. *Ibid.*

124. V. Bogićević, *Sarajevski atentat*, Annex.

125. *Ibid.*, p. 403.

126. *Ibid.*

127. Jevdjević, p. 46.

128. V. Bogićević, "Zločinac koji je objesio trojicu ucesnika Sarajevskog atentata-zvanični dželat Kraljevine Jugoslavije," *Oslobodjenje*, February 24, 1952. The executioner Alois Seifried, according to V. Bogićević, remained in Yugoslavia after 1918 in his function as state executioner.

129. V. Bogićević, "Zločinac koji . . . ," *loc. cit.*

130. M. Mratinković, "Poslednji casovi narodnih mucenika Veljka Čubrilovića, Miška Jovanovića i Danila Ilića," *Narodno jedinstvo*, May 9 and 10, 1919.

131. *Ibid.*

132. W. Glück, "Kako je Ivasjuk saznao imena ostalih zaverenika," *Politika*, November 22, 1933.

133. M. Krnić, "Na grobovima heroja," *Zvono*, February 7, 1920.

CHAPTER XVI   *pages 351–365*

1. J. Dangić, "S Gavrilom Principom od Sarajeva do Terezina," *Nova Evropa*, March 26, 1940.

2. *Ibid.*

3. *Ibid.*

4. *Ibid.*

5. KA, 41–15–34.

6. *Ibid.*

7. *Ibid.*

8. KA, 41–35–34, Finanzministerium to Theresienstadt und Möllersdorf.

9. C. Jandrić, "Smrt Gavrila Principa," *Politika*, March 18, 1926.

10. Kranjčević, *Uspomene*, p. 127.

11. As told to this writer by Dr. Vukosava Branisavlević-Čabrinović.

12. F. Werfel, "Tschabrinovitsch," *Die Neue Rundschau*, May 2, 1923.

13. KA, 14 A 59–I–2 Strafl Schädel Präparierung-Kriminalbüro Sarajevo Überlassung.

14. KA, 14 A 59–13 of February 16, 1916.

15. KA, 14 A 59–13/1,2 Finanzministerium to k.u.k. Kriegsministerium, April 13, 1916.

16. S. Žakula, *Od Terezina do Sarajevo*, pp. 11–12.

17. Dr. A (pseudonym), "Bogdan Žerajić," *Nedeljni sarajevski list 7 dana*, July 2, 1953.

18. Žakula, p. 6.

19. Jandrić, *op. cit.*

20. Pappenheim, "Conversations with Princip," pp. 701–2.

21. *Ibid.*, p. 702.

22. *Ibid.*, p. 703.

23. *Ibid.*, pp. 703–5.
24. *Ibid.*, p. 705.
25. *Ibid.*, p. 706.
26. *Ibid.*
27. Kranjčević, *Uspomene*, pp. 126–29.
28. *Ibid.*, p. 126.
29. *Ibid.*, p. 132.
30. *Ibid.*, p. 135.
31. C. Popović, "Prilog istoriji Sarajevskog atentata," *Politika*, April 5, 1928.
32. As told to the author by Vaso Čubrilović.
33. B. Zagorac, "Proljeće na robiji," *Narodna odbrana*, May 6, 1934, pp. 289–90.
34. Kranjčević, p. 139.
35. D. Dimović, "Kod Karla Habzburga," *Politika*, April 7, 1922.
36. KA, k.u.k. KM zu Ant. r/I Nr. 3264.
37. KA, 4 A 3–2/3
38. P. Nikitsch-Boulles, *Vor dem Sturm*, pp. 226–27.
39. *Ibid.*
40. S. Gavrilović, "Smrt Gavrila Principa," *Politika*, March 20, 1926.
41. Kranjčević, p. 128.
42. Dr. Špatni, "Lutanje sarajevskih mucenika," *Zvono*, April 9, 1919 (translated from *Češko slovo*).
43. Dr. A. Marsch, "Princip in Theresienstadt," *Die Zeit* (Prague), June 29, 1937.
44. V. Bogićević, *Sarajevski atentat*, Annex.
45. F. Löbl, "Tamnovanje i smrt Gavre Principa," *Zvono*, February 14, 1919.
46. N. Trišić, *Sarajevski atentat*, p. 89.

CHAPTER XVII   *pages 366–400*

1. Besides three published collections of Austro-Hungarian documents on the events leading to the First World War and its beginning (see Bibliography), the Austrian State Archives are open for academic research. The Archduke Franz Ferdinand's *Nachlass*, as well as the papers of his *Militärkanzlei*, are of a particular importance for the study of this period of history.

2. German archives captured during the Second World War offer great research possibilities for the 1903–1914 period, particularly as far as relations between Germany and Serbia for that period are concerned (Catalogue of German Microfilms). The Archives of the Foreign Ministry in Bonn have the documents in full, particularly those which had not been microfilmed. The destruction of a part of the Archives of the German Supreme Headquarters for the First World War is a serious handicap for historians.

3. The Serbian government published only one collection of its diplomatic papers of 1914 (see Bibliography). A greater part of the Serbian Court Archives, Archives of the Ministry of Foreign Affairs and Archives of other Serbian government agencies were captured during the First and the Second World Wars. One part of these archives was restored to Yugoslavia, after 1945, but some of the most important documents are still abroad. One part of the Serbian diplomatic papers has been published by private individuals (see Bibliography). In the Archives of the State Secretariat for External Affairs in Belgrade (DSIP) the archives which were returned from Austria are available for academic research.

4. V. Dedijer, *Prilozi za biografiju Josipa Broza-Tita* (Belgrade, 1952), p. 38.
5. Dumba, *Memoirs of a Diplomat*, pp. 218–19.
6. Ćorović, *Odnosi izmedju Srbije i Austro-Ugarske*, pp. 93–94.
7. AA, Reel 57, UM Ser.
8. AFR, FR–231 FA St. Petersburg—MAE.

9. J. Cvijić, "Značaj Bosne i Hercegovine za srpski narod," *Cviji-
ćeva Knjiga* (Belgrade, 1927).

10. *Ibid.*, pp. 80–83.

11. National Archives, Washington (NA), State Department NF
724607270, 1906–1910, February 27,
1909. The Swedish minister in
Rome, historian Bildt, on the other
hand expressed a different opinion.
In his report to Stockholm of November 1, 1908, he said: "The Serbs
in Serbia are not so brave as the
Serbs in Montenegro and will not
rush at the Austrian cannons with
bared chests, but the Serbs in Belgrade are ready to assassinate poor
Forgach (the Austrian minister in
Belgrade) or to put fire in the Austrian legation. One can imagine
what complications could arise."
(SA—Archives of the Swedish
Ministry of Foreign Affairs.)

12. DSIP, *Zbirka Vojislava Jovanovića.*

13. At the beginning, the action
of *komite* in Macedonia and Kosovo was led by a private committee headed by Dr. Milorad Godjevac. But after heavy losses of *komite* units in the encounters with
the Turkish army, the whole *komite* action at the end of 1904 came
under the supervision of the state
and public authorities of Serbia, as
the archives in Belgrade show.
There existed a central committee,
composed of public figures, in addition to a principal committee,
which was centered in the Consular
Department of the Ministry of Foreign Affairs. At the Turkish border, at Vranje, an executive committee, headed by officer Ljuba
Vulović, took care of the training
of the members of *komite* units and
their dispatch over the border.

14. Vemić's diary was written in
pencil on sixty-nine pages of graph
paper, size 16 by 10 centimeters.
The authenticity of this diary has
yet to be established; the handwriting appears to be Vemić's, but the
diary was rewritten or rearranged
by him sometime between 1915
and 1917, since the years do not
follow consecutively.

15. DSIP, *Zbirka Vojislava Jovanovića.*

16. *Ibid.*

17. *Ibid.*

18. S. Jovanović, *Moji savremenici,* pp. 36–39.

19. DSIP, *Solunski proces.*

20. *Ibid.*

21. M. Milenović, *Narodna Enciklopedija Srpsko-hrvatsko-slove-
načka,* Vol. II, p. 171.

22. DSIP, *Zbirka Vojislava Jovanovića.*

23. DSIP, *Solunski proces.*

24. O. Tartalja, *Veleizdajnik
Moje Uspomene,* pp. 24–26.

25. M. Živanović, *Pukovnik
Apis,* p. 657.

26. "Narodna odbrana," a bro-
chure issued by the Central Committee of Narodna Odbrana (Belgrade), pp. 6–7.

27. M. Bogićević, *Procès de Salonique,* pp. 33–34.

28. M. Živanović, p. 202.

29. *Ibid.*

30. S. Stanojević, *Ubistvo austriskog prestolonaslednika Ferdinanda,* p. 39.

31. DSIP, *Zbirka Vojislava Jovanovića.*

32. AFR FMB-MAE, November
20, 1911.

33. M. Bogićević, *Procès de Salonique,* p. 3.

34. DSIP, *Solunski proces.*

35. DSIP, *Zbirka Vojislava Jovanovića.*

36. *Ogledi i pisma,* pp. 309–13.

37. *Ibid.*, pp. 86–87.

38. S. Jovanović (*Moji savremenici,* p. 59) claimed that the Serbs
outside Serbia represented the majority of the Ujedinjenje ili Smrt
members.

39. DSIP, *Zbirka Vojislava Jovanovića.*

40. DSIP, *Solunski proces*, Colonel Apis's statement at the Salonika trial.

41. D. Stojadinović, "Srbija i Nemačka u Svetskom ratu," p. 418.

42. DSIP, *Solunski proces*.

43. *Ibid.* Colonel Apis was the source of the information about his alleged relations with Milovanović. In Milovanović's papers, as this writer was told by Dr. D. Djordjević, there is no evidence of these relations. Milovanović's family even doubts that Milovanović was poisoned.

44. D. Djordjević, *Milovan Milovanović*, p. 157.

45. DSIP, *Zbirka Vojislava Jovanovića*.

46. AFR FFI FMB-MAE, July 28, 1904.

47. AFR FA III FMB-MAE, January 16, 1909.

48. AFR V 28 FAV-MAE, October 18, 1908.

49. *Politika*, March 25, 1909.

50. DSIP, *Solunski proces*.

51. M. Živanović, *Pukovnik Apis*, p. 79.

52. *Ibid.*, p. 548.

53. *Ibid.*, p. 549.

54. *Ibid.*

55. *Ibid.*, p. 34.

56. *Ibid.*, p. 549.

57. DSIP, *Zbirka Vojislava Jovanovića*.

58. AFR V 105 FMB-MAE, February 16, 1911.

59. See B. Nešković, *Istina o solunskom procesu*, p. 20; M. Bogićević, *Le Colonel Dragoutine Dimitriewitch-Apis*, p. 33. After King Alexander's death a book was published in Belgrade under the title *Blaženi borac—Milan Djordjević*, signed by the pseudonym Talica. Its author was Talica Djordjević, the daughter of a former prime minister of Serbia, Vladan Djordjević. The main topic of the book is the relations between Alexander and General Petar Živković, par-

ticularly their alleged intimacy. According to some rumors, the publication of the book was financed by General Ljubomir Marić, an enemy of General Živković.

60. The papers of Aca Blagojević (AB).

61. *Ibid.*

62. NEFF, Letters, Box 2.

63. AB.

64. Prince Djordje left the detention house only in 1941.

65. About Bela Ruka activities, S. Jovanović (*Moji savremenici*) gives a general assessment of its relations with Colonel Apis. The Serbian press from about 1910 remains the most valuable source about the conflict between the two wings of the Serbian officer corps. The still unpublished memoirs of General Miloš Božanović, the former minister of war, might contribute to this controversial issue.

66. S. Jovanović, *Moji savremenici*, p. 36.

67. *Ibid.*, pp. 34–44.

68. *Ibid.*

69. *Ibid.*, pp. 44, 45, 47, 48, 56, 57.

70. D. Stojadinović, p. 157.

71. M. Bogićević, *Procès de Salonique*, p. 9. The diplomatic representatives of France, Russia and Austria-Hungary in Belgrade sent several detailed reports about the struggle between Pašić and Colonel Apis. (DDF 3 Ser. X, 207, 233, 285, 331, 394, 437, 451; Oe-U, VIII, 9649, 9673, 9702, 9734, 9809, 9819; IB, III, 143, 145, 280, 281, 282; and MO, 3 Ser. IV, 103.)

72. DSIP, *Solunski proces;* also M. Živanović, *Pudovnik Apis*, p. 215.

73. M. Živanović (pp. 214–49) is of the opinion that Colonel Apis did not envisage a *coup d'état* in the full sense of the term; S. Jovanović (*Moji savremenici*, p. 34) is of the opinion that Colonel Apis on that occasion did not wish to make a *coup d'état* in Belgrade, but only

a take-over by the military authorities in Macedonia.

74. This document was found in Belgrade during the First World War by the Austro-Hungarian authorities and was sent to Sarajevo, where it was incorporated into the juridical files on Gavrilo Princip and his accomplices. It was discovered during the Second World War by Dr. Hedwig Übersberger-Fleischhacker while she was working on her book about the Sarajevo investigation and trial. (Bittner, Hajek and Übersberger, *Serbiens Aussenpolitik*, p. 10 fn.) A facsimile of the complete document was presented in *Serbiens Aussenpolitik* (pp. 6–9). The document is also reproduced in the unfinished manuscript of Dr. Hans Übersberger's collection of captured Serbian documents (DSIP, *Zbirka Vojislava Jovanovića*). Dr. Übersberger, in his *Österreich zwischen Russland und Serbien*, p. 265, reproduced only the first part of the document.

Analysis of the outside verification of this document suggests that it was not forged. It is true that some words are spelled in the *ijekavski* dialect of the Serbo-Croat language (used in Bosnia, but not in Serbia), and there are some obvious grammatical mistakes. However, these were made by the copyist of the Bosnian *Landesregierung*, where the original had been retyped.

The typist erred in not copying the date of the document. Übersberger suggested that the document dates between June 2 and June 13, 1914. But June 2 seems too early, because Jakov Milović, as the document says, brought the pupils on June 2. To return to Serbia and come to Šabac, Milović needed at least two days, and then some time intervened before Boža Milanovic informed Belgrade, so the document could not have been written before June 5.

The inner evaluation of the document reveals several clues which prove its authenticity. The names of the peasant guides who took Princip and Grabež from Serbia to Bosnia are right (Jakov Milović and Miloš Milošević), as are the names of further links—trusted agents—in the "kanal" of Narodna Odbrana (the teacher Veljko Čubrilović and M. J. [Miško Jovanović] in Tuzla.)

Jakov Milović did not catch Princip's name, but he mentioned Grabež's nickname, "Triša." Milović correctly named the border guard people who helped Princip and his group to cross the frontier —Rade Popović, Kosta Todorović and Sergeant Grbić—as well as the island of Mladen Isaković on the river Drina, where they spent the night before the crossing.

Also, the name of the head of the Šabac district of Narodna Odbrana is right—Boža Milanović.

In its second part, the document mentions Milan Vračarić, a peasant from Badovince, a confidant of Narodna Odbrana, who is mentioned in other documents in connection with Princip's crossing into Bosnia.

There are several other minor points which prove the authenticity of the document. It says that Major Dimitrije Pavlović sent six boxes of hand grenades to Bosnia before the war (obviously the Balkan War) and that four of these were found in the river Sava, near Brcko.

This document also speaks of Rade Malobabić, the most controversial person in the whole story of the assassination. Malobabić after the summer of 1913 was Apis's chief secret agent, operating deep within Austria-Hungary and Bulgaria.

75. Pašić's note was reproduced

in *Serbiens Aussenpolitik*, p. 6;
Übersberger's *Osterreich zwischen
Russland und Serbien*, p. 265. Pašić's
note is written in rather illegible
handwriting in Cyrillic script, and
it consists of five lines:

Line 1: 2 pupils h. [higher] c.
[classes] of gimn. [high
school] Trisa [Trifko
Grabež] Mladenov [name
of Drina island]. [The last
word on the line is illegible.]
Line 2: 6 hand-grenades, 4 rev.
[revolvers] From Narodna
Odbrana, Jankovic
Line 3: Boža Milanović and Tankosić's
Line 4: trusted agent, [then comes
an illegible word] and this
returned, in Trnovo, in
Priboj.
Line 5: in Tusla, in Sarajevo.

The experts do not question the
authenticity of Pašić's handwriting.
The date of the note is missing, and
several deductions might be postu-
lated; perhaps Pašić made this summary of Milović's report after June
28, 1914. This writer believes that
Pašić made this summary in the
first days of June—after the fourth
or fifth, but not much later.

Pašić's summary is not clear on
one rather important point: lines 2
through 4 seem confusing, although
in all probability Pašić was describing how the news came to him
through Narodna Odbrana by
Jakov Milović, who happened to
be at the same time the agent of
Boža Milanović and Tankosić.

76. This writer has found in the
Austrian archives two documents
which confirm that the Serbian authorities stopped two groups of
armed men at the frontier in the
summer of 1910. The Headquarters
of the 15th Corps in Sarajevo informed Vienna on July 9, 1910,
how the Serbian gendarmes dis-

armed and arrested five *komite*
who tried to cross into Bosnia.
(KA, PF/8RES.)/10

77. During the First World War,
Italian writer Luciano Magrini
heard from Major Milan Djordjević that Pašić learned about the
plot early in June 1914, and he tried
his best to obstruct the plan of the
conspirators. (Magrini, *Il Dramma
di Sarajevo*, pp. 106–7.) Also in S.
Stanojević's book on the Sarajevo
assassination, there are some hints
that the Serbian government knew
something about the plot. Ljuba
Jovanović, a member of Pašić's
government, wrote in 1924 a leading article in a *Festschrift* called
Krv Slovenstva (Blood of Slav-
dom), in which he said: "I do not
remember whether it was at the
end of May or the beginning of
June, when one day M. Pašić said
to us (he conferred on these matters more particularly with Stojan
Protić, who was the minister of the
interior; but he said this much to
the rest of us) that there were people who were preparing to go to
Sarajevo to kill Franz Ferdinand,
who was to go there to be solemnly
received on Vidovdan . . . On the
afternoon of Vidovdan I was in my
house on the Senjak. About five
o'clock an official telephoned to me
from the press bureau, and told me
what had happened at noon at Sarajevo. Even though I knew what
had been prepared there, nevertheless I felt, as I held the receiver, as
though some one had dealt me an
unexpected blow."

This statement of Ljuba Jovanović was interpreted by Edith Durham to mean that the Serbian government was involved in the conspiracy against the Archduke.
After Seton-Watson's letter in *The
Times* on February 16, 1925, appealing to Pašić and Ljuba Jovanović to reveal the whole truth,
Ljuba Jovanović gave an interview

in *Politika,* April 17, 1925, repeating his narrative, adding that Pašić gave an interview on July 7, 1914, in which he said that the Serbian government had informed the Viennese government in time about the dangers in Sarajevo. He also mentioned that the Serbian government took adequate measures at the frontier and quoted the special order of Minister of War General Dušan Stefanović that frontier units should stop the crossing of the border by armed persons. Ljuba Jovanović also published in the review *Novi Život* (Nos. 1 and 2, 1925) a lengthy article with a similar substance. In 1926 the debate became more vehement, when Ljuba Jovanović and Pašić started to fight over the leadership of the Radical Party. Djurdje Jelenić accused Ljuba Jovanović as a traitor in an open letter to the Central Committee of the Radical Party (*Politika,* March 26, 1926). Milan Zečević, a friend of Jovanović, answered in *Politika,* March, 29, 1925, stating that Ljuba Jovanović did not write that Pašić made the statement about young men carrying weapons at the Cabinet meeting—but in private conversations afterwards. Pašić himself expressed his views both in private letters and publicly. On August 16, 1925, he wrote a letter to Momčilo Ninčić, the foreign minister of Serbia, answering his queries about Ljuba Jovanović's statement: "We have already spoken about it, and I told you already then that I am waiting for Mr. Ljuba Jovanović to deny what he wrote, and what is not true. Thus I am obliged to write a denial and to say that Serbia at that time did everything possible to improve our relations with Austria-Hungary after the annexation of Bosnia and Hercegovina, after the Balkan wars, when Serbia had avenged Kosovo, so that Austria-Hungary

would spare us and leave us at peace, because we knew what it had undertaken against us during the Balkan wars and during the peace negotiations with Bulgaria." (DSIP, *Zbirka Vojislava Jovanovića.*) At a meeting of the Central Committee of the Radical Party, on April 25, 1926, Pašić made a public statement on the matter which was reported in *Politika* on April 26, 1926:

Foreign Correspondents had asked him [Pašić] if he had known that the Austrian heir apparent was to be murdered. This he had repudiated. He had requested Mr. Jovanović to deny this, for it was not true that he, Pašić, had asserted this at a meeting of the council of ministers . . . He had even asked his colleagues: Friends, have I not perhaps forgotten that I said this? And all of them had affirmed that he had really not said this. . . . I do not know why Ljuba Jovanović has said it, but he has said what is not true. He has done all this on his own initiative, and if any one has done this, independently of an agreement with his colleagues, it is dangerous.

Ljuba Jovanović, as *Politika* reported on April 26, 1926, answered Pašić at the same meeting, charging that he had not read his article at all, and that he had not said that Pašić made his communication at a meeting of the government but that he had done so in a private conversation. Ljuba Jovanović was read out of the Radical Party, but the discussion over this issue flared up again in 1931. The only two members of the Serbian government of 1914 who were alive at that time, Velizar Janković and Dušan Stefanović, gave their versions. Janković wrote in the *Poli-*

tika of July 9 and 10, 1931, that at a meeting of the government in May 1914 Minister of the Interior Stojan Protić reported that some young men from Bosnia came to Serbia and then returned to Bosnia, under the protection of the Serbian frontier authorities. Consequently the government took measures, through Minister of the Interior Protić, to stop this dangerous traffic, as well as to remove the members of Ujedinjenje ili Smrt from all important positions in the army. It was also decided that Pašić should in the best possible way advise someone in Vienna to pay attention to the Bosnian youth during the army maneuvers in Bosnia. Janković also stated that the Minister of War was not present at this meeting. Minister of War Dušan Stefanović had a different version. He stated in *Politika* on August 13 and 15, 1931, that he had never heard anything about the preparations for the Sarajevo assassination, but he quoted his talks with Pašić in February 1925 in connection with Ljuba Jovanović's article and said that Pašić had told him: "According to some private reports I guessed that something was being prepared in Sarajevo, and I had a talk with Stojan Protić about it. He sent a directive for the police authorities to keep an eye on the Drina frontier so that suspicious persons do not cross from our country to Bosnia." (See also A. von Wegerer's comments on these two statements, in "Die Erinnerungen des Doktor Velizar Janković," *Berliner Monatshefte*, September 1931, pp. 851–69; and in "Der ehemalige serbische Kriegsminister über den Ausbruch des Weltkreieges," *Berliner Monatshefte*, October 1931, pp. 990–98.

78. This document was copied by Major Kosta Todorović in his diary, which was captured by the Austrian army in 1914. It was sent to Bosnia and it was used at the trial, in Banja Luka in 1916, of the leading Serbs of Bosnia and Hercegovina. Ćorović found this document in the Archives of the Supreme Court in Sarajevo (Ćorović, *Odnosi*, p. 607). The document was also reproduced by Pfeffer *Istraga u Sarajevskom atentatu*, p. 113–14). Ćorović also published (p. 608) a report written by Captain Jovan Prvanović on June 27, 1914, to the Commander of the Fifth Frontier Section: "I have heard lately that the police authorities, as well as customs authorities, on the basis of a higher order, are supervising and controlling the personnel of this company. The chief of the Jadar District received two confidential orders from the Chief of Podrinje Region to keep an eye on men from this company and to report at once everything he learns. The same one has interrogated the chief of the customs station at Šipačka Ada. The Chief of the Azbukovica District ordered the village authorities, as well as the chief of Ljubovija customs, to inform him at once about the work of our men. All this has been done without the knowledge of the undersigned, as the commander of his men, and this is all true because several county presidents at the border informed him about it."

79. DSIP, *Solunski Proces.*

80. M. Bogićević, *Le Colonel Apis*, p. 97.

81. DSIP, *Solunski proces.*

82. *Ibid.*

83. *Ibid.*

84. B. Nešković, *Istina o solunskom procesu*, p. 260.

85. *Ibid.*, pp. 266–67.

86. V. Bogićević, *Sarajevski atentat*, p. 117.

87. *Ibid.*, pp. 296–97.

88. Č. Popović, "Vidovdanska tajna-o Sarajevskom atentatu," *No-*

vosti (Belgrade), June 28, 1924; and "Sarajevski atentat i organizacija 'Ujedinjenje ili smrt,'" *Nova Evropa*, July 26, 1932.

89. S. Jovanović, *Moji savremenici*, pp. 66–67.

90. C. Popović, "Vidovdanska tajna-o Sarajevskom atentatu," and "Sarajevski atentat i organizacija 'Ujedinjenje ili smrt.'"

91. P. Kašiković, "Sarajevski Vidovdan," *Politika*, July 4, 1929.

92. *Ibid.*

93. *Ibid.*

94. As told to the author by Dr. Vaso Čubrilović.

95. V. Bogićević, "Prilog istoriji Sarajevskog atentata," *Nin*, July 20, 1952.

96. Glück, *Sarajewo* pp. 187–89; V. Bogićević, "Narodna odbrana i sarajevski atentat," *Krug*, February 19, 1938; D. Lončarević, *Jugoslaviens Entstehung* (Zurich, Leipzig and Vienna, 1929); K. Krajšumović, "Sarajevski Vidovdan 1914," *Politika*, July 1, 1929.

97. D. Ljubibratić, *Gaćinović*, pp. 144, 146, 147, 150.

98. L. Albertini, *Origins of the War of 1914*, p. 63; B. Čerović, *Bosanski omladinci*, p. 76; letter of J. Jovanović to Jules Isaac, in J. Isaac, *Un Débat historique*, p. 237.

99. On June 29, 1914, *The New York Times* published the following dispatch from the London *Daily Mail*:

Before the Archduke went to Bosnia last Wednesday, the Serbian Minister here expressed doubts as to the wisdom of the journey, saying the country was in a very turbulent condition and the Serbian part of the population might organize a demonstration against the Archduke. The Minister said if the Archduke went himself he certainly ought to leave his wife at home, because Bosnia was no place for a woman in its present disturbed state. The Minister's word proved correct.

Štampa, of Belgrade, on June 30, 1914, claimed that the Serbian minister in Vienna had visited Berchtold and advised him against the Archduke's visit to Sarajevo. The Serbian minister in St. Petersburg, Spalajković, in an interview for the paper *Novoye Vremya*, June 30, 1914, declared that a warning had been given. Miloš Bogićević, in his *Procès de Salonique*, p. 139, claimed that Pašić, in an answer to a deputy in the Skupština, had stated that he had sent a warning to Vienna. Poletika gave the same version in his book on Sarajevo, p. 352. The French consul in Budapest sent a dispatch to Paris on June 30, stating that the Serbian government had warned Vienna of the dangers awaiting the Archduke in Bosnia. (DDF, 3d Ser., X, 463.) The Serbian minister in Paris, Vesnić, said to an official of the French Ministry of Foreign Affairs on July 1, 1914, that the Serbian government had warned the Vienna government that it had got wind of the plot. (DDF, 3d Ser., X, 466.) *Le Temps*, of Paris, stated on July 10, 1914, that Pašić confirmed that a warning had been given. During the First World War, French historian Ernest Denis (*La Grande Serbie*, Paris, 1915) came out again with this story, as did Stanoje Stanojević, in his book on Sarajevo, p. 61. The Italian journalist and historian Luciano Magrini, in his book on Sarajevo, pp. 115–16, wrote that the Serbian military attaché in Vienna at the time of the Sarajevo assassination, Colonel Lešjanin, told him during the First World War that the Serbian minister in Vienna, Jovanović, had delivered the warning. The *Wiener Montagsblatt*, June 23, 1924, published the news item that the Serbian minister in Vienna, Jovanović, had been instructed to deliver the warning. This information was attributed to Djordje Josimović, a Serbian diplomat in Vienna in 1914; but he denied it later.

100. Pašić's denials appeared on July 7 in the Budapest paper *Az Est* and on July 20 in the Paris edition of *The New York Herald*.

101. The Austro-Hungarian government twice denied the story of a Serbian warning—on July 1 and on July 2 (Oe-U, VIII, 9952). Count Berchtold issued another denial in a letter dated May 9, 1917 (Leopold Mandl, *Die Habsburger und die serbische Frage*, p. 152).

102. In the Serbian Ministry of Foreign Affairs dispatch book, July 4, 1914, under the number A/I 3-2431, a telegram sent to the Serbian legation in Vienna was summarized as follows: "Some newspapers mention that you drew attention to the danger of the journey to Sarajevo." In the same book, for the same day, under A/I 3-2481, an answer from Vienna was summarized in this way: "Reports that at the end of last month he told some of the ambassadors that maneuvers in Bosnia look like a demonstration." These documents were captured by the German army during the Second World War. They were published in the *Serbiens Aussenpolitik*, 9 and 10, together with a photostat of the Serbian Ministry of Foreign Affairs dispatch book. The editors of *Serbiens Aussenpolitik*, in footnotes on pages 18 and 19, claim that the originals of both of these telegrams were taken from the Archives of the Serbian Ministry of Foreign Affairs in 1926 by Dr. Vojislav Jovanović. Übersberger, in his *Österreich zwischen Russland und Serbien*, p. 261, also cites

the paraphrase of the two documents.

103. Jovan Jovanović, in a letter to the *Neues Wiener Tageblatt*, June 28, 1924, stated that on his own initiative he visited Bilinski on June 5, 1914, and expressed his fear that "among the Serb youths there might be one who will put a ball cartridge in his rifle and he may fire it." Jovanović repeated his story of this meeting several times—in *Politika*, December 4, 1925; in *Srpski književni glasnik*; in two letters to the French historian Jules Isaac, December 31, 1932, and January 25, 1933; and in a letter to Italian author Luigi Albertini, on January 21, 1938. Bilinski, in his memoirs, p. 277, said simply that the rumors that he had warned the Emperor Franz Josef that the Archduke should not visit Sarajevo were not true—"because I had no right to interfere in military affairs." But P. Flandrak, an official in Bilinski's office, confirmed that Bilinski had spoken to him about Jovanović's visit. According to Flandrak, Jovanović asked Bilinski not to consider his statement as an official communication and that Bilinski see in it neither an open nor a veiled warning. (P. Flandrak, "Bilinskis Eingreifen in die auswärtige Politik," *Neues Wiener Journal*, April 26, 1925.)

104. DSIP, *Solunski proces*.

105. *Ibid*.

106. S. Jovanović, *Moji savremenici*, p. 57.

107. There is not yet any direct evidence that Alexander ordered the execution of Colonel Apis to protect the interests of the Karadjordjević dynasty in connection with the request of the Austrian Emperor Karl. It is an open question whether Alexander knew about these negotiations before Colonel Apis was sentenced and

executed. Prince Sixte de Bourbon (*L'Offre de paix separée de l'Autriche*, p. 55) gives the main points of the February 12, 1917, memorandum in which the conditions for Serbia were mentioned. Also, on page 59 he mentions Czernin's note of the same date, which in Point 2 says that Austria-Hungary did not intend to destroy Serbia, but that it was necessary to take for the future all the guarantees against "political agitation which brought about the Sarajevo assassination." The theory that Alexander effectively murdered Colonel Apis in the interests of the Karadjordjević dynasty was advanced by several writers, among them Svetozar Pribićević (*La Dictature du roi Alexandre*, pp. 273–319) and S. Jovanović (*Moji savremenici*, p. 64), who expressed the opinion that Alexander eliminated Colonel Apis to give proof of his desire for future correct relations with Austria–Hungary. See also Talica, *Blaženi Borac—Milan Djordjević*, p. 329.

108. As established at the retrial of Colonel Apis and his friends in Belgrade, June 2–13, 1953.

109. DSIP, *Solunski proces*.

110. M. Živanović, *Pudovnik Apis*, pp. 175–78.

111. DSIP, *Solunski proces*.

112. *Ibid.*

113. *Ibid.*

114. Übersberger, *Österreich zwischen Russland und Serbien*, p. 295.

115. From the Serbian edition of Sarrail's *Beleške generala Saraja*, p. 281; also M. Bogićević, *Procès de Salonique*, p. 18.

116. D. Stojadinović's letter to the author, May 22, 1962.

117. M. Živanović, p. 592.

CHAPTER XVIII   *pages 401–419*

1. HHSTA IB 1902 639/4.

2. *Ibid.*

3. AFR, ASI–25 FA Vienna–MAE.

4. Jaszi, *Dissolution of the Habsburg Monarchy*, p. 127.

5. V. Jelovac, "Neobelodanjeni Dogadjaj," *Republika*, October 16, 1956.

6. HHSTA IB 1903 515/4.

7. HHSTA IB 1906 2816/4.

8. HHSTA IB 1907 3075/4.

9. S. Stanojević, *Ubistvo austriskog prestolonaslednika Ferdinanda*, p. 43.

10. DSIP, *Solunski proces*.

11. MKEFF ME/21/11.

12. *Ibid.*

13. *Ibid.*

14. MKEFF Me/252/1912.

15. Oe-U.

16. MKEFF 68–3/21–2 ad x.

17. KA KM 58–5/1913.

18. HHSTA IB 1–21–1913.

19. *Ibid.*

20. *Ibid.*

21. See Chapter XII.

22. Funder, *Vom Gestern ins Heute*, p. 446.

23. *Ibid.*

24. *Ibid.*, p. 484.

25. T. Zurunić, "Odgovornost za rat," *Politika*, August 27, 1931.

26. Bilinski, *Wspomnienia i dokumenty*, p. 211.

27. Gottlieb von Jagow, *Ursachen und Ausbruch des Weltkrieges* (Berlin, 1919), Chapter IX.

28. Oe-U, VIII, 6693, 6694, 9893, 9963.

29. *Ibid.*

30. *Ibid.*

31. A. Urbanski von Ostrymiecz, "Conrad von Hötzendorf und die Reise des Thronfolgers nach Sarajevo," *Berliner Monatshefte*, May 1929.

32. Eisenmenger, p. 178.

33. *Ibid.*

34. *Ibid.*

35. NEFF, Letters, Box 17.

36. Conrad, *Aus meiner Dienstzeit*, Vol. III, p. 700.

37. Max Hohenberg, in interview, *Paris-Soir-Dimanche*, July 4, 1937.

38. Sosnosky, *Franz Ferdinand der Erzherzog-Thronfolger*, p. 196.

39. Bardolff, *Soldat im alten Österreich*, p. 131.

40. Eisenmenger (English edition), p. 158; Nikitsch-Boulles, *Vor dem Sturm*, p. 130; HHSTA IB 1902 639/4.

41. MKEFF 15–2/5.

42. Chlumecky, *Erzherzog Franz Ferdinands Wirken und Wollen*, p. 363.

43. Margutti (English edition), p. 178.

44. Oe-U, VIII, 10029.

45. BD, XI, 70.

46. V. Bogićević, "Austriske vlasti i Sarajevski atentat," *Nova Evropa*, July 26, 1934.

47. *Ibid.*

48. NEFF, *Sarajevo Prozess.*

49. *Ibid.*

50. Bilinski, p. 282; also Sosnosky, p. 207.

51. Glück, "Sarajevo juna 1914 godine-Opste prilike pre atentata," *Politika*, November 16, 1933.

52. *Ibid.*

53. *Ibid.*

54. *Ibid.*

55. Glück, *Sarajewo*, p. 137.

56. *Ibid.*

57. *Ibid.*, p. 140.

58. MKEFF, Nr. 1261, May 28, 1914.

59. *Ibid.*, 15–2/5–14.

60. *Ibid.*

61. Kranjčević, *Uspomene jednog učesnika u sarajevskom atentatu*, pp. 65–66.

62. *Ibid.*

63. H. W. Steed, "The Pact of Konopischt," *The Nineteenth Century*, 1916, pp. 265ff.; also *Through Thirty Years*, pp. 400–3.

64. The Belgrade *Balkan*, July 1, 1914, said that in October 1913, when Čabrinović had arrived in Belgrade, the local police, through the Austro-Hungarian consulate, inquired of the Sarajevo police whether the facts given by Čabrinović in his application for permission to stay in Belgrade were correct. Dr. Gerde, the Sarajevo police official, answered that the facts were correct; but he failed to mention that Čabrinović had been expelled from Sarajevo for five years because of his anarchistic activities. On July 4 *Balkan* accused Čabrinović of being a secret agent of Austria–Hungary. Nikola Pašić also mentioned in an interview for *Az Est* of July 7, 1914, that the Serbian police had inquired about Čabrinović and had received a satisfactory answer from the Austro-Hungarian authorities. The British representative in Belgrade, Crackanthorpe, affirmed that Secretary General Dr. Slavko Grujić of the Serbian Foreign Office had told him on July 18, 1914, about the action of the Belgrade police in connection with Čabrinović and about their having received "satisfactory information on this point." (BD, XI, 80.) Throughout Europe the press commented on *Balkan's* allegation about Čabrinović, and on July 8, 1914, the Austro-Hungarian authorities gave their version of the story (Oe-U, VIII, 10123, 10124, 10139, 10152, etc.). During the First World War the story that the Hungarian authorities had organized the plot and that Čabrinović had been an Austro-Hungarian secret agent was several times repeated—by Nikola Stojanović, Gottfried Beck, Jules Pichon, Janež Žibert, Vladislav Savić, and others.

In the 1920's the whole story was revived. According to documents in the Serbian Ministry of Foreign Affairs, one of the leaders

of the Radicals, Dr. Lazar Marković, recommended to Momčilo
Ninčić, Minister of Foreign Affairs, that a certain newspaperman,
Dušan Tvrdoreka, conduct research and write a book on the
Sarajevo assassination. Tvrdoreka
was appointed an official of the
press section of the Ministry of
Foreign Affairs, and with letters
of recommendation from Momčilo Ninčić he went through Serbian archives, collecting all the
documents on the Sarajevo plot.
After one year Tvrdoreka published a series of four articles, under the title "Odgovornost za rat,"
in Jovan Jovanović-Pižon's paper,
Novosti, in Belgrade, September 1
to 25, 1926. His main thesis was
that Nedeljko Čabrinović was an
agent of the Austro-Hungarian
police and that in such capacity he
threw his bomb at the Archduke.
This writer has gone through
Tvrdoreka's files and has established that Tvrdoreka falsified
some documents in order to prove
his thesis. Dr. Vojislav Jovanović,
head of the Historical Department
of the Yugoslav Ministry of Foreign Affairs, wrote a long memorandum on Tvrdoreka, and subsequently Tvrdoreka was arrested
and all his archives were seized.
Nevertheless, Bora Jevtić continued publishing articles in which
he abused Čabrinović as a coward
who betrayed his friends.

65. S. Pribićević, *La Dictature
du roi Alexandre,* quoted from D.
Stojadinović, "Srbija i Nemačka u
Svetskom ratu," p. 457.

66. Muret, *L'Archiduc François-
Ferdinand,* p. 337.

67. *Ibid.*

68. M. Bogićević, *Le Colonel
Apis,* pp. 25–26; also Bogićević,
Causes of the War, p. 12.

69. M. Bogićević, *Le Colonel,*
p. 26.

70. *Ibid.* Also Jovan Jovanović's
letter to Jules Isaac (Isaac, *Un Débat historique,* p. 255).

71. See AFR FFI–301 FMB–
MAE, April 6, 1904, April 30, 1904,
October 14, 1905, May 30, 1906;
AFR AII–76, Fr.Amb. Vienna-
MAE, June 2, 1906; AFR II–151
FMB-MAE, July 21, 1906, August
6, 1906; AFR FF II–81 FIF to
MAE, November 29, 1906; *Neue
Freie Presse,* October 5, 1906.

72. Conrad sent the Archduke
a confidential report on December
6, 1909, about how regicides headed
by Apis and Damjan Popović were
preparing a conspiracy to overthrow the Karadjordjević dynasty
(KA MKEFF P/71 RES/09).
Vemić's diary confirmed the main
points of Conrad's report. (Vemic's
diary, October 23, 1909, DSIP,
Zbirka Vojislava Jovanovića.)

73. Albertini, *Origins of the
War of 1914,* Vol. II, pp. 65–66;
Bittner, article in *Berliner Monat-
shefte,* X, pp. 55–61.

74. S. Pribićević, quoted from
D. Stojadinović, p. 451.

75. S. Jovanović, *Moji savremenici,* p. 59.

76. AFR V 136 FMB-MAE.

77. D. Stojadinović, pp. 173,
176–177, 199, 203, 204.

78. *Ibid.,* pp. 57–82.

79. Quoted by N. Trišić, *Sarajevski atentat,* p. 369.

80. Prince Ludwig Windischgraetz, *My Memoirs,* p. 49, quoted
by Hamilton Fish Armstrong, "A
Letter of Count Tisza's," *Foreign
Affairs,* April 1928, p. 501.

81. Albertini, II, p. 127.

82. Letter from the Archives of
the Joint Ministry of Finance, Vienna, quoted by Hamilton Fish
Armstrong, "A Letter of Count
Tisza's," *Foreign Affairs.*

83. Oe-U.

84. Conrad, IV, pp. 30–1.

85. Oe-U, VIII, 10018.

86. *Ibid.*

87. *Ibid.*

88. RBII (*Republik Österreich: Staatsamt fur äussere diplomatische aktenstucke zur Vorgeschichte des Krieges 1914*), p. 52; also Oe-U, VIII, 10253. See also Pfeffer, in *Obzor*, July 22, 1926; Pfeffer, *Istraga u Sarajevskom atentatu*, pp. 111–112, 153, 163. Wiesner challenged his own views from 1914 in *Reichspost*, June 28, 1924, and particularly in "Die Unwiderlegt Gebliebene Begrundung fur das Ultimatum Österreichs an Serbien von Juli 1914," in *Kriegsschuldfrage*, June 1927, pp. 492–543.

89. Bülow, III, p. 156. *Memoirs*, Vol. III, p. 156.

90. SPK Ministarstvo Inostranih Dela, *Diplomatska prepiska o srpsko-austriskom sukobu* (Niš, 1914).

91. *Ibid.*

92. *Ibid.*

CHAPTER XIX   *pages 420–427*

1. M. Hohenberg, in interview for *Paris-Soir-Dimanche*, July 4, 1937.

2. *Ibid.*

3. NEFF, VI, *Zeitungsartikel bzw. Ausschnitte.*

4. Literature on M. Bogićević is rare. He explained his political acts in his *Causes of the War* and in the Introduction of his *Auswärtige Politik Serbiens*. In the reviews of some of his books (for instance, *Nova Evropa*, July 26, 1927, reviewing his *Procès de Salonique*) assessments of his political activities were made, but often they were one-sided. Dr. Milutin Jovanović, the former Secretary of the Serbian legation in Berlin, 1911–1914, gave to this writer two statements of Bogićević's activities in

Berlin at that time. In both the German and French archives there is little material on Bogićević, as is true also of the Serbian archives. M. Bogićević's file in the archives of the German Supreme Command and the documentation covering his death have not yet been found. According to some rumors M. Bogićević left all his papers with his wife in Vienna.

5. In *Jugoslovenska enciklopedija*, Vol. III, V. Vić wrote a short biography of the Bogićević family.

6. D. Stojadinović, p. 394.

7. M. Živanović, *Pukovnik Apis*, p. 645.

8. M. Bogićević, *Colonel Apis*, p. 12.

9. *Ibid.*

10. *Ibid.*, p. 12.

11. *Ibid.*

12. DSIP, *Vemićev Dnevnik.*

13. D. Stojadinović, "Srbija i Nemačka u Svetskom ratu," p. 23.

14. Lj. Jovanović, "Crnorukci pre Crne ruke," *Samouprava*, December 26, 1919.

15. *Ibid.* See also an answer to Jovanović's charges in *Pravda* (Belgrade), January 14 to February 2, 1920.

16. D. Stojadinović, p. 212.

17. *Ibid.*, p. 21.

18. *Ibid.*, Chapter XIII.

19. *Ibid.*

20. Stojadinović has elaborated this thesis in Chapters III, IV, V, VI, VII, VIII and IX of his manuscript.

21. I. J. Kolar, *Preporodovci 1912–1914, 1914–1918*, p. 48.

22. *Vreme*, July 8, 1938; *Jugoslovenska enciklopedija*, Vol. III, Vič article on Bogićević family; in a letter to the author, D. Stojadinović maintains that the Nazis killed Bogićević.

23. M. Živanović, *Pukovnik Apis*, p. 7.

24. Letter in the possession of the author.

25. M. Živanović, *Pukovnik Apis*, p. 76. S. Jovanović (*Moji savremenici*, p. 57) recorded that Lj. Jovanović himself told him that Colonel Apis was planning an assassination attempt against the Kaiser.

26. M. Živanović, *Pukovnik Apis*, pp. 306, 463.

27. *Ibid.*, pp. 314–21. Also N. Trišić, "Uspomene na Muhameda Mehmedbašića," *Pregled*, July–August 1953, pp. 57–59. S. Jovanović, *Moji savremenici*, p. 75.

28. M. Živanović, *Pukovnik Apis*, pp. 322–24.

29. S. Stanojević, *Ubistvo austriskog prestolonaslednika Ferdinanda*, pp. 42, 44.

30. D. Stojadinović, "Srbija i Nemačka," p. 61.

31. *Jugoslovenska enciklopedija*, Vol. III, V. Vić article on Bogićević family.

32. From the collection *Tsarskaya Rossiya v Mirovoi Voine* (Leningrad, 1926), p. 82—as quoted by K. Vinogradov, *Burzhoazna Istoriografiya Pervoi Mirovoi Voini*. (Moscow, 1962), p. 78.

33. S. Jovanović, *Moji savremenici*, p. 45.

34. *Ibid.*, p. 50; also *Politicki Glasnik*, July 30, 1925.

35. D. Stojadinović, Introduction.

CHAPTER XX   *pages 428–443*

1. The accusation against the Russian Foreign Minister Sazonov appeared in H. E. Barnes, *Genesis of the World War*, p. 96, and in Hermann Lutz, "Zum Mord von Sarajevo," *Kriegsschuldfrage*, July 1925, pp. 445–50. It is based on Czernin's interpretations of the talks between the Rumanian king and Sazonov at the beginning of June 1914. The charges against Russia were repeated by Poletika in an article in *Istorik Marksist*, November 1929, and in his *Sarayevskoye Ubiistvo* (Leningrad, 1930), p. ix, in which he stated flatly that the "Sarajevo assassination was organized by the Serbian secret service on orders from Russia." Poletika repeated his thesis in 1935 in his *Vozniknovenie Mirovoi Voini*, p. 285; but he changed these views thirty years later in his revision of the same book, *Vozniknovenie Pervoi Mirovoi Voini*, pp. 236–37.

2. *Pijemont*, September 3, 1911.

3. AFR, FR 281; FA, Vienna-MAE.

4. *Ibid.*

5. Živanović, *Pukovnik Apis*, p. 667.

6. AFR FR 300 FMB-MAE. Dr. Branko Pavićević found a dossier on Apis in the Soviet archives. It had been compiled by Russian intelligence at the Tsar's request. It ran to more than 700 pages and gave a history of regicides. The Tsar had read the whole dossier and had written in longhand that it should be preserved for historical studies. After June 28, 1914, right-wing monarchist papers in St. Petersburg (*Soyuz Russkovo Naroda, Russkaya Znamia, Grazhdanin Zyemshchina*) attacked the "Serbian murderers of tsars" and demanded that no aid be sent to Serbia. (Poletika, *Vozniknovenie Pervoi Mirovoi Voini*.)

7. *Pijemont*, December 3, 1913.

8. M. Bogićević, *Procès de Salonique*, p. 20; also M. Živanović, *Pukovnik Apis*, pp. 535–36. Übersberger (*Österreich zwischen Russland und Serbien*, pp. 305–14) published some documents from the Archives of the Serbian Ministry of Foreign Affairs dealing with the intervention of Tereshchenko.

9. The Bulgarians never published the alleged document. Wegerer in his *Der Ausbruch des Weltkrieges* mentions this news item from *Neue Freie Presse*, but he too does not quote the alleged document.

10. Nikola Nenadović (pseudonym of Mustafa Golubić), "Tajna beogradske kamarile," *La Fédération Balkanique*, December 1, 1924, p. 109.

11. V. Serge, "La Vérité sur l'attentat de Sarajevo," *Clarté*, May 1925, p. 210.

12. L. Mandl, article in *Neues Wiener Abendblatt*, June 27, 28, 1924.

13. M. Bogićević, article in *Kriegsschuldfrage*, July 1925, pp. 388–90; L. Albertini, *Origins of the War of 1914*, Vol. II, pp. 82–84.

14. M. N. Pokrovsky, "Kak Nachalas' Voina 1914 g.," *Prolyetarskaya Revolutsiya*, No. 30, p. 27. Quoted from Poletika, *Sarayevsko Ubiistvo*, p. ix.

15. E. V. Tarle, *Evropa v Epoku Imperiyalizma—1871–1919* (Moscow, 1928).

16. See Note 1 of this chapter.

17. This confirms the Soviet collection of Russian diplomatic papers from 1914 (see Bibliography). But Übersberger in his *Österreich zwischen Russland und Serbien*, pp. 297–98, claimed that Hartvig's dispatches from Belgrade for the crucial period between May and July 1914 were taken by an unidentified person from the archives of the Russian Foreign Ministry and destroyed during the first days of the October Revolution in 1917. However, Übersberger could not prove his allegations.

18. DSIP, *Solunski proces*.

19. L. de Trywdar-Burzynski, *Le Crépuscule d'une autocratie* (Florence, 1926), p. 127; see also Cartagene, *Erinnerungen an meine Botschafterzeit in Russland 1914* (Berlin, 1934), pp. 113–14. A similar thesis was held by Michael Taube, *Der grossen Katastrophe entegen* (Leipzig, 1937). Artamonov on four occasions answered these charges. He told Bernadotte Schmitt in 1928 that it was true that he had given some money to Colonel Apis for intelligence purposes and that he had not been informed about the plot against Archduke Franz Ferdinand (Schmitt, "New Evidence in the Sarajevo Assassination," *Journal of Modern History*, December 1955). Artamonov repeated the explanation in a letter to D. Stojadinović ("Srbija i Nemačka u Svetskom ratu," p. 170), then in an article, "Erinnerungen an meine Militärattachezeit in Belgrad" (*Berliner Monatshefte*, July–August 1938), and later in a statement to Albertini (*Origins of the War of 1914*, pp. 85–86).

20. *Malaya Sovietskaya Entsiklopediya*, Vol. I (Moscow, 1930), p. 115.

21. *Ibid.*

22. DSIP, *Solunski proces*. The report of Colonel Apis to the commander of the Third Serbian Army, October 8, 1916, p. 202; quoted also in M. Bogićević, *Procès de Salonique*, p. 79. Colonel Apis in this document stated that he had recommended Malobabić to "the military attaché of a friendly country, now allied, which with my help used Malobabić's services."

23. M. Živanović, p. 439.

24. Kiszling, *Erzherzog*, p. 296; also Čerović, *Bosanski omladinci*, p. 74.

25. Cited from Trišić, *Sarajevski atentat*, p. 22.

26. As told to this writer by Stevan Dedijer.

27. *Ogledi i pisma*, p. 213.

28. *Ibid.*

29. Gradski muzej Sarajeva, Lebedev papers.

30. M. Čurčin, "Nov momenat u sarajevskom atentatu," *Nova Evropa*, July 26, 1937, pp. 244–46; A. von Wegerer, "Das Attentat von Sarajevo und die Bolschewisten," *Berliner Monatshefte*, January 1938; S. M. Stedimlija, *Partizani o sebi.*

31. People's Commissariat of Justice of the U.S.S.R. Report of Court Proceedings in the case of the Anti-Soviet (Trotskyite Center) heard before the Military Collegium of the Supreme Court of the U.S.S.R., Moscow, January 23–30, 1937. Verbatim report. Morning session, January 29. Last pleas of the accused, Radek, p. 543.

32. Wegerer, *Der Ausbruch des Weltkrieges*, p. 6.

33. During World War II the Nazis got hold of the Serbian state papers, including the Salonika trial documentation. Among other documents they found Apis's statement on the Sarajevo plot. Deutsche Institut für aussenpolitische Forschung, an agency of the German Ministry of Foreign Affairs, instructed Übersberger in a letter of May 11, 1943 (Reichsarchiv in Vienna, No. 1339/1943; copy of letter in DSIP, *Zbirka Vojislava Jovanovića*) as to how Apis's document should be used. In this letter it was stated that Ribbentrop had said that "Russia is a permanent disturber of the peace in Europe—both Tsarist and Bolshevik." In *Auswärtige Politik*, July 1943, Übersberger published an article, "Das entscheidende Aktenstück zur Kriegsschuldfrage 1914," pp. 429–38, in which he not only repeated the above-mentioned thesis, but also falsified the translation of Apis's statement. He reported that Apis said that he had communicated his plans for the assassination to the Russian military attaché in Belgrade, although in the facsimile of Apis's statement it is clear that Apis wrote that he had not informed Artamonov. Übersberger's falsification was exposed by Nešković (*Istina o Solunskom procesu*, p. 42); Gavrilović and Bernadotte Schmitt, "New Evidence in the Sarajevo Assassination," *Journal of Modern History*, December 1955, pp. 410–14. Übersberger himself admitted his falsification, in his *Österreich zwischen Russland und Serbien*, p. 289.

34. Ljubibratić, *Gaćinović*, p. 202.

35. A. Berkman, *Now and After: The A.B.C. of Communist Anarchism*, p. 16.

36. V. Bogićević, *Sarajevski atentat*, p. 40.

37. *Ibid.*, p. 42.

38. *Ibid.*, pp. 74–75.

39. *Ibid.*, p. 108.

40. *Ibid.*, p. 293.

41. *Ibid.*

42. *Ibid.*, p. 294.

43. *Ibid.*, p. 296.

44. Cited from Trišić, *Sarajevski atentat*, p. 45.

45. Mousset, *Un Drame historique*, Introduction.

46. V. Bogićević, *Sarajevski atentat*, Introduction.

47. NEFF, Memoranda.

48. E. Ludendorff, *Vernichtung der Freimaurerei durch Enthüllung ihrer Geheimnisse*, and *Wie der Weltkrieg 1914 'gemacht' wurde.*

49. Ludendorff, *Wie der Weltkrieg*, p. 33.

50. *Ibid.*, p. 34.

51. *Ibid.*

52. *Politika* (July 4, 1931).

53. D. Nikolajević, "Ratna odgovornost i g. Ludendorf," *Politika*, October 20, 1928.

54. *Ibid.*

55. E. Reventlow, *Kriegsschuldlüge und Kriegsschuldlügner* (Munich, 1929).

56. Quoted from B. Bratić,

"Sarajevski atentat i nacionalno-socijalistčka propaganda," *Pregled*, February 1938, pp. 116–19.

57. Auswärtiges Amt 1939/41, Nr. 7, *Dokumente*, p. 3; also Dr. Werner Frauendienst, *Jugoslawiens Weg zum Abgrund* (Berlin, 1941).

58. Albertini, II, p. 59.

59. Nešković, *Istina o Solunskom procesu*, pp. 113–14.

60. "Izjava g. dr. Radovana N. Kazimirovića profesora," *Politika*, February 26, 1932.

61. Kazimirović wrote an article in *Pijemont*, March 25, 1913, about the negotiations between the Serbian government and the Vatican for the conclusion of a Concordat, expressing himself in principle for the Concordat but warning against too much privilege to the Catholic Church.

62. AFR, FF II 148, FMB-MAE of October 4, 1911, mentioned that a third Freemason lodge was formed in Belgrade and that it had links with Germany.

63. Czernin, *In the World War*, p. 46.

64. In 1908 Aehrenthal kept up a long correspondence with his ambassadors in Paris, Madrid, Lisbon and Berlin, in connection with confidential reports that in Paris there existed a secret society which had organized the unsuccessful attempt in 1905 against the king of Spain and the successful one against the king of Portugal and his son in Lisbon in 1908. The source of information was the Spanish ambassador in Paris. The secret society according to him was headed by a certain Malato, "a friend of the French politicians, who are all Freemasons." The Spanish ambassador further claimed that three quarters of all police agents in Paris were Freemasons, and that "the government therefore protects the assassins." (HHSTA IB Attentäter Anarchisten 209/08)/579.

CONCLUSION *pages 445–447*

1. V. Masleša, *Mlada Bosna*, p. 45.

2. J. Tomašević, *Peasants, Politics and Economic Change in Yugoslavia* (Stanford, 1955), pp. 223–225; also V. Stanojević in *Enciklopedija Srba, Hrvata i Slovenaca*, Vol. III, p. 449.

3. The author is working on an essay about the similarities among the secret societies of Bosnia, Ireland and India before 1914.

BIBLIOGRAPHY

I. PRIMARY SOURCES

A. *Unpublished*
1. State and Public Archives
   AA Archives of the German Foreign Ministry 1867–1920 (microfilm), Waddon Hall, England.
   AAA Archives of the German Foreign Ministry, Bonn.
   AFR Archives of the French Ministry of Foreign Affairs, Paris.
   DAS Državni arhiv, Sarajevo.
   DSIP Državni sekertarijat inostranih poslova, Istoriski arhiv, Belgrade.
   GMS Gradski muzej Sarajevo.
   HHSTA Haus-Hof-Staatsarchiv, Vienna.
   HI Hoover Institution on War, Revolution and Peace, Stanford University, California.
   HL Houghton Library, Cambridge, Massachusetts.
   KA Staatsarchiv-Kriegsarchiv, Vienna.
   MKEFF Militärkanzlei Erzherzog Franz Ferdinand, Österreichisches Staatsarchiv-Kriegsarchiv, Vienna.
   MS Arhiv Matice Srpske, Novi Sad.
   NA National Archives, Washington, D. C.
   NEFF Nachlass Erzherzog Franz Ferdinand, Haus-Hof-Staatsarchiv, Vienna.
   SA Archives of the Swedish Foreign Ministry, Stockholm.
   UB Univerzitetska biblioteka, Belgrade.
   VU Archives of Vienna University.

2. Private Papers and Archives
   A B   The papers of Major Aca Blagojević, Belgrade.
   Lj J   The papers of Professor Ljubo Jurković, Ljubljana.
   M S   The papers of Marinko Stojanović, Serbian legislator, Belgrade.
   P S   The papers of Professor Pero Slijepčević, Belgrade.

3. Correspondence of the contemporaries with the author
   Dr. Vukosava Branisavljević-Čabrinović, Sarajevo
   Dr. Vid Gaković, Belgrade
   Professor Ljubo Jurković, Ljubljana

Professor Ivan Janež Kolar, Ljubljana
Dragiša Stojadinović, Belgrade
Professor Božidar Tomić, Belgrade

4. Monographs, including unpublished documents
Stojadinović, Dragiša, "Srbija i Nemačka u Svetskom ratu," MS deposited at St. Anthony's Library, Oxford, England.

Übersberger, Hans, Unfinished MS on the Salonika trial, 1917, worked on during the Second World War, in Vienna. (A part of the galley proofs is in DSIP, Belgrade.)

Übersberger-Fleischhacker, Hedwig, Unfinished MS on the investigation and trial of Gavrilo Princip and his accomplices, started during the Second World War, in Vienna. (A part of the galley proofs is in DSIP, Belgrade.)

B. *Published*
  1. Diplomatic Papers (official editions)
  BD *British Documents on the Origins of the War, 1898–1914,* 11 vols., edited by G. P. Gooch and H. W. V. Temperley. London: His Majesty's Stationery Office, 1926–38.

  DDF Ministère des Affaires Étrangères, Commission pour la publication des documents relatifs aux origines de la guerre de 1914–1918, *Documents diplomatiques français, 1871–1914,* 11 vols.; 3d series, 1911–1914. Paris: Imprimerie Nationale, 1929–36.

  DI Ministero degli Affari Esteri, Commissione per la Pubblicazione dei Documenti Diplomatici, *I Documenti diplomatici italiani,* 12 vols.; 4th series, 1908–1914. Rome: Libreria dello Stato, 1952–64.

  GP *Die grosse Politik der europäischen Kabinette, 1878–1914: Sammlung der diplomatischen Akten des Auswärtigen Amtes,* 40 vols. Berlin: Deutsche Verlagsgesellschaft für Politik und Geschichte m. b. h., 1922–27.

  IB *Die internationalen Beziehungen im Zeitalter des Imperialismus: Dokumente aus den Archiven der zarischen und der provisorischen Regierung,* edited by the commission of the Central Executive Committee of the Soviet Government headed by M. N. Pokrovsky; German edition prepared in the name of Deutsche Gesellschaft zum Studium Osteuropas by Otto Hoetzsch, 5 vols.; 1st series, 1914 to the outbreak of the war. Berlin: Reimar Hobbing, 1931.

  MO Komissiya C.I.K. SSR po izdaniyu dokumentov epokhi imperiyalizma pod predsedatelstvom M. N. Pokrovskovo, *Mezhdunarodniye Otnoseniye v Epokhu Imperiyalizma: Dokumenti iz Arkhivovo Tsarskovo i*

BIBLIOGRAPHY 519

Vremennovo Pravitelstvo, 1878–1917 gg., 10 vols.; 3d series, 1914–1917. Moscow: Gosudarstvenoye Sotsialno-ekonomicheskoye Izdatelstvo, 1930–1932.

Oe-U *Österreich-Ungarns Aussenpolitik von der bosnischen Krise 1908 bis zum Kriegsausbruch 1914: Diplomatische Aktenstücke des österreichisch-ungarischen Ministeriums des Äussern*, edited by Ludwig Bittner, Alfred Francis Pribram, Heinrich von Srbik, and Hans Übersberger, 8 vols. Vienna and Leipzig: Österreichischer Bundes Verlag, 1930.

RBI K.u.K. Ministerium des Äussern, *Diplomatische Aktenstücke zur Vorgeschichte des Krieges 1914*. Vienna: Staatsdruckerei, 1915.

RBII Republik Österreich, Staatsamt für äussere diplomatische Aktenstücke zur Vorgeschichte des Krieges 1914, *Ergänzungen und Nachträge zum Österreichisch-ungarischen Rotbuch*. Vienna: Staatsdruckerei, 1919.

SPK Ministarstvo Inostranih Dela, *Diplomatska prepiska o srpsko-austriskom sukobu*. Niš, 1914.

2. Diplomatic Papers (private editions)
Bittner, Ludwig, Hajek, Alois, and Übersberger, Hans, *Serbiens Aussenpolitik, 1908–1918*, Vol. III (May 26 to August 6, 1914). Vienna: Adolf Holzhauses Nachfolger, 1945.
Boghitschewitsch (Bogićević), Miloš, *Die auswärtige Politik Serbiens*, 3 vols. Berlin: Brückenverlag, 1928–31.
Ćorović, Vladimir, *Diplomatika Prepiska Kraljevine Srbije, 1902–1914*, Vol. I (1902–May 1903). Belgrade: Državna Štamparija, 1935.
Geiss, Immanuel, *Julikrise und Kriegsausbruch 1914*, 2 vols. Hanover: Verlag für Literatur und Zeitgeschehen, 1963.
Übersberger, Hans, *Österreich zwischen Russland und Serbien: Zur Südslawischen Frage und der Enstehung des ersten Weltkrieges*. Cologne and Graz: Hermann Böhlaus Nachfolger, 1958.

3. Government Documents, Law Courts, etc. (official)
Obtožnica proti Luki Jukiću i Drugovima, prilog Narodnih novina, broj 168, Zagreb, 1912.
Obtužnica i obrazloženje protiv Gavrila Principa i drugova radi atentata Njeg. C. i Kr. visosti Prestolonasljednika Nadvojvode Franje Ferdinanda i Visoke Mu supruge. Sarajevo: Naklada Knjižare, D. S. Kajon, 1914, p. 52.
Osuda Okružnog suda u Sarajevu po zavrsenoj raspravi protiv Gavrila Principa i drugova, Radi Atentata Njeg. C. i Kr. visosti Prestolonasljednika nadvojvode Franje Ferdinanda i Visoke Mu Supruge. Sarajevo: Naklada Knjižare, D. S. Kajon, 1914, p. 61.
Tajna Prevratna Organizacija, Izveštaj sa procesa u Vojnom sudu

za oficire u Solunu, Po beleškama vodjenim na samom procesu.
Solun: Velika Srbija, 1918, p. 636.

4. Government Documents, Law Courts, etc. (private)
Brandenburg, E., *Der Sarajevo Prozess*. Berlin: Arbeitsausschuss
Deutscher Verband, 1933.
Bogićević, Vojislav, *Sarajevski atentat: Stenogram Glavne Ra-
sprave Protiv Gavrila Principa i Drugova*. Sarajevo: Drž. Arhiv
Nrbih, 1954.
Mousset, Albert, *Un Drame historique: l'attentat de Sarajevo—
documents inédits et texte intégral des sténogrammes du pro-
cès*. Paris: Payot, 1930.
*Official Shorthand Minutes of the Trial of the Trotskyite Center,
The*. Moscow: 1937.
Pharos, Professor (pseudonym of Anton Puntigam), *Der Prozess
gegen die Attentäter von Sarajevo, nach dem amtlichen Steno-
gramm der Gerichtsverhandlung*. Berlin: Decker, 1918.
Übersberger, Hans, *Der Saloniki Prozess*. Berlin: 1933.

5. Monographs and memoirs in which some previously unpublished
state and other documents were revealed
Allmayer-Beck, Johann Christoph, *Ministerpräsident Baron Beck:
Ein Staatsmann des alten Österreich*. Munich: R. Oldenburg,
1956.
Bilinski, Leon von, *Wspomnienia i dokumenty 1846–1922*, 2 vols.
Warsaw: F. Hoesicka, 1924–25.
Boghitschewitsch (Bogićević), Miloš, *Le Colonel Dragoutine
Dimitriewitch-Apis*. Paris: Delpeuch, 1928.
Bogićević, Miloš, *Causes of the War*. Amsterdam: Langenhuysen,
1919.
———, *Le Procès de Salonique*. Paris: 1928.
Bourbon-Parma, Sixte de, *L'Offre de paix separée de l'Autriche*.
Paris: Plon, 1920.
Čerović, Božo, *Bosanski omladinci i Sarajevski atentat*. Sarajevo:
Trgovačka Štamparija, 1930.
Chlumecky, Leopold von, *Erzherzog Franz Ferdinands Wirken
und Wollen*. Berlin: Verlag für Kulturpolitik, 1929.
Conrad von Hötzendorf, Franz, *Aus meiner Dienstzeit 1906–
1918*, 5 vols. Berlin, Leipzig, Munich: Rikola, 1922–25.
Ćorović, Vladimir, *Crna Knjiga, Patnje Srba Bosne i Hercegovine
za Vreme Svetskog Rata 1914 to 1918*. Belgrade and Sarajevo:
Dj. Djurdjević, 1920.
———, *Odnosi izmedju Srbije i Austro-Ugarske u XX veku*. Bel-
grade: Državna Štamparija, 1936.
Eisenmenger, Victor, *Archduke Francis Ferdinand*. London: Sel-
wyn, 1931.
———, *Erzherzog Franz Ferdinand: Seinem Andenken gewidmet
von seinem Leibarzt*. Zurich, Leipzig and Vienna: 1929.

Ernst, Otto, *Franz Joseph as Revealed by His Letters*. London: Methuen, 1927.

Hantsch, Hugo, *Leopold Graf Berchtold*, 2 vols. Graz, Vienna, Cologne and Styria: 1963.

Jovanović, Jovan, *Stvaranje zajedničke države Srba, Hrvata i Slovenaca*, 3 vols. Belgrade: Srpska Književna Zadruga, 1928–1930.

Kiszling, Rudolf, *Erzherzog Franz Ferdinand von Österreich-Este: Leben, Pläne und Wirken am Schicksalsweg der Donaumonarchie*. Graz and Cologne: Hermann Böhlaus Nachfolger, 1953.

Krv-Slovenstva, 1914–1924: Spomenica desetogodišnjice Svetskog Rata. Belgrade: Radenković, 1924.

Magrini, Luciano, *Il Dramma di Sarajevo, origini e responsibilità della guerra europea*. Milan: Athena, 1929.

Margutti, Albert von, *The Emperor Francis Joseph and His Times*. London: Hutchinson, 1921; New York: Doran, 1921.

———, *Kaiser Franz Josef: Persönliche Erinnerungen*. Vienna, Leipzig and Mainz: 1924.

———, *La Tragédie des Habsbourgs: Mémoires d'un aide de camp*. Vienne: Rhombus, 1923.

———, *Vom alten Kaiser: Persönliche Erinnerungen an Franz Josef I*. Leipzig and Vienna: Leonhardt, 1921.

Nešković, Borivoje, *Istina o solunskom procesu*. Belgrade: Narodna Knjiga, 1953.

Nikitsch-Boulles, Paul, *Vor dem Sturm: Erinnerungen an Erzherzog-Thronfolger Franz Ferdinand von seinem Privatsekretär*. Berlin: Verlag für Kulturpolitik, 1925.

Pfeffer, Leo, *Istraga u Sarajevskom atentatu*. Zagreb: Nova Evropa, 1938.

Pribićević, Svetozar, *La Dictature du roi Alexandre: Contribution à l'étude de la démocratie*. Paris: Bussuel, 1932.

Redlich, Josef, *Emperor Francis Joseph of Austria*. London and New York: Macmillan, 1929.

———, *Kaiser Franz Josef von Österreich: Eine Biographie*. Berlin: Verlag für Kulturpolitik, 1928.

Sosnosky, Theodor von, *Franz Ferdinand der Erzherzog-Thronfolger: Ein Lebensbild*. Munich and Berlin: Oldenburg, 1929.

Stanojević, Stanoje, *Ubistvo austriskog prestolonaslednika Ferdinanda*. Belgrade: Izdavačka Knjižarnica Napredak, 1923.

Živanović, Milan, *Pukovnik Apis: Solunski Proces Hiljadu Devetsto Sedamnaeste*. Belgrade: Kultura, 1955.

6. *Festschrifte* of members of the South Slav secret societies in which some unpublished documents of their activities were revealed

Bogićević, Vojislav, *Mlada Bosna pisma i prilozi*. Sarajevo: Svjet-lost, 1954.

Današnjica i Mlada Bosna—Uloga i značaj Vladimira Gaćinovića. Sarajevo: Biblioteka Vladimir Gaćinović, 1937.

Gaćinović, Vladimir, *Ogledi i pisma*, edited by Todor Kruševac. Sarajevo: Svetlost, 1956.

Slijepčević, Pero, drugovi, *Napor Bosne i Hercegovine za oslo-bodjenje i ujedinjenje*. Sarajevo: Narodna Odbrana, 1929.

Spomenica Danila Ilića, edited and published by his friends. Sara-jevo: 1929.

Spomenica Vasilja Grdžića. Sarajevo: Prosveta, 1935.

Spomenica Vladimira Gaćinovića, edited by Pero Slijepčević. Sa-rajevo: published by comrades and friends, 1921.

Trotsky, Leon (under pseudonym T.L.), *Ispovest Vladimira Gaćinovića—Sarajevski atentat*. Belgrade: Svetlost, 1922.

C. *Newspapers and Journals*
   1. Newspapers and journals of the South Slav secret societies, and periodicals to which their individual members contributed

Bosanska Vila, Sarajevo
Kievskaya Misl, Kiev, Russia
Narod, Mostar
Novi Val, Zagreb
Pijemont, Belgrade
Politika, Belgrade
Pregled, Sarajevo
Preporod, Belgrade
Preporod, Ljubljana
Sloboda, Split
Slovenski jug, Belgrade
Srpska omladina, Sarajevo
Srpska riječ, Sarajevo
Val, Zagreb
Vihor, Zagreb
Zora, Vienna
Zora, Prague
Zvono, Sarajevo

   2. Contemporary newspapers and journals

Arbeiter Zeitung, Vienna
Balkan, Belgrade
Berliner Tageblatt, Berlin
Bosnische Post, Sarajevo
Budapeszt Hirlap, Budapest
Danzers Armee Zeitung, Vienna
Gross Österreich, Vienna
Hrvatski Dnevnik, Sarajevo

Istina, Sarajevo
Neue Freie Presse, Vienna
Neue Rundschau, Berlin
Neues Abendland, Vienna
Neues Wiener Tageblatt, Vienna
New Europe, London
Obzor, Zagreb
Pester Lloyd, Budapest
Pravda, Belgrade
Reichspost, Vienna
St. Petersburg Gazette, St. Petersburg
Samouprava, Belgrade
Srbobran, Zagreb
Srpske novine, Corfu
Srpski književni glasnik, Belgrade
Ujedinjenje, Geneva
Zabavnik, Corfu
Zastava, Split
Zeit, Vienna
Zukunft, Vienna

II. SECONDARY SOURCES

A. *Bibliographies*
Trišić, Nikola, *Sarajevski atentat u Svjetlu Bibliografskih Podataka*. Belgrade: Veselin Masleša, 1960.
Wegerer, Alfred von, *Bibliographie zur Vorgeschichte des Weltkrieges*. Berlin: Quaderverlag, 1934.

B. *Memoirs*
Auffenberg-Komarow, Moritz, *Aus Österreichs Höhe und Niedergang: Eine Lebensschilderung*. Munich: Drei-Mosken-Verlag, 1921.
Baernreither, Joseph Maria, *Fragmente eines politischen Tagebuches: Die Südslawische Frage und Österreich-Ungarn vor dem Weltkrieg*. Berlin: Verlag für Kulturpolitik, 1928.
———, *Fragments of a Political Diary*. New York: Macmillan, 1930.
Bardolff, Karl, *Soldat im alten Österreich: Erinnerungen aus meinem Leben*. Jena: E. Diederichs, 1938.
Bartulović, Niko, *Od revolucionar omladine de Orjune*. Split: published by the author, 1925.
Bülow, Bernhard von, *Memoirs of Prince von Bülow*, 4 vols. Boston: Little, Brown, 1931.
Burian, Stephan von, *Austria in Dissolution*. New York: Doran, 1925.

Cistler, Rudolf, *Kako sam branio Principa i drugove 1914, godine.* Ljubljana, 1937.

Ćurić, Hajrudin, *Jedan Nacionalni Revolucionar iz Hercegovine* (special print from Kalendar Gajreta). Sarajevo: Gajret, 1938.

Czernin, Ottokar, *In the World War.* New York: Harper, 1920.

Djordjević, Talica, *Blaženi Borac—Milan Djordjević.* Belgrade, 1939.

Dumba, Constantin, *Memoirs of a Diplomat.* Boston: Little, Brown, 1932.

Franz Ferdinand Erzherzog von Österreich-Este, *Tagebuch meine Reise um die Erde, 1892–1893,* 2 vols. Vienna, 1896.

Funder, Friedrich, *From Empire to Republic.* New York: Albert Unger, 1963.

———, *Vom Gestern ins Heute.* Vienna: Herold, 1952.

Glück, Wladyslaw, *Sarajewo: Historija Zamachu Sarajewskiego* Krakow: Gebethner-Wolf, 1935.

Grey of Fallodon, Viscount, *Twenty-Five Years—1892–1916,* 2 vols. London: Hodder and Stoughton, 1925–26.

Jevdjević, Dobrosav, *Sarajevski atentatori.* Zagreb: Binoza, 1934.

Jevtić, Borivoje, *Sarajevski atentat.* Sarajevo: P. N. Gaković, 1923.

Jovanović, Slobodan, *Moji savremenici* (reprint of essays from *Glas Kanadskih Srba,* August 2, 9, 16, and October 18, 1962), Windsor, Canada: Avale Printing and Publishing Co., 1962.

Kolar, Ivan Janež, *Preporodovci* 1912–1914, 1914–1918. Kamnik: Izdanje Štamparije A. Slatnar, 1930.

Kranjčević, Ivo, *Uspomene jednog učesnika u sarajevskom atentatu.* Sarajevo: Svjetlost, 1954.

Ljubibratić, Drago, *Gavrilo Princip.* Belgrade: Prosveta, 1959.

———, *Vladimir Gaćinović.* Belgrade: Nolit *Prosveta,* 1961.

Mandić, Velimir (pseudonym of Maneli, V. G.), *Bosna u lancima ili povodom atentata Gavrila Principa.* Sarajevo: Štamparija Bosanske Pošte, 1919.

Pappenheim, Martin, "Dr. Pappenheim's Conversations with Princip," translated with an introduction by Hamilton Fish Armstrong, *Current History* (New York), August 1927, pp. 701–706 —offprint. (From the original German—*Gavrilo Princips Bekenntnisse: Ein geschichtlicher Bettrag zur Vorgeschichte des Attentats von Sarajevo.* Vienna: Lechner Sohn, 1936.)

Sieghardt, Rudolf, *Die letzten Jahrzehnte einer Grossmacht: Menschen, Völker, Probleme des Habsburger-Reichs.* Berlin: Ullstein, 1932.

Spitzmüller-Harmersbach, Alexander, *. . . und hat auch Ursach, es zu leben.* Vienna, Munich, Stuttgart, Zurich: Wilhelm Frick, 1955.

Stedimlija, S. M., *Partizani o sebi.* Zagreb: 1944.

Steed, Henry Wickham, *Through Thirty Years, 1892–1922: A Personal Narrative.* London: Heinemann, 1924.

Tartalja, Oskar, *Veleizdajnik Moje Uspomene iz Borbe Protiv Ornozutog Orla.* Zagreb and Split: Srepel, 1928.

Zakula, Stevan, *Od Terezina do Sarajevo*. Belgrade: Naklada Piš-
čeva, 1930.

C. *Newspapers and Periodicals of Special Interest in Relation to 1914
Events*
    Auswärtige Politik, Berlin
    Berliner Monatshefte, Berlin
    Borba, Belgrade
    Češko slovo, Prague
    Clarté, Paris
    Current History, New York
    La Fédération Balkanique, Vienna
    Foreign Affairs, New York
    Gajret, Sarajevo
    Glas naroda, Sarajevo
    Glasnik Jugoslovenskog profesorskog društva, Belgrade
    Glas Zadra, Zadar
    Godišnjak istoriskog društva Bosne i Hercegovine, Sarajevo
    Harvard Slavic Studies, Cambridge, Massachusetts
    Historijski Zbornik, Zagreb
    Hrvatski narod, Zagreb
    Istorik Marksist, Moscow
    Istoriski zapisi, Cetinje
    Jugoslavenska njiva, Zagreb
    Jugoslovenska Pošta, Sarajevo
    Jugoslovenski list, Sarajevo
    Književna Republika, Zagreb
    Književnik, Zagreb
    Književni sever, Subotica
    Književnost, Belgrade
    Kriegsschuldfrage, Berlin
    Krug, Belgrade
    Letopis Matice Srpske, Novi Sad
    Manchester Guardian, Manchester
    Mitteilungen des österreichischen Staatsarchivs, Vienna
    Le Monde, Paris
    Narodna odbrana, Belgrade
    Narodno jedinstvo, Sarajevo
    Nedeljni sarajevski list 7 dana, Sarajevo
    Neues acht Uhr Blatt, Vienna
    Neues Wiener Journal, Vienna
    Neues Wiener Abendblatt, Vienna
    Nin, Belgrade
    Nineteenth Century and After, The, Edinburgh
    Nova Evropa, Zagreb
    Nova misao, Belgrade
    Novi Srbobran, Zagreb
    Novi Život, Belgrade

Novo Doba, Split
Novosti, Zagreb
Observer, The, London
Oslobodjenje, Sarajevo
Österreichischer Wehrzeitung, Vienna
Paris-Soir-Dimanche, Paris
Pogledi na savremena pitanja, Zagreb
Politički Glasnik, Belgrade
Prosvjeta, Sarajevo
Radikal, Belgrade
Razvitak, Banja Luka
Republika, Belgrade
Riječ, Zagreb
Ruski Arhiv, Belgrade
Slavonic Review, London
Štampa, Belgrade
Večernja pošta, Sarajevo
Völkischer Beobachter, Berlin
Vrbaske novine, Banja Luka
Vreme, Belgrade
Zeit, Prague
Život, Sarajevo

D. *Monographs*

Albertini, Luigi, *The Origins of the War of 1914*, translated and edited by Isabella M. Massey, 3 vols. London and New York: Oxford University Press, 1952–57.

Almira, José Stevan Giv, *Le Déclic de Sarajevo*. Paris: Editions Radot, 1927.

Barnes, Harry Elmer, *The Genesis of the World War*. New York: Alfred A. Knopf, 1926.

Beck, Gottfried, *La Responsibilité de la Hongrie*. Paris: Librairie Payot, 1917.

Berkman, Alexander, *Now and After: The A B C of Communist Anarchism*. New York: Vanguard Press, The Jewish Anarchist Federation, 1929.

Bloch, Camille, *Les Causes de la Guerre Mondiale: Précis historique*. Paris: Paul Hartmann, 1933.

Burgess, John William, *Political Science and Comparative Constitutional Law*, 2 vols. Boston and London: Ginn, 1890.

Čubrilović, Vaso, *Istorija Političke Misli u Srbiji XIX Veka*. Belgrade: Prosveta, 1958.

Cvijić, Jovan, *Balkansko Poluostrvo i Jugoslovenske Zemlje*, 2 vols. Belgrade: Državna Štamparija, 1922.

Djordjević, Dimitrije, *Milovan Milovanović*. Belgrade: Prosveta, 1962.

Durham, Edith, *The Sarajevo Crime*. London: George Allen and Unwin, 1925.

Evans, Arthur John, *Illyrian Letters*, a revised selection of letters to the *Manchester Guardian* in the year 1877. London, 1878.

———, *Through Bosnia and Hercegovina on Foot*. London: Longmans, Green, 1876; 2d ed. (enlarged, revised), 1877.

Falkenegg, S., *Erzherzog Franz Ferdinand von Österreich Este*. Berlin, 1908.

Fay, Sidney Bradshaw, *The Origins of the World War*, 2 vols. New York: Macmillan, 1930.

Franz, Georg, *Erzherzog Franz Ferdinand und die Pläne zur Reform der Habsburger Monarchie*. Brno, Munich, Vienna: Verlag G. D. W. Callwey, 1943.

Gooch, George Peabody, *Before the War: Studies of European Diplomacy*, 2 vols. London and New York: Longmans, Green, 1936–38.

Grünberg, Karl, *Die Agrarverfassung und die Grundlastungsprobleme in Bosnien und der Herzegowina*. Leipzig, 1911.

Heller, H., *Franz Ferdinand*. Vienna, 1911.

Herbert, Eugenia, *The Artist and Social Reform—France and Belgium, 1885–1898*. New Haven: Yale University Press, 1961.

Isaac, Jules, *Un Débat historique: Le Problème des origines de la guerre*. Paris: Les Éditions Rieder, 1931.

Jägerskjöld, Stig, *Tyrannmord och motståndsrätt 1792–1809*. Stockholm: Scandinavian Studies in Law, 1964.

Jászi, Oscar, *The Dissolution of the Habsburg Monarchy*. Chicago: University of Chicago Press, 1929.

———, and Lewis, John D., *Against the Tyrant: The Tradition and Theory of Tyrannicide*. Glencoe, Illinois: Glencoe Free Press, 1957.

Jovanović, Jovan, *Odgovornost Srbije za svetski rat*. Belgrade: Franjo Bah, 1927.

———, *Stvaranje Zajednicke Drzave Srba, Hrvata i Slovenaca*, 3 vols. Belgrade: Srpska Književna Zadruga, 1929.

Kann, Robert, *The Multinational Empire: Nationalism and National Reform in the Habsburg Monarchy*, 2 vols. New York: Columbia University Press, 1950.

Kanner, Heinrich, *Der Schlüssel zur Kriegsschuldfrage*. Munich: Sudbayerische Verlagsgesellschaft, 1926.

Kristoffy, Josef, *Magyarország Kalvariája*, 2 vols. Budapest, 1928.

Krug von Nidda, Richard, *Der Weg nach Sarajevo*. Vienna: Amalthea Verlag, 1964.

Kruševac, Todor, *Petar Kočić*. Belgrade: Prosveta, 1951.

Kunzelmann, F., *Erzherzog Franz Ferdinand*. Berlin, 1916.

Lammasch, Marge, and Sperl, Hans, *Heinrich Lammasch: Seine Aufzeichnungen, sein Wirken und sein Politik*. Vienna and Leipzig: Deuticke, 1922.

Lazarević, Dobrivoje, *Die Schwarze Hand*. Lausanne: Librairie Nouvelle, 1917.

Lennhoff, Eugen, *Die Freimaurer*. Zurich, Leipzig, Vienna: Amalthea Verlag, 1929.

———, *Politische Geheimbunde*. Zurich, Leipzig, Vienna: Amalthea Verlag, 1931.

Ludendorff, Erich, *Vernichtung der Freimaurerei durch Enthüllung ihrer Geheimnisse*. Munich, 1928.

———, *Wie der Weltkrieg 1914 "gemacht" wurde*. Munich: Ludendorff Verlag, G. m. b. H., 1935.

Maitron, Jean, *Histoire du mouvement anarchiste en France 1880–1914*. Paris: Société Universitaire d'Éditions et de Librairie, 1951.

Mandl, Leopold, *Die Habsburger und die Serbische Frage: Geschichte des staatlichen Gegensatzes Serbien zu Österreich-Ungarn*. Vienna: Moritz Perles, 1918.

Masleša, Veselin, *Mlada Bosna*. Belgrade: Kultura, 1945.

Muret, Maurice, *L'Archiduc François-Ferdinand*. Paris: Grasset, 1932.

Pelagić, Vaso, *Borba za Oslobodjenje: Istorija Bosansko-Hercegovacke Bune u Svezi Srpsko-Vlasko-Bugarsko i Rusko-Turksim Ratom*, 3d ed. Belgrade, 1882.

Pichon, Jules (under pseudonym Jules Chopin), *Le Complot de Sarajevo (28 juin 1914): Étude sur les origines de la guerre*. Paris: Éditions Bossard, 1918.

Pisarov, J., *Osvoboditelnoye Dvizhenie Yugoslavyansky Narodov Avstro-Vengrii*. Moscow, 1962.

Poletika, Nikolai, *Sarayevsko Ubiistvo*. Leningrad: Krasnaya Gazeta, 1930.

———, *Vozniknovenie Mirovoi Voini*. Moscow: Gosudarstvennoye Sotsialno-ekonomicheskoi Izdatelstvo, Marksa-Lenina, 1935.

———, *Vozniknovenie Pervoi Mirovoi Voini*. Moscow, Misl, 1964.

Popovici, Aureli, *Die vereinigten Staaten von Gross-Österreich: Politische Studien zur Lösung der nationalen Fragen und staatsrechtlichen Krisen in Österreich-Ungarn*. Leipzig, 1906.

Schmitt, Bernadotte, *The Coming of the War 1914*, 2 vols. New York and London: Charles Scribner's Sons, 1930.

Seton-Watson, Robert William, *Sarajevo: A Study in the Origins of the Great War*. London: Hutchinson, 1926.

Skalnik, K., *Dr. Karl Lueger: Der Mann zwischen den Zeiten*. Vienna and Munich: Herold, 1954.

Škerović, Nikola, *Crna Gora na osvitku 20 vijeka*. Belgrade: Srpska Akademija Nauka, 1963.

Wegerer, Alfred von, *Der Ausbruch der Weltkrieges*. Hamburg: Hanseatische Verlagsanstalt, 1939.

Wendel, Hermann, *Die Habsburger und die Südslawenfrage*. Belgrade and Leipzig: Geca Kon, 1924.

Woodcock, George, *Anarchism*. New York: Penguin Books, 1962.

Žibert, Janež A., *Der Mord von Sarajevo und Tiszas Schuld an dem Weltkriege*. Vienna, 1918.

Zwitter, Fran, with the collaboration of Jaroslav Šidak and Vasa Bogdanov, *Les Problèmes nationaux dans la monarchie des Habsburg*. Belgrade, 1960.

INDEX

ABOUT THE AUTHOR

Vladimir Dedijer, whose official biography of Tito has been published
in thirty-seven languages throughout the world, was an officer in the
Partisan forces which drove the Nazis out of Yugoslavia. As an experienced newspaperman he became the best-known chronicler of that
movement. As a historian, he has taught at some of the world's leading
universities, including Stockholm, Oxford and Manchester in England,
Harvard and Cornell in the United States. He now lives and writes in
Ljubljana, Yugoslavia.